The Jews of Polai
Between Two World Wars

Published for Brandeis University Press by
University Press of New England
Hanover and London

The Jews of Poland Between Two World Wars

Edited by
Yisrael Gutman,
Ezra Mendelsohn,
Jehuda Reinharz,
and Chone Shmeruk

Assistant Editor
Sylvia Fuks Fried

© 1989 by the Trustees of Brandeis University

Printed in the United States of America
∞

Library of Congress Cataloging-in-Publication Data

The Jews of Poland between two world wars.

   (The Tauber Institute for the Study of European
Jewry series; 10)

   Papers from the International Conference on
the Jews of Poland Between Two World Wars held
Apr. 12–15, 1986 at Brandeis University, Waltham,
Mass.

   Includes index.

   1. Jews—Poland—History—20th century—Congresses.
2. Poland—Ethnic relations—Congresses.
I. Gutman, Yisrael.   II. International Conference
on the Jews of Poland Between Two World Wars
(1986 : Brandeis University)   III. Series.
DS135.P6J47   1989   943.8'004924   88–40349

ISBN 0–87451–446–0

5   4   3   2   1

The Tauber Institute for the Study of European Jewry, established by a gift to Brandeis University from Dr. Laszlo N. Tauber, is dedicated to the memory of the victims of Nazi persecutions between 1933 and 1945. The Institute seeks to study the history and culture of European Jewry in the modern period. The Institute has a special interest in studying the causes, nature, and consequences of the European Jewish catastrophe and seeks to explore them within the context of modern European diplomatic, intellectual, political, and social history. The Tauber Institute for the Study of European Jewry is organized on a multidisciplinary basis, with the participation of scholars in history, Judaic studies, political science, sociology, comparative literature, and other disciplines.

The Tauber Institute for the Study of European Jewry Series
Jehuda Reinharz, General Editor

Contents

Historiography

Acknowledgments

The International Conference on the Jews of Poland Between Two World Wars was organized under the auspices of the Tauber Institute for the Study of European Jewry at Brandeis University, Waltham, Massachusetts, and the Center for Research on the History and Culture of Polish Jews at the Hebrew University, Jerusalem, in cooperation with the YIVO Institute for Jewish Research, New York.

The conference was sponsored by the Valya and Robert Shapiro Endowment at Brandeis University. We are deeply grateful to Mr. and Mrs. Robert Shapiro for their generous support of our efforts. For the timely support of the publication of this volume, we wish to thank Mrs. Toni Greenberg and the Jacob Perlow Estate. We would also like to extend our gratitude to Mrs. Alice S. Dorn, Dr. Morton Godine, Mrs. Dorothy S. Kassel, Professor George L. Mosse, Mr. and Mrs. Isadore Rosenberg, Mr. and Mrs. James Sassower, the Abraham Shapiro Charity Fund, Mr. and Mrs. Sidney Shapiro, Mrs. Eugenia Shrut, Mr. Marcus Smith and the Joseph and Anna Smith Foundation, Mr. and Mrs. George Szabad, Rabbi Samuel Chiel and the Temple Emanuel Special Fund, and Mr. and Mrs. Gerald Tishler.

We extend our thanks to Dr. Ann Hofstra Grogg, who meticulously copyedited the volume and prepared the index, and to Sylvia Fuks Fried, Assistant Director of the Tauber Institute, who, as assistant editor of the volume, oversaw all stages of editing. We express our thanks also to the editors and staff of the University Press of New England, and Dr. John R. Hose, governor of Brandeis University Press, whose energy and wisdom have contributed greatly to the Tauber Series.

The Editors

The Jews of Poland Between Two World Wars

POLAND BETWEEN THE WARS

Baltic   Sea

LITHUANIA

GERMANY

VILNA
• Vilna

POMORZE

GERMANY

NOWOGRÓDEK

U.S.S.R.

• Nowogródek

Toruń

BIAŁYSTOK
• Białystok

POZNAŃ
• Poznań

WARSAW
Warsaw •

POLESIE
• Brześć nad Bugiem

Łódź •

ŁÓDŹ

LUBLIN

VOLYNIA
• Łuck

Kielce •

• Lublin

KIELCE
• Katowice

LWÓW
Lwów •

TARNOPOL
• Tarnopol

ŚLĄSK

• Cracow

CRACOW

• Stanisławów
STANISŁAWÓW

CZECHOSLOVAKIA

HUNGARY

RUMANIA

Ezra Mendelsohn

Introduction: The Jews of Poland Between Two World Wars—Myth and Reality

For many individuals belonging to the small nations of Eastern Europe, the years between the two world wars have attained the status of a golden age, an all-too-brief period during which the attainment and exercise of national independence more than made up for the prevalence of economic misery and political instability. A good case for this assessment could certainly be made with regard to the Baltic peoples—the Lithuanians, Latvians, and Estonians—whose twenty years of unexpected, scarcely-dreamed-of political sovereignty, wedged in between tsarist and Soviet oppression, greatly facilitated their success in joining the family of modern nations and is of great importance in their efforts to maintain their national existence today. Then there are the Czechs, who in 1918 played the leading role in establishing a state that, while it may not have been loved by its various minority nationalities, was nonetheless one of the most successful and admired of the successor states of Eastern Europe. Finally, consider the Poles, whose political independence had come to an end in the late eighteenth century and whose resurrection as a modern nation-state was often hailed as one of the great achievements of the post–World War I settlement. Poland of the years 1918–39 may not have been a model society, but despite the failure to solve basic social, economic, and political problems, Polish achievements during this time were considerable, and these achievements helped make certain that the state would continue to exist, in some form or other, after World War II. Nostalgia in today's Poland for the Republic of the 1920s and 1930s is a perfectly understandable phenomenon, for this was the time when an independent, democratic, pluralistic, Western-oriented, Catholic Poland finally regained her rightful place among the states of Europe.

1

What of the Jews of interwar Eastern Europe? Can we speak in their case, too, of a golden age of national achievement despite widespread poverty and the evils of antisemitism? Of course there are problems in comparing their fate and the fate of the territorial peoples of the region. Nevertheless, the Jews certainly shared the hopes of all these peoples—hopes in some cases fulfilled—that the end of the terrible war and the establishment of the new order would lead to a new and happier era. The Jews in particular hoped that the new environment would be conducive to the flourishing of Jewish cultural and religious life, and they also hoped to be recognized as equal citizens in the new states of the region. Many of them—the nationalists—wanted some form or other of autonomy that would enable them, among other things, to prepare the Jewish youth to take up the great national tasks devolving upon the Jewish people, such as the building of a national home in Palestine.

It became clear rather early on that at least some of these hopes could not be realized in the Soviet Union, where the regime stifled a wide range of autonomous Jewish activities from the very beginning and where, by the late 1930s, precious little in the way of specifically Jewish cultural (not to mention political) life was allowed to exist. But what of the smaller successor states of the region, where there also resided important Jewish communities and where political conditions were much more favorable than those prevailing in the Soviet Union? And what, above all, of Poland, in which resided by far the largest Jewish community in noncommunist Europe, a community heir to the great traditions of Russian and Habsburg Jewries, a community whose heritage of religious, cultural, and political creativity was unmatched, a community that Jews of every stripe—Hasidim, Zionists, socialists, Yiddishists, Hebraists—regarded as the leading cultural and political (if not financial) force in the Jewish Diaspora? The leaders of this community certainly expected that the combination of a large and truly "Jewish" (that is, nonassimilated and to an extent nonacculturated) community and favorable political conditions existing in the new state would lead to great things. As early as 1917, even before the establishment of independent Poland, the Zionist Rabbi Yitzhak Nisenbaum predicted that Polish Jewry would soon take its rightful place as the leader of world Zionism, as it had once taken the lead in Torah studies during the previous "golden age" at the time of the medieval Polish Commonwealth.[1] And such predictions were a commonplace in the early years of Polish independence.

Were these hopes realized? Were the interwar years in Poland a "golden age" for Jews, or at least for some of them, just as interwar, independent Lithuania was a golden age for Lithuanians?

There is no doubt that many Jews have regarded, and continue to regard, these years as a luminous era of Jewish achievement. One reason, of course, is that the interwar period was not only an important chapter in recent Jewish history (of this there can be no doubt) but also the last important chapter in Polish-Jewish history and, indeed, probably the last important chapter in the history of the unique Eastern European, Yiddish-speaking, Ashkenazi Jewish civilization (we do not know what the future has in store for Soviet Jewry, but it would be rash to predict the revival of such a civilization in that country). Lithuanian history goes on, as does Polish history, but Polish-Jewish history has come to an end—and a terrible, violent, unnatural end at that.

But this is not the only reason why Jews have tended to look to this period with special reverence. Beyond the trauma caused by the unparalleled catastrophe of Polish Jewry, a trauma that has led to the production of countless memorial books celebrating a world which no longer exists, lies the conviction shared by the "folk" and by many intellectuals that this was a time when many great ideologies and movements born in the old multinational Russian and Habsburg empires came of age and won over large numbers of followers. For Zionists this was an age when the Zionist movement finally emerged as a great force that both dominated Jewish political life in Poland and rescued the Palestinian Yishuv (Jewish community) by sending to it tens of thousands of idealistic pioneers. For Bundists this was an age when the Jewish proletariat, under the Bund's leadership and allied with the Polish working class, fearlessly held up the banner of Jewish socialism and, in the 1930s, led the struggle against antisemitism. For Yiddishists this was the period in which a secular Yiddish school system, the Yiddish press, Yiddish theater, and Yiddish literature flourished, and when the great majority of Polish Jewry declared Yiddish to be its mother tongue, while

1. Yitzhak Nisenbaum, speech at the Third Polish Zionist Conference, Warsaw, October 1917, printed in *Hatzefirah*, November 8, 1917, p. 10.

Hebraists took pride in the flourishing of Tarbut schools, which allowed Jewish children to obtain a modern, first-class education in Hebrew from kindergarten through high school. For Orthodox Jews this was a period when the great Hasidic courts still held sway, when somewhat modernized Orthodox schools proliferated, and when their political organization, Agudat Israel, became a force to reckon with. And one could go on and on. True, hopes for equal status with non-Jews (in fact, not in theory) and for the decline of antisemitism were certainly not entirely fulfilled, and in this respect the situation deteriorated in the late 1930s. But there were great compensations.

Along with the tendency of Jews from various, often competing camps to regard the history of interwar Polish Jewry as one of great, even unique achievement, we also have the tendency to regard this period as one of heroic struggle, a tendency linked to the very rise of antisemitism, which seemed to dash Jewish hopes for true equality. Antisemitism and the deteriorating economic situation may have pushed the Jews to "the edge of destruction," as the title of Celia Heller's book on this period would have it,[2] but they fought back with tenacity and skill, thus writing a glorious page in the history of Jewish resistance. It is no accident that some of the most important scholarly books on this period contain in their titles the word "struggle,"[3] drawing on a tradition established by Yitzhak Gruenbaum, who published a well-known book called *Milhamot yehudei Polanyah* (The Wars of Polish Jews).[4] In the heroic struggle for their civil and national rights the Jews might not always have emerged victorious. But the struggle itself was of great moral significance and was something of a prelude to the heroism of the ghetto fighters during the Holocaust and of the Yishuv in its struggle for survival and political independence.

This is not the place to deal at length with the question of the accuracy of those assessments that emphasize the flourishing of Jew-

2. Celia S. Heller, *On the Edge of Destruction: Jews of Poland between the Two World Wars* (New York, 1977).

3. Thus Shlomo Nezer, *Maavak yehudei Polin al zekhuyoteihem ha-ezrahiyot ve-ha-leumiyot, 1918–1922* (The Struggle of Polish Jews for Their Civil and National Rights, 1918–1922) (Tel Aviv, 1980); Emanuel Melzer, *Maavak medini be-malkodet: Yehudei Polin, 1935–1939* (Political Strife in a Blind Alley: The Jews in Poland, 1935–1939) (Tel Aviv, 1982); Moshe Landa, *Miut leumi lohem: Maavak yehudei Polin ba-shanim 1918–1928* (A Fighting National Minority: The Struggle of Polish Jews, 1918–1928) (Jerusalem, 1986).

4. Yitzhak Gruenbaum, *Milhamot yehudei Polanyah* (Jerusalem, 1941).

ish cultural, religious, and political movements and the heroism of the community. Suffice it to say that they should be regarded with caution. Zionism was a strong movement, but it by no means "conquered" Polish Jewry, and its achievements in the area of *aliyah*, for example, should not be exaggerated. Yiddishist and Hebraist school systems failed to attract large numbers of Jewish children. Polish Jewry was in general undergoing a significant process of Polonization, which may not have led to assimilation but which did undermine some of the more extravagant hopes of the champions of autonomy and the promoters of Yiddish and Hebrew culture. Orthodoxy was on the decline, though we do not know exactly to what extent. Jewish leaders may have "struggled" for Jewish rights, but the community was hopelessly divided and bitterly at war with itself.

Wherever the truth may lie, the time has come to make a new evaluation of this period, an evaluation unencumbered by the various mythologies that have emerged in the post-Holocaust period. This was, in fact, an objective of the 1986 conference, "The Jews of Poland Between Two World Wars." The scholars who assembled at Brandeis University represented various generations and various schools. There were Jewish scholars born in Poland and educated in Israel, scholars from present-day Poland (whose presence demonstrates a new and most welcome interest among non-Jewish scholars in the Polish-Jewish past), and a new generation of mostly American-born researchers whose appearance is of great significance for the future of Polish-Jewish studies. These scholars are engaged in taking a fresh look at the interwar years. Their assessments of the nature of Gentile-Jewish relations and of Jewish politics, culture, and economic life represent an attempt to analyze events and trends and place them in proper perspective without recourse to the rhetoric of the age and to the ideological preoccupations of an earlier generation.

The fruits of their labor are collected in this volume, the burden of which is, perhaps, that the kind of question posed at the outset of these remarks is not the kind of question we should be asking. Rather than wondering if the interwar period was a golden or heroic age, we should be concentrating on less grandiose but more meaningful issues: the complex question of relations between the Jewish minority and the Christian-Polish majority, the constraints under which Jewish political and cultural activists labored, and the tensions between Jewish ideologies and cultural-religious positions (such as nationalism, integrationism, and Orthodoxy) and the realities of Polish-Jewish life in the 1920s and 1930s. The essays in this book take up these and other questions. They constitute, together, a volume that, I believe, will come to be seen, along with other recent publications, as ushering in a new period of research on the modern history of Polish Jews.

The Political Arena

Ezra Mendelsohn

Jewish Politics in Interwar Poland: An Overview

To present an overview of Jewish politics in interwar Poland in the brief space available to me is a difficult, if not impossible, task. Simply enumerating all the Jewish political parties, youth movements, and nonpolitical organizations (associations of merchants, industrialists, and artisans, for example) that played a role in Jewish politics would require a good many pages. This kind of list might be of some interest, as it would demonstrate the remarkable richness, creativity, inventiveness, and fragmentation of Jewish political life. But rather than indulge in such an exercise, however entertaining, I propose to attempt an analysis of several aspects of Jewish politics and to consider the "lessons" that the Jewish political experience in Poland offer to those interested in modern Jewish history.

Let me begin by presenting two contradictory descriptions of Polish-Jewish political life. Consider, first, the testimony of Alexander Goldstein, a veteran Russian Zionist who came to Poland in 1930 to collect funds for Keren Hayesod (Foundation Fund). In Grodno he addressed a meeting "so overfilled that several hundred people could not get in." In Vilna, "the poorest and most ruined city" (we should keep in mind that the Great Depression, which so devastated Poland, was now in full swing), "a wave of real enthusiasm" greeted his arrival in town. In Równe, Goldstein tells us, "My arrival . . . had the character of a great holiday. Thousands of people met me at the station and followed my auto in the streets. . . . All the meetings I addressed were so overcrowded that hundreds had to be turned away."[1] Three years later David Ben-Gurion arrived in Poland, and

1. Alexander Goldstein to "Dear Friends," May 13, 1930, Central Zionist Archives, Jerusalem (hereafter CZA), KH4/B/2164; Goldstein to ?, February 2, 1930, CZA, KH4/B/2161/1. The reader should allow for a certain degree of exaggeration in Goldstein's reports.

he, too, was astonished by the tremendous enthusiasm his presence generated. In Białystok more than a thousand people were unable to gain admission to a lecture he gave in the morning, which was attended by 1,100 supporters.[2]

Now consider the remarks of yet another Zionist emissary to Poland, Shmuel Czernowitz, who visited the country in 1927. He writes, "We find everywhere here not a Zionist organization but a corpse, a few Zionists who are ashamed of Zionism . . . we have to begin all over again." Polish Zionism, the great hope of the World Zionist movement and of the Palestinian Yishuv (Jewish community), was characterized by "complete emptiness, an organizational vacuum."[3] A year later the Hebrew poet and Keren Hayesod leader Leib Jaffe, also in Poland for fund-raising purposes, went to speak with the Polish socialist leader Ignacy Daszyński. The latter, though not unfriendly to the idea that Jews should go to Palestine, spoke with contempt of the impotence of Polish Zionism. Jaffe, unable to contradict him, wrote in shame to Arthur Hantke that even the Gentiles were aware of the movement's terrible weakness. His own impressions are summed up in the following words: "I am confronted with such apathy and lack of faith as I could never imagine to myself."[4]

What is the historian of Jewish politics (and in particular Zionism) to make of these conflicting reports? The answer is not clear, but the question prompts me to attempt some general comments on the nature of Jewish politics and its impact on the Jewish community. I shall begin with a few remarks on the "political culture" of Polish Jewry, a vague but useful term that provides a framework in which to organize some broad generalizations concerning the essential features of Jewish political life.

My first generalization derives directly from the material cited above. I would suggest that one basic characteristic of Jewish politics in Poland was the oscillation between the extremes of euphoria and despair, a kind of "manic-depressive" quality (although admittedly by the end of the 1930s depression had taken over almost entirely).

2. David Ben-Gurion, *Zikhronot*, vol. 1 (Tel Aviv, 1971), p. 603.

3. Shmuel Czernowitz to Leib Jaffe, April 2, 1927, CZA, KH4/B/2144; Czernowitz, "Ha-ziyonut be-Polanyah," July 28, 1927, CZA, KH4/B/2143.

4. For Ignacy Daszyński's comments, see the report dated October 17, 1928, CZA, KH4/B/2154; Leib Jaffe's letter to Arthur Hantke of October 19, 1928, is in ibid; the final quotation is from Jaffe to Keren Hayesod, Jerusalem, October 14, 1928, also in ibid.

There were, for example, many occasions when Jewish politicians (of various persuasions) were convinced that a "new era" had begun in Polish-Jewish relations: in 1919 after the Allied Powers meeting in Versailles agreed on the need to safeguard Jewish minority rights; in 1922 after the success of the Minorities Bloc in elections to the Sejm (House of Deputies) and the Senate; in 1926 after Józef Piłsudski's *coup d'état*. But such joy was almost always followed by despair and by the rather hasty conclusion that the whole political enterprise, the struggle for civil and national rights, was worthless (a sentiment more common, of course, in the 1930s than in the 1920s).[5] The Ugoda of 1925, when Jewish leaders in the Koło Żydowskie (Jewish Parliamentary Club) reached an agreement with representatives of the Polish government designed to improve the Jewish condition, is an excellent illustration of this phenomenon. Grossly exaggerated hopes for a new period of goodwill and cooperation between Poles and Jews all too quickly gave way to utter despair when the agreement failed to live up to the high expectations of its Jewish architects.[6] Another example is the Zionist conviction in 1920, after the San Remo Conference, that a Jewish state would shortly be established in Palestine, followed by gloom when the miracle failed to take place.[7] And then there was the case of the Fourth Aliyah, in the mid-1920s, when the feeling among some Zionists that "the beginning of redemption" was under way was soon transformed into a feeling of helplessness in the face of insurmountable obstacles.[8]

The cycle of euphoria and depression is well expressed in the fate of Jewish political organizations in interwar Poland. The Zionist movement went up and down like a yo-yo—up in the early 1920s,

5. Even Agudat Israel, probably the most stable of Jewish parties, fell prey to despair in the 1930s. Thus the lament of A. M. Rogovy in "Vi Homen dem greger . . . ," *Dos yidishe togblat*, February 7, 1935, p. 3: "There are no more illusions, one knows that everything, even the strongest words, are nothing more than a voice crying in the wilderness."

6. These expectations are lampooned in a cartoon in *Haynt*, July 17, 1925, which shows a downtrodden Jew confronted by a smiling Leon Reich, leader of the Eastern Galician Zionist Federation and a supporter of the agreement. The caption reads: "Er brengt im di yeshue" (He is bringing him salvation).

7. For an example of Zionist euphoria (not limited to Poland, of course), see the April 29, 1920, issue of *Haynt*. It includes Yitzhak Gruenbaum's article "S'blozt der shoyfer fun geule," p. 1.

8. So unhappy were some Zionists after the failure of the Fourth Aliyah that they actually placed it "on trial" for its sins against Zionism. This is reported in *Hatzefirah*, October 12, 1926, p. 4.

down with a thud in 1926–28, up again in the mid-1930s, and down again in the late 1930s. The Halutz (Pioneer movement) attracted thousands of recruits and lost them almost overnight.[9] Youth movements rose, fell, and rose again. A similar phenomenon can, I believe, be observed in the case of the Polish Bund. The Folkspartei was a force for a few years and then collapsed. And so on.

I would certainly not claim that the "neurosis" I have described was unique to Jewish politics in Poland, but it was a very striking phenomenon. What explains it? The "national character" of the Jews, and more specifically of the Eastern European Jews, may have something to do with it (as some German-Jewish observers of the Polish-Jewish scene certainly believed), but I would be happier with an explanation emphasizing the status of the Jews as a relatively powerless minority whose political fortunes were inextricably tied to outside forces over which they had little control. This condition (shared by other minorities) certainly had something to do with the cycle of exaggerated hope and deep depression that I perceive to be an integral part of Jewish political culture.

A second, somewhat related characteristic of Jewish political culture in Poland is the yawning gap between Jewish political rhetoric and Polish reality. Jewish politicians and activists propagated slogans and programs that sounded splendid but could hardly be implemented. A few examples must suffice. Some Zionists (associated with the Tarbut movement) held high the banner of "Hebraization of the Polish Diaspora" at a time when even Yiddish, the language of the Jewish masses, was fighting for its life against the ever-increasing inroads of Polish in Jewish public and private life.[10] Many Zionists clung to the hope that the Jewish Question in Poland would be eventually solved through *aliyah,* although it became more and more clear as the years passed that the number of Jews departing for the Holy Land could not possibly decrease in any dramatic way the number of Jews in Poland, which the Zionists believed was far too great (this fact was pointed out by many non-Zionists and anti-Zionists).[11] The slogan of Jewish "evacuation" from Poland was put

9. For Halutz membership figures, see Yisrael Otiker, *Tenuat Hehalutz be-Polin, 1932–1935* (Tel Aviv, 1972), pp. 26–48.

10. A conference of Tarbut teachers in Wołyń in 1936 admitted that the great hope of Hebraization had not been fulfilled. See "Yediot ha-vaad ha-merkazi," *Mesilot,* January 1936, pp. 23–31.

11. Daszyński pointed this out to Jaffe in 1928. See the material in CZA, KH4/B/2154, as cited in note 4, above.

forward by Revisionist politicians at a time when even the limited *aliyah* of the early and mid-1930s was giving way to virtually no *aliyah* at all.[12] Jewish leaders promoted the idea that Poland should be a "nationalities state" (rather than a "nation-state") at a time when it was perfectly clear that Polish public opinion was overwhelmingly opposed to such a definition.[13] Agudat Israel clung to its slogans calling for the preservation of premodern Orthodoxy during a period of growing secularization; the Bund stuck stubbornly (some might say dogmatically) to its time-honored opposition to Jewish *aliyah* to Palestine (to the amazement even of some of its Polish socialist allies) and to its equally traditional belief in the salutary process of Jewish proletarianization, even in the late 1930s. Nor did the Bund and other Jewish political forces ever abandon their slogans calling for some form of Jewish national autonomy, very much of a "nonstarter" in interwar Poland.[14]

The inflated rhetoric of Jewish politicians was accompanied by another prime attribute of Polish-Jewish political culture, namely extreme divisiveness, factionalism, personal hatreds, and the like. This aspect is very well known, and I do not have to rehearse here the endless procession of splits and the willingness to fight to the end over the finest points of doctrine (of interest, one might have thought, only to the theologian). As the Vilna Zionist leader Yaakov Vygodsky put it, in Polish-Jewish politics every compromise was regarded as "the greatest sin."[15] Nahum Sokolow remarked in 1933, during a visit to Poland, that "Polish Zionism is like a page of Rambam" (this was not meant to be taken as a compliment). "I could learn this great *'toyre',*" he continued, "but I leave it to you."[16] It does, in fact, require something of a talmudic mind to understand the differences between Left Poalei Zion and Right Poalei Zion in Eastern Galicia, Right Poalei Zion in Congress Poland, Zeirei Zion, Hitahdut, and Dror (all these parties belonged to the Zionist Left).

12. See the excellent treatment of this subject in Emanuel Melzer, *Maavak medini be-malkodet: Yehudei Polin, 1935–1939* (Tel Aviv, 1982), pp. 148–57.

13. See Yitzhak Gruenbaum, "Undzere politishe shtrayt fragn," *Haynt*, April 4, 1923, p. 2, which calls for the transformation of Poland into a nationalities state.

14. The well-known writer and socialist Andrzej Strug told Jaffe in 1934 that he could not understand why the Bund still opposed emigration to Palestine. He spoke of the "dead dogmatism of the Bund." "Mi-yomano shel L. Jaffe," March 4, 1934, CZA, KH4/B/2176.

15. Yaakov Vygodsky, in *Haynt*, April 4, 1934, p. 4.

16. Nahum Sokolow, in *Haynt*, December 26, 1933, p. 2. Sokolow also said that in Poland there are "more opinions than people." *Haynt*, November 23, 1933, p. 4.

Factionalism was accompanied by bitter feuds. Yitzhak Gruenbaum accused the Galician Zionists of being *shtadlanim* (intercessors, one of the nastiest words in the Zionist vocabulary) and went so far as to call Leon Reich, leader of the Eastern Galician Zionist Federation, a "traitor" to Zionist principles. No wonder he was prevented from speaking at Reich's funeral in Lwów in 1929.[17] Gruenbaum himself was frequently accused of being a "dictator" by his fellow General Zionists, and when he left Poland for Palestine in 1933, Revisionists shouted at him as he boarded his train, "Down with the traitor Gruenbaum."[18] The Western Galician Zionist Federation waged a ferocious campaign against the "bolsheviks" of the formidable youth movement Hashomer Hazair (which was committed to sending its graduates to Palestine while most Galician Zionist leaders remained in Poland), and the Mizrahi fought furiously against pioneers accused of eating unclean food during their passage to Palestine.[19] Nor should we forget the remarkably nasty things said about the "bourgeois" elements who made their way to Palestine during the days of the so-called Grabski Aliyah of the mid-1920s.[20] On the whole, Jewish politics in Poland resembled the proverbial "war of all against all." This cursed factionalism shocked and dismayed foreign observers and made some of them despair of anything positive ever developing from the undeniably great political energies of Polish Jewry.[21]

Empty slogans, dogmatism, endless splits—Polish Jewry enjoyed no monopoly over these facts of political life. Nonetheless it is remarkable to observe a beleaguered minority, rather homogeneous in its social structure, so much at odds with itself. Explaining this state of affairs, among other things, were the lack of political responsibility and experience that constituted the inevitable condition of a politically weak (though economically influential) minority. It

17. "Der protses Gruenbaum-Reich farn kongres-gerikht," *Haynt*, August 8, 1929, p. 3; *Haynt*, December 3, 1929, p. 1.

18. *Haynt*, November 28, 1933, p. 2.

19. On accusations against Hashomer Hazair, see the material in CZA, Z4/3234/I. On the issue of pioneers and *treyfe* food, see Jaffe to Bernard Hausner, November 20, 1933, CZA, KH4/B/2171.

20. See, for example, Gruenbaum's speech, as reported in *Hayom*, March 4, 1925, p. 4.

21. Jaffe is eloquent on this point. See also Czernowitz's letter to Jaffe of January 29, 1927, in which he bewails the "disputes and dissension" that lead to apathy and worse. CZA, KH4/B/2140.

was this state of affairs that drove the true moderates among Jewish politicians, like Yehoshua (Osias) Thon, nearly mad.[22]

Even less edifying was a fourth characteristic of Jewish political culture, again closely related to those mentioned above. I have in mind the emergence, in the 1930s, of physical violence (as opposed to verbal mudslinging) as part and parcel of the Jewish political scene. The Revisionists (and especially their organization Brit Ha-hayal) were usually singled out for their particularly conspicuous role in the political riots of this period, but others—*halutzim* (Zionist pioneers) and Jewish communists, for example—were also involved. In the 1930s fund raisers working for Keren Hayesod were beaten up by Revisionist sympathizers, and when Ben-Gurion visited Poland in 1933, he had to be protected by scores of bodyguards.[23]

This aspect of Jewish political life was, of course, a reflection of the general tendency toward violence in Eastern European political life. And it was surely less pronounced among the Jews than among their neighbors. But it was, for all that, an important phenomenon, which should be understood in the context of economic decline, of psychological despair, and perhaps also of strong acculturating tendencies among the youth.

Let me conclude this section by mentioning a more "positive" characteristic of Polish-Jewish politics, namely its "heroic" nature. I have in mind the courage of Gruenbaum speaking in a hostile Sejm in defense of Jewish rights, of Bundists standing up to the hooligans of the extreme Polish Right, of Rabbi Yitzhak Rubinstein denouncing antisemitism in the dark period of the late 1930s. This aspect of Eastern European Jewish politics—standing up to the hostile Gentile world—may perhaps be understood as the other side of the coin of Jewish political dogmatism and lack of realism. It was associated, I think, with another heroic aspect of Jewish politics, namely the obsession among some Jewish political organizations with the need to create the "new Jewish man" (or woman) who would, among other things, be able to look the Gentile in the eyes and win his (or her) respect. This motif was particularly evident in the Bund and in the Zionist youth movements, both of the Left and the Right.

It would surely be of great interest to consider the influence of

22. See Yehoshua (Osias) Thon's remarks, in *Haynt,* March 29, 1935.
23. On the fate of one unfortunate Keren Hayesod worker, see the material in CZA, KH4/B/2169.

these characteristics of Polish-Jewish politics on postwar Jewish politics, particularly in Israel. But that would constitute another article. I must go on now to discuss another question touched upon in my introductory comments, namely the impact of Jewish politics on Polish-Jewish society.

How deeply rooted in Jewish life were the various Jewish political organizations? Did they win over the hearts and minds of large sections of the Jewish public? Did they succeed in mobilizing great support? It is far from easy to answer these questions. What follows are a few thoughts on the subject.

Any discussion of the impact of Jewish politics must begin by mentioning the regional factor. I do not have to dwell on the well-known point that Jewish national politics (but not Jewish Orthodox politics) were on the whole much more appealing in the eastern borderlands than in central Poland. There was, by and large, more politicization in the small and medium-sized towns of the kresy than in the big cities in the ethnic heartland of the Polish state. It is perhaps not entirely accidental that the reports by Goldstein and Ben-Gurion quoted above were from such cities as Grodno, Vilna, and Białystok—all located in historic Jewish Lithuania.[24]

Leaving aside regional considerations, there is little doubt that in general there was an impressive degree of politicization among Polish Jews. Sokolow described it well. In the old days, he wrote, Jews would sharpen their minds by studying the rabbinic literature; today they engage in politics.[25] Particularly impressive was the politicization of previously untouched (or nearly untouched) sections of the Jewish population, above all the Orthodox. The success of Agudah in mobilizing support among the Hasidic masses of Congress Poland was significant. The Bund, too, had success in spreading its message among the Jewish working class (this process had begun, of course, well before World War I). There is little doubt that interwar Poland was an ideal environment for Jewish political mobilization (since it offered a combination of democracy, nationalism, and antisemitism) and that Polish Jewry was ideally suited for po-

24. Documentation on this point is abundant. See, for example, the report of Gershon Hanokh, "Darkei tenuatenu ba-golah," *Hapoel Hazair,* January 7, 1926, p. 16, where much is made of the "emptiness" of Jewish life in Congress Poland as opposed to the kresy.

25. Nahum Sokolow, in *Haynt,* November 23, 1933, p. 4.

litical mobilization (since it was a community deeply rooted in Jewish traditional life but undergoing a process of modernization).

On the other hand, historians of Polish-Jewish politics cannot fail to be struck by the endless complaints concerning the absence of "activists," of people to run the schools, the fund-raising campaigns, the party press. Hantke wrote a memorandum on the state of Galician Zionism in 1928 in which he deplored the fact that there were too many "jobs" and too few people.[26] A survey of Polish Zionism in the early 1920s revealed that the whole movement (surely the largest and most influential of all Jewish political movements in the country) was run by a mere handful of party stalwarts.[27] There were, to be sure, a remarkable number of organizations, but their imprint was often extremely superficial. Sometimes they sprang to life during elections, only to lapse back into inactivity after the campaign. There were always leaders prepared to be candidates for the Sejm and Senate, and even for the city council and *kehillah* (Jewish community council), but this by no means indicates widespread appeal.

I have already suggested one reason for this phenomenon—the frequent collapse of organizations as a result of some external event that led to despair and to the disappearance of party and youth movement activists. The Zionist movement (particularly the Halutz) naturally suffered from the loss of many of its leaders and supporters via *aliyah*. Let me suggest a possible additional factor: the rapid process of acculturation among Polish Jews, particularly in the second decade of the interwar period. It is certainly true that acculturation in Poland proceeded at a slower rate than in the two other great centers of Eastern European Jewry, the Soviet Union and the United States. It is also true that acculturation did not preclude the acceptance of one or another variety of Jewish nationalism. On the contrary. Nonetheless, Polonization as a major sociological process in Polish-Jewish life may have had something to do with the failure of Jewish political parties to root themselves more firmly within the community. This hypothesis should certainly be investigated more thoroughly. It is interesting, in this connection, that in tiny, independent Lithuania, where there was much less Jewish acculturation,

26. Arthur Hantke, "Bericht über die Keren Hajessod Arbeit in Ostgalizien, Westgalizien u. Schlesien," November 30, 1928, CZA, Z4/3566/1.
27. "Anketa al ha-misrad ha-histadruti be-shnat tarpa," 1921, CZA, A/127/172.

Zionism was a greater factor within the Jewish community than it was in Poland.[28]

Nevertheless, despite the ravages of despair and the impact of Polonization, Jewish politics did make a profound impression upon some members of one crucial section of the Jewish population, namely the youth. Indeed, while the Polonization process may well have reduced the number of young people drawn into specifically Jewish political movements, and while the number of Jews who joined the youth movements may not have been all that impressive, it was they who provided the man power and inspiration to keep the organizations going in times of general collapse. They are often described as the only source of light in the midst of darkness—this was certainly the case if one considers the Zionist movement during the period of sharp decline between the collapse of the Fourth Aliyah and the beginning of the Fifth.[29] Thus Ben-Gurion, dismayed with the state of Polish Jewry in 1933, consoled himself with the vision of tens of thousands of youthful idealists and wondered, "Where does this youth come from, these numerous young people so blessed with enthusiasm?"[30] It is apparent that Jewish youth were particularly vulnerable to the appeal of politics, whether Jewish or non-Jewish, since these were times of crisis in the Jewish world, when parents and the traditional religious leadership were able to offer little guidance and when youth movements and political parties often provided a much more attractive cultural and social environment than was available in the home. Thus the phenomenon of entire classes of Jewish schoolchildren joining a youth movement *en masse*.[31] But not all remained, and not all found in youth movements the solution to their problems as young Jews with little or no future in an antisemitic state. This is reflected in Ben-Gurion's prescient remark in 1933: "What will happen to this youth? . . . what can these thousands of people, the best of our youth, expect in the

28. See my "Zionist Success and Zionist Failure: The Case of East Central Europe between the Wars," in *Vision Confronts Reality: Historical Perspectives on the Contemporary Jewish Agenda,* ed. Ruth Kozodoy, David Sidorsky, and Kalman Sultanik, *Herzl Yearbook,* vol. 9 (London, 1988), pp. 190–209.

29. See, for example, the letters of Natan Bistritski in CZA, KKL5/700.

30. Ben-Gurion, *Zikhronot,* 1:640. Many of these young people eventually found their way into the ranks of the underground Komunistyczna Partia Polski (KPP, Polish Communist Party).

31. See the evidence for this in the collection of autobiographies of Polish-Jewish youth in the archives of the YIVO Institute for Jewish Research, New York.

near future?"[32] Even he could not foresee what lay in store for most of them.

This leads me to my concluding remarks, and to my final question: What can the historian of modern Jewish politics learn from the interwar Polish experience? Let me suggest a few "lessons." First, despite the fact that interwar Poland constituted an ideal environment for Jewish Diaspora politics, it can be said without too much fear of contradiction that all the Jewish "isms" failed. Autonomism, Yiddishism, Hebraism, Bundism, Agudism, and Zionism—all proved impotent to one degree or another in the face of Polish reality and the international situation. Second, the search for allies, which played so important a role in Polish-Jewish politics (as it does in Jewish Diaspora politics everywhere) was also marked by failure. What all this means is that if we assume that interwar Poland was the great testing grounds for the classic varieties of Diaspora Jewish politics, then Jewish politics failed the test. It may well be that, generally speaking, the only Jewish political doctrine that has really proven itself successful in the Diaspora (though certainly not everywhere in the Diaspora, and not at all times) is that which preaches some form of Jewish integration. In Poland, as is well known, there was no Jewish "integrationist" political force to speak of, and that is no wonder given the fact that most Poles did not think of Jewish integration as possible or desirable.[33] But neither could the various national and Orthodox political solutions put forward be implemented. Therein lies one of the tragedies of Polish-Jewish history in the 1920s and 1930s.

32. Ben-Gurion, *Zikhronot,* 1:640.
33. Polish Communists (Jewish and non-Jewish) may have constituted an exception. See Moshe Mishkinsky, "The Communist Party of Poland and the Jews," in this volume.

Gershon C. Bacon

Agudat Israel in Interwar Poland

The appearance of the Orthodox party Agudat Israel on the Polish-Jewish political scene culminated the politicization of Polish Jewry that spanned several decades. Under the relatively liberal (at least regarding political activity) German occupation of Polish territory during World War I, forces and trends that had only partial expression under the Russian regime, even during the Duma elections, now came to the surface. Political agitation and organization began in earnest, as Jews and Poles prepared for the coming of Polish independence, which had been promised by both sides battling in the Great War.[1]

In the highly politicized atmosphere of Polish Jewry, the Orthodox were late, reluctant entrants to party politics. Internal Jewish developments, rather than external factors, proved decisive in spurring some elements in the Orthodox community to organize politically. Despite its late start, Agudah fairly quickly demonstrated significant vote-getting ability, achieving a distant second-place ranking to the Zionists in elections to the Sejm (House of Deputies) and a dominant position in many *kehillot* (Jewish community councils), including long periods of control of the major communities of Warsaw and Łódź. As a major factor in Polish-Jewish politics, Agudah merits our serious attention, and it certainly deserves more balanced treatment than it has received in many vituperative contemporary and retrospective accounts of interwar Jewish politics. Of late, as we can contemplate the events of those years with a bit more historical perspective, a reconsideration of Agudah's role in that era is in order as part of a more general rethinking of our approach to the politics

This is a revised version of my essay, "The Politics of Tradition: Agudat Yisrael in Polish Politics, 1916–1939," in *Studies in Contemporary Jewry,* ed. Peter Y. Medding, vol. 2 (Bloomington, Ind., 1986), pp. 144–63.
    1. See, e.g., Yitzhak Nisenbaum, *Alei heldi* (Jerusalem, 1969), pp. 323–26

of Polish Jewry at that time. Within the limits of space allotted to me, I propose to summarize the results of research on Agudah dealt with in greater detail elsewhere[2] and to offer some more general comments on Polish-Jewish politics seen through the perspective of the specific case of Agudat Israel.

Origins

It should be stressed at the outset that Agudah never succeeded in uniting all of traditional Jewry under its banner. Beside the religious Zionists who remained within the framework of the Zionist movement, important elements of the Orthodox community continued to oppose any political organization on the part of Orthodox Jews. Such politicization, they claimed, represented too great a compromise with the secular values and ideologies that Orthodox parties supposedly came into existence to combat. Those rabbinic and lay leaders who eventually founded Agudat Israel countered that the interests and feelings of the "silent majority" of traditional Jews should not go unrepresented.

Given this deep and abiding opposition within Orthodoxy to political involvement, the political organization of Polish Orthodoxy proceeded at a slow pace. The first actions in the political sphere came after much hesitation and with obvious feelings of ambivalence. Once the decision to embark on a full-fledged partisan course was made, the mechanics of electioneering, fund raising, and canvassing for membership had to be learned. The cautious, moderate political stance that Agudah would exhibit stemmed in part from these ambivalent feelings about politics in general. If circumstances forced the Orthodox into politics, they would do their utmost to transfer age-old modes of Jewish political behavior into the realm of modern parliamentary politics.

Though representatives of Polish Jewry participated in the founding conference of the world Agudat Israel movement in Katowice in May 1912, serious organizational efforts in Poland began only in 1916, during the German occupation. The fact that the initiative for founding Agudah came from Frankfurt Orthodoxy, and that two German rabbis, Pinhas Kohn and Emanuel Carlebach, promoted po-

---

2. See Gershon C. Bacon, "Politics of Tradition," and Bacon, *Agudat Yisrael in Poland, 1916–1939: The Politics of Tradition,* forthcoming.

litical action by the Orthodox during the occupation,[3] has led some commentators to brand Agudah as a foreign implant of the separatist spirit of Frankfurt Orthodoxy in Poland.[4] While the organizational skills of these German rabbis and their connections with the German occupation regime contributed much to the formation of Agudat Haortodoksim (as Agudah was then called), what has not been adequately stressed is that their call to organize fell on willing ears. Among the followers of the Gerer Rebbe in particular they found a receptive audience. That Hasidic group had a long history of struggle against modernist tendencies in Judaism and viewed with concern the rise of Zionist and Jewish socialist parties. The founding of an Orthodox daily newspaper in 1907 with the full support of the Gerer Rebbe attests to the feeling that the traditional forces had to organize to face the secularist threat.[5] In Lithuania as well, the early years of the twentieth century witnessed several abortive attempts by major rabbinic figures at founding an Orthodox political movement.[6] Thus the founding of Agudat Haortodoksim had significant local causes that the German rabbis catalyzed and used for their own interests.[7]

Though the German rabbis may have had their own agenda, deriving from German interests in the region as well as internal Jewish issues relevant to both Germany and Poland, the Polish Agudah quickly developed an independent style and stance that had as much in common with its Zionist and Bundist opponents as it did with Frankfurt Orthodoxy. It wanted no part of the hallmark of Frankfurt Orthodoxy, namely the formation of a separatist Orthodox community. Polish Orthodoxy turned to politics not in order to preserve a dwindling minority group, as in Germany, but to provide a spokesman for a hitherto silent majority. Nor did the Polish Agudah condone any separation of religion and nation. Religion served as the basis of Jewish nationality; but it was a nationality all the same,

3. Alexander Carlebach, "A German Rabbi Goes East," *Leo Baeck Institute Year Book* 6 (1961): 62. On the activities of the German rabbis, see Mordecai Breuer, "Rabbanim-doktorim be-Polin-Lita bi-yemei ha-kibush ha-germani, 1914–1918," *Bar-Ilan* 24–25 (1989): 117–53.

4. Salo Wittmayer Baron, *A Social and Religious History of the Jews* (New York, 1937), 2:393.

5. *Meir einei ha-golah* (Brooklyn, N.Y., 1969–70), pt. 1, pp. 121–22, pt. 2, pp. 89–92; Lucy Dawidowicz, *The Golden Tradition* (Boston, 1968), pp. 210–11.

6. Hayim Oyzer Grodzinski, *Ahiezer: Kovez igerot* (1939; reprint Bnei Brak, 1970), 1:257–65, 281.

7. See *Morgn-zhurnal* (New York), August 10, 1941, p. 5.

even if Agudah rarely used the term "national minority rights" so resented by the Poles. In other areas—the realms of ideology and education—German orthodoxy did have lasting, if more subtle influences on the development of the Polish Agudah. The ideological writings of German Agudah thinkers were translated into Yiddish[8] and Hebrew and appeared regularly in Polish Agudah publications. German or German-trained Jews served in important positions in the educational system and contributed to pedagogic and children's periodicals. With all their influence, however, Agudah's ideology and educational system in Poland still retained a style and flavor of its own.

Constituency

It is difficult to identify with statistical precision the exact social and religious strata of the Polish-Jewish community that supported Agudah. Researchers have done district-by-district analyses of voting patterns in several elections,[9] but neither these nor analyses of the Polish censuses of 1921 and 1931 provide data concerning the voting patterns or demographic makeup of the various Hasidic groups that loomed so large in the Agudah camp. Ezra Mendelsohn has noted a peculiar kind of "ticket splitting" by Polish Jews that complicates the task still further: the same individual who supported the Zionists in the Sejm elections might support Agudah in the *kehillah* elections and the Bund in municipal or union elections, in each case reflecting his weighing of his own interests and of the strengths and weaknesses of the various parties.[10]

A related problem is that of evaluating the size of the pool of potential Agudah voters who did not exercise their franchise. Figures from the 1919 elections show, for the sake of illustration, that in heavily Jewish districts of Warsaw only 55 percent of eligible Jewish males and 48 percent of eligible Jewish females voted, as compared with 73 percent of non-Jewish males and 71 percent of non-Jewish females in the same districts. Beyond this extreme case in the capital, in every district surveyed (with the unexplained exception of the city of Kutno) Jewish voter participation fell below

8. E.g., Isaac Breuer, *Di shpurn fun meshiekh* (Warsaw, 1922).

9. See Ludwik Hass, *Wybory warszawskie, 1918–1926* (Warsaw, 1972).

10. Ezra Mendelsohn, "Polin," in *Ha-tefuzah: Mizrah Eropah,* ed. Yaakov Tsur (Jerusalem, 1976), p. 207.

that of non-Jewish voters. The author of the survey attributes the lower Jewish turnout to harassment of Jewish voters at polling stations by gangs of Polish nationalists.[11] In addition, I would cite the lack of political consciousness among some sectors of the Jewish population. It would seem reasonable to assume that among religious Jews, who were visible targets for antisemitic taunts, and among religious women, whose political consciousness was even lower than that of religious males, the full political potential would not be reached, but for the present this must remain a working hypothesis.

These cautionary notes aside, the general pattern that emerged in the 1919 elections remained more or less stable throughout the interwar period, even if the areas where the 1919 elections were contested did not include all the territories eventually included in the reborn Polish state. Of the 396,807 votes cast for Jewish parties in former Russian Poland, Agudah received 97,293 (24.5 percent), second only to the Zionist-dominated Tymczasowa Żydowska Rada Narodowa (Temporary Jewish National Council) list, which received 180,234 votes (45 percent).[12] Agudah deputies were returned from the Łódź and Lublin districts (Rabbis Moshe Eliahu Halpern and Abraham Perlmutter). Lack of a vote-sharing agreement with the Zionists prevented the election of a third Orthodox deputy (from the capital). Thus despite garnering one-fourth of the votes for Jewish parties, Agudah was somewhat underrepresented with two of the eleven Jewish deputies, or 18 percent of the total.[13]

Agudah's electoral strength lay mostly in the area of former Congress Poland. In this area lived the Gerer Hasidim and some other smaller Hasidic groups that, according to contemporary and retrospective accounts, formed the backbone of Agudah's support. In later elections, when voting took place in all of the Polish territory, the general picture changed little, though the Agudah did develop pockets of support in Eastern Galicia and Polish Lithuania. With some local variations (e.g., the strong popularity of the Folkspartei and its leader Noah Pryłucki in Warsaw), Agudah established itself

---

11. I. Minzin, "Di bateyligung fun di yidn in di valn tsu di poylishe seymen (1919, 1922)," *Bleter far yidishe demografye, statistik un ekonomik* (Berlin), April 15, 1932, no. 2, pp. 89–90.

12. Aleksander Hafftka, "Zycie parlamentarne Zydow," in *Żydzi w Polsce Odrodzonej*, vol. 2, ed. Ignacy (Yitzhak) Schiper, Aryeh Tartakower, and Aleksander Hafftka (Warsaw, n.d.), p. 289.

13. Hass, *Wybory warszawskie*, table 17 (between p. 68 and p. 69).

in a solid, if distant second place to the Zionists in former Congress Poland. If Agudah's claim to speak for the majority of Polish Jewry did not reflect political realities, it had established itself as a significant factor on the Polish-Jewish political scene.

In trying to understand Agudah's limited appeal in other regions of Poland, we must note first that in Congress Poland, the most developed area of the country, the struggle between traditional and modernist ideologies was most intense and lines were more clearly drawn. Thus, for example, religious Jews found a more congenial atmosphere in the Zionist movement in Galicia and Polish Lithuania than in Congress Poland.[14] Another factor contributing to Agudah's weakness in Galicia was that large segments of Orthodox Jewry in that region maintained an apolitical or antipolitical stance, preferring to leave politics to non-Jews or to secularist Jews. Personal factors also played a role in Agudah's poor showing outside Congress Poland. The Belzer Rebbe, leader of Galician Hasidism, did not wish to yield to the leadership of the Gerer Rebbe. Non-Hasidic Lithuanian Orthodox Jews may have avoided associating with a party so clearly under Hasidic domination, even if the heads of major Lithuanian *yeshivot* also participated in Agudah rabbinical councils.

Leadership

All Jewish political parties, Agudah included, chose their candidates with an eye toward presenting a distinct party image to the Jewish voting public. In Agudah's case, those men chosen as candidates for the Sejm, Senate, or local offices represented the special political approach of Agudat Israel. This approach combined the aura of religious tradition, a rabbinic stamp of approval, and the age-old image of the Jewish *shtadlan* (intercessor), the proud, dignified figure who went to the corridors of power to plead the case of his people. To fulfill these ends and others, Agudah ran three major types of candidate.

Prominent among them were, first of all, rabbis, particularly in the first election campaigns of 1919 and 1922 but continuing throughout the period. Beside making the obvious point about the religious nature of the party, rabbinical political candidates trans-

14. Ezra Mendelsohn, *Zionism in Poland: The Formative Years, 1915–1926* (New Haven, Conn., 1981), pp. 177–78.

mitted other messages as well. Traditionally garbed, long-bearded rabbis sounding patriotic declarations in eloquent Polish harked back to the idyll of Polish-Jewish cooperation during the Polish re- volts against Russian rule, a not unimportant symbol in the period of Poland's rebirth, when Jewish demands for minority rights were denounced as unpatriotic by Polish spokesmen. Indeed, Agudah played upon this association by sending to the Sejm Rabbi Abraham Perlmutter,[15] a student and colleague of the legendary patriotic figure Rabbi Dov Berish Meisels of Warsaw. The Agudah leaders also be- lieved that rabbinical candidates served an important educational function. Such Jewish deputies in the Sejm showed Orthodox Jewish youth that they could continue in the old ways yet still be part of a modern state.[16] In some cases (e.g., the noted Rabbi Meir Shapira, who ran and was elected in 1922), the rabbinic candidates were not even fluent in Polish. Finally, Agudah maintained that rabbinic fig- ures made the best *shtadlanim* in times of crisis, since their dignified demeanor and bearing best expressed Jewish anguish.

The second type of Agudah candidate and deputy, the mainstay of the party leadership, was the wealthy Orthodox businessman and communal leader. These men, who combined traditional education with some (usually informal) secular knowledge, had the where- withal to devote most of their time to communal work. In the nine- teenth century they had often been in the shadow of the even wealthier assimilationists who dominated the *kehillah* councils. In the more democratic *kehillah* regime that prevailed after Polish in- dependence, the Orthodox plutocracy came into its own. The feeling of an obligation to serve the public was a strong one, and we can find the same man serving simultaneously in the Sejm, on the city council, and on the local *kehillah* council.[17] This phenomenon also meant that the leadership would remain a small group, but within Agudah circles this situation did not arouse public criticism. Both the rabbi and businessman-type deputies were cautious, conserva- tive figures who wished to continue the "old politics" of *shtadlanut*

15. *Der moment*, February 9, 1919, pp. 3–4.

16. Dr. Hillel Seidman, former secretary to the Agudah Sejm delegation, interview with author, New York, January 29, 1976.

17. For personal data on Agudah deputies, see Tadeusz Rzepeccy and Witold Rzepeccy, *Sejm i Senat, 1922–1927* (Poznań, 1923), pp. 186, 297, 305, 334, 375–76. See also Hillel Seidman, *Ishim she-hikarti* (Jerusalem, 1970), pp. 271–75; personal archive of Lejzor Sirkis, Central Archives for the History of the Jewish People, Je- rusalem, microfilm HM 9976.

in the newer forums of the democratically elected *kehillah* and the Sejm.

Upon the formation of Agudat Israel, there emerged a third type of leader. This was the party functionary, the young Orthodox Jew recruited by the German rabbis during World War I or who had grown up in Agudah or the Agudah youth movement.[18] These young men, some of whom even possessed university degrees, took to partisan politics much more naturally than did their elders. They functioned in editorial, secretarial, educational, and other staff capacities. The rise of this younger element into the party hierarchy and elective office took time and was not without its tensions. By the 1930s younger party activists made their political debut on the local level, in the *kehillot* and in city councils.

Political Orientation and Strategy

Jewish political strategy in independent Poland took two major directions: cooperation and confrontation. With some exceptions, the Galician Zionists, the merchant groups, and Agudah tried to protect Jewish interests through cooperation with the government, while the Congress Poland Zionists, Bundists, and Folkists adopted oppositionist tactics of one form or another.[19]

Within this general framework, Agudat Israel took its stand as a proud representative of the "old" Jewish politics and the accumulated political wisdom of past centuries. This approach stemmed both from the generally conservative, religiously oriented nature of Agudah's leadership and from their assessment of Jewish political clout as severely limited. Thus Agudah, with the major exception of its joining the Minorities Bloc in 1922, pursued a minimalist political strategy based on the premise that Jews still lived in a hostile environment. Legal emancipation and democratic elections did not alter the fact that the Jews were a people in exile, the tent-dwelling Jacob dependent on the good graces of his wild brother Esau for survival.

Agudah spokesmen contended their stance was the most sensible one for Polish Jewry. Opposition for the sake of opposition was

18. See, e.g., *Eleh ezkerah* (New York, 1956), 1:110.
19. See Ezra Mendelsohn, "The Dilemma of Jewish Politics in Poland: Four Responses," in *Jews and Non-Jews in Eastern Europe, 1918–1945,* ed. Bela Vago and George Mosse (New York, 1974), pp. 203–19.

useless. In an undated memorandum to the American Jewish Joint Distribution Committee (which appears to be from the early period of Polish independence), the Polish Agudah defined its position in a slightly different manner. Agudah represented Jews who wished to regulate all aspects of life according to tradition. Jewish tradition obligated Jews to maintain a loyal attitude of peace and goodwill to the state. Jewish nationalist parties aimed at stimulating a secular national consciousness and weakening the hold of religion. Their struggle for national minority rights brought them into conflict with the policies of the state. This involved grave risks, particularly in a young state like newly independent Poland.[20]

Opponents of Agudah denounced its stance as a shameful relic of a bygone era. The Zionist leader Yitzhak Gruenbaum regarded quiet diplomacy and personal intervention as nothing more than craven submission by men who lacked the strength to speak in a loud voice about their suffering and could "only look with begging eyes at the Polish lord."[21]

For its part, Agudah regarded personal *shtadlanut* (intercession) as a necessary and honorable part of the work of any dedicated Jewish representative. It set as its goal the defense of Jewish rights in every way possible, whether the particular injustice at hand involved an individual Jew or an entire community. If circumstances demanded, personal intercession was a proper activity for a Jewish politician who daily heard the pleas and cries of the wronged.[22] This attitude may explain in part why Agudah had some Sejm deputies not overly fluent in Polish. Since an important part of their job was providing a sympathetic ear for Jews' personal difficulties, here the rabbis were admirably suited for the task.

I might comment at this juncture that this emphasis on behind-the-scenes intercession as one of Agudah's major activities makes it difficult to evaluate Agudah's overall success or failure in the interwar period. It is usually impossible to disprove or to substantiate Agudah's claim that its major successes lay in *preventing* even worse things from happening.[23]

In the Sejm, Agudat Israel pursued a general policy of cooperation

20. "Poland—Culture and Religion," n.d., Archives of the American Jewish Joint Distribution Committee, New York, file 346.

21. Yitzhak Gruenbaum, *Milhamot yehudei Polanyah* (Jerusalem, 1941), p. 289.

22. *Der moment*, February 14, 1922, p. 3.

23. Seidman interview.

with other Jewish parties while reserving for itself freedom of action and making no programmatic commitments. Thus in the Sejm, Agudah joined the Zionists and Folkists in the so-called Fraye Fereynikung fun Deputatn fun Yidishn Natsyonalitet (Free Union of Deputies of Jewish Nationality), but it would not accede to Zionist requests for an agreed-upon political program beyond a list of short-term goals, such as gaining placement of Jewish deputies on key Sejm committees.[24]

From the outset Agudah questioned one of the axioms of the new Jewish politics, namely, that the progressive forces of the Polish Left were natural allies of the Jews and therefore Jews should support the Left on general political and social questions.[25] The stalemate among Left, Center, and Right in the Sejm that produced a series of unstable coalition governments might offer the chance of concessions from either side in exchange for a handful of Jewish deputies' votes, as was proven by the events surrounding the election of the marshal of the Sejm. Even if this case of concessions granted by the Right to the Jews was an exception, Agudah argued that *a priori* identification of the Jews with one Polish political camp weakened any potential Jewish political leverage. In addition, Agudah leaders wondered whether Jews necessarily had common interests with the Left. After all, the Jews were mostly small businessmen and artisans, and their interests could often clash with those of workers and peasants. Furthermore, they argued, when it came down to basics, neither the Left nor the Right would support the Jews. The socialists might sign a few appeals or parliamentary questions, but for their own ideological reasons they, too, opposed Jewish national aspirations. Full implementation of the socialist program would lead to economic ruin of the Jewish community. Agudah therefore advocated a pragmatic, case-by-case approach to politics, voting sometimes with the Left, sometimes with the Right, but always determined by a view of what was best for Jewish interests.[26]

In speeches from the Sejm rostrum, Agudah deputies tried to

24. Jacob Shatzky (Szacki), "Yidishe politik in Poyln," in *Algemeyne entsiklopedye* (New York, 1950), vol. 9, col. 219; *Haynt*, February 10, 1919, p. 2, February 19, 1919, p. 3.

25. Yitzhak Gruenbaum, "Yidishe politik," in *Haynt yubiley-bukh* (Warsaw, 1928), pp. 64–65; Leopold Halpern, *Polityka żydowska w Sejmie i Senacie Rzeczypospolitej, 1919–1933* (Warsaw, 1933), p. 15.

26. *Der yid*, November 2, 1920, pp. 3–4, October 21, 1920, p. 2, November 17, 1920, p. 3, November 24, 1920, p. 2, November 12, 1920, p. 4.

exemplify the ideal of *shtadlanut* by combining statements of Jewish demands in nonprovocative language with expressions of confidence in the goodwill of the Polish majority. Agudah's approach, which preferred intercessionary activities, dictated that the party not take a determined public stand on every issue. Though they supported their Jewish colleagues in almost every case, Agudah deputies themselves took a public stand only when they believed a fundamental matter of Jewish dignity was at stake.[27] Otherwise, they tried to win concessions at the committee level or through intervention with public officials. Of course, Agudah deputies also took the rostrum as representatives of the Jewish deputies whenever issues arose in connection with matters under discussion in the committees on which they served.

While working in their own way to promote general political goals, Agudah representatives made special efforts to defend the interests of the Orthodox community against perceived threats. These included such matters as a proposal to exclude clerics from the Sejm and a motion to make public schools completely secular.[28] Interventions with government officials might involve protection of the sanctity of synagogues requisitioned during the Polish-Soviet War or complaints of harassment of religious Jewish soldiers.[29] Agudah's one major success in the religious field was its achieving official recognition of its *heder* system as fulfilling the requirements of the compulsory education law.[30]

The single significant deviation from Agudah's established political approach took place in 1922. Lack of government action on even minimal Jewish demands, in addition to an election law clearly designed to limit minority representation, led a reluctant Agudat Israel to join the Minorities Bloc. On numerous occasions Agudah spokesmen noted that joining the bloc was a last resort and that they preferred a united Jewish list, even if that meant reduced representation, to an association with other minority groups that openly expressed their hostility to the Polish state. Only when it became convinced that a separate Jewish list would lead to electoral disaster

27. See, e.g., the speech by Rabbi Abraham Perlmutter, in *Sprawozdanie Stenograficzne Sejmu Ustawodawczego*, February 24, 1919, col. 183.

28. *Der yid*, October 29, 1920, p. 4, March 17, 1921, p. 3.

29. *Der yid*, October 10, 1920, p. 4, October 11, 1920, p. 4.

30. Hillel Seidman, *Żydowskie szkolnictwo religijne w ramach ustawodawstwo polskiego* (Warsaw, 1937), pp. 14–17.

did Agudah assent to a purely technical bloc with no binding pro-grammatic aspects.[31] Even within the proposed Koło Żydowskie (Jewish Parliamentary Club), Agudah demanded the right to follow its own views on matters of principle.

Both in the Sejm and in the Koło Żydowskie, Agudah usually preferred to do its work quietly. In the period before Józef Piłsudski's *coup d'état* of 1926, Agudah deputies spoke infrequently from the Sejm rostrum and generally did not embark on policy initiatives. They did dissent vigorously if policies under consideration directly threatened Orthodox interests. On such matters they continued to lobby government officials and to propose amendments in commit-tee or in the Sejm chamber.

Agudah's one major political initiative in the interwar period was its alliance with the Piłsudski camp in the wake of the 1926 *coup*. Although the new regime did not alleviate any of the principal Jew-ish grievances, the change in atmosphere at least, plus confidence in Piłsudski himself, led Agudah to seek an alliance with the regime as an alternative to its reluctant membership in the Minorities Bloc. This alliance did not mean, however, that Agudah abandoned in-dependent politics altogether. In the elections of 1928 and 1930 we find the somewhat anomalous situation of Agudah running its own independent list while at the same time Agudah candidates were running on the list of the Bezpartyjny Blok Współpracy z Rządem (BBWR, Nonparty Bloc for Cooperation with the Government). This mixed strategy fit with Agudah's general aim of seeking an accom-modation with the Polish majority while still standing up for Jewish interests. From its point of view, Agudah saw little future for a Minorities Bloc strategy. Despite the impressive electoral achieve-ments of 1922, the bloc had gained little on the legislative front, while deputies working in private had done much to better the sit-uation of Jews. Jewish deputies elected on a list the government considered hostile could not expect much success in intercessionary activity.[32]

The alliance between Agudah and the Sanacja was based on a mixture of perceived common values, optimism, and wishful think-ing. As a conservative, business-based, "nonpartisan" Jewish po-litical movement, Agudah did not find it difficult to identify in

31. *Der yid,* October 13, 1922, p. 6.
32. *Der yid,* December 16, 1927, p. 6[?].

principle with a regime that preached nonpartisan, competent government for the nation and made frequent, if imprecise declarations about a just Polish society.[33] For its part, the BBWR wished to line up sympathetic representatives of the national minorities behind its call for national solidarity.

Though still pessimistic about the possibilities of immediate far-reaching changes in the Jewish situation in Poland, Agudah regarded the invitation to join the BBWR list as an unprecedented action by a major Polish group, a move toward ending chauvinistic politics and carrying out the provisions of the Polish Constitution.[34]

The moderate, loyalist stance of Agudah may have misled the Piłsudski camp into thinking that Agudah had no significant political demands of its own. Government reports and publications on Jewish political groups stressed that Agudah regarded loyalty to the government as a religious duty and that its ideology was dominated by the religious factor to the virtual exclusion of social and economic matters.[35] In the long run neither side got what it expected from this pact. Agudah could not "deliver" the Jewish vote for the Sanacja, while it continued to voice frequent criticism of government policies. The Piłsudski camp, though it was far preferable to the Endecja, still did little to deal with long-standing Jewish political grievances. Nevertheless Agudah continued to regard the alliance with the Sanacja as the best possible option. Its deputies pursued a policy of careful cataloging of Jewish needs and grievances accompanied by expressions of trust in the goodwill of the Piłsudski camp. The Agudah press blamed the failure of the government to act on any number of factors: the heritage of the pre-*coup* era, interference by lower-echelon bureaucrats, or preoccupation with the economic crisis.[36] In the final analysis Agudah deputies could only express hopes for fulfillment of the ideal of Polish-Jewish cooperation and redouble their efforts at intercession to aid individuals in distress.

After the death of Piłsudski in 1935, the alliance with the Sanacja

33. Joseph Rothschild, *East Central Europe between the Two World Wars* (Seattle, Wash., 1974), pp. 57–59. See *Der yid,* September 26, 1927, p. 6.

34. Halpern, *Polityka żydowska,* pp. 32–33; *Der yid,* January 29, 1928, p. 6, March 27, 1928, p. [?].

35. See the report on Jewish political parties entitled "Żydowskie Ugrupowanie Polityczne," in the Archiwum Akt Nowych, Warsaw, Interior Ministry, Organizational Department, Nationalities Divison, file 1062. See also S. J. Paprocki, ed., *Minority Affairs and Poland* (Warsaw, 1935), pp. 148–49.

36. *Dos yidishe togblat,* February 12, 1932, p. 2, November 8, 1934, p. 4, March 4, 1932, p. 4.

lost much of its luster and finally broke down when its successor movement, the Obóz Zjednoczenia Narodowego (OZON, Camp of National Unity), became openly anti-Jewish. The final blow to the policy of trust in the regime was the 1936 campaign waged against *shehitah* (ritual slaughter), which culminated in restrictive legislation.[37] Agudah regarded the legislation as a direct blow at the Jewish religion, the very "turf" it saw as its own. It suffered a great defeat in this affair, and it is not surprising that it suffered reversals in the *kehillah* elections of 1936 as the electorate sounded a protest vote against all the Jewish parties that had deputies in the Sejm by giving unprecedented support to the Bund at their expense. Until the outbreak of the Second World War, the few remaining Agudah deputies continued their activities of intercession, although with greatly lowered expectations. In the Sejm and the city councils, they sounded the Jewish cry of distress.

Agudat Israel, the party of tradition, followed political tactics used throughout centuries of Diaspora Jewish history. *Shtadlanut* aimed at protecting Jewish interests in a hostile political atmosphere. By patiently, proudly, but tactfully presenting Jewish needs and demands, Agudah hoped to meet some of those needs or, failing that, to protect Orthodox institutions and prevent any further erosion of the Jewish position.

The preceding short survey of the activities of the Agudat Israel party in interwar Poland leads me to several conclusions or, perhaps better, reflections on Agudah, on Orthodox Jewry in Poland, and on Jewish politics in Poland:

First, Agudah's appearance on the political scene symbolizes the end of the long-standing political alliance between the Orthodox and assimilationists that characterized *kehillah* politics in the nineteenth century. Those Orthodox Jews who preached political involvement reasoned that Zionism and Jewish socialism presented dangers that had to be met by an organized Orthodox counterforce.

Second, Agudah's debut coincided with the eclipse of *assimilationism* as a political force within the Jewish community. This fact, however, does not free us from the responsibility of making a fuller evaluation of *acculturation*, linguistic and otherwise, which contin-

---

37. *Dos yidishe togblat,* February 27, 1936, p. 2, March 6, 1936, pp. 1–2, 10, 12, March 19, 1936, p. 6.

ued, spurred onward by public education and other forces. Regional and other differences also have to be weighed in the process.

Third, the loyalist, low-key tactics of Agudah yielded little more than the more militant tactics of other Jewish parties. Agudah's failure was part of a more general failure of all the Jewish parties, Right and Left, Zionist and non-Zionist, socialist and nonsocialist, and it reflects the failure of the Second Polish Republic to reach an acceptable *modus vivendi* with the numerous minorities within its borders.

Fourth, the limited chances for major political achievements dictated that the Zionists would have to indulge in the very same intercessionary work that Agudah devoted itself to so fully. Jewish politics in Poland was conducted on two different planes: an "exalted" plane that dealt with minority rights, government subsidies, and equal participation in all aspects of Polish life, and an everyday plane that dealt with bureaucratic discrimination and softening the impact of burdensome legislation on individual Jews and Jewish institutions. The difference between Agudah and its adversaries lay more in their respective attitudes to this activity.

Fifth, Polish Orthodoxy, as opposed to its contemporaries in Germany and Hungary, stands out in its willingness to work within the framework of a unified *kehillah* and within the various unions of Jewish deputies. It may have had its hesitations; it may have refused to make any programmatic commitments in its dealings with other parties; but it was not separatist in its orientation.

Sixth, the experiment of Jewish participation in the BBWR, despite its failure in the long run, deserves further elucidation as an unprecedented gesture. Perhaps further access to archival material will reveal more on the motivations of both sides in this matter.

Seventh, the activities of Agudah, perhaps more than those of any other party, point up the all-embracing nature of Jewish political parties in interwar Poland. At every step of the way, controversy raged within Agudah circles, but eventually there developed a full range of satellite organizations (workers, youth, women, education, loan banks) that existed in the competing camps. Agudah absorbed more than a little of the methods and the approach of its secularist opponents. Even such a major point as the stress on maintaining the traditional Jewish dress in Agudah youth circles, noting that this is the "uniform" of the Jew, shows the power of the notion. The Orthodox had to "play the game" in the battle for the youth.

Finally, Agudah leaders, even if their wider political plans never materialized, felt that they had performed their religious mission as faithful emissaries of the community and, as such, served as an "address" and rallying point for traditional Jews trying to cope with political, economic, and ideological upheaval.

Edward D. Wynot

The Polish Peasant Movement and the Jews, 1918-1939

The relationship between peasant and Jew in Poland has presented a complex picture of mutual dependency and ambivalent feeling for centuries. Each needed the other for economic survival, yet simultaneously each often regarded the other with suspicion, mistrust, and, occasionally, loathing and fear. Nonetheless, until the emergence of a formally organized peasant movement in the late nineteenth century, it was extremely difficult to measure the actual perceptions and attitudes the peasantry held regarding the Jews. This essay will trace the evolution of the stance toward the Polish Jews adopted by the peasant movement in the independent Polish Republic between the two world wars. It will note the passage of this stance from varieties of political indifference and economic concern through a phase of overt antisemitism to the final stage of deemphasizing the Jewish Question as a major factor in the political program and strategy of the movement.

The relationship between the organized Polish peasant movement and the non-Poles inhabiting common territory concerned the movement's leaders well before the advent of national independence. The first recorded program declaration in 1886 called for the establishment of ethnically homogeneous and independent states on the basis of national self-determination, under which each nationality would be free to govern its own destiny. Without mentioning specific

I would like to thank the director and staff of the following institutions for their assistance in researching this subject: the Archiwum Akt Nowych, Zakład Historii Ruchu Ludowego przy Naczelny Komitet Wykonawczy Zjednoczowego Stronnictwa Ludowego, and the Main Library of Warsaw University, all of Warsaw; the Russian and East European Institute and Main Library of Indiana University, Bloomington, Indiana; and the Russian and East European Center and the Library of the University of Illinois, Champaign-Urbana, Illinois.

ethno-religious groups by name, the declaration noted that "the extension of Polishness [*polskość*] at the expense of other peoples" would be "harmful for the national future, for in this fashion we will create for ourselves enemies where we could have friends."[1] Nearly twenty years later, in 1903 in Austrian Galicia the first real peasant political party—the Polskie Stronnictwo Ludowe (PSL, Polish Peasant Party)—issued its initial program and spoke more directly to the question of interethnic relations. After expressing its desire that complete freedom of worship be extended "in equal measure to the believers of all religions and sects," the party focused on individual ethno-religious groups. It called for a future system that would permit the Lithuanians and Ruthenians (Ukrainians) to "stand as equals in the area of political rights," while assuring "not one but all three peoples of complete freedom for their national development." The Jews were singled out for special attention. The PSL perceived two distinct types of Polish Jew. One, "having a sense of national affinity for the Polish community, wanting to be set apart from the larger society only by religion," would be a welcome member citizen of the New Poland. Quite the opposite case was presented by the Jew who was a member of a "tribe" (*szczep*) adhering by custom to Germanic culture, a tribe which considers itself alien to Poland and which we also consider as such"; the party preferred to remove this type of Jew from Poland through the emigration to Palestine espoused by the Zionist movement.[2]

The attitude of the peasant movement took a more extreme turn as World War I approached. Several factors combined to produce an environment hostile to the emergence of amicable peasant-Jewish relations. One was the increasing economic development under way throughout the Polish lands, which made the Jews appear to pose a major obstacle to the survival, let alone the prosperity, of a peasantry caught up in the changing agrarian structure. Indeed, one scholar has observed, "Much more than the waning power of the landowners, the passing of the Jewish economic domination spelt the end of the near feudal system in the Polish countryside." In these

---

1. "*Przegląd Społeczny*," 1886–1887, ed. Krzystof Dunin-Wąsowicz (Warsaw, 1955), p. 64, quoted in Czesław Wycech, "Polityczna myśl ludowa w świetle programów stronnictwo chłopskich," *Roczniki Dziejów Ruchu Ludowego* 1 (1959): 14.

2. "Program Polskiego Stronnictwa Ludowego w Galicji," in *Materiały źródłowe do historii polskiego ruchu ludowego* (hereafter *MZHPRL*), vol. 1: *1864–1918*, ed. Krzystof Dunin-Wąsowicz et al. (Warsaw, 1966), doc. 16, pp. 76–77.

circumstances the logical step for the populist leaders was in a direction designed "to accomplish what they had always thought of doing and to take over the economic life of the villages completely."[3] At the same time the outbreak of severe anti-Jewish violence in Russian Poland fostered an atmosphere in which antisemitic words and deeds were viewed as positive statements of discontent with the traditional Jewish role in Poland. Moreover, the tendency of the infant peasant movement to ignore the landless proletariat and poor smallholders opened the opportunity for the socialists to gain adherents among these groups. In both Russian and Austrian Poland, the Polska Partia Socjalistyczna (PPS, Polish Socialist Party) agitated in the rural areas and achieved some notable electoral success in Austrian Poland. Since some of the PPS activists were Jewish, both aristocratic and peasant leaders reacted to this threat by publicly equating socialists and Jews as sworn enemies of the Polish–Roman Catholic peasant.

The growing anti-Jewish outlook among certain segments of the peasant movement erupted into the open following a major split within the PSL on the eve of World War I. In 1913 its leader, Jan Stapiński, seceded with its more radical members and formed a new party called the PSL–Lewica (Left). The remaining members, dominated by more conservative elements, reconstituted into the PSL–Piast, recalling the mythical peasant who had founded the first Polish dynasty. This party with its new leader, a prosperous farmer of moderate views and sound political instincts named Wincenty Witos, was destined to play a major role in future Polish political life.[4] The division of the peasant movement into two rival wings—one moderate, aiming its message at the growing peasant middle class and hence willing to cooperate with the bourgeoisie, the other more radical and ready to align with the workers' movement—became a constant factor in independent Poland. More to the point of this essay, it made an immediate impact on the attitude of the peasant

3. Olga Narkiewicz, *The Green Flag: Polish Populist Politics, 1867–1970* (London, 1976), p. 149. There is ample evidence of this line of reasoning in the articles by early PSL leaders Bolesław Wyslouch and Jan Stapiński in their weekly publication, *Przyjaciel Ludu*, and in the words of a local peasant official, Jan Słomka, whose memoirs have been translated into English as *From Serfdom to Self-Government: Memoirs of a Polish Village Mayor, 1842–1927*, trans. W. J. Rose (London, 1941).

4. For details on the split, see Andrzej Garlicki, *Powstanie Polskiego Stronnictwa Ludowego Piast* (Warsaw, 1966). The best biographical study of Wincenty Witos is by Andrzej Zakrzewski, *Wincenty Witos: Chłopski polityk i mąż stanu* (Warsaw, 1977).

movement toward the Jews. Desiring to obtain effective political allies for the pending electoral struggles, Witos turned to the Narodowa Demokracja (National Democracy, its adherents the National Democrats, or Endeks) for support. This socially and politically conservative movement featured rabid antisemitism among its main doctrines. Rather than being uneasy over a partnership with this type of organization, Witos apparently felt ideologically as well as politically comfortable, even retrospectively. In his memoirs he asserted that, although the Endeks "could be criticized for their social ideals, their national ideals were, in my opinion, beyond reproach; they stood above the others, because they had the courage of their convictions and were not afraid to voice them in public." Not coincidentally, antisemitic articles began to appear shortly thereafter in the main newspaper of the Witos party, *Piast*. Perhaps the best exposition of the PSL–Piast stance was an editorial entitled "Ludowcy a Żydzi" (Populists and the Jews), published in the first issue of 1914, for it presented the essence of the main Polish peasant party's views on the Jewish Question: "Populists are not antisemites in the sense that they would like to expel, even through forceful means, the Jews from Polish territory. . . . But they aspire to the expulsion of the Jews from the countryside, and will aspire to this until it has been accomplished."[5]

The outbreak of World War I brought two important developments to the Polish peasant movement, although neither had an immediate effect on the peasant-Jewish relationship. One was the formation of a new populist party in late 1915 through the merger of three smaller peasant groups active in the Russian zone. The result was the Polskie Stronnictwo Ludowe (PSL, Polish Peasant Party), later officially renamed the PSL–Wyzwolenie (Liberation) to distinguish it from its Austrian counterpart, with which it differed on many key points. Its program, which one eminent historian of this period has called "a curious blend of intelligentsia radicalism and anti-clericalism which adopted the patriotic slogans of [Józef] Piłsudski," completely omitted mention of the party's stance toward the non-Polish population, apart from a generally stated commitment to "equality of all citizens before the law." It did call, however, for the formation of agricultural, commercial, and credit cooperatives to

5. Wincenty Witos, *Moje wspomnienia*, vol. 2 (Paris, 1964), p. 36; "Ludowy a Żydzi," *Piast*, January 4, 1914, no. 1. See also the issues for January 11, 25, 1914, nos. 2, 4, for samples of anti-Jewish party opinion.

end the "exploitation by the middlemen" of the peasantry and promote the "social and economic development of the people."[6] It soon became apparent that the PSL–Wyzwolenie was an affiliate of the Piłsudski movement designed to rally the peasants to that political orientation. Not surprisingly, the conservative and Endek circles in Russian Poland countered with their own rural party. In February 1917, with the active backing of the Roman Catholic hierarchy and the above-mentioned groups, several rural activists created the Zjednoczenie Ludowe (Peasant Union). Its staunch political and social conservatism was matched only by its overt Catholicism. After declaring that other religions, "in keeping with the tradition of the nation, will have guaranteed toleration," the party program asserted that "the Roman Catholic church, as the dominant religion, should be surrounded with special care by the government and community"; among other ways, this could be accomplished through the "universal, compulsory, and free education in elementary schools in the Catholic and national spirit." The program was even more direct in assessing the need to establish rural cooperatives "for the effective fight against usury, immorality in trade, cheating, and exploitation."[7] The Peasant Union competed quite successfully with the Wyzwolenie for mass rural support until some of their key leaders defected to the Piast in 1918.

The armistice of that year, together with the formal establishment of the independent Polish Republic, brought a new dimension to the peasant-Jewish relationship. Witos noted that it "was not a surprise" that in many rural areas the Jewish Question surfaced "with utter ferocity," for "if the population had many reasons for disliking the Jews before the war, during the conflict these reasons increased considerably." While stating his disapproval of the rise of violent antisemitism among the peasantry, he nonetheless asserted, "It is essential to note that the Jews themselves contributed much to this" through their black-marketeering and profiteering activities, along with the perceived preferential treatment accorded them by the occupying authorities. Consequently, "It is not surprising that the de-

6. Stefan Kieniewicz, *The Emancipation of the Polish Peasantry* (Chicago, 1969), p. 242; "Program Polskiego Stronnictwa Ludowego w Królestwie Polskim," in *MZHPRL*, vol. 1, doc. 141, pp. 422–26. For an in-depth examination of the formation of the PSL–Wyzwolenie, see Jan Molenda, *Polskie Stronnictwo Ludowe w Królestwie Polskim, 1915–1918* (Warsaw, 1965).
7. "Program Zjednoczenia Ludowego," in *MZHPRL*, vol. 1, doc. 142, pp. 426–28.

sire for revenge was aroused among the masses, and when the opportunity arose, they wished to carry it out."[8]

Meanwhile, the 1919 elections to the Sejm (House of Deputies) had returned deputies of the two main peasant parties to this legislative body, and both used its initial sessions as a forum to outline their positions on the major issues facing the infant state. Given the earlier association between the National Democratic and Piast movements, together with the recent infusion of some activists from the Peasant Union to the latter, the moderate views expressed in the declaration by Piast president Witos are somewhat surprising. Without referring directly to the ethno-religious minorities, he stated that, while "standing on a Catholic foundation, we respect the freedom of all religions." Conversely, the Wyzwolenie had drawn closer to the left wing of the Piłsudski camp, a development reflected in the statement by its president, Błażej Stolarski. Speaking directly of the minority inhabitants of the Polish eastern provinces, Stolarski called for a "union of peoples—free with free, equal with equal." Turning to religious affairs, he conceded that Wyzwolenie recognized that "the huge majority of the nation" was Roman Catholic, but nevertheless was "against the abuse of the position and influence of the church in political and social matters"; he further pledged that his party would work to see that other religions "are granted guarantees of complete freedom."[9]

Shortly thereafter Piast adopted its first formal program in independent Poland. Although it made no specific reference to the national minorities, the program opened by stating the party's total commitment to "guaranteeing and safeguarding real power for the Polish people [lud], the lawful steward of the state." It emphasized that "freedom of convictions and freedom of religion must be assured" to all citizens, but underscored the vital need to shape a "healthy and honest Polish mercantile class" to ensure prosperity. The former Piast colleagues now reconstituted in the PSL–Lewica

8. Witos, *Moje wspomnienia*, 2:184–85. Witos added that the Polish authorities tried to suppress the anti-Jewish outbursts and restore order but faced a difficult dilemma, since the people began to believe that the officials "were in league with the Jews and conspiring to oppress and exploit the peasant together."

9. "Deklaracja PSL Piast w Sprawach Ogólnych, Złożona, przez Prezesa Stronnictwa Wincentego Witosa na Posiedzeniu Sejmu Ustawodawczego," in *MZHPRL*, vol. 2: *1918–1931*, ed. Stanisław Giza and Stanisław Lato (Warsaw, 1967), doc. 1, pp. 9–12; "Deklaracja PSL–Wyzwolenie w Sprawie Stosunku do Rządu, Złożona przez Prezesa Stronnictwa Błażeja Stolarskiego na Posiedzeniu Sejmu Ustawodawczego," in ibid., doc. 2, pp. 12–16.

had issued their program a few weeks earlier, and they had been more direct in addressing the minorities issue. The program favored granting the non-Poles equal rights, but would only guarantee them "those rights which the Polish nation will have in the mother countries of those minorities." The party was less circumspect than Piast had been on the question of the largely Jewish merchants and creditors in rural Poland, as it called for "the complete elimination of private commercial intermediaries" and their replacement by cooperatives, in order to "remove the profiteering and speculation of the middlemen."[10]

The Wyzwolenie party program, which did not appear until March 1921, was predictably more liberal in its attitudes toward the minorities than had been its Piast or Lewica rivals. Article 3 demanded complete freedom for the minorities to develop their own distinctive cultures and to use their native languages in educational, administrative, and judicial settings; it also endorsed the granting of territorial autonomy where concentration of a minority warranted it. Article 13 dealt with civil and legal rights. After affirming that the party considered "the safeguarding of the rights of man and the citizen" as one of its "most pressing tasks," Wyzwolenie insisted that no citizen could be deprived of his or her rights for reasons of "social standing, religion, or nationality, whether this deprivation is the result of law or the customs of privilege enjoyed by another social class, religion, or nationality." A further article (article 52) acknowledged the "absolute right to the free national development of all peoples, who wish to develop themselves independently." At the same time the party urged the rapid establishment of credit as well as commercial cooperatives for small peasant farmers but refrained from speaking of "parasitic middlemen" or in other antisemitic innuendos.[11]

The earlier, more tolerant stance of Piast changed abruptly under the stress of the Polish-Soviet War, during which Witos served as prime minister. His memoirs record his own personal bitterness and disgust, as well as that of the Polish peasants, at the extent to which the Jews openly supported the Bolsheviks as the Red Army drove

10. "Program Polskiego Stronnictwa Ludowego Piast," in ibid., doc. 5, pp. 25–29; "Deklaracja i Program Polskiego Stronnictwa Ludowego Lewica," in ibid., doc. 4, pp. 19–25.

11. "Program Polskiego Stronnictwa Ludowego Wyzwolenie," in ibid., doc. 13, pp. 49–58.

into Poland. The party's central press organ regularly featured articles and editorials denouncing Jewish conduct as disloyal, with Witos himself penning some of the more overtly anti-Jewish pieces, even after hostilities had ceased.[12] Not surprisingly, this outlook found expression in the revised party program issued in 1921. Although it stated the Piast desire to live with the minorities "according to the principles of justice and harmonious cooperation" and pledged the party to work for the "statutory guarantee of full and free development of their cultural and national life" (article 14), the program contained several qualifying provisions. It announced the party's wish to "apply Christian principles in private, social, and state life" (article 4) and demanded that the cities become "vital centers of Polish national culture and Polish economic life" (article 10). It also called for the establishment of cooperatives as the best way to develop trade "in a direction meeting the interest of the people" (article 28) and promoted the "creation and development of Polish industry and handicrafts as a basic condition for guaranteeing the nation and state their true independence" (article 12). Finally the party targeted the "formation of national cultural values as one of its most urgent tasks" (article 12, part 2). Although never stated outright, an anti-Jewish bias was clearly implied in all references to the economic or cultural development and well-being of the "Polish nation." This attitude found echo in a small regional competitor, the Chłopskie Stronnictwo Radykalne (Radical Peasant Party). Its program pledged commitment to the defense of individual liberties, including religion, "without exception" (article 11), but made this broad statement of tolerance conditional to the extent that the ethno-religious minorities "will not act with any hatred in their relationship to the Republic."[13]

The entire complex question of national minorities in Poland, including the situation of the Jews, became a major political issue with the signing of an agreement among the Piast, National Democratic, and Chrześcijańska Demokracja (Christian Democracy) parties in May 1923 to create a parliamentary majority and form a

---

12. Witos, *Moje wspomnienia*, 2:307–8, 323–24, 391–92. See also Witos's editorials: "Żydzi a Polska," *Piast*, October 9, 1921; "Jeszcze Żydzi a Polska," *Piast*, October 23, 1921.

13. "Program Polskiego Stronnictwa Ludowego Piast," in *MZHPRL*, vol. 2, doc. 14, pp. 58–71; "Program Chłopskiego Stronnictwa Radykalnego," in ibid., doc. 15, pp. 71–80.

stable government. Generally known as the Łanckoroński Pact, this lengthy document pledged its signatories to strive for Polish ethnic and Roman Catholic religious domination over every facet of the country's life, especially in gaining a monopoly over the economic, political, and administrative systems. Of particular concern to the Jews was the pact's specific call for the establishment of a *numerus clausus* in education, public sector employment, and the awarding of government contracts.[14]

The progressive elements within the peasant movement reacted promptly to this overt swing of Piast to the antisemitic Right. After numerous statements denouncing the pact and its signatories, in November 1923 Wyzwolenie joined forces with the Jedność Ludowa (Peasant Unity), a small radical group. Its program dealt extensively with the ethno-religious minorities and their relationship to the peasantry. After committing the new organization to "removing misunderstandings or struggles between nations through mutual familiarity and cooperation" (article 21) and noting the constitutional guarantees of minority rights, it demanded that there be "no discrepancy between the Constitution and life" (article 23). This included observing the constitutional promise of access for all children to education in their native tongue and the complete equality for all religions and religious organizations. Turning to individual minority groups, the party recognized the need to extend to the Jews "the full rights of which all citizens of Poland can take advantage," since "genuine concern for the guarantee to the minorities of their citizenship rights is not just a liberal slogan, but an act of creative state policy" (article 28). However, this concern did not prevent the new organization from repeating the standard call for the development of cooperatives to "do away with the middlemen" (article 107). Nor did it hinder one of the group's deputies in the Sejm, Józef Putek, from castigating the Koło Żydowskie (Jewish Parliamentary Club) for supporting the proposed Concordat with the Vatican to settle the status of the Roman Catholic church in Poland.[15]

14. "Zasady Współpracy Stronnictwa Polskiej Większości Parlamentarnej w. Sejme r. 1923, Tak Zwany Pakt Łanckoroński," printed in its entirety in ibid., vol. 2, doc. 16, pp. 80–92.

15. "Program Polskiego Stronnictwa Ludowego Wyzwolenie i Jedność Ludowa," in ibid., doc. 20, pp. 116–34; *Sprawozdanie Stenograficzne Sejmu Rzeczypospolitej,* March 26, 1925, cols. 3–34. Among other things, Józef Putek declared that "we are not and have not been an antisemitic party, and we do not need to be an antisemitic party, but it does not follow from this that we are supposed to be some kind of *Judenschutztruppe* and cover up the political mistakes made by the Koło Żydowskie on its own authority."

The peasant movement soon had more pressing matters before it. On May 12, 1926, Piłsudski staged a successful *coup d'état* against a newly formed Center-Right government headed by Witos. Piłsudski, who had withdrawn from active political life in 1923 rather than accept the dominance of his National Democratic rivals, seemed the ideal person to end the problems facing Poland's minorities, especially the Jews. By 1926 he was avowedly nonpartisan, yet with a leftist past that appeared to preclude an antisemitic orientation and simultaneously assure the hostility of the Right and Center. Not surprisingly, the Jews were at first among his most avid supporters. Of the peasant parties, Piast was the most immediately affected by this shift in political power.[16] It devoted the next few years to condemning the programs and actions of the various Piłsudski-sponsored governments. If its words of criticism were consistent, however, the party's stance on the minorities was not. The revised program adopted in November 1926 illustrates the Piast ambivalence on this particular issue. On the one hand, the party sharpened its ethno-religious chauvinism. The article dealing with religion continued to endorse the principle of complete religious freedom but also declared that Piast stood for "Christian principles and their observance in private, social, and state life, proceeding from the premise that the Christian world view, deeply imbedded in the life of the community, can only prolong peace and the harmonious coexistence of people and nations" (article 6). The program also stated the determination to work for "the implementation of proper changes in the Constitution and the adoption of such an electoral ordinance that would guarantee that the Sejm will be an expression of the will of the majority of the Polish nation" (article 3). Yet simultaneously that portion of the program dealing specifically with the minorities was far more positive and conciliatory than the 1921 version. After reaffirming the earlier commitment to the principle of equality for all citizens, the party added that, "standing on the position of the unity of the Polish Republic," it recognized "the right of all nationalities residing in the state to their free cultural and economic development" and announced the Piast intent to cooperate "economically and culturally with the farmers of the national minorities" (article 9).[17]

16. The best study of the Piast party during this critical period between Piłsudski's *coup* and the Depression is Józef Szaflik, *Polskie Stronnictwo Ludowe "Piast": 1926–1931* (Warsaw, 1970).
17. "Program Polskiego Stronnictwa Ludowego Piast, Uchwalony na Nadzwyczajnym Kongresie w Krakowie," in *MZHPRL*, vol. 2, doc. 38, pp. 216–41.

These lofty ideals notwithstanding, Piast maintained an anti-minority stance, thereby suggesting the tactical nature of the above sentiments. An example of this continued hostility was the press campaign against a proposed change in the local government electoral ordinance. Press analyses claimed its passage would strip the Polish population from any local posts in certain parts of the country, thereby "depriving it completely of influence over the *gmina* [community] and county" and would "thrust the Polish minority out beyond the limits of life, consigning it to the role of helots in its own state."[18] Witos frequently complained of the preferential treatment accorded the national minorities, including the Jews.[19] The emergence of another competing party, the Stronnictwo Chłopskie (Peasant Party), with a far more conciliatory approach to the minorities, and the continued prominority position of Wyzwolenie further accented Piast's ethnic chauvinism.[20]

The second decade of independence brought new challenges and fresh opportunities to the Polish peasant movement. Chief among the former was the Great Depression, which hit Poland harder than most other countries and lasted longer there. It proved particularly devastating for the agrarian sector, which felt its effects earlier than the industrial or commercial branches of the national economy. This was especially true for the peasantry, as living conditions declined to primitive levels in most areas of rural Poland. In the midst of this mass suffering, which saw membership support for the various peasant parties fall precipitously, the Piłsudski regime launched an offensive against the leaders of the chief opposition groups. The so-called Brześć Purges hit Piast especially hard, as Witos and other key officials were arrested and tried for treason. Upon their convictions, they were offered the choice of prison or exile, with Witos

18. Wincenty Witos, "O ustawach samorządowych," *Wola Ludu,* January 16, 1927. See also the articles by Witos—"Moje spostrzeżenia w Małopolsce Wschodniej," *Wola Ludu,* June 19, 1927; "Na drodze ku anarchii," *Piast,* January 16, 1927—in which he expressed the fear that the removal of ethnic Poles from positions of local governmental power will "open the gates to anarchy and, following that, Bolshevism."

19. See especially his speech to the Sejm on January 26, 1927, in which he recounted examples of this preferential treatment and concluded, "Gentlemen from the national minorities, you complain about wrongs done you, but you see that you are, in fact, privileged." *Piast,* February 6, 1927.

20. For example, see the program of the Stronnictwo Chłopskie adopted in June 1927, "Program Stronnictwa Chłopskiego," in *MZHPRL,* vol. 2, doc. 41, pp. 261–67; and the electoral platform statement of Wyzwolenie for 1928, *Wyzwolenie,* January 22, 1928.

and several others choosing the latter. The levels of social, economic, and political tension rose to new highs in the beleaguered country, which faced a resurgence of popular antisemitism. The National Democrats, quick to exploit the situation for political advantage, opened a major campaign to blame the Jews for all of Poland's ills; indeed, after charging the government with drawing its chief backing from the Jews, a leading Endek observed in July 1931 that "Polish public opinion representing all social segments will turn against the Jews, and this will be solely the result of their own policies."[21]

The reaction among those Poles not as committed to antisemitism as a fundamental element of their program appeared to validate this observation and provided a grim harbinger of things to come. This was especially true of the peasantry. In the face of concerted political and economic pressures, the three main parties—Piast, Wyzwolenie, and Stronnictwo Chłopskie—finally ceased their bickering and merged to form a single organization—the Stronnictwo Ludowe (SL, Peasant Party) in March 1931. Its program reflected the compromises inherent in such a fusion. This merger was clearly evident in the sections dealing with issues affecting the minorities. The more liberal Wyzwolenie and Stronnictwo Chłopskie views emerged in the article governing civil rights, wherein the party pledged "to defend tirelessly that equality before the law guaranteed all citizens by the Constitution" (article 4), and in the article on religion, which excluded the traditional Piast recognition of the special place that Christianity, especially Roman Catholicism, should occupy in public as well as private life (article 6). Article 9 dealt specifically with the party's relationship to the minorities. After restating its endorsement of complete civil and legal equality for all ethnic and religious groups, the SL advocated the right of "all minorities inhabiting the state to their cultural and economic development, along with the use in full of the local governments as defined by state laws in the limits of the entire Republic." It further condemned "all oppression and lawlessness" directed against the non-Poles but insisted that they consent to "a sincere fulfillment of their obligations to the state." Working within this framework the SL promised to "strive for cooperation, particularly in the economic realm, with the farmers of other nationalities in the state." In return for accepting these

21. R. Rybicki, "Polityka żydowska," *Gazeta Warszawska*, July 19, 1931.

formulations on minority relations, Piast received inclusion in the new program of its usual assertion that urban centers had to become "vital centers of Polish culture and economic life" (article 10). In addition, the section treating education and culture (articles 11–16) omitted the other parties' call for public-funded instruction for all minorities in their native languages and retained the Piast definition of the role of culture as a prime vehicle for shaping "national cultural values" (*narodowe wartości kulturalne*). Finally, without mentioning the Jews by name, the program incorporated the standard demand for the development of extensive producer, commercial, and credit cooperatives to remove the largely Jewish middleman from economic life (article 23).[22]

Unhappily, this generally enlightened position could not long withstand the mounting internal pressures against the Jews. Within two years the Polish peasants were displaying evidence that the ceaseless National Democratic hammering away at the Jews as the source of all the country's evils was bearing fruit among the rural masses. In 1933 the Instytut Gospodarstwa Społecznego (Institute of Social Economy)—what today might be termed a "liberal think tank"—in conjunction with the SL conducted a survey to gather personal testimonies from peasants regarding their past experiences and present circumstances in depression-wracked Poland. The first volume of selected responses revealed overt antisemitism in nearly one-fourth of those surveyed. Although actual wording varied according to the individual authors, the general viewpoint expressed was consistent on certain points: The Jew was a parasitic middleman who exploited the naive, ignorant peasants by paying submarket prices for farm products and then charging exorbitant ones for manufactured goods or essential raw materials, often dealing dishonestly with them in the process; the Jew was an archetypal "loan shark" who deceived the peasants into overextending their credit at usurious rates, then foreclosing on their land; the Jew was responsible for using his influence abroad to knock the bottom out of the international market for Polish agricultural products. The second volume contained fewer peasant contributions, but more than one-half of those expressed anti-Jewish feelings to some extent.[23]

---

22. "Program SL" [1931], in *MZHPRL*, vol. 3: *1931–1939*, ed. Jan Borkowski and Józef Kowal (Warsaw, 1966), doc. 2, pp. 13–23.
23. *Pamiętniki chłopów*, nos. 1–51 (Warsaw, 1935); *Pamiętniki chłopów*, ser. 2 (Warsaw, 1936).

The subsequent activities of the peasant movement reflected its awareness of the current mood of its constituents. The chief council of the SL approved as "proper" the government declaration in September 1934 that it would no longer feel bound to honor the 1919 Minorities Treaty.[24] The party's next moves appeared to validate Witos's observation from exile that by 1935 the substitute head of the SL, Stanisław Mikołajczyk, had drawn closer to the National Democrats in outlook and was even discussing the possibility of merging the youth organizations of both parties. The refusal of the Jewish parties to join in the general opposition boycott of the 1935 parliamentary elections in protest against the undemocratic nature of the newly revised electoral ordinance may have been the final determining factor in altering the SL attitude toward the Jews.[25] This attitude was fully demonstrated in the new program adopted at the party congress held in early December 1935. After restating its commitment to the "full equality of citizens before the law," it called for "absolute respect" for the "principles of Christian morality in public life" (section IV). Section VII dealt extensively with the minorities issue. It opened with the general statement that "all citizens of the state, without regard for their nationality and religion, are to be guaranteed equal rights" and then devoted specific attention to each major ethno-religious group in turn. The segment treating the Jews is sufficiently significant to warrant direct quotation:

> In view of the fact that historical circumstances have not permitted the Polish nation to develop its own middle class, which could take over as trade and credit intermediaries, and these social functions have fallen into the hands of a *Jewish element* more powerful on a percentage basis than in any other European country, whereas the slogans of assimilating this element have appeared unrealistic and the Jews in Poland today constitute a consciously alien nation—*the most vital interest of the Polish nation and state demand that the above functions pass over in an increasingly greater degree to the hands of Poles.* It is necessary to achieve this not through fruitless acts of violence, which lead to the impoverishment of the nation's soul, but primarily *through the development of cooperatives, the organization of producers and their direct contact with consumers, and the support of the Polish element in all economic life.* Standing

---

24. "Uchwały Rady Naczelnej SL w sprawach politycznych, międzynarodowych, oświatowych i gospodarczych (September 30, 1934)," in *MZHPRL*, vol. 3, doc. 59, pp. 172–78.

25. Wincenty Witos, *Moje tułaczka, 1933–1939*, ed. Józef Szaflik (Warsaw, 1967), p. 219. Witos bitterly asked, "Did the Jews give this help [to the regime] for nothing, or maybe will their privileges go so far that not only peasants but all Poles will again feel themselves foreigners in their own Fatherland?" *Moje wspomnienia*, 2:402.

on the basis of equal citizens' rights possessed by the Jews, it is essential to strive to settle the Jewish Question through supporting with all our strength the emigration of Jews to Palestine and those other areas which should be obtained for Jewish colonization by means of an international accord.

It appeared that several members of the left wing in the SL who seceded from that party and formed a reconstituted Stronnictwo Chłopskie were correct in commenting that "the former Piast, with its Endek attitudes, has triumphed in the battle for control" of the SL.[26]

Meanwhile anti-Jewish violence, sparked chiefly by the National Democrats, was spreading rapidly throughout Poland, especially in the rural areas. To compound the problem, the government had embarked on a course of action designed to give official sanction to antisemitism in a vain attempt to retain its power following Piłsudski's death in May 1935.[27] Consequently anti-Jewish excesses that in some cases resembled minipogroms increased throughout the first half of 1936. These activities drew sharp retorts from some elements within the peasant movement, although the SL remained silent. The Stronnictwo Chłopskie issued strong denunciations of the "chauvinistic anti-Jewish uproar" as "shameful work of determined enemies of the rural people, intended to demoralize and disunify the masses while diverting them from the class struggle against fascism and capitalism."[28] More significant, the SL youth group Wici joined with its socialist counterpart to demand state-funded private elementary schooling "in the native tongue of the child" and called for the free development of their culture for all minorities, reminding the authorities that " 'the nation which opposes other nations cannot be free itself.' "[29] Prodded by this rebuke from its youth movement and a letter from Witos, the central office

26. "Program SL" [1935], in *MZHPRL*, vol. 3, doc. 92, pp. 249–54, italics in the original; "Uchwały CKW Stronnictwa Chłopskiego (Grupa Stawiarskiego) w Sprawach Politycznych," in ibid., doc. 93, pp. 254–55.

27. This subject is discussed in detail in Edward D. Wynot, " 'A Necessary Cruelty': The Emergence of Official Anti-Semitism in Poland, 1936–1939," *American Historical Review* 76 (1971): 1035–58.

28. See "Rezolucje CKW Stronnictwa Chłopskiego w Sprawach Politycznyck i Wewnętrznych," in the party's newspaper, *Chłopskie Jutro*, January 12, March 29, 1936.

29. "Deklaracja Praw Młodego Pokolenia Polski (Ogłoszenie)," in *MZHPRL*, vol. 3, doc. 100, pp. 266–70. The full name of the youth group was Związek Młodzieży Polskiej (ZMP, Union of Polish Youth), known popularly as Wici from the title of its official journal.

of the SL issued a directive to its provincial and county leaders ordering them to avoid any cooperation with either the regime or the Endeks, since the latter "stand even more clearly on the basis of a fascist dictatorship."[30]

This disavowal of joint activity with the National Democrats did not mean the peasant movement was ready to abandon its hostile stance toward the Polish Jews. The Wici indicated as much with its program of May 1936. The political section repeated the warning against cooperation with the Right, but the economic portion re-affirmed the parent party's position on the Jewish Question. It opened by drawing attention to the fact that "an overwhelming majority of sales in trade and industry" were handled by "elements alien to the country," a fact that gravely threatened state security. The logical solution to this serious problem was the development of producer, commercial, and credit cooperatives, which would replace "the present irrational system of small town retail markets, which facilitate the exploitation of disorganized agriculture by parasitic retail traders."[31]

Several smaller peasant parties formed by activists dissenting from the SL were more direct. The Stronnictwo Chłopskie insisted that "trade should be Polonized and socialized" through the use of co-operatives and, where they did not exist, "it is essential to support private Polish trade." A revived Wyzwolenie, formed by peasant activists in favor of cooperation with the regime, demanded that the government "remove the dominance of alien elements over Polish forces in all sectors of life" and specifically asserted that "the Polish element must take over the entirety of economic life in Poland, and the population must be aided in this task" by "creating conditions conducive to this." The most militant stance came from the Rady-kalna Partia Chłopska (Radical Peasant Party), which was created in June 1936 out of a split within the Stronnictwo Chłopskie. After calling for a struggle against "rapacious middlemen," the party program devoted a separate section to discussing the Jewish Question (part 8):

> There is for the Polish nation the question of the existence of hundreds of thousands of peasants seeking supplementary and basic

30. *Zielony Sztandar,* May 3, 1936.
31. The program statements were printed in two issues of the journal *Wici*: the political section was in May 24, 1936, no. 21; the economic portion in July 12–19, 1936, nos. 28–29.

incomes in trade and artisan activities that the Jews have seized. Wholesale trade, banking, and industry are equally under their influence, and well known is Jewish solidarity, which struggles with subtle cunning and the negation of all ethics against each action designed to place trade in Polish hands. Today we see that the Jews are already developing activity aimed at buying up land and settling on it. The consciousness of the broad peasant masses is being aroused, and finally is erupting. We are far from applying any violence, but we must mount an economic struggle, and we will aspire to a law guaranteeing the Polish element liberation from economic dependency on those who today play the dominant economic role and already are going after our land. We will defend ourselves from the influences that the Jews exert over the Polish mentality through the destruction of social foundations, the negation of national roots, the development of communist antistate activity, and the undermining of moral relations at every step.[32]

Given the above sentiments, it no doubt came as a major shock that the national SL congress concluded its deliberations in January 1937 without passing any resolutions specifically focusing on the Jews, although it did devote one to the Ukrainian minority.[33] When the nationalist press chided the party for ignoring this "vital issue," *Piast* replied on behalf of the SL, "We do not regard the Jewish problem as the main axis around which everything revolves in Poland. The chief enemy of the Polish peasant today is the ruling party, the regime which oppresses him morally, materially, politically, and culturally. The Polish peasant will not permit this struggle against the regime to be undermined by the Jewish Question." It concluded that the party did not intend to compete with the nationalists in anti-Jewish violence but instead would realize its goals "in this field by organizing cooperatives and our own shops," a method "both more effective and more cultured than the smashing of Jewish windows."[34]

The SL continued to deemphasize the Jews as a main focal point for its grand political strategy. Six months after the congress, its central press organ *Zielony Sztandar* dismissed the regime's growing antisemitism as a transparent device to gain backing from the nationalist Right and to prolong Poland's real evil, "the gentry's ex-

---

32. "Rezolucja Zjazdu Działaczy Stronnictwa Chłopskiego w sprawach politycznych i gospodarczych," *Sztandar Chłopski*, September 27, 1936; "Rezolucje Uchwalone przez Zjazd Grupy 'Wyzwolenia,'" *Wyzwolenie*, October 11, 1936; "Tezy Programowe," *Polska Ludowa*, June 28, 1936.

33. The resolutions, which were severely censored from the SL press, are printed in their entirety, "Uchwały Nadzwyczajnego Kongresu Stronnictwa Ludowego," in *MZHPRL*, vol. 3, doc. 126, pp. 327–32.

34. *Piast*, January 31, 1937.

ploitation of the peasants."[35] The party's determination to avoid being diverted from its true political purposes by an anti-Jewish crusade became evident during the peasant strike that erupted in late August 1937. The official document summoning the farmers to halt deliveries of foodstuffs to the market reminded them that "this strike is not directed against any other social stratum" and warned against being "provoked into any other outbursts"; instead, they were urged to conduct themselves "peacefully and act calmly in the event of unrest."[36] Evidently the peasants heeded this admonition, for neither internal Polish government nor Western press and diplomatic reports contain any reference to violence directed against the Jews, although there were numerous incidents of attacks on both person and property.

This strike seemed to mark the opening of a new, final phase in the peasant movement's attitude toward the Jews. Except for continued emphasis on the need for the expansion of a cooperative system, subsequent public pronouncements and internally circulated documents—including letters from the exiled Witos—avoided discussion of the Jewish Question. The peasantry had come to realize that its real enemy was the increasingly totalitarian regime and not the Polish Jews. Its true need was for a thorough restructuring of the agrarian system and genuine political reform; driving the Jews out of Poland was of distinctly secondary importance. Indeed there appeared to be an inversely proportionate relationship between the increasingly antisemitic character of the regime after 1935 and the decreasing urgency of the Jewish Question in peasant political thought and action.

Clearly the militant oppositionist stance of the peasant movement inclined it to reject whatever the government advocated. But perhaps there are other explanations for the peasantry's refusal to embrace openly political antisemitism. The National Democrats provided the main competition for votes and financial support in most areas of rural Poland, and the peasant parties may well have viewed strident antisemitic agitation as a major Endek organizing tool, the success of which could only harm the SL and other genuine populist groups.

35. *Zielony Sztandar,* July 11, 1937. The editorial concluded with the statement, "When the peasants will have cleansed Poland of all the sad remnants of the *szlachta*-lord times, they will also have solved the Jewish Question in a suitable manner."
36. "Odezwa SL Proklamująca 10-dniowy Strajk Chłopski," in *MZHPRL*, vol. 3, doc. 137, pp. 343–44.

In like fashion, the growing tendency of the Roman Catholic church, from its national hierarchy down to the lowliest parish priests, to adopt an increasingly overt antisemitic profile in the latter half of the decade might well have triggered an opposing reaction from the peasant movement. Despite their avowedly Catholic religious outlook, virtually all peasants—from movement activists to ordinary rural residents mired in abject poverty—shared a deep-rooted anticlerical feeling that inclined them to resist staunchly any public manifestations of clerical involvement in political or socioeconomic life. In short, the peasants probably reasoned that if the regime, the National Democrats, and the clergy all favored organized antisemitism, then it was clearly in the best interest of rural Poles to oppose it.

Finally, the average Polish peasant may well have wondered what all the anti-Jewish uproar meant in the first place. After all, over the course of centuries the Polish Jew and peasant had developed a personal and economic relationship based on mutual need and dependency that bound them to one another in a tie sufficiently strong to challenge the cultural, religious, linguistic, or other differences separating them. For most rural inhabitants, a pathologically racist or opportunistically political antisemitism simply did not make sense; as a Jewish observer noted in early 1939, "The peasant, with his rather primitive, apolitical, and unsophisticated mind finds it difficult to comprehend why the Jew should suddenly be taken out beyond the pale of citizenship when both he and the Jew have lived and worked on the same soil for centuries and can continue to do so."[37]

That is not to say that the SL and other peasant organizations abandoned their long-standing goals of gaining ultimate control over the rural economy for the Polish peasant; this remained a basic objective of the movement. But it is clear that political antisemitism ceased to play a role in the leading parties' programs after 1937. The same observation cannot be made for many other political movements in interwar Poland. Perhaps the same observer quoted above was correct when he commented:

> Despite huge antisemitic propaganda, the peasants have not been won over to the antisemitic front. The peasant still maintains a per-

37. Joel Cang, "The Opposition Parties in Poland and Their Attitude towards the Jews and the Jewish Problem," *Jewish Social Studies* 1 (1939): 251.

spective of realities and fair qualities of judgement. He is able to distinguish between his real and unreal grievances. . . . It should be stated to the credit of the Polish peasant that his attitude towards the Jew, happily for him, for the Jew, and for Poland, is still guided by a sufficient dose of common sense which not even all the evil spirits freely amuck in Poland today have been able to destroy.[38]

38. Ibid., pp. 250–51.

Moshe Mishkinsky

The Communist Party of Poland
and the Jews

The parties of the international communist movement knew many tragedies. But it is no accident that "the tragedy of Polish communism"[1] has achieved special fame as a description of the fate of the Komunistyczna Partia Polski (KPP, Communist Party of Poland) between the two world wars.[2]

The KPP was one of the parties that established the Comintern at the beginning of 1919, and afterward it was one of the most active bodies in it. Members of the KPP were integrated into the party and state apparatus of Soviet Russia, and some reached very high levels. Representatives of the party held important positions in the Com-

---

1. Isaac Deutscher, "La tragédie du communisme polonais entre les deux guerres," *Les Temps modernes*, no. 145 (March 1958): 1632–77. An authorized English version (with minor changes) was published in mimeograph form as "The Tragedy of Polish Communism between the Wars" by the Socialist Labor League, n.d.

2. From its founding at the end of 1918 until 1925 the Communist Party of Poland was known as the Komunistyczna Partia Robotnicza Polski (KPRP, Communist Workers' Party). The decision to change the name, taken at the Third Party Convention at the beginning of 1925, was an effort to emphasize the fact that the party represented not only the interests of the proletariat, but the interests of farmers and other populist classes as well. Formerly the rubric Sekcja Międzynarodówki Komunistycznej (Section of the Communist International) had been added to the party name in parentheses. From then on the party would be called KPP and KPRP interchangeably. For convenience, KPP has been used to designate the party throughout this essay. Throughout the entire period, the party was illegal. Franciszka Świetlikowa, *Komunistyczna Partia Robotnicza Polski, 1918–1923* (Warsaw, 1968), deals mainly with the "organizational politics" of the party. See also the well-documented article by Tadeusz Szafar, "The Origins of the Communist Party in Poland, 1918–1921," in *War and Society in East Central Europe*, ed. Ivo Banac (Brooklyn, N.Y., 1983), pp. 5–52. Specific monographs on the history of the KPP include M. K. Dziewanowski, *The Communist Party of Poland: An Outline of History* (Cambridge, Mass., 1976), more than half of which deals with the period after the outbreak of the First World War; Henryk Cimek and Lucjan Kieszczyński, *Komunistyczna Partia Polski, 1918–1939* (Warsaw, 1984); and Antoni Czubiński, *Komunistyczna Partia Polski (1918–1938): Zarys historii* (Warsaw, 1985). A chapter on the history of the KPP is also included in Jan B. de Weydenthal, *The Communists of Poland* (Stanford, Calif., 1978), pp. 1–33.

intern and acted as its emissaries to various other communist parties. In 1937, however, Moscow began to suppress the KPP. In 1938 the party was officially disbanded by the Comintern, and its activities ended gradually over the course of that year. These actions were accompanied by general accusations of duplicity, provocation, espionage, and treachery. The leaders of the KPP were morally and physically liquidated, having been either resident in the Soviet Union or invited and entrapped there for that purpose.[3] This process had actually begun to take shape at the beginning of the 1930s, but its particular significance had not been noted, hidden by the more general Stalinist terror against the Old Bolsheviks that began shortly thereafter. From its beginnings, however, the KPP had been placed in a tragic situation on account of the deep political and ideological contradictions by which it was eventually consumed.[4]

Not least of the manifestations of the KPP's tragic history is our topic here: the relation of the party and the Jews. The last echo of this story was heard only in 1967 and 1968, thirty years after the disbanding of the KPP and twenty-six years after the establishment of its successor, the Polska Partia Robotnicza (PPR, Polish Workers' Party). A crisis that grew out of a fight within the ruling party

3. On the breakup of the KPP, see Marian Malinowski, "Przyczynek do sprawy rozwiązania KPP, *Z Pola Walki* (hereafter *ZPW*) 11, no. 3 (1968): 3–24; Józef Kowalski, *Komunistyczna Partia Polski, 1935–1938* (Warsaw, 1975), pp. 376–85, 398–437; Dziewanowski, *Communist Party of Poland*, pp. 146–54. Dziewanowski's study is the only one of these works that includes Soviet foreign policy as an explanation for the dissolution: Joseph Stalin feared that any future deal with Adolf Hitler would arouse opposition within the ranks of the KPP, partly on account of the large number of Jews in the party (p. 154). This hypothesis has been repeated by others. There is a tragic-ironic ring in the juxtaposition of the concluding slogans of the final proclamations put out in the name of the Central Committee of the KPP (which had already, in fact, ceased to exist) in April and June 1938: "Long Live the KPP" and "Long Live Stalin [with his usual titles attached]," the man who more than anyone was responsible for the party's actual destruction. Severyn Ajzner et al., eds., *Dokumenty Komunistycznej Partii Polskiej* (Warsaw, 1968), docs. 62, 63. Only in 1956 was the KPP "rehabilitated," through the joint announcement of several communist parties: no honest explanation was given for its dissolution. The "rehabilitation" of activists continued into the 1960s. Recent monographs on the KPP from the years 1984–85 (see note 2, above) also avoid explaining the true reasons for its breakup and liquidation.

4. Ludwik Grosfeld, "Polskie partie polityczne wobec Rewolucji Październikowej," *ZPW* 1, no. 1 (1958): 69. Compare also Józef Kowalski, "Z zagadnień strategii i taktyki KPRP i PPS na przełomie lat, 1918–1919," *ZPW* 1, no. 1 (1958): 97–98, on the slogan of the Socjal-Demokracja Królestwa Polskiego i Litwi (SDKPL, Social Democracy of the Kingdom of Poland and Lithuania) during the turning point in 1917–18 for the unification of Poland with revolutionary Russia. The KPP was the result of a merger of the SDKPL with the Polska Partia Socjalistyczna–Lewica (PPS–Lewica, Polish Socialist Party–Left).

created a wave of antisemitism, called "anti-Zionism" but not without racist overtones.[5] It was no accident that over the debate hung the historical question of the Jews and the KPP and that the question should be resurrected.[6] Even after official antisemitism in Poland had withered, Polish historiography made no serious attempt to deal with the antisemitic forces that had left their mark even on the interpretation of the history of the KPP.[7]

The subject of the KPP and the Jews has thus suffered in the past from neglect.[8] There has been, for example, no systematic collection of documents on the topic. In the historiography of the KPP, whether written in Poland or elsewhere, there are fragmentary references to certain aspects of the subject, but there has been no attempt clearly

5. A great deal has been written about this subject. See Paul Lendvai, *Anti-Semitism without Jews* (New York, 1971), pp. 89–239, which also refers to the anti-Jewish notions that accompanied the political and party crisis of 1956.

6. A clear mixture of contemporary antisemitism and historical explanation, including charges of damage Jews allegedly did to the KPP, can be found in the article most widely quoted in this connection, written by a member of the Central Committee of the Polska Zjednoczona Partia Robotnicza (PZPR, United Polish Workers' Party): Andrzej Werblan, "Przyczynek do genezy konfliktu," *Miesięcznik Literacki*, 1968, no. 6, pp. 61–72. See also note 7, below. A critical discussion of these ideas is included in chapter 4 (pp. 145–203) of Leszek Krzemień, *Szkice polemiczne* (Warsaw, 1974), a book that is primarily polemical. The title of this chapter—"Izaak Gutkind wstepuje do KPP"—is based on "Księżyc z ulicy Pawiej" (The Moon of Pawia Street), a poem by the well-known procommunist Polish poet Władysław Broniewski that describes the life of his prison mate, a young Jewish tailor who joined the KPP.

7. See, for example, Marian Żychowski, *Polska, naród, ojczyzna* (Warsaw, 1968), pp. 78–80. The author adopts the approach of Werblan, "Przyczynek do genezy konfliktu," though in a more camouflaged form. The debate about the KPP also caused the renewal of the polemic about SDKPL and its relation to the Polish national question. Thus a tendency arose, whether open or disguised, to split the "more" and the "less" national-minded according to a division between Poles and Jews. Compare also the note about the "one-sided composition" of the directorate of SDKPL (1906) from the aspect of the nationality of its members (as if they were chosen according to an ethnic criterion) and a parallel observation between "extremist internationalist stands" and a "patriotic-internationalistic stand" in Norbert Michta's introduction to his edition of Julian B. Marchlewski, *Ludzie, czasy, idee* (Warsaw, 1973), p. 36; also see Michta's comments in his edition of Marchlewski, *Polska-naród-socjalizm* (Warsaw, 1975), p. 458. In retrospect, a different perspective appears in Feliks Tych, *Socjalistyczna Irredenta* (Cracow, 1982), and in a review of the book by I. Kancewicz, in *ZPW* 27, no. 3 (1984): 154–69.

8. Archival material on the KPP concerning the Jews is registered in Marian Naszkowski et al., eds., *Komunistyczna Partia Polski-Informator z lat 1918–1939* (Warsaw, 1970). The documents published in three volumes in the 1950s (*KPP Uchwały i rezolucje*, vols. 1–3 [Warsaw, 1953–56]) also include material concerning the Jews. But the entire publication is problematic because of the way the documents were chosen for inclusion and the general reliability of the texts published at that time. See Henryk Malinowski, "Problemy historiografii KPP," *ZPW* 12, no. 1 (1969): 107. The author states that research into the KPP within the Jewish community is "in the preliminary stage" (p. 106).

to define the range of the subject and certainly no attempt at a general synthesis. In Yiddish there are a number of works that bring together documents, memoirs, bio-bibliographical material, and historical interpretation.[9] Although these are of some value, they are unsystematic, apologetic, and tendentious, whether because of the influence of old dogmatic stances or political pressures at the time of their publication. In the 1970s several important articles were published in Polish on various specific topics, but these, too, are somewhat marked by adherence to conventional terminology, axiomatic definitions, and ideological biases.[10] There is also a literature of memoirs, both books and articles, of Jewish Communists and ex-Communists, active at various levels and in different sectors of the KPP or its peripheries. If one bears in mind the caution always required in using autobiographical material, these need not be rejected out of hand.[11]

There are various reasons that the subject of the KPP and the Jews has been ignored in the general historiography of the KPP. In part, it has not been seen as a serious, distinct topic. But to some extent we might say that the neglect is a direct result of the exaggerated importance given to the topic by the identification of communism with the Jews made by the antisemitic Polish right wing and other

9. Szymon Zachariasz, *Di komunistishe bavegung tsvishn der yidisher arbetndiker bafelkerung in Poyln* (Warsaw, 1954); Zachariasz et al., eds., *Unter der fon fun KPP* (Warsaw, 1959); Zachariasz, *Mentshn fun KPP* (Warsaw, 1964). A dissertation on the work of the KPP within the Jewish community in 1918–26 (mentioned in *35 lat dzialałnośći Żydowskiego Instytutu Historycznego w Polsce Ludowej* [Warsaw, 1980], p. 41) has not yet been published. In May 1968 the directorate of the institute decided on the publication of two volumes to note fifty years of the KPP, but the plan was never implemented, for "internal and external reasons" that were not spelled out (p. 34). On the stand of the KPP on Jewish issues, see Celia S. Heller, *On the Edge of Destruction: Jews of Poland between the Two World Wars* (New York, 1977), s.v. "Communist Party of Poland" in the index; Edmund Silberner, *Kommunisten zur Judenfrage* (Opladen, Federal Republic of Germany, 1983), pp. 220–39.

10. The following are pertinent: Gereon Iwański, "Żydowski Komunistyczny Związek Robotniczy Kombund w Polsce, 1921–1923," *ZPW* 17, no. 4 (1974): 43–76; Iwański, "Powstanie i działalność Komunistycznej Organizacji Młodzieży 'Cukunft' w Polsce: Styczeń 1922–Kwiecień 1923 r.," *Pokolenia* 74, no. 3 (1974): 41–62; Larysa Gamska, "Lewica żydowskich partii socjalistycznych wobec III międzynarodówki i KPRP (1918–1923)," *Biuletyn Żydowskiego Instytutu Historycznego* (hereafter *BŻIH*), no. 97 (1976): 61–75; Gamska, "KPP wobec problemów kulturalno-oświatowych ludności żydowskiej w okresie od I zjazdu do IV Konferencji," *BŻIH*, no. 103 (1977): 35–47.

11. Some of the memoirists include: Bundists who went over to the KPP—Hersh Mendel (Shtokfish), Yiddish and German; Pinkus (Alexander) Mintz, Yiddish; H. Metalovetz (Bekerkunst), Yiddish; former Fereynikte—Yitzhak Gordin; former Poalei Zion—Gershon Dua-Bogen (immigrated to Palestine and emigrated again in 1922), Yiddish; Hersh Smolar, Yiddish and Hebrew.

sectors of the Polish public and government before the Second World War. We must add also the resurrection of this stereotype in postwar Poland that accompanied the growth of chauvinism within communism itself. These factors, no doubt, created a psychological block among historians and made them hesitant to study the issue. There is also an essential difficulty deriving from the continual oscillation between the desire to emphasize the multiethnic character of the party, uniting many peoples, and the desire to emphasize its specifically Polish identity. One may add a major technical problem: the inability of Polish historians (with rare exceptions) to use an important part of the sources—namely, those in Yiddish[12]—or the secondary literature in that language and in Hebrew. Another substantial hindrance is an ignorance of patterns of life within the Jewish community.

It seems, however, that the major reason for neglect of the issue has been the conceptual problems attached to it. The dominant approach has been to see the issue of the KPP and the Jews as a part of the history of the KPP, under two main aspects: first, the party's position on the Jewish Question, and, second, the party's position on what was called, within the party, "Jewish work." Even on these questions there is room for controversial approaches. But we need also to attempt to view matters from another perspective altogether, that is, to view communism among the Jews in the context of the autonomous history of the Jews in the Second Polish Republic. That is to say, we must examine all the various elements that allow us, with all due caution, to define Jewish communism as a separate trend within the political and ideological spectrum of Jewish life.[13] This approach is two dimensional: vertical (historical or diachronic) and horizontal (contemporaneous or synchronic). Our analysis must take cognizance of (1) the special relationship of Jewish communism to the development of the Jewish socialist labor movement in the different regions that had been included in Poland after World War I; (2) the crisis that Polish Jewry was experiencing in this period, and in particular the changes occurring among the workers,

12. Jerzy Holzer, in *ZPW* 21, no. 4 (1978): 127.
13. I can account for the limitations of the grounds of this contention: concentration on one period of time in the history of the KPP and lack of access to a significant number of primary sources. Nonetheless, the existing material and also a cursory reading of the later history of the affair make possible some formulation and examination, however preliminary, of the said contention.

the lower classes, the intelligentsia, and the youth; (3) the relationship of the development of Jewish communism to events within the Jewish socialist parties of the Soviet republics in the first years after the war and also to those of other countries in which there was a new split within the movement in the wake of the Bolshevik Revolution and the establishment of the Communist International and its affiliated parties.

Likewise within the context of the close ideological, political, and organizational ties and attachments of Jewish communism to the KPP and the Comintern and in view of the deep contradictions that these gave rise to, we should not ignore the attempts of Jewish communism in Poland to give answers to the particular problems of the Jewish working population. We must also consider whether and to what degree it attempted, amid the twisting and turning of its development, to sketch out the possibility of a collective Jewish existence in the future. The bitter end of Jewish communism and the illusions that were bound up with it do not release us from the need to study and evaluate it within the context of the particular conditions of its time and place, that is, if our study is to be historical and not merely ideological.

Jews in the KPP and the KPP among the Jews, 1918–1923

There are several aspects to the question of the place of the Jews in the KPP and its periphery. First there is the quantitative question: What was the absolute and relative number of Jews among the members of the party and the various organizations under its direction? And likewise: What was the strength of the party among the Jews, as evidenced by election returns?

The statistics as to the number of members of the KPP in general and the Jews among them in particular are far from precise.[14] But on the basis of data for some of the regional organizations of the party and the circles (later called "cells") and also on estimates of the number of affiliates from other Jewish socialist parties, we may

---

14. Świetlikowa, *Komunistyczna Partia Robotnicza Polski*, pp. 274–77. An interesting comparison can be found in Józef Ławnik, "Represje policyjne wobec Komunistów w Polsce, 1918–1939," *ZPW* 21, no. 3 (1978): 27–28; Ławnik, *Represje policyjne wobec ruchu robotniczego, 1918–1938* (Warsaw, 1979), pp. 134–42. Even after this, the confusion on numbers continues. Compare, in relation to 1918 and 1923: Cimek and Kieszczyński, *Komunistyczna Partia Polski*, p. 53; Czubiński, *Komunistyczna Partia Polski*, pp. 30, 89; de Weydenthal, *Communists of Poland*, p. 137.

assume that by the end of 1923, about 20 percent of members of the KPP were Jews.[15] One should note the proportion (higher than in the party) of Jewish members of the Związek Młodzieży Komunistycznej w Polsce (ZMKWP, Union of Communist Youth in Poland), of the trade unions,[16] and the scope of communist publications in Yiddish.[17]

As to the scope of communist influence in the Jewish community, one may compile some comparative data, relatively continuous for the period under discussion, with regard to the capital, Warsaw, a city with a special place in the history of KPP. These are the results of elections within the Jewish trade unions to the Rady Delegatów Robotniczych (Councils of Workers' Delegates) at the end of 1918, the Committees of Health in 1921 and 1923, and the Sejm (House of Deputies) in 1922.[18] There are also partial and fragmentary results for other places.

15. Franciszka Świetlikowa, "Liczebność okręgowych organizacacji KPP w latach 1919–1937," ZPW 13, no. 2 (1970): 183–201; Kowalski, Komunistyczna Partia Polski, p. 90; Gereon Iwański et al., eds., II Zjazd Komunistycznej Partii Robotniczej Polski (19.IX–2.X.1923), protokoły obrad i Uchwały (Warsaw, 1968), pp. 82, 94, 96. Slightly different figures appear for Warsaw in Zbigniew Szczygielski, "Warszawska organizacja KPP," Studia Warszawskie 1 (1968): 180, 191.

16. In a special monograph on the KPP within the trade union movement, only a few pages, with little real content, are devoted to the Jewish unions. Edward Kołodziej, Komunistyczna Partia Robotnicza Polski w ruchu zawodowym, 1918–1923 (Warsaw, 1978), pp. 157–59. See also Świetlikowa, Komunistyczna Partia Robotnicza Polski, pp. 197–98. A sizable amount of material is dispersed throughout various journals. The subject in its totality still awaits proper treatment. A description of the situation in the Jewish unions and the communist influence on them is included in articles by Zalmen Kratko: "Di yidishe profesyonele bavegung in Kongres-Poyln in der tsayt fun der ershter velt-milkhome," Gal-Ed 2 (1975): 113–44; "Fareynikung un shpaltung-protsesn in der yidisher profesyoneler bavegung in farmilkhomedikn Poyln," Gal-Ed 4–5 (1978): 311–43. His survey on Kwartalnik Historii Ruchu Zawodowego (of which he was co-editor before he left Poland for Israel), in Asufot, 1971, no. 2, pp. 121–22, is of particular interest. See also S. M. Zigelboym, "Di profesyonele bavegung fun di yidishe arbeter," and Sholem Hertz, "Di profesyonele fareynen fun di yidishe arbeter," in Di geshikhte fun Bund, ed. Sholem Hertz et al. (New York, 1960–81), 4:179–217, 219–83, respectively.

17. Maria Meglicka, Prasa KPRP, 1918–1923 (Warsaw, 1968), pp. 311–17, 334–44. The author identified forty-eight periodical and single-issue publications (which are, it seems, the majority) in Yiddish; of these, thirty-eight came out during 1922–23. This accounts for approximately one-third of all the communist publications of those types during that time. Compare also a later article by the same author in Prasa KPP w latach 1918–1938: Z dziejów polskiej prasy robotniczej (Warsaw, 1983), p. 109. Little data exist on the number of editions of the journals and their distribution. Additional bibliographical details on the publications of the KPP in Yiddish can be found in a listing by Yisrael Szajn, in Unter der fon fun KPP, pp. 323–39; Szajn, Bibliografye fun oysgabes aroysgegebn durkh di arbeter parteyen in Poyln, 1918–1939 (Warsaw, 1963), pp. 13–28.

18. Ludwik Hass, Wybory warszawskie, 1918–1926 (Warsaw, 1972).

With due caution, one may arrive at two general conclusions. First, only a small minority of Jews ever belonged to the KPP or supported it. Within the KPP, on the other hand, the Jews were a substantial minority. There were Jews in the other Polish parties as well, but none had a percentage of Jewish members close to that of the KPP. Yet the KPP saw itself essentially as a multiethnic party.

Second, the KPP did wield political and ideological influence among the Jews, and especially among labor, albeit never the influence of the Bund. Thus it established a foundation for the party to become a fixed part of Jewish labor and a focus for public antagonisms, exerting a constant pull on youth, the intelligentsia, and the lower classes in general.

But quantity is only one aspect of the question of the KPP and the Jews. The other is the impact of the political and organizational influence of the Jews in the KPP. This influence can be measured by identifying individual Jews in the ideological, political, and organizational leadership and apparatus of the party. Of all the questions included in our topic, this one has suffered the greatest degree of mystification.

First of all, there is simple exaggeration. One may read, for example, that "the Jewish communists assumed a pivotal position in the leadership of the KPRP and the KPP, occupying most of the seats in their Central Committees."[19] Lists of the members of these committees disprove this assertion.

Likewise one must question the very common assumption that the Jewishness of the Jews who held important positions in the party apparatus determined the party's stance on the political aspect of the Polish national question. First of all, those Jews never acted as a collective unit. Like their Polish colleagues, they, too, were divided by the bitter and extended internal party strife over all the basic questions that the party faced. Second, Jews were among the leaders (often in fact the most prominent and most diligent leaders) of the KPP who challenged the traditional Luxembourgian stances against demands for Polish independence and on the issues of "export of

---

19. De Weydenthal, *Communists of Poland,* p. 26. In this way, the author "Judaizes" a veritable Pole like Julian Leński (Leszczyński), who was for a long time the secretary general of the party. As for the real state of things, compare Franciszka Świetlikowa, "Centralne instancje partyjne KPP w latach 1918–1938," *ZPW* 12, no. 4 (1969): 139–45.

revolution" from the Soviet Union, the agrarian question, and sectionalism in the relations with other labor parties.

Last, but not least, we must examine the nature of the Jewish identity or sense of belonging of Jewish members and supporters of the KPP, and especially its leadership. Clearly this matter is closely tied to an understanding of the variety of motives that led Jews to attach themselves to the party and the communist movement. As with the socialist movement before it, so now with communism: Jews came to the movement from many different directions and, having joined, continued to follow separate paths. One can accept only with substantial reservations the view that the process of radicalization was necessarily an expression of desire not only for acculturation but for complete assimilation into the Polish nation.[20] It is correct for a fraction of Jewish party members, particularly those (and not all of them) in the party higher levels. Symptomatic is the fact that of the fifty-one Polish delegates to the Second Party Convention in 1923, fourteen identified themselves as being "of Jewish origin" and seven others as Jews (probably the former members of Jewish socialist parties).[21] But the proportion of the latter to those "of Jewish origin" at the convention did not reflect their proportion among the rank and file. There the overwhelming majority of Jews saw themselves as Jews, retained their ties to the Jewish community, and felt a special responsibility for the plight of the Jewish masses. The affiliation of Jews with the KPP stemmed from the conditions that encouraged the spread of communism in general: the experience of the First World War and the Russian Revolution, messianic expectations of a world revolution, and the internal division of the socialist movement. But particular aspects of Jewish life were also

20. See the comments of Maria Turlejska, in "Internacjonalizm—patriotyzm—nacjonalizm w dziejach polskiego ruchu robotniczego," ZPW 13, no. 2 (1970): 158–59. The author asserts her opinion about communization and the desire for complete national self-negation specifically against the claim of the National Democrats (Endeks) that the workers "of Jewish origin" imposed a "non-Polish" atmosphere on the revolutionary movement in Poland. The total identification of the Jewish communists with the assimilationists can also be found in R. V. Burks, *The Dynamics of Communism in Eastern Europe* (Princeton, N.J., 1961).

21. Iwański et al., eds., *II Zjazd KPRP,* pp. 307–12, 648–58. Among these were three members who came to the KPP from Poalei Zion: Saul Amsterdam [Henrykowski], Aharon Lewartowski, Mendel Michrowski; two of the Fereynikte: Yitzhak Gordin (Lenowicz), Pinchas Bukshorn; Shlomo Miller, a former anarchist; and Ludvik Rosenberg, who represented the Komunistyczna Partia Galicji Wschodniej (Communist Party of Eastern Galicia) at the convention. Since he had come to the KPP indirectly, he was not included among those coming from Poalei Zion, to which he had formerly belonged. See note 31, below.

at work. Events in the Jewish socialist parties of Poland and of the neighboring and also more distant countries exerted a remarkable influence; so did the situation of the Jews in Poland as an oppressed national minority.[22] Antisemitism and pogroms cast their shadows on the Jews, especially at the outset of Polish independence. But more than negative factors were involved. Jewish workers hoped to break their isolation and to attach themselves to the Polish proletariat by means of the multiethnic KPP, which recognized, in fact, the national identity of the Jews. Within an atmosphere heavy with the expectation of impending revolution, Jews looked for a comprehensive solution of all of the world's problems, not only an end to antisemitism and pogroms but also the chance for the continuation of Jewish collective existence and cultural distinctiveness as they understood it.

Antisemitism as a Political, Social, and Intraparty Problem

Antisemitism was a fixed part of the history of the Second Polish Republic. But it went through ups and downs, and its two peak periods were at the very beginning of the Republic and at its very end, on the eve of the Second World War.[23] Both periods were marked by the incidence of anti-Jewish attacks and pogroms. The first period was, in fact, even worse than the second, with a larger scope of destruction and a greater number killed and wounded. Furthermore, in some if not actually the majority of the cases, the military was responsible for, or at least participated in, the incidents. The pogroms were also accompanied by anti-Jewish activities on the part of various arms of the government and incitement by the press. Poland being independent, it was now impossible to shift responsibility for the violence onto foreigners—the occupying powers—as had been done in the past. This realization came as a psychological shock, especially for the Jews in ethnic Poland, whose relations with the Polish majority had deep roots.

22. To substantiate his thesis on the attraction of national minorities to communist parties, Burks points to the role of Jews in Eastern European communist parties, including the KPP. *Dynamics of Communism*, pp. 158–65. Some of his data warrant further examination.

23. See the recent overviews of the situation of the Jews in interwar Poland: Ezra Mendelsohn, *The Jews of East Central Europe between the World Wars* (Bloomington, Ind., 1983), pp. 11–83; Paweł Korzec, "Antisemitism in Poland as an Intellectual, Social, and Political Movement," in *Studies on Polish Jewry, 1919–1939*, ed. Joshua A. Fishman (New York, 1974), pp. 12–104.

Both violent antisemitism and Jewish self-defense on the one hand, and the regulation of the group status of Polish Jewry on the other, had extensive international implications. It was in this situation that the term *Żydo-komuna* (Judeo-communist)—identifying one with the other—captured a central place in the vocabulary of propaganda. It was a two-edged sword, which used old and widespread anti-Jewish feelings in order to discredit the communists and at the same time used anti-Bolshevik feelings to justify antisemitism. The term *Żydo-komuna* seemed particularly manipulative and useful, because it joined together old stereotypes and brand new ones.

The old accusation that "Litvaks"—Jews from White Russia and Lithuania but extended to include all Russian Jews—were acting to Russify Poland was now shaped into a condemnation of the Jews acting to support Bolshevism, which was presented as the heir of Russian imperialism. The international aspect of the Jewish Question was paralleled to the universal character of communism, and the joining of the two fit very well with the notion of the "international Jewish conspiracy" as promoted by *The Protocols of the Elders of Zion*, which experienced worldwide revival at this time and had been translated into Polish. The term and stereotype *Żydo-komuna* also connected with the centrality of the Jewish Question in the doctrine of the chief pan-antisemitic ideologue, Endek leader Roman Dmowski. There was also the attachment of long standing to the clustered accusations of "Jewish exploitation" and "Jewish radicalism." Furthermore, opposition to communist atheism could be grafted onto the living roots of Christian motifs in popular antisemitism. Accompanying all of these was a tendency to reverse causes and effects. Antisemitism was explained or justified at the time (and later) in the sympathy that developed among the Jews for Soviet Russia during its war with Poland (1919–20), even though that support came first of all as a result of Polish pogroms and antisemitic violence.

At its founding convention the KPP passed a special resolution protesting and denouncing pogroms and nationalist incitement against the Jews. The resolution placed responsibility for the actions on the "proprietary classes" and on the government (headed by Jędrzej Moraczewski), the "silence" of which "implies consent." To put an end to these outrages, the resolution looked forward to the "dictatorship" (of the proletariat) and the "destruction of capitalism" (both of which were seen as imminent).[24]

The complexity and also the seriousness of the problem of antisemitism became apparent in the Rady Delegatów Robotniczych that were set up in various cities from 1918 (some of them before the establishment of the KPP) and existed until July 1919.[25] The Polish and Jewish socialist workers' parties participated in the councils; so did the workers' organizations of the Polish Center and Right. The issues of antisemitism came up at the councils in four central contexts: (1) whether there should be mixed Polish-Jewish councils; (2) reactions to the pogroms and the administrative actions against the Jews; (3) various evidences of antisemitism, both political and cultural, within the councils themselves; (4) the attitude of the trade unions to the employment of Jewish workers and their acceptance into the rank and file.

The question of the structure of the councils came up especially in major cities such as Warsaw and Lublin. Jewish socialist parties supported the idea of a joint Polish-Jewish council. Opposition or evasive stances on the question arose from the pressure of antisemitic tendencies among the workers, who did not want accommodation with Jews. The KPP supported the concept of united councils in theory and, generally, also in practice.

The question of pogroms and anti-Jewish incitement was discussed frequently by the Warsaw Council and others. In these discussions the initiative was generally taken by the Jewish parties, but the KPP took part in working through the resolutions and in certain cases even took the initiative itself.

The issue of Yiddish was striking in anti-Jewish propaganda and popular feelings. The question of the status of Yiddish, in both theory and practice, for example, and the right to its use at meetings and in publications of the councils were also disputed. The positions of the representatives of the KPP on this question were weak and unclear, something that we shall see more of further on.

Most of all, however, the Warsaw Council was concerned with the dismissal of thousands of Jewish railway workers who had been

24. Tadeusz Daniszewski, ed., *KPP: Uchwały i rezolucje*, vol. 1 (Warsaw, 1953), p. 54.
25. *Rady delegatów robotniczych w Polsce*, vol. 1 (Warsaw, 1962), vol. 2 (Warsaw, 1965).

employed during the war. The Polish trade union showed a sharp hostility toward the discharged employees, and the KPP worked for a change of the union's policy toward the discharge and toward rights of the dismissed workers to membership in the union.

In 1920 a new edition of the pamphlet *Antysemityzm a robotnicy* (Antisemitism and the Workers) appeared in Warsaw,[26] the work of Julian Marchlewski, a veteran leader of the Socjal-Demokracja Królestwa Polskiego i Litwy (SDKPL, Social Democracy of the Kingdom of Poland and Lithuania) who was known as a theoretician and a man of great political and organizational experience. The pamphlet, however, made several assumptions that undercut its declared purpose, which was to explain the need for struggle against antisemitism. First, a goal was treated as a fact by assuming that the working class had already turned its back on anti-Jewish incitement. Furthermore, the author mechanically equated outrageous antisemitism with "Jewish nationalism" that had a basis in self-defense. And finally, he opposed Yiddish, a position that could feed antisemitic attitudes. On the other hand, a small work written in 1922 (and published in 1924) by Henryk Lauer, one of the major figures in the leadership of the KPP, painted a very different picture.[27] Lauer recognized the strength of antisemitism among the workers and even the existence of prejudices within the party itself on the questions of Yiddish and the rights of Jews to work in factories. In his opinion, the majority of the party opposed those primitive ideas but was not ready to fight against them.

The KPP's Second Party Convention, in September–October 1923, was the first broad forum of the party in which the question of antisemitism was discussed at length. The convention completed the turnabout that the party had made on a variety of basic questions. Among these was a reevaluation of the Polish national question, of the attitude taken toward the *petit bourgeois* classes, and of the tactic

26. J. B. Marchlewski, *Antysemityzm a robotnicy,* 3d ed. (Warsaw, 1920). It is included in Marchlewski, *Ludzie, czasy, idee,* pp. 318–439. There is no reference to Marchlewski's pamphlet in Michta's very extended introduction. Compare K. Dolindowska, *"Książka" i "Tom": Z dziejów legalnych wydawnictw KPP, 1918–1937* (Warsaw, 1977), pp. 61, 202. Marchlewski's essay is the most comprehensive work on Jewish matters from the pen of a prominent SDKPL and KPP leader and deserves a more extensive discussion.

27. Ernest Brand [Henryk Lauer], *Głos w kwestii żydowskiej: Czy stosunek do kwestii żydowskiej jest dla komunisty sprawa drażliwa (Z notatek więźnia)* (Warsaw, 1924). See Silberner, *Kommunisten zur Judenfrage,* pp. 227–28. There should be no doubt about the identity of the author.

of a united front with the other workers' organizations. Gregory Zinoviev, the chairman of the Comintern's Executive, emphasized that the Communists had still to prove to the Jewish workers and *petit bourgeoisie* that they had freed themselves from antisemitism. Various party leaders touched on different facets of the problem. The speech of Yitzhak Gordin, one of the most active figures in the Jewish work of the party, is of special interest. He dealt with antisemitism in a relatively comprehensive way, emphasizing both its special importance in the political life of the country and the need to fight it more actively than had been done previously.[28] Actually, Gordin's speech implied that one should not interpret "internationalism" to mean that Jewish Communists are only obliged to denounce what is called Jewish nationalism or social-nationalism, but that Jewish Communists had no special role in the fight against the antisemitic chauvinism and discrimination found in Polish nationalism.

The convention drew up a resolution against antisemitism, oppression of the Jewish and the German minorities, and discrimination against them by the administrative, judicial, and educational systems. The resolution did not, however, reflect the voices that had been heard in the course of the convention—especially Gordin's— stressing the grave danger of antisemitism. Nor was any outline drawn for a well-defined program to lead a systematic and intensive fight against it. Echoes of the discussions were, however, heard afterward in the public pronouncements of the party.

In sum, the KPP from its beginning took a principled stand against antisemitism and the pogroms and gave expression to that stand in its official documents and in the positions its representatives took within broader political and communal bodies. This stance certainly put the party in the first rank of the opponents of antisemitism in Polish society. It is impossible, however, to find any sign of a systematic consideration of antisemitism by the KPP or of any comprehensive, tangible program for its elimination. Nor was the party free of opportunism, expressed in underestimating or ignoring manifestations of antisemitism. The KPP put the question of public and official antisemitism into the framework of class warfare, chauvinist incitement, discrimination, and the oppression of non-Polish minorities. Changes that occurred in the KPP's assessment of

28. Iwański et al., eds., *II Zjazd KPRP,* pp. 29–30, 343–47.

the general social and political situation are also reflected in changes in its approach to antisemitism.

Within the party, there were conflicting opinions as to the particular significance of antisemitism in Polish political life and the scope and depth of its influence among the Polish proletariat. Hence there could be no agreement as to the place that the fight against antisemitism should take in the actual policy of the party and its propaganda. The sensitivity of the KPP to the issues of antisemitism, as it developed, stemmed from the pervasive influence of the *Żydokomuna* stereotype in Polish society on the one hand and, on the other, from the fact of its being a party, a large fraction of whose members and adherents were Jewish, and which was concerned with activity among Jews. In practice, however, incidents of antisemitism occurred on the periphery of the party and even within its ranks. For all that the KPP recognized this fact and the need to combat it, there is no record of any systematic or continued activity, only of recurrent sporadic efforts. The Polish-Jewish mixture of the party, and its efforts within two essentially separate spheres, Polish and Jewish, which it tried to combine or even to join, made antisemitism a daily problem for the KPP. The party's opposition both to Polish nationalism and to Jewish nationalism, which stemmed from its ideology, often caused it not to distinguish between their different natures. It therefore tended to equate a nationalism that sought to oppress minorities with a minority nationalism that was partly, or even essentially, a mode of self-defense.

Within this context, the nucleus of Communists active within the Jewish community recognized the need to spur the party on to a definition of its struggle against antisemitism that would acknowledge the centrality of that struggle in the framework of its goals and assigned tasks. This need was already expressed to some degree at a meeting of the Jewish party activists in September 1921. Thus a link was made within the specific conditions of the KPP to the heritage of the Jewish labor movement, for which the question of antisemitism had been a prime motivating factor.

Positive Demands and the Question of Organization

Gradually, however, the need arose for the KPP to take stands not only on antisemitism but also on the positive aspects of Jewish existence: the collective identity of the Jews and their equal rights as a national, cultural, and religious minority. The KPP was forced to define both the acceptable modes and the limits of self-assertion and self-activity by the Jewish proletariat; these, in turn, determined the form and the content of the Jewish work of the party and the place of Jewish cadres within its organizational structure.

The KPP recognized the collective national identity of the Jews. But one should not conclude therefore, as has been done frequently in the literature, that this stance was unproblematic.[29] In *Antysemityzm a robotnicy,* Marchlewski took a stance unequivocally in favor of assimilation: he identified internationalism as applied to the Jewish proletariat with the complete loss of national identity. We may presume that this attitude did not vanish entirely among members of the KPP, even if it was not officially recognized. In the course of time, the party made positive demands on the issues of Yiddish and education for the Jews. It took these steps without applying any theoretical analysis of assimilation, whether historical, contemporary, or future; rather, it operated out of a new *de facto* evaluation of the dichotomy of nationalism and internationalism. "Proletarian internationalism" was now understood not as a cosmopolitan notion, but rather as allowing room for a Jewish national existence.

The gradual formulation of positive demands on Jewish issues accompanied changes in the KPP's stance on questions of nationality in general and on the questions of evolving partial demands within the existing capitalist regime, establishing a united front with other workers' parties, and weighing the interests of classes other than the proletariat, especially of the lower middle classes that prevailed in the Jewish community. Particularly decisive, however, was the gradual joining, continuously throughout this period, of groups and factions from the Jewish socialist parties to the KPP.[30] This amalgamation was influential in two ways. It strengthened recognition of the need to develop activities directed at the Jews, and it created an active internal body that influenced the character of that work. Thus the KPP arrived at a positive attitude toward the Tsentrale Yidishe Shul Organizatsye (TSYSHO, Central Yiddish School Orga-

29. The misunderstandings in this respect are connected with a too hasty generalization of the factual situation (Silberner, *Kommunisten zur Judenfrage,* pp. 226–27), eventually with an ideological preconception (Gamska, "Lewica żydowskich partii socjalistycznych," p. 37).

30. This crucial development is barely touched upon here. It deserves a comprehensive treatment, first of all, in the context of the history of the Jewish labor movement.

nization).[31] The KPP's Second Party Convention adopted a general formula for free national development for the Jewish population. The right to free use of Yiddish within the judicial and administrative systems was demanded, as was the establishment of state and municipal secular Yiddish-language schools. In the wake of the convention one may note a desire for the party to take part in daily constructive organizational work, both cultural and economic, and also a desire to move beyond the bounds of the working class. The principles of "self-help" and "self-activity" were attached from the beginning to the Jewish workers' movement.[32] In this period they found expression, albeit limited and beset by contradictions, within the KPP as well.

A second line of policies was drawn in another sphere, that of organization. Two points served as the primary bases for the independent development of Jewish labor socialism. The first was the need to conduct propaganda and indoctrination in Jewish languages. The second was the demand for a special organization of Jewish workers and socialists of the intelligentsia involved in the Jewish community. Specific ideologies and platforms that joined socialist or class and national orientations in various ways were arrived at, whether sooner or later, as the organization developed; the fact of institutional existence shaped in a substantive way the consciousness of individuals and the organization as a collective body.

In the broad perspective of the historical meeting of socialism and Jews, the strength of the principle of organization may also be seen along another line, outside of the limits of the independent Jewish labor movement. In Polish parties, such as the Polska Partia Socjalistyczna (PPS, Polish Socialist Party) and the Polska Partia Socjal-Demokratyczna (PPSD, Polish Social-Democratic Party) in Galicia, unassimilated Jewish members demanded the establishment of special Jewish bodies. This same tendency was also expressed in the

31. On this and other aspects of the Jewish work of the KPP, see the sharp debate originally appearing in *Nowy Przegląd*: Karolski [A. Wajcblum], "Bolączki roboty żydowskiej KPRP i jak je usuwać," and A. Duński [Saul Amsterdam] and E. Czarnecki [Yitzhak Gordin], "Krytyka czy jątrzenie (w sprawie naszej roboty żydowskiej," reprinted in *Nowy Przegląd, 1924–25* (Warsaw, 1959), pp. 195–230 and 253–71, respectively. Karolski was a central figure in the Jewish work of the SDKPL and the KPRP between 1916 and 1920, and Duński and Czarnecki were active between 1921 and 1924. See note 21, above.

32. See Moshe Mishkinsky, *Reshit tenuat ha-poalim be-Rusyah: Megamot yesod* (Tel Aviv, 1981), pp. 76, 156.

parent parties of the KPP—the SDKPL and the Polska Partia Socjalistyczna–Lewica (PPS–Lewica, Polish Socialist Party–Left).

The KPP was committed to centralization and did not accept any principle of organizational autonomy for party members who also belonged to a national minority, especially those groups that were not concentrated in any territory. From its beginning, however, the KPP established special forms of organization for its Jewish work. A central body, the Jewish department, was even appointed by the Central Committee and operated under its aegis. For the nationwide coordination of Jewish work, meetings of Jewish cadres were also occasionally set up. The statutory position of these groups, however, was not well defined, and they were generally conceived as no more than technical executive bodies. In reality, however, these bodies addressed all of the problems that were related to Jews, including Jewish trade unionism.

The centrality of the question of Jewish organization within the KPP stood out in the extended process of contacts with the various factions of the Jewish socialist parties. The question was especially important in the history of the dealings of the communist wing of the Bund and, later, the independent Kombund Party with the KPP before their union in early 1923. It was characteristic that even after agreement had been reached on the large political and ideological questions, such as the proletarian world revolution and the affiliation with the Communist International, controversy over questions of organization continued. The pendulum swung between the desire for the existence of a special Jewish communist party, at least provisionally (an idea that was by no means an anathema to the Comintern leadership), and special statutory demands in the event of union with the KPP. When this union actually occurred, the Kombund demanded the establishment of Jewish sections within the KPP and of a central bureau that would have authority in all Jewish matters and would enjoy the authorization of party institutions. The statutes of the Jewish section show that a compromise was actually reached. A central Jewish bureau, elected by Jewish cadres, was set up, but without official recognition of its autonomous rights. Parallel provincial and local sections were also set up. The final authority of the party's ruling bodies was thus preserved. During the period of increased emphasis on positive demands on behalf of the Jewish proletariat and the Jews in general, these particularist bodies began to play an active political organizational role among the Jews. And likewise their specific weight increased in the working out of the KPP party line on Jewish questions.

With the changes that were made in party tactics in the spring of 1924, the reversal of decisions of the Second Party Convention, and the shift in party leadership, changes were also made in the position of the party and the Jewish section on questions involving the Jews.[33] A full examination of these changes is beyond the scope of this study. But in conclusion one must point out that even after the twistings and the contradictions of the KPP later on, the influence of processes that had been at work during the formative period could still be seen: stances in favor of a more consistent struggle against antisemitism; headway toward the formulations of positive demands on behalf of the Jews; and the establishment of institutional forms that would serve to organize the Jewish communist cadres internally and to shape them into autonomous factors in activities of the Jewish labor movement and in the Jewish community generally.

33. These changes are reflected outspokenly in the articles mentioned in note 31, above.

Abraham Brumberg

The Bund and the Polish Socialist Party in the Late 1930s

I

Relations between the Bund and the Polska Partia Socjalistyczna (PPS, Polish Socialist Party) in interwar Poland were characterized by intermittent friction, mutual suspicion, and occasional collaboration alternating with repeated failures to work out common platforms and programs of action. At first blush it might seem astonishing that these two parties could not work in tandem: both drew on similar constituencies—in the case of the Bund, the Jewish proletariat; in the case of the PPS, the Polish workers and (at least according to its program) the "working peasantry"; both were Marxist in their orientation; both were in principle dedicated to the abolition of the capitalist order and the creation of a socialist system.[1]

Yet, in fact, these similarities were more apparent than real. For one thing the Bund, even though it considered itself a "class party," was nevertheless vocal in demanding cultural, personal, and administrative autonomy for the Jewish community as a whole. For some Bundists, the espousal of equal rights for the Jewish minority in Poland—the right to maintain schools, theaters, newspapers, and

---

1. The Marxism of the PPS was more eclectic than that of the Bund. In the words of the Polish historian Jan Żarnowski, although "admittedly the official ideology of the PPS was that of Marxism and scientific socialism," there were considerable differences within the party "as to which concepts of Marxism, and which of its elements constitute the storehouse of scientific socialism." *Polska Partia Socjalistyczna w latach 1935–1939* (Warsaw, 1965), p. 182. Many PPS leaders were not Marxists, and belief in Marxism was not a condition for membership in the party. On the other hand, the party's educational materials were, according to Żarnowski, based largely on Marxist theories. See pp. 182–211; Jerzy Holzer, *PPS: Szkic Dziejów* (Warsaw, 1977), pp. 153–67.

other institutions in the Yiddish language, indeed the need to encourage the growth of an autonomous Jewish secular culture—was of paramount importance, a goal not more, but certainly not less, important than the triumph of socialism. For other Bundists cultural autonomy was an objective to be attained regardless of whether it would lead to the flourishing of Jewish secular culture or assimilation and—eventually—the loss of a Jewish identity.

The PPS, in contrast, was hostile to the very idea of cultural and administrative autonomy for the Jews. The platform adopted by the party at its Seventeenth Congress in 1919, and even more explicitly four years later, gave full support to the right of minorities to run their own institutions and to receive government subsidies for this purpose. But the party flatly rejected the national demands put forward by the Bund and other Jewish political parties. The rationale—strikingly similar to V. I. Lenin's view on the subject—was that the Jews were not a nationality and that the solution of the Jewish Question lay only and exclusively in secularization and eventual assimilation into the surrounding populace. Indeed, it was the PPS deputies in the first and second Sejms (Houses of Deputies) who, sometimes more vigorously than their right-wing rivals, opposed the "excessive" claims of the Jewish deputies. Bitter disputes raged not only over cultural rights but over economic matters as well—for example, over the bill stipulating Sunday as the only rest day for the entire population of the country and the attempts to deprive Jewish workers of access to equal employment. The Bund was never represented in the Sejm, so its clashes with the PPS over some of these questions took place in the various city councils in which both parties were represented, in the press, and sometimes at trade union gatherings.[2]

2. On the role of the Bund and of the Landrat fun Yidishe Profesyonele Fareynen (National Council of Jewish Trade Unions), dominated by the Bund, in the struggle against economic discrimination, particularly through the Byuro far Rekht oyf Arbet (Bureau for the Right to Work), organized by the trade unions in 1925, see Sholem Hertz, "Der Bund in umophengikn Poyln, 1926–1932," and Emanuel Nowogrodzki, "Kamf far rekht oyf arbet," in *Di geshikhte fun Bund*, ed. Sholem Hertz et al. (New York, 1960–81), 5:93–101, 145–66, respectively. In the early 1920s the Bund had few allies, among either the Poles or the Jews, in its efforts to force private enterprises and government-run institutions to hire Jewish workers or to resist the passage of laws specifically aimed at depriving Jews from equal access to employment. In *Lodzer veker,* March 10, 1921, the Łódź Bundist leader Shmuel Milman bitterly complained that "both the PPS and the Communists remain silent on this matter . . . fearing that they be accused, God forbid, of friendship toward the Jews." Quoted in Hertz, "Der Bund in umophengikn Poyln, 1926–1932," p. 96. The attitude changed somewhat

The problem of Polish nationalism also contributed to the tension between the two parties. Until 1918, the Bund's stance toward Polish independence was lukewarm. Once the Polish state came into being, the Bund proclaimed its loyalty to it, while insisting, in keeping with its principle of *doikeyt* (literally, "hereness") that since Jews, no less than any other nationality, considered Poland their rightful home, they were entitled to the same rights as all other citizens. There was an essential difference between what might be termed the evolving "Polish patriotism" of the Bund and the unabashed nationalism of the PPS. The Bund, for instance, refused to support Józef Piłsudski's attempt to incorporate the Western Ukraine and Belorussia into the Polish state (not to speak of a good part of Lithuania), while the PPS supported its old party chief wholeheartedly in his expansionist appetites. The nationalist fervor that gripped the Polish population during the Polish-Soviet War in 1919–20, especially in the wake of the so-called Miracle on the Vistula when Polish troops routed the Soviet forces, infected the Polish socialists as well. Later on, in the mid-1920s, the Bund was openly disdainful of the "collaborationist" attitude of the PPS (which participated in the government immediately preceding Piłsudski's *coup* of May 1926), of its initial support of the *coup*, and of its willingness to

---

starting in 1926, after the formation of the Byuro far Rekht oyf Arbet and the special Arbeter Kongres far Glaykhe Rekht oyf Arbet (Workers' Congress for Equal Labor Rights), organized by the Jewish trade unions. See S. M. Zigelboym, "Di profesyonele bavegung fun di yidishe arbeter," in *Die geshikhte fun Bund*, 4:196–200. The attitudes of the Jewish parties toward the problem of the Sunday Rest Law are summarized in Joseph Marcus, *Social and Political History of the Jews in Poland, 1919–1939* (New York, 1983), pp. 213–15. The Bund was opposed to the attempts to permit Jewish workers to work on Sundays, on the grounds that this would constitute an infringement of the forty-eight-hour week. Yet another reason, according to Marcus, was ideological. He paraphrases Wiktor Alter, a leader of the Bund, as saying that "the small traders are nothing else than a 'lumpen proletariat,' and their shops must sooner or later perish; so it would be wrong to prolong their existence by allowing them to trade on Sundays. The sooner these people became real proletarians, the better, said Alter" (p. 214, no source given). Nowogrodzki offers a less ideologically colored explanation of the Bund's position on this matter: "When the antisemites wanted to break the traditional Sabbath rest day, the Bund came out in defense of the right of Jews to a rest day on Saturday. However, when Jewish workers and employees began to make efforts to be employed in other [than Jewish] branches of industry or in national and municipal enterprises, the problem of their rest day was placed in a different light. To cling obstinately to the Sabbath would have meant, in practice, that the doors of those enterprises would be closed to Jewish applicants. There was no other choice, then, but to recommend that Jewish workers change their rest day from Saturday to Sunday. This was indeed the position adopted by the National Council of Jewish Trade Unions, which was directed by leaders of the Bund." Nowogrodzki, "Kamf far rekht oyf arbet," p. 155. See also Frank Golczewski, "The Problem of Sunday Rest in Interwar Poland," in this volume.

work with parties, such as the Polskie Stronnictwo Ludowe–Piast (PSL–Piast, Polish Peasant Party–Piast), the largest peasant party, whose nationalism was infused with a potent dose of antisemitism—all of which scarcely made for an amicable, let alone intimate, working relationship between the two parties.

Another factor that precluded systematic cooperation was the Bund's insistence on maintaining its ideological purity and organizational independence. The fear of ideological contamination did not, of course, characterize only the Bund; to a larger or lesser extent it was part, as many historians have noted, of the ethos and the *modus operandi* of all Jewish political parties in interwar Poland. But no other party was as determined to guard its freedom of action as was the Bund, and no other party was as fiercely opposed to entering into even temporary alliances with other political movements, Jewish or Polish. The only Jewish group with which the Bund maintained close and cordial relations was the Left Poalei Zion. So unalloyed was the Bund's hostility to all the Jewish parties (religious and Zionist) that it lumped them together with Polish right-wing parties in the same "reactionary camp." Its objections to the PPS were, to be sure, far less intense. In fact, the Bund made repeated efforts to enlist the cooperation of the PPS, but never in any manner that would imply either the blurring of its own organizational lines or its subordination (however temporary or tactical) to the latter.[3]

Ideologically, the PPS and the Bund were separated by a number of contentious issues, even apart from what the Bund perceived as the PPS's "nationalist deviation." The Bund was more aggressively "Marxist," more radical and contemptuous of social democratic parties stained by the sin of "reformism"—that is, by a less dogmatic approach to the problems of seizure of power, the need of instituting a "proletarian dictatorship" (or, as the Bund, ever conscious of doctrinal subtleties, maintained for a brief time, a "dictatorship of the revolutionary classes"). It was—as noted before—resolutely opposed to any idea of collaborating with bourgeois parties. Until it entered the Second Socialist International in 1930, it had been af-

---

3. The question of collaboration with Communists was shaped as much by the attitude of the Bund toward the Soviet Union and the Cominform as by the latter's policies, which the Polish Communists followed obediently. During the period 1928–35, in keeping with the line laid down by the Sixth Congress of the Communist International, the Bund found itself alternately wooed and attacked—not only verbally, but physically—by the Communists. For the Bund's attitude toward the popular front, see below.

filiated first with the so-called Two and a Half International head-quartered in Vienna, and then with the Paris Bureau of Revolutionary Parties. Once it joined the Socialist International, the Bund staked out for itself a position to the left of that occupied by most of the other member parties.[4]

Between the early 1920s and the mid-1930s both the Bund and the PPS underwent an ideological evolution, the former gradually shedding its unabashed leftist (and cautiously pro-Soviet) orientation, the latter eventually relinquishing its residual sympathy for Piłsudski (who embarked on his political career as a member of the PPS) and for his Sanacja associates. The influence of their respective left-wing factions (the PPS–Lewica [Left] and the so-called *tsveyers* [seconds] in the Bund) exemplifies these processes. In the Bund, the *tsveyers* in effect succeeded in capturing the party immediately after World War I, and although by 1925 they were reduced to a small if vocal minority, they nevertheless continued to exert an influence on the Bund's perception of the Soviet Union for more than another decade or so. The PPS–Lewica, on the other hand, remained until the end a small group of highly gifted intellectuals and political activists, with hardly any base of support within the party. Even after the first serious break between the PPS and Piłsudski, following his *coup* of May 1926, as well as after the beating and incarceration of numerous PPS leaders (and other opponents of Piłsudski) in September–October 1930, the party did not choose to embrace the more radical principles of the PPS–Lewica, sticking as it had in the past to its moderate, reformist guns. Characteristically, too, the Bund's youth groups, Tsukunft and Ogniwo, remained loyal constituent members of the parent organization throughout all of the latter's ideological vicissitudes, while the PPS-affiliated youth organizations, more radical than the PPS proper, retained their organizational and ideological autonomy.

The differences between the PPS and the Bund are strikingly illustrated by their respective attitudes toward the popular front. In the mid-1930s, the (illegal) Komunistyczna Partia Polski (KPP, Communist Party of Poland), in response to Comintern directives, issued a call for a popular front aimed against fascism and reaction.

---

4. On the debates preceding the Bund's entry into the Socialist International, see Sholem Hertz, "Der Bund in umophengikn Poyln, 1918–1925," in *Di geshikhte fun Bund*, 4:51–93; Bernard K. Johnpoll, *The Politics of Futility: The General Jewish Workers Bund of Poland, 1917–1943* (Ithaca, N.Y., 1967), pp. 136–41.

The PPS, though it had occasionally cooperated with the Communists in the past, unequivocally rejected the appeal. The Bund, despite its hostile attitude toward the Soviet Union, nevertheless considered a common front with the Communists both feasible and desirable. Thus Wiktor Alter, one of the principal leaders and theoreticians of the Bund, closed an article scathingly critical of the Moscow trials with the following words: "As in the past, so today it is our opinion that there is much in common between the socialist and communist workers; they should belong to one organization, in which conflicts can be resolved in a democratic manner, on the basis of freedom of thought and the discipline of action."[5]

A year later, illusions of the feasibility of a popular front discarded, Alter and the Bund fully endorsed the position of the PPS. The Bund (with the exception of its recalcitrant *tsveyers*) could no longer have any doubts that the Communist conception of a popular front was one which was to be controlled, dominated, and manipulated by the local Communists, which is to say, by the Comintern in Moscow. Yet it tells us something about the ideological orientations of the two parties that as late as 1936 Alter could criticize the PPS daily *Robotnik* for saying that "there exists an abyss between socialists and communists" and that "there can be no unity between them." The idea of a common bond between communist and socialist workers, both of them "struggling against fascism and capitalism," was for many years an article of faith, even for a man like Alter, his loathing of the Stalinist terror in the Soviet Union and of the Comintern's "organizational principle that leads to a dictatorship over the masses" notwithstanding.[6]

Finally, the problem of antisemitism. It was difficult for many Bundists, reared as they were on the dogma of proletarian internationalism, to acknowledge that hatred of the Jews was not confined only to the Polish middle classes, to segments of the intelligentsia, or (with minor exceptions) to the Catholic church, and indeed to nearly all of the political parties, but to a good part of the working class as well. Yet the Bundist press of the 1920s and early 1930s is full of reports on antisemitic incidents involving PPS workers. The heated disputes on the subject between the two parties, as

5. Wiktor Alter, "Di moskver ekzekutsyes," *Folkstsaytung* (Warsaw), September 1936, reprinted in *Henrik Erlikh un Viktor Alter,* ed. Viktor Shulman et al. (New York, 1951), p. 378.
6. Ibid., p. 375.

well as the written and oral reminiscences of various Bundist leaders,[7] clearly suggest that antisemitism in the working class was not
a marginal phenomenon. Although the leadership of the party
(among which were a number of prominent assimilated Jews) was
generally untouched by it and tried to counteract it, the leaders
would frequently find themselves hostage to the rank and file, which
resented any joint actions with a Jewish party and tended to regard
those who favored such cooperation as little more than flunkies of
the Jews.

This issue festered throughout the entire interwar period, most
conspicuously in the 1920s and early 1930s. In 1919–20, when a
wave of pogroms swept the country, the Bundist press bitterly attacked the PPS for failing to take decisive action against the mas-
sacres and for being reluctant to conduct a vigorous campaign
against antisemitic prejudices among the workers. Thus *Głos Bundu,*
in its issue of June 13, 1919:

> The stronger the influence of antisemitism, the more feeble and quiet
> are the protests of the Polish socialists. It is no exaggeration to say that
> in this respect their behavior amounts to ideological capitulation. . . .
> Antisemitism finds a fertile soil among the Polish working masses . . .
> [above all] because of the deeply rooted concept that a Jew, even a
> Jewish worker, is some kind of a creature deserving scorn and con-
> tempt. . . . The Polish socialists do little to counteract it. Although they
> condemn the pogroms, and pass appropriate resolutions (frequently
> halfheartedly) [*mit a halbn moyl*], they lack the courage openly and
> consistently to defend the idea that a Jew (literally a Jew, and not a
> Pole of Mosaic faith) has full rights in all areas of public life. Even
> worse, not only in the country as a whole, but in working-class in-
> stitutions, which base themselves on the class principle, Polish social-
> ists treat the Jewish workers as second-class citizens. . . . This tactic
> objectively helps to confirm in the Polish masses the conviction that
> Jews constitute a kind of caste, and that it is justifiable to persecute
> them.[8]

Charges of this sort were flung with monotonous regularity in the
succeeding years. The refrain was always the same: the PPS, out of
fear of the antisemitic attitudes of its constituents, refused to take
a strong stand on antisemitism, either on its own or in collaboration
with the Bund. In July 1923 the Bund managed to conclude an

---

7. This was confirmed to me by several Bundist leaders whom I interviewed in
preparation for this paper, including Sholem Hertz, Abraham Faynzilber of Vilna,
and Arthur Nonberg, who had worked in Galicia and Warsaw.

8. *Głos Bundu*, June 13, 1919, quoted in Hertz, "Der Bund in umophengikn Poyln,
1918–1925," p. 46.

agreement with the PPS to work in concert against "fascism, nationalism, and antisemitism." The agreement remained—as the Bund charged then and as latter-day historians concur—a dead letter; the PPS turned a deaf ear to the Bund's pleas that it be implemented.[9] Even in the one organization in which the Bund and the PPS coexisted, the Polish Zjednoczone Klasowe Związki Zawodowe (ZKZZ, Trade Union Movement), clashes about antisemitism were no novelty. In 1920 the Bund proposed a merger of the extant Jewish and Polish labor unions into centralized industrial unions "without regard to national or party identity." The PPS rejected the proposal, on the grounds that "a complete fusion is impossible at the present moment because of the antisemitic mood that reigns among many Polish workers."[10]

It should be noted that within the ZKZZ the ideological differences between the PPS and the Bund were less pronounced, and collaboration between them far more frequent than within the framework of party-to-party relations. For instance, although the PPS firmly rejected the notion of cultural autonomy for the Jews, the Third Congress of the ZKZZ, held in Warsaw in 1925, unanimously adopted a resolution demanding for all national minorities—"Ukrainians, White Russians, Jews, Germans, and Lithuanians"—the right to maintain, at the expense of the government, schools in their native languages, and the right "to employ these languages in the courts of the land."[11] Yet it was symptomatic that at the same congress a railroad worker from Vilna, Franciszek Stonrzowski, delivered a speech bristling with antisemitic invective. The Jewish delegates kept protesting, but to no avail; the chairman of the meeting, another Vilna railroad worker named Adam Kurilowicz, refused to call Stonrzowski to order.[12]

II

To sum up, then: despite ideological similarities, despite similar "proletarian" constituencies, and despite their tacit recognition of a common enemy, the PPS and the Bund had not managed to work

9. Ibid., p. 110.

10. Henryk Erlich, as quoted in Sholem Hertz, "Di profesyonele fareynen fun di yidishe arbeter," in *Di geshikhte fun Bund*, 4:270.

11. Quoted in ibid., p. 274.

12. *Undzer folkstsaytung* (Warsaw), June 16, 1925, p. 5.

out either a common political platform or a joint program of action. By 1936, however, the situation began to change and continued to do so until the outbreak of the Second World War—so much so that the period 1936–39 forms a distinct chapter in the relations between the PPS and the Bund.

Precipitated by the death of Marshal Józef Piłsudski in May 1935, economic deterioration and increasing political instability marked Poland in the late 1930s. If Piłsudski, even as he withdrew into sullen isolation during the last years of his life, was still able to impart a certain direction to the country's domestic and foreign policies, little—if any—of it was evident under the reign of his Sanacja successors. Internecine quarrels among the "Colonels" and frequent changes of government betrayed the bankruptcy of an elite whose only political credentials were their ties and loyalty to their late *Wódz* (Leader). The rise of Adolf Hitler helped spawn semifascist groups such as the Falanga and the Obóz Narodowo Radykalny (ONR, National Radical Camp) and spurred the growth of racist antisemitism within the ruling Obóz Zjednoczenia Narodowego (OZON, Camp of National Unity) no less than within the mainstay of the Endecja movement (which did not need much encouragement). By 1938 nearly all of the political parties in Poland, with the exception of the PPS, the miniscule Stronnictwo Demokratyczne (Democratic Party), and the KPP, adopted programs calling for the elimination of Jews and "Jewish influence" from Poland.[13] The hate campaign was accompanied by calls for an "economic boycott" (spearheaded by the Endeks and sanctioned by most of the Catholic clergy), by attempts to force Jewish students (whose access to higher education had already been severely restricted under Piłsudski) to occupy special "ghetto benches" at the universities, by a growing number of discriminatory measures, and by brute physical violence.

The PPS, faced by the growing fascist and antisemitic rampage,

---

13. See Edward D. Wynot, "'A Necessary Cruelty': The Emergence of Official Anti-Semitism in Poland, 1936–1939," *American Historical Review* 76 (1971): 1035–58. In fairness, it must be noted that the Stronnictwo Ludowe (SL, Peasant Party), which in its program adopted in December 1935 termed the Jews "a consciously alien nation" in Poland and supported economic boycott and Jewish emigration "with all our strength," dropped any reference to the Jews in the resolutions passed at its next congress in January 1937. "Six months after the congress, [the SL's] central press organ *Zielony Sztandar* dismissed the regime's growing antisemitism as a transparent device to . . . prolong Poland's real evil, 'the gentry's exploitation of the peasants.'" Edward D. Wynot, "The Polish Peasant Movement and the Jews, 1918–1939," in this volume, pp. 52–53.

became radicalized, by and large abandoning its hopes of influencing the policies of the Sanacja regimes. At its Twenty-Fourth Congress in February 1937 it adopted a series of resolutions that identified the Sanacja as no less an enemy of democracy than its traditional foe, the Endecja. Another resolution called for a concerted struggle against antisemitism and for the recognition of cultural autonomy and equal rights not only for the Ukrainian, Belorussian, Lithuanian, and German minorities, but specifically and explicitly for Poland's three and one-half million Jews. Passage of this resolution alone eliminated—or at least should have eliminated—one of the major obstacles to joint action with the Bund.

For the Bund, too, 1936 was a turning point. Until then the Bund could not be considered a mass party; its influence had been confined almost entirely to the Jewish working class and a part of the Jewish intelligentsia. Now it became, in the eyes of the majority of Polish Jews, a party defending the interests of the Jewish population at large. The single event most overtly responsible for this remarkable change of perception was the pogrom of March 9, 1936, in the town of Przytyk, near Radom. In several hours of wanton violence, two Jews were killed, twenty more seriously injured, and Jewish homes and property were put to the torch. While the pogrom was neither the first nor the worst of the furious attacks on Jews that spread throughout the country in the late 1930s, it was seen as a symbol of the virulence and strength of antisemitism, hitherto kept under control (more or less) by the Piłsudski regime. Shocked by its magnitude, as well as by the passivity (if not tacit encouragement) of the local police, Jewish political parties responded with anger against not only the Endeks (who had organized the pogrom), but the Sanacja regime as well. Even the traditionally conciliatory Agudat Israel was forced to revise its attitude: henceforth, *shtadlanut* (intercession) was to give way to political activism.

But by far the most spectacular initiative came from the Bund. In a passionate appeal, it called upon Polish Jews to stage a half-day protest strike on March 17. The response was overwhelming. On the scheduled day, hundreds of thousands of workers, shopkeepers, businessmen, and even factory owners laid down their tools and closed their establishments. Hundreds of protest meetings took place throughout the country. The morning after, all the Yiddish papers (as well as some Polish ones) paid tribute to the success of the strike no less than to its organizers.[14]

14. Paweł Korzec, "Antisemitism in Poland as an Intellectual, Social, and Political

The militant stand of the Bund thus won it adherents even from the ranks of those inhospitable to its general program and ideology. Their numbers grew as the Bund's self-defense squads—Ordener-Grupes and Tsukunft-Shturem—went into action to guard May Day demonstrators against attacks by antisemitic hooligans, to defend shopkeepers, to protect Jewish students from razor-wielding Endeks at the universities, and to organize resistance in towns threatened by pogroms.[15] Nor was this all: when the government tabled a new law banning ritual slaughter, clearly designed to present Jewish religious practices in the most odious light and to deprive thousands of Jews of their livelihood, the Bund rose to their defense. The growing constituency of the Bund soon translated into electoral victories. In 1936 and again in 1938 the Bund gained impressive majorities in local *kehillot* (Jewish community councils)—which the Bund had boycotted until then—and in various city councils. Its most striking success came in the elections to the Warsaw city council in 1938, where it won seventeen out of the twenty-one seats claimed by the Jewish parties.

According to one historian, the Bund "put itself in the forefront of 'the struggle against antisemitism'" purely out of a desire "to make capital out of the anxieties of the people."[16] The charge has no substance. True, the Bund continued to reject the concept of a *kol-yisroel* party. It continued to refuse collaboration with parties it deemed to be tools of "clericalism" and the "bourgeoisie." It remained bitterly opposed to Zionism. In view of British policy at the time, it could—and did—claim that the Zionist option of mass emigration was more illusory than ever. But its policies were as much an outgrowth of the Bund's traditional claim to represent the interests of the Jewish masses as a direct and altogether logical response to the raging antisemitic tide that began to engulf Poland in the mid-1930s and that the Bund singled out as the greatest threat not only to the Jews but to democracy in general. Its position was as compatible with its image as a Jewish party as with its loyalty to the concept of "proletarian solidarity."

What, then, of "proletarian solidarity"? The time was certainly ripe, more than ever before, for the two socialist parties to subsume

Movement," in *Studies on Polish Jewry, 1919–1939,* ed. Joshua A. Fishman (New York, 1974), p. 87; Johnpoll, *Politics of Futility,* p. 213.

15. On the Bund's self-defense squads, see Leonard Rowe, "Jewish Self-Defense: A Response to Violence," in *Studies on Polish Jewry,* pp. 105–49.

16. Marcus, *Social and Political History,* p. 360.

their differences in a closing of ranks before their joint enemy. And so they did, up to a point. In fact, as time went on, the Bund and the PPS collaborated in a manner that would have been unusual, if not unthinkable, five or ten years earlier. What follows is a partial yet representative list of actions undertaken jointly by the Bund and the PPS:

First, the half-day protest strike against the Przytyk pogrom. While designed as a specifically Jewish manifestation, it was fully endorsed by the PPS, some of whose leaders addressed rallies and meetings organized on that day by the Bund.

Second, the Arbeter Kongres tsum Kamf mitn Antisemitizm (Workers' Congress for the Struggle against Antisemitism), scheduled for June 13, 1936, though eventually prohibited by the Polish authorities. The Bund made a concerted effort to involve Polish workers in the preparations for the congress (sponsored by the Bund and the Landrat fun Yidishe Profesyonele Fareynen [National Council of Jewish Trade Unions]) and was aided in this effort by the PPS. According to the Bund newspaper *Naye folkstsaytung*, "thousands of workers, both Jewish and Polish," took part in the numerous meetings held in the first months of 1936. The PPS printed and distributed half a million copies of an appeal to Poles to support this action. Local PPS organizations produced similar leaflets.[17] A special supplement to the *Naye folkstsaytung*, called *Arbeter kongres tsum kamf mitn antisemitizm*, May 24, 1936, carried endorsements from Mieczysław Niedziałkowski, editor-in-chief of *Robotnik*; a long article by the secretary of the PPS, Kazimierz Pużak; and one by Jan Kwapiński, chairman of the Central Committee of the ZKZZ.

Third, the strike organized by Polish peasants for "freedom, democracy, and an end to dictatorship," held August 15–25, 1937. Work on the fields and transport of produce to the cities came to a halt. Thousands of peasants flocked to mass rallies throughout the country. The police were dispatched to suppress the strike, in the course of which fifty peasants were mowed down by police bullets. The PPS and the Bund sent speakers to the rallies, raised funds for the peasants, and staged memorial demonstrations.[18]

Fourth, joint actions undertaken at universities on the initiative of the Bund's youth organizations, Tsukunft and Ogniwo and the

17. *Naye folkstsaytung* (Warsaw), April 19, 1936, p. 7. Some of these leaflets can be found in the Bund Archives, New York.
18. Jacob Pat, *Der oysveg in Poyln* (New York, 1938), pp. 16–17.

youth groups close to the PPS, especially the left-oriented Związek Niezależnej Młodzieży Socjalistycznej (Union of Independent Socialist Youth). A detailed study of the student movements in the 1930s, published in Warsaw in 1972, provides a grim picture of the difficulties faced by left-wing student groups (among them groups associated with the left wing of the Polskie Stronnictwo Ludowe–Wyzwolenie [PSL–Wyzwolenie, Polish Peasant Party–Liberation], the Stronnictwo Demokratyczne, and the underground KPP) in combatting antisemitism at the universities. The majority of students either belonged to various Endek and extreme right-wing groups (such as ONR and Falanga) or was strongly under their influence. The clamor for introducing a so-called Aryan Paragraph in the universities also found a sympathetic echo within the academic and administrative staffs. In 1935 and 1938, the congresses of the Union of Polish Academic Corporations passed resolutions demanding that universities adopt the *numerus nullus* principle in their admission as well as in their hiring policies. Bowing to pressure from students and professors alike, the government by late 1937–early 1938 in effect sanctioned the introduction of "ghetto benches" at the universities and the further restrictions on admission of Jewish students, though it balked at the demand for a *numerus nullus* and feebly condemned the physical attacks on Jewish students. Nonetheless, the protest actions organized by the left-wing youth groups—mostly the production and dissemination of leaflets, but also the staging of several protest rallies—helped to strengthen the morale of the rapidly dwindling and beleaguered Jewish student body.[19]

Fifth, the general response to antisemitic violence. The Bund's self-defense units frequently worked hand in glove with the PPS militia, especially its paramilitary formation called Akcja Socjalistyczna (Socialist Action).[20]

Sixth, May Day demonstrations. Rare in the 1920s and early 1930s, after 1936 joint demonstrations became far more frequent. In some cases they were banned by the authorities. In those cases where the PPS and the Bund joined forces, the Bund—true to its

19. For details, see Andrzej Pilch, *Studencki ruch polityczny w Polsce w latach 1937–1939* (Warsaw, 1972), pp. 157–71; *Tsvey yor arbet un kamf: Barikht fun der varshever organizatsye fun Yugnt-Bund "Tsukunft" in Poyln, 1937–1939* (Warsaw, 1939).
20. Jerzy Holzer, *Mozaika polityczna Drugiej Rzeczypospolitej* (Warsaw, 1974), p. 507; Bernard Goldstein, *Tsvantsik yor in varshever "Bund," 1919–1939* (New York, 1960).

principles—always insisted on marching under its own banners rather than those of the PPS. Both the PPS and the Bund detachments, however, were protected by mixed militia groups drawn from both parties. At the end of the marches the participants joined together in public meetings addressed by the Bund, PPS, and trade union leaders alike.

Seventh, city council elections. In 1936, and even more in 1937 and 1938, the two parties, despite the PPS's rejection of the Bund's proposal for a united ticket, worked far more closely than ever before. In some cases the Bund asked its supporters to vote for the PPS candidates in districts where the Bund did not field its own candidates. In areas where the PPS knew it was bound to lose to its right-wing Polish rivals, it asked the voters to support the Bund ticket. In Warsaw and Łódź, where the two parties scored substantial electoral victories in 1936 and 1938, the municipal councils became a major arena in which the parties collaborated on specific legislative projects.

Finally, publications dealing with antisemitism. Both the Bund and the PPS published a number of brochures on this subject, some of them under joint sponsorship. Judging by references in the *Naye folkstsaytung*, the PPS press, daily and periodical, also carried more articles on this subject. In the past antisemitism had been treated warily by a party anxious lest it be accused (by its own members) of excessive "philosemitism." Now that Polish antisemitism was no longer seen as a mere species of nationalism but as part of an explicitly racist and fascist political program, embraced in part or *in toto* by nearly all of the political parties in Poland, the time had come to speak plainly on this issue. "Contemporary antisemitism has an altogether different character"—thus Adam Próchnik, one of the leaders of the PPS. "It is racism, reborn in Hitlerism." Its chief exponents are the "Hitlerite sections of the Endecja, such as the various ONRs," but also the "official Endecja," with the "government camp and the peasant camp" trailing behind them. "The wave of antisemitism is rushing on, devastating everything on its way, and threatening to cause even more terrible devastation in the future. Who will resist it in the Polish political world? None but the camp of social justice."[21]

---

21. Adam Próchnik, "Polskie stronnictwa polityczne a antysemityzm," in *O Żydach i Antysemityzmie*, published by the Bund (Warsaw, 1936), pp. 35–38.

Yet another new note was that of sympathy for the national and cultural demands of the Bund. In an article published in the PPS newspaper *Dziennik Ludowy,* the left PPS leader Zygmunt Zaremba denounced the notion that Polish Jews, because of their distinct culture and language, were indifferent to the fate of Poland. He praised the efforts "to cultivate the Yiddish mother tongue and to maintain schools with Yiddish as the language of instruction." Such schools, said Zaremba, not only do not alienate the "Jewish child from Poland" but, in fact, by using the child's own language, help to instill in him a loyalty to his homeland.[22] One need hardly point out that it was not exactly the chief function of the Yiddish schools to inculcate Jewish children with the spirit of Polish patriotism. Nonetheless, Zaremba's words were a far cry from the "assimilationist" position advocated by the PPS in the past.

III

The evidence, then, suggests a marked improvement in the relationship between the PPS and the Bund in the years 1936–39. Yet two questions arise: First, what was the actual magnitude of the collaboration between the two parties, and second, to what degree did it reflect a change in the average Polish worker's attitude toward Jews and antisemitism?

These questions derive, to begin with, from the political climate in Poland in the late 1930s. As mentioned earlier, not only did the largest political movement, the Endecja, pledge itself to render the country *Judenrein,* whether by means of economic boycott, emigration, or physical violence, but so did most of the other parties. In addition, the antisemitic campaign was abetted and encouraged by a good part of the Catholic clergy.[23] Was it reasonable in such circumstances to expect the average worker to remain impervious to the relentless hate campaign, to the notion that his own lot would vastly improve if only the parasitic and exploitive three and one-half million Jews would somehow vanish from the scene?

The Bundist sources, from which most of the evidence in this

22. Zygmunt Zaremba, in *Dziennik Ludowy* (Warsaw), July 25, 1939, as reported in *Naye folkstsaytung,* July 26, 1939.
23. See Korzec, "Antisemitism in Poland"; Edward D. Wynot, "The Catholic Church and the Polish State, 1935–1939," *Journal of Church and State* 15 (1973): 223–40.

paper is drawn, also invite some skepticism. If the Bund had trouble accepting the full reality of working-class antisemitism in the 1920s, it found it even more difficult to concede its existence once the PPS adopted a more forceful attitude toward antisemitism. The difficulty faced by the contemporary researcher lies not in the accuracy of the reports on specific joint actions and declarations but rather in some of the general claims advanced by the Bund at that time. A case in point is the pamphlet entitled *Der oysveg in Poyln* (The Way Out in Poland), written by the Bund leader Jacob Pat and published by the Jewish Labor Committee in New York in 1938. The pamphlet deals with the spreading orgy of anti-Jewish violence in Poland and with the resistance to it mounted by the Bund and the PPS. The facts, as related by the author, speak for themselves. But what of the author's more rhetorical assertions? Was it true that "the Polish masses are becoming ever more conscious of the danger posed by antisemitism to them no less than to the Jews"? Or that "tens of thousands of Polish workers" joined "the Jewish masses on March 17, 1936, in their protest strike against pogroms"? In January 1937, the Sixth Congress of the Farband fun Profesyonele Klasn-Fareynen–Yidishe Opteylung (Union of Professional Trade Unions–Jewish Section), held in Warsaw, was addressed by, among others, the PPS leader Antoni Szczerkowski. "I stretch my hands out to you, Jewish workers"—according to Pat—"the hands of a Polish worker and I cry out in the name of the entire working class of the country: 'Long live the brotherhood of the Jewish and Polish workers!' "—at which point "the audience rose with enthusiasm; hearts and banners fluttered in unison."[24] A stirring scene; but how representative?

The evidence indicates that Pat was engaging in that venerable and altogether understandable human proclivity for wishful thinking. There is no concrete proof, for instance, that "tens of thousands of workers" participated in the Przytyk protest strike. A detailed study, published by the Jewish Historical Institute in Warsaw in 1972, carefully avoids giving any figures on Polish participation. It cites Jan Kwapiński, head of the Polish trade unions, who was asked by the Jewish union leadership to urge his constituents to participate in the strike. Kwapiński expressed his general "solidarity" with the

24. Pat, *Der oysweg in Poyln,* pp. 7, 8, 10. The pamphlet mistakenly dates the Sixth Congress to December 1935; it took place in January 1937.

plea but added "that the situation has not matured sufficiently for common action because part of the working class has yielded to nationalist slogans."[25] The Communist historian T. Berenstein concedes that while "90 percent of all Jewish workers and more than two-thirds of the Jewish population" participated in the strike, the Polish representation was low—due, ostensibly, not only to "the nationalist separatism of the right-wing leaders of the PPS" but also to the refusal of the Bund to work together with the KPP. (Since the influence of the KPP among Polish workers was minimal, Berenstein's claim has little to recommend it.)[26]

An article in the Yiddish daily *Haynt*, which appeared one day after the strike, also sheds some light on the question of Polish participation. The author, while expressing his admiration for the work of the Bund, went on to indulge in some ironic comments. The strike, he concluded, did not exactly prove the Bund's assertion that antisemitism is merely the "product of capitalist relations," for "on the whole the Polish working class, the socialist working class, remained a passive onlooker, refusing to take part in the demonstration."[27] The author was an opponent of the Bund; still, his observations seem far more congruent with the assessments quoted above than with the rather inflated claims of the Bund.

In addition, the elections to the Łódź municipal council in 1936 and 1938 have been depicted as remarkable victories not only for the Bund and the PPS separately, but also for their newly forged alliance. The facts suggest a somewhat different conclusion. In 1936 the PPS firmly refused to run on a joint ticket with the Bund, on the grounds that to do so would compromise it in the eyes of many workers and would seriously damage its ability to defeat the Endek candidates. Instead the PPS proposed two tickets: one consisting of the PPS and the Polish trade unions, the other of the Bund and the Jewish unions. The Bund grudgingly agreed (though not, as a later memoir by one of its local leaders conceded, without "pain and bitterness"),[28] only to be faced with a new demand that the Bund withdraw and urge its constituents to vote for the PPS list. The

25. Marian Grinberg, in *Biuletyn Żydowskiego Instytutu Historycznego*, no. 24 (1972): 28–52, quotation from Jan Kwapiński on p. 47.

26. T. Berenstein, "Walka KPP przeciwko pogromom," *Biuletyn Żydowskiego Instytutu Historycznego*, nos. 15–16 (1956): 50.

27. A. Eynhorn, in *Haynt*, March 18, 1938.

28. Shmuel Milman, "Der Bund in Lodz fun 1912 biz 1939," *Undzer tsayt*, 1947, nos. 3–4, pp. 107–12.

conflict finally died down, largely as a result of representations made
by the central authorities of the PPS,[29] but it flared up again two
years later when the PPS again refused to work jointly with the
Bund "because of antisemitic sentiments which make it impossible
for Jewish names to appear on the same list with the PPS."[30] After
the 1938 elections there was another unpleasant incident. The Bund,
which had won eleven out of the seventeen Jewish seats, demanded
one of the two vice-presidential posts in the council. The request
was rejected. Kwapiński stated bluntly that "the PPS cannot allow
a Jew to hold such a position, not because the Jews do not deserve
it, but because of the reaction of the Polish masses." If we go along
with the request, he added, "we shall simply lose many of our supporters." No doubt he was right.[31]

Other examples of the resilience of antisemitic feelings among
Polish workers and its inhibitive impact on PPS's relations with the
Bund can be found in the study of the PPS by the Polish historian
Jan Żarnowski.[32] A somewhat different, yet revealing illustration of
this attitude is the pamphlet by the PPS writer J. M. Borski, called
Sprawa żydowska a socjalizm: Polemika z Bundem (The Jewish Problem
and Socialism: A Polemic with the Bund).[33] The pamphlet was published in 1937 by the PPS newspaper *Robotnik*. Borski did not occupy
any position of authority in the party, but he was one of its major
publicists and a regular contributor to *Robotnik* on both domestic
and international issues. The pamphlet, ostensibly a defense of the
Poalei Zion position on the Jewish Question, was a forceful and frequently acrid attack on the position of the Bund, particularly as
enunciated by Wiktor Alter in his major article "O Żydach i Antysemityzmie" (About Jews and Antisemitism). According to Alter's
orthodox Marxist interpretation, antisemitism, a product of the capitalist order, would automatically disappear with the establishment
of a socialist state.[34] Not so, said Borski: Alter's analysis of the

29. *Der yidisher arbeter klas in yor 1936* (Łódź, 1937), p. 253.
30. Milman, "Der Bund in Lodz."
31. Efraim Lazer (Zalmanovitsh), "Der Bund in Lodz," *Undzer tsayt,* 1947, nos.
3–4, pp. 117–18.
32. Żarnowski, *Polska Partia Socjalistyczna.* After listing several cases where PPS
leaders refused to join the Bund in united May Day demonstrations, Żarnowski
writes: "In most localities the authorities forbade joint May Day demonstrations of
Polish and Jewish organizations. In many cases the PPS greeted these orders with
relief" (p. 245).
33. J. M. Borski, *Sprawa żydowska a socjalizm: Polemika z Bundem* (Warsaw, 1937).
34. "In other words, antisemitism is the armor of the capitalist order. As long as

causes of antisemitism is flawed, and his prognosis little more than a chimera. Anti-Jewish hatred in Poland, in Borski's view, is not rooted in economic rivalry and exploitation. Rather, it stems from the fact that the Jews constitute "an alien element," culturally, religiously, linguistically, and even physically. Jews have never considered Poland as their homeland, they have "no tradition" and "no history as a nation in Poland." They remain and will remain steeped in their "medieval" and "backward" ways and customs whether Poland stays capitalist or turns socialist. And since they will never assimilate or be accepted as equals, their only alternative is to emigrate.[35]

It is of course legitimate to argue that Borski's advocacy of emigration is no more "antisemitic" than that of the Zionists. Indeed, Borski notes in his introduction that "in the struggle between the Bund and the Poalei Zion" he "leans toward the program of the Poalei Zion."[36] Yet in fact Borski's position falls more within the rubric of what was known at that time as "emigrationism" than emigration as understood by most Zionist parties (including Poalei Zion).[37] All Zionist parties remained wedded to emigration as the fundamental and eventual solution to the Jewish Question. Few, however, considered a mass exodus in the mid-1930s as a realistic option. The right of, and elimination of all obstacles to, free emigration to Palestine, they maintained, must go hand in hand with the struggle for equal rights for Poland's Jews (a subject Borski mentions only in passing). Moreover, it was precisely the notion of the Jews as an "alien" element—"backward," "medieval," "ob-

---

capitalism exists, antisemitism will exist and flourish. And the other way around: Antisemitism can be defeated only and exclusively by the abolition of the capitalist system." Wiktor Alter, "O Żydach i Antysemityzmie," in *Tsu der yidn-frage in Poyln* (Warsaw, 1937), pp. 8–28, quotation on p. 18.

35. Borski, *Sprawa żydowska a socjalizm*, pp. 10–12.

36. Ibid., p. 3.

37. Apparently the Right Poalei Zion found Borski's brochure embarrassing, judging from an article by the editor of the Poalei Zion newspaper *Naye vort* (Warsaw), April 9, 1937, as cited in *Naye folkstsaytung*, April 10, 1937, p. 5: "To be sure, there are passages [*psukim*] in Borski's brochure that are false and even dangerous. Not a single Jew will leave Poland in order to deprive the Endeks of a basis for their reaction and antisemitism. It is also a mistake to maintain that Jewish emigration can have this result." Nevertheless, the author goes on, "It is a distortion of the facts to accuse Borski of sinning against socialism only because he identifies emigration as part of the Jewish problem." To which the *Naye folkstsaytung* comments, with rather evident *Schadenfreude*: "Mr. Helman [the editor] cannot, poor fellow, swallow the bone. On the one hand—it is indeed a Poale Zion bone, but on the other a rather hard and thorny one."

scurantist"—that was the stock in trade of all the antisemitic parties and the *ultima ratio* for their advocacy of mass emigration—to Palestine, Madagascar, or the putative "colonies" that Poland was suddenly discovered to be in need of. All of which helps to explain why the Bund found Borski's pamphlet not a legitimate polemic but a profoundly offensive diatribe.

Was *Sprawa żydowska a socjalizm* a mere aberration? Possibly. It was repudiated by the PPS (and bitterly condemned by the Bund); it was in startling contrast to the resolutions approved by the PPS at its Twenty-Fourth Congress in February 1937. But it also illustrates the tenacity of antisemitic stereotypes even within the ranks of the PPS intelligentsia and the fragility of the very idea of ethnic diversity and pluralism as a principle of modern nationhood.[38]

In sum, then, the period 1936–39 was indeed one in which the two socialist parties in Poland gravitated toward each other. In the face of the growing menace of fascism, externally and internally, erstwhile feuds were forgotten and common goals reasserted. The evidence of concerted actions and of a generally healthier and more cordial relationship between the PPS and the Bund cannot be gainsaid.

Yet when all is said and done, it is difficult not to agree with the Polish historian Żarnowski, who in his study of the PPS during this crucial period notes, "On the one hand the official struggle waged by the PPS against antisemitism, perceived as an integral part of the struggle against the Endecja, and on the other hand the growth of antisemitism within the very ranks of the party."[39] Whether the struggle against antisemitism and fascism might have borne fruit had it not been for the war and the cataclysmic fate that befell the entire Jewish community of Poland is a question no one can answer. What seems to be true, however, is that at a time when Poland was moving toward totalitarianism, the Jewish population as a whole and the Bund in particular found it possible to influence neither the policies of the regime nor even the fundamental attitudes of its closest ideological ally, the Polish Socialist Party.

38. The fact that Borski was of Jewish origin in no way vitiates this judgment. Borski was not the first Jew to internalize antisemitic stereotypes, such as Jewish "backwardness" or lack of "tradition."
39. Żarnowski, *Polska Partia Sojalistyczna*, p. 245.

Antisemitism

Yisrael Gutman

Polish Antisemitism Between the Wars: An Overview

The phenomenon of modern, or political, antisemitism, which dates from the 1870s and has left its mark on a variety of countries, stands at the center of a long-lasting scholarly debate. The preeminent question in this debate is, Is it possible to identify common sources or processes throughout Europe that stirred and fed the wave of Jew-hatred which crested and overflowed almost simultaneously in societies as different from one another in pace of development, in cultural and economic system, and in political regime as Germany, France, Austria, Hungary, and Russia? Or were the outbreaks of antisemitism in each country related to indigenous factors and their contemporaneity merely coincidental?

One does not need to tackle this complex and thorny question in all its ramifications in order to provide a historical assessment of the phenomenon of Polish antisemitism. Antisemitism in Poland, which began gathering momentum in the 1880s, derived from changes within the Polish national movement and was affected by developments throughout Europe. Following the trauma of the failed Uprising of 1863, the Poles as a nation engaged in deep soul searching. Hope for liberation from foreign domination and for restoration of Polish independence through an act of force diminished and, in some cases, was wholly abandoned. To a great extent, the Poles lost faith in the compelling power of European liberal nationalism, with its appeal to the right of self-determination for all peoples in general and for the Poles in particular. National impulses began to be redirected toward other, more realistic, goals, such as promoting greater social solidarity among the various strata of the Polish society within a framework that questioned the privileged position of the gentry. In the economic sphere there were calls for pragmatism, for fostering entrepreneurship and urban economic development. In the political sphere new tactics were developed that stressed maneuvering among the partitioning powers and exploiting the political and military crises that beset them, as well as uniting the Poles formerly split by the Partition into one national-acting community. The Narodowa Demokracja (National Democracy, its adherents the National Democrats, or Endeks), which took shape during the early 1890s, spoke of "national egoism," and, while viewing Prussia as Poland's most formidable enemy, it regarded Otto von Bismarck as a model statesman to be emulated.

This wing of Polish nationalism adopted an antisemitic position from the outset. The National Democrats' platform of 1903 stated that the Jews ought to be completely subordinated to the Polish national interest and removed from the key positions in Polish economic life and that their influence in Polish society and culture must be curtailed.[1] Roman Dmowski, the prominent leader of this party, had been an outspoken antisemite since his youth, and his expressly stated anti-Jewish position formed an integral part of his passionate political writings, of his career as a statesman, and of his leadership of an ideological and political movement. From his first pamphlet, *Separatyzm Żydów i jego źródła* (Separatism of the Jews and Its Sources),[2] until the end of his political career in the late 1930s, his anti-Jewish views grew increasingly extreme and harsh. According to some historians, Poland's social and political structure between the two world wars was shaped above all by the influence of two dominant figures: Józef Piłsudski and Roman Dmowski. According to Dmowski, the Jews formed an alien body in Poland and, with the exception of some individuals, they were neither capable nor deserving of being integrated into the Polish nation. For him, mass assimilation of Jews was undesirable, as it would undermine the Polish mentality and the unique national character of the Polish people. The Jews only took advantage of the political and social weakness of Poland in order to penetrate the country. In times of trial they had always joined forces with Poland's enemies, and they constituted not merely a foreign element but a kind of subversive force. When in 1912 the Jews refused to support Polish candidates

1. For parts of the program concerning Jews, see Barbara Toruńczyk, ed., *Narodowa Demokracja: Antologia myśli politycznej "Przeglądu Wszechpolskiego"* (London, 1983), pp. 121–22.

2. Roman Dmowski, *Separatyzm Żydów i jego źródła* (Warsaw, 1909).

with an openly anti-Jewish outlook in the elections for the Fourth
Duma, a parliamentary body in tsarist Russia, an anti-Jewish economic boycott and a brutal, demagogic campaign against the Jews
were launched by Dmowski and his party.[3]

The existence of antisemitism in interwar Poland is an incontro-
vertible fact. Scholars differ, however, in their assessments of the
extent and intensity of Polish antisemitism in comparison to that in
other European countries at the time, and recent investigations have
sought to identify *leitmotifs* of the animosity toward the Jews in order
to develop a typology of antisemitism and to assess its relative
strength and impact among various social strata and political parties
and on Polish foreign policy.

An examination of the roots of Polish antisemitism lies outside
the framework of this paper. It goes without saying that the oft-
repeated observation about all Poles at all times being Jew-haters
is unfounded. However, antisemitism in Poland has remained, in
Julian Marchlewski's words, "powerful and beastly for ages."[4]

In the period between the two world wars the historical tradition
of Polish antisemitism exerted a considerable influence on the web
of relations between Poles and Jews. The negative image of the Jew
had been temporarily discredited in the 1860s, especially during
the Uprising of 1863, when one could even discern some signs of
rapprochement between the two peoples. From the turn of the century until the First World War, however, the polarization of Jews
and Poles increased, and Polish opposition to the Jews mounted.
The negative image of the Jew had been undergoing changes in still
another sense. In the past, the image of the Jew as peddler, innkeeper, and middleman had been an individual stereotype. Now it
became a collective stereotype, referring to the Jews as a whole.
Here the Jews emerge as wielding enormous power in Poland and
the world at large, as representing their own particularistic and
national interests, and as devising dark plots against Poland and
Christian society in general.

At the same time, however, it should be emphasized that Jew-
hatred in Poland, while fed by contempt and by prejudices of religious background and superstitions portraying the Jew as swindler

---

3. For more details on the background of the boycott, see Frank Golczewski,
*Polnisch-jüdische Beziehungen, 1881–1922: Eine Studie zur Geschichte des Antisemitismus in
Osteuropa* (Wiesbaden, 1981), pp. 101–20.

4. Julian B. Marchlewski, *Antysemityzm a robotnicy* (Chicago, 1913), p. 54.

and exploiter in business, never assumed the a-human or antihuman dimensions of racism in its German rendition. In contrast to Poland, antisemitism in Germany became the pivot of a whole world view and provided legitimacy for administrative structures designed to implement remorselessly antisemitic policies. Polish antisemitism could lead to disturbances and even violent outbursts, but not to systematic destruction and total extermination.

Józef Piłsudski is credited with saying that as a Pole he would be ashamed if pogroms had taken place in Poland. It is conceivable that the international press presented an overblown account of anti-Jewish excesses in the years 1918–20. At the same time, however, one cannot ignore the wave of pogroms that swept over newly independent Poland, in places such as Kielce, Lwów, and Pinsk, as well as blood libels, murders, and executions in which the army was also involved. During the First World War the Jews were accused of being pro-German and therefore disloyal. At the end of the war and during the restoration of Polish independence, they were accused of supporting the Ukrainians in Eastern Galicia and of being allied with the Bolsheviks.

In Polish interwar historiography the Jews and their supporters were often portrayed as prime movers behind the Minorities Treaty the victorious powers imposed on the new and enlarged countries of Central and Southern Europe. To a great extent the Poles were justified in maintaining that this treaty expressed lack of confidence in the ability and will of certain countries to guarantee equal treatment of their minorities. In fact, Polish Jews were not greatly benefited by this treaty, as authorities in Poland, and in other countries as well, always managed to find a way to circumvent its terms. At the same time, I believe that the Polish policy toward the minorities in general and Jews in particular vindicated *post factum* those who were suspicious of the Polish intentions and demanded the imposition of the Minorities Treaty in principle.

Some scholars argue that one cannot speak of antisemitism *per se* as a premeditated anti-Jewish government policy in interwar Poland. This argument crops up in the contemporary Polish historical scholarship. According to this view all minorities suffered from discrimination; the Jews were not an exception, and their plight did not stem directly from specifically antisemitic policies. In other words, if I may use the formulation recently put forward by Jerzy Tomaszewski, the country was torn between competing conceptions: a "commonwealth of many nations" (*rzeczpospolita wielu narodów*) on the one hand or a "Poland for the Poles" on the other.[5] What happened was that the second view gained the upper hand.

Now this argument is correct so far as it goes. Unquestionably the Ukrainians and the Belorussians were discriminated against and denied rights in interwar Poland. In my view, however, the situation of the Jews and the treatment they received were unique. In the case of the Ukrainians and the Belorussians, proposals were advanced for various forms of federation and autonomy on the one hand, and for forced assimilation and linguistic-cultural Polonization on the other. None of those proposals, however, denied these minorities the very right of settling and living on the land their forefathers had occupied for generations. The Jews fared very differently. They were denied the elementary right of residing on Polish land. Centuries of settlement and involvement in the Polish economy and other areas of Polish life did not, apparently, earn them this right. In the 1920s one section of Polish society and the Polish political system denied the Jews this right, whereas other forces came out in defense of the Jews' status as citizens with equal rights. In the 1930s, especially after the death of Piłsudski and the tightening of ties with Nazi Germany, the majority of the Poles began leaning toward the "exclusivist" position. By this time exclusivism was upheld not merely as a theoretical assumption but as a policy to be pursued; it took the form of a public campaign whose radical fringes resorted to violence. Bogusław Miedziński, editor of the government's *Gazeta Polska* and a leader in the camp of Piłsudski's heirs, quipped in the Sejm (House of Deputies) in 1937 that he personally liked Danes very much but if there had been three million Danes in Poland he would want to get rid of them as soon as possible. Władysław Pobóg-Malinowski, who was far from being close to the Endek's views, observed in the second volume of his history of modern Poland, written after the Second World War, that the Jews, unlike the Ukrainians and Belorussians, had not been an indigenous population; they simply had found haven in Poland from persecutions or were settled in the country by the hostile tsarist power.[6]

There is also another theory I would like to mention here. It holds that the maltreatment of the Jews in interwar Poland was caused by

5. Jerzy Tomaszewski, *Rzeczpospolita wielu narodów* (Warsaw, 1985).
6. *Gazeta Polska*, January 12, 1937; Władysław Pobóg-Malinowski, *Najnowsza historia polityczna Polski* (London, 1967), 2:806.

the conditions of poverty in a country which struggled incessantly with grave social problems and chronic economic crisis. Due to their numbers, patterns of congested residence in large urban centers, and preponderantly backward occupational structure, the Jews found themselves in the focus of Polish sensitivities. As a consequence of this constellation of unfortunate circumstances, they bore the brunt of attempts of social change, progress, and development in the country. It cannot be denied that this assessment provides a reasonably adequate account of the factual conditions of the country in general and of the Jews in particular. Some Jewish scholars regard the "struggle for bread," as Jacob Lestschinsky put it, or competition in the framework of an impoverished economy as the main cause of Polish antisemitism in the interwar period. It seems to me, however, that here, too, only one side of the coin is being examined. In his essay dealing with this aspect of antisemitism in Poland, Raphael Mahler wrote:

> The propaganda of "nationalization" of Polish economy by ousting the Jews from their positions acquired a new pretext under the conditions of regained independence. Until now, it was argued, we have been occupied with the struggle for our political freedom, now that we have obtained political power, the other half of the task—the economic liberation from the Jews—has to be taken up.[7]

In any event, none of the programs for reforming the economy and solving the plight of one or another socioeconomic stratum in Poland bespeak a concern for and an attempt to address the changing needs of Polish Jews and to integrate them in the process of social transformation and development.

Political writings and propaganda from the period in question abound with the image of the Jews as exercising control over financial markets and the key branches of the Polish economy. In reality the proportion of Jews in the Polish financial-industrial oligarchy did not exceed their proportion in the population generally. The overwhelming majority of Jews in the cities and *shtetlekh* in central and eastern Poland, including those registered as independent wage-earners and merchants, lived under conditions of dire and deepening poverty. Their income lagged behind the average income of an industrial worker.

7. Raphael Mahler, "Antisemitism in Poland," in *Essays on Antisemitism*, ed. Koppel S. Pinson (New York, 1946), pp. 165–66.

In addition to the systematic anti-Jewish economic boycott launched and managed by various factions of the Endecja and their political affiliates throughout the period in question, one should not pass over the anti-Jewish line of official policy. One of its expressions was an effort to introduce an official *numerus clausus* in the universities; when this attempt ran into difficulties, ways were sometimes found to implement the policy in a covert manner. One of the early laws mandated the closing of all businesses on Sunday. Although this legislation was ostensibly progressive, it was nonetheless directed against the predominantly observant Jewish population, which was thereby forced to idleness two days a week. Taxation and credit policies and official monopolies of certain branches of the economy and trade were all accompanied by latent or manifest anti-Jewish tendencies or outcomes. Numerous articles were written about Jewish artisans who were deliberately made to fail the tests required for professional licenses. Likewise ostensibly progressive were the new regulations forbidding ritual slaughter, but, in actual fact, the real issue was the removal of the Jews from one of the last areas of the economy where they still maintained a considerable foothold. It is true that in the 1920s these regulations and methods were hesitantly implemented out of some concern for the democratic image of the country and the reaction of public opinion abroad. The anti-Jewish tendency was significantly moderated, at least in terms of public atmosphere, in the first years after the Piłsudski *coup* in May 1926 and particularly during the first term of Kazimierz Bartel as head of the government. But this relatively stable situation, like every aspect of Polish life, began to deteriorate with the deep economic crisis that set in at the beginning of the 1930s. Conditions were further aggravated when the radical wing of young Endeks split off from the parent party and adopted the ideological principles and methods of the fascists. At about that time the heirs of Piłsudski, divided and afraid of losing power, turned to overt antisemitism as a means to shore up wide popular support and to divert public attention from real and glaring social contradictions. In 1937 the Polish prime minister, Gen. Felicjan SławojSkładkowski, declared that although he opposed violence in the anti-Jewish campaign, he gave his blessings to the economic boycott.

It should be made clear that political antisemitism and anti-Jewish economic policies did not impinge on the considerable freedoms the Jews enjoyed in their organizational life and social and cultural activities. The Jews were free to set up their own political organizations, to bring up their children as they saw fit, to publish a whole range of newspapers and literary works relatively free of outside interference, and to present their cause in the Sejm and before the court of public opinion. Furthermore, Jews—mostly assimilated ones—occupied important positions in Polish literature, art, and the theater. In Polish poetry of this period the formidable presence of poets such as Bolesław Leśmian, Julian Tuwim, Antoni Słonimski, and Józef Wittlin was in no way diminished by frequent attacks containing unveiled, often nasty, references to their Jewish origins. It should also be borne in mind that throughout the interwar period many political bodies, particularly on the liberal Left, opposed antisemitism and were not deterred from voicing their views in public. Their voice was of particular importance during the hooligan excesses and the anti-Jewish terror waged by strong student unions active in most Polish universities in the 1930s. Jewish students were required to sit only in specially designated seats, called "ghetto benches," in the lecture halls. Rather than acquiesce in their segregation, they remained standing during their classes, joined by some of the most prominent Polish scholars in an expression of solidarity. Polish students and university lecturers were beaten together with the Jews, and a number of them resigned in protest, refusing to be swept up by the ugly wave of antisemitism.

Some young Polish contemporary scholars argue that Polish antisemitism should be regarded primarily in terms of confrontation between two national, or nationalistic, ideals. According to this view, Polish nationalist extremists found themselves facing advocates of extreme Jewish nationalism. The conflict, so the argument goes, reflected the clash of two fanatical forms of nationalism rather than a social reality of wide strata of the population.[8] In my opinion this strange theory is based wholly on either a lack of knowledge or a misunderstanding. It envisions Polish-Jewish relations in terms of the conflict that did, in fact, exist between the Poles on the one hand and the Ukrainians and the Belorussians on the other. By contrast, the aims of Jewish nationalists, by whom I mean Zionists and particularly the radical Revisionist Zionists, in one way concurred with those of the Polish nationalists and antisemites, who recognized that immediate mass emigration to Palestine would help rid Poland of

8. This view was presented in the most vulgar fashion in a book rich in antisemitic tendencies and anti-Jewish libels: Józef Orlicki, *Szkice z dziejów stosunków polsko-żydowskich, 1918–1949* (Szczecin, 1983).

Jews. It is no coincidence that Vladimir Jabotinsky's evacuation plan and the Revisionist movement as a whole gained sympathy and support among political heirs of Piłsudski.

The last years of the Polish Republic, from the mid-1930s on, were marked by grave escalation in the antisemitic public mood and of anti-Jewish policies. Even a cursory examination of the Polish press from those years produces an impression that the Jewish Question stood among the central problems preoccupying the Polish society and the government. The goal of decreasing the Jewish population in Poland by immediate mass emigration became something of a national consensus. Only the Left expressed reservations, and even there some regress could be observed in its position on this question. I should mention in this context that some members of the Polish intelligentsia and the Polish Left encouraged emigration of the Jews, particularly emigration to Palestine, out of a positive approach and avowed sympathy for the Zionist venture in that land. Those liberal sympathizers always took care to make it clear that they did not want pressure put on the Jews to leave Poland and that the decision should be taken by individual Jews themselves.

Early in 1937 the Obóz Zjednoczenia Narodowego (OZON, Camp of National Unity), which was founded as a movement of regime supporters, advocated the division of the Polish population into two categories: Christians and non-Christians. OZON demanded mass emigration of Jews to Palestine and other countries, but at the same time it voiced reservations regarding violent means to speed up the process, not only out of humanitarian concerns but also out of fear that violence might destabilize the political order and result in anarchy. The option of emigration did not, of course, depend entirely on the will of the Poles and the Jews in Poland, as many of the countries thought of as possible destinations for the would-be *émigrés* had closed their doors to newcomers. The radical wing of the Endecja and other extremist political forces of the radical variety were not satisfied with declarations about the necessity for boycotting the Jews and removing them from the country. They argued that pressure must be applied to the Jews by initiating a campaign of violence, including pogroms. Jacob Lestschinsky mentions hundreds of victims in scores of cities and towns swept by a wave of anti-Jewish outbursts in the years 1935–37.[9] Trials conducted in the aftermath

9. Jacob Lestschinsky, "Ha-praot be-Polin (1935–1937)," in *Dapim le-heker ha-shoah ve-ha-mered*, vol. 2, ed. Nahman Blumental (Tel Aviv, 1952), pp. 37–72.

of those disturbances—the arguments put forward by the defense
as well as the sentences given the offenders—also reflect the spirit
of the times.

A separate question that merits further systematic research concerns the extent of the influence of National Socialism and the Third
Reich on the antisemitic public climate in Poland and the anti-
Jewish policies pursued during the interwar years. Szymon Rudnicki's recent study of the Obóz Narodowo Radykalny (ONR, National Radical Camp), makes a significant contribution in that
direction.[10] Polish antisemitism is often portrayed, as explained
above, as lacking a racist component. One of the reasons that race
was not a factor was the relatively small number of Jewish converts
to Christianity in Poland, as opposed to the much higher numbers
in Germany and Austria. Another, and perhaps more important reason was that the Roman Catholic church regarded racism as a deviation from Christian doctrine, although this view should not
obscure the part played by the church in fanning antisemitic sentiments or at the least in not restraining such sentiments. In actual
fact, many priests supported the Endeks. One church leader, Cardinal August Hlond, condemned physical violence against the Jews
in his 1936 pastoral letter, but at the same time he went to great
lengths to underscore the sins committed by the Jews as a collec-
tivity. In this view the Jews were seen as speculators, dealers in
unfair trade practices, spreaders of permissivism and atheism, and,
worse of all, supporters of the Left in general and communism in
particular. The most extreme among the anti-Jewish priests, such as
Stanisław Trzeciak in Warsaw, did not refrain from seeking justification for racism in Christian doctrines.

More pronounced, however, was the influence of Nazi Germany
in the political sphere. It can be seen in attempts to emulate Nazi
legislation and to adapt German methods of harassing Jews to Polish
conditions. Thus, for example, in September 1938, one year before
the German invasion of Poland, Adolf Hitler told Józef Lipski, the
Polish ambassador to Germany, of his intention to deport European
Jews to colonies, indicating that Poland was to be a part of this plan.
Lipski did not regard this matter as a strictly Polish internal affair,

10. Szymon Rudnicki, *Obóz Narodowo-Radykalny: Geneza i działalność* (Warsaw,
1985).

and he went so far as to declare that should the Nazi leader succeed, the Poles would erect a magnificent statue in his honor in Warsaw.[11]

The Endeks, as a traditionally anti-German party, regarded Germany as a constant threat to Poland. Consequently they preferred to follow the example of Italian fascism, though not in its lack—until 1938—of a pronounced antisemitic component. However, the contemporary Polish writer Andrzej Micewski remarked in his biography of Dmowski that the Nazi's anti-Jewish policy confused the ardent views of the Endek leader. Dmowski was a profound political thinker, and his anti-German stand remained a constant component in his analysis of the Polish political situation. But Dmowski believed, according to Micewski, that "German imperialism was promoted by freemasonry and the Jews. Since Hitler has crushed these forces, Germany is no longer a threat."[12] The OZON, which went to great lengths to draw in the young generation that had allied with the radical splinter of the Endeks, did not flinch from for a time joining forces with fascist and fanatically antisemitic groups. There is no shortage of racist articles, pamphlets, and legislative proposals, copying elements of the Nuremberg Laws submitted in those years to the Sejm.

In summary, I do not think that Polish antisemitism should be regarded as a phenomenon *sui generis*, unaffected by developments throughout Europe and by the social and political dynamics of the interwar period. Antisemitism was deeply embedded in the tissue of Polish-Jewish relations as they developed over centuries. If one disregards the radical fringes, the anti-Jewish themes that had been crystallizing in the course of many generations in Poland did not evolve into forms of aggressive political action with genocidal overtones. Popular antisemitism, however, when combined with the objective conditions prevailing in interwar Poland (such as the sheer numbers of the Jews, the economic plight, and so forth) and with outside influences, particularly the rapprochement with Nazi Germany and the inspiration it provided, turned Polish antisemitism into a combustible mixture, especially in the late 1930s.

In the last months before the outbreak of the Second World War, there was some movement toward reconciliation between Poles and

11. See Józef Lipski, *Diplomat in Berlin (1933–1939)*, ed. Wacław Jedrzejewicz (London, 1968), p. 411.

12. Andrzej Micewski, *Roman Dmowski* (Warsaw, 1971), p. 367.

Jews as they perceived the threat posed by a common enemy. This reconciliation was, however, temporary and short lived. Yet I summarily reject the thesis that portrays the Poles as playing a part in initiating and implementing the extermination of Jews in the Holocaust. There is no documentary evidence to support the contention that the extermination camps were built in Poland because of the intensity of Polish antisemitism. At the same time I do not accept the opposite argument that antisemitism ceased to exist, or at least was significantly weakened, in Nazi-occupied Poland. In my view antisemitism was an active factor and to some degree had an adverse effect on the situation of the Jews in Poland, on the possibilities of Jewish defense, and on the extent of rescue of the Jews during this period.

In support of my view I would like to quote from the diary of the historian and chronicler Emanuel Ringelblum. The following was written in the Warsaw ghetto in August 1940:

> August 22. An Endek newspaper was published [clandestinely] containing the following: Jews are being beaten up and the Poles are being killed; the Jews are given several days to move out, whereas several hours were given to Poles in Poznań. The Jews are being rounded up, but the Poles are being shot at. We congratulate you [the Jews] for your new ally.[13]

This excerpt from an Endek paper is a good illustration of antisemitism beclouding the mind in a way that, in critical periods, may lead to grave consequences.

13. Emanuel Ringelblum, *Ksovim fun geto*, vol. 1: *Togbukh fun varshever geto (1939–1942)* (Warsaw, 1961), p. 134.

Antony Polonsky

A Failed Pogrom: The Demonstrations in Lwów, June 1929

In 1929 the Catholic festival of Corpus Christi fell on Thursday, May 31. On the succeeding Sunday, as was traditional, processions of the faithful, following the consecrated host, took place all over Poland. One of these was held in Lwów. Its route passed along Zygmuntowska Street, where a large private Jewish girls' *gymnasium* was located. As in other private Jewish schools, the girls were in the school because Sunday was a regular school day. It happened that the procession passed the school during a break between two classes, so fair numbers of children were playing noisily in the school courtyard and could be heard in the street. One of the smaller girls, in order to get a better view of the procession, stood on a stool, which fell over, causing her to cry out loudly and her companions to laugh in amusement. Those at the back of the procession took these harmless occurrences as a Jewish profanation of the Catholic religion. A number of Catholics gathered at the school and attempted to provoke a disturbance, but they were quickly dispersed by the police.

NOTE ON SOURCES: It proved a difficult and frustrating task to try to establish what actually happened in Lwów and elsewhere in Poland in the first two weeks of June 1929. A search of the Archiwum Akt Nowych, Warsaw, did not reveal any material on the subject. It is possible that some of the documents were overlooked, or that the material was destroyed during the Second World War, or that it has been removed to the Soviet Union. The records of the Polish Embassy in London also contained nothing of significance, as was the case with the British Foreign Office files in the Public Record Office and those of the British Board of Deputies in Woburn Place. The only archival document I was able to find was the confidential quarterly issued by the Polish Ministry of the Interior, *Sprawozdanie z życia mniejszości narodowych* (Report on the Life of the National Minorities), a microfilm copy of which is in the library of Warsaw University. In the absence of primary documentation, I had to rely extensively on newspapers, above all those published in Poland, but also on the *Jewish Chronicle* and the dispatches of the Jewish Telegraphic Agency.

The incident soon assumed a much greater significance, for it occurred at a time of heightened political tension in Poland. Relations between the government of Marshal Józef Piłsudski and the Sejm (House of Deputies) were moving toward a decisive confrontation. Piłsudski had seized power in May 1926, with the support of sections of the army and the parties of the Left, in order to forestall a right-wing *coup* that he believed to be imminent. Though he had originally hoped to cooperate with the Sejm, his autocratic temperament soon led to growing discontent, which came to a head over the methods the government had employed to obtain a relative majority in the elections of March 1928. The parties of the moderate Left—Polska Partia Socjalistyczna (PPS, Polish Socialist Party), Stronnictwo Chłopskie (Peasant Party), and Polskie Stronnictwo Ludowe–Wyzwolenie (PSL–Wyzwolenie, Polish Peasant Party–Liberation)—were now deeply alienated, and they made common cause with Center groups such as the Narodowa Partia Robotnicza (National Workers' Party), the Chrześcijańska Demokracja (Christian Democracy), and the Polskie Stronnictwo Ludowe–Piast (PSL–Piast, Polish Peasant Party–Piast)—to impeach Gabriel Czechowicz, the minister of finance, for making a relatively small sum available from government funds to aid the election campaign of the government party. The trial before a Sejm tribunal was to begin on June 26.[1]

The Right also hoped to make use of the growing clash between Piłsudski and the Sejm to regain the ground it had lost since 1926 and in particular in the elections of March 1928, in which the parties of the Right had done relatively badly. The principal ideological force on the Right was the veteran antisemite Roman Dmowski, who in the mid-1920s had come out clearly in favor of the establishment of an Italian-style fascist regime in Poland. He was, in fact, abroad when Piłsudski seized power, attempting to prepare opinion in the West for a right-wing take-over in Poland. In December 1926, disgusted with the weak response of the Związek Ludowo-Narodowy (Popular National Union), the principal right-wing parliamentary group, to the *coup*, Dmowski established the radical profascist Obóz Wielkiej Polski (OWP, Camp for a Greater Poland), which was to lay the basis for a transformation of the ideological climate in Poland

---

1. On these developments, see Antony Polonsky, *Politics in Independent Poland, 1921–1939* (Oxford, 1972), pp. 234–327; Andrzej Garlicki, *Od maja do Brześcia* (Warsaw, 1981).

and facilitate the return of the Right to power.[2] The OWP soon emerged as a significant force, particularly among university students, and when the Związek Ludowo-Narodowy was reorganized in 1928 as the Stronnictwo Narodowy (SN, National Party), it became a part of the new group while preserving its autonomy. It was determined to provoke a clash with the government, and the issue of the defense of the Catholic religion was one on which it believed it could count on the support of broad circles of the Right. This was also the view of the more moderate deputies of the SN. Since the May *coup* the right-wing opposition, presenting itself as the only defender of Catholic values in Poland, had consistently attacked the government for its alleged neglect of Catholic interests. In the electoral campaign of 1928, when the Polish bishops had issued a letter stressing that "division in circumstances such as those in which we find ourselves weakens the Catholic and national camp," the party had immediately responded and resolved to place itself "on the ground indicated by the bishop's pastoral letter," declaring itself favorable "to an electoral campaign pursued by a united national camp."[3] On this occasion the government was successful in inducing an important section of the church hierarchy to distance itself from the Narodowa Demokracja (National Democracy, its adherents the National Democrats, or Endeks). But this did not prevent the party in the following year from again attempting to present itself as the principal spokesman for Catholic interests. The National Democrats had thus opposed attempts in the Sejm to limit the scope of Catholic religious instruction in the schools and had supported the university authorities in Warsaw when they had ordered Professor Szymanowski, the dean of the Veterinary Faculty, to replace a crucifix that he had taken down in a lecture theater. The National Democrats also strongly criticized the government in the summer of 1928, when the cabinet had refused to increase the subsidy to the Catholic University of Lublin, and had also accused the government and its supporters of secretly supporting the Mariawites, a sect that had seceded from the Catholic church and was being bitterly attacked

2. For the evolution of the Right, see Roman Wapiński, *Narodowa Demokracja, 1893–1939* (Warsaw, 1980); Szymon Rudnicki, "Narodowa Demokracja po przewrocie majowym: Zmiany organizacjyne i ideologiczne (1926–1930)," in *Najnowsze Dzieje Polski, 1914–1939*, vol. 11 (Warsaw, 1967), pp. 352–69; Antony Polonsky, "Roman Dmowski and Italian Fascism," in *Ideas into Politics*, ed. R. J. Bullen, H. Pogge von Strandmann, and Antony Polonsky (London, 1984), pp. 130–46.

3. *Gazeta Warszawski Poranna*, December 12, 1927.

by the Catholic hierarchy.[4] The new party program adopted in October 1928 stressed the role of the National Democrats as the defenders of the Catholic religion. It affirmed,

> the National [Democratic] Party makes it an attitude of principle that the Roman Catholic religion should occupy the leading place in Poland, that the Roman Catholic church should be governed by its own laws, and that relations with the state should be regulated by an agreement with the Holy See. The laws and actions of the state, in particular regulations relating to the family and marriage, which are the foundation of society, as well as to education, must conform to the principles of the Roman Catholic religion, whose principles must also imbue public life in Poland.[5]

Lwów seemed in several respects an ideal place to initiate a major campaign designed to establish the national camp as the defender of the country's Catholic faith. It was a nationally heterogeneous city. According to the census of 1931, of the town's 312,000 inhabitants (which made it the third largest city in Poland), 63.5 percent gave their mother tongue as Polish, 7.75 percent gave Ukrainian, 3.5 percent gave Ruthenian, and 24 percent gave Yiddish, and there were small groups of Russian, German, and Czech speakers. These figures certainly understated the Ukrainian presence; a better indication can be gained from the 15.9 percent who gave their religion as Greek Catholic (Uniate). A fair proportion of Jews gave their mother tongue as Polish, Hebrew, or German, and the Jewish community almost certainly numbered nearly 100,000.[6] The bitter conflict between Poles and Ukrainians, which dominated Eastern Galician politics in the latter part of the nineteenth century, had led to a Polish-Ukrainian war for the province in the years 1918–19 in which Lwów had been one of the main battlefields.[7]

---

4. On religious education in the schools, see *Gazeta Warszawska*, June 28, 29, July 2, 5, 1928; *Kurjer Warszawski*, June 25, 1928; *Robotnik*, June 27, 1928; *Dzień Polski*, June 27, July 10, 1928. On the incident in the Veterinary Faculty, see *Gazeta Warszawska*, October 3, 1928. On the subsidy for the Catholic University of Lublin, see *Epoka*, October 9, 1928; *Robotnik*, October 10, 1928. On the Mariawites, see *Robotnik*, October 10, 14, 1928; *Gazeta Warszawska*, October 3, 9–10, 14, 1928.

5. *Gazeta Warszawska*, October 16, 1928.

6. *Statystyka Polski*, ser. C (Warsaw, 1938), fasc. 94a.

7. For the Ukrainian view of this conflict, see Matthew Stachiw and Jaroslaw Sztendera, *Western Ukraine at the Turning Point of Europe's History, 1918–1923* (New York, 1969–71); Stefan Ripets'kyi, *Ukrainian-Polish Diplomatic Struggle, 1918–1923* (Chicago, 1983). For the Polish side, see Eugeniusz Wawrzkowicz and Józef Klink, eds., *Obrona Lwowa 1–22 listopada 1918: Organizaga listopadowej obrony: Lwowa. Ewidencja uczestników walk* (Lwów, 1939); Rosa Bailly, *A City Fights for Freedom: The Rising of Lvov in 1918–1919* (London, 1956).

The war had led to heightened national feelings among the Polish population who, though they constituted the majority in Lwów, were in a minority in the province as a whole.

It is true that the leadership of the Jewish community, whether Zionist or assimilationist, looked for the most part on the rising Ukrainian national movement as a much greater threat to their position than anything they could expect from the Poles. The emancipation of the Jews in the mid-nineteenth century and their access to higher education had also led to a considerable degree of acculturation and the adoption of the Polish language and culture. As early as the 1890s, for instance, the sermon in the Reformed Temple in Lwów was given in Polish.[8] However, Polish-Jewish relations in the town had been severely exacerbated by the Jewish desire to maintain a neutral position in the Polish-Ukrainian conflict. In Lwów itself, the existence during the worst of the conflict of an armed Jewish militia, which had acted against both Polish and Ukrainian troops who had attempted to loot Jewish property, stimulated accusations that the Jews had taken the Ukrainian side. Shortly after the Poles freed Lwów of Ukrainian rule, large-scale disturbances had broken out, in which at least seventy Jews had been killed, many more wounded, and much Jewish property destroyed.[9] In the mid-1920s the Jews had also been greatly agitated by the trial of Leon Steiger, who was accused by the Polish authorities of attempting to murder the Polish President Stanisław Wojcie-chowski during his visit to Lwów in 1924. In fact the assassination attempt had been the work of Ukrainian nationalists, one of whom finally confessed his responsibility in 1925. But the trial had been accompanied by many accusations against the Jews as a whole, which had alarmed the Jewish leadership.[10] This leadership, headed

8. See Majer Bałaban, *Historia Lwowskiej Synagogi Postępowej* (Lwów, 1937). On Jewish assimilation and acculturation in Lwów, see Ezra Mendelsohn, "Jewish Assimilation in Lvov: The Case of Wilhelm Feldman," *Slavic Review* 28 (1969): 577–90; Mendelsohn, "From Assimilation to Zionism in Lvov: The Case of Albert Nossig," *Slavonic and East European Review,* 49 (1971): 521–34.

9. On the events in Lwów, see J. Bendow (Tenenbaum), *Der Lemberger Judenpogrom: November 1918–January 1919* (Vienna, 1919); *Les pogroms anti-juifs en Pologne et en Galicie en novembre et decembre 1918: Faits et documents* (Stockholm, 1919). Jerzy Tomaszewski has reprinted the report of the two officials sent by the Polish Foreign Ministry to investigate the incident in *Przegląd Historyczny* 2 (1984): 215–20. The episode is also intelligently discussed in Ludwik Hass, "Stosunki polsko-żydowskie," *Dzieje Najnowsze* 17 (1985): 208–9.

10. Paweł Korzec, "The Steiger Affairs," *Soviet Jewish Affairs* 3, no. 2 (1973): 38–57.

by the Zionist Leon Reich, a veteran Jewish parliamentarian, a member of the Comité des Délégations Juives at the Versailles Congress, and a member of the World Zionist Organization,[11] had adopted a policy of conciliation *vis-à-vis* the Polish state. Reich and his followers had bitterly disagreed with the political strategy of Yitzhak Gruenbaum, leader of the Zionists of the Congress Kingdom, who had argued that the Jews should aim to transform Poland from a national state into a state of nationalities in which Jews would enjoy national rights. Reich dissented strongly from Gruenbaum's conclusion that the Jewish interest lay with the other national minorities. He argued, to the contrary, that the Jews had nothing in common with these groups. The Germans were irredentist and the Ukrainians and Belorussians wanted at the least territorial autonomy and at the most independence. What the Jews required was the full implementation of rights to which they were entitled under the Constitution and the Minorities Treaty. To secure these, a direct approach to the government was required, and this dictated the strategy that led to the Ugoda with the government of Władysław Grabski in the summer of 1925.[12]

In the elections of March 1928, the National Democrats had not done particularly well in Lwów (see table 1), reflecting their loss of support in the country as a whole. In Lwów 61.12 percent of the electorate had voted, a slightly lower percentage than for Poland as a whole (63.9 percent), which may have reflected the residual unwillingness of some Ukrainians to vote in a Polish election (Ukrainian parties had boycotted the previous election of November 1922). The largest share of the vote had in fact been won by the Galician Zionists; the Bezpartyjny Blok Współpracy z Rządem—the government bloc—had come in second; and the Komitet Katolicko-Narodowy, the National Democratic list, third. The PPS was a close fourth. Interestingly the other Jewish lists (the Bund, Poalei Zion, Agudat Israel) had all done very badly, as had the Blok Mniejszości Narodowych w Polsce (Bloc of National Minorities in Poland), which was not supported by the Jews in Galicia and reflected the weak-

11. On Leon Reich, see the article in the *Encyclopedia Judaica*; Nathan Michael Gelber, *Toldot ha-tenuah ha-ziyonit be-Galizyah* (Jerusalem, 1958), 2:833–34.

12. On this dispute, see Paweł Korzec, "Der Block der Nationalen Minderheiten im Parlamentarismus Polen des Jahres 1922," *Zeitschrift für Ostforschung* 24, no. 2 (1975): 193–230; Korzec, "Das Abkommen zwischen der Regierung Grabski und der judischen Parlamentsvertretung," *Jahrbucher für geschichte Osteuropas* 3 (1972): 331–66.

TABLE 1

Election Results in Lwów, March 1928

Lists	Valid votes	Percentage
Jewish National Union in Malopolska (Galicia)	28,411	29.3%
Nonparty Bloc for Cooperation with the Government	24,715	25.5%
Catholic National List (National Democrats)	13,829	14.3%
Polish Socialist Party	12,993	13.4%
Bloc of National Minorities in Poland	9,617	9.9%
Worker-Peasant Union (Communists)	3,592	3.7%
Bund	2,188	2.3%
General Jewish National Electoral Bloc in Poland (Agudat Israel)	787	0.8%
Poalei Zion	690	0.7%
Worker-Peasant Union—Left (Dissident Ukrainian Communists)	106	0.1%

SOURCE: Tadeusz Rzepeccy and Karol Rzepeccy, *Sejm i Senat, 1928–1933* (Poznań, 1928).
NOTE: Of the 159,016 eligible to vote, 97,197 voted, or 61.12 percent. Of those, 96,928 votes were valid.

ness of Ukrainian national sentiment in Lwów. The Communists—represented by the Jedność Robotniczo-Chłopska and Jedność Robotniczo-Chlopska–Lewica—also did poorly. Of the four seats assigned to the city, two went to the Galician Zionists, one taken by Reich himself and the other by Dr. Maurycy Leser. The government seat went to Eugeniusz Kwiatkowski, the minister of trade and industry, and that of the National Democrats to a veteran Endek lawyer, Dr. Jan Pieracki.

Thus the Corpus Christi incident offered the National Democrats an opportunity to reestablish their position in Lwów and to put the government on the defensive. The Jewish leadership, too, quickly realized the seriousness of the situation they faced. Leon Reich, in Berlin for a meeting, was summoned back to Lwów. In his absence the question of how to deal with the crisis fell to Maurycy Leser and another Jewish deputy from Galicia, Henryk Rosmaryn. They decided the best course of action would be to try to keep news of the incident out of the press until the expected police report could be published, a plan they hoped would defuse the crisis by showing that no sacrilege was intended. This proved to be an error. They did persuade the Jewish, progovernment, and left-wing Polish papers to print nothing about the incident. To their horror, however, on Monday morning a highly colored and exaggerated attack on Jewish sacrilege appeared in the main Endek paper, *Lwowski Kurjer Poranny.*

The article claimed that some of the Jewish girls had thrown crusts of bread and bits of rubbish at the procession. One had thrown an inkwell, and some had spat at the Host. These incidents had continued throughout the entire period of more than fifteen minutes that the procession had been passing the school. Jewish sources were subsequently to claim that the *Lwowski Kurjer Poranny* was actively involved in organizing the disturbance that now occurred and that this was proved by a document found in the newspaper offices by the police.[13]

It is certain that as a result of the provocative newspaper article and the rumors of Jewish sacrilege, a crowd of several hundred, mostly university students, converged on the offices of the principal Polish-language Jewish newspaper in Lwów, *Chwila*, and the branch of the Yiddish paper *Der moment*. They entirely destroyed the premises of these newspapers before the police arrived, and they moved on to Legionów and Kopernik streets, breaking windows of several synagogues. The police appealed to the crowd to disperse and, when there was no response, dispersed the demonstrators with a baton charge. A second crowd assembled on Zygmuntowska Street. After invading the girls' *gymnasium*, where a fair amount of damage occurred, and beating up a number of Jewish students, the crowd repaired to the Dom Studencki (Jewish Students' Club) on St. Teresa Street, which it also demolished. The police again intervened to stop the disturbances. More than forty demonstrators were arrested, a strong police presence was established in the streets, and by ten in the evening the town was quiet. Later that night a delegation of students went to the *starosta* (district head), a man named Klotz, asking him to release those imprisoned on bail and promising to maintain order if he agreed. The request was categorically rejected, the *starosta* affirming that any further demonstrations would be met with maximum force.

The following day the rectors of all establishments of higher education in Lwów appealed without success to Klotz's superior, the *wojewoda* (provincial governor), a man named Goluchowski, to release the students. In all, thirty-eight were interrogated by the police, and thirty-one were charged with various offenses. The Związek Narodowy Polskiej Młodzieży Akademickiej (National Union of Polish Students) responded by calling a students' strike in Lwów

13. *Lwowski Kurjer Poranny,* June 4, 1929; *Jewish Chronicle,* June 21, 1929, p. 25.

on June 5. The strike was not universally observed, and violent incidents occurred as the nationalists attempted to prevent students from attending lectures. These involved not only Jewish students but also members of the left-wing Związek Polskiej Młodzieży Demokratycznej (Union of Polish Democratic Students). That evening a mass meeting of five thousand students demanded the closing of the girls' *gymnasium* on Zygmuntowska Street.

The government quickly realized that it had a major crisis on its hands. As early as June 5 the Ministry of the Interior announced that a special commission, led by Kazimierz Stamirowski, head of the ministry's political department, had been set up to deal with the situation. Infantry and cavalry patrols were instituted in Lwów to preserve order, and Jewish institutions were defended by armed police with bayonets. In addition on Wednesday, June 6, in a telephone conversation, the Minister of the Interior Felicjan Sławoj-Składkowski assured Rosmaryn in the name of the government that the security of the Jewish community would be maintained.[14]

The Jews also attempted, perhaps on the suggestion of the *starosta*, to defuse the situation by a direct approach to the Catholic hierarchy. On June 6, an official communiqué of the *starosta* was published in all Lwów papers, describing a meeting between Rabbis Freund and Levin with Monsignor Franciszek Lisowski, the suffragan bishop of Lwów. It concluded:

> The rabbis expressed their regret, while asserting that it was impossible that the schoolchildren involved had intended an act of desecration. Msgr. Lisowski told them that from the outset he had not believed in the possibility of any desecration and had regarded the children's behavior as a simple act of hooliganism. For his part he expressed his regret at the unpleasant incidents that had occurred and had led to the destruction of Jewish cultural property.[15]

This well-meant initiative backfired. The Catholic hierarchy in Lwów, and in particular Archbishop Józef Teodorowicz, the Armenian metropolitan and a zealous supporter of the National Democrats, were unwilling to forgo the advantages they saw as resulting from the incident. Msgr. Lisowski was thus forced to make a humiliating retraction. On the afternoon of June 6 the *Lwowski Kurjer Poranny* published a special edition containing a communiqué of the Archepiscopal Curia and signed by Msgr. Bolesław Twardowski,

14. *Nasz Przegląd*, June 6, 1929.
15. *Nasz Przegląd*, June 6, 1929.

metropolitan archbishop of the Latin Rite; Archbishop Józef Teodorowicz, the Armenian metropolitan; and Msgr. Lisowski. The communiqué, which took the form of an open letter to *Wojewoda* Goluchowski, claimed that the statement issued by *Starosta* Klotz and published that morning "did not correspond to reality." The rabbis' words had been placed in Msgr. Lisowski's mouth, and neither he nor the rabbis expressed any regret. The letter concluded that the character of the incident on Zygmuntowska Street was "clear to all," even the authorities, and that if "immediate and severe" action had been taken against those responsible, the subsequent incidents, which were the result of "outraged religious sentiment" faced with an act of sacrilege "perhaps unprecedented in Poland," would not have occurred.[16]

The special edition of *Lwowski Kurjer Poranny* containing these inflammatory assertions was seized by the police, and, when a second illegal edition was produced, the printer was arrested. This led to a new wave of demonstrations. Groups formed in the street to listen to public readings of the Archepiscopal Curia's communiqué, and a procession marched to the Catholic archepiscopal palace to congratulate the hierarchy on its stand. On the following day, processions were organized in all Catholic churches. They came together to form a demonstration twenty-five thousand strong, at the head of which marched two archbishops.

The situation was now quite alarming. On June 6, the progovernment radical newspaper *Epoka* observed:

> The attitude of the Jewish youths involved, even if it demonstrated a lack of respect in relation to the Catholic procession, cannot be regarded as scandalous. It is difficult to believe that young Jewish girls would attempt to provoke a Catholic crowd. . . . We see today to what savagery university students can descend under the influence of ethnic and confessional hatred! We are returning to the seventeenth century, when pupils of the Jesuits attacked Protestant churches, beat up nonconformists, and created the unhappy question of the dissidents, which led to the ruin of Poland.[17]

The progovernment *Głos Prawdy,* a weekly that was shortly to become a daily and the main spokesman of the radical wing of the government camp, was in no doubt about the political goals of those who were encouraging the anti-Jewish agitation. The right wing,

---

16. *Lwowski Kurjer Poranny,* special ed., June 6, 1929.
17. *Epoka,* June 6, 1929.

having lost much of its influence in the country, the paper claimed on June 7, was attempting to find a new basis for support among the students. "We are sure," the paper wrote with heavy irony, "that the National Democrats will soon accuse us, for Jewish gold, of crucifying Christ and will produce fifty eyewitnesses to support their claims. These methods did not convince." Addressing its right-wing opponents, the paper wrote:

> We cannot tolerate your base propaganda you cynical demagogues. We see your goal clearly. You aim in the first place to create the impression that the Catholic religion does not enjoy in Poland the protection to which it is entitled from the governmental authorities. In the second place you aim to provoke disturbances that will allow people to doubt the existence of internal order in our country. You have not achieved either goal. You have only created a situation in which Poland is obliged to furnish to the entire world feeble explanations for the excesses that have occurred in Lwów and in Poznań so as to safeguard the reputation of our civilization.[18]

This was also the view of the government. On June 7 the minister of the interior flew into Lwów. He took a very tough line, asserting "the government will not yield to terror." The police were encouraged to act firmly against demonstrators, and a number of police officers, accused of sympathy with the rioters, were relieved of their posts. The minister refused to meet either a delegation of the heads of institutions of higher learning in the city or one from the students. On his return to Warsaw, his ministry issued an official communiqué that affirmed, "There can be no possible talk of a conscious desire on the part of the Jewish girl students to undertake any sort of desecration of religious observances."[19]

The government's strong stand exercised a calming influence. It is true that on the evening of June 8 there were further disturbances in several parts of the city. The police reacted strongly, arresting thirty-eight people and injuring several demonstrators. In subsequent days violence tailed off, although there were a number of cases of Jewish students being attacked or windows of Jewish houses being broken. By June 10, *Nasz Przegląd*, the principal Polish-language Jewish daily in Poland, could report: "Peace reigns in Lwów."[20] An important role in the end of the disturbances must be attributed to the decision of the archbishops of Lwów to use their

18. *Głos Prawdy*, June 7, 1929.
19. *Nasz Przegląd*, June 8, 1929.
20. *Nasz Przegląd*, June 10, 1929.

influence on the students. On June 9 they issued a public appeal to them to end both their agitation and their strike. This issue was discussed at a stormy meeting of students on June 11, where it was decided by a fair majority to end the strike and to appeal to students elsewhere in Poland to do the same.

Efforts had certainly been made to spread the agitation to other university centers. These had been most successful in the National Democratic stronghold of Poznań in western Poland. There, on June 8, after a meeting at the university, a mob had invaded the small Jewish quarter of the town, breaking the windows of the synagogue, the offices of the Jewish community, and a number of shops. In Vilna the anti-Jewish agitation was incited by the National Democratic *Dziennik Wileński,* and fear of disturbances led to an armed guard being placed outside the Jewish students' club. Although a number of Jewish students were attacked, the agitation had less success than elsewhere, and the students' union voted against calling a strike.

Students were most deeply divided in Warsaw. There about four thousand students on June 8 voted to condemn "the attitude of the government press, which supports the Jews against Poles," and to call for "the need to undertake a campaign in favor of the *numerus clausus* and a boycott of the Jews."[21] The students did not, however, call for a strike. After the meeting antisemitic students attacked the offices of the progovernment newspaper *Kurjer Poranny,* breaking several windows before they were dispersed by the police. The antisemitic agitation among the students did not go unchallenged. The Związek Polskiej Młodzieży Demokratycznej strongly criticized the whole campaign, while on June 10 a number of student organizations of various political complexions united to issue a declaration condemning the violence. These included the Uniwersytecki Związek Pacyfistów (University Union of Pacifists), the Koło Uniwersytecki Czerwonego Krzyża (University Circle of the Red Cross), the Młodzież Uniwersytecka Ludowa w Polsce (Peasant University Youth of Poland), the Związek Niezależnej Młodzieży Socjalistycznej (Union of Independent Socialist Youth), and the Organizacja Młodzieży Konservatywnej (Conservative Youth Organization). It was perhaps because of the presence of a number of center and right-wing groups

21. *Gazeta Warszawska,* June 9, 1929.

among the signatories that the declaration attempted in a rather spurious way to be evenhanded. It affirmed:

> We must recognize as morally responsible for these brutalities the popular nationalist newspapers both Jewish and Polish, which are the instruments of political groups on the wane and which are hoping to preserve such influence as they still possess from final shipwreck by exploiting ethnic and confessional hatreds.[22]

This resolution was, in fact, fairly characteristic of the Polish reaction, and though by and large the Jews had reason to be satisfied, not only with the response of the government, but also with that of Polish society, there were some disquieting features in the reaction of political groupings. The large landowning conservatives, who were in alliance with the government, took a rather disappointing line. While condemning anti-Jewish violence and the role of the National Democrats, who, they argued, were exploiting the incident to improve their popularity, they also criticized the Jews. They were in no doubt that sacrilege had occurred, and they criticized the Jewish community, which "has not been able to find one word of criticism for the instigators of the incident." *Czas,* the main conservative paper wrote on June 9:

> For some time one has observed the worsening of relations between the Jews and Polish society. What is the cause of this unfortunate phenomenon? Is it not partly the result of the intensified action of Zionists, who are working systematically to place the Jews on the margin of the society in which they live? Originating as an idealistic conception, it has degenerated with time into a nationalism as aggressive as that of its enemies. Not content with arousing the conscience of the Jewish masses, the leaders of Zionism have inspired in the youth of their faith a dangerous pride and an excessive sensitivity that makes difficult the necessary coexistence with the Polish element and can easily provoke irritated or violent responses.[23]

The socialists, anxious to win as much support as possible for their campaign against the government, also hesitated to attack the Endecja too openly. The fault, they claimed, lay rather in the educational system, which was assailed in very general terms. According to *Robotnik* on June 17: "The youth of a democratic country, which has an immense task to accomplish and should imbue them with the spirit of progress, has been formed according to the principles of nationalism, clericalism, and reaction."[24]

22. *Czas,* June 10, 1929.
23. *Czas,* June 9, 1929.
24. *Robotnik,* June 17, 1929.

One of the reasons the government acted so firmly against the agitation was its fear of the reaction abroad in both Jewish and non-Jewish circles. The elections of March 1928 had created a delicate situation within the Koło Żydowskie (Jewish Parliamentary Club), with six deputies following the conciliatory line of Reich, six following Gruenbaum, and one independent. The government was thus determined to demonstrate that it would act firmly against anti-Jewish violence, particularly when it occurred in the hometown of the leader of one of the Jewish groups with which it hoped to reach an accommodation. There was also a widespread awareness within the government of the damage that had been done to the Polish cause by the anti-Jewish riots marking the first years of independence. The confidential quarterly *Sprawozdanie z życia mniejszości narodowych* (Report on the Life of the National Minorities) issued by the Ministry of the Interior, reported in its issue for the second quarter of 1929: "Jewish public opinion in Poland and abroad holds that the excesses were provoked by the National Democrats, whose whole program is antisemitism, and has expressed its gratitude to the government for its energetic action in quickly liquidating the crisis."[25]

This was an accurate summary of Jewish opinion both inside and outside Poland. The London *Jewish Chronicle* of July 14, 1929, wrote:

> It is not easy to unravel the confused and tangled story of the cause of the attacks, which however were clearly premeditated and carefully organised. But it is at least gratifying to note that there was not the least encouragement of the excesses on the part of the Polish government, which on the contrary has taken commendably prompt measures for their suppression and for the punishment of the malefactors concerned in them.[26]

As regards the general reaction abroad, the government was embarrassed by the fact that the agitation coincided with the Madrid meeting of the League of Nations, which was to consider the question of minorities. Certainly the Soviets, who were not yet members of the League, stigmatized the whole affair as another example of the intolerant treatment meted out to its minorities by the Polish state. According to *Pravda*, "The oppression of the Belorussian, Ukrainian, and Jewish minorities has produced more sad results in

25. *Sprawozdanie z życia mniejszości narodowych*, 1929, no. 2, microfilm, Warsaw University Library, Warsaw.
26. "The Lemberg Anti-Semitic Riots," *Jewish Chronicle*, July 14, 1929, p. 14.

the form of the Lwów pogrom." A similar reaction was provoked in Germany, where, for instance, the socialist *Volkstimme* protested strongly against the disturbances, which it referred to as "stain on the conscience of the Polish nation."[27]

It was in Paris that the greatest controversy was aroused. Here the procommunist International League for the Struggle against Antisemitism, together with the Union of Jewish Students, called a meeting to protest at the events in Poland. This move led Sholem Asch to write a bitter article in *Parizer haynt* entitled "Yidish blut gehert nisht tsu yenem, nor tsu yidn" (Jewish Blood Does Not Belong to Anybody, Only to Jews), in which he attacked the International League, arguing that it was acting in the Soviet interest and that its behavior would harm the efforts undertaken to reach an understanding between Poles and Jews. The affair seems to have aroused less interest in the United Kingdom. There were articles in the *Times, Daily Herald,* and *Manchester Guardian* of a brief and factual nature, but no editorial comment. Polish fears that the incident would lead to a great deal of anti-Polish propaganda, as had been provoked by the anti-Jewish excesses in the years 1918–20, were in this respect misplaced.

The whole affair ended somewhat inconclusively and was indeed swallowed up by the growing conflict between the government and the parliamentary opposition of the Centrolew, the union of the six parties of the Center and the Left, which came to a head in 1930. Although the government announced in late July that it would prosecute thirty-two students for their part in the disturbances, in the end fears of an embarrassing show trial caused it to abandon these plans. The fact that fourteen prominent National Democratic lawyers led by the National Democratic deputy for Lwów, Jan Pieracki, offered their services to the students free of charge must have given the government pause and led to the conclusion that no good would be served by further actions. This was probably also the view of the Jewish leadership, which was well satisfied by the behavior of the authorities. The balance within the Koło Żydowskie was in fact tilted in favor of the more conciliatory Galician Zionists, although their influence diminished with the death of Leon Reich in late 1929.

Throughout that year the Koło Żydowskie took a neutral position in the clash between the government and the opposition and tried

27. Both quoted in *Sprawozdanie z życia mniejszości narodowych,* 1929, no. 2.

to resolve the conflict within the framework of the Constitution. The internal report on the minorities for the third quarter of 1929 was reasonably satisfied with this outcome. Its author wrote that the Jewish attitude to the government had to be assessed on two levels: on the way the Jews felt they were treated as citizens and on the way they were treated as members of a national minority. On the latter question there were criticisms, particularly because of the feeling that the government should do more to help the Jews in the economic sphere. But

> as regards the treatment of the Jews as citizens of the state, represen-
> tatives of the Jewish community have in letters to the central admin-
> istration and in their press often expressed their sincere gratitude. As
> special examples of the friendly attitude of the government toward the
> Jews, they have singled out the way the government handled anti-
> Jewish demonstrations in the Poznań region . . . the Kielce region . . .
> and in Lwów. The action of liquidating the disturbances has strength-
> ened the popularity of the government among the Jews, who have
> expressed their sincere gratitude to the minister of the interior.[28]

What conclusions can be drawn from this whole episode? The first is that the Lwów disturbance, as was so often the case with anti-Jewish disturbances, has to be seen in the framework of the conflicts taking place within Polish society. The Jews were a convenient tool for the National Democrats in trying to mobilize anti-government sentiment. On this occasion, because of the strong government response, their campaign did not succeed. By the middle of the 1930s, however, the situation in Poland had changed. The severe impact of the Great Depression had drastically undermined the economic position of the Jewish community. At the same time the speed with which the Nazis had been able to take away the rights of one of the wealthiest and best assimilated communities in Europe acted as a great stimulus to antisemitism. The failure of the international community to respond in any significant way to the Nazis' actions also did not go unnoticed. In the years after 1935, when the death of Marshal Piłsudski robbed the government of its political cohesion and when its divisions made it increasingly vulnerable to opposition attacks, the temptation to exploit popular antisemitism as a means of winning the support of the Right became too great to be resisted. It is a sad irony that Felicjan Sławoj-Skład-

---

28. *Sprawozdanie z życia mniejszości narodowych,* 1929, no. 3.

kowski, who as minister of the interior in 1929 had acted so strongly in defense of Jewish rights, commented as prime minister in 1936 that, while he opposed violence against Jews, he believed that economic boycott was justified (*owszem!*).[29]

29. *Sprawozdanie Stenograficzne Sejmu Rzeczypospolitej*, June 4, 1936, col. 7.

Emanuel Melzer

Antisemitism in the Last Years of the Second Polish Republic

The years 1935–39 constitute a distinct period in the history of interwar Poland as well as in the history of the country's Jewish community, three and one-half million strong at that time. These were the last and the most fateful years of Polish Jewry. This period before the Holocaust was marked by the radicalization of Polish antisemitism after the death in May 1935 of Marshal Józef Piłsudski, the charismatic personality whose influence on the domestic and foreign policy of his country following his *coup d'état* of May 1926 was most decisive. In April 1935 a new Constitution replaced the Constitution adopted in March 1921. Its aim was to strengthen the ruling camp of Piłsudski's followers—the Sanacja—and to weaken the authority of the two legislative houses—the Sejm (House of Deputies) and the Senate. In July 1935 a new electoral law restricted the ability of opposition parties and the national minorities to nominate their candidates to the Sejm freely. It pushed Poland one step further toward a semitotalitarian state. For the majority of Polish Jewry, Piłsudski's death proved quite a shock. Many Jews believed that his quasi-dictatorial rule had been the only restraint against Poland's deeply ingrained antisemitism.[1]

The weakness of the Sanacja government after Piłsudski's death, together with the increasing intensity of anti-Jewish sentiments and pressures to compete with the nationalist Endecja camp, led to a radicalization of antisemitism within the former. The Sanacja leaders hoped to prevent the disintegration of their camp by officially sanctioning anti-Jewish activity while expressing no more than mild disapproval of its extreme and violent manifestations.

1. Majer Bałaban, "U trumny budowniczego," *Nasz Przegląd*, September 15, 1935.

The crisis within the Sanacja camp was visible in its political body, the Bezpartyjny Blok Współpracy z Rządem (BBWR, Nonparty Bloc for Cooperation with the Government). This bloc, headed by Col. Walery Sławek, had been organized in 1928 as a wide political spectrum that embraced various social groups among the population, including some Jews, especially from assimilationist and Orthodox circles. Piłsudski's purpose in establishing the bloc was to cut into the political power of the Endecja. Here two conflicting conceptions clashed: on one hand was the view of Piłsudski, characterized by an anti-Russian orientation and, originally, by the notion of the superiority of the state over the nation; on the other hand was the view of Roman Dmowski, which was anti-German and considered the Polish nationality as the supreme bearer of the state's sovereignty.[2] In the last years of Piłsudski's rule, the Sanacja came closer ideologically to the basic Endecja conception of a national state.

The coming of the Nazis to power in Germany in January 1933 undermined the base of both political trends. Sanacja circles were aware of the threats to Poland inherent in the Nazis' revisionist aims toward the German-Polish borders. On the other hand, the victory of antisemitic ideology in Germany prompted some circles within the Endecja, especially among its younger groups, to reevaluate their traditional anti-German attitude. These groups left the Endek Stronnictwo Narodowe (SN, National Party) in 1934 and founded the Obóz Narodowo Radykalny (ONR, National Radical Camp), whose extreme political attitudes and anti-Jewish policy was based on the Italian and German model. The ONR organized special assault groups (Bojówki) to carry out violent attacks on Jews.[3] Although it was legally active only during a few months in the spring of 1934, the ONR carried on its activities until the beginning of the Second World War in 1939.

The signing of the ten-year Polish-German nonaggression pact in January 1934 also had considerable impact on attitudes within Poland, and especially official Polish policy toward the Jews. In September 1934 the Polish government renounced its obligations

2. On Roman Dmowski's political orientation and his antisemitic ideology, see Roman Dmowski, *Myśli nowoczesnego Polaka* (Lwów, 1907); Dmowski, *Niemcy, Rosja i kwestja polska* (Warsaw, 1914).

3. J. J. Terej, *Rzeczywistość i polityka* (Warsaw, 1971), pp. 10, 75; Józef Kowalski, *Trudne lata* (Warsaw, 1966), p. 557.

deriving from the 1919 Minorities Treaty. This action was clearly a result of a rapprochement between Poland and Germany.[4]

After Piłsudski's death, the influence of President Ignacy Mościcki and of General (later Marshal) Edward Rydz-Śmigły, who had been appointed head of the army, grew. Following the failure of Sanacja in the Sejm elections of 1935, in which only 46.5 percent of the electorate voted and which were boycotted by the opposition parties of the Right and the Left, Colonel Sławek's government resigned and the BBWR was subsequently dissolved.[5] The era of the rule of the "Colonels" who had been closest to Piłsudski came to an end.

Under the weak government of liberally inclined Prime Minister M. Z. Kościałkowski, anti-Jewish propaganda increased, and in some localities the atmosphere was clearly conducive to economic boycott and pogroms. The government lacked the courage to take effective measures against the wave of antisemitic actions that swept over the country. At the same time, government circles were keen to make apologetic statements in the official press denying allegations that the government was friendly toward the Jews.[6]

In May 1936 Gen. Felicjan Sławoj-Składkowski, the appointee of the strongman Rydz-Śmigły, was nominated to head the new government. This time the new prime minister outlined an anti-Jewish economic policy in an official statement in the Sejm: "Economic struggle—by all means, but without causing any harm."[7] Thus the government expressed a favorable attitude toward the anti-Jewish economic boycott.

The Roman Catholic church also promoted this economic boycott as part of its official policy in Poland. Its attitude was clearly defined in the pastoral letter of February 1936 of Cardinal August Hlond,

4. The attitude of the Polish government was that the Minorities Treaty should be applicable to all countries with national minorities. See Jan Lemański, "Generalizacja zobowiązań mniejszościowych a Polska," *Sprawy Narodowościowe* 8, no. 5 (1934): 527–36.

5. On the inter-Jewish party polemic in Poland over whether to boycott the 1935 elections, see Emanuel Melzer, *Maavak medini be-malkodet: Yehudei Polin, 1935–1939* (Tel Aviv, 1982), pp. 46–50.

6. M. Z. Kościałkowski himself admitted his government's lack of courage to oppose the wave of antisemitic acts. Jan Szembek, *Diariusz i teki Jana Szembeka*, ed. Tytus Komarnicki (London, 1965), 2:129–30.

7. *Sprawozdanie Stenograficzne Sejmu Rzeczypospolitej*, June 4, 1936, col. 7. This statement was entirely different from the declaration on July 19, 1926, of Kazimierz Bartel, the prime minister after Piłsudski's *coup d'état* the previous May, that his government opposed anti-Jewish economic discrimination. See Andrzej Chojnowski, *Koncepcje polityki narodowościowej rządów polskich w latach 1921–1939* (Wrocław, 1979), p. 69.

the primate of the Catholic church in Poland. This letter, which was to be read from the pulpits of all the churches in the country, presented the majority of Jews as freethinkers and bolsheviks who spread pornographic literature, practiced usury, and dealt in white slavery. Although this letter warned against anti-Jewish acts of violence and described racist ideology as un-Christian and contrary to Catholic ethics, it nevertheless resembled the kind of antisemitism propagated by the official circles that in the end had led to violence.[8] There was, in fact, a close relationship between the Endecja and the hierarchy of the Polish-Catholic clergy, and the clergy as spokesmen for the church often promoted Endecja policy. A synod of Polish bishops, for example, resolved in 1937 to demand that Jewish children be segregated in schools and that Jews be prohibited from teaching Polish children.[9]

The anti-Jewish excesses and pogroms in the years 1935–37 had their specific characteristics and dynamics. Usually they resulted from the killing of a Pole by a Jew, either as an act of self-defense or as a criminal act of an individual committed out of personal revenge. For this killing the entire local Jewish community was held collectively responsible. The pogroms in Grodno (1935), Przytyk (1936), Mińsk Mazowiecki (1936), Brześć nad Bugiem (1937), and Częstochowa (1937) all followed this pattern.

In other cases the Endeks used anti-Jewish violence as a means for undermining the authority of the government. These acts of violence were motivated by the political rivalry between the Endecja and the Sanacja. For example, in June 1936 an Endek group headed by Adam Doboszyński, one of the leaders of the SN in the Cracow region, assaulted the small town of Myślenice near Cracow, destroying the residence of the *starosta* (district head), overpowering the local police station, and demolishing Jewish shops.[10]

This anti-Jewish atmosphere in different regions of the country occurred together with acts aiming to deprive Jews in Poland of their rights and undermine their economic position. This was the

---

8. Celia S. Heller, *On the Edge of Destruction: Jews of Poland between the Two World Wars* (New York, 1977), pp. 112–14. A similar statement was made by the archbishop of Cracow, Adam Stanisław Sapieha, in April 1936, in which he advocated an anti-Jewish economic boycott and accused the Jews of spreading communism in Poland. *Tygodnik Polski,* April 5, 1936.

9. Heller, *Edge of Destruction,* p. 110.

10. Władysław Pobóg-Malinowski, *Najnowsza historia polityczna Polski, 1864–1945* (London, 1967), 2:834.

case during the deliberations over the bill banning ritual slaughter introduced in the Sejm by a member of Sanacja, Janina Prystor, in February 1936. The bill was an attempt to force Jews out of the meat trade and to limit their religious freedom. Its sponsors also sought to create a legal precedent for impairing the constitutional rights of the Jewish community. The amended law, as finally passed in January 1937, put severe restrictions on ritual slaughter.[11]

Similar motives prompted increasing numbers of anti-Jewish acts of violence in Polish institutions of higher learning. In December 1935, the Lwów Politechnic became the first academic institution to establish a segregated seating policy, restricting Jews to what were called "ghetto benches." Subsequently pressure to introduce ghetto benches in all academic institutions grew, and two years later, in September 1937, the minister of education authorized the rectors to publish official administrative instructions concerning special seats for Jewish students.[12] Although there were already certain cases of compulsory segregation of Jews in markets and railroad carriages, the issue of the ghetto benches can be seen as the first official attempt to "ghettoize" Polish Jewry. Therefore the resistance of the Jewish students to segregation in ghetto benches was of the utmost importance to later events in the history of Polish Jewry. The Jewish students who stood through their classes rather than acquiesce in discrimination were the vanguard of the resistance to the violent antisemitic offensive, and their stand was at that time stronger and more resolute than that of other Jewish sectors. They were joined in their opposition by a small group of liberal Polish students and professors.

As of 1935 Jewish emigration had been presented by the authorities as the only realistic solution to the Jewish Question in the country, and to all the political, economic, and social problems that were troubling the country as well. Moreover, Jewish emigration was also presented as one justification, among others, for Poland's demands for colonies and mandate territories, which would help to absorb Jewish immigration. The demand for Jewish mass emigration demonstrates how antisemitism in all its forms was used politically

11. On the whole subject of the legislation on ritual slaughter in Poland, see Melzer, *Maavak medini be-malkodet*, pp. 97–110, 243–50.

12. "Prof. Zygmunt Szymanowski ó żółtej łacie na Politechnice Lwowskiej," *Chwila*, December 16, 1935; Andrzej Pilch, *Studencki ruch polityczny w Polsce w latach 1932–1939* (Warsaw, 1972), p. 154.

in the internal as well as in the external affairs of the state.[13] At the same time, however, potential destinations for Jewish emigration were virtually nonexistent, so the solution was not realistic at all. Yet it relieved government circles of the apparent need to initiate constructive socioeconomic reforms.

Even two rival Zionist leaders—Yitzhak Gruenbaum and Vladimir Jabotinsky, both living permanently outside of Poland in 1936 while planning and supporting a large-scale emigration of Jews from Poland to Palestine—spoke of "objective" causes of antisemitism,[14] which they related to the specific economic and social structure of Polish Jewry. These explanations met with sharp criticism from Jewish public opinion in Poland, especially in the Bund and wider Zionist circles. The Jewish public also noticed the discrepancy between the urgent need for free emigration and emigrationism as a political slogan, which implied that the Jews were an alien and unreliable element in the country. The Zionists demanded that all official plans for Jewish emigration from Poland be accompanied by a declaration ensuring that equal constitutional rights of the Jews in Poland would be preserved. The Polish authorities were not, however, willing to make this declaration, under pressure from extremist antisemitic circles who sought to use discrimination, an intensification of anti-Jewish economic measures, and the encouragement of violent acts as means for imposing emigration on the Jews.

The Polish government was, of course, aware that its emigrationist policy would not solve the Jewish Question in Poland. But it tolerated violent antisemitism in the hopes that such activities would keep this problem in the minds of the Western powers, so that they would eventually be obliged at least to alleviate it.[15] Yet these policies succeeded neither in opening new countries to absorb Jewish emigration nor in increasing the number of Jewish emigrants from the country.

After the dispersal of the BBWR there was a vacuum in the camp

13. Emanuel Melzer, "Ha-diplomatyah ha-polanit u-baayat ha-hagirah ha-yehudit ba-shanim, 1935–1939," *Gal-Ed* 1 (1973): 211–49.

14. Yitzhak Gruenbaum, *Milhamot yehudei Polanyah* (Jerusalem, 1941), p. 413; Vladimir (Zeev) Jabotinsky, *Ketavim*, vol. 7: *Ba-saar* (Jerusalem, 1953), pp. 223–27. On the objective ideological causes of Polish antisemitism, see Paweł Korzec, "Antisemitism in Poland as an Intellectual, Social, and Political Movement," in *Studies on Polish Jewry, 1919–1939*, ed. Joshua A. Fishman (New York, 1974), p. 14.

15. Cable from Józef Beck, the Polish foreign minister, to Edward Raczyński, the Polish ambassador in London, May 12, 1939, Hoover Institution Archives, Stanford, Calif., Ambasada U.S. 66-8-039.

of support for the government in Poland until the Obóz Zjedno-czenia Narodowego (OZON, Camp of National Unity) was formed in February 1937. Headed by Col. Adam Koc under the patronage of President Mościcki and Marshal Rydz-Śmigły, it was intended to stabilize the political situation in Poland and provide a convenient way out of the impasse that followed the death of Piłsudski. Its founding, however, constituted another step in the decline in the political position of the Jews in Poland. Koc endeavored to attract the extreme antisemitic youth from the ONR/Falanga, formally dis-solved in 1934, by establishing, within the OZON, the Związek Mło-dej Polski (ZMP, Union of Young Poland), led by Jerzy Rutkowski, a former ONR leader.

The official ideological position of the OZON was stated in Colonel Koc's declaration of February 21, 1937. Although it opposed acts of anti-Jewish violence, it advocated "the instinct of cultural self-defense and the natural aspiration of the Polish nation to economic independence." This declaration in fact constituted a break with the traditional policy of the Sanacja toward the Jews. Contrary to the policy of the BBWR, the OZON was closed to Jewish membership.[16]

In January 1938 internal opposition to the radical right-wing course of the OZON succeeded in toppling its leadership. Colonel Koc was replaced by Gen. Stanisław Skwarczyński. This change sig-nified the severance of links between OZON and ONR members who were eliminated from the ranks of the ZMP.[17] Koc's policy to win over the Endecja had failed, as the majority of the Endecja was interested in liquidating the regime rather than in joining it. But the new leadership attempted to demonstrate that nothing had changed in the OZON's attitude toward the Jews. In May 1938 the Supreme Council of the OZON adopted a thirteen-paragraph resolution on the Jewish Question in Poland. It described Polish Jews as aliens, opposed their assimilation and integration into Polish society, and proposed mass emigration as the solution to the Jewish Question. While the resolution opposed acts of physical violence directed against Jews, it stressed the necessity for reducing the Jewish influ-ence on economic and cultural life through special legislation. Al-though detailed drafts of the discriminatory legislation were pre-

16. Pobóg-Malinowski, *Najnowsza historia polityczna Polski*, pp. 797–801. On the close relations between the OZON and the ONR, see Szymon Rudnicki, *Obóz Naro-dowo-Radykalny: Geneza i działalność* (Warsaw, 1985), pp. 312–18.

17. *Gazeta Polska*, April 21, 1938.

pared in OZON headquarters, the deteriorating political situation postponed implementation of this policy.[18]

The OZON's initial shift toward an explicit antisemitic policy and association with factions of the ONR/Falanga on the one hand, and the influence of Nazi racist ideology on the other, prompted the SN to radicalize its antisemitism even further. Although large circles within this party genuinely admired the achievements of antisemitism in Nazi Germany, the official attitude in the years 1938–39 remained anti-German.

The Stronnictwo Ludowe (SL, Peasant Party) had not at the time clearly defined its attitude toward the Jewish Question, but its platform did not include a paragraph supporting the exclusion of Jews from their economic positions. The Polska Partia Socjalistyczna (PPS, Polish Socialist Party) was the one party that consistently stood up against antisemitism in all forms, although some inkling of the antisemitic mood could be felt in those years within the lower ranks of the party. The PPS was especially active in attacking the antisemitic policy of the government. Similarly, the small Stronnictwo Demokratyczne (Democratic Party) and from 1937 the Kluby Demokratyczne (Democratic Clubs), composed mostly of intelligentsia, opposed the antisemitism of the ruling circles as a deviation from Piłsudski's principles.[19]

In the meantime, the anti-Jewish boycott had been intensified by a systematic, well-planned, and institutionalized campaign. The Kongres Kupiectwa Chrześcijańskiego (General Congress of Christian Merchants) was convened in Warsaw in November 1937 under the patronage of the Polish authorities, and its opening session was attended by President Mościcki and members of the government. The congress's resolutions stressed the importance of the "Polonization of commerce in the country for economic and security reasons." Polish authorities were asked to be involved directly in the anti-Jewish boycott in Poland. The principle of Polonization was, in

18. This was also the opinion of Hans von Moltke, the German ambassador in Warsaw, in his report to the German Foreign Ministry, November 22, 1938. *Documents on German Foreign Policy 1918–1945*, ser. D. v. V (Washington, D.C., 1953), doc. 103, p. 132. The full text of the thirteen-paragraph resolution of OZON is printed in *Sprawy Narodowościowe* 12, no. 3 (1938): 278–79.

19. For a more detailed analysis on the attitude of the SL, the PPS, and the Stronnictwo Demokratyczne toward the Jewish Question at that time, see Melzer, *Maavak medini be-malkodet*, pp. 191–95, 341. For the attitude of the peasant parties, see Edward D. Wynot, "The Polish Peasant Movement and the Jews, 1918–1939," in this volume.

fact, synonymous with the intention to destroy the economic positions of Jews in the country.[20]

Polish authorities began to subsidize, through low-interest credits obtained from state banks, the transfer of Polish merchants from the western to the eastern provinces of the country in order to replace Jewish merchants. This transfer left important economic positions in western Poland open to the intensified activity of the German minority.[21]

The wave of anti-Jewish riots that swept over Poland in 1937 in a way complemented the economic boycott. The two most violent anti-Jewish outbreaks in 1937 took place in Brześć nad Bugiem and Częstochowa. In Łomża and Kielce the existence of defense groups composed of Jewish and Polish workers prevented the outbreak of riots.[22]

Polish authorities still preferred to discriminate against Jews by means of indirect legislation or by administrative decrees.[23] They tried to convince the Polish people that the policy of systematic and controlled anti-Jewish discrimination was preferable and more effective than violent and sporadic anti-Jewish outbreaks, which merely united the Jews in organizing assistance toward the rehabilitation of the affected Jewish communities.

As we have seen, Polish antisemitism was a strong political factor in its own right, but it was also greatly influenced directly and indirectly by the victory of racial ideology in Germany at the time of a political rapprochement between the two states.[24] In the coming years the tension within the Endecja between its ideological antisemitic identification with Nazi Germany, on the one hand, and its traditional enmity against Germany on the other, continued stronger than ever.[25] Antisemitism was, in fact, regarded as something of a

20. *Nasz Przegląd*, November 16, 1937. Compare also the report of H. W. Kennard, the British ambassador in Warsaw, to the British Foreign Ministry, November 17, 1937, Public Record Office, London, FO371, file 20765.

21. *Haynt*, June 24, 1938; *Nowy Dziennik*, February 24, 1938.

22. "Kegn der panik," *Folkstsaytung*, September 17, 1937.

23. Dyrektywy Ministra Becka w sprawach żydowskich na konferencji w M.S.Z., February 15, 1939 [top secret classified], Archiwum Akt Nowych, Warsaw, MSZ, file 9908.

24. This view is contrary to the thesis that the growth of antisemitism in Poland during the 1930s was unaffected by antisemitic racist ideology and practice in Germany, as presented in Edward D. Wynot, " 'A Necessary Cruelty': The Emergence of Official Anti-Semitism in Poland, 1936–1939," *American Historical Review* 76 (1971): 1037.

25. See Jolanta Niemunis, "Stronnictwo Narodowe wobec Hitleryzmu jako prądu

bridgehead over the abyss of historical enmity between the two countries.

Relations between the two states were also strongly influenced by the German minority in Poland, which occupied important economic positions, especially in the western regions, and had strong political bonds with its mother country. Most of the German organizations in Poland underwent a process of Nazification in 1933–35. The German press in Poland frequently published antisemitic propaganda that originated in *Weltdienst,* the journal of the Antisemitic International in Erfurt.[26] The leaders of the German minority organizations in Poland were careful, however, to refrain from large-scale direct and public anti-Jewish propaganda and incitement. They were fully aware that Polish antisemitism was a major force in itself, deriving from specific political, social, and economic conditions in Poland. Nevertheless, the impact of the influence of German antisemitism on Polish antisemitism in light of Germany's political successes during those years should not be ignored.

The close connection between an extreme pro-German political orientation and antisemitism can best be illustrated by the activities of two influential Polish personalities at that time, both from Vilna—Stanisław Cat-Mackiewicz, editor of the conservative daily *Słowo,* and Prof. Władysław Studnicki. Studnicki advocated strengthening the political and economic position of the German minority in Poland, maintaining that this would effect the process of "de-Judaizing" (*odżydzenie*) Poland.[27] Mackiewicz openly stated, "We are racists" (*Jesteśmy rasistami*) in opposing the acceptance of converted Jews as Poles.[28] At that time an increasing number of professional organizations in Poland took formal antisemitic action by inserting restrictive paragraphs in their membership bylaws, using such terms as "Aryan," "Christian by birth," and "of Jewish descent." Although based on Nazi ideology and the Nuremberg Laws, such definitions were in many cases endorsed by Polish authorities.[29] They

---

ideowo-politycznego w latach 1933–1939," *Gdańskie Zeszyty Humanistyczne* 10 (1967): 99–122.

26. B., "Liga przeciwko zniesławieniu Żydów," *Chwila,* November 14, 1935.

27. Władysław Studnicki, *Sprawa polsko-żydowska* (Vilna, 1936), pp. 88–90. Compare also "W. Studnicki w świetle dokumentów Hitlerowskich II Wojny Światowej," *Zeszyty Historyczne* (Paris) 11 (1967): 3–4, 42; A., "W świetle prasy," *Chwila,* August 3, 1937.

28. Stanisław Cat-Mackiewicz, in *Słowo,* reprinted from *Warszawski Dziennik Narodowy,* April 24, 1937.

29. On anti-Jewish discrimination in various liberal professions in Poland, see

were noted in Germany as well. The German journal *Osteuropa*, for example, expressed its satisfaction with the progress of Aryanization in Poland as a result of the OZON's "thirteen Jewish Paragraphs."[30]

The months between the complete German occupation of Czecho-slovakia in March 1939 and the outbreak of the Second World War in September were characterized by a serious crisis in Polish-German relations and by a parallel rapprochement between Poland and the Western democracies. In that period of political tension there was a temporary decrease in the antisemitic campaign, al-though it again gained in intensity during the summer of 1939. In the spring, when Poland's situation was deteriorating in view of the immediate danger of a German invasion, Poland had been eager to obtain security guarantees from Britain. Even then, however, the Polish government insisted that the agenda of Polish Foreign Min-ister Józef Beck's official visit to London in April 1939 should in-clude the question of emigration of the Jews from Poland.[31] Thus public opinion in Poland was indoctrinated that even in those critical days the problem of how to get rid of the Jews was of vital impor-tance to the interests of the state.[32]

After the Nazis came to power in Germany, the German embassy and consulates in Poland followed all anti-Jewish manifestations throughout Poland with special interest and sent home detailed re-ports about them. German propaganda succeeded in making capital of Polish antisemitism and endeavored to portray the anti-German line in Poland as a "Jewish policy,"[33] thereby hoping to undercut Poland's preparedness and its power of resistance in those critical months before the invasion. On the other hand, the Endek anti-semitic propaganda, while depicting both the Germans and espe-cially the Jews as the enemies of Poland, diverted public opinion from the real and sole danger facing the country, namely Nazi Ger-many. The Endek press even accused the Jews of standing behind

---

Raphael Mahler, "Jews in Public Service and the Liberal Professions in Poland, 1918–1939," *Jewish Social Studies* 6 (1944): 291–350. Both Prime Minister Felicjan Sławoj-Składkowski and Foreign Minister Józef Beck mention in their later memoirs the considerable influence of Nazi antisemitism on Poland at that time. See Felicjan Sławoj-Składkowski, *Nie ostatnie słowo oskarżonego* (London, 1964), p. 225; Józef Beck, *Final Report, 1926–1939* (New York, 1957), p. 32.

30. Werner Markert, "Übersichten-Polen," *Osteuropa* 13 (1937–38): 766.

31. Melzer, *Maavak medini be-malkodet*, pp. 341–43, 346–47.

32. Paweł Korzec, "Documents on the Jewish Problem in Poland on the Eve of World War II," *Michael* (Tel Aviv) 6 (1980): 115–48.

33. Melzer, *Maavak medini be-malkodet*, pp. 340, 345.

the anti-Polish Ribbentrop-Molotov Pact signed on August 23, 1939.[34] This kind of propaganda penetrated deeply into the consciousness of elements of the Polish population.

In conclusion, the atmosphere prevailing in the last years of the Second Polish Republic, on the eve of the Holocaust, was characterized by a radicalization of antisemitism in all its various manifestations within Polish society and within the country's ruling circles. Building upon traditional Polish anti-Jewish attitudes—which derived from religious myths, nationalistic ideology, and economic interests—antisemitism increased during the period in question and became in addition a central political issue in interparty struggles, especially in the confrontation between the post-Piłsudski Sanacja and the Endecja.

An additional feature of antisemitism in Poland at this time was its institutionalized and official character. The new political body behind the government, the OZON, had drafted anti-Jewish legislation but postponed introducing these laws as the situation shifted. The official hierarchy of the Catholic clergy in Poland likewise adopted a newly declared anti-Jewish line by openly supporting the economic boycott while opposing racist ideology and acts of violence against the Jews.

Despite these indigenous influences, the radicalization of antisemitism in Poland was directly, and especially indirectly, affected by the German model and in many cases was patterned on Nazi ideology and practice. The process of Aryanization in different forms in various organizations and professional unions continued apace in Poland in the late 1930s. Nazi forms gave antisemitism in Poland both legitimacy and prestige. On the other hand, the Polish political parties and individuals who opposed antisemitism at this time were placed on the defensive.

The end of Polish Jewry during the Holocaust was abrupt and of course not a direct outcome of the processes at work during the period under discussion. The anti-Jewish atmosphere prevailing in the country on the eve of the war had, however, serious implications for the relations between Poles and Jews during the Holocaust.

34. *Warszawski Dziennik Narodowy,* August 23, 1939; *ABC,* August 24, 1939.

Economic and Social Spheres

Jerzy Tomaszewski

The Role of Jews in Polish Commerce, 1918-1939

An examination of the role of Jews in Polish commerce between the world wars requires a look at statistical data. The most complete figures concerning the professional and social structure of the Polish population were gathered in 1931, during the general census, and classified according to religion. While religious beliefs do not necessarily correlate with national identification, the difference between adherence to the Mosaic faith and expression of Jewish national feelings can be overlooked for the practical aims of this study. It is important to remember, however, that in all statistical tables based on the census material cited in this essay there is a tacit assumption that religion and national identification are identical. Thus the figures are only approximate.

The figures also reflect errors introduced when the data were processed by the Główny Urząd Statystyczny (GUS, Central Statistical Office). The totals taken from the tables concerning particular provinces or cities do not necessarily add up to the same figures presented by GUS for Poland as a whole. For large classes of the society the differences are, as a rule, due to minor errors in arithmetic. The discrepancies can be much more troubling, however, for small professional groups. In this study they are also troubling for mobile occupations like peddling. The inevitable errors cannot, however, distort the general conclusions.

I have taken data concerning the economically active population so as to indicate the Jewish share of commerce. These data do not agree with the number of enterprises found in the Ministry of the Treasury sources, which is based on tax statistics.[1] There are some

---

1. Zbigniew Landau and Jerzy Tomaszewski, *Druga Rzeczpospolita: Gospodarka—społeczeństwo—miejsce w świecie (sporne problemy badań)* (Warsaw, 1977), pp. 176–78. See also M. Zajdenman, "Udział Żydów w handlu Polski Odrodzonej," in *Żydzi w Polsce Odrodzonej*, vol. 2, ed. Ignacy (Yitzhak) Schiper, Aryeh Tartakower, and Aleksander Hafftka (Warsaw, n.d.), p. 465.

reasons for these discrepancies. The largest enterprises were organized as joint-stock companies. In 1930 there were in Poland 137 such companies in commerce; Jews held an important or controlling interest in 39 of them. Precise information concerning the religion or nationality of the owners is not, of course, available. My estimate is based on the names of directors and board members and on available information about some of the best-known businessmen of the period. It is generally known, for example, that the Szereszowski family was Jewish. While arbitrary and serendipitous, this information in particular cases is all we have to go on, and the margin of error is probably no more than plus or minus 10 percent. There were also commercial enterprises organized by large industrial corporations (in some cases by individual businessmen) as limited liability companies, and Jews played an important role in some of them. I have not found enough information on these companies, however, to draw any conclusions about Jewish participation. Sometimes two or more merchants were partners in one enterprise. As the census classified all partners as economically active, the number of individuals active in commerce is somewhat higher than the number of enterprises.

With these reservations, the data concerning joint-stock companies (table 1) provide a picture of the role of Jews in large-scale commerce (mainly wholesale) in Poland, and the figures for the economically active population (table 2) offer the information about medium-sized and small commercial enterprises. Table 3 compares the percentage of Jews in commerce to the agricultural population as a whole. The figures given in the tables are represented graphically in the map showing the geographical distribution of Jewish commerce in Poland. All figures are estimates only, based on the general data concerning the whole country.

As the tables and map demonstrate, Jews constituted the overwhelming majority of peddlers, shopkeepers, and merchants in the southeastern and eastern regions of the Polish Republic. The same was true for Lublin province; in Białystok province Jews still constituted a majority, but not by such a large margin. In other central provinces the percentage of people in commerce who were Jews was significantly lower. In the western provinces Jews were the insignificant minority.

The general picture that emerges from table 3 is that Jews dominated commerce in Poland's economically backward, primarily ag-

TABLE 1

Joint-Stock Companies in Polish Commerce, 1930

Legal seat (city and province)	Total number	Number probably controlled by Jews
Warsaw	85	27
Poznań	10	–
Cracow	7	3
Lwów	6	2
Katowice	5	–
Łódź	3	2
Vilna	2	2
Lublin	2	–
Będzin (Kielce province)	1	1
Bydgoszcz (Poznań province)	1	–
Częstochowa (Kielce province)	1	–
Grodno (Białystok province)	1	–
Inowrocław (Poznań province)	1	–
Kołomyja (Stanisławów province)	1	–
Lubliniec (Śląsk province)	1	1
Nowa Wieś (Śląsk province)	1	–
Ostrowiec (Kielce province)	1	–
Pabianice (Łódź province)	1	–
Płock (Warsaw province)	1	–
Radom (Kielce province)	1	–
Radomsko (Łódź province)	1	–
Rawa Mazowiecka (Warsaw province)	1	–
Siedlce (Lublin province)	1	–
Toruń (Pomorze province)	1	–
Włocławek (Warsaw province)	1	–
Totals for all of Poland	137[a]	39

SOURCE: Tadeusz Szober et al., *Rocznik informacyjny o spółkach akcyjnych w Polsce,* 1930.
[a]Four of these are subsidiaries of foreign companies.

ricultural regions.[2] Where the economic structure shifted in favor of industry, the Jewish share of commerce diminished. The explanation for this distribution is rooted in the history of the Polish lands, especially in the policies pursued by the former rulers of Austria and Russia. Jews were sometimes forced to pursue nonagricultural occupations, and, in the purely agrarian regions, the most important avenue open to them was commerce. The development of industry offered Jews new kinds of work, and many Jews in industrial areas abandoned commerce for these new opportunities.

2. It was so not only in Poland. See Ezra Mendelsohn, *The Jews of East Central Europe between the World Wars* (Bloomington, Ind., 1983).

TABLE 2

Economically Active, Self-Supporting Persons in Polish Commerce, by Province, 1931

| | Commerce | | Retail trade | | Wholesale trade | | Mobile trade | |
| | | | | | Branches of commerce | | | |
Provinces and cities	Employing personnel	Not employing personnel	Employing personnel	Not employing personnel	Employing personnel	Not employing personnel	Employing personnel	Not employing personnel
Tarnopol								
Total	713	18,954	656	18,464	53	157	4	333
Number of Jews	595	17,603	559	17,713	36	125	—	305
Percentage of Jews	83.5%	92.9%	85.2%	95.9%	67.9%	79.6%	0.0%	91.6%
Stanisławów								
Total	1,026	15,775	950	15,290	72	192	4	293
Number of Jews	880	14,580	820	14,172	58	167	2	241
Percentage of Jews	85.8%	92.4%	86.3%	92.7%	80.6%	87.0%	50.0%	82.3%
Polesie								
Total	384	9,136	364	8,499	54	256	8	1,675
Number of Jews	354	8,294	336	7,730	52	246	8	1,502
Percentage of Jews	92.2%	90.8%	92.3%	91.0%	96.3%	96.1%	100.0%	89.7%
Volynia								
Total	630	23,237	602	21,078	28	182	—	1,977
Number of Jews	507	21,099	484	19,100	23	159	—	1,840
Percentage of Jews	80.5%	90.8%	80.4%	90.6%	82.1%	87.4%	—	93.1%
Lwów exclusive of city								
Total	1,963	34,953	1,840	33,402	114	335	28	3,296
Number of Jews	1,556	31,692	1,465	30,322	84	268	18	3,052
Percentage of Jews	79.3%	90.7%	79.6%	90.8%	73.7%	80.0%	64.3%	92.6%
Nowogródek								
Total	317	7,963	298	7,455	—	—	1	447
Number of Jews	272	7,075	254	6,613	—	—	1	409
Percentage of Jews	85.6%	88.8%	85.2%	88.7%	—	—	100.0%	91.5%
Vilna exclusive of city								
Total	218	7,142	197	6,639	—	—	—	418
Number of Jews	188	6,230	171	5,840	—	—	—	308
Percentage of Jews	86.2%	87.2%	86.8%	88.0%	—	—	—	73.7%

	Col 1	Col 2	Col 3	Col 4	Col 5	Col 6	Col 7	Col 8
Lublin								
Total	1,048	36,767	975	32,943	68	173	5	3,651
Number of Jews	675	32,093	631	28,464	42	154	2	3,475
Percentage of Jews	64.4%	87.3%	64.7%	86.4%	61.8%	89.0%	40.0%	95.2%
Białystok								
Total	762	15,592	714	14,392	46	132	2	1,068
Number of Jews	625	13,192	592	12,197	32	116	1	879
Percentage of Jews	82.0%	84.6%	82.9%	84.7%	69.6%	87.9%	50.0%	82.3%
Lwów city								
Total	1,819	7,010	1,763	6,356	51	59	5	595
Number of Jews	1,496	5,523	1,453	4,957	38	45	5	521
Percentage of Jews	82.2%	78.8%	82.4%	78.0%	74.5%	76.3%	100.0%	87.6%
Kielce								
Total	1,927	41,536	1,824	36,625	86	282	17	4,629
Number of Jews	1,282	32,199	1,221	28,111	48	239	13	3,849
Percentage of Jews	66.5%	77.5%	66.9%	76.8%	55.8%	84.8%	76.5%	83.1%
Cracow city								
Total	1,520	4,705	1,382	4,157	136	106	2	442
Number of Jews	1,165	3,554	1,040	3,116	123	91	2	347
Percentage of Jews	76.6%	75.5%	75.3%	75.0%	90.4%	85.8%	100.0%	78.5%
Cracow exclusive of city								
Total	1,852	21,076	1,719	19,312	122	216	11	1,548
Number of Jews	1,279	16,080	1,187	14,682	82	151	5	1,247
Percentage of Jews	69.1%	76.3%	69.1%	76.0%	67.2%	69.9%	45.5%	80.6%
Vilna city								
Total	713	4,965	692	4,452	—	—	1	495
Number of Jews	594	3,678	577	3,355	—	—	—	310
Percentage of Jews	83.3%	74.1%	83.4%	75.4%	—	—	0.0%	62.6%
Warsaw city								
Total	5,784	28,126	5,630	22,950	146	147	8	5,029
Number of Jews	3,882	21,547	3,782	17,075	96	109	4	4,363
Percentage of Jews	67.1%	76.6%	67.2%	74.4%	65.8%	74.1%	50.0%	86.8%
Łódź city								
Total	1,929	15,640	1,850	13,263	75	75	4	2,302
Number of Jews	1,446	11,565	1,384	9,743	59	61	3	1,761
Percentage of Jews	75.0%	73.9%	74.8%	73.5%	78.7%	81.3%	75.0%	76.5%

TABLE 2 (Cont.)

	Branches of commerce							
	Commerce		Retail trade		Wholesale trade		Mobile trade	
Provinces and cities	Employing personnel	Not employing personnel	Employing personnel	Not employing personnel	Employing personnel	Not employing personnel	Employing personnel	Not employing personnel
Warsaw exclusive of city								
Total	1,356	29,897	1,292	27,931	53	112	11	1,854
Number of Jews	686	21,188	654	19,594	32	88	—	1,506
Percentage of Jews	50.6%	70.9%	50.6%	70.2%	60.4%	78.6%	0.0%	81.2%
Łódź exclusive of city								
Total	1,131	25,763	1,047	22,361	64	157	20	3,245
Number of Jews	553	16,316	510	13,907	37	116	6	2,293
Percentage of Jews	48.9%	63.3%	48.7%	62.2%	57.8%	73.9%	30.0%	70.7%
Three western provinces (Poznań, Pomorze, Śląsk)								
Total	9,408	34,791	8,757	30,941	634	317	15	323
Number of Jews	1,462	4,543	1,353	3,214	116	26	•	•
Percentage of Jews	15.5%	13.1%	15.5%	10.4%	18.3%	8.2%	•	•
Poland								
Total	34,500	383,028	32,552	346,510	1,802	2,898	146	33,620
Number of Jews	19,497	288,051	18,473	259,905	963	2,161	61	25,985
Percentage of Jews	56.5%	75.2%	56.7%	75.0%	53.4%	74.6%	41.8%	77.3%

SOURCE: All figures are based on the official results of the 1931 census, published by the Główny Urząd Statystyczny in the volumes of *Statystyka Polski*, ser. C (Warsaw, 1936–38).

NOTE: • indicates that the figures are lacking; — indicates that there are no persons.

TABLE 3

Percentage of Jews among Economically Active Persons in Commerce
Compared to the Percentage of Agricultural Population among All the
Inhabitants of Poland, 1931

Provinces and cities	Number of economically active persons in commerce	Percentage of Jews in that number	Percentage of agricultural population in the total population
Tarnopol	19,667	92.5%	79.6%
Stanisławów	16,801	92.0%	74.7%
Polesie	9,520	90.8%	80.6%
Volynia	23,867	90.5%	79.4%
Lwów exclusive of city	36,916	90.0%	76.1%
Nowogródek	8,280	88.7%	82.4%
Vilna exclusive of city	7,360	87.2%	84.8%
Lublin	37,815	86.7%	71.0%
Białystok	16,354	84.5%	69.9%
Lwów city	8,829	79.5%	1.1%
Kielce	43,463	77.0%	56.8%
Cracow city	6,225	75.8%	0.9%
Cracow exclusive of city	22,928	75.7%	65.7%
Vilna city	5,678	75.2%	2.6%
Warsaw city	33,910	75.0%	0.4%
Łódź city	17,569	74.1%	0.3%
Warsaw exclusive of city	31,253	70.0%	60.8%
Łódź exclusive of city	26,894	62.7%	63.0%
Three western provinces (Poznań, Pomorze, Śląsk)	44,199	13.6%	38.1%
Poland	417,528	73.7%	60.6%

SOURCE: *Statystyka Polski,* ser. C.

The more detailed figures reveal that the Jewish share of the retail
trade was overwhelming. Except for some large industrial centers,
this branch of commerce was associated strictly with villages. In
many regions Jews were known mainly as village shopkeepers or
peddlers. The peasants in these regions included Poles, Belorussians,
Ukrainians, and Lithuanians. No matter how good the relations
between shopkeepers and their customers seemed, there was always
some level of distrust. In the traditional values of the villagers, manual work in the fields was the main—or even the sole—worthy
occupation; all other professions and occupations were considered
to exploit the hard labor of the peasants. This distrust grew during
economic disturbances, when peasants received less for the goods
they produced. After 1918 an additional problem arose in the eastern provinces with the introduction of the metric system of measures

DISTRIBUTION OF JEWISH COMMERCE
IN POLAND, 1918–1939

Baltic Sea

LITHUANIA

VILNA

GERMANY

POMORZE

NOWOGRÓDEK

U.S.S.R.

GERMANY

BIAŁYSTOK

POZNAŃ

WARSAW

POLESIE

ŁÓDŹ

LUBLIN

VOLYNIA

KIELCE

ŚLĄSK

CZECHO-

CRACOW

LWÓW

TARNOPOL

STANISŁAWÓW

SLOVAKIA

RUMANIA

Percentage of Jews among the economically active
population engaged in commerce:

More than 85 percent.

62–85 percent.

Number of Jews so small that they were not
included in the percentage results of the census.

SOURCE: Official results in the 1931 census published by Głowny Urząd Statystyczny in the volumes of *Statystyka Polski*, ser. C.

and weights. Traditional country people used the old—Russian— system. As they often did not understand the difference between the two systems and were not able easily to convert the traditional units into the legal ones, they believed that they were cheated by the merchants. A similar problem occurred in connection with the introduction of instruments for weighing and measuring, such as balances. Traditionally peasants sold some goods by approximate weights; a wandering purchaser of pigs and cows, for example, did not as a rule use a balance. Even those peasants who possessed balances knew in most cases only the old system of weights. It is impossible to know how often their accusations of cheating were justified and how often not.

The tension between a merchant and a producer, though origi- nating in the economic sphere of life, was also related to differences in faith, language, habits, and dress. Such vast differences made tensions volatile. At the same time Jewish merchants were in many regions the only link between the village producer and the distant market. Peasants could—and did—travel to the nearest town and sell their products there. The needs of the local towns were small, however, and surplus goods had to be sent to larger, regional mar- kets. It was not an easy task. Peasants sold in small quantities—a little corn here, a few animals there—and the quality of their prod- ucts varied widely. Such goods might be suitable for the local mar- ket, but they were of no use for export without a developed network of local peddlers and merchants who gathered the products, tried to standardize them, and sent them to large commercial centers.[3] It is true that the dispersion of commerce and the enormous number of local tradesmen became a heavy burden for the producers of agricultural goods. Jacob Lestschinsky considered that the number of merchants in central and eastern Poland was greater than the economic life really required.[4] On the other hand, the primitive economy of these regions could develop exchange of goods in no other form. The backwardness of agricultural practices made this primitive kind of commerce inevitable.[5] Commerce could not take

3. Kazimierz Sokołowski, *Koszty pośrednictwa* (Warsaw, 1938), pp. 62–63.
4. Jacob Lestschinsky, cited in Aryeh Tartakower, "Zawodowa i społeczna struk- tura Żydów w Polsce Odrodzonej," in *Żydzi w Polsce Odrodzonej*, 2:391.
5. Andrzej Hodoly and Wacław Jastrzębowski, *Handel wiejski w Polsce międzywojen- nej: Liczby i fakty* (Warsaw, 1957).

a different course without the introduction of modern forms of agriculture and a thorough revision of the Polish economy as a whole.

The detailed figures in table 2 suggest that in most regions Jewish
merchants represented a relatively small amount of capital and
owned relatively small enterprises that did not employ personnel.
Only in Polesie province, in some big cities, and in the western part
of Poland was the percentage of Jewish merchants employing personnel higher than those not employing personnel. These data provide evidence that Jewish trade was relatively dispersed as compared
with other national groups in Poland. At the same time, the proportion of joint-stock companies in which Jews held controlling interests was even smaller, with some regional exceptions of minor
importance.

The most important exception was the relatively high percentage
of Jewish merchants employing personnel in the western parts of
Poland. It would be interesting to consider this question in a special
study. At this time I can present only a preliminary hypothesis.
Between 1918 and 1929, there were two categories of Jews in the
western provinces. The first comprised the people of Mosaic faith
and German culture who lived there before 1918 and remained after
the Polish Republic was reborn. There are reasons to think that
among them were businessmen of some wealth who hesitated to
emigrate to Germany and start all over again. The second category
included immigrants from other parts of Poland who settled in the
western provinces hoping to pick up where the liquidated German
enterprises had left off. Commerce in this part of Poland was distinguished by high standards and relatively strong organization. Newcomers had to bring some capital with them in order to compete
successfully.

After 1929, under the impact of the Great Depression, a third
category of Jewish tradesmen immigrated to the western provinces.
Diminishing revenues and increasing poverty created a demand for
cheap goods of poor quality and a reduction in the costs of trade.
For the first time the economy of western Poland was open to poor
Jewish peddlers. At the same time professional commercial journals
in Poznań and other cities of the region denounced Jewish tradesmen who tried to sell their goods from house to house and even
from office to office. The tragic economic crisis of 1929–35 made
the most economically developed region of Poland take a backward
step.

It is also necessary to point out, however, that in certain branches of commerce Jewish merchants took advantage of their traditional business connections to combine their small capital resources and promote Polish industry. The most important case was the reconstruction of the textile industry after 1918; Jewish capital rebuilt devastated textile factories and restored their productivity.[6] In the following years, however, such financial opportunities diminished. With the Great Depression, large commercial enterprises suffered severe losses and lost ground to the rapidly developing peddler trade. Under worsening economic conditions, shops that had depended on a well-to-do clientele to meet high overhead costs could not compete with more primitive forms of commerce. This growing competition explains, in part, the noisy anti-Jewish propaganda seen in the professional journals of Poland's western provinces.

The splintering of Polish trade actually boosted Jewish commerce in the 1930s. It is true that there were large Jewish companies with developed networks of representatives and international connections. Although these companies were often cited as evidence of the importance of Jewish commerce in Poland, they were but a minority. (And they were also not that important; one must remember the relative value of the word "large"). The bulk of Jewish merchants and peddlers belonged to another economic category altogether. In a poor society only a poor shopkeeper with minimum overhead could survive. As a professional journal put it in 1929, "If the Jewish shopkeeper can live on his insignificant profits, it is only owing to his minimal standard of living, so low that no Polish shopkeeper could survive on it."[7]

Jewish shopkeepers and peddlers in eastern Poland had to use every ingenuity to make a living under these difficult conditions. They took advantage of family networks to export agricultural products from Poland. For lack of market, peasants asked relatively low prices for their products. A local merchant whose relatives had emigrated and owned an enterprise in another country might be able to purchase eggs or other goods from peasants and organize their export for sale abroad. Taking advantage of family connections kept costs low and eliminated competition from other merchants. Thus

6. Zajdenman, "Udział Żydów w handlu Polski Odrodzonej," p. 468; Ignacy (Yitzhak) Schiper, *Dzieje handlu żydowskiego na ziemiach polskich* (Warsaw, 1937), pp. 580–81.

7. "Pierwsze joskółki," *Przegląd Kupiecki* 12, no. 22 (June 7, 1929): 3–4.

Polish goods found their way into the wider world. The scope and importance of this kind of trade has not yet been explained, and sources for this kind of study may not even be available.[8]

At the same time the primitive nature of Jewish commerce in Poland was an important reason for the relative weakness of Jewish merchants. Shopkeepers and peddlers earned only the barest minimum to support themselves; capital accumulation was out of the question.[9] Inevitable changes in the Polish economy found them unprepared. They could maintain their way of life as long as pre-capitalist or semicapitalist agriculture and a well-marked traditional division of professions existed. After 1918 agriculture in the central and eastern regions of the Polish Republic began to change. The development of general and professional education for young men was of great importance, as well as the peasants' increasing participation in political life. Such trends resulted in the growth of the cooperative movement, and cooperative shops were established in some villages. Polish peasants considered the cooperatives as a way to reduce the costs of trade. Ukrainian cooperatives had a political importance, too, for the Ukrainian cooperative movement created the economic basis for various social, cultural, and political activities. Sometimes the cooperative movement is regarded as anti-Jewish action, but that is not true despite the tinges of antisemitism one can find in cooperative literature. The cooperative movement competed with all private shopkeepers regardless of religion and nationality. If the shopkeepers were Jews, then they might have perceived the cooperative movement as directed against them. It is interesting, however, that Polish shopkeepers also saw themselves as victims, attacking the cooperatives as a threat to the Polish middle class.[10]

Studies organized by the Jewish institutes in Poland revealed that with the opening of village cooperatives the Jewish share in local commerce diminished. Jacob Lestschinsky investigated eighty-one towns, and in almost all of them the percentage of Jewish shops had

8. Some documents can be found among the diplomatic reports from France in the Archiwum Akt Nowych, Warsaw.

9. Aryeh Tartakower, "Pauperyzacja Żydów polskich," *Miesięcznik Żydowski*, 1935, nos. 3–4, p. 113; Ada Kalecka, "Badania ankietowe sprzedawców ulicznych," *Statystyka Pracy*, 1934, p. 237; Stefan Baum, *Handel uliczny w Warszawie* (Warsaw, 1930), p. 36; Jacob Lestschinsky, *Di ekonomishe lage fun yidn in Poyln* (Berlin, 1932).

10. For some interesting data, see Hodoly and Jastrzębowski, *Handel wiejski w Polsce międzywojennej*, pp. 151–52.

diminished in the period 1932–37.[11] It seems that the development of the cooperative movement was one of the most important reasons for this trend.

In the 1930s a new political factor influenced the situation of Jewish shopkeepers and merchants. The Narodowa Demokracja (National Democracy, its adherents the National Democrats, or Endeks) exploited antisemitism as a way to gain the support of backward elements in Polish society and to attack the government, which enjoyed the support of some Jewish parties in the Sejm (House of Deputies). National Democrats named Jews as responsible for Poland's economic disasters. Pogroms occurred, organized by radical nationalists and criminals. Studies indicate that some Jewish shops liquidated during the period were probably destroyed in pogroms.[12]

Professional unions of Christian tradesmen engaged in anti-Jewish propaganda, seeing it as a means for competing with Jewish trade. Even serious professional weeklies such as *Tygodnik Handlowy* and *Kupiec—Świat Kupiecki* began to publish anti-Jewish articles with religious arguments, some of them with a racist tinge. The daily *Mały Dziennik*, published by Franciscans and edited by radical nationalists, became notorious for its antisemitism.

From 1936 on there was an active campaign to boycott Jews in trade and social relations, especially in the western provinces and Lublin and to some extent in other towns. At the same time a new program was formulated, backed by the Christian professional unions of shopkeepers and artisans, to settle Polish shopkeepers and artisans from the western provinces in the eastern borderlands.[13] The results were rather limited, largely because of the important economic differences between the western and eastern provinces. The settlers encountered many difficulties because they did not understand the economic conditions in these unfamiliar regions. Some lost their money; others gave up; and it seems the whole idea

11. Jacob Lestschinsky, "Der yidisher handl inem kleynem shtetl fun Poyln," *Yidishe ekonomik* 1, no. 1 (May 1937); Tartakower, "Zawodowa i społeczna struktura Żydów w Polsce Odrodzonej," p. 390; Zajdenman, "Udział Żydów w handlu Polski Odrodzonej," p. 465.

12. Menahem Linder, "Der khurbn funem yidishn handl in bialystoker rayon," *Yidishe ekonomik* 1, no. 2 (June–July 1937): 13–14, 24; Lestschinsky, "Der yidisher handl inem kleynem shtetl fun Poyln," pp. 17–18.

13. Jerzy Tomaszewski, "Handel prywatny w Polsce w latach 1936–1939," in *Drobnomieszczaństwo XIX i XX wieku*, ed. Stefania Kowalska-Glikman (Warsaw, 1984), pp. 221–25, 229–32.

ended without any significant success. Probably no more than one thousand shopkeepers and artisans, in all, were resettled.

It is very difficult to appreciate the impact of all these activities on Jewish commerce in Poland. The boycott and other programs were noisily promoted, but the Polish economy as a whole probably had a more important effect. Jews generally offered cheaper goods than their Christian competitors. The low prices made a big difference to people with modest incomes, especially in the villages, where even the popular opinion that the Jews sold goods of poor quality did not deter sales.[14] Christian shopkeepers were criticized by the Polish nationalist press for buying from Jewish wholesale dealers while placing anti-Jewish slogans on their front doors.[15] In the eastern provinces inscriptions such as "The Polish Shop," displayed as an instrument of the anti-Jewish boycott, often had quite the opposite effect on Belorussian and Ukrainian peasants.[16]

Taking all these and related facts into consideration, I think anti-Jewish propaganda and the boycott had a relatively minor impact on Jewish commerce in Poland. The main reasons for the decline of Jewish commerce were the Great Depression, the social changes that it brought, and the very slow recovery in the next years. In a poor country where the number of shops was growing together with the percentage of unemployed and overpopulation in the agricultural sector, the revenues in the tertiary sector could not be sufficient to maintain those who tried to live on them.

Certain government policies contributed more directly to the decline of Jewish commerce. The best-known case is the anti-*shehitah* (ritual slaughter) law passed by the Sejm and the Senate in 1936.[17] The law was not initiated by the government, however, but by some deputies in the Sejm who belonged to the government's majority while embracing the brand of nationalism espoused by the National Democrats. Irrespective of political considerations, some ministers and officials feared possible economic consequences of the new law,

14. "Es-e, Na fałszywym torze?" *Tygodnik Handlowy* 20, no. 7 (April 1, 1937): 180.
15. "Ze Związku Tow. Kup. w Poznaniu," *Kupiec—Świat Kupiecki*, 1936, no. 7, p. 83; "Obserwator" [Observer], "Bądźmy czynnymi patriotami," *Kupiec—Świat Kupiecki*, 1938, no. 1, p. 7.
16. See, e.g., Wanda Wasilewska, "Szukam antysemityzmu," *Wiadomości Literackie*, September 26, 1937, no. 40, p. 3.
17. Tomaszewski, "Handel prywatny w Polsce w latach 1936–1939," p. 227; Czesław Bobrowski, *Wspomnienia ze stulecia* (Lublin, 1985), pp. 93–94.

which put some restrictions on ritual slaughter (it did not prohibit it, as is sometimes claimed). As Jews were important buyers of meat, the law might hurt the meat trade, with dire consequences for the peasants. Therefore some rabbis and officials from the Ministry of Agriculture secretly cooperated in circumventing the most severe regulations.

Other government policies contributing to the decline of Jewish commerce were, in fact, associated with a general plan for Polish economic development. In the sphere of commerce the government tried to stimulate the modernization of shops and the entire trade system.[18] The new regulations introduced—with many difficulties— in the 1930s required some hygienic improvements in the trade with alimentary goods, such as glass cases (to protect against houseflies), separate storage areas for different kinds of goods, the separation of the shop space from living quarters (in poor shops the two were often identical), and others. Even in the relatively wealthy western provinces these new regulations were protested by Polish merchants, who argued that the economic crisis made investment impossible and renovating shops to meet the regulations could lead to bankruptcy. The authorities postponed introducing some of the regulations but did not alter the imperatives; many shopkeepers were forced to find money to buy new equipment and even renovate their shops. For some of them it was absolutely impossible.

Another problem was the growing level of state intervention in the Polish economy.[19] This intervention resulted from the inadequate capital strength of private businessmen as well as the situation on the international market. Organizing export of some goods necessitated compulsory cartels and the establishment of special privileges for some groups or even individual enterprises. A trade agreement with Austria, for example, required that an organization of Polish exporters of pigs be set up. This kind of requirement was not unusual. In other cases the government tried to make Polish exports more profitable by standardizing produce like butter and eggs and some industrial wares. Only goods that met specified standards were allowed to be exported; others were slapped with very high export taxes. This policy favored companies with the best equipment and most experienced staff and restrained the export

18. Zbigniew Landau and Jerzy Tomaszewski, *Gospodarka Polski międzywojennej, 1918–1939,* vol. 3: *Wielki kryzys, 1930–1935* (Warsaw, 1982), pp. 343–44.

19. Ibid., passim.

trade of many small merchants. Cooperatives received some additional privileges.

There is no doubt that Polish commerce—internal as well as international—was often financially weak and professionally unskilled and inadequately equipped.[20] Competition on the international market required a general strengthening of Polish trade. At the same time, this branch of the national economy suffered heavily in the years 1929–35, especially from lack of capital. State intervention aimed at promoting Polish trade caused many troubles for poor merchants and pushed some of them out of the market altogether. That was true irrespective of nationality or religion, but as most of the poor merchants were Jews, this class of society suffered the most. Moreover, the deplorable state of the Polish economy—in spite of all government efforts—made alternative occupations unavailable. It should be pointed out that the government invested—or promoted private investments—in the modern branches of industry where some special professional skills were required, but former shopkeepers and even artisans did not possess these skills. They had little choice but to become unskilled laborers, and even in this work they faced growing competition from pauperized peasants.

The economic as well as the political situation in Poland led, therefore, to the diminishing role for Jews in Polish commerce. The modernization of the Polish economy, the increase in state intervention, the development of cooperatives, and changes in agriculture were all part of this trend.

In this light it is necessary to discuss some projects concerning the solution of the Jewish Question in Poland. Emigration was only one of the theoretical possibilities, and, given the international situation, not the most important one. The Polish government used every opportunity to promote the emigration movement. At the end of the 1930s some agreements for accepting Polish immigrants were negotiated and signed with Latin American countries, but these countries expected peasants, not shopkeepers, and often did not accept Jews at all. An agreement with Afghanistan permitted the immigration of a small number of textile and highway engineers and foremen, but to find an outlet for Jewish emigration outside of Palestine (where the British mandatory authorities also placed strict

20. Hodoly and Jastrzębowski, *Handel wiejski w Polsce międzywojennej*, pp. 107–8, 233–37.

regulations on immigration) was really a very difficult task. Polish diplomats, with the help of some distinguished Jewish leaders, even tried to frame plans for the immigration of Polish Jews in the program of the Evian Conference, but with no success.

The other solution to the Jewish Question in Poland was to increase the so-called productiveness of Jews. The idea of providing Jewish youth with professional training in fields outside traditional commercial and tailoring trades was related in part to the long-standing contempt with which noblemen and peasants regarded merchants and shopkeepers. There were also, however, some rational arguments for such projects. The modernization of the Polish economy left little place for the traditional kind of commerce and so the professional reconstruction of Polish Jewry was of considerable importance. But the real impact of these plans was limited by inadequate funds and widespread unemployment in Poland.

These troubles were not limited to Polish-Jewish tradesmen. Unemployment, the lack of alternative occupations, and the effects of the state intervention shaped the lives of all Polish citizens. Jews had their full share of these difficulties, however, and their future was full of fears and doubts.

Frank Golczewski

The Problem of Sunday Rest
in Interwar Poland

The problem of Sunday, or Sabbath, rest in Poland must be considered in the context of its development and with recognition of its far-reaching implications. It is not simply an issue of Polish history. It needs to be examined in the broader context of regulations on days and hours of work and the intellectual history of the Western world, generally, during the industrial era.[1]

The Religious Context

Although the injunction for Sabbath rest is included in the Decalogue (Exodus 20:8–11), the forbidding of labor on this day did not retain the force of sanctification when early in the Christian era the "Sabbath" was moved from Saturday to Sunday. As the modern German Catholic theologian Reinhold Bärenz puts it, "The Sunday rest is a positive church commandment that could be repealed by the church at any time." The most important element of the Sunday rest commandment is participation in Holy Mass; it was included in the so-called Five Church Commandments outlined by Antony of Florence in the late Middle Ages. Even then, however, the injunction was not formalized. Bärenz explains that these commandments were "practical pastoral directions for the shaping of a Christian life." In Martin Luther's teachings, of course, the observance of Sunday rest became—theoretically at least—primarily an individual de-

1. The issue of Sunday rest in Poland might be fruitfully compared with the issue of prohibition in the United States. Both marshaled religious and social arguments, and both were used as political tools by groups whose position statements cannot be taken at face value.

cision. To Luther this duty was more an expression of love of neighbor than the fulfillment of a commandment.[2]

Not until 1917–18 was the obligation of Sunday observance included in canonic law and thus a binding order for the whole of the Catholic world. Why, we must ask, did the question of Sunday rest become an important issue during the period of the Polish Republic when before it had not been so?

The Social Context

The question of whether one should refrain from work on a specific day of the week was not relevant during the Middle Ages, nor did it pertain prior to widespread industrialization. In premodern Christian society, the peasant had to work every day, all week long, in order to till his fields properly, and where he was under feudal obligation to an overlord, Sunday was sometimes the only day in which the peasant was allowed to work his own plot.[3] Moreover trade, as the German word *Messe* (meaning both "fair" and "mass") suggests, was in many cases conducted when Christian people gathered to attend religious services. No contradiction was perceived between trade and worship; people often did both on Sunday or church holidays. The premodern Jew, however, was bound by a strict commandment for Sabbath rest, and observance of the Sabbath constituted a fundamental difference between premodern Christian and Jewish societies.

Thus the question of Sunday rest must be seen as a problem of the modern era. When early industrial shops tended to exploit human labor to the utmost, the workers' movement argued for a weekly day of rest at the same time it sought to reduce the number of hours in the workday. This socialist demand for a weekly day of rest coincided with similar demands from other quarters. In Germany Otto von Bismarck's social security legislation sought to alleviate worker distress, and Adolf Stöcker's Christlichsoziale Arbeiter

2. Reinhold Bärenz, *Das Sonntagsgebot: Gewicht und Anspruch eines kirchlichen Leitbildes* (Munich, 1982), pp. 58, 42, 45.

3. Christoph Deutschmann terms the precapitalist structure of work time as "organic," for nature dictated the organization of labor as opposed to the abstract "timetable" set by man after the industrial revolution. *Der Weg zum Normalarbeitstag* (Frankfurt a.M., 1985), p. 73, after A. J. Gurjewitsch, *Das Weltbild des mittelalterlichen Menschen* (Munich, 1980). Thus the Jewish way of organizing time might be thought of as more abstract, more "capitalist," or more modern.

Partei (Christian-Social Workers' Party) of 1878 linked benefits for
workers with antisemitic slogans directed against Jews as representatives of liberalism and thus responsible for worker exploitation.
At the same time the Catholic church, which also promoted Sunday
rest, denounced both liberalism and socialism with Leo XIII's en-
cyclical *Rerum novarum* (1891). The church was fighting very hard
to retain its position in the face of increasing secularism and atheism. Common demands by workers and the clergy evidenced not so
much a joining of ranks as an effort by both the church and various
political parties to win over the emerging workers' movement.

I mention these familiar episodes of world history to show that
the links between workers' demands and antisemitism on the one
hand and church politics on the other are not surprising. Many
workers' demands in the late nineteenth and early twentieth centuries had more of a religious base than those who focus only on
leftist workers' movements acknowledge. In any case, the issue of
Sunday rest was debated on various sides throughout the Western
world.

Sabbath or Sunday?

One additional issue arose in English-speaking areas of the West.
Some English and American sects emphasized the importance of
observing the original Sabbath (Saturday) instead of the traditional
Christian Sunday, and debate over the proper rest day was lively
where these sects were active. It was marked by arguments based
more on religious loyalties than on reason. For example, a statement
before the National Sabbath Convention meeting at Saratoga, New
York, in 1863, argued:

> It is an undeniable fact that the two nations which keep the Sabbath
> most strictly—Great Britain and the United States—are the wealthiest
> and freest on earth. Sabbath-rest is the condition of successful week-
> labor for man and beast and successful labor is the parent of wealth.
> . . . Yeah, the end of the Sabbath would be for America the beginning
> of the unlimited reign of the infernal idol-trinity of Mammon, Bacchus
> and Venus and overwhelm us at last in temporal and eternal ruin.[4]

Philip Schaff, the author of this statement, openly asserted that the
sanctification of the correct (in his case the Sabbath) day would

4. Philip Schaff, "The Anglo-American Sabbath," in *The National Sabbath Convention*
(Saratoga, N.Y., 1863), doc. 26, pp. 11, 32.

ensure material blessings for the observant. In Schaff's viewpoint and its widespread acceptance we can see some of the emotion that fueled arguments for Sunday rest in Poland. Some Poles also believed that observance would magically bring material benefits, and it is important to understand that in order to understand the intensity of Polish commitment in the debate.

By the end of the nineteenth century, Sunday rest had become an important issue, appearing on the agenda of most legislative bodies in the Western world. Between 1875 and 1915 Christian groups organized a series of International Lord's Day congresses in both the United States and Europe. Their proceedings were published, and the persistence of these efforts alone points to the prominence of Sunday rest as an international issue. In most of the Western world, however, the issue was primarily religious and social. Here the Polish context differs, for in Poland Sunday rest evolved as a political issue.

Rest-Day Legislation in Poland before World War I

In Polish lands under Prussian rule, a law of June 1, 1891, declared Sunday rest obligatory for industry and craft workers (*Gewerbe*) and technical employees *(Angestellte)*. Commercial workers and office clerks were specified in legislation passed on February 25, 1919, when Polish Prussia was still formally under German jurisdiction.[5] Some kinds of work, such as transportation and innkeeping, were excluded from the legislation, and local bylaws also exempted those providing specific services to the public. As German Jews tended to be less strict than Jews elsewhere about keeping the Sabbath, the issue did not assume political proportions in Prussian Poland.

The rulings in Russian Poland were liberal in that they allowed for work on Sundays if another day of rest was observed, leaving decisions in such instances to the local authorities. In 1907 Warsaw governor Georgij Skallon approved Sunday work providing no work was done between 10 A.M. and 2 P.M. so church services would not be disturbed.

The most elaborate legislation pertaining to Sunday rest was in

5. *Arbeitszeitordnung*, commentary by Johannes Denecke, 9th ed. (Munich, 1976), p. 246.

Austrian Poland, where laws applicable only to Galicia and Bukovina allowed Jews to work on Sundays so long as specific requirements were met. Employers who were Jewish or who employed only
Jewish workers had to submit, on a regular basis, lists of those who
worked on Sundays, including their names, places of employment,
and types of work performed. Such workers could work on Sundays
if a twenty-four-hour rest period were enforced on Saturdays and
if the Sunday work were not performed in public and did not produce a loud noise (*grösseres Geräusch*) to disturb the quiet of the
Lord's Day. These restrictions did not apply, however, to kosher
butchers and sausage makers (*Koscherselcherei oder Koscherwursterzeu-
gung*), who were allowed to sell their products on Sundays although
that gave them an advantage over Christian butchers, who could
not sell to rural people coming into town on Sundays to attend
church.[6]

While such provisions may seem restrictive rather than liberal to
us, we must remember that they were often loosely enforced. Jewish
Sunday commercial activity in trade, innkeeping, and other areas
was both visible and lively, and the object of verbal attack from the
Catholic clergy as well as right-wing and populist politicians.

The Political Situation after World War I

The question of Sunday rest must also be seen in the context of
increasing interest in the so-called Jewish Question in the years
immediately preceding and following World War I. In the prewar
period economic boycott brought the economic aspect of Polish-
Jewish relations to the top of the political agenda, though not solely
for economic reasons. In Galicia the cooperative movement had a
long history of anti-Jewish activities.[7] After the war, however, the
issue took on different ramifications.

The economic misery of Poland at this time was overwhelming.
Too many people were competing for the same few resources, and
in this environment controversies between Poles and Jews, like

6. Laws of January 16, 1895 (Reichsgesetzblatt 21) and July 18, 1905 (Reichs-
gesetzblatt 125), published also as *Vorschriften über die Sonntagsruhe im gewerblichen
Betriebe Österreichs* (Vienna, 1909), as a special supplement of the *Soziale Rundschau*,
December 1909, pp. 82, 83.
7. See Frank Golczewski, *Polnisch-jüdische Beziehungen, 1881–1922: Eine Studie zur
Geschichte des Antisemitismus in Osteuropa* (Wiesbaden, 1981), pp. 60–84, 90–120.

those in Częstochowa and in several areas of Galicia, came to a head. At the same time, the Polish people were free for the first time in more than a century to shape a modern Polish nation. During decades of foreign domination, some of it non-Catholic, generations of Poles had continued to think of themselves as Polish and Catholic, so with the establishment of the Polish Republic it was natural that they should make their new nation both strongly Polish and strongly Catholic. Even the adherents of Józef Piłsudski, less religiously fervent than most interwar politicians, acquiesced in shaping the state in accordance with Catholic principles, though they insisted on guaranteeing civil rights and freedom of worship to all national and religious groups. Piłsudski's followers no doubt remembered that the Cracow archbishop Adam Stanisław Sapieha had warned in 1914 that Piłsudski's Naczelny Komitet Narodowy (Central National Committee) was bound to build a "socialist and Jewish" Poland,[8] and Piłsudski had had to accommodate himself to both the clergy and the Narodowa Demokracja (National Democracy, its adherents the National Democrats, or Endeks), which had strong support from the clerical hierarchy in Poland.

Only slowly did the new Polish Republic unify the various legal systems inherited from the partitioning powers. Sunday rest laws were but one element in these systems, and not a very important one, yet the issue of Sunday rest was one on which all the important parties could agree. No doubt that is one reason it was placed on the agenda of the Sejm (House of Deputies) as early as 1919 and discussed in the broader context of labor law.

Even earlier the issue had been raised at the Versailles Peace Conference, where, with others, Jewish representatives had tried to ensure a multilateral guarantee of Jewish religious, cultural, and political rights. A memorandum delivered by the Comité des Délégations Juives on May 10, 1919, coincided with news of antisemitic atrocities committed in Vilna, Lida, and Pinsk during Piłsudski's northeastern campaign. Consequently the memorandum was received by the Allied Powers with more interest than previous documents. Article 8 stated:

> Persons for whom the day of rest is not Sunday, but any other day, cannot be forced on this day or on any other feast to do work their

---

8. See also Bożena Krzywobłocka, *Chadecja, 1918–1937* (Warsaw, 1974), p. 46.

religious commandments consider a sin; neither will they be forbidden to work on Sundays or other holidays.

An elaboration added support:

> This article . . . is concerned with an object of first-rank importance from the point of view of religious freedom and economic equality. . . . Jews in Poland, for example, are 14 percent of the country's population. Their festive day is Saturday. If they would not be allowed to exercise their respective trades on Sundays they would thus lose one sixth of their economic potential; this again would be a serious injury in their fight for a living. In addition it is a principle in accordance with all perceptions of justice that one should not force Jews to profane the day their forefathers held sacred for ages.[9]

Sunday rest was not the main issue on the Jewish agenda. Even though the Allied Powers were to a certain degree friendly toward some Jewish demands, they did not include a guarantee of Jewish immunity from Sunday rest legislation in the Minorities Treaty that Polish representatives were forced to sign on June 28, 1919, in order to receive the other benefits of the Versailles Treaty.

But even the minor victory the Jews won in having some of their cultural rights guaranteed by the League of Nations—whose ineffectiveness was not yet apparent—set off a wild political storm in Poland. One thing is clear: the primarily right-wing political parties ruling Poland were definitely unwilling to grant Jews any favors not required by the Minorities Treaty.

The left-wing parties, on the other hand, took this opportunity to draft a Sunday rest law that would emphasize workers' rights without alienating either right-wing or bourgeois groups and could therefore be passed by the legislative bodies and enforced throughout Poland. After the signing of the Minorities Treaty, therefore, prospects for resisting a strict Sunday rest law looked dim indeed.

The Sunday Rest Law before the Sejm

When the bill enforcing Sunday rest came before the Sejm, the arguments advanced by various groups did not always reflect their real motives. Thus Rabbi Moshe Eliahu Halpern, the Agudah representative, emphasized that it was necessary to work longer hours

---

9. "Memoriał Komitetu Delegacji Żydowskich przy Konferencji Pokojowej," May 10, 1919, in Izaak (Yitzhak) Gruenbaum, *Żydzi jako mniejszość narodowa: Materiały w sprawie żydowskiej w Polsce*, vol. 2 (Warsaw, 1919), pp. 40, 45.

in times of need than in "normal" times, including "some hours" on Sundays. In fact, his arguments for observance of the Sabbath differed little from those of the Catholic clergymen who supported Sunday rest. "The betrayal of religious duties and traditions," he claimed, "leads our people to the loss of all feelings of duty toward all rites and all traditions, leads . . . to extreme radicalism not only from the religious point of view but also from the moral-ethical one, leads to subversion and anarchy."[10]

It seems obvious that Halpern's statement on behalf of the Koło Żydowskie (Jewish Parliamentary Club) might as well have represented the stand of the clerical Catholic Right. It definitely had no chance of success—even if one thinks that legislators' minds can be changed by a speech. But Halpern does not seem to have been aware that the two points of view were mutually exclusive. Both operated to the same extent out of moral and ethical principles that imbued ritual observance with a magical quality. As the numerical strength of the so-called Sunday party was greater, the outcome of this confrontation was never in doubt.

For Feliks Perl, who spoke for the Polska Partia Socjalistyczna (PPS, Polish Socialist Party), the religious context was clearly irrelevant. He was interested only in *a* day of rest: "The principle of one day of rest in a week is intended to give the worker one day for himself alone, for his family, for social life, for social, cultural, and political activities." Whether that day were Sunday or Saturday did not matter to Perl; for him it was the thirty-six hours of uninterrupted rest that was important. Yet he recognized that government and large enterprises could not afford two days of rest, so, as most Poles were Catholics, it was logical that Sunday should be the appointed day. "Thus, of course, in all societies, in which the big majority of the population traditionally rests on Sundays, only Sunday can be that day of rest," he concluded.[11]

In addition to this deduction, however, Perl added a political perspective, one that inspired "hilarity," as the Sejm stenographer noted. Perl introduced to the discussion the new term *odpoczynek zbiorowy* (collective rest): "Only then the individual rest acquires additional strength . . . when it is observed together at the same time. This is an important psychological motive, that makes it nec-

10. *Sprawozdanie Stenograficzne Sejmu Ustawodawczego*, November 20, 1919, cols. 18–19.
11. Ibid., cols. 21, 22.

essary to have one *common* day of rest, and not an optional one."[12] Where Perl stressed that, among other activities, he had it in mind to arrange joint meetings and demonstrations among Jewish and Christian workers, it seems clear that he advocated the "religious" quality of the day of rest not out of belief in revelation but from expediency. Perl's statements about the solidarity of Jewish and Christian workers could not obscure that he was essentially in line with socialist thought—and of course the entire European socialist movement was a part of the Judeo-Christian tradition, a way of thinking called in German *abendländisch*.

Perl was not only Occidental, but he was also a socialist of Jewish origin and, like many of similar background and interests, an atheist. Thus he saw no need to conceal his delight that pressing economic need should compel Jews to work on Saturdays. "If Jews will work on Saturdays due to this [legislation], this will be no calamity! In any case this will be an escape from the 'ghetto.'"[13] In 1927 Apolinary Hartglas called Perl's statement "assimilatory bolshevism."[14]

Sunday rest was also linked with modernization. While Halpern applauded the liberal Sunday rest provisions of the Russian and Austro-Hungarian empires, Perl dismissed those states as reactionary and pointed to the relevant legislation in Germany and Czechoslovakia as modern—though in other connections German and Czech examples did not hold much favor in the Polish political scene. Replying to Halpern, Perl declared that it was not so much the religious question that mattered to Jewish politicians as their desire to keep Polish Jews in the ghetto.[15]

Here the question of Sunday rest throws light on another aspect of Polish-Jewish relations. While the PPS favored acculturation and the assimilation of Polish Jewry into the mainstream of Polish culture (of which Perl was an impressive example), the Zionists as well as Jewish Orthodox circles (who had little in common on other issues) supported a separate development for Jews in Poland. This phenomenon and the constant strife between assimilationists and

12. Ibid., col. 22.
13. Ibid., col. 23. Though not present in the Sejm, Bundist politicians professed similar views.
14. Apolinary Hartglas, "Ustawa o odpoczynku niedzielnym a Żydzi," *Natio*, June 6, 1927, p. 15.
15. *Sprawozdanie Stenograficzne Sejmu Ustawodawczego*, November 20, 1919, cols. 25–26.

Jewish nationalists in interwar Poland actually strengthened the position of the PPS.

Ignacy (Yitzhak) Schiper, representing Poalei Zion, was in a difficult position. On the one hand, he could not contradict Perl's argument that religious demands were of no importance to Jewish workers; on the other, he had to keep in mind the actual situation in Poland. After all, Jewish society continued to be shaped largely, if not by Jewish Orthodoxy, at least by a respect for Jewish traditions, of which Sabbath observance was one. In the end Schiper allied himself with the statement of a 1918 trade union conference in Bern, which affirmed an obligatory day of rest but declared it should not be restricted to Sunday, warning that Jewish employers might fire Jewish workers if these workers were to have two days off.[16] The prediction came true, aggravating the problems of Poland's Jews, who were ousted from positions in the intermediary and state monopoly sectors and forced to seek new avenues of employment, only to run up against Sunday rest laws.

Yitzhak Gruenbaum, the leader of the Zionist faction in the Sejm, entered into the intra-Jewish strife when he called Perl, the socialist speaker, an "assimilationist," one who firmly showed the face of "assimilationism" and demonstrated that assimilationism was an ally of the anti-Jewish forces. Gruenbaum insisted that Jewish socialists had a long tradition of planning demonstrations for Saturdays, and this tradition together with other antipathies prevented them from joining Christian socialist demonstrations on Sundays. Perl would have accused Gruenbaum of defending the "ghetto," but Gruenbaum declared that any other point of view was naïve. In this he was not altogether wrong. He further introduced a broader political view in stating that current Sunday rest legislation would alienate the Jewish population from the Polish state even further, thus preventing their identification with non-Jewish Poles.[17]

Yet another perspective was introduced by Józef Pietrzyk, the Dą-

16. Ibid., cols. 27–30. For the Jewish Orthodox employer, the difficulties arising from employing Jews and forcing them to work on Saturdays seemed insurmountable. As religion forbade allowing Jews to work on Saturdays, Orthodox Jews preferred to employ Christians, to whom the restriction would not apply; thus they got an extra day of work from their employees. Such situations contributed to the economic distress of working-class Jews. See Zbigniew Landau and Jerzy Tomaszewski, *Robotniczy przemysłowi w Polsce* (Warsaw, 1971), pp. 118–19.

17. *Sprawozdanie Stenograficzne Sejmu Ustawodawczego,* November 20, 1919, cols. 31–37.

browa Basin deputy of the Narodowy Związek Robotniczy (NZR, National Workers' Union), a national socialist party historically linked to the traditions of the Polish Right.[18] Members of the NZR were not known for close cooperation with the PPS, whom they often stigmatized as "Judaized." The NZR openly linked class demands to nationalist demands, and in this case that connection posed no problem, for the Sunday rest question made a deviation from normal party lines possible. The NZR speaker openly applauded the PPS speaker, but he did something else, too. When the Jewish deputies stressed the injustice such laws would do to the Jewish employee, he stressed the injustice the lack of such laws would do to the non-Jewish employee. He argued against any exceptions to Sunday work, because "if any Jewish shop or workplace will be open on Sundays the worker will be there against his will . . . and this will not be a real holiday or rest day." He pointed to Jewish shops that were open on Saturdays, stating they demonstrated that "the Jews are able to circumvent the Saturdays, too. If we would allow them to work on Sundays, their shops would always be open."[19] It is interesting that the NZR used the Jewish deputies' line of reasoning to argue the case against Jewish demands.

None of the amendments or alternatives proposed by Jewish deputies was considered in the main, second reading of the bill. When the vote was taken, the Sejm marshal did not even have to count the votes individually; those favoring any relaxation of the most rigid interpretation of the Sunday rest law were clearly in the minority. The division remained unaltered at the bill's third reading, when questions of common interest attracted more attention than the Sunday rest issue. Debate focused, for example, on a work week of forty-six or forty-eight hours.

Joshua Farbstein gave a long speech arguing that the Jews would suffer an economic decline if the obligatory Sunday rest were implemented,[20] but the hecklings directed at him indicated that he made no great impression on either the Right or the Left. The Sejm marshal swiftly closed debate, and the law was passed, the vote demonstrating that there was no support for Jewish arguments from either side.[21]

18. For a more complete history, see Teresa Monasterska, *Narodowy Związek Robotniczy, 1905–1920* (Warsaw, 1973).

19. *Sprawozdanie Stenograficzne Sejmu Ustawodawczego*, November 20, 1919, col. 31.

20. Ibid., December 18, 1919, col. 30.

21. The law was published in the *Dziennik Ustaw*, 1920, no. 2.

The Sunday Rest Law in Operation

The law was never fully implemented.[22] A 1923 circular from the Ministries of the Interior and Labor clarified that the law did not apply where all employees of an enterprise were members of the employer's family. The Ugoda of 1925 included a provision for the abolition of some parts of the law,[23] but that provision was never implemented. Later, working on Saturday evenings was permitted.[24]

In the following years, as Polish-Jewish hostilities grew and took more radical forms, the question of Sunday rest paled beside the harsher setbacks Polish Jews suffered. Only to complete the picture do I need to mention that in 1925 the then totally isolated Noah Pryłucki, from the tiny Folkspartei, tried to have the Jews included in the categories of employees allowed to work on Sundays.[25] Hartglas tried the same thing in 1927, but the exceptions continued to apply only to Christian enterprises.[26]

The relaxation of tensions after Piłsudski's *coup d'état* led to a reexamination of the Sunday rest question by a commission of experts. They recommended that the Sunday restriction not apply to self-employed tradesmen and craftsmen, but this recommendation was never seriously considered in the legislature.[27]

The national minorities had had great hopes for the Piłsudski regime, as it promised to end the Endeks' domination, but those hopes were disappointed. In order to gain public support, Piłsudski and his adherents had to prove that they were not "in the Jewish pocket," and supporting economic antisemitism seemed a good way to combat that impression. Thereafter and through the 1930s the

22. Paweł Korzec is not correct in asserting that the Sunday rest law was constantly criticized by the Jews. *Juifs en Pologne* (Paris, 1980), p. 104.

23. See Hartglas, "Ustawa o odpoczynku niedzielnym a Żydzi," pp. 20–22; Paweł Korzec, "Das Abkommen zwischen der Regierung Grabski und der jüdischen Parlamentsvertretung," *Jahrbuch für Geschichte Osteuropas*, n.s., 20 (1972): 331–36.

24. See Harry M. Rabinowicz, *The Legacy of Polish Jewry* (New York, 1965), p. 70.

25. See Joseph Marcus, *Social and Political History of the Jews in Poland, 1919–1939* (Berlin, 1983), p. 213.

26. See Hartglas, "Ustawa o odpoczynku niedzielnym a Żydzi," pp. 24–28. Hartglas explains (p. 10) that the exceptions dealt mostly with Christian businesses, such as florists and merchants of milk products, whereas the former Austrian provisions for Jewish tradesmen were abolished. Most of these exceptions lost their relevance with the introduction of refrigeration.

27. See Marcus, *Social and Political History*, p. 214. In the years 1924–25 a campaign to reduce the number of *Christian* holidays caused considerable agitation in concerned political circles. See Landau and Tomaszewski, *Robotniczy przemysłowi w Polsce*, pp. 349–50.

Sunday rest issue lost its political importance. Except for a few large enterprises, no visible efforts were made to enforce the letter of the Sunday rest law. Local policemen were often bribed to look the other way when Jewish shops were open on Sunday, and operating a shop through the rear door, while the front door remained officially closed, was common practice. Sunday rest as a political issue practically disappeared.

Conclusions

The question of Sunday rest was heatedly debated during the first years of the Polish Republic. This intense interest in the question lagged only a few years behind similar debates in other countries. In Poland the arguments grew out of workers' concerns for the regulation of the workday and work week and, more generally, from widespread demands that policy be shaped by ideology, specifically Catholic principles.

On these bases the Polish Left and the Polish Right met. It should be pointed out, however, that the explicitly Jewish Left—the Bund— had no interest in eliminating restrictions on Sunday trade. In 1928 Wiktor Alter saw the Orthodox Jewish tradesmen and craftsmen as a dying breed that should not be allowed to impede the progress of history. One more compulsory day of rest would only increase their pauperization and thus speed their proletarization and, generally, the progress of history.[28]

One might wonder if this point of view really accorded with the demands of Jewish workers. After all, the Bund was not a force to be reckoned with in those days (it would be stronger in the 1930s, when Sunday rest as an issue had disappeared). But the issue clearly divided Jews from Poles in political circles.

In reality the law did have a negative effect on Jewish workers, for even Jewish factory owners preferred Christian workers, who could be counted on to be fully productive six days a week. Yet the effect of the law did not generate much debate. The Jewish workers' movement remained divided over the issue and found no way to fight against its uneven enforcement.

Thus the Sunday rest issue actually undermined the unity of the Jewish socialist movement. After all, Sabbath observance was one

28. Marcus, *Social and Political History,* p. 214.

of the most visible ways in which Jews were different from non-Jews, but very few socialists observed the Sabbath in any case. As atheists, most of them regarded Sunday rest as a minor issue. It mattered only that the worker be free of work one day a week, and those interested in solidarity upheld the choice of Sunday.

The socialists did see Sunday rest as a way to foster worker solidarity, but in this they were proven wrong. There was not much Christian-Jewish solidarity in Poland's working classes immediately after World War I. The Polish Right saw Sunday rest as a way to reduce ''Jewish supremacy'' in the Polish economy, to use the strong words of the Jesuit priest Henryk Haduch. But at the same time the Right stressed its religious, not its economic motives. Haduch interpreted the Jewish ''profanation'' of the Sunday as the intentional undermining of the spiritual values of Poland's Catholics, and thus a weapon the Jews were using in their fight against Poland. Against that weapon, he argued, the Poles must be allowed to defend themselves.[29]

Thus while Jewish socialists could not do much about the implementation of Sunday rest, they did undermine their position among the Jewish working class. For most of Poland's working-class Jews, Sabbath rest was important, and the Jewish socialist position on the issue turned working-class Jews away from socialism and toward alliance with bourgeois Jews, who seemed to argue for Sabbath rest. Whether this was a sincere stand on the part of Poland's bourgeois Jews we cannot evaluate at present.

The vast array of arguments on the Sunday rest issue makes it difficult to draw conclusions. Even the Jewish side presented economic axioms not grounded in reality. Aside from the fact that in large areas Sunday rest was not enforced, the results of Sunday rest were not at all what Jewish national politicians had feared. Joseph Marcus states in his controversial *Social and Political History of the Jews in Poland* that Sunday rest did not impoverish the Jews. First, he points out, the law was not implemented. Second, Jewish producers and tradesmen catered largely to the Jewish community. Third, ''the Jewish artisans, allegedly condemned to idleness for an extra day of the week, far more often suffered from lack of demand than from lack of time to work.''[30]

29. See Henryk Haduch, *Ustawa o spoczynku niedzielnym a żydzi* (Poznań, 1923), pp. 14, 24.
30. Marcus, *Social and Political History,* p. 215. I should like to dispute Marcus's

In conclusion it may be said that the general political atmosphere in Poland colored the discussion of the Sunday rest issue. Viewed from this perspective, the issue of Sunday rest provides considerable insight into the nature of politics in interwar Poland. Outside of Poland, political disputes over Sunday rest were less heated, and Jewish respect for Sunday rest was achieved with little effort.[31] In Poland, however, the issue of Sunday rest served as a convenient political tool and provided yet another arena in which Polish-Jewish antagonism was played out. The contest was not based on facts or reality, but rather stemmed from the need for each side to promote its particular political agenda. The socialists wanted to demonstrate the Polish (i.e., non-Jewish) quality of their party. In those stormy days, the Right was not convinced. The Right wanted to stress the Polish-Catholic quality of the newborn state. With the exception of the Orthodox, the Jewish national politicians took their stand as a symbolic defense of Jewish standards.

---

contention that Jewish producers and tradesmen catered largely to the Jewish community.

31. Though there were complaints and incidents and a fairly strict enforcement of the law in former years, the question of Jewish Sunday rest never, to my knowledge, acquired a larger political significance in the United States. See Albert M. Friedenberg, *The Sunday Laws of the United States and Leading Judicial Decisions Having Special Reference to the Jews* (Philadelphia, 1908).

Shaul Stampfer

Marital Patterns in Interwar Poland

I

Marital patterns are important social indicators. Factors such as the age at which people marry and the length of time they are married exert a wide-ranging influence on fertility, family structures, and the individual psyche. Since marital patterns are themselves the product of interaction among social, intellectual, economic, and other factors, changes in marital patterns over time and from one region to another are important indicators for other, often less measurable developments in a community.

An analysis of marital patterns is a particularly useful way of approaching the history of Poland between the world wars. Many interesting questions about interwar Poland—the human price of national and economic development, for example, or the degree of national integration achieved after independence—are difficult to answer. Data suggest a wide variety of behavior patterns in Poland in the interwar period, and that they often changed rapidly. An analysis of three of the most interesting measures of marital behavior—the extent of early marriage, the proportion of people who marry, and age at widowerhood or widowhood—can shed light not only on demographic questions but provide new insights into the larger, more basic questions about interwar Poland as well.[1]

The research for this essay was generously supported by a grant from the Wolf Foundation, administered by the Israeli Academy of Sciences.

1. The most important book-length studies relevant to this topic are Raphael Mahler, *Yehudei Polin bein shtei milhamot ha-olam* (Tel Aviv, 1968); Szyja Bronsztein, *Ludność żydowska w Polsce w okresie międzywojennym: Studium statystyczne* (Wrocław, 1963); Joseph Marcus, *Social and Political History of the Jews in Poland, 1919–1939* (Berlin, 1983). A recent relevant article is Lucjan Dobroszycki, "The Fertility of Modern Polish Jewry," in *Modern Jewish Fertility*, ed. Paul Ritterband (Leiden, 1981), pp. 64–77. These studies contain references to all the relevant literature. For understandable reasons they devote more attention to the thorny problems of how *many* Jews there were in Poland and their fertility rather than their family patterns. A fascinating and

The importance of paying attention to regional variations should be emphasized at the outset. Most studies have dealt with Poland as a whole or, at best, with a breakdown of the newly independent nation into four regions. Summarizing data without noting the degree or significance of deviance within regions inevitably creates the misleading impression that behavior was uniform over wide areas. This impression, in turn, makes it more difficult to uncover those factors that had the greatest impact on behavior. This study is based on Polish census data, with the breakdown according to province as well as urban-rural settlement patterns. Census data do not permit breakdown into smaller geographical units, but analysis of the urban-rural categories can be further refined by taking into account the size of the urban community. That step was not necessary for the current study, but it remains an avenue worth exploring.

The reborn Polish state, established in November 1918, comprised lands that had been under Russian, Prussian, and Austrian rule since the Partitions of the late eighteenth century. During the nineteenth century significant differences developed in the economic, social, and political conditions of the three areas, in part the result of differences in governmental policies of the three partitioning powers. These differences compounded earlier differences—determined by geography as well as other factors—so that the new Polish state could most easily be divided into regions defined by their previous rulers. At the same time, there was much that united the three regions, including a common language and national heritage. What is difficult to measure are the degree of similarity among the regions and how quickly, if at all, the new national political unity was translated into other spheres during the interwar period.

The largest part of the new Polish state comprised lands that had previously been under tsarist rule. In part they had been governed as the semiautonomous Kingdom of Poland, or Congress Poland, and in part they had been included in the western provinces of the Russian Empire. The tsarist regime had been unable or unwilling to invest significantly in the economic infrastructure of Poland—in

---

sophisticated article, which for perfectly good reasons does not deal directly with Jewish marital patterns, is June Sklar, "The Role of Marriage Behaviour in the Demographic Transition: The Case of Eastern Europe around 1900," *Population Studies* 28, no. 2 (1974): 231–47. Sklar's paper indicates that at the turn of the century, delayed marriage was typical for Poles. Among others, she points out the significance of sexual imbalances as a factor in determining marital behavior. For our purposes, it existed but apparently did not have a major role.

part out of strategic concerns as well as anti-Polish sentiment. On the other hand, the existence of a large hinterland, the lack of a well-developed alternative industrialized zone within the empire, and protective tariffs provided entrepreneurs with a large market and led to the formation of a large textile industry as well as a food-processing industry, while agriculture fared poorly.

The portion of the new state that had been under Habsburg rule was mainly Galicia. A relatively neglected corner, it had had little to offer in an empire that already had more developed industrial regions and richer agricultural lands. Galicia was a byword for poverty, and it may well be claimed that its main export was human beings—people who emigrated to seek a living. As Zbigniew Landau and Jerzy Tomaszewski put it, "From an economic point of view the Austrian partition was in many respects the least favourable *vis-à-vis* the other Polish territories."[2] The lands under German rule had enjoyed the best market conditions for agricultural produce of all the Polish lands while importing most of their industrial needs from Germany.

Data from the post-Partition period indicate that it was precisely in the unpromising agricultural areas of Galicia that there was the highest population density of peasants, while the lowest density was to be found in the relatively well-developed western areas. The central and eastern regions were somewhere in the middle. In other words, demographic pressures compounded economic pressures.[3]

II

Early and universal marriage was a well-recognized characteristic of traditional Jewish society,[4] owing in large part to religious concerns for morality as well as to the economic environment. As urban dwellers, Jews did not have to delay marriage until land should be available, as was common in some peasant societies. Among

2. Zbigniew Landau and Jerzy Tomaszewski, *The Polish Economy in the Twentieth Century* (New York, 1985), p. 16. This classic work deals in a number of places with the question of regional characteristics. For the purposes of this essay, the discussion in chapter 1 is most relevant.

3. Jack Taylor, *The Economic Development of Poland, 1919–1950* (Ithaca, N.Y., 1952), p. 24, citing Wilbert Moore, *Economic Demography of Eastern and Southern Europe* (Geneva, 1945), p. 203.

4. The standard article on this topic is still Jacob Katz, "Family, Kinship and Marriage among Ashkenazim in the Sixteenth to Eighteenth Century," *Jewish Journal of Sociology* 1 (1959): 3–22, or chapters 14 and 15 in his *Tradition and Crisis* (New York, 1961).

nineteenth-century Polish Jewry, child marriage was not unknown, and a significant proportion were married in their teens. According to the 1921 census, however, there were almost no married Jewish males or females under the age of seventeen. There is no reason to suspect false reporting to census takers, as there are no contemporary reports of marriage among fifteen- and sixteen-year-olds, and had such a practice existed, it surely would have attracted attention. The once-common practice of child marriage was apparently long forgotten. Even more significant was the very low level of marriage among Jews in the late teens. This shift away from traditional marital patterns demonstrates that by 1921 all sectors of Jewish society had undergone significant changes in family life, even Orthodox circles who claimed that they were the unchanging sector of the community and sought to demonstrate their adherence to tradition through their attire, language, and religious practice. There is less reason to think that marital patterns among Roman Catholics in 1921 were significantly different from past patterns.

Even a cursory glance at the patterns of teenage marriage outlined in table 1 reveals a significant degree of variation among Poland's population groups. It is immediately clear that male patterns differ from female patterns. Moreover, while the data involve relatively small numbers, regional variations also clearly emerge. The lowest levels of male teenage marriage were reported from the western provinces, areas formerly part of Prussian Germany and under intensive Western influence while enjoying relative prosperity. The southern provinces had only slightly higher rates of male teenage marriage, while the eastern and central provinces had the highest levels. This pattern holds for Jews and Roman Catholics alike. Except for the east, there was usually a higher level of teenage marriage among urban male Jews than among urban male Roman Catholics. For rural male Jews, the pattern varied from province to province except for the central provinces, where teenage marriage was more common among Jewish males than among Roman Catholic males. The differences between urban and rural patterns within a population group were generally not large. The low level of marriage of teenage Jewish males is not radically different from the picture we have of the Jews of European Russia, where in 1902 less than 5 percent of the marriages contracted between Jews involved a groom under the age of twenty.[5]

5. See S. Rabinowitsch-Margolin, ''Die Heiraten der Juden im europäischen Russ-

The behavior of women was quite different from that of men. The age differences between the sexes in any given area were far greater among Roman Catholics than among Jews, suggesting that there was a greater tendency among Catholics for younger women to marry older men than among Jews. The differences between behavior in urban and rural regions were also larger among Roman Catholic women than among Jewish women. Less expected, perhaps, is that the highest levels of early marriage among Jewish women tended to show up in the same areas that had the highest levels of early marriage among Roman Catholics and not necessarily where the highest levels of early marriage for Jewish males were found. Thus, while levels for males were low in all the southern provinces, that was not the case for women. It should be noted that while in certain places, such as urban Warsaw, the percentage of married males was higher than that of females, that does not mean that young Jews were marrying older women; in these cases the pool of males was smaller than that of females.

The table shows that among men the most important factor affecting the rate of teenage marriage was the region, then religion, and then urban or rural residence. For women the most important factor was religion, then urban or rural residence for Roman Catholics and region for Jews. It seems that a differing set of causal factors—or, to be more precise, a different weighting of common causal factors—was at work for men as opposed to women. The low male levels in the south can probably be attributed to economic conditions, while those in the west to German influences. Since women were expected to supplement the family income but not to serve as the main breadwinners, economic factors should have had less of an impact on female marriage patterns. It appears that while it was influenced by economics, female behavior (more than male behavior) was significantly affected by cultural values and standards—which in human terms is probably equivalent to greater dependence on the wishes of parents. This assumption explains the similarity of the levels of early marriage of Jewish women in the

---

land von Jahr 1867 bis 1902," *Zeitschrift für Demographie und Statistik der Juden* 5 (1909): 180. On early marriage, see Jacob Goldberg, "Die Ehe bei den Juden Polens im 18. Jahrhundert," *Jahrbuch für Geschichte Osteuropas* 31 (1983): 481–515. Readers of Hebrew who are interested in the topic may find something of interest in my article, "Ha-mashmaut ha-hevratit shel nisuei-boser be-Mizrah-Eropah ba-meah ha-18," in *Studies on Polish Jewry: Paul Glikson Memorial Volume*, ed. Ezra Mendelsohn and Chone Shmeruk (Jerusalem, 1987), pp. 65–77.

TABLE 1

Percentage of Population Married, Ages Eighteen and Nineteen, 1921

Region	Jewish male	Roman Catholic male	Jewish female	Roman Catholic female
Center				
Warsaw				
urban	2.5	1.2	2.1	8.8
rural	2.1	1.3	3.2	8.0
Kielce				
urban	2.6	1.1	2.4	8.7
rural	2.7	1.1	3.1	10.4
Lublin				
urban	3.2	1.3	2.8	10.0
rural	4.9	1.6	5.4	10.1
East				
Białystok				
urban	1.7	1.5	2.5	8.5
rural	1.9	2.0	3.2	7.8
Vilna				
urban	2.0	1.1	1.7	9.4
rural	2.9	1.5	2.4	7.9
Nowogródek				
urban	3.4	1.3	3.9	12.6
rural	0.9	2.1	3.5	7.3
Polesie				
urban	3.3	1.8	3.4	7.5
rural	3.5	5.0	3.9	15.8
Volynia				
urban	2.1	2.1	5.5	9.9
rural	2.8	3.4	5.2	19.3
South				
Cracow				
urban	0.5	0.3	1.7	5.4
rural	0.3	0.4	2.4	6.3
Lwów				
urban	0.6	0.5	3.0	6.8
rural	0.8	0.6	4.1	7.0
Stanisławów				
urban	0.5	0.3	3.5	6.7
rural	0.6	0.6	0.7	14.1
Tarnopol				
urban	0.6	0.5	4.9	10.6
rural	0.4	0.8	5.7	14.6
West				
Śląsk				
urban	0	0.2	1.5	3.8
rural	0	0.2	8.6	8.0
Pomorze				
urban	2.3	0.3	0	6.5
rural	0	0.5	2.5	3.7

SOURCE: This and other tables for 1921 are based on *Statystyka Polski*, published by the Głowny Urząd Statystyczny (GUS, Central Statistical Office) (Warsaw, 1926–27), vols. 15, 17–23, 25–31. Although I did not have a full set of census records at my disposal, relatively few volumes were missing and the data were consistent (or inconsistent, as the case may be). It is therefore highly unlikely that the missing material would lead to any changes in the argument. The Polish census of 1931 was based on a pool slightly different from that for the census of 1921, but that variation should not affect the conclusions either. For technical reasons, not all of the tables could be constructed to the same degree of precision. In these tables, where a separate figure for *city* is given, *city* indicates the city proper, *urban* indicates urban settlements in the province exclusive of the capital city, and *rural* indicates rural settlements.

south to that of Jewish women in other regions of Poland despite the differences in male patterns. There were greater differences between the behavior of urban Roman Catholic women as compared to nonurban Roman Catholic women than was the case for Jewish women, a relationship probably explained by the fact that for Roman Catholics the place of residence usually reflected occupation and social circumstances. The nonurban Roman Catholic was usually a peasant, and peasant society was, of course, quite different from society in towns. Among Jews, the differences in occupation and social values between town dwellers and country people were, of course, far less pronounced, as even in nonurban settings Jews were concentrated in commercial and craft activities.

In some regions—as in the south in the case of males—behavior in the various provinces was quite similar; in other regions there were wide variations. Clearly data should be disaggregated as much as possible or feasible. One additional cautionary note: the tables that accompany this essay compare Jewish behavior with that of Roman Catholics and not that of the total population or the total non-Jewish population. This approach makes it possible to identify differences between two national groups, but the presence of additional national groups should not be ignored. There are socio-economic implications here, because in purely Polish areas the peasantry was all Roman Catholic and, correspondingly, rural Roman Catholics were mainly peasants. In other areas, especially in the east, a lower percentage of the Roman Catholic rural population was made up of peasants.

In the course of the 1920s, a number of interesting developments took place with regard to teenage marriage, as table 2 shows. In order to make comparison of tables 1 and 2 convenient, the data were weighted, based on the assumption that of the fifteen- to nineteen-year-olds married, most were older rather than younger.

Table 2 clearly indicates different patterns of development between Polish Roman Catholics and Polish Jews. Among males of both groups there was a drop in teenage marriage during the decade 1921–31. What was once a distinctive pattern of the south was now typical for Poland as a whole. However, while among Jews the female rates dropped along with the male rates, the reverse was true with regard to Roman Catholic females. The rise in early marriages among rural Roman Catholic women since 1921 can only be described as spectacular. In this group, the ratio between early rural

TABLE 2

Percentage of Population Married, Ages Eighteen and Nineteen, 1931

Region	Jewish male	Roman Catholic male	Jewish female	Roman Catholic female
Center				
Warsaw				
city	0.9	1.8	2.5	10.0
urban	0.8	1.3	1.8	15.0
rural	2.0	1.5	2.5	17.5
Łódź				
city	1.0	1.8	2.5	12.5
urban	0.8	1.3	1.8	10.0
rural	1.4	1.0	2.5	12.5
Kielce				
urban	0.9	1.1	2.0	15.0
rural	1.1	1.3	2.5	17.5
Lublin				
urban	1.1	1.0	2.0	12.5
rural	1.3	2.0	1.5	20.0
East				
Białystok				
urban	0.8	1.3	1.9	10.0
rural	1.3	1.9	2.5	15.0
Vilna				
city	1.3	0.8	2.5	7.5
Nowogródek				
urban	0.4	1.6	2.5	12.5
rural	1.0	2.3	2.3	15.0
Polesie				
urban	1.0	1.3	1.5	12.5
rural	1.4	2.5	2.5	25.0
Volynia				
urban	0.5	1.5	2.5	17.5
rural	1.9	2.4	2.5	25.0
South				
Cracow				
city	0.5	0.3	1.8	2.5
urban	0.4	0.5	0.9	7.5
rural	0.4	0.8	1.9	12.5
Lwów				
city	0.4	0.5	2.5	7.5
urban	0.3	0.4	1.0	7.5
rural	2.3	1.1	1.6	12.5
Stanisławów				
urban	0.3	0.9	2.0	12.5
rural	1.8	2.5	1.8	33.0
Tarnopol				
rural	0.8	2.5	2.5	30.0
Poland				
urban	0.8	0.9	2.0	10.0
rural	1.0	1.3	2.0	15.0

SOURCE: This and other tables for 1931 are based on *Statystyka Polski*, ser. C, published by GUS (Warsaw, 1936–38), vols. 36, 48–49, 54, 57–58, 64–65, 67–68, 70–71, 75, 78, 81, 83, 85–88.
NOTE: Table 1 deals with a two-year cohort; table 2 with a five-year cohort, though most of those married were among the eighteen- to nineteen-year-olds. Adjustments make it possible to compare tables 1 and 2, but the figures should be used with caution.

female marriages and early urban marriages was maintained. There was no external pressure for early rural female marriages, so it appears that the increase for this age group resulted from the lifting of social and economic barriers that had previously restrained early marriage.[6] Independent Poland must have offered new opportunities; for some the economic growth reported for the mid and late 1920s had very significant human implications. At the same time, the rates of early marriage were declining for Jews, implying that Jews were not benefiting from Poland's economic growth; on the contrary, they seemed to be suffering from it.

A comparison with patterns of mature marriage makes it possible to test this thesis. Teenage marriage is just one end of the age spectrum, and the other end is equally interesting. By the age of thirty, peak fertility has been reached, so that delaying marriage to this point and beyond has a very significant effect on fertility rates. Moreover, intuition says that by age thirty most people wanted to be married, and if they did not marry, it was not for lack of desire. In traditional Eastern European Jewish society in the nineteenth century, a vast majority of the population, both male and female, was married at age thirty. That was not the case in Poland in 1921, as is shown in table 3.

The first point to be noted is the large number of unmarried people among both Jews and Roman Catholics, a development far removed from traditional Jewish patterns. As for patterns of male behavior, the central region stands out as having the highest levels of marriage. Moreover, while in all other regions the levels of marriage for Roman Catholic males were higher than those for Jewish males, the reverse was true in the center. In the south there was little variation in the levels for urban males, while in the east there were considerable differences from province to province in the levels of marriage of males. In general, among Jewish males the level of marriage was higher in urban areas, while the reverse was true for Roman Catholics. Assuming that traditionally Jewish males had been married by the age of thirty, these figures indicate that the changes in male Jewish marital behavior were more radical in the countryside than in the cities—a rather unanticipated finding. One

---

6. In peasant societies it is common for marriage to be delayed until land becomes available. Thus new occupational opportunities would nullify this factor. See John Hajnal, "European Marriage Patterns in Perspective," in *Population in History,* ed. David Glass and D. E. C. Eversly (Chicago, 1964), pp. 101–46.

TABLE 3

Percentage of Population Married, Ages Twenty-five to Twenty-nine, 1921

Region	Jewish male	Roman Catholic male	Jewish female	Roman Catholic female
Center				
Warsaw				
urban	58.6	57.6	69.1	65.8
rural	59.6	54.5	75.2	73.4
Kielce				
urban	62.8	56.5	69.6	67.0
rural	63.7	53.0	63.7	78.3
Lublin				
urban	63.1	53.4	73.6	65.5
rural	68.1	54.1	84.4	75.3
East				
Białystok				
urban	42.1	49.2	65.4	64.4
rural	47.7	37.9	68.7	71.7
Vilna				
urban	32.2	36.8	61.2	60.4
rural	20.8	37.3	57.5	66.1
Nowogródek				
urban	36.9	41.9	65.8	67.2
rural	24.5	36.4	65.5	68.0
Polesie				
urban	42.5	46.9	67.5	69.1
rural	40.3	48.0	75.0	76.5
Volynia				
urban	50.7	49.2	67.4	68.9
rural	44.0	56.4	69.6	77.0
South				
Cracow				
urban	42.1	42.2	51.8	49.1
rural	35.5	46.0	50.2	57.6
Lwów				
urban	43.9	41.4	54.1	50.6
rural	42.2	49.4	60.7	63.5
Stanisławów				
urban	42.1	44.8	54.9	56.6
rural	40.0	55.0	36.2	71.0
Tarnopol				
urban	46.4	46.9	56.7	60.6
rural	42.1	59.0	61.8	73.4
West				
Śląsk				
urban	31.6	36.1	48.4	41.9
rural	49.1	54.7	51.9	60.5
Pomorze				
urban	33.3	55.9	26.4	61.0
rural	13.0	50.2	9.1	54.5

SOURCE: *Statystyka Polski.*

cannot jump to the conclusion that there was a faster rate of social change in the villages than in the cities. It seems far more likely that other factors were at work, such as the tendency for talented and ambitious young Jewish men to move away from rural areas, leaving ne'er-do-wells behind who, of course, would have found it hard to find a bride wherever they lived. While Roman Catholics generally show large differences in the behavior of urban males as compared to the rural males, this is true for Jews only in the east, not in the south or the center. Since the rural-urban division was, of course, more significant in a socioeconomic sense for Roman Catholics than for Jews, these figures are in line with the earlier suggestion that male marriage behavior was closely linked to economic patterns.

Among all women, the south displayed the most distinctive patterns, with a particularly low level of marriage for both urban and rural women. These figures seem to reflect the severity of the economic crisis rather than a difference in values among regions. It should be recalled from tables 1 and 2 that the south did not have very distinctive female rates of teenage marriage; among Jews alone (male and female) the center had distinctively high levels. As noted, the center was the most developed industrial area in Poland. Thus the Jewish pattern indicates a significant relationship between the possibility of getting married and economic modernization or industrialization. In the center, the percentage of Jewish women married was also generally higher than that of Roman Catholic women, while the reverse was true in the east. In most cases the rate of marriage among rural Roman Catholics was higher than among rural Jews. The variations in marriage rates from province to province were generally greater among rural Jewish women than among urban Jewish women. Similarly, the difference between urban behavior and rural behavior was generally greater among Roman Catholics than Jews.

The percentage of women married at ages twenty-five to twenty-nine was uniformly higher than that of men. There was no simple correlation, however, between male and female behavior. The low levels of married women in the south were not matched in the male population, while the distinctively high levels of married males in the center were matched by a high but not as distinctive a level among women. In the east the rates of marriage of urban Jewish males varied widely, while that of females remained relatively stable, but in the center the reverse was true. In the center and south, shifts in rates of married males corresponded to similar shifts among women, but there seems to have been little connection between the two in the east. The northeastern provinces (Vilna, Nowogródek, and Białystok) showed distinctive male patterns, with lower percentages married, as compared with southeastern provinces (Polesie and Volynia). The behavior patterns of urban women in both the northeast and the southeast were similar, but rural women in the southeast had higher levels of marriage. In short, it is clear that no simple framework or model can explain all the regional and provincial variations.

Ten years later this cohort had undergone significant changes, as table 4 shows. It is clear that during the decade 1921–31 many marriages had occurred involving parties in their thirties. In every case the rate of marriage among Jewish women aged thirty-five to thirty-nine was higher than that of Roman Catholic women. The same was generally true of males as well. Regional differences had begun to blur, and already one can talk of a developing national pattern. In Jewish society the traditional marital pattern of universal marriage had been recreated, but at a later age. If the reason for delays of the previous decade were the economic dislocations of the war and postwar period, then this table suggests a greater continuity in values than one might have thought. Figures for the twenty-five- to twenty-nine-year-olds in 1931 give the impression that deep changes in marital patterns among Jews were under way and that the rise in the age of marriage, with all that it entails, was not a passing phenomenon.

Table 5 looks closely at the cohort of twenty-five- to twenty-nine-year-olds, the traditional age in which most Jews were married. It indicates that some significant changes had occurred between 1921 and 1931, with contrary trends taking place among Jews and Roman Catholics. Among Jews the rates of marriage, when compared with the same age group in 1921, are lower in almost every case. These lower rates are surprising, for rates in 1921 might be expected to reflect the instability of the war and immediate postwar years, while the rates for 1931 to reflect a decade of relative quiet. One of the few exceptions to this pattern was the rise in the percentage of married men in the east, the region that suffered most heavily during World War I.

The shift seen in table 5 is dramatic. In the south, only one-third

TABLE 4

Percentage of Population Married, Ages Thirty-five to Thirty-nine, 1931

Region	Jewish male	Roman Catholic male	Jewish female	Roman Catholic female
Center				
Warsaw				
city	87	82	79	66
urban	93	89	87	76
rural	94	91	91	85
Łódź				
city	88	89	82	73
urban	91	90	86	77
rural	92	91	91	91
Kielce				
urban	93	89	87	77
rural	95	92	92	85
Lublin				
urban	94	87	88	76
rural	96	91	91	84
East				
Białystok				
urban	88	88	84	76
rural	89	89	90	82
Vilna				
city	88	84	79	67
Nowogródek				
urban	90	85	86	75
rural	86	88	89	82
Polesie				
urban	89	87	86	81
rural	90	89	90	87
Volynia				
urban	92	86	84	79
rural	93	91	89	87
South				
Cracow				
city	85	80	83	58
urban	91	85	87	69
rural	85	88	84	78
Lwów				
city	85	81	81	63
urban	88	91	88	81
rural	89	87	85	73
Stanisławów				
urban	89	87	83	75
rural	90	93	87	81
Tarnopol				
rural	90	94	87	85
Poland				
urban	89	86	84	72
rural	91	90	89	82

SOURCE: *Statystyka Polski,* ser. C.

TABLE 5

Percentage of Population Married, Ages Twenty-five to Twenty-nine, 1931

Region	Jewish male	Roman Catholic male	Jewish female	Roman Catholic female
Center				
Warsaw				
city	45	49	47	50
urban	49	61	56	69
rural	56	63	66	79
Łódź				
city	48	61	46	59
urban	48	60	48	66
rural	47	61	58	76
Kielce				
urban	51	57	54	65
rural	56	62	65	77
Lublin				
urban	53	54	59	66
rural	59	63	72	77
East				
Białystok				
urban	52	56	57	69
rural	53	56	69	75
Vilna				
city	47	46	50	53
Nowogródek				
urban	48	48	60	72
rural	45	54	67	76
Polesie				
urban	50	50	57	71
rural	52	60	67	80
Volynia				
urban	49	53	58	74
rural	52	61	67	82
South				
Cracow				
city	32	36	47	36
urban	37	48	44	54
rural	31	54	45	65
Lwów				
city	32	42	46	47
urban	31	47	41	47
rural	30	56	46	68
Stanisławów				
urban	37	49	47	64
rural	37	67	58	79
Tarnopol				
rural	38	72	58	78
Poland				
urban	44	51	51	58
rural	47	58	62	72

SOURCE: *Statystyka Polski*, ser. C.

of Jewish men aged twenty-five to twenty-nine were married. In the center male rates were down by 10 percent in just a decade. The drop was not as drastic for women as for men, but it was still significant. Jewish women displayed greater urban-rural variations in behavior than men. In almost every case fewer of those in urban settings were married, perhaps reflecting differing values and stronger traditionalism in villages or simply that unmarried women gravitated to cities to look for mates, leaving their married sisters behind. Among Roman Catholics the rates of marriage in this age group were generally higher than a decade earlier. The only significant exception is again in the south.

The most reasonable explanation for this shift in marital patterns was that the economic climate was making it possible for Polish Roman Catholics to marry earlier than before while at the same time making it less possible for Jews to marry. This sheds light on one of the issues of interwar Polish history: whether the burdens of economic and political modernization fell more heavily on Jews than on the Roman Catholics. In a recent article, Ezra Mendelsohn surveys the relevant literature and concludes that "more than one answer is possible." With regard to the impact of economic conditions and developments on Jews and Poles, it is difficult to provide a simple answer.[7] The data we have support the subjective reports of Polish Jews, then and now, that the burdens of economic and political development were unequal. In fact, data on marital behavior appear to be a good, quantifiable measure of the differing impact of independent Poland on the various populations of the state. The marital behavior of Jews suggests that they were under more economic pressure than were Roman Catholic Poles.

The evidence of marital patterns is paralleled by the data on shifts in the numbers of those who never married. The traditional patterns of marital behavior in Poland are reflected in table 6. Since most individuals marry before the end of their thirties, we can assume that the characteristics of those people in their forties for 1921 were the product of their behavior in the prewar years. The rarity of old bachelors and spinsters among Jews, as compared to Roman Catholics, is striking. Regional variations are also not without signifi-

7. Ezra Mendelsohn, "Interwar Poland: Good for the Jews or Bad for the Jews," in *The Jews in Poland*, ed. Chimen Abramsky, Maciej Jachimczyk, and Antony Polonsky (Oxford, 1986), pp. 130–39, quotation on p. 139. See also Mendelsohn's introduction to this volume.

TABLE 6

Percentage of Population Never Married, Ages Forty to Forty-nine, 1921

Region	Jewish male	Roman Catholic male	Jewish female	Roman Catholic female
Center				
Warsaw				
urban	1.6	6.0	1.1	10.1
rural	1.4	4.4	1.0	5.2
Kielce				
urban	1.3	5.0	1.0	9.1
rural	1.0	3.3	1.6	4.5
Lublin				
urban	1.0	6.6	1.1	10.2
rural	0.8	4.3	0.8	4.9
East				
Białystok				
urban	3.5	7.6	6.6	12.6
rural	3.2	7.3	1.2	8.7
Vilna				
urban	5.2	11.2	3.0	13.0
rural	8.6	11.6	2.1	10.6
Nowogródek				
urban	2.6	9.7	1.6	10.8
rural	5.6	9.2	1.6	8.0
Polesie				
urban	1.8	7.8	0.6	8.8
rural	2.5	7.5	1.5	4.8
Volynia				
urban	2.2	9.5	2.1	9.2
rural	1.5	5.5	1.0	4.1
South				
Cracow				
urban	4.4	11.0	2.3	19.7
rural	4.5	7.3	3.3	10.2
Lwów				
urban	3.6	9.6	2.7	14.1
rural	2.7	4.4	1.8	6.1
Stanisławów				
urban	3.0	7.4	1.9	8.3
rural	2.8	3.8	1.1	4.2
Tarnopol				
urban	3.0	6.5	1.8	8.5
rural	2.4	2.8	1.7	3.3
West				
Śląsk				
urban	8.8	9.8	7.8	21.9
rural	3.6	7.9	3.8	10.3
Pomorze				
urban	17.7	18.6	18.9	11.4
rural	27.0	6.1	30.0	7.5

SOURCE: *Statystyka Polski.*

cance. The lowest levels for Jews were in the center, the industrial region. There is almost no correlation between levels of bachelorhood and spinsterhood between Jews and Roman Catholics in the various provinces. The highest levels for individuals who were never married in these age groups were found in precisely those areas where emigration had been highest in the prewar years. Emigration itself created sexual imbalances that contributed to individuals' not finding marital partners. Moreover, the most important cause of emigration was economic distress, which of course also had a negative effect on marriage rates. Thus directly or indirectly, economic factors had a major role in determining levels of bachelorhood and spinsterhood.

The behavior of individuals aged forty to forty-nine in 1931, shown in table 7, reflected the realities of life in interwar Poland. It is not surprising that in this category, as well, the situation had changed in the course of a decade. Among Jewish males and females, the general tendency was for a rise in the numbers of those who had never married, as it was for Roman Catholic females, though their rise was proportionately lower than the rise among Jewish women. On the other hand, there was a clear decline in the number of Roman Catholic males in this age group who had never married. The south had distinctively high levels of bachelorhood and spinsterhood in 1931—as had been the case a decade before. However, the differences between the south and other regions were smaller. It is clear here that in the course of the 1920s more Jews were marrying than were Roman Catholics, but that the direction of change among the Jews was less favorable to marriage than among the Roman Catholics.

The portion of the population widowered and widowed at any given age is an important determinant of the social life of a community. Since a married couple acts as an efficient economic and social unit, while singles, especially older singles, tend to need help from communities, the degree of widowerhood and widowhood has an impact on the number of dependents in a society. Table 8 shows a consistently low level of widowerhood (about 20 percent) among all men as compared with levels of widowhood among women. Among women, the levels of widowhood are lower among Jewish women than among Roman Catholic women. This difference could be a function of a lower death rate among Jewish males than among Roman Catholic males or of a greater tendency of Jews to remarry.

TABLE 7

Percentage of Population Never Married, Ages Forty to Forty-nine, 1931

Region	Jewish male	Roman Catholic male	Jewish female	Roman Catholic female
Center				
Warsaw				
city	4	9	6	18
urban	2	5	2	11
rural	1	4	2	6
Łódź				
city	3	4	4	12
urban	2	5	3	10
rural	2	4	2	5
Kielce				
urban	2	5	2	11
rural	1	4	1	5
Lublin				
urban	1	5	2	11
rural	1	4	0	5
East				
Białystok				
urban	4	7	2	13
rural	4	7	2	9
Vilna				
city	4	8	5	21
Nowogródek				
urban	4	9	3	11
rural	5	7	3	9
Polesie				
urban	2	8	2	9
rural	2	6	1	5
Volynia				
urban	2	8	3	10
rural	1	5	1	4
South				
Cracow				
city	5	11	5	27
urban	3	8	3	17
rural	7	7	4	13
Lwów				
city	5	10	5	19
urban	3	7	2	13
rural	3	5	1	8
Stanisławów				
urban	4	6	3	11
rural	3	4	3	5
Tarnopol				
rural	4	3	3	4
Poland				
urban	3	7	3	14
rural	3	5	2	7

SOURCE: *Statystyka Polski*, ser. C.

TABLE 8

Percentage of Population Widowered and Widowed, Age Sixty Plus, 1921

Region	Jewish male	Roman Catholic male	Jewish female	Roman Catholic female
Center				
Warsaw				
urban	19.8	17.8	50.6	58.9
rural	18.8	19.2	45.9	53.9
Kielce				
urban	18.9	17.7	48.2	63.3
rural	20.2	21.8	43.1	56.9
Lublin				
urban	21.2	20.7	54.2	59.4
rural	19.5	26.1	44.8	57.2
East				
Białystok				
urban	19.1	18.7	50.6	58.6
rural	18.9	23.4	43.1	54.6
Vilna				
urban	22.7	22.9	50.0	67.9
rural	22.4	26.8	43.9	62.3
Nowogródek				
urban	20.4	20.7	52.7	68.9
rural	18.1	26.8	41.5	61.8
Polesie				
urban	20.3	23.9	52.9	65.1
rural	20.7	25.9	44.6	60.3
Volynia				
urban	22.0	25.4	59.7	67.8
rural	22.1	27.2	52.9	60.7
South				
Cracow				
urban	18.3	19.0	49.6	56.9
rural	19.2	20.5	45.8	51.4
Lwów				
urban	21.5	19.8	56.1	63.5
rural	22.9	22.9	47.7	55.2
Stanisławów				
urban	21.0	21.5	57.3	66.2
rural	24.8	22.6	51.4	59.7
Tarnopol				
urban	24.1	24.3	55.9	66.8
rural	23.6	26.9	51.4	63.6
West				
Śląsk				
urban	19.2	19.4	55.8	53.8
rural	18.0	18.2	44.6	55.7
Pomorze				
urban	20.5	19.4	41.9	50.2
rural	25.0	19.6	50.0	45.9

SOURCE: *Statystyka Polski.*

However, the fact that Roman Catholic men tended to marry women much younger than themselves no doubt also had an effect on the levels. A large age gap between husbands and wives with similar patterns of life expectancy means that many husbands will die long before their wives. Among Jews, the age gap was apparently not generally large. This Jewish marital pattern had a positive by-product in that it tended to limit the potential claimants for support. Once again, it should be emphasized that these data for 1921 reflect prewar patterns that were compounded by the impact of the war itself.

Marital behavior underwent significant changes between 1921 and 1931. The data in table 9 show changes in the rates of widow-erhood and widowhood but a relative absence of change in the *patterns* of widowerhood and widowhood—the relation of statistics for Jewish males to those for Roman Catholic males, and of statistics for Jewish females to those for Roman Catholic females—during the course of the decade. There were relatively small differences among regions or rates for males from province to province, implying that the factors playing such an important role in determining marriage rates, which were apparently related to economics, did not play a role here. Widowerhood and widowhood appear to have been mostly a product of biology and mate selection patterns.

The relative advantage of Jewish women over Roman Catholic women is clearly expressed in table 10, which details the spread of young widowhood. But beyond this, the high level of widowhood in general should be noted. Most of these young widows probably had children. Thus, this pattern of widowhood meant that in both Jewish and Roman Catholic society, there was a large body of "po-tential candidates" for whatever welfare aid there was. Here, as above, male patterns were quite similar, irrespective of religion or province. Regional variations and religious variations among women were significant. The simplest explanation for the differences be-tween Jews and Roman Catholics again is the greater difference in age of the Roman Catholic partners.

Ten years later, despite the many changes in other areas of Polish life, the same patterns were in effect, as demonstrated by table 11. The low male levels of widowerhood and the lack of regional dif-ferentiation in these levels had not changed. The consistently lower rates among Jewish women, when compared with Roman Catholic women, were still present.

TABLE 9

Percentage of Population Widowered and Widowed, Ages Sixty to Sixty-five, 1931

Region	Jewish male	Roman Catholic male	Jewish female	Roman Catholic female
Center				
Warsaw				
city	12	10	38	49
urban	13	13	41	46
rural	11	10	54	44
Łódź				
city	12	8	42	49
urban	13	9	37	47
rural	13	12	36	45
Kielce				
urban	12	10	?	49
rural	11	13	36	50
Lublin				
urban	13	13	37	48
rural	13	11	42	50
East				
Białystok				
urban	12	10	40	49
rural	12	20	38	67
Vilna				
city	10	10	49	53
Nowogródek				
urban	10	15	44	56
rural	12	15	41	55
Polesie				
urban	11	12	43	59
rural	12	16	38	47
Volynia				
urban	12	11	47	58
rural	13	13	44	48
South				
Cracow				
city	10	10	41	45
urban	11	10	35	43
rural	12	13	33	40
Lwów				
city	12	8	45	49
urban	12	11	39	43
rural	15	14	35	44
Stanisławów				
urban	14	8	46	52
rural	13	14	38	53
Tarnopol				
rural	12	13	40	53
Poland				
urban	12	10	42	46
rural	13	12	38	44

SOURCE: *Statystyka Polski,* ser. C.

TABLE 10

Percentage of Population Widowered or Widowed, Ages Forty to Forty-nine, 1921

Region	Jewish male	Roman Catholic male	Jewish female	Roman Catholic female
Center				
Warsaw				
urban	3.7	3.3	15.2	18.6
rural	3.6	2.7	12.4	15.0
Kielce				
urban	2.8	3.9	13.5	19.4
rural	3.1	3.0	13.8	13.5
Lublin				
urban	4.1	4.0	15.9	18.7
rural	3.8	3.6	15.3	17.8
East				
Białystok				
urban	3.1	3.2	14.6	20.1
rural	3.4	3.4	13.3	16.6
Vilna				
urban	3.7	5.9	14.8	21.7
rural	3.3	3.9	15.6	18.8
Nowogródek				
urban	4.3	4.4	16.3	21.2
rural	3.1	3.7	13.8	19.5
Polesie				
urban	4.2	5.6	17.4	21.2
rural	3.1	4.5	15.1	19.7
Volynia				
urban	3.5	4.2	18.5	21.6
rural	4.1	4.7	17.2	19.9
South				
Cracow				
urban	2.3	3.3	11.7	17.5
rural	2.4	2.8	10.4	14.6
Lwów				
urban	3.1	3.6	14.7	20.7
rural	3.4	3.0	13.9	16.0
Stanisławów				
urban	3.6	3.6	18.3	22.6
rural	3.7	3.2	16.4	22.7
Tarnopol				
urban	3.9	4.0	17.8	23.1
rural	4.4	3.6	17.0	23.2
West				
Śląsk				
urban	1.1	3.3	11.7	17.4
rural	2.4	2.0	7.6	15.4
Pomorze				
urban	5.4	2.1	20.6	12.6
rural	2.7	2.0	4.0	9.9

SOURCE: *Statystyka Polski.*

TABLE 11

Percentage of Population Widowered or Widowed, Ages Forty to Forty-nine, 1931

Region	Jewish male	Roman Catholic male	Jewish female	Roman Catholic female
Center				
Warsaw				
city	2	2	14	20
urban	2	2	14	20
rural	2	2	13	17
Łódź				
city	2	2	12	18
urban	2	2	13	19
rural	2	2	13	17
Kielce				
urban	2	2	14	19
rural	2	2	13	19
Lublin				
urban	3	2	15	21
rural	2	3	14	19
East				
Białystok				
urban	2	2	15	21
rural	2	4	13	29
Vilna				
city	2	2	18	22
Nowogródek				
urban	1	3	19	23
rural	2	3	17	23
Polesie				
urban	1	2	17	20
rural	2	3	18	17
Volynia				
urban	1	3	20	23
rural	2	2	18	19
South				
Cracow				
city	2	2	12	18
urban	2	2	13	28
rural	3	2	14	17
Lwów				
city	2	2	15	20
urban	2	2	15	20
rural	2	2	15	19
Stanisławów				
urban	2	2	18	24
rural	2	2	16	24
Tarnopol				
rural	1	2	16	23
Poland				
urban	2	2	15	19
rural	2	2	15	18

SOURCE: *Statystyka Polski,* ser. C.

III

The scope of this study precludes a detailed analysis of the many subregional differences that are evident in the data presented here. Such an analysis would no doubt be best undertaken with the aid of specialists in local history. Even this survey of the data, however, makes it possible to perceive the tremendous impact that the realities of life, especially economic conditions, had on the most intimate aspects of individual lives. In the intersection of traditional values and current opportunities, both Jews and Roman Catholics changed their patterns of marital behavior. By examining the changes in this behavior, it is possible to assess in a convincing way the relative burden on various populations of the difficult years of interwar Poland.

A rise in the age at marriage is familiar from various Jewish communities undergoing modernization. One may claim that Polish Jewry was undergoing modernization, depending on the definition of modernization that one chooses to use. However, there is no simple equation between modernization and a rise in the age at marriage. In German Jewry such a rise has been tied to the entry into bourgeois society and was very possibly related to longer periods of study and preparation before entry into certain occupations. Such factors are not relevant in the Polish context, where there was no massive entry of Jews into higher education. Moreover, there is little evidence for widespread premarital intercourse along with the use of birth control methods that could explain a decreased desire or pressure to marry. Given the traditional patterns of early marriage, the only convincing explanation for delay in marriage is that many saw it as economically untenable. Since this delay differed from earlier patterns, it is clear that Jews were postponing marriage while Roman Catholic Poles were marrying at an earlier age. These data offer solid evidence that the Jews bore a disproportionate share of the burden of economic development in interwar Poland. The drop in Jewish fertility that has been carefully described by Lucjan Dobroszycki and others was no doubt related to the economic conditions of the Jews.[8] However, this picture of the Jews of Poland should be

---

8. Lawrence Schafer, ''Emancipation and Population Change,'' in *Revolution and Evolution: 1848 in German Jewish History,* ed. Werner Mosse, Arnold Paucker, and Reinhard Rürup (Tübingen, 1981), pp. 63–89, esp. pp. 79–87; Marcus, *Social and Political History,* p. 241; Dobroszycki, ''Fertility of Modern Polish Jewry.''

balanced by their vitality and will to create families, as is strikingly demonstrated by the large numbers who married even in their thirties.

These conclusions should not be misinterpreted as suggesting that there was any difference between Jews and Roman Catholics as to the desire to marry and raise families. If more Jewish women married (and fewer were widowed), that was in part a product of traditional patterns of mate selection that, in turn, may well have been affected by occupational factors. In a peasant society where males delay marriage until they can get possession of land, there is a clear advantage to choosing a young woman who has many working years in front of her. Merchants and artisans who reach maximum income levels early in life can marry earlier and chose women their own age. In neither case did the desires of women seem to play much of a role.

The continued dynamism of Polish Jewry up to its end, and in spite of the growing economic crisis of the 1930s, had its roots in many factors. One that is indicated by the findings of this study is that Jewish marital patterns minimized the number of dependents on the limited welfare resources of the community. While not the product of conscious decision or even unconscious pressures, this demographic pattern contributed to the communities' abilities to utilize their resources to the utmost.

Surprisingly little work has been done on interwar Polish demography, Jewish and general, and the data presented here may have raised more questions than they have answered. The rich mix of nationalities, regionalities, and cultures so characteristic of interwar Poland, as well as the drive for economic modernization, should reward additional demographic work on the period with a better understanding of the many issues in interwar Polish history.

Samuel D. Kassow

Community and Identity in the Interwar *Shtetl*

The *shtetl* confronts the historian of interwar Poland with the daunting problem of reconciling symbolism with reality, implied uniformities with unmistakable diversity, assumed national exclusivity with the growing presence of another nation for whom the term *shtetl* meant absolutely nothing. Indeed the historian is tempted to plead academic rigor and leave the *shtetl* to the literary critics.

To complicate matters, finding satisfactory sources is a major task. Secondary literature is sparse and unsatisfactory.[1] Memorial books give vital information but only when used with great care and, if one hopes to document major trends, in great quantity.[2] Oral history offers possibilities, but many survivors were only adolescents at the beginning of the war and would therefore have much less to say about communal institutions than, for example, about youth movements. (This situation affects the memorial books as well.) The central Yiddish press reported events in the small towns but not in much detail. Yet useful sources do exist. While the memorial books are uneven, some contain important information. The archives of the Joint Distribution Committee in New York, the Jacob Lestschinsky Archives at the Hebrew University in Jerusalem, and the youth autobiographies in the archives of the YIVO Institute for Jewish Research in New York are quite important, as are contemporary articles in such journals as *Folkshilf* and *Dos virtshaftlekhe lebn*. Moreover some *shtetl* newspapers—such as a full run of the *Gluboker lebn*

---

1. Two secondary works on the *shtetl* are Mark Zborowski, *Life Is with People* (New York, 1950); and Rachel Ertel, *Le shtetl: La bourgade juive* (Paris, 1982). Zborowski's *shtetl* is an abstract composite. Ertel makes good use of memorial books and provides a helpful discussion of youth movements but makes little reference to the Polish and Yiddish press. Furthermore, the book fails to provide an adequate historical context.

2. See Jack Kugelmass and Jonathan Boyarin, "*Yizker Bikher* and the Problem of Historical Veracity: An Anthropological Approach," in this volume.

and the *Gluboker shtime*—have survived.[3] These are a priceless resource, especially when the historian remembers their limitations.[4] All these sources, when used with care, enable the historian to examine the major contours of social and communal life in the interwar Polish *shtetl*. The subject needs attention. While political history and the Jewish political parties have been studied by historians of Polish Jewry, there has been relatively little written about Jewish life on the local level, about the interplay of people and communal institutions.

Such an examination, albeit tentative and preliminary, will show that the *shtetl* was a much more dynamic community than many have supposed, that its institutions and inhabitants were closely intertwined with outside organizations and influences, and that its network of communal institutions reflected a remarkable degree of social and attitudinal flexibility. Above all, the *shtetl* should not be studied in a vacuum but should rather be seen in a specific historical and legal context.

Given the realities of Polish Jewry in 1938, it is both ironic and revealing that Mordechai Gebirtig, in writing "Undzer shtetl brent" (Our *Shtetl* Is Burning), chose the *shtetl* to symbolize endangered Polish Jewry. After all, on the eve of World War II one out of four Polish Jews lived in the five largest cities and 40 percent lived in settlements of more than ten thousand Jews. The city, not the *shtetl*, was the center of the new political parties, trade unions, newspapers, youth organizations, credit associations, and cultural networks that were transforming Polish-Jewish life. But be it Gebirtig's song, Sholem Asch's sentimentalism, Y. L. Peretz's depressing travel sketches, I. M. Weissenberg's brilliant treatment of the *shtetl* in revolutionary upheaval, or L. Rashkin's pitiless analysis of the demoralization of the wartime *shtetl*, the small town maintained its hold on the imagination of Eastern European Jewry.[5]

---

3. The archives of the YIVO Institute for Jewish Research in New York have full runs of the *Gluboker lebn* (1930–36) and the *Gluboker shtime* (1936–39), as well as issues of the *Gluboker vokh* (1934–36). By coincidence, these newspapers cover the area where my parents lived.

4. The editor of the *Gluboker lebn* tried to downplay events that would undermine the image of the *shtetl* among the American *landslayt*. Moreover, to avoid fomenting further controversy, the paper deemphasized ideological disputes as well as the conflict over who should be the town rabbi. It also appears—especially after the advent of a competing newspaper in 1934—that the *Gluboker lebn* was not overanxious to offend the local Polish authorities.

5. Mordechai Gebirtig, "Undzer shtetl brent" (1938), in Gebirtig, *Ha-ayarah boeret/*

It is as a symbol of a certain kind of Jewish community that the *shtetl* claims its place in Jewish history. And given the peculiar position of Polish Jewry, the institutions, customs, and communal patterns developed in the small towns reflected crucial social and political processes in a people who occupied a double position: often a majority on the local level, a decided minority on the national level. Historically a Jew could identify far more easily with a specific town than with a province or country, and it was local structures—the rabbi, the *bes-medresh* (study house), or the *bikur kholim* (community hospital)—that touched his or her life far more than provincial and national organizations.[6]

As an *ideal type,* the *shtetl* was a form of settlement based on a market that served as a contact point between the Jewish majority and a Gentile hinterland whose social composition and cultural level minimized the threat not only of assimilation but even of acculturation. Even in a *shtetl* with a sizable Polish population, the Jews lived in a compact mass, usually in the streets around the marketplace.[7] The *shtetl*'s economic function dictated a specific interplay of time and space, with the market day and the Sabbath as the two main events of the week, as well as an economic relationship with the Gentiles that was complementary rather than competitive, although in practice competition from Gentile merchants, artisans, and cooperatives became more severe during the interwar period. The market day itself tended to divide into the morning hours, when the peasants sold their products, and the afternoon, when they went into the Jewish shops to buy goods. On nonmarket days the *shtetl* was eerily quiet.[8]

Undzer shtetl brent (Tel Aviv, 1967), pp. 8–11; Sholem Asch, *A shtetl* (New York, 1909); Y. L. Peretz, "Rayze bilder," in Peretz, *Geklibene verk,* ed. David Pinski, vol. 2 (New York, 1920), pp. 3–285; I. M. Weissenberg, "A shtetl," in Weissenberg, *Geklibene verk,* vol. 1, ed. Pearl Weissenberg (Chicago, 1959), pp. 287–355; L. Rashkin [Shaul Fridman], *Di mentshn fun Godlbozhits* (Warsaw, 1936). See also Dan Miron, *Der imazsh fun shtetl* (Tel Aviv, 1981).

6. A fine essay discussing this point is Abram Menes, "Di kemerlekh fun tsibur lebn bay yidn," *YIVO bleter* 2 (1931): 193–99.

7. One supplement to the overwhelming evidence on this point contained in memorial books and interviews is the archives of Mińsk Mazowiecki, which contain a street-by-street breakdown of the Jewish and non-Jewish population in 1932. Ninety percent of the Jewish population lived on six streets adjoining the marketplace. See Population Registry, 1932, Archiwum Mińska Mazowieckiego, Otwock, file 112.

8. An excellent description of a *shtetl* on a nonmarket day can be found in a report on Węgrów in the late 1930s. See Bezalel Botchan, report on the Węgrów *gemiles khesed kase* (free-loan society), 1937, Jacob Lestschinsky Archives, Hebrew University, Jerusalem, file 258.

The state of communications and transportation dictated a static market: the *shtetl* mainly served peasants who could come to town with their horse-drawn wagons and return home on the same day.[9] Unless there was a major river system or railroad, entrepreneurial opportunities were rare and credit was a persistent problem, so much so that a major function of communal organization was often the extension of credit to buy goods to sell on the market day.

Yet while the market has come to be seen as the focal point of the *shtetl*'s economic existence, there were in fact wide variations in the economic physiognomy of various *shtetlekh*, especially during the interwar period. While a *shtetl* in Polesie or the Vilna area might have conformed to the classic pattern of the market town and suffered greatly from the crisis of its agricultural hinterland, other *shtetlekh*, such as Kałuszyn in Warsaw province, found a modicum of economic security as centers of specialized handicrafts or as transfer points between larger cities and the surrounding countryside.[10]

The *shtetl* had enough Jews to support a basic network of community institutions—a *mikveh* (ritual bathhouse), a *bes-medresh*, a *khevre kadisha*, (burial society), and a rabbi or *moreh-horaah* (religious judge). In this way it differed from smaller types of settlement such as villages, and the differences between *yishuvnikes* (village Jews) and *shtetl* Jews figured prominently in the *shtetl*'s collective sense of humor. But the Jewish community was not so big that most inhabitants were not known, ranked, exposed to social pressures, and most often fixed in the community's mind by an apt nickname.[11] Social differences were clear and strong. Seating arrangements in the synagogue, *aliyes* (calls to the Torah), and burial sites in the cemetery all served as a constant reminder of social gradations: *sheyne yidn* (upper-class Jews), *balebatim* (well-to-do Jews), *bal-melokhes* (artisans), *proste* (lower-class Jews), and so forth. Even within such comparatively modest categories as artisans, there were definite distinctions of status based on the nature of the tailoring or

9. For a discussion of this point, see Hayim Sosnov, "Kalkalah ve-hevrah be-Kolno bein shtei milhamot ha-olam," in *Sefer zikaron le-kehillat Kolno,* ed. Isaac Reinba and Benjamin Halevi (Tel Aviv, 1971), pp. 28–42. In the 1930s Sosnov collected data on economic conditions in various *shtetlekh* for YIVO.

10. On Kałuszyn, see S. Gotlib, "A yidish shtetl vu ale hobn parnose," *Varshever radio,* October 16, 1936.

11. On the role of nicknames, see, besides the memorial books, Hirsh Abramovich, "A yidish shtetl in Lite," in *Oyf di khurves fun milkhomes un mehumes: Pinkes fun gegnt-komitet EKOPO,* ed. Moshe Shalit (Vilna, 1931), pp. 362–84.

the shoemaking being performed. Watchmaking ranked higher still.[12]

But if the *shtetl* nursed a strong sense of social gradation, it also maintained important "safety valves," counters to the humiliations of the caste system. *Bal-melokhes* could gain prestigious *aliyes* by the simple expedient of starting their own *minyan* (quorum for public prayer), which also doubled as a fraternal organization.[13] If a rich man showed little social responsibility, or gave too little to charity, his heirs might well face a hefty bill from the *khevre kadisha*. Especially in Congress Poland and Galicia, Hasidism was a powerful social force that established subcommunities marked by close contact between rich and poor—although often at the expense of women and family life.[14]

If social differences and prejudices were real, they still lacked clear legal and moral underpinnings. The *shtetl* culture was pluralistic and flexible enough to nourish new social attitudes, and this tendency was especially marked in the interwar period. After World War I youth movements introduced new ferment into the *shtetl*'s life and sharply attacked the traditional *shtetl* bias toward *mishker* (trade) and against physical labor and craftsmanship. New organizations like the *handverker fareynen* (artisans' unions) fought hard to counteract this traditional prejudice by emphasizing the dignity of physical labor—*melokhe iz melukhe* (having a trade is power). The massive influx of aid from the United States after World War I gave new

12. On the question of status distinctions among artisans, see Note Koifman, "Dos yidishe ekonomishe lebn in Sokolov," in *Sefer ha-zikaron: Sokolow Podlaski*, ed. M. Gelbart (Tel Aviv, 1962), pp. 156–70. See also Moshe Kligsberg, "Di yidishe yugnt bavegungen in Poyln tsvishn beyde velt-milkhomes: A sotsyologishe shtudye," in *Studies on Polish Jewry, 1919–1939*, ed. Joshua A. Fishman (New York, 1974), pp. 143–44.

13. For a good explanation of why artisans wanted to start their own *minyanim*, see Yaakov Malanvanchik, "In katsevishn bes-medresh," in *Sefer yizkor le-kehillat Shedletz*, ed. A. Wolf Jasny (Yasni) (Buenos Aires, 1956), pp. 581–84. In 1938 the Głębokie tailor's *minyan* was in danger of being closed down on the grounds that it violated sanitary regulations. The *Gluboker shtime* reported: "Yes, this was a *minyan* for workers, for artisans, for those toilers [*horepashnikes*] who felt a sense of self-respect there. They did not have to wait for the second-class *aliye*, for the thin *maftir* [weekly *haftorah* portion] that were thrown to them in other synagogues. They elected a president [*gabai*] from among their own . . . and became in their own eyes the equal of everybody else." See S. Agus, "Shtol," *Gluboker shtime*, August 12, 1938.

14. Yekhezkiel Kotik, *Mayne zikhroynes* (Warsaw, 1913), pp. 399–415, offers an excellent discussion of the social impact of Hasidism in the late nineteenth century. Much of what Kotik observed was still relevant for the interwar period. A fictional treatment of how Hasidism affected family life can be found in I. J. Singer, *Di brider ashkenazi* (New York, 1951). See also Jacob Katz, *Tradition and Crisis* (New York, 1961).

leaders a chance to come forward and take a prominent role in the relief effort. In the process they contested the position of the prewar elite in the *shtetl*'s politics.[15]

This tension between social discrimination and countervailing safety valves provides a basic key to understanding the interwar *shtetl*. Another was a growing structure of organizational links between the *shtetl* and the wider Jewish community. The *landsmanshaft*, the Joint Distribution Committee, the central headquarters of the political party or youth group, the touring Yiddish theater troupe, or the daily newspaper coming from Warsaw or Vilna all helped integrate the *shtetl* into a wider network of allegiances and loyalties. The interplay of economic deprivation and these new outside currents imparted its own logic to social organizations in the *shtetl*. Young people could not afford books and newspapers but developed libraries within the framework of youth organizations, which in turn transformed patterns of social life, especially in the area of male-female relationships. The growing need for credit gave the Joint Distribution Committee (JDC) the opportunity to begin a new kind of democratic credit organization, the *gemiles khesed kase* (free-loan society), which also came to play a very important social role. Alongside traditional social events such as the banquets of long-established societies, new rituals, such as annual firemen's parades (a good example of Jewish-Gentile cooperation), Passover fund-raising bazaars (which connected the youth movements with adult politics), and amateur theater performances (often linked to the fund-raising needs of the local Tarbut or TSYSHO school) helped to mark the evolution of the interwar *shtetl* and create a sense of community.

If one accepts such integration as an index of "modernization," where traditional communities fall under the influence of universal symbols and mobilizing influences from the outside, then the interwar *shtetl* was clearly undergoing such a process. Yet in fact there was no straight linear evolution from "tradition" to "modernity." The influence of outside institutions on the *shtetl* was filtered through traditional social organizations. While the *shtetlekh* on the eve of World War II had both caftaned Agudaniks and militant young

---

15. A prime example was the role of the Evreiskii Komitet Pomoschi Zhertvam Voyny (EKOPO, Jewish Relief Committee for War Victims) in distributing Joint Distribution Committee (JDC) money in northeastern Poland. The EKOPO recruited local committees to ensure that the relief funds were spent fairly.

Bundists or *halutzim* (Zionist pioneers) in blue shirts tramping off to soccer matches on Sabbath afternoons, one should not forget that most Jews in the *shtetl* fell somewhere between these two extremes. All *shtetlekh* had a *khevre shas* (study society) or its equivalent. At the same time, in most *shtetlekh* Jews could peruse advertisements for the screening of *King Kong* (a *tsvantsik meterdike malpe!* [an ape twenty meters high!]), *Captains Courageous*, and *The Blue Angel*—not to mention such uplifting rituals as "Miss Głębokie" (or Dęblin or Kazimierz), complete with all the latest vicarious glitter from Atlantic City.

Traditional patterns and organizations remained strong and reflected the intertwining of social and religious issues. One example was the conflict over electing new rabbis; poorer Jews could work through organizations such as the *handverker fareyn* to ensure the election of a rabbi they perceived to be friendly to their interests.[16] Artisans could wield power by gaining control of the *khevre kadisha*. Traditional *minyanim* and *khevres* often assumed a particular political complexion or even ran their own candidates in *kehillah* elections. One measure of their importance was that they often were the major distributors of *moes khitim* (Passover relief) and other funds sent to the *shtetl* by *landsmanshaftn* abroad.[17] The hold of religion, if only in the form of *haltn shtat* (doing things for appearance' sake), remained strong—until the very end.

Contrary to popular perceptions, the *shtetl* saw its share of violence and chicanery. Chaim Grade's account in *Tsemakh Atlas* of a local *balebos*'s hiring thugs to destroy a library[18] accords with real-life accounts of violence during *kehillah* elections, disputes over new rabbis and funerals, and arguments over taxes. Grudges and grievances often interrupted Sabbath prayers and even led to fights in the synagogue.[19] Incidents such as that which occurred in Mińsk Ma-

16. An example is the controversy surrounding the election of a rabbi in Mińsk Mazowiecki in the early 1930s. Efraim Shedletzky, interview with author, Jerusalem, July 1982.

17. "Vi azoy zaynen farteylt gevorn di 300 doler," *Gluboker lebn*, April 15, 1932. A committee in the *shtetl* would receive a sum from the American *landsmanshaftn* and distribute most of it to the *minyanim* to help the neediest cases. Certain sums were, of course, reserved for communal institutions or for Jews who were not associated with a particular *minyan*.

18. Chaim Grade, *Tsemakh Atlas* (New York, 1968), 2:141.

19. Shloyme Bagin, "Shande! Shande!" *Gluboker lebn*, September 25, 1931: "Other peoples like to fight in bars. . . . We prefer to fight in *shul* [synagogue]. All disputes, all lowly feelings, all kinds of crazy behavior are saved for the synagogue on the Sabbath or on a holiday. . . . If somebody bears a grudge against somebody else . . . then he waits until Saturday." The paper pointed out that on the previous Saturday, Shabes tshuve, there had been fights in three synagogues.

zowiecki in the 1930s, when the local butchers assaulted a respected Zionist delegate to the *kehillah* after he raised the meat tax
to pay for the local Tarbut school, were not uncommon. Bribery to
fix elections of new rabbis was rampant, and the disgruntled party
often brought in its own candidate, thus leading to serious conflicts
that split families and friends.

Quite often these conflicts went to the Polish courts, a point suggesting a higher degree of Jewish-Gentile contact than one would
assume from reading the memorial books. An incident in Głębokie
on Yom Kippur in 1932 was not atypical. In that case, a conflict
arose in the Starosielsker *minyan* over who would lead the *musaf*
(additional) prayers. When Rabbi Menakhem-Mendl Kuperstock
began to intone "Hineni he-ani," a fistfight broke out. His opponents, still draped in prayer shawls, ran to adjoining synagogues to
rally reinforcements. A mass brawl ensued, and as Polish police
arrived *en masse* to quell the fighting, the leader of the pro-
Kuperstock faction was seen escaping through a window. Twenty-
five Jews, including many of the prominent community leaders,
faced a public trial, which ended in suspended sentences. The editor
of the local newspaper had pleaded with the opposing parties to
settle their differences before the trial began. For a time it seemed
that he had succeeded, but as soon as the court session started,
charges and countercharges—in a broken Polish that caused waves
of laughter from the spectators—began flying back and forth.[20] In
Mińsk Mazowiecki, a sharp battle over the rabbi's position went all
the way to the Polish Najwyższy Trybunal Administracyjny (Supreme Administrative Tribunal).[21]

Indeed the *shtetl* did not accord a rabbi automatic respect. That
had to be won through force of personality; it did not come with
the office. Sometimes a forlorn rabbi had to beg the *kehillah* for his
salary and even run a stall in the marketplace to eke out a precarious living.[22] Yet in other cases the rabbi would be not only a religious leader but an organizer of philanthropy, a mobilizer of the
community in crisis, and an intermediary with national Jewish organizations.[23] In short, generalizations are difficult.

20. "Arum dem yom-kipur protses," *Gluboker lebn*, June 2, 1933. One should note
that there is no mention of this incident in the memorial book.

21. *Nasz Przegląd*, July 2, 1936.

22. On this point, see, aside from obvious literary references, Abramovich, "A
yidish shtetl in Lite," pp. 380–81.

23. For example, see Elkhanan Saratzkin, "Der lebnsveg fun ha-Rav Zalmen Sar-

Thus while the *shtetl* as an "ideal type" has a certain heuristic value, no two *shtetlekh* were alike. Each *shtetl* had its own particular economic characteristics and its own particular occupational patterns. A common feature, though, was the prevalence of "secondary occupations" as a supplemental source of income, especially for those Jews dependent on trade.[24]

Regional differences were reflected in institutional, educational, and political patterns. In *shtetlekh* in the eastern, formerly Russian provinces (the kresy) a much larger percentage of Jewish children attended private, nongovernment schools than was the case in Congress Poland or Galicia.[25] Over time, however, economic pressures caused a tendency for more parents to send their children, especially girls, to government schools. Voting patterns also showed marked differences depending on the size of the settlement and region. For example, *shtetlekh* in the central provinces were a stronghold for the Agudat Israel, while their counterparts in the eastern provinces favored the various Zionist parties.[26]

In addition to regional differences, personal factors and relationships played a key role in the development of particular political organizations and educational trends. One *shtetl* might have a Tarbut school for its children, while a neighboring one would support a Yiddishist school of the Tsentrale Yidishe Shul Organizatsye

---

atzkin," in *Pinkes Zhetl,* ed. Borukh Kaplinski (Tel Aviv, 1957), p. 233. In Głębokie," Rabbi Yosef Halevi Katz played a major role in the creation of the town bank. In Mińsk Mazowiecki, Rabbi Jacob Kaplan halted a Sabbath service and ordered Jews to go home and bring money to help the victims of fire in a nearby town. See Yehoshua Budvitzki, "Bein noar dati," in *Sefer Minsk Mazowieck,* ed. Efraim Shedletzky (Jerusalem, 1976), p. 93.

24. This becomes quite clear in the various JDC reports. One example is Probużna, in Galicia. Of the 1,104 Jews in the town, 40.2 percent of those employed depended on trade, and 26.8 percent were in crafts and manufacturing. Of the 185 families engaged in trade, 62 had a secondary occupation. Of 121 families dependent on crafts, 17 had secondary occupations. The more modest the type of commercial activity, the more likely the Jew was to have a secondary occupation. Of the 38 market stall owners, all but 8 had another occupation. Report on Probużna, 1934, Joint Distribution Committee Archives, New York, Poland, Reconstruction, Localities, Probużna.

25. "Uczniowie Żydzi w szkolach powszechnych," *Biuletyn Ekonomiczno-Statystyczny,* September 1937. In the central provinces 81.9 percent of Jewish children attended state schools, while 18.1 percent attended the various Jewish schools (Tarbut, TSYSHO, Yavneh, etc.). In four eastern provinces, 58 percent attended state schools, while in Galicia 95 percent were in state schools. In Vilna province itself, 56.3 percent of Jewish children attended Jewish schools. Ibid.

26. Leon Ringelblum, "Di valn tsu di shtotratn in Poyln in 1934," *Dos virtshaftlekhe lebn,* 1934, nos. 8–9, pp. 1–12.

(TSYSHO, Central Yiddish School Organization).[27] Adjoining *shtet-lekh* would support a totally different constellation of youth organizations. Sokołów Podlaski was a Poalei Zion stronghold, while nearby Łuków's major organization was Hashomer Hazair. These differences arose not from economic or social factors but from purely personal reasons. In fact the *shtetl* was heavily dependent on a small core of people—both young people and adults—who gave their time and effort to run communal institutions, youth organizations, and cultural events. When such individuals emigrated, tired of their task, or, in the case of young people, married and withdrew into private concerns, the community often had considerable difficulty replacing them.[28]

A major difference between the structure of communal life in the bigger cities and in the *shtetlekh* stemmed from the role and functions of the *kehillah*. During Partition, the various parts of Poland had different legislation concerning Jewish community councils.[29] The common denominator of the pre-1914 councils was restricted suffrage and purely religious competence. While reform of the *kehillah* was a major concern of both Zionists and Bundists before World War I, little in fact happened until the German occupation and the subsequent period of Polish independence.[30] By 1928 new *kehillah* legislation allowed all males over twenty-five to vote. While their function remained primarily religious, the councils were allowed, if they wished, to spend money on social needs.[31] In short, the *kehillah* became a catalyst for the development of political activity that embraced all strata of the population—a situation markedly different from that of the prewar period. Political parties, coalitions of *min-yanim* and Hasidim, personal cliques, and occupational organizations all contested the elections. The campaigns were often marked

27. For an informative survey of education in forty-nine *shtetlekh* in Vilna province in 1929, see Moshe Shalit, "Ankete vegn der tsol kinder in di shuln fun Vilne un gegnt in lernyor 1929–1930," in *Oyf di khurves*, p. 688.

28. Y. V., "Miz zaynen orem in gezelshaftlekhe tuer," *Gluboker shtime*, March 3, 1939; Yankev Dokshitski, "Tsurik in di reyen," *Gluboker vokh*, February 16, 1934.

29. On the details of *kehillah* legislation, see Michał Ringel, "Ustawodawstwo Polski Odrodzonej o gminach żydowskich," in *Żydzi w Polsce Odrodzonej*, vol. 2, ed. Ignacy (Yitzhak) Schiper, Aryeh Tartakower, and Aleksander Hafftka (Warsaw, n.d.), pp. 242–48.

30. For a valuable account of the importance of this issue in pre-1914 Jewish politics in the Russian Empire, see Genrikh Sliozberg, *Dela Minuvshikh Dnei* (Paris, 1934), 3:263–64.

31. Ringel, "Ustawodawstwo Polski Odrodzonej o gminach żydowskich," pp. 246–48.

by violence, especially when the Agudah turned to local authorities to void Bundist and left-wing Zionist election victories.[32]

Depending on the inclinations of the *wojewoda* (provincial governor) and whether the Jewish component of a particular town had been diluted by annexations of adjoining villages, the Jewish community could often use its delegates on the local town council to win needed financial support for local institutions like Jewish schools, the *linas hatsedek* (hospice for the poor), the Towarzystwo Ochrony Zdrowia Ludności Żydowskiej (TOZ, Society for the Safeguarding of Health of the Jewish Population), or for even sending needy individuals for rest cures at sanatoriums. Local politics was a key area of Jewish-Gentile interaction, and the results were sometimes, although not always, positive.[33]

But political realities forced the Jews into compromises even when they formed a majority of the voters and paid 80 percent of the taxes. Since the *wojewoda* could change budgets approved by the town councils, Jewish council members often settled for far lower subsidies than they felt Jewish institutions deserved. In Głębokie, even when the Jews formed two-thirds of the town council, they did not push their claims to generous subsidies. In the local elections of 1935 the Jews faced a choice of joining with the government bloc and accepting minority status on the council (seven of fifteen delegates) or contesting the elections on a separate Jewish list. Many Jews wanted to fight it out, but the newspaper editor reminded his readers that the risk of stirring up antisemitism was too high a price to pay. The local authorities could always assure a Gentile majority by annexing adjoining villages. Besides, the town council had com-

---

32. This happened often. Article 20 of the election statute disqualified those who openly proclaimed their hostility to religion. In Sokołów Podlaski, after the Agudah joined forces with the *handverker fareyn* in voiding a Left Poalei Zion victory, the Poalei Zion supporters hurled rocks through the windows of the home of the Agudah leader and invaded the *kehillah* building, overturning desks and chairs. See Peretz Granatshtein, *Mayn khorev gevorene shtetl Sokolov* (Buenos Aires, 1946), p. 66.

33. In interwar Zdzięciół (in Yiddish, Zhetl), the Jewish majority managed to reverse a decision diluting the Jewish hold on the local town council by incorporating nearby villages. Thus the Jewish delegates were able to use local taxes (mostly paid by the Jews themselves) for the well-being of the town. See Moyshe Mendel Layzerovitsh, "Zhetl un der zhetler handverker," in *Pinkes Zhetl*, pp. 134–35. The interwar archives of the Mińsk Mazowiecki town council, where as a result of incorporation the Jewish delegates were in a minority, record the constant struggle to retain town subsidies to Jewish communal institutions. While the subsidies were small, they continued throughout the interwar period, as did the practice of subsidizing the sanatorium expenses of poorer citizens.

paratively little power. After many stormy public meetings and much argument, the Jewish community accepted the Polish offer.[34]

The politicization of the *shtetlekh* was also affected by new organizations developed by *amkho* (poor Jews) after the First World War. At that time, in addition to political parties, new craft organizations began to mobilize previously dormant groups in the *shtetl*. One of the most important was the *handverker fareyn*. In some *shtetlekh*, depending on personal and local factors, the *handverker fareyn* collaborated with the Agudah, in others with the Bund or the Zionists. What mattered was the effort of the *fareyn* to give the Jewish artisan a new sense of self-respect and inspire him to play a more assertive role in the affairs of the *shtetl*.[35] The *handverker fareyn* played on long years of pent-up resentment against the *balebatim*. But in many *shtetlekh* organizers found artisans intimidated, too unsure of themselves, to start contesting *balebatim*'s control of the *kehillah*.[36] One of the ways the *fareyn* tried to build up spirit was through song.

Handverker fun ale fakhn
glaykht di rukns oys
derloybt nisht mer fun aykh tsu lakhn
geyt shtolts, mutik un faroys
zingt un loybt glaykh mit laytn
di arbet nor iz undzer makht
fargest di alte, alte tsaytn
der handverker hot tsurik ervakht
amol is geven a groyser khet
tsu zayn a blekher, shloser, shmid
yeder yakhsn hot zikh tseredt: bal melokhe, nidriker yid
inem klal fun lebn keyn onteyl genumen
fun ale gevezn farakht
gey fun vanen du bist gekumen
vi a nidrike brie hot yeder getrakht.[37]

Artisans of all trades
Stand tall
Don't let them laugh at you
Go proudly forward
Sing, praise, just like everyone else
It's work that is our one great strength
Forget the old times

34. Shloyme Bagin, "Tsu an eynhaytlekher yidish-kristlekher liste tsu di shtotrat valn," *Gluboker lebn*, May 18, 1934.

35. A useful, if biased, source on the *handverker fareyn* is Elimelekh Rak, *Zikhroynes fun a yidishn handverker tuer* (Buenos Aires, 1958).

36. For example, see Yaakov Rag, "Tsvey khevres," in *Sefer Ratne*, ed. Yakov Batoshanski and Yitzhak Yanosovich (Buenos Aires, 1952), pp. 141–47.

37. Rak, *Zikhroynes fun a yidishn handverker tuer*, p. 151.

The artisan has awakened
Once it was a great sin
To be a tinsmith or a locksmith
The rich Jews thought an artisan is a lowly Jew
We took no part in communal life
All taunted us
Go back where you came from, they said
They thought we were a lower form of life.

The development of new organizations in the interwar *shtetl* also led to calls for a change in the position of women. In February 1934 an angry article in the *Gluboker vokh* pointed out that while women bore much of the burden in running charitable organizations, they had no representation in the *shtetl*'s major institutions. In a later issue of the same newspaper an article ridiculing this claim called forth a bitter rebuttal from the *froyen fareyn* (women's union), which played a growing role in Głębokie and other *shtetlekh*. [38]

Another general feature of the transformation of the *shtetl* in interwar Poland was the integration of previously autonomous societies into the organizational structure of the *kehillah*. While this did not happen everywhere, there was a tendency for the *kehillah* to assert its control over the *khevre kadisha* and the slaughter of meat. [39] After World War I it became more common for the *khevre kadisha* to share burial fees with the *kehillah*.

During the interwar period the *khevre kadisha* remained a focal point of conflict, and communal political alignments and tensions were often reflected in the *khevre*. In Mińsk Mazowiecki, where the *handverker fareyn* managed to bring the *khevre* under its effective control, rich families who had been at odds with the *fareyn* often had to bargain for a few days before their relatives could be buried. [40] Another source of tension was funerals for leftists. In Kazimierz (in Yiddish, Kuzmir) a shoving match at a funeral (over the issue of wearing *yarmulkes*) resulted in the president of the *khevre* being pushed into an open grave. In Dęblin (in Yiddish, Demblin) violence broke out after the *khevre* buried a member of the Poalei Zion near

---

38. M. Rubin, "Vi halt es mit der froy in undzer gezelshaftlekhn lebn," *Gluboker vokh*, February 2, 1934; letter to the editor, *Gluboker vokh*, February 9, 1934.

39. For example, see Zalmen Saratzkin, "Zhetl in der tsayt fun mayn rabones," and anon., "Hevres un institutsyes," *Pinkes Zhetl*, pp. 97–109, 177–79, respectively.

40. Esther Rokhman, interview with author, Tel Aviv, August 6, 1981; Efraim Shedletzky, interview with author, Jerusalem, August 7, 1981.

the fence of the cemetery. His friends disinterred the body, reburied him, and guarded the grave.[41]

A major difference between the *kehillot* in large cities and those in small towns was in how they spent their money. While revenue sources were largely the same—the meat tax, the poll tax (*etat*), and burial fees—*kehillot* in large cities spent a much larger proportion of their budgets on education and social welfare. In the smaller towns, to the great chagrin of many *shtetl* residents, the major concern of the *kehillah* continued to be the rabbi's salary and the upkeep of traditional religious institutions.[42] This became a major issue of small-town politics, as various groups called for more disbursements to help particular schools, credit unions, or the needs of the poor.

Pressures on the *shtetl kehillot* to provide support for the poor increased during the Great Depression. For obvious reasons, Polish authorities encouraged the attitude that Jewish poverty was a Jewish problem rather than a charge on public relief funds. But here the *shtetl kehillah* faced unforeseen problems. In 1933 the Głębokie *kehillah* tried to organize a public campaign to help the poor. But the "masses" became deeply suspicious when the printed appeal emphasized the plight of *gefalene balebatim* (well-to-do Jews who had lost their economic status), and the *kehillah* had to reassure an unruly crowd gathered in the main synagogue that social status was not a criterion in allocating aid. Unfortunately the appeal failed to raise enough money, and a crowd of destitute Jews staged another demonstration in front of the *kehillah* building.[43]

One reason for the difference in the *kehillah* budgets was that conditions in the larger cities already required the extensive institutionalization of social services, while the *shtetl* still relied on personal, more direct forms of philanthropy. There was very strong social pressure on well-off individuals to give not only money but time as well.[44] Passover relief and dowries for poor brides would be

41. David Shtokfish, ed., *Pinkes Kuzmir* (Tel Aviv, 1970), p. 195; Shtokfish, ed., *Sefer Demblin-Modzice* (Tel Aviv, 1969), p. 127.

42. "Sotsyale arbet in Poyln," June 1936, JDC Archives, Poland, General, no. 326a; Y. Bornshteyn, "Di struktur fun di budzshetn fun di yidishe kehiles in Poyln," *Dos virtshaftlekhe lebn*, 1934, nos. 1–2, pp. 16–18.

43. "Hunger demonstratsye bay der yidisher kehile in Glubok," *Gluboker lebn*, February 12, 1933. When the Polish police arrived, the Jews asked to be arrested, arguing that at least in jail they would be fed.

44. Moshe Zisserman, interview with author, Holon, Israel, August 27, 1981. Zisserman was the president of the *linas hatsedek* in Mińsk Mazowiecki in the late 1930s.

organized by local rabbis or individuals.[45] Health organizations such as the *linas hatsedek* would raise money by staging traditional Purim plays. The *shtetlekh* tried to keep their traditional "social safety net" in place: the synagogue stove (which warmed the very poor), the *hekdesh* (poorhouse), *nedoves* (alms) for wandering beggars. After *havdole*, the ceremony marking the end of the Sabbath, volunteers would collect slices or loaves of bread in a *torbe* (pail) to distribute to the poor (*lekhem evyonim*, or "bread of the poor").

In 1929 Hirsh Abramovich, a statistician of the Vilna Evreiskii Komitet Pomoschi Zhertvam Voyny (EKOPO, Jewish Relief Committee for War Victims), wrote a revealing, strongly negative report on the decline of his nearby *shtetl*. But he emphasized that Jews in the *shtetl* still gave a much higher proportion of their disposable income to charity than did Jews in the larger cities and that the bonds of social responsibility remained strong, especially during major illnesses, when the Jews contributed to send their ailing townsperson to city hospitals.[46] The *Gluboker lebn* regularly featured open appeals, where the givers publicly challenged specific individuals to match their gift. A typical case was Libe Kraut, a widow with six children who had nowhere to live. Leading *balebatim* led a campaign to fix her house.[47] Charity even extended to the public schools. When a Jewish woman ran off with a Gentile, leaving her husband and children and taking the family's savings, the children's classmates raised twenty-five *złotys* in the local *szabasówka*, a Polish-language public school intended exclusively for Jewish children.[48]

Yet the interwar period saw growing sentiment for a basic change in the structure of *shtetl* philanthropy. The traditional reliance on personal giving, *lekhem evyonim*, and so forth, was sharply criticized, especially by those who argued that many needy Jews who were too proud to take alms from individuals might accept help if it were properly organized and institutionalized.[49] Taking food collected in a pail was cited in particular as a custom badly needing reform.[50]

45. "Sotsyale arbet in Poyln." The 1934 report on Probużna (see note 24, above) mentions that all charity was organized by the rabbi. Hayim Sosnov recalls that in Kolno his father objected to the institutionalization of the town's philanthropy on the grounds that "it was not Jewish." See "Kalkalah ve-hevrah be-Kolno," pp. 28–42.
46. Abramovich, "A yidish shtetl in Lite," pp. 381–84.
47. "Retungs-keyt tsu endikn di kleyn shtibele fun der almone mit di yesoymim Kraut," *Gluboker vokh*, July 6, 1934.
48. "A familyen tragedye vos iz farlofn in Glubok," *Gluboker shtime*, April 15, 1938.
49. "Arbet un sotsyale hilf," *Gluboker lebn*, January 29, 1932.
50. [Shloyme Bagin?], "Arum der Gluboker lekhem evyonim," *Gluboker lebn*,

TABLE 1

Passover Relief, 1937

Size of community	Percentage from local Jews	Percentage from foreign sources
Less than 2,000	22.6%	77.4%
2,000–5,000	44.2%	55.8%
5,000–10,000	77.7%	22.3%
10,000 +	81.6%	19.4%

SOURCE: Hersh Shner, "Ankete vegn pesakh shtitse in di yorn 1935–37," *Yidishe economik* 1 (1937): 65. The figures for communities of 10,000 plus add up to more than 100 percent.

In the interwar period the bonds of place became particularly apparent in the crucial relationship between the *shtetlekh* and the *landsmanshaftn*. According to one JDC report, the worse off a *shtetl* had been before World War I, the more help it was likely to get from this source, since it was the poorest *shtetlekh* that provided the highest proportion of emigration before World War I.[51] Figures published in 1937 on Passover relief illustrate just how important the *landsmanshaftn* were (see table 1).

For Głębokie, donations from the United States were of critical importance. A few key *landslayt*—Barney Rappaport of Hartford, Connecticut; Morris Cepelowicz of Buffalo, New York; and Judah Pollak of New York City—regularly organized appeals to support Passover relief, the TOZ, the Kinder Shutz (Society for the Protection of Children), the *gemiles khesed kase,* and the local Tarbut school. An important factor in maintaining contact between Głębokie and *landslayt* overseas was the weekly *Gluboker lebn,* which was regularly sent to the United States. (Głębokie, in turn, had the chance to read extensive articles about the exploits of Barney Rappaport in the Connecticut legislature.) Not counting funds sent to individual relatives, American money probably provided for 60 percent of the resources used to maintain these public institutions. The distribution of the American moneys often led to bitter conflicts.

The help from the United States, nourished by the weekly arrival of the *Gluboker lebn*, came at a price. The *Gluboker lebn* faithfully

---

November 10, 1933: "A beggar might take a piece of bread in a pail, but not *gefalene balebatim* or someone who has lost his job." The newspaper argued that philanthropy was the responsibility of both the town council and the *kehillah.*

51. For a discussion of this point, see the report on Sokółka, 1937, JDC Archives, Poland, Reconstruction, Localities, Sokółka.

reported the growing poverty in the town but tried to play down incidents such as the Yom Kippur brawl for fear of jeopardizing the inflow of dollars. American *landslayt* regularly visited Głębokie and heard complaints from those who felt that they had been slighted in the distribution of funds. Some Jews resented the groveling tone supposedly taken by the *Gluboker lebn* toward the *landslayt*. In 1934 a *coup* ousted Shloyme Bagin as the editor. His successor, Yonah Berkman, announced to the readers that henceforth the newspaper would be written in proper Yiddish rather than the Americanized "jargon" favored by Bagin. American visitors would be treated with dignified respect, but the *shtetl* would also remind them that Głębokie was more than just a *shnorrers'* association.[52]

The *shtetl* suffered greatly from the Great Depression and the structural problems of the Polish economy. In addition, the problem of economic boycott for the Jew in the small town took a different cast. The Jew in the *shtetl* could not be an anonymous economic actor. His economic position was conspicuous and personal and depended to a large extent on a specific relationship with individual Gentiles. Nor could the Gentile easily hide the fact that he was buying from a Jew.

On the other hand, one must keep in mind Joseph Marcus's argument that the issue of Jewish poverty must be seen in the context of the living standards of the non-Jewish population.[53] Another important point is that the effectiveness of economic boycott depended on two fundamental factors: the attitudes of the Polish local authorities and the ability of newly minted Gentile merchants to compete effectively over time. Jacob Lestschinsky filed a dispatch describing how, in the aftermath of the 1936 pogrom, the Jewish share of commerce in Mińsk Mazowiecki had fallen from 81 percent to 63 percent.[54] But four months later a reporter for the *Varshever radio* wrote that the Jews were holding their own in the town and that while the Polish townspeople felt strong social pressure to avoid Jewish shops, the peasants were ignoring the boycott. Many of the new Gentile shopkeepers could not retain peasant business, and the

52. Yonah Berkman, "Der sakhakl fun a yor arbet," *Gluboker lebn*, June 28, 1935.
53. Joseph Marcus, *Social and Political History of the Jews in Poland, 1919–1939* (New York, 1983), p. 243.
54. Jacob Lestschinsky's account of his visit to Mińsk Mazowiecki can be found in the Lestschinsky Archives, file 286. For another unpublished eyewitness account of the pogrom, see Moshe Rozenberg's entry in the 1939 YIVO youth autobiography contest, YIVO Archives, Youth Autobiographies, 143644/3753.

new *starosta* (district head) forbade close picketing of Jewish stores.[55] *Shtetlekh* fortunate enough to have a *starosta* determined to keep order suffered much less from the boycott than towns where the local authorities were less sympathetic.

Besides help from the *landsmanshaftn*, a major weapon against economic crisis was the credit union—especially the JDC-sponsored *gemiles khesed kase*. The development of these *kases* played a key role in the economic life of the interwar *shtetl*, not only as an economic lifeboat but also as a social institution counterbalancing the centrifugal influence of political parties and ideologies.

Credit had always been important in the traditional *shtetl*, both *gemiles khesed* (free loans) and more conventional loans. But the traditional organization of credit had depended largely on private individuals. Interest rates on conventional loans were high, and the traditional *gemiles khesed kases* had required the posting of articles as security.[56]

In 1926 the Joint Distribution Committee laid the groundwork for the establishment of a network of *gemiles khesed kases*, which by 1937 included 870 towns and cities out of a total of 1,013 settlements of more than three hundred Jews. The *kases* were to give small, free loans (they averaged ninety-five *złotys*) to Jewish artisans or traders who needed money to buy wares for the market day and somewhat larger loans for the purchase of a horse or an artisan's license. In order to force members of the Jewish community to work together and avoid the party strife that plagued Jewish local politics, the JDC stipulated that "all social and economic groups in the town be united in the *kase*'s work . . . and that there exist no *kases* for special groups." The JDC gave a town seed money after ascertaining that a suitable committee, able to command the respect and trust of the community, was ready to manage the enterprise. The town had to supplement the JDC's capital with its own contributions and eventually to pay the JDC back. The strategy was successful. The *kases* won the trust and respect of the Jewish public, and the JDC's share of the total *kase* capital declined from 58 percent in 1929 to

---

55. S. Gotlib, "Der emes vegn di straganes," *Varshever radio*, October 7, 1936.

56. "Sotsyale arbet in Poyln." In *Yunge yorn* (New York, 1918), Sholem Asch describes Leybl, a traditional moneylender who enjoyed walking around the *shtetl* intimidating all his debtors. For a good description of a Jewish credit bank before World War I, see B. Mintz, "Di antviklung fun yidishn kredit vezn in Shedletz," in *Sefer Shedletz*, pp. 425–48. One constant problem in the organization of credit in the *shtetl* was the tension between the needs of the artisans and those of the small merchants.

47 percent in 1936. In that year the total capital of the *kases* amounted to ten million *złotys*. The smaller the town, the higher proportion of the Jewish population dependent on the *kase*. A survey in the late 1930s showed that Jewish small traders obtained half their total credits from the *kases*, 20 percent from private money-lenders, 10 percent from private banks, and 5 percent from commercial savings institutions. Thirty-three percent of all borrowers were artisans, and 50 percent were small traders.[57]

In many *shtetlekh* more than 90 percent of the working population joined the *kases*, whose membership elected the supervising committee each year. The committee met once a week, usually on Sunday, to hear requests for loans. Each loan applicant went to the *kase* and made his or her case for a loan, which was to be repaid in not less than three and not more than twelve months. The records of the *kases* provide a valuable glimpse into the problems of *shtetl* life. The following case, taken from the *kase* report of Węgrów, was typical.

> A woman enters with tears in her eyes. "Jews," she says, "you know that my husband is a scribe and makes eight *złotys* a week. Of course you know that one can't live on that wage. My children don't have any bread. . . . I would like to open a soda-water stand . . . some soda water, some apples, and I'll be able to make do [*Ikh vel zikh an eytse gebn*]. But a license costs twenty-eight *złotys*. . . . Please Jews, lend me twenty-five *złotys*. I'll pay back one *złoty* a week."[58]

The JDC went to great lengths to investigate any charges of corruption or personal bias. Unlike the credit cooperatives for more well-to-do merchants, the *kases* were relatively free of charges of favoritism or corruption.[59]

Along with the new *kehillot* and the political parties, the *kases* were institutions that mobilized groups previously uninvolved in the communal affairs of the *shtetl*. Unlike the first two types of organizations, however, the *kases* engendered a spirit of communal cooperation rather than competition.

Of all the new changes affecting the interwar *shtetl*, one of the

---

57. Internal memorandum, April 15, 1943, JDC Archives, Poland, Reconstruction, Gemiles Khesed Kases, no. 398; "Sotsyale arbet in Poyln."

58. Botchan, report on the Węgrów *gemiles khesed kase*.

59. Internal memorandum on *gemiles khesed kases*, April 11, 1938, JDC Archives, Poland, Reconstruction, General, 1938.

most significant was the advent of the youth movements.[60] Although the great ideological movements that swept Eastern European Jewry had begun before World War I, they did not become mass movements until the postwar period, and their vital core was the youth organizations. While the latter were certainly not rebelling against the leadership of the adult parties, the fact remains that Jewish parliamentary politics in interwar Poland could not really improve the condition of Polish Jewry. But in creating a framework for new social networks and youth organizations, the political parties were more successful.

It would not be too farfetched to say that literature and theater played almost as large a role in the Jewish youth movements as ideology. Discussions of literary as well as ideological questions and an intense interest in amateur theater gave the youth movement in the *shtetlekh* its own peculiar cast—that of a counterculture, a home away from home.[61]

A major determinant of the youth movements was the progressive decline of economic opportunity. Traditional options for young men in the *shtetl* had included taking a dowry and starting a store; going to a master, either in the *shtetl* or in a larger city, and learning a trade; studying in the *bes-medresh* in the hopes of impressing a prospective father-in-law; entering the parent's business; or emigrating. If a young woman did not marry, there was the choice of going to a larger city and becoming a maid or finding some sort of factory work. Many of these options narrowed after World War I. Economic conditions often meant that dowries which earlier would have sufficed to start a business no longer covered these costs.[62] Only a small proportion of Polish-Jewish youth had entered trade schools, and hard-pressed artisans were taking on fewer youths as apprentices.[63] In Głębokie a 1931 survey showed that 61 percent of the boys and

60. An indispensable source for any discussion of the youth movements is Kligsberg, "Di yidishe yugnt bavegungen in Poyln," pp. 137–228. Much of the discussion below is based on Kligsberg as well as on extensive interviews conducted in 1981 and 1982 with participants in the youth movements.

61. On this point, see the excellent treatment by Ertel, *Le shtetl*, pp. 243–98. On this aspect of the youth movements, I owe much to a conversation with my late uncle, Lazar Kraut, who was a member of Hashomer Hazair in Głębokie.

62. On this point, see Abramovich, "A yidish shtetl in Lite," pp. 371–72.

63. There are many discussions of this point in *Folkshilf* as well as in *Dos virtshaftlekhe lebn*. A spot survey taken by the JDC in Ostróg, a *shtetl* in Volynia, in the late 1930s showed that of forty-two youngsters between age fourteen and sixteen, three had a contract with a master to learn a trade. Report on Ostróg, 1937, JDC Archives, Poland, Reconstruction, Localities, Ostróg.

83 percent of the girls between ages sixteen and twenty had no work.[64] Another product of the economic situation may have been a trend toward later marriage.[65] To some extent the economic pressure on Jewish youth had been counterbalanced by the demographic impact of World War I, but the number of Jewish children turning thirteen increased from twenty-four thousand in 1930 to forty-five thousand in 1938, heightening competition for limited economic opportunities.[66]

The youth organizations offered hope and dignity, evenings and Saturday afternoons of intense discussion about moral values, literature, and politics, and opportunities to engage in amateur theater and to travel.[67] There was always the chance, however slim, that years of backbreaking *hakhsharah* (pioneer training) might eventually lead to a coveted Palestine emigration certificate. Youths from poorer families often found in the Bundist (and communist) youth organizations a supportive environment that not only encouraged respect for the dignity of their labor but gave them the chance to raise their self-esteem through cultivation of their dramatic and cultural talents in the language they knew best—Yiddish.

Regardless of ideology, the structure of the youth organizations was largely the same. A rented room—the *lokal*—was the center of the organization's activities. The *lokal* would probably have a library where books—too expensive for most youths to afford on their own—would be available and serve as the basis for *kestl ovntn* (debates) and discussions. The organizations sponsored amateur plays,

64. Shaul Yididovich, "Di yidishe bafelkerung fun Glebok in tsifern," *YIVO bleter* 2 (1931): 414–20. Of those "employed," most helped out in their parents' shops. For the town as a whole, 53.6 percent of the Jewish population depended on crafts and 26.2 percent on trade.

65. In Horodno, of forty-four young people in the twenty-five to twenty-nine age group, thirty-three were unmarried. See A. Tzinaman and L. Shlamovitsch, "Di yidishe bafelkerung in Horodno," *Dos virtshaftlekhe lebn*, 1935, nos. 8–9, pp. 92–105. Of course overall generalizations are difficult to make on the basis of such fragmentary evidence. See also Shaul Stampfer, "Marital Patterns in Interwar Poland," in this volume.

66. Jacob Lestschinsky, "Vegn a konstruktivn plan fun hilf far di poylishe yidn," *Yidishe ekonomik* 2 (1938): 12.

67. Granatshtein, *Mayn khorev gevorene shtetl Sokolov,* provides excellent material on the youth organizations in Sokołów Podlaski. In one chapter (pp. 142–48) he recalls going to neighboring Sterdyń with other members of the Poalei Zion to attend the wedding of some friends. The leader of the Sterdyń Poalei Zion youth group wanted to use the wedding to recruit new members. The brother of the bride, a Bundist, objected to the political speeches and suggested that everyone relax and have a good time. When the Sokołów Poalei Zion supported this suggestion, the whole Sterdyń group got up *en masse* and left the wedding!

trips to neighboring *shtetlekh,* and long hikes. All but the religious youth organizations scheduled trips on the Sabbath, thus straining relations between young people and religious parents.

As Moshe Kligsberg points out, the values encouraged by the youth movement provided a powerful antidote to traditional *shtetl* attitudes that denigrated manual work and valued commerce.[68] If the youth movements did not entirely eliminate social divisions, they at least provided a new structure in which young people from different classes could meet on equal terms. On the whole there was more social integration in the Zionist than in the Bundist youth organizations; the latter remained primarily working class.

The youth movements played a major role in changing relationships between young men and young women. Hikes, discussion groups, and *kestl ovntn* provided opportunities for young people to meet away from the supervision of parents. Parents often tried to stop their daughters from joining youth organizations, but few succeeded. A hapless father in a *shtetl* near Vilna, told that his daughter was going on picnics in the woods on Saturday afternoon and even carrying baskets of food, replied, "Male vos zey trogn in vald iz nor a halbe tsore. Di gantse tsore vet zayn ven zey veln onheybn trogn fun vald" (I'm more worried about what she'll be carrying out of the forest than what she carries into it).[69]

This survey has attempted to show that there were in fact wide variations among the Jewish *shtetlekh* in interwar Poland as well as some basic common trends. The interwar *shtetl* was undergoing a process of political and social transformation. Social tensions and conflicts were a constant feature of *shtetl* life, and these conflicts often became quite bitter. Yet the overall tendency was for the *shtetl* to reflect wider trends in the history of interwar Polish Jewry and to develop new institutions and organizations that involved and mobilized a larger proportion of the population and provided some antidote—moral if not financial—to a declining economic situation. Above all, the *shtetl* developed institutions and attitudes that counterbalanced traditional prejudices and provided the community with underlying social flexibility and even resilience. Personalities mattered as much as institutions. Power and authority in the *shtetl* did

68. Kligsberg, "Di yidishe yungt bavegungen in Poyln," pp. 137–228.
69. Abramovich, "A yidish shtetl in Lite," p. 370. *Trogn* means both "carry" and "be pregnant."

not flow automatically from the rabbinate and the *kehillah* but reflected the ability of specific personalities to gain respect and prestige by working through particular structures. While economic pressures affected the *shtetl,* overall generalizations have to be counterbalanced against local factors. The Jewish struggle for economic survival was not entirely unsuccessful. The attitude of local authorities, help from the United States, the ability of Jewish merchants to hold on to peasant business, and the continuing social pressures to help less fortunate members of the community all point to at least a partial revision of the widespread view that, on the eve of the war, Polish Jews were waiting for their death.

Patterns of Religious Life

Ephraim E. Urbach

The History of Polish Jews after World War I as Reflected in the Traditional Literature

In 1853 the *Monatsschrift für Geschichte und Wissenschaft des Judentums* carried an article entitled "Zur Geschichte der Juden in Polen" (On the History of the Jews in Poland) by a certain Hermann Sternberg, who introduces himself as a "Pole familiar with the language, history, ways, and customs of his fatherland." The article includes an editorial note by the journal's outstanding editor, Zachariah Frankel, which states: "The historiography of Poland suffers from a complete disregard for the sources of rabbinical literature. True, its investigation demands a great effort, but it is bound to yield a rich crop."[1]

During the 135 years that have passed since Frankel's complaint, many advances have been made. The discovery of important manuscripts has enabled us to gain more exact information about the beginnings of rabbinical literature and a more colorful picture of its categories, trends, and character. We still lack, however, a comprehensive history of rabbinical literature in Poland that covers the whole range of its topics and themes. Such an overview would, of course, have to include the traditional literature produced after the First World War. It would make possible a far more reliable answer to the subject under discussion: To what extent and in what way are the changes in the history of Polish Jews in the interwar period reflected in the traditional literature?

If we look through the extensive list of publications and of bibliography concerned with the history of the Jews in Poland during the interwar period, we can find no reference to rabbinical litera-

1. Hermann Sternberg, "Zur Geschichte der Juden in Polen," *Monatsschrift für Geschichte und Wissenschaft des Judentums* 2 (1853): 211–24, 263–69, 304–10, 369–85. Zachariah Frankel's editorial note is on p. 211.

ture.[2] Scholars who write on the religious institutions and parties in this period base their work mainly on the press, conference proceedings, pamphlets, and other materials preserved in archives or in memorial books. References to rabbinical literature are very rare. For other periods, this traditional literature has served as the main source for the internal history of Jewish life, its institutions, its economic and social tensions, and its ideological struggles. Of course the relevant material has had to be disentangled from the mass of commentaries on passages of the Bible or the Talmud, from homilies and moral treatises, and especially from collections of responsa— the written answers and decisions of rabbinical authorities in response to submitted questions. Neglect of this kind of evidence for contemporary history can be explained by the abundance of new material easily accessible in sources that do not require extreme efforts of interpretation or identification and thus do not put an additional burden upon the historian. As we know, the shift in the sources of Jewish history also resulted from changes in Jewish society in Poland wrought by the Haskalah, a movement that reached the Orthodox strata only during the interwar period.

One must admit, too, that the writings on the works and activities of figures in the rabbinical world and on religious institutions and concerns are even more inclined to take a romanticized view of the destroyed past than are other biographies and histories. In traditional literature inner strife, shortcomings, and failure are frequently covered by a thick layer of pious phraseology. Biographies tend to become hagiographies. While reading such descriptions one might be inclined to recall the words of Malcolm Muggeridge: "How fascinating to live long enough to meet one's own world as history and to find it barely recognisable." The lack of a critical approach blurs all the differences among varied personalities and prevents a realistic evaluation of the performance of both individuals and institutions. However, a method of research that recognizes these characteristics

2. *Studia Historyczne* 14, no. 4 (1972), published by the Instytut Historii Polskiej Akademia Nauk (History Institute of the Polish Academy of Sciences), which concentrates on Warsaw during the Second Polish Republic (1918–39), includes a short article by Bernard Mark (better known as Berl Mark) entitled "Zarys rozwoju literatury żydowskiej w latach 1918–1939," p. 138. It is concerned exclusively with modern Jewish poetry and prose. An editorial states that the article is taken from a larger work by the late Professor Mark on Jewish literature in Poland from its origins to the present. I have not been able to find out anything about the content and character of the work.

of rabbinical literature has made it useful for studying Jewish history and, applied to interwar rabbinical literature, can make this material an additional source of valuable information for the period.

Traditional literature embraces works of a variety of categories and types, but for the present essay I shall limit consideration to halakhic works and especially to responsa. In this category I shall examine the class of responsa that open with a question about a specific case and give a full description of the matter concerned. These queries are usually directed by rabbis of small communities to a recognized authority, often also a rabbi in a small community who had an extensive fund of knowledge and a fertile and versatile mind capable of drawing many analogies to the question under discussion or of supplying precedents from similar cases. In these features the responsa literature of the period clearly indicates the strength of continuity and the persistence of tradition. Jewish politics and the divergent approaches of various Jewish parties are barely evident. Instead we learn from the responsa much about the problems faced by individuals in everyday life. Thus far there have been no attempts to explore this rich material,[3] and that seems to me an urgent task. These sources will supply us not only with evidence from another segment of the population, but also with evidence of a different type. While in general creative writers invest events with an individual perspective, often shaped by religious circles and parties, the halakhic literature presents the facts as reported by eyewitnesses or others who have no particular point of view to uphold.

At the same time, we as historians cannot ignore changes in halakhic literature resulting from the influence of external events—in this case those connected with the First World War. The prevailing view is that since the war, the world is no longer the same, echoing the popular distinction between "before the war" and "after the war." Much less is reflected in this literature of the changes wrought by the amalgamation of three different parts of a country whose population had lived under different regimes for more than a century. Connections between rabbinical scholars in the different parts of Poland had been maintained during the Partitions, while the ma-

---

3. Wolff Glicksman has performed this service for Yiddish literature in his two articles: "Cultural and Social Trends as Reflected in Yiddish Literature," *Gal-Ed* 2 (1975): 373–92; "Jewish Poverty in Poland as Reflected in Yiddish Prose," *Gal-Ed* 4–5 (1978): 461–84.

jor ideological differences that had shaped the peculiar character of Polish-Jewish communities also remained in force during the decades of the Second Polish Republic.

Where we find differing responses to modernization, we must take a closer look at the characters and positions of the protagonists. Before I get to this, however, let me make a general remark about the standards applied in the evaluation of rabbinical works by the circles from which they stem. Here the highest appreciation is reserved for *Torah li-shmah* (study for its own sake). The main criterion is not the nature of the decision given but the method applied and the principles discovered during a long itinerary starting with an analysis of the problems posed and continuing with the citation of sources and interpretations that at first glance seem not really related to the questions at issue. Besides the temptation to parade intellectual skills, another danger now derived from the organized Orthodox religious parties and affiliations that originated in the prewar period and continued to be influential during the years of the First World War.

Divisiveness was deeply ingrained, and calls for unity failed time and again. Evidence of early efforts is found in *Raboteinu she-ba-golah* (Our Teachers in Exile), a neglected treatise edited by Nahum Nata Leiter, the son of the rabbi of Dunajów in Galicia. It contains contributions by rabbis who fled to Vienna when their towns and villages were occupied or destroyed by the invading Russians. The book opens with a list of ninety-four rabbis and Hasidic rebbes who lived in Vienna, a compilation that itself constitutes an important record. It is followed by an article entitled "Bein tikvah le-yeush" (Between Hope and Despair) by Rabbi Moses Leiter of Zawałów describing the preparations for the great assembly scheduled to take place in Frankfurt in Elul 1914. "And in our dreams we have already seen," Leiter writes, "a well-organized traditional Judaism." The outbreak of the war had put an end to all such plans, bringing instead disasters and persecutions by the Russian "Amalekites" with their wild and terrifying actions in Galicia and Bukovina. Leiter movingly describes the precarious situation of the Jews in Poland and Lithuania who suffer from the allegations of their Polish "friends," the followers of Roman Dmowski and his Polish nationalists. The news from the Holy Land is distressing, too: vital young people and workers are leaving the country; the locust is laying waste the farms and Jewish colonies; the old Yishuv (Jewish community) is frustrated. "The ground of the dispersion is shaken and the building of Eretz Israel is falling."[4]

Rabbi Leiter goes on to describe the inner religious and moral crisis that he sees as an even greater threat to Jewish existence. The remedy, he says, lies in creating an active rabbinical organization that will reach out to those who have become alienated. In his opinion the only hope for creating an orderly rabbinical council rests within the World Organization of Agudat Israel. Although he well knows that many of its undertakings and activities are subject to criticism, at present it is the only framework available. But even this project will not be enough. Leiter finds the time ripe for an organization that will embrace all the communities in the Austro-Hungarian Empire. His primary call is for national unity. In commending the aid extended by the community of Vienna to the refugees from Galicia, he writes: "The two factions of our people—the religious and the emancipated—can each learn from the other. The emancipated and the semiemancipated may learn love of Judaism, adherence to Jewish values, and the warmth of religious feelings, but there is equal room for the Orthodox to learn from the emancipated about orderly behavior, decency, and philanthropy." Only a well-organized union of the Jewish community can prevent damaging changes. Leiter calls on "the great and holy men in Israel" to press the secular leaders and the active rabbis to accept his proposal. On the necessity of creating a united front of all Jewish parties and groups, he writes, "When the angel of death [the Russians] entered our country, he made no distinction between Zionist and Orthodox, between them and assimilationists."[5]

The hopes raised by Leiter were not in vain, at least with regard to organizational activities. Inner Jewish life in reunited Poland displays a conspicuous vitality, but the dreamed-of unity never materialized. The first national conference of Agudat Israel convened in Warsaw in December 1918, but significant segments of the Orthodox community and many Hasidic groups remained aloof from the new organization and began to oppose it.

The first rabbinical conference took place in Warsaw on 23–25 Tevet 1922. The chairman was Rabbi Ezekiel Lifschitz of Kalisz, who delivered the opening address. A representative of the Polish gov-

4. Nahum Nata Leiter, ed., *Raboteinu she-ba-golah* (Pressburg, 1915). Moses Leiter's article, "Bein tikvah le-yeush," is on pp. 13–24.
5. Ibid.

ernment also greeted the conference, and welcoming speeches were delivered by Dr. Mordechai Nurok of Riga on behalf of an organizing committee of a conference of Russian rabbis; Rabbi Shlomo Aronson on behalf of the rabbis in the Ukraine; Dr. Mateusz Mieses in the name of the army chaplaincy; Rabbi Isaac Meir Levin from Agudat Israel; Rabbi Dr. Yaakov Freiman of Poznań; Joshua Farbstein, a deputy in the Sejm (House of Deputies) from the Mizrahi; Rabbi Menahem Zemba of the Metivta; Dr. Meir Balaban of the Tahkemoni; and Rabbi Meir Shapira of Sanok in the name of the rabbis of Galicia. In his inaugural speech the Mizrahi leader Farbstein expressed the hope that the new Agudat Harabbanim (Association of Rabbis) in Poland would contribute to peaceful relations among the religious parties. Such a hope seemed plausible, given the collection of speakers that morning and the list of the four hundred members of the association included in the conference proceedings. Among them are well-known leaders and activists in the Mizrahi, including Rabbi Jehuda L. Kowalski of Włocławek, Rabbi Samuel Brodt of Lipno, and Rabbi Yehuda Isaac Trunk of Kutno, grandson of the famous Rabbi Joshua Trunk of Kutno and son-in-law of the second Sochaczewer Rebbe, the Shem Mishmuel. Rabbi Yehuda Isaac Trunk had been a prominent participant in Iyar 1919 at the second conference of the Mizrahi in Poland, which had for its theme the Jewish community. He had proposed an interesting program for community organization and for raising the standard and independence of the rabbinate. This lecture, rich in ideas and modest in presentation, contained some of the practical resolutions afterward adopted by the conference of Agudat Harabbanim. In reality, however, the hopes for unity were not fulfilled. The proceedings reveal that the organization was already becoming a tool of Agudat Israel. When Rabbi Trunk of Kutno expressed surprise that the issue of Eretz Israel did not appear on the agenda of the conference, Rabbi Joel Fuks of Blaszki, himself close to the Mizrahi, replied that until the organization had stabilized, only items on which there were no differences of opinion would be included on the agenda.[6]

It is time to turn to the main question: Are these ongoing organizational activities and party affiliations reflected in the responsa of the great rabbinical authorities? The answer is clearly no. While

6. The conference proceedings were published by Agudat Harabbanim as *Kovez drushim* (Piotrków, 1923).

the responsa relate to numerous queries concerned with the social and economic problems resulting from political pressures, the replies are completely free of the ideological doctrines. There is no trace of the *daat Torah* ideology that, as Gershon C. Bacon rightly claims, developed into something similar to the doctrine of papal infallibility.[7] *Daat Torah* ideology has never been based upon authoritative halakhic sources, and, as far as I know, recourse has never been made to it in halakhic debate. As a tool for demanding absolute obedience to a political organization or religious institution, there was no place for it in halakhic decisions. In studying Halakhah, stress was placed, as always, on the basic methodology of sifting sources and tradition. The *ad hoc* usage was, however, directly related to the personality of the rabbinical scholar and dependent on his intellectual ability and knowledge. In the period under consideration no rabbi, including Hasidic rabbis, when considering halakhic questions and decisions, claimed divine revelation of any kind as his source. The famous rebuttal of such a claim by Rabbi Joshua at the beginning of the second century—''we pay no heed to a heavenly voice''—still prevailed. Even those who referred to divine revelation in their political and educational activities avoided such claim in the halakhic sphere, recognizing that argumentation in the accepted mode would be more impressive to leading authorities.

A case in point is the energetic Rabbi Meir Shapira, a person of abundant initiatives. His activities in the Agudah, as a deputy in the Sejm, in the founding of Yeshivat Hakhmei Lublin, and in introducing the *daf yomi* are well known and have been widely described and discussed. Less attention has been paid to his responsa *Or ha-meir* published in Piotrków in 1926, just two years after the laying of the cornerstone of Yeshivat Hakhmei Lublin. The introduction to the volume—an exposition of the value and centrality of Torah study in Jewish life—includes the inaugural speech delivered at the Lublin ceremony.[8]

Very few of the responsa in *Or ha-meir* are composed in answer to actual questions. They typify responsa of a certain genre, being sometimes no more than an exchange of correspondence initiated by a younger or less-renowned author and addressed to an eminent

---

7. Gershon C. Bacon, *Agudat Yisrael in Poland, 1916–1939: The Politics of Tradition*, forthcoming.

8. Meir Shapira, introd. to *Or ha-meir* (Piotrków, 1926), pp. 1–2.

authority, consisting mostly of comments on or objections to a work by that authority. If the illustrious person thus addressed was gracious and responded to the comments and questions raised, the recipient felt himself entitled to include them in his publication, thus heightening its value. So we find that responsum 3, written by Shapira in Sanok in 1924, is addressed to Rabbi Israel Meir Hakohen, the Hafez Hayim. One need not say that he had no cause to spare honorifics and expressions of reverence to the highly respected and saintly man. The letter postulates critical remarks concerning the *Likutei halakhot* of the Hafez Hayim on the tractates Zebahim and Menahot. The Sage of Raduń sends a brief reply in which he addresses Shapira by all the usual titles and additionally as "deputy of the Sejm." He thanks Shapira for his valued comments and expresses his joy that a great man of Shapira's stature has read his work. Weakness of eyesight, however, prevents him from reacting duly, and he sends his blessings that the Lord may grant Rabbi Shapira strength to study and search out his Torah and to accomplish his work in the "tents of Japhet," an allusion to his activity in the Sejm. Shapira prefaces this letter with the remark, "The words of the Gaon, the *saba kadisha* [old holy man], long may he live, are of special worth in the world of Judaism for our days and for future generations, and therefore I am reproducing his answer word for word." Rabbi Menahem Yosef, the son-in-law of the Hafez Hayim, had replied to the questions referred to the Hafez Hayim, and Shapira then continues with his responses to the reaction of the son-in-law, which was not very complimentary.[9]

The book also contains letters in a vein similar to those of other celebrated authorities, such as Rabbi Meir Arik of Tarnów, Rabbi Meir Yehiel Halevi Halshtik of Ostrowiec, and Rabbi Avraham Menahem Steinberg of Brody as well as to lesser-known scholars, some of them Rabbi Shapira's students and colleagues going back to his own years of study in Tarnopol or to his first years in the rabbinate of Glinyany. The responsa on practical issues, of which there are only a few, disclose his own estimate of himself as well as his principles and convictions. In a responsum dated Kislev 1912, he addresses a question raised by a rabbinical assessor in Glinyany as to whether one is permitted to sell one's house to people who are going to turn it into a church. The extensive answer, covering six pages,

9. Ibid., no. 3.

reaches the conclusion that there are reasons for allowing the sale of the house to a non-Jew. However, as this is a very serious decision, he recommends that the inquirer should be advised to move his own place of dwelling elsewhere and promises success if this advice is heeded. In an additional note to this responsum, Shapira remarks that later, when he accepted his appointment as a rabbi of Glinyany, he was informed that the inquirer had done accordingly and fared well in all his affairs.[10]

Before I turn to the few responsa dealing with more practical issues, I should like to mention Shapira's curious reply to an observation of literary criticism made by Rabbi Gershon Lange, an assessor at the rabbinate of Frankfurt. Lange expressed his surprise at a comparison proposed by the Maggid of Kozienice between the view of Maimonides and a passage in the Zohar. According to Shapira, there can be no reason for surprise because there are many places in the code of Maimonides whose source is the Zohar.[11]

A strict adherence to commonly held views characterizes the few responsa concerning public and private affairs. One from Sanok dated 15 Adar 1924 is addressed to Rabbi Joseph Moshkowicz of Istryk, who reported about a woman married to a certain Rabbi Judah. The woman had fallen in love with a Gentile, by whom she had a daughter, but she now desired to return to Jewish ways, claiming that the Gentile had bewitched her. Her husband and family were ready to take her back, because they were afraid that if her husband divorced her she would convert to Christianity. Shapira answers that she cannot be granted permission to return to her husband but that the family should support her with a sum of money so that she can accept a divorce and be able to remarry and repent properly.[12]

A letter dated Elul 1925, and thus written in Piotrków, is addressed to the great rabbis "Hasidim and men of praxis" in Cracow. It deals with the question of autopsies. The head of the Prosectorium had demanded that Jewish corpses be supplied. Jewish students also asked permission to perform autopsies on Jewish bodies, arguing that autopsies were designed to advance medical studies and so help to save human lives, and that a refusal would result in the exclusion of Jewish students from the schools of medicine and consequently

10. Ibid., no. 6.
11. Ibid., no. 31, and addition in the index.
12. Ibid., no. 38.

weaken their attachment to Judaism. Shapira answers that the issue had been discussed the previous year at a conference in Warsaw attended by a committee of the rabbis of Warsaw. He writes, "We decided in the negative," and "I wrote at that time an extensive responsum and I am copying here parts of it." He quotes, of course, the responsa by Rabbi Yehezkel Landau, the famous Noda Beyehudah, and that of Rabbi Jacob Ettinger of Altona and also the view of "anonymous," a *lek* (trivial man) who was satisfied if parts of the body were buried after the examination. Shapira firmly opposes such permissiveness. He concludes his deliberations with a sharp rebuttal of the argument that refusing to supply autopsies might alienate students from Judaism. If this demand were met, it could result in the wholesale abolition of all religious restrictions and commandments. The strength of the Torah has proved itself in face of greater dangers.[13] These words recall the intervention of Rabbi Shapira during the second convention of the Agudah in 1923. When the speaker A. Z. Frydman sounded an impassioned plea that the living Torah be adapted to today's needs, Shapira interrupted him and said that surely he meant that life had to adjust to Torah.[14]

I found a reaction to this view on autopsy in the collection of responsa *Porat Yosef* by Rabbi Joseph Halevi Zweig of Potok Złoty. In his introduction the author describes the plight and sufferings of his community during the war years and the difficulties he faced after the war in sustaining his family, so that he was forced to turn to townspeople of the city who had emigrated to the United States and had invited him to that country and supported him. In his letter to Shapira dated 1928, Zweig writes that although he had read his attack upon the rabbi who had expressed a different opinion, he does feel obliged to propose a partial solution to the question raised, especially as the situation had gotten worse and the opposition to autopsies was already serving as pretext for acts of terror against Jewish students. In an additional note he explains that in 1932 legislation was passed regarding the supply of Jewish corpses for Jewish students.[15] The stand taken by Rabbi Shapira may demonstrate that involvement in organizational and religious party life did not necessarily create greater acquiescence to "problems of the day" than seen in rabbis removed from any such involvement.

---

13. Ibid., no. 74.
14. Quoted in Bacon, *Agudat Yisrael in Poland*, forthcoming.
15. Joseph Halevi Zweig, *Porat Yosef* (Bilgoraj, 1933), no. 17.

To this category belongs certainly Rabbi Avraham Yaakov Horowitz of Probużna in the area of Tarnopol. Born in 1864, he lived to
witness the first outrageous weeks of the Nazi occupation. Two
weeks after his death in 1942 his entire family was deported to
Bełżec. The rich collection of his responsa, *Zur Yaakov*, is in the best
classical tradition. He does not withhold his opinion under the pretext of *yirat horaah* (fear of decision). One responsum is directed to
Rabbi Meir Shapira. Horowitz thanks Shapira for sending him his
book, but his reaction to the proposed interpretations are not more
favorable than those of the above-mentioned son-in-law of the Hafez
Hayim.[16]

Rabbi Horowitz's responsa, reflecting varied aspects of life and its
perplexities, are a mine of information. In a responsum to an inquiry by Rabbi Israel Landau of Złoczów, Horowitz takes a strong
stand against a rabbi (*hakham ehad*) who wanted to allow battening
of fowl despite the custom that forbids it. This rabbi reasoned that
if the practice were not permitted, those with commercial interests
would persist in it and would not perform the *shehitah* (ritual slaughter). In his reply Horowitz states that there is no reason to care
about the religious well-being of transgressors. The principle to be
applied is "batten the wrongdoer and let him die."[17]

Such expressions of a principle are rare in Rabbi Horowitz's responsa. Most of them reflect the problems of individuals, a number
of which are aberrations or have a sensational character. There is a
case of a young woman who found life with her husband impossible
and left him and returned to the house of her parents in Olesko.
After two years she was asked to appear before a local rabbinical
court, but she refused. Her family, violent people, threatened the
local rabbi. Horowitz advised that she be summoned before the
court of the rabbi of Lwów or of Brody. The local court followed
this advice but without success. The registered letters were returned
with the statement that the addressee had refused to receive the
postcard on which the summons was written. The question faced
by the court was whether such a refusal would be sufficient grounds
for declaring the husband exempt from the *herem* (ban) of Rabbi
Gershom and allowing him to remarry. Horowitz recalls that many
years ago he received a responsum from the Gaon of Brzeżany,

16. Avraham Yaakov Horowitz, *Zur Yaakov* (Bilgoraj, 1936), no. 50.
17. Ibid., no. 6.

Rabbi Shalom Mordechai Shvadron of blessed memory, in which he quoted the author of the codex *Knesset ha-gedolah,* Rabbi Hayim Benvenisti, that absolution from the *herem* may be granted only if the woman refused to appear before a court in the presence of two witnesses. While Rabbi Moses Sofer accepts this view, Horowitz, following a distinction formulated by Rabbi Hayim Halberstam, the Sandezer Rebbe, considers the *herem* of Rabbi Gershom not as a Torah-based *herem* but only a ban of the Sages, which means that in case of doubt a lenient attitude is justified. Horowitz states that the view of Rabbi Hayim Benvenisti may be disregarded concerning the ban of Rabbi Gershom, like similar opinions of Sephardi codifiers, because, he explains, "We Ashkenazim are better informed about it." A refusal in the presence of one witness, or even of a Gentile who reports it inadvertently, suffices to justify an absolution from the *herem.*[18]

In another case concerning the *herem,* Rabbi Horowitz takes a much stricter stand. A case brought to his attention by Rabbi Joshua Widerkehr of Przemyśl concerns a Jewish prisoner of war in Moscow who met a non-Jewish girl. She agreed to marry him, and he brought her to an enlightened rabbi, who converted her on the basis of her declaration that she would be faithful to Judaism. But when the young Jew took her with him to Przemyśl, she continued to behave like a Christian. She then fell ill and was confined in a hospital for the insane in Lwów. The rabbi of Przemyśl visited her in the hospital and was informed by the physician in charge that she was suffering from an incurable illness. The husband wanted to remarry, and the rabbi of Przemyśl was inclined to grant his permission without invoking the required confirmation of a hundred rabbis, but he asked Rabbi Horowitz for his opinion. Horowitz's answer proves again that he was sensitive to the realities of life. He states that he knows many cases of mixed marriages in which a Jew asks for the conversion of his intended bride only because of the insistence of his parents. Such conversions are not of much worth, but in the present case the man himself took the initiative, so it would seem that at the time of the marriage the couple had decided to lead a Jewish life. Subsequent developments cannot impinge upon the act of the past. Besides, Horowitz declares, he does not know much about the religious character of the man (thus indicating the

18. Ibid., no. 12.

possibility that he was trying to discredit his wife and was not asking for the divorce out of religious conviction). Horowitz therefore is of the opinion that the permission of a hundred rabbis is to be required.[19]

In a responsum to Rabbi David Reis of Kołomyja, Horowitz reiterates this position. He states that under the prevailing conditions, he rejects the decision of Rabbi Reis in a case of a husband who accused his wife of failure to observe the laws of purity. Reis regarded this as a reason to allow the husband to remarry without the necessary approbation of a hundred rabbis. Horowitz argues that the complaint cannot be genuine as the husband himself belongs to progressive circles. A different argument once used by the Noda Beyehudah, he says, cannot be applied to the modern people of our own day. Horowitz gives similarly negative answers to Rabbi Aryeh Leib of Zaleszczyki and to Rabbi David Zeiman of Dukla.[20]

The conversion of Gentile women married to Jews, which Horowitz mentions in passing, appears in several responsa in the collection *Ahiezer* of Rabbi Hayim Oyzer Grodzinski of Vilna. In the latest, from 1934, Grodzinski takes a position different from that at the beginning of the century. Although he approves the opinion of the inquirer that an honest court should not perform such conversions, he advises him and other "rabbis of this generation" not to raise their voice against them, since the lay people will consider such protest as *hilul ha-shem* (desecration of the name of God).[21]

Much more attention than that paid to the demands of husbands of the kind mentioned is given in numerous responsa to the plight of women who lived in uncertainty about the fate of their husbands who had served in World War I and later in the Polish army during the Bolshevik invasion of Poland in 1920. The problem of the *agunot* (anchored women) and questions connected with the means of legally establishing the deaths of missing spouses fill volumes of responsa in different periods and countries, but it became acute in the aftermath of the First World War. The correctness of reports of comrades on the battlefield and of prisoners of war who returned from Russia and the reliability of official documents and death certificates are all widely discussed in the collection of Rabbi Horowitz's correspondence with rabbis in various towns and countries.

19. Ibid., no. 24.
20. Ibid., nos. 17, 75, 76.
21. Hayim Oyzer Grodzinski, *Ahiezer,* vol. 3 (Vilna, 1939), no. 28.

In all these responsa Rabbi Horowitz's inclination is clearly discernible. He adopts the rule formulated by Rabbi Meir Arik: "In all questions concerning *agunot* we should proceed in the ways of our Holy Sages and not look for superfluous restrictions, which may lead to the chaining of thousands of women."[22] But leniency was not a matter of principle with either of them. In a letter to Rabbi Hayim Oyzer Grodzinski, Horowitz strongly opposes proposals published in a pamphlet by a certain Rabbi Joseph Shapotshnik in London on the topic of *halizah* (levirate), refuting each of his arguments in turn. Horowitz voices similar criticism of a decision given in a case concerning a *halizah* that occurred in Sosnowiec.[23] Rabbi Meir Arik shares the same approach on this question. Complete disregard of religious law and Jewish ways by a person living in New York is not recognized by him as sufficient reason for acquitting the widow of his brother from the duty of *halizah,* as even an extreme transgressor is considered as a Jew.[24]

Neither strictness nor leniency consistently characterize traditional literature in interwar Poland. Rabbi Horowitz approves the action taken by Rabbi Shraga Willig of Buczacz, who refused to allow the circumcision of a child born to a *kohen* who had married a divorced woman despite the prohibition and refused to divorce her. On the other hand, he permits an abortion to be performed in a case where expert opinion has shown that the birth would endanger the mother. On another occasion he was consulted by members of a *shtibl* (prayer house) that prohibited members who shaved their beards from being called up to the Torah. This rule caused opposition and quarrels, and Rabbi Horowitz was asked whether it could be abolished. His answer was that if the rule caused strife in the synagogue, the peace should be preserved, for "great is peace."[25]

The economic stress of the postwar and depression years also figures in the work of Rabbi Horowitz and his contemporaries. In a responsum dated 12 Marheshvan 1925, Horowitz deals with the question of Rabbi Eliezer Joshua of Raków as to whether a person who is in great need is allowed to sell a Torah scroll in his private possession. Rabbi Horowitz answers that only if the man has ab-

---

22. Meir Arik, *Imre Yosher,* vol. 2 (Cracow, 1925), no. 145.
23. Horowitz, *Zur Yaakov,* no. 128. Rabbi Joseph Shapotshnik declared in *Herut olam* (London, 1928) that his proposals had been distorted by the press.
24. Arik, *Imre Yosher,* vol. 2, no. 126.
25. Horowitz, *Zur Yaakov,* nos. 93, 141, 100.

solutely nothing with which to sustain himself should the principle
of *pikuah nefesh* (obligation to save life) be applied, but even then
only with certain stipulations. Some of the money realized from the
sale should be used for buying books. The man might also ask for
a loan or pawn the scroll in the hope that his situation will improve
and he can repay the loan and recover the scroll.[26]

The restabilization of the *złoty* in 1926 is reflected in a question
from that time concerning a person who agreed to acquire a sum
of dollars from another at the rate of eleven *złotys* per dollar. Subsequently the purchaser reneged on his agreement, as the value of
the dollar dropped.[27] The change in the monetary system in the first
years after the war prompted many such questions. Collectors of
donations for the poor in Eretz Israel had failed to exchange German
marks at the date fixed by the government. Rabbi Meir Arik declares
the collectors responsible for the loss incurred and obliges them to
refund the money. In another responsum directed to Rabbi Hayim
Graff in the Hague, Rabbi Meir Arik deals with a much more complicated business transaction in which the currency of the Nether-
lands, German marks, old Russian rubles, and the new worthless
currency of Russia are invoked.[28]

In the 1920s railroad passengers were often plagued by theft.
Rabbi Aron Hoffen of Jezupol inquired of Rabbi Horowitz whether
it is permitted to use a *talit* (prayer shawl) and *tefillin* (phylacteries)
bought from people suspected of dealing in stolen goods. The rightful owner would have reason to expect that no one but Jews would
buy such items and therefore would neither lose hope of regaining
them nor relinquish claim to ownership. On the other hand, he
might relinquish it if he assumed that the thieves would burn such
objects.[29]

An interesting example of the effect of inflation on religious matters that also reflects moral sensibility is a responsum of Rabbi Meir
Arik. Rabbi Yehezkel Landau of Leżajsk asked about a person who
vowed during the illness of his wife that, if she recovered, he would
pay for the wedding of a young orphan virgin. Due to inflation, the
amount had now reached a very high sum, and he asked whether
he would have fulfilled his vow if he supplied the need of a divorced

26. Ibid., no. 1.
27. Ibid., no. 67.
28. Arik, *Imre Yosher,* vol. 2, nos. 145, 151.
29. Horowitz, *Zur Yaakov,* no. 66.

relative who was about to remarry. Rabbi Arik's decision was negative. A divorced woman, even if she is an orphan, is supposed to know how to take care of herself and does not fall in the category of orphans. The person who took the vow is obliged to fulfill it as it stands and if necessary should even sell some of his possessions in order to obtain the requisite sum.[30]

A similar sensibility formulated as Halakhah is displayed in a responsum of Rabbi Zvi Aryeh Frommer, known as the Kozilgower Rav because he served for a time as rabbi of this community. The Gerer Rebbe, Abraham Mordechai Alter, asked his opinion whether a person who entreats another for a gift is transgressing the commandment "Thou shall not covet." That is the opinion of Rabbi Jonah Girondi in his treatise *Shaarei teshuvah,* but the Gerer Rebbe asks whether it could not be regarded as the single opinion of a moralist. The Kozilgower Rav replies that even if this decision had not been uttered by Rabbi Jonah, it is self-evident and a logical conclusion from the decisions of Maimonides and the Shulhan Arukh that a person who covets an object in the possession of someone else and importunes him or sends friends to induce him to sell it to him is transgressing the Tenth Commandment. If this is the case when he pays for the object, how much more so if he induces the owner to give it to him as a gift.[31]

The responsa in the collections discussed thus far prove that their authors remain in the tradition of the great respondents of the sixteenth and seventeenth centuries in Poland, like Solomon Luria, Moses Isserlein, and Joel Sirkis, who followed their predecessors in medieval Germany and Spain. They combine a thorough analysis of the sources with an eye on changing conditions in everyday life, the social order, and contemporary psychology, and, above all, they all evince a determination not to shrink from giving decisions. The same may be said about the responsa *Mahze Avraham* by Rabbi Avraham Menahem Steinberg of Brody, the three-volume responsa *Ahiezer* by Rabbi Hayim Oyzer Grodzinski of Vilna, and *Zekan Aharon* by Rabbi Aharon Walkin of Pinsk.[32]

I have found these observations valid for responsa in the sphere of private law, family life, the laws of marriage, divorce, inheritance,

---

30. Arik, *Imre Yosher,* vol. 2, no. 98.
31. Zvi Aryeh Frommer, *Eretz ha-zvi* (Lublin, 1938–39), no. 3.
32. Avraham Menahem Steinberg, *Mahze Avraham* (Brody, 1927); Grodzinski, *Ahiezer;* Aharon Walkin, *Zekan Aharon* (Pinsk, 1932).

and others of that nature, as well as in those concerned with issues resulting from the critical economic situation. For Jews, Poland's economic problems were aggravated by legislation aimed against them, such as the restrictions on ritual slaughter that were ostensibly imposed for humanitarian reasons but actually motivated by a wish to exclude the Jews from the meat trade. Legislation declaring Sunday as the sole day of rest likewise exacerbated the economic difficulties Jews faced and prompted deliberations about the religious status of those who could not observe the Sabbath. Some difficulties were caused by local anti-Jewish initiatives. Encouraged by the clergy, Gentiles in Kosów refused to do any work for Jews on the Sabbath; the local clergy ordered, for example, that no one should milk cows owned by Jews. In a responsum of 1925, Rabbi Walkin of Pinsk tries very hard to find a way that could help to ease the situation, but he asks the support of other authorities for his proposed solution.[33]

Problems connected with new inventions and technology increasingly find their way into the responsa: the use of electricity on the Sabbath and holidays, especially when Jews shared the ownership of an electricity plant;[34] leaving the radio switched on on the Sabbath in order to listen to music.[35] These kinds of questions were asked mainly by Orthodox rabbis in the West.[36] Rabbi Israel Yitzhak Piekarski of Zurich asked Rabbi Frommer whether a *kohen* is permitted to fly in an airplane that may pass over cemeteries. The respondent puts forward many reasons for permitting the flight and implies that he thinks the question trivial. The speed, he writes, of the airplane leaves no time for the impurity of the cemetery to spread to the airplane because—and he quotes Proverbs 23:5—''before your eyes are upon that, it is no more.''[37]

On the question whether poultry produced by artificial incubation is kosher, the Kozilgower Rav cites the investigations of scientists in order to distinguish between the results of this process and that of natural hatching. This modern approach does not prevent him from adding a kabbalistic explanation of his position.[38]

---

33. Walkin, *Zekan Aharon*, no. 17.
34. Arik, *Imre Yosher*, vol. 2, no. 25; Grodzinski, *Ahiezer*, vol. 3, no. 60.
35. Frommer, *Eretz ha-zvi*, no. 64.
36. Walkin, *Zekan Aharon*, no. 13.
37. Frommer, *Eretz ha-zvi*, no. 93.
38. Ibid., no. 104.

Questions concerning community organization or the status of rabbis *vis-à-vis* the communities and their leaders do not take up much space in the responsa. I could find only few examples. A responsum in *Zur Yaakov* deals with the questions whether the rabbi, the *av bet din* (presiding judge), has the authority to introduce ordinances without the consent of the chosen representatives of the community and whether the representatives may adopt such regulations without asking the opinion of the rabbi. Horowitz answers that the rabbi is authorized to issue temporary regulations without the consent of the community if circumstances demand it, but he is not permitted to do so on a permanent basis unless he was given the mandate at the time of his appointment to introduce ordinances without asking for the consent of the majority of his community.[39]

Rabbi Horowitz's responsum does not mention the name of the petitioner, but it is addressed to the "noble, God fearing community of Frankfurt." We are, however, in a position to identify the petitioner as the *Austrittsgemeinde* (separatist community), as the same question appears in *Zekan Aharon*. Dated Shavuot 1929, it is directed to "my friend Rabbi Yaakov Rosenheim in Frankfurt," leader of the Agudah, who was well known to Rabbi Walkin of Pinsk. More details of the question are given in *Zekan Aharon*. The community council proposed to include in the contract with the newly appointed rabbi a paragraph stating that decrees and bylaws, especially those concerning the relations with other communities and organizations (*Gemeinde politische Angelegenheiten*) should not be adopted by the rabbi without the consent of the community. But some members objected to this condition because it contradicted an older standing rule that said the elected rabbi is the only legal religious authority in the community (*Die einzige religionsgesetzliche Autorität der Gemeinde*).[40]

The decision given by Rabbi Walkin differs from that of Rabbi Horowitz. Walkin says he can see no reason for preventing the present community council from introducing a new regulation that abolishes a previous one, even if those who issued it were "greater in wisdom and in number" (*gedolim ba-Torah u-ve-minyan*). Only if the intention of the previous regulation was to construct "a fence around the law" is the community not allowed to abolish it. But if

---

39. Horowitz, *Zur Yaakov,* no. 47.
40. Ibid.; Walkin, *Zekan Aharon,* no. 54.

refusing to introduce the new clause in the contract is likely to provoke quarrels and conflicts and to endanger the peace of the community, then it would be better to concede to the demand for a new regulation, especially as, in his opinion, the clause does not contradict the older provision. *Die einzige religionsgesetzliche Autorität* cannot mean that the rabbi is an absolute ruler who does not need to consult the elders and nobles of the community. Such a measure of authority was not even granted to Moses. It can only mean that in case of differences of opinion between the rabbi and the community leaders, the rabbi's view, based upon *daat Torah* and *daat notah*, is the final one. Walkin assumes that this is also the intention of the party which asks for the new provision. This approach is correct for purely religious affairs in which the opinion of the rabbi is decisive, but also, "I am convinced," Walkin writes,

> that you should not think differently even when interests that are not directly religious are involved. But, when the rabbi is convinced that it may have negative results in the future, you will not deny his claim to your obedience. Only when *politische Angelegenheiten* are concerned should you propose that the leaders of the community be consulted, and even then you should not deny him the right of decision when a difference of opinion occurs. . . . But if you find that there is a contradiction between the established rule and the new proposal, the council of the community is entitled to abolish the old rule.

Walkin concludes, "You are entitled to introduce the new paragraph into the contract."[41]

The differences between Horowitz and Walkin are not over competence and tradition. They are, rather, the result of different attitudes toward political-religious organization, which in itself was an adaptation of a kind of modernity but often resulted in a professed antimodernity.

The question of inheritance of the post of rabbi has a long history. The rabbinical dynasties in many communities have been the subject of numerous conflicts. Such conflict is dealt with in a responsum by the Koziglower Rav dated 1920. His approach reflects the change taking place in rabbinical status. Rabbi Frommer says that he is well aware of the differences of opinions among those who decide about the right of inheriting "the crown of Torah" (the position of rav). But, notwithstanding the position of his distinguished and admired teacher, the Sochaczewer Rebbe, he is of the opinion that "the crown

41. Walkin, *Zekan Aharon*, no. 54.

of Torah" was heritable in the times when it had not been a source of livelihood but a post of authority based exclusively on recognition. In our days, however, it has become a source of salary, and the rabbinate is no longer a source of "honor and esteem." On the contrary, he says, one who is a scholar and not a rabbi is even more highly respected today because he is independent. The rabbinate is falling into disrespect, and, even for those few rabbis who are respected, their main reason for accepting the position as rav comes out of necessity. They are therefore not different from other community employees, cantors, and ritual slaughterers.[42]

There are similar complaints from Rabbi Aharon Walkin of Pinsk. He, however, accuses the prevailing curriculum in the *yeshivot* of concentrating on only one or two treatises of the Babylonian Talmud and neglecting all the others. He testifies that it has been his sad experience that rabbis were not ashamed to ask him for *semikhah* (ordination) although their knowledge was limited to one part of the Shulhan Arukh—the Yoreh Deah. Not surprisingly, Walkin blames the inclination of rabbis to modernity, as expressed in their sermons. He himself was not untouched by modernity, as his Hebrew style is clearly influenced by modern literature. He was, after all, a student in Wołożyn until 1893. As far back as 1914 he had traveled to the United States, together with Rabbi Meir Hildersheimer of Berlin, on behalf of the Agudah. After the war he used to go to Bad Nauheim and was in close contact, as we have already noticed, with Orthodox rabbis and community leaders in the West. His stand against modernity appears mainly in the responsa sent to them.[43]

The great organizational issues in interwar Poland are sparingly treated in the responsa literature. But this is not to say that, besides interesting themselves in the problems of daily life, with all the difficulties, sorrows, and anxieties encountered by individuals, the authors of the responsa were not affected by the general situation in Poland and the pogroms, riots, and assaults upon Jews. We can discern in their writings the impact of the general atmosphere of political despair in the conduct of Jewish affairs and the rapid pace of secularization and assimilation, even in responsa dealing with specifics. More general allusions are found in the introductions to these collections, some of which read like sermons bearing more or

42. Frommer, *Eretz ha-zvi*, no. 103.
43. Walkin, *Zekan Aharon*, nos. 6, 54.

less comforting messages connected with the national renaissance in Palestine.[44] But others propose practical solutions for the problems facing Polish Jewry. Here let us return for a moment to Rabbi Avraham Yaakov Horowitz. While emphasizing that he knows how difficult economic distress is making it for most Jews to dedicate themselves to the duty of learning Torah, he urges them not only to care for the education of their own children but also for those of others by enabling them to study. The introduction to volume 3 of the responsa of Rabbi Hayim Oyzer Grodzinski was written in 1939, on the edge of destruction. It emits a mournful sound and a feeling of helplessness. "The events we witness," he writes, "are worse than the darkest days of the Middle Ages. Even the beam of light which seemed to shine from the East, from the land of our yearnings, the Holy Land, is now darkened by a heavy cloud." These words refer both to the deterioration of the Jewish situation throughout Europe and to the anti-Jewish outbreaks in Palestine since 1936. The only remedy that Grodzinski has to propose is establishing more traditional schools, and courses for young people and workers and, primarily, strengthening the great *yeshivot* in Lithuania and Poland.[45]

It is a fact that in these difficult interwar years Torah studies in Poland reached a very high standard. Some of the authors of responsa literature, while dealing with practical issues, extend the range of their discussions and the variety of their sources to the point that the works become independent treatises. The responsa of the Kozilgower Rav belong to this category. We have seen that collections given the title of responsa may actually be no more than an exchange of correspondence. The more profound, however, contain discussions of difficult passages in talmudic and rabbinical literature that at first sight may seem to have nothing to do with any applicable results. But a deeper investigation reveals that, although dealing with abstract concepts and topics immaterial to the day, they disclose principles that can also answer practical questions. An outstanding example of this type of work are the responsa *Zera Avraham*, an exchange of correspondence between Rabbi Menahem

44. Following the declaration of the San Remo Conference, we find such homilies in *Kovez drushim*, nos. 1 and 5, by Rabbi Segalowicz of Mława, and in nos. 2 and 18 by Abraham Halevi Epstein of Sokoły. See also Meir Yehiel Halevi Halshtik, *Meir einei hakhamim*, ed. Yehiel Reuven Mandelbaum (New York, 1950), p. 52.
45. Horowitz, introd. to *Zur Yaakov*, p. 1; Grodzinski, *Ahiezer*, introd. to vol. 3 (1939), n.p.

Zemba, head of the Metivta in Warsaw, and Rabbi Abraham Luftbir, the son-in-law of the famous Rabbi Meir Simha of Dvinsk, the author of the *Or sameah*.[46]

On another plane, an exaggerated quasi-scientific phraseology is used by a Rabbi Samuel Fliskin in the jubilee volume dedicated to the *rosh yeshivah* (principal) of Grodno, Rabbi Shimon Yehudah Shkop, whose depth of mind, clarity of logic, and sharpness of intellect are described as "a tele-microscope which discovered the atom of reason"; "while probing the microbes of logic," he is no more or no less than a "talmudic Koch."[47] There is no need to point out the naïveté of this "modern" description of the method used by Rabbi Shkop, who followed methods introduced by Rabbi Hayim Soloveichik. We do not know the reaction of Rabbi Shkop to such a description, but we may deduce it from the short contribution of Rabbi Hayim Oyzer Grodzinski to the volume. Rabbi Grodzinski writes that he is fully convinced that the publication of a jubilee volume as such—a type of celebration not known to the elder rabbis—is also not to the taste of Rabbi Shkop, but as Shkop has taken upon himself the burden of caring for the *yeshivah*, he will suffer it if it brings additional support.[48]

Rabbi Isser Yehudah Unterman, the late chief rabbi of Israel, contributed to the volume reminiscences from his student years at the *yeshivah* in Malecz. He describes in a quite different style the crisis that broke out over the spell cast by the socialist parties upon the young people, who were inclined to be influenced by its slogans and propaganda. Rabbi Shkop realized that there was a need for a new method of learning with an intellectual challenge that could withstand the attractions of profane literature.[49]

As we know, the type of literature described in this essay differs in many ways from modern Hebrew and modern Yiddish literature, yet it represents in no lesser measure a culture and spiritual values not only deeply rooted in tradition and therefore held in high esteem but also enjoyed as an exercise of intellectual endeavor and an op-

46. Menahem Zemba and Abraham Luftbir, *Zera Avraham* (Bilgoraj, 1920).

47. Samuel Fliskin, "Ha-mamzi ha-talmudi," in *Sefer ha-yovel le-Rav Shimon Yehudah Shkop* (Vilna, 1937), p. 72. The reference is to the famous Nobel Prize–winning bacteriologist Robert Koch, whose experiments and observations led to great discoveries in medicine.

48. Hayim Oyzer Grodzinski, "Maamar Gaon Israel," in ibid., p. 11.

49. Isser Yehudah Unterman, "Torah mahzeret al akhsanya shelah," in ibid., pp. 12–20.

portunity to display the capacity for concentration and innovation although relating to sources that have been studied through many generations. This yardstick certainly applies to *Zera Avraham*. The work is introduced by a kind of approbation from the pen of Rabbi Meir Yehiel Halevi Halshtik, the Ostrowiecer Rebbe. After short sentences of praise for both authors, Halshtik continues, "In order that my letter should not be devoid of Torah content, I write what came to my mind when I read responsa 11 and 30."[50] To a stranger the issues involved will appear perhaps oversophisticated or trivial, but to the initiated they were a source of enjoyment and intellectual satisfaction, such as described in the preface to Halshtik's *Meir einei hakhamim*, published posthumously by his pupil Yehiel Reuven Mandelbaum.[51] The same applied to the work of one of his first pupils, Rabbi Samuel Brodt of Lipno and leader of the Mizrahi. His posthumously published collection of responsa, *Sugiot be-kodshim*, is totally faithful to the methods applied by his teacher and known as "the Ostrowiecer way."[52]

An example of enthusiasm and devotion to a specific methodology may be seen in *Mekabzael*, a journal published by a group of students at Yeshivat Hakhmei Lublin in 1937. They write in the introduction:

> We have decided to publish the lectures of our teacher, Rabbi Aryeh Frommer, lest they be lost and forgotten by us, but we do it also for the benefit of students in other places in order to offer them an opportunity to acquaint themselves with the truth of Yeshivat Hakhmei Lublin. Thus they, like ourselves, will come to recognize the difference between our previous way of learning, which lacked order and was full of thistles, and our present way, which we acquired since we drank from the well of living water of our teacher.[53]

This essay has touched on only one segment of the traditional literature and has not exhausted even that segment in scope or quantity. A thorough, critical study of the traditional literature of interwar Poland, in all its ramifications, is an urgent task. At present we still stand before a relatively unexplored territory. This literature offers a perspective that should be opened up and integrated in a consistent way into our view of the history of Polish Jewry during the interwar period. While it is only natural that scholars should be

50. Meir Yehiel Halevi Halshtik, introd. to Zemba and Luftbir, *Zera Avraham*.
51. Mandelbaum, preface to Halshtik, *Meir einei hakhamim*.
52. Samuel Brodt, *Sugiot be-kodshim* (Jerusalem, 1969).
53. Introd. to *Mekabzael*, 1937, n.p.

primarily occupied with research in their own field, it seems essential to consider how to build bridges that may lead to a reworking of some of our conceptions concerning social and cultural changes and the aspects of tradition. The pieces of knowledge that our different approaches contribute cannot be used simply as historical additives. But awareness of their existence, and efforts to integrate them into the main structure, may diminish the tendency to flatten out historical processes into a one-dimensional frame.

The richness of Jewish life in interwar Poland and its tragic fate are richly documented. The continuing impact of this history upon large segments of our people, notwithstanding all the manifold changes occurring since, make it imperative to keep the record free, so far as possible, from prejudice, distortion, or mythology. We owe this obligation to the past, but no less to our present and future.

David E. Fishman

The Musar Movement in Interwar Poland

To date, the study of Jewish Orthodoxy in interwar Poland has focused on the ideology and activity of its political organization, Agudat Israel, whose primary function was to represent Orthodox Jewish interests in public forums such as the Sejm (House of Deputies), local municipalities, and *kehillot* (Jewish community councils).[1] The religious life and thought of Orthodoxy—its Hasidic courts and Lithuanian *yeshivot*; its synagogues, *khevres* (fraternal societies), and the rabbinate; developments in mysticism, messianism, and talmudic learning—have yet to receive scholarly attention. This essay attempts to sketch the portrait of one Orthodox religious current in interwar Poland, the Novaredok Musar movement.[2] The discussion will focus on the structure and scope of the Novaredok movement and on certain new developments in its religious ideology and practice during the interwar period.

The name Novaredok is usually associated with an anecdote about *yeshivah* students entering an apothecary to ask the clerk for nails or, more happily, with Chaim Grade's great novel *Tsemakh Atlas* (published in English as *The Yeshiva*) (1967–68), which revolves around the figure of Tsemakh Atlas, a tormented Novaredok Musarist. Both the folklore surrounding Novaredok and Grade's monumental writings in prose and poetry offer vivid images of this

1. Ezra Mendelsohn, "The Politics of Agudas Yisroel in Inter-War Poland," *Soviet Jewish Affairs* 2, no. 2 (1975): 47–60; Gershon Bacon, *Agudat Yisrael in Poland 1916–1939: The Politics of Tradition*, forthcoming.
2. Although the study of Musar and the cultivation of religious-ethical sensibilities were pursued in most of the large interwar *yeshivot* (e.g., Mir, Raduń), only Novaredok can be considered a *bona fide* Musar movement. This point will be developed at length below. To date, the only survey of Novaredok in interwar Poland has been a rather uncritical overview by one of the movement's own adherents: Yehudah Leyb Nekritz, "Yeshivot Beit Yosef Novaredok," in *Mosdot Torah be-Eropah*, ed. S. K. Mirsky (New York, 1956), pp. 247–90. Rabbi Nekritz headed the Novaredok *yeshivah* in Brooklyn, New York.

current in Jewish religious life, but neither takes the place of historical documentation and analysis. On the contrary, I would argue that the historical study of Novaredok has the added benefit of clarifying and illuminating Grade's unique personal vision of Novaredok Musarism.[3]

The Novaredok *Yeshivah:* Basic Features and Institutions

The *yeshivah* in Novaredok (in Polish, Nowogródek; in Russian, Novogrudok, Minsk gubernia) was founded and headed by Rabbi Yosef Yoizl Hurwitz, a former businessman who had been converted to Musarism by its founding father, Rabbi Israel Salanter.[4] Hurwitz, who studied extensively with Salanter's disciples in Kowno (in Russian and Yiddish, Kovna) and Slobodka, first achieved a measure of notoriety in the 1880s when for several years he secluded himself in a hut in the Zoshen forest. He refused to set foot outside the hut during that time and was fed by a kindly old woman who slid food into his hut through two holes—one for *milkhiks* (dairy) and one for *fleyshiks* (meat). While Salanter's major disciples dissociated themselves from Hurwitz's behavior and viewed him as a misguided eccentric, Hurwitz maintained that his extended isolation from society was necessary in order to combat his evil instincts and passions.[5]

In founding his own *yeshivah* in 1896, Hurwitz was following the lead of other disciples of Salanter who had established schools in Grobiṇa (in Yiddish, Grobin), Slobodka, and elsewhere, where the study of religious-ethical texts was incorporated into the daily regime alongside the study of the Talmud. These schools also featured a new type of religious mentor, the *mashgiekh,* who presented periodic *Musar shmuesn* (discourses on religious ethics) to the students and supervised their religious-ethical growth. The latter might divide responsibilities with a *rosh yeshivah,* who presented the traditional *shiurim* (talmudic discourses). Hurwitz built on the model of the Musar *yeshivot* in Grobiṇa and Slobodka, a model that would

3. I hope to follow this line of inquiry in a separate paper.

4. On Salanter's life and thought, see Immanuel Etkes, *Rabi Israel Salanter ve-reshitah shel tenuat ha-Musar* (Jerusalem, 1982).

5. The major works on Yosef Yoizl Hurwitz are Dov Katz, *Tenuat ha-Musar,* vol. 4 (Tel Aviv, 1963), pp. 179–351; M. Gertz [Gershon Mowshowitz], "Der alter fun Novaredok," in *Musernikes* (Riga, 1936), pp. 21–37; Esriel Karlebach, "Mussar," *Jahrbuch der Jüdisch-Literarischen Gesellschaft* 22 (1931–32): 374–86.

soon spread to *yeshivot* in Telšiai (in Yiddish, Telz), Slutsk, Łomża, Mir, and Raduń as well.[6]

From the very outset, Hurwitz's *yeshivah* in Novaredok differed from the other Musar *yeshivot* in one important respect. There was no *rosh yeshivah* in charge of its talmudic studies. Hurwitz devoted himself to guiding the students' religious-ethical growth through private meetings with them and weekly *Musar shmuesn*, but he did not give *shiurim*. The students studied the Talmud informally, in pairs and small groups. When formal *shiurim* were eventually instituted during the early 1900s, they were delivered by a number of senior students. There was no mentor-model in talmudic learning.[7] This fact, coupled with Hurwitz's dominant presence as mentor in religious-ethical perfection, signaled a clear shift in the traditional scale of values, with religious-ethical perfection taking precedence over the mastery of Torah knowledge.

The *yeshivah*'s curriculum and regime evolved over the years, and became increasingly distinct from those of other *yeshivot*. By the eve of World War I, the differences between Novaredok and Slobodka were substantial. The time formally allotted for the study of Musar was an hour and a quarter[8] (rather than the half hour in other Musar *yeshivot*), and a range of unique Musar activities were conducted regularly. These included:

1. The *birzhe* (literally, stock market), a daily hour designated for the free-wheeling peripatetic exchange of Musar insights. The students would "stroll in pairs across the length and breadth of the hall, full of enthusiasm and lively gesticulation," discussing matters of Musar.[9]

2. The *vaad* (committee): "All the *yeshivah* students were divided

---

6. Shaul Stampfer, "Shalosh yeshivot litaiyot ba-meah ha-19" (Ph.D. diss., Hebrew University, Jerusalem, 1981); and, generally, the essays in Mirsky, ed., *Mosdot Torah be-Eropah*.

7. Katz, *Tenuat ha-Musar,* 4:197–198, 329; Joshua Uvsay, *Reshimot ve-maamarim* (New York, 1946). Uvsay, who studied in Novaredok in 1900, relates: "It was estimated that Hurwitz's level of Torah knowledge was that of an average rabbi. I say 'estimated' because he rarely spoke words of Torah and never stressed his learning" (p. 123).

8. Katz, *Tenuat ha-Musar,* 4:217.

9. The descriptive quotations are from Moshe Silberg, "Kat ha-novardokaim," *Haaretz,* December 26, 1932, p. 2, December 28, 1932, p. 2, published in Yiddish as "Di novardoker," *Yidisher kemfer,* September 1985, Rosh Hoshanah 5746 no., pp. 30–35. Silberg studied in the Novaredok *yeshivah* in 1916, shortly after its relocation to Homel.

into various groups that met once a week to discuss matters of
Musar. Each *vaad* was headed by one or two students . . . who were
its spiritual guides and main speakers."[10]

3. *Protim* or *peules,* exercises designed to cultivate certain positive
character traits or eradicate negative ones. Students were expected
to engage in acts that would forge those moral virtues in which they
found themselves lacking.[11] The proverbial asking for nails in an
apothecary was an exercise in modesty or alternately in developing
the inner fortitude to withstand ridicule.

4. *Asiri koydesh,* a day devoted by the individual student to intro-
spection and self-criticism in seclusion, observed every ten days.
This practice, although not mandatory, was viewed as a sign of one's
devotion to religious-ethical improvement.[12]

Taken together, the expanded time for Musar study, the daily
birzhes, the weekly *vaad* meetings, weekly *Musar shmuesn,* the *asiri
koydesh* once every ten days, and the involvement in *protim* constituted a structured and highly demanding program of Musar activity
that was unparalleled in any other *yeshivah.*

The religious-ethical ideals Hurwitz inculcated in his students
were in themselves quite traditional—kindness, humility, love and
fear of God, and so forth. His novel contribution was a philosophy
of moral extremism. Hurwitz was convinced that the improvement
of one's religious-ethical character could be achieved and sustained
only through radical and extreme acts, not through gradual moderate change. The forces of evil in the human soul were too strong
to allow for any accommodation, no matter how minimal or temporary. Evil traits must either be crushed and uprooted entirely,
through acts of moral heroism, or they would reign supreme. There
was no in-between.[13]

Hurwitz's philosophy of moral extremism guided and permeated
the life-style of the Novaredok *yeshivah.* Its students, taking various
religious and ethical ideals to unrestrained extremes, behaved in an
unconventional manner viewed by outsiders as bizarre, if not insane.

10. Ibid., December 26, 1932, p. 2.
11. Katz, *Tenuat ha-Musar,* 4:255–58.
12. Ibid., p. 219.
13. Ibid., pp. 231–40, 252–61, and passim. I have argued elsewhere that these
Musar activities and the ideology of moral extremism that accompanied them were
adaptations of practices and ideas found in the Jewish labor and revolutionary movement about 1905. See David E. Fishman, "Musar and Modernity: The Case of Novaredok," *Modern Judaism* 8, no. 1 (February 1988): 41–64.

For instance, they adhered to Hurwitz's doctrine of *bitokhn* (confidence in God), which called for *bitokhn le-lo hishtadlus* (confidence in God without any human effort) regarding the satisfaction of material needs such as food, clothing, and lodging. Consequently the students pursued a life of poverty, economic inactivity, and indifference toward material needs. They wore tattered and torn clothes and ate extremely sparse meals, since devoting attention to acquiring money, fine clothing, or food would have indicated a lack of *bitokhn*. The *yeshivah*'s poverty was perpetuated by Hurwitz himself, who was reluctant to engage in active fund raising, since this, too, would have reflected a lack of *bitokhn* on his part.[14]

The ideal of *prishus* (aloofness from the world) was also taken to a new extreme, and contact with the world outside the *yeshivah* was reduced to a minimum. Outsiders were viewed as being utterly immersed in sinfulness, since they did not devote themselves totally to the study of Musar and the improvement of their religious-ethical personality. Hence interaction with them could have a harmful influence on the aspiring Musarist. Religious Jews were no better than heretics in this regard; they, too, were unwittingly enslaved to their evil passions. Hurwitz publicly praised those students who refrained from leaving Novaredok to visit their parents and siblings. He viewed them as having reached a higher level of devotion to Torah and Musar, since even home visits could prove harmful to one's religious-ethical growth. As a result, "All notion of father and mother, wife and child, relatives and family was alien to the Novaredok students."[15]

At this juncture it should be noted that the Novaredok *yeshivah* in many ways resembled a religious sect. It consciously withdrew itself from the world and from society in order to pursue its unique religious agenda; its attitude toward the external world was hostile and uncompromising; it demanded a high level of devotion and involvement from its members—all features characteristic of sectlike religious bodies.[16]

14. Silberg, "Kat ha-novardokaim," *Haaretz*, December 28, 1932, p. 2; Katz, *Tenuat ha-Musar,* 4:336.

15. Katz, *Tenuat ha-Musar,* 4:206; Avrohom Joffin, *Ha-Musar ve-ha-daat*, vol. 2 (Jerusalem, 1973), p. 1; quotation from Silberg, "Kat ha-novardokaim," *Haaretz,* December 28, 1932, p. 2.

16. J. A. Winter, *Continuities in the Sociology of Religion* (New York, 1977), pp. 105–16.

Development and Change: 1915–1922

The years of and immediately after the First World War were a period of important institutional and ideological change for Novaredok. Decisions made at that time, in reaction to the war crisis, had an enduring impact, and they determined basic features of Novaredok Musarism in interwar Poland.

As for the *yeshivah* itself, Hurwitz and the majority of its estimated three hundred students fled from the war zone in 1915, resettling in the Belorussian city of Homel. Shortly thereafter, the *yeshivah* was divided into four groups, three of which were sent on to other cities, where they were headed by Hurwitz's foremost disciples—in Kiev, by Rabbi Dovid Bliacher; in Kharkov, by Rabbi Yisroel Yankev Lubchansky; and in Rostov, by Rabbi Avrohom Zalmanes. The decision to disperse was a tactical necessity. Many of the students were subject to the Russian military draft, and a large assembly of young men would have been conspicuous, prompting repeated searches, arrests, and forced inductions. The dispersal was viewed as a temporary measure, and it was understood that the *yeshivah* would be reunited following the end of hostilities.[17] In fact, however, the division into four "central" *yeshivot* remained intact until 1939.

Meanwhile, a related change occurred in Hurwitz's Musarist ideology. Sensing that the war threatened utterly to destroy the remaining vestiges of Torah and Musar in Jewish society at large, Hurwitz abandoned his doctrine of aloofness and isolation, transmuting it into a doctrine of extreme aggressiveness in the dissemination of Musarism throughout Jewish society. This radical break in Hurwitz's thinking was recalled by his son-in-law, Rabbi Avrohom Joffin, in the following terms:

> What is most wondrous is that at the beginning of the first [world] war, he "altered his order of study." . . . He spoke to [the students] and emphasized to them, that besides their desire and devotion to raise themselves higher in Torah and *yirah* [piety], the time precipitated, and the hour demanded, that they consider themselves men of responsibility and stand in the breach with great courage. And he explained to them, based on the Talmud and common sense, that the fate and survival of the Torah lay in their hands. Most, if not all of them volunteered, and undertook to do all in their power, even to risk their lives, for the sake of the eternal survival of Torah and *yirah*.[18]

17. Katz, *Tenuat ha-Musar*, 4:211–12, 218.
18. Avrohom Joffin, introd. to Yosef Yoizl Hurwitz, *Madregat ha-adam* (Jerusalem, 1964), pp. 3–4. The introduction was first published in the New York, 1947 edition of Hurwitz's book.

In practice, Hurwitz called upon his students in all four centers "to create . . . *yeshivot* and *kibutzim* [study collectives] everywhere—in the cities, the towns, and the villages; to bring the entire younger generation under the banner of Torah and *yirah*." "At this hour," he wrote, referring to the time of war and pogroms, "it is impossible for a person, no matter who he may be, to look only after his own soul."[19]

In response to their master's orders, the Novaredokers threw themselves into an active campaign to recruit students for the four central *yeshivot* (through door-to-door canvasing, public addresses, and so forth) and to establish new *yeshivot* throughout Belorussia and the Ukraine. The Kiev *yeshivah*, for instance, established "branches" in Pereyaslav, Belaya Tserkov, Nezhin, Konotop, and Zolotonosha. According to one estimate, thirty Novaredok *yeshivot* were established in Belorussia and the Ukraine (including a few east of the Volga) between 1915 and 1921.[20] In this period the name Novaredok became synonymous with evangelism for the cause of Torah and Musar. Previously an isolationist religious sect, it now became an aggressive, expansionist religious sect. As one of Hurwitz's disciples put it, "Before the world war, the *yeshivah* was in a period of seclusion, as he [Hurwitz] had been in his first period. . . . But with the outbreak of the world war, it [began] to perform marvels in order to turn the many unto righteousness."[21]

In December 1919, Hurwitz died, and the leadership of his *yeshivah* network was assumed by his scattered disciples, with the Homel *yeshivah* coming under the direction of his son-in-law, Rabbi Avrohom Joffin. In 1921 Soviet authorities initiated an exerted campaign to close the Novaredok *yeshivot*. After consultation, the *yeshivot* decided to cross over into Poland. In the winter of 1921–22 approximately six hundred Novaredok students, from all four centers, smuggled themselves across the Soviet-Polish border—roughly twice as many students as had evacuated to the Ukraine some seven years

19. The quotations are from Hurwitz's letter "to all the Novaredok *yeshivot*" entitled "Mezake et ha-rabim" (To Turn the Many unto Righteousness), which he wrote in 1919. It was subsequently included as the final section in his collected *Musar shmuesn: Madregat ha-adam*. See *Madregat ha-adam*. (Jerusalem, 1970), pp. 235, 237.

20. Y. Shayn, "Yeshivat Mezritsh ha-merkazit ba-tekufah bein shtei milhamot ha-olam," *Kol Israel* (Jerusalem), April 26, 1946, p. 2. The series of articles under this title deal mainly with the history of the Międzyrzec *yeshivah*'s forerunner, the Novaredok *yeshivah* in Kiev.

21. *Or ha-Musar* (reprint, Bnei Brak, 1965), 1:172–73.

earlier. The very last Novaredok stronghold in the Soviet Union, the Berdichev *yeshivah*, crossed over to Poland in 1925.[22]

From *Yeshivah* to Movement

Following their border crossings into Poland, the Novaredok central *yeshivot* did not reunite but remained separate and autonomous institutions. The Homel *yeshivah*, headed by Joffin, settled in Białystok, and the Kiev *yeshivah* reestablished itself in Międzyrzec (in Yiddish, Mezritsh). A third center was created in Warsaw by Rabbi Avrohom Zalmanes (formerly head of the Rostov *yeshivah*), and a fourth, led by Rabbi Shmuel Weintraub (formerly head of the Berdichev *yeshivah*), wandered from one city to another until it settled in Pinsk in 1928. All four named themselves Beys Yosef after their master Rabbi Yosef Yoizl Hurwitz.

It is interesting that no serious consideration was given to returning to the prewar structure of *one* Novaredok *yeshivah*. Several factors rendered such reunification extremely difficult, if not impossible. First, the financial burden of maintaining a single *yeshivah* with six to seven hundred (nearly twice the size of the renowned *yeshivah* in Mir at its peak), would have been formidable. Furthermore, there was no clear-cut agreement as to which of Hurwitz's sons-in-law (Joffin, Lubchansky) or disciples (Bliacher, Zalmanes, and others) should succeed him as the spiritual leader of "all Novaredok." Institutional rivalry and inertia favored the perpetuation of the existing *yeshivot*, with their separate leadership structures. Finally, Novaredok's ideological commitment to "turn the many unto righteousness" seemed to be best served by maintaining a decentralized structure.

In interwar Poland, the name Novaredok referred not to a single *yeshivah* in the town by that name but to its heirs, the four central Beys Yosef *yeshivot*, each in a different province and with its own satellite *yeshivot ketanot* (junior *yeshivot*) under its supervision. Each center was essentially autonomous and self-sufficient, caring for its own financial needs and setting its own institutional policies.

Nonetheless the *menahelim* (educational and administrative heads) and students did feel bound to each other by virtue of their common master and his teachings. Their shared aloofness from the world

22. Katz, *Tenuat ha-Musar,* 4:221–29.

outside their *yeshivot* also helped preserve their sense of cohesion. It is therefore not surprising that the four central *yeshivot* maintained ties with each other after their resettlement in Poland.

The most important forum for contact between the four central *yeshivot* and an affirmation of their spiritual unity were the periodic Novaredok conventions. These events, ten of which were held in the interwar years, were attended by the *menahelim* of the central *yeshivot* and Hurwitz's other major disciples. The idea itself was not new; Hurwitz had convened a similar gathering in Homel in December 1917 in order to bring together his dispersed disciples. But in interwar Poland the Novaredok convention became a regular institution.[23]

A Novaredok convention was more than a great big *birzhe* at which Musar insights were exchanged among those in attendance. Its programs consisted of more than a series of *Musar shmuesn* by the *menahelim*. (Needless to say, both such events were featured as well.) It was the forum at which the Novaredokers attempted to set a common spiritual agenda: what religious-ethical characteristics required special attention; where, when, and how the study of Musar should be conducted; where new branch *yeshivot* should be set up; what sort of ties should exist between the branch *yeshivot* and their centers; and so on.

In many respects the conventions bore an uncanny resemblance to the conventions of modern Jewish movements and organizations. Each *yeshivah* was represented by its own official delegates. The gathering featured deliberations and debates that culminated in the passage of resolutions. The Novaredok Musar calendar, for example, discussed at length below, was passed as a resolution at the March 1925 convention. A *vaad ha-poel* (executive committee) was appointed to supervise the enactment of decisions, and specialized *komisyes* (commissions) were formed to deal with particular problems.[24] These formal and procedural elements vividly reflected the transformation of Novaredok into a religious *movement*, with the trappings of a modern movement or political party. But unlike Agudat Israel, the Novaredok movement restricted itself to questions of religious-spiritual life as it was to be lived by its members.

23. For a report on the first convention in Poland in the summer of 1923, see *Or ha-Musar*, 1:52–53. On the 1917 convention, see Katz, *Tenuat ha-Musar*, 4:216–19; Silberg "Kat ha-navardokaim," *Haaretz*, December 28, 1932, p. 2.
24. *Or ha-Musar*, 1:167–70.

The transformation of Novaredok from a *yeshivah* into a movement was also reflected in the creation of an internal hierarchical structure. The leaders and activists of the Beys Yosef *yeshivot* were now formally organized in *agudot* (councils) beginning with the Agudah Merkazit (Central Council) or Agudah Rishonah (First Council), which consisted of the *menahelim* of the central *yeshivot*. Further down the line, each individual *yeshivah* had a council made up of its faculty (the *menahel, rosh yeshivah,* and so forth), and a second council for its senior students. All such councils, whether central or local, held periodic meetings to examine their personal spiritual conditions as well as the spiritual state of their *yeshivah* or *yeshivot*. The meetings routinely ended with the passage of resolutions concerning its members as individuals and their respective *yeshivot*.[25]

Besides adopting certain institutional and structural features of a modern movement, Novaredok also adopted the standard medium of internal communication for a modern movement—the official organ or in-house journal. Entitled *Or ha-Musar* (The Light of Musar), the Hebrew-language journal presented itself (on its title page) as the "organ of the holy Beys Yosef *yeshivot* of Novaredok in Poland; devoted to matters of piety, Musar, and work among the public; edited by the Central Council of the Novaredok *yeshivot* . . . Warsaw." Fifteen issues of *Or ha-Musar* appeared between 1922 and 1933.[26] They featured Musar discourses by the *menahelim* of the central *yeshivot*, writings by Rabbi Israel Salanter and other founding fathers of Musarism, and—last but not least—Novaredok news. *Or ha-Musar* regularly reported on the latest convention, printed the text of its resolutions, noted the meetings of the Central Council (and other high-level councils), and announced the establishment of new *yeshivot*. It was succeeded by another in-house journal of similar content, *Hayei ha-Musar* (The Life of Musar) (1935–39).

The creation of conventions, officers (for that is what the council members were), and in-house journals transformed Novaredok into a modern organization. One need only compare the Novaredok Musarists to the numerous Hasidic groupings in interwar Poland to appreciate the novelty of such practices. With the exception of Lu-

25. See the report of the meetings of the Central Council and other councils in *Or ha-Musar,* 2:54, 99–100.

26. The first seven issues of *Or ha-Musar* were in hectograph and are rare collectors' items. Numbers 14 (April 1931), 15 (1933), and 16 (September 1938) were published by the Beys Yosef center in Palestine.

bavitch, no Hasidic group, no matter how numerous or scattered its Hasidim, resorted to such modern tools as conventions or in-house journals to unify its adherents. It is striking that Novaredok, a stridently sectarian group that kept the outside world at a distance and viewed it with hostility, imitated—whether consciously or unconsciously—the organizational structure of worldly movements and political parties. This feature suggests the pervasive influence of modernity in Polish-Jewish society in the 1920s, even in its most "unworldly" corners.

Expansion and Growth

The new generation of Novaredok leaders who crossed over into Poland held fast to the ideology of aggressive evangelism that Hurwitz had embraced in 1915. There were apparently no voices in favor of returning to the isolation and introversion of prewar Novaredok. The sense of crisis regarding the survival of Torah and Musar that had become an ingrained feature of Novaredok thinking during the years of war, pogroms, and Soviet rule did not dissipate following the migration to Poland. In fact, the tenor of Polish Jewish life that the Novaredokers discovered in 1922 may only have intensified their sense of crisis. The secular currents in Jewish politics, culture, and education had grown by leaps and bounds between 1915 and 1922, owing to the relative freedom afforded Jews under the German occupation and the new Polish state. Most ominous from the Novaredokers perspective were the secular Jewish schools—Tarbut, Tsentrale Yidishe Shul Organizatsye (TSYSHO, Central Yiddish School Organization), and others—which now openly competed with traditional forms of Jewish education. The latter may have come to the Novaredokers as a jolting shock, since they had been cut off from Poland and its Jews during the years when these new educational institutions had come into being and multiplied. To their minds, the mortal danger to Torah and Musar had not subsided at all but had assumed a new and more treacherous form. Writing in 1937, Joffin recalled: "We saw that the education of the youth had fallen greatly. The old *heder*—where Jewish children were raised on the Bible, Talmud, and commentaries, and aspired to go to a *yeshivah*—had become a forgotten word. In its place came the schools of the secularists, which do not teach the Bible or Mishnah, and, furthermore, stuff [the children] with deceitful opinions and secular views." The only proper Novaredok response was the one practiced in Russia. "The hour has come," an early issue of *Or ha-Musar* editorialized, "to build and plant *yeshivot* in all the dispersion of Israel . . . and to save from death, God forbid, the youths who are caught in the trap of the secularists."[27]

The *menahelim* of the four central *yeshivot* used *Musar shmuesn* and other public appearances to energize their students into action. They portrayed the creation of *yeshivot* as an act of salvation, which had the power of rescuing whole communities from spiritual destruction and damnation.

> If a *yeshivah* had been founded in the city where the boy named Trotsky grew up—may his name and memory be erased; his political machinations have caused the destruction of a third of the world's Judaism—then perhaps we would not have reached such a state of devastation. And if this is so, then those who could have built a *yeshivah* there and did not do so will be judged for the consequences of their laziness. For perhaps the *yeshivah* would have saved that boy.

> We must not be satisfied with rescuing the individual, just as he [Hurwitz] was not satisfied with "working on himself." He did not seclude himself, for he saw that the hour was not suited for it. He devoted himself tirelessly [to rescuing others] in his old age. . . . How much more so should we, in our youth, awaken our souls to work endlessly, to stand in the breach and bring benefit to others. For he who rescues them is likened to one who rescues a person from the lion's mouth.[28]

Throughout the interwar years, the Novaredok centers expended strenuous efforts on establishing Beys Yosef *yeshivot ketanot*, for boys between thirteen and seventeen years of age, in towns across Poland. The foot soldiers in this campaign were the older students of the central *yeshivot*, who set out on missions to various destinations, either individually or in groups. Some of them were designated by the centers as the future *menahelim* or *rashei yeshivot* of the schools they would found, while others assisted in the initial stages of the schools' formation and then returned to their *yeshivah*. According to one memoirist, the central *yeshivot* were abuzz with students coming and going to and from various towns, and it was virtually prohibited

27. Avrohom Joffin, "Oz nidabru" (1937) in *El ha-mevakesh* (reprint, Bnei Brak, 1964), p. 136; "Me-hayei ha-yeshivot," *Or ha-Musar,* 1:54.

28. Dovid Bliacher, *menahel* of Międzyrzec center, quoted in Chaim Ephraim Zaytchik, *Ha-meorot ha-gedolim,* 3d ed. (Jerusalem, 1967), p. 382; David Budnik, "Yudzayin Kislev," *Or ha-Musar,* 1:32–33. Budnik was head of the Warsaw center (with Zalmanes) until his departure for Latvia in 1931.

for an older student to remain in the *yeshivah* without interruption, even if he so wished.[29]

The efforts of the four central *yeshivot* to "turn the many unto righteousness" through the establishment of new *yeshivot ketanot* was spurred on by a healthy measure of institutional rivalry among them. Each branch *yeshivah* (called a *snif*) remained under the close supervision of the center that founded it and was required to send its most advanced students to the center for further study. Thus the establishment of new branch *yeshivot* served as the means by which the *menahelim* in Białystok, Międzyrzec, Pinsk, and Warsaw broadened their respective spheres of influence and enlarged their pools of potential students.

The manner in which the Beys Yosef *yeshivot* were established and maintained and the relations between them and the local Jewish communities are complex subjects that cannot be examined at length in this context. Here I will touch on only a few salient points.

A common tactic employed by the Novaredokers in the establishment of new branches was to simply "occupy" one of the town's study houses or synagogues, often in the middle of the night, without consulting community members or requesting their permission. Congregants might arrive for the regular morning services to find a group of youths occupying some of their seats or benches and announcing that this was the place of a new *yeshivah*. The town residents were usually extremely reluctant to evict youths engaged in Torah study from a study or prayer house. Once the Novaredokers felt that the "captured" position was secure, members of the group would go out to recruit students for the *yeshivah*. With the *yeshivah* firmly in place and local youngsters in attendance, the *menahel* would proceed to seek out local financial support.[30]

The quality of the relations between the Beys Yosef *yeshivot* and their host communities varied considerably, depending on a range of factors (e.g., the personalities of the *menahel* and the local Ortho-

29. Mordkhe Shtrigler, "Farshverer," *Yidisher kemfer,* no. 1551 (April 10, 1964): 8–9. This unfinished historical novella, based on Shtrigler's experiences as a student in the Beys Yosef *yeshivah* in Łuck during the 1930s, contains valuable information and insights on the Novaredok movement in interwar Poland. It appeared in serialized form in *Yidisher kemfer,* nos. 1550–58 (March 27–May 29, 1964), nos. 1572–80 (September 9–November 6, 1964).

30. For instances of such "occupations," see "Yeshivat Beit Yosef," in *Piotrkow Trybunalski ve-ha-sevivah,* ed. Yaakov Malts and Naftali Lavi (Lau) (Tel Aviv, 1965), pp. 329–30; A. Z. Tarshish, "Ha-yeshivah be-Pinsk," in *Pinsk,* ed. Nahman Tamir (Mirski) vol. 2 (Tel Aviv, 1966), pp. 259–60; Karlebach, "Mussar," pp. 384–86.

dox leaders), but on the whole the ties were either tenuous or strained. The Novaredok leaders usually spurned contact with local *balebatim* (leading citizens), and the *kehillot* generally did not support the Novaredok schools. The latter were usually dependent upon the aid of a few generous donors, and lack of local support appears to be one reason why so many of the *yeshivot* relocated from one town to another. In at least one instance, in Oszmiana, relations between *yeshivah* and community deteriorated so badly that residents informed on the *yeshivah* to the Polish police, contending that it harbored illegal immigrants from the Soviet Union. (The charge itself was most likely true, since the Novaredokers had crossed the border illegally in 1921–22.) The Beys Yosef *yeshivah* fled town shortly thereafter.[31]

Despite formidable obstacles, the Novaredok *yeshivah* network grew at a remarkably rapid pace between 1922 and 1939. According to figures cited in the movement's internal publications, there were eleven Beys Yosef *yeshivot* (the centers included) in 1924, thirty-five in 1933, and sixty in 1937.[32] The retrospective estimate of Rabbi Ben Zion Bruk that on the eve of the Holocaust the Beys Yosef network encompassed seventy *yeshivot* and three thousand students does not appear to be farfetched.[33] The total number of locales in Poland that housed Novaredok *yeshivot* at one time or another during the interwar years exceeds ninety (see table 1).

A cursory review of table 1 reveals two patterns in Novaredok's spread across Poland. First, Beys Yosef *yeshivot ketanot* were generally established in towns and not in larger urban centers. Notice the absence of Novaredok *yeshivot* in Cracow, Lublin, Lwów, Vilna, Grodno, Slutsk, and Brześć nad Bugiem (in Yiddish, Brisk). This tendency may be due to the fact that a Novaredok *yeshivah* was more capable of generating local support (from the rabbi and others) in

31. Shtrigler, "Farshverer," *Yidisher kemfer,* no. 1557 (May 22, 1964): 8. The hostile relations between the *menahel* of a Beys Yosef *yeshivah* and local *balebatim* are the focus of Shtrigler's story "Yeshivah baah la-ayarah," in *Hadoar* 35, nos. 36–40 (August 17–October 12, 1956). The story, based on events that occurred in Shtrigler's hometown of Zamość, culminates with a violent struggle between the two parties for control over a local study house. On Oszmiana, see Ben Zion Bruk, *Gevilei esh* (Jerusalem, 1973), p. 89.

32. "Me-hayei ha-yeshivot," *Or ha-Musar* 1:52–54, 2:145; Joffin, "Oz nidabru," p. 136.

33. Bruk, *Gevilei esh,* p. 17. Bruk, Novaredok *rosh yeshivah* in Jerusalem, died in 1984. Nekritz's estimate of one hundred *yeshivot* is exaggerated. "Yeshivot Beit Yosef Novaredok," p. 268.

TABLE 1

Beys Yosef *Yeshivot* in Poland, 1922–1939

Place	Number of students	Year	Source
Białystok Center	187	1926	VH, no. 1115
	199	1929	VH, no. 1115
	230	1935	VH, no. 1104
	222	1938	VH, no. 1104
Bielsk Podlaski	60	1926	VH, no. 1116
	52	1929	VH, no. 1116
	44	1938	VH, no. 1104
Brańsk	106	1929	VH, no. 1104
	70	1935	VH, no. 1104
Brody	—		Nekritz, p. 268
Buczacz	—		Nekritz, p. 268
Bursztyn	—		Nekritz, p. 268
Ciechanowiec	—		*OH*, 2:99
Częstochowa	—		Joffin, 2:91
Grajewo	46	192?	VH, no. 1125
	50	1935	VH, no. 1104
	48	1938	VH, no. 1104
Horochów	36	1938	VH, no. 1104
Horodenka	—		Nekritz, p. 268
Jadów	—		Nekritz, p. 268
Kołki	—		Nekritz, p. 268
Kołomyja	—		Joffin, 2:91;
			Nekritz, p. 268
Kosów	—		Nekritz, p. 268
Krynki	60	1935	VH, no. 1104
Luboml	45	1935	VH, no. 1104
	43	1938	VH, no. 1104
Łuck	70	1929	VH, no. 1139
	85	1935	VH, no. 1104
	82	1938	VH, no. 1104
Maków	—		*OH*, 2:145
Ostrów Mazowiecka	ca. 100	1925	*OH*, 1:107
Piotrków	—		Nekritz, p. 268
Przasnysz	—		Nekritz, p. 268
Puławy	—		Nekritz, p. 268
Rożyszcze	—		Nekritz, p. 268
Skidel	38	1929	VH, no. 1104
	40	1935	VH, no. 1104
Sokółka	—		*OH*, 2:53
Święciany	30	1934	*DV,* November 2,
			1934, p. 4
	40	1935	VH, no. 1104
	35	1938	VH, no. 1104
Świsłocz	—		*OH*, 2:145
Szczuczyn	—		Nekritz, p. 268

TABLE 1 (cont.)

Place	Number of students	Year	Source
Tomaszów Lubelski	ca. 80	1925	*OH*, 1:107
Włodzimierzec	143	1926	VH, no. 1164
	155	1932	VH, no. 1104
	120	1938	VH, no. 1104
Wysokie Mazowieckie	ca. 100	1925	*OH*, 1:107
	57	1926	VH, no. 1167
	55	1929	VH, no. 1104
	70	1935	VH, no. 1104
	40	1938	VH, no. 1104
Międzyrzec Center	150	1926	VH, no. 1141
	187	1929	VH, no. 1141
	220	1935	VH, no. 1104
	219	1938	VH, no. 1104
Biłgoraj	—		Nekritz, p. 268
Chmielnik (formerly in Radom)	—		*OH*, 2:53
Dęblin	—		Nekritz, p. 268
Kałuszyn	ca. 100	1928	*OH*, 2:54
Kielce	ca. 100	1928	*OH*, 2:54
Kinsk	ca. 100	1928	*OH*, 2:54
Końskie	—		Nekritz, p. 268
Kowel	45	1938	VH, no. 1104
Łęczyca	—		*OH*, 2:145
Libawno	—		Nekritz, p. 268
Łódź	—		Nekritz, p. 268
Łosice	—		*OH*, 2:54
Lubartów	—		Nekritz, p. 268
Ostrowiec (formerly in Biala Podlaska)	ca. 100	1925	*OH*, 1:107
Paryśow	—		Nekritz, p. 268
Piaski	—		Nekritz, p. 268
Siedlce	ca. 100	1925	*OH*, 1:107
Staszów	—		*OH*, 2:145
Szydłowiec	—		*OH*, 2:99
Tomaszów Mazowiecki	—		Nekritz, p. 268
Włodawa	ca. 100	1925	*OH*, 1:107
Żełechow	—		*OH*, 2:146
Zwoleń	—		Nekritz, p. 268
Pinsk Center	ca. 200	1930	VH, no. 1146
(formerly in	125	1935	VH, no. 1104
Iwia, Siemiatycze)	130	1938	VH, no. 1104
Aleksandrowsk	—		*OH*, 2:145
Brasław	—		Nekritz, p. 268
Dąbrowica	—		*OH*, 2:99
Dawidgródek	—		Wischnitzer, p. 28
Gorlice	—		Nekritz, p. 268

TABLE 1 (cont.)

Place	Number of students	Year	Source
Janów Poleski	—		*OH,* 2:99
Kałusz	—		Wischnitzer, p. 28
Lachowicze	33	1938	VH, no. 1104
Lida	—		Wischnitzer, p. 28
Olkieniki	—		*OH,* 1:108
Ożarów	—		Wischnitzer, p. 28
Pinsk (*yeshivah ketanah*)	70	1929	VH, no. 1104
	45	1935	VH, no. 1104
Poczajów	—		Wischnitzer, p. 28
Prużana	—		*OH,* 2:145
Raków	—		*OH,* 1:108
Sambor	—		Wischnitzer, p. 28
Siemiatycze	—		Nekritz, p. 268
Tuczyn	35	1938	VH, no. 1104
Wiśniowiec Nowy	—		*OH,* 1:108
Wołkowysk	70	1938	VH, no. 1104
Zamość	—		Nekritz, p. 268
Zdzięcioł	—		Nekritz, p. 268
Warsaw Center	—		—
Będzin	—		Nekritz, p. 268
Falenica	—		Nekritz, p. 268
Izbica Kujawska	—		Nekritz, p. 268
Lubcz	—		*OH,* 1:145
Mława	—		*OH,* 2:54
Nowogródek	87	1929	VH, no. 1104
	55	1935	VH, no. 1104
	52	1938	VH, no. 1104
Ostrołęka	ca. 100	1925	*OH,* 1:107
Pabianice	—		Nekritz, p. 268
Płońsk	—		Nekritz, p. 268
Pułtusk	ca. 100	1928	*OH,* 2:53
Sandomierz	—		Nekritz, p. 268
Skieriewice	ca. 100	1926	*OH,* 1:169
Węgrów	ca. 100	1928	*OH,* 2:54
Włocławek	ca. 100	1925	*OH,* 1:107
Wołomin	—		Nekritz, p. 268
Wyszków	ca. 50	1925	*OH,* 1:169

SOURCES:

DV: Dos vort, a Vilna Orthodox weekly
Joffin: Avrohom Joffin, *Ha-Musar ve-ha-daat,* vol. 2 (Jerusalem, 1973)
Nekritz: Yehudah Leyb Nekritz, "Yeshivot Beit Yosef Novaredok," in *Mosdot Torah be-Eropah,* ed. S. K. Mirsky (New York, 1956), pp. 247–90
OH: Or ha-Musar
VH: Vaad Hayeshivot Archives, YIVO Institute for Jewish Research, New York
Wischnitzer: Mark Wischnitzer, "Di banayung fun di yeshives in Mizrekh Eyrope nokh der ershter velt-milkhome," *YIVO bleter* 31–32 (1948): 9–36

locations where there were no existing *yeshivot* for boys between thirteen and seventeen. Since a good number of *yeshivot* were situated in Poland's larger cities, the Novaredokers may have gravitated toward smaller settlements where they were, more often than not, the "only show in town."

Second, a surprisingly high proportion of Beys Yosef *yeshivot* were established outside the Lithuanian provinces, that is, outside the native territory of Salanterian Musar. (Note the proliferation of *yeshivot* in Galicia and central Poland.) This distribution may likewise reflect a tendency for Beys Yosef *yeshivot* to fill in preexistent voids. Jewish communities in central Poland did not have a strong tradition of maintaining formal *yeshivot* for teenage boys. Instead, they supported *shtiblekh* (prayer and study houses), where the hours and programs of study were flexible and set by each student independently. Thus there were few existing *yeshivot* in the towns of the central provinces. Novaredok's success in spreading throughout these heavily Hasidic regions may also owe something to certain phenomenological affinities between the Hasidic and Musarist brands of pietism.[34]

In Lithuania, on the other hand, the Novaredokers encountered a considerable degree of opposition, particularly among the rabbinical elite. The cities of Brześć nad Bugiem and Vilna were effectively closed to them because the leading rabbinical figures objected to Novaredok Musar as a perversion of Judaism and refused to tolerate Beys Yosef *yeshivot* in their midst. Elsewhere opposition was motivated by self-interest rather than religious principle. Existing *yeshivot* protested loudly whenever they felt that the Novaredokers were encroaching on their territory, claiming that the competition for students and funding would threaten their continued existence. When, for instance, a group of Novaredokers settled in Pinsk in 1922 (shortly after crossing over the Soviet border into Poland), they were brought before a rabbinical court by another *yeshivah* on charges of *hasagat gevul* (trespassing). The court ruled against the Novaredokers and ordered them to leave town. As a rule, Novaredok's expansion into Lithuania was modest and cautious.[35]

34. Compare S. Schachnowitz, "Zwei Erkentnisse und Ein Bekenntnis," in *Festschrift für Jacob Rosenheim*, ed. Heinrich Eisenmann (Frankfurt a.M., 1931), pp. 126–30.

35. A. S. Hershberg, *Pinkas Bialystok*, vol. 2 (New York, 1950), p. 338; Shtrigler, "Farshverer," *Yidisher kemfer*, no. 1551 (April 10, 1964): 8, no. 1552 (April 17,

Taken as a whole, the growth of the Novaredok movement in interwar Poland as measured in the number of *yeshivot* (from four to seventy) and number of students (from six hundred to three thousand) is quite impressive. To appreciate the significance of these figures one must view them in their proper context and recall the following points: First, the Novaredok *yeshivot ketanot* were the rough equivalents of high schools, not elementary schools. The figure of three thousand students therefore compares quite favorably with the student figures at the high school level of the modern Jewish school systems. Second, the branch *yeshivot* received no direct financial support from the centers, and each *yeshivah ketanah* made its own financial arrangements. Third, the Novaredokers were total strangers and outsiders to the communities they "infiltrated" in order to establish schools. *A priori* they had no local members or supporters. The figure of seventy *yeshivot* is therefore all the more impressive. Finally, the Novaredok schools were sectarian religious institutions. Demands on students in terms of time and energy were very great. Enrollment in a Novaredok *yeshivah* involved considerable sacrifices, such as material impoverishment and dissociation from one's family and friends.

Much of the credit for Novaredok's growth must be attributed to the zeal and energy of its youthful vanguards, who resembled in this regard current-day Lubavitch *shelikhim* (emissaries). In fact, Novaredok in the interwar period may be viewed as the historical antecedent of contemporary Lubavitch, in that it was the first aggressively expansionist Orthodox movement in modern times.

Viewed within its immediate historical context, Novaredok should also be considered one of the many youth movements that swept across Polish Jewry in the interwar years. Novaredok's activists were young men in their late teens and twenties; the four central *yeshivot* were their *lokals,* their movement meeting halls. The central *yeshivot* constituted a separate realm in which the activists lived, studied, debated, strived, planned, and built, far away from their parents and the older generation. Their sense of "chosenness" and of their mission to remake themselves, the younger generation, and eventually the world according to their shared vision was comparable to the

---

1964): 11–12. The historical veracity of this and the previously mentioned events, as well as the names of the places in which they occurred, were confirmed by Shtrigler in an interview with the author, New York, May 28, 1987.

élan that existed in the various Zionist and socialist youth movements of the period.[36]

In the aftermath of the Holocaust, Rabbi Avrohom Joffin looked back nostalgically (and with some exaggeration) at the interwar years as the golden era of Novaredok: "All of Poland was in our hands, from Swienzian [Święciany] on the border with Lithuania, to Kołomyja on the Rumanian border, Pinsk on the Soviet border, and Częstochowa . . . And just in our last year there we had great success in our work of spreading Torah and Musar. But suddenly we fell from our high peak. The calamity is very great . . . our territory was taken from us."[37]

Changes in Religious Life

To this point I have examined developments in Novaredok's structure and scope. I now turn to its internal religious life, which underwent changes of a more limited kind.

The regime of Musar activities followed in the Beys Yosef *yeshivot* was identical to the one established by Hurwitz in Novaredok—daily *birzhes*, weekly *vaadim*, work on *protim* or *peules*, *Musar shmuesn* twice weekly, and the *asiri koydesh* for those most totally involved. The work on achieving religious-ethical perfection continued along much the same lines as before the war.

But something important had in fact changed, at least for the upper echelon of students in the central *yeshivot*. The pursuit of religious-ethical perfection had become more difficult and problematic, because Musar activity had lost its exclusive pride of place. Many students at the four central *yeshivot* now divided their time between "working on themselves" and "turning the many unto righteousness," that is, establishing new *yeshivot ketanot*. There was a built-in tension between these two highly valued types of activity, and one necessarily took time and energy from the other. The interwar generation of Novaredokers had to struggle with reconciling and balancing these activities. According to Joffin:

36. Moshe Kligsberg, "Di yidishe yugnt bavegungen in Poyln tsvishn beyde velt-milkhomes: A sotsyologishe shtudye," in *Studies in Polish Jewry, 1919–1939,* ed. Joshua A. Fishman (New York, 1974), pp. 137–229; Ezra Mendelsohn, "Jewish Politics in Interwar Poland: An Overview," in this volume.
37. Joffin, *Ha-Musar ve-ha-daat,* 2:91.

Our Master bequeathed to us his teachings and set down for us the path of our activity: to work on ourselves and to work on behalf of the many to the utmost. We always had a great struggle about how to join these two aspects, so that they could coexist as one. How can one fulfill the side of attaining high moral virtues, of being immersed constantly in examining one's deeds and the purity of one's soul . . . when at the same time he is obligated to engage in work on behalf of the many, which of necessity distracts him, particularly if he must leave and journey to outlying areas [to fortify the branches of the *yeshivot*]?[38]

The conflict between these two values was felt most acutely by the *menahelim* of the new branch *yeshivot*, who were burdened with considerable administrative responsibilities. Only recently they had been students in the central *yeshivot*, immersed in problems of Musar. Now they were preoccupied with problems of student recruitment, financing, room and board, relations with the local community and with the central *yeshivah*, and so forth. Their personal work on themselves decreased dramatically and they were acutely aware of the spiritual losses they had suffered because of their "public work." In order to address the need of the *menahelim* for spiritual growth and regeneration, a new Novaredok practice was instituted—retreats for groups of *menahelim*. Called *kolelim*, these gatherings lasted for a week's time, during which the participants focused together on "prayer, the study of Musar, and reviewing each and every one's [spiritual] condition" away from the pressures of their respective *yeshivot*.[39]

Another practice that may have been instituted in response to the new problem of sustaining both inner spiritual growth and public activity was the Novaredok calendar. The calendar, passed at the March 1925 convention, divided the year into six seasons, each devoted to working on a different moral virtue or vice: contentment with one's lot, confidence in God, consistency between thought and deed, kindness, pride, and repentance were the original six. In subsequent years the calendar was expanded to nine different seasons, with some minor differences instituted among the central *yeshivot*.[40] This calendar, which helped provide guidance and direction to the Musar activity in Novaredok *yeshivot*, had a number of positive results. It forged an additional link between the scattered Beys Yosef

38. Ibid.
39. Ibid., p. 37; *Or ha-Musar*, 2:54.
40. *Or ha-Musar*, 1:167–69; Katz, *Tenuat ha-Musar*, 4:257–58; "Kuntrus Hasde Dovid," anonymous biography (by Aharon Surasky?), in Dovid Bliacher, *Divrei binah ve-Musar* (Tel Aviv, 1970), pp. 46–48.

yeshivot and ensured a certain sweep and comprehensiveness to each student's "work on himself." But it also assisted students and *menahelim* in employing their personal Musar time more effectively, since the theme for the month was set and well defined. It thereby helped ease their frustration that a portion of their time was being "swallowed up" by the work of establishing and maintaining *yeshivot ketanot*.

A third religious value, besides the cultivation of Musar and the establishment of new *yeshivot*, came to prominence during the interwar years—talmudic learning. As mentioned earlier, Talmud had not been a major concern in the original Novaredok *yeshivah*. Hurwitz's virtual disregard of this discipline, the core of the traditional *yeshivah* curriculum, had disturbed a great many Lithuanian rabbis and created tensions between Novaredok and the mainstream Lithuanian *yeshivot*. In the interwar years, the gap between the Novaredok central *yeshivot* and Mir, Kleck, and Raduń was narrowed with regard to the relative weight ascribed to talmudic study and the actual caliber of learning.

In the interwar years all the Novaredok centers had *rashei yeshivot* on their staffs, that is, scholars whose prime responsibility was to give *shiurim* and supervise the talmudic studies on the premises. This was a significant departure from the prewar practice in Novaredok, where senior students, without formal credentials or known reputations, had given the *shiurim*. The Białystok and Międzyrzec centers maintained two *rashei yeshivot* each and conducted *shiurim* on two and occasionally three different levels. Attendance was not compulsory, and only a small fraction of students "belonged" to a *shiur*. But the mere presence of a *bona fide* mentor in talmudic learning constituted an elevation of its status.[41] In most branch *yeshivot* as well, the staff consisted of both a *rosh yeshivah* and *menahel*.

The Białystok center, under the leadership of Rabbi Avrohom Joffin, broke most clearly of all with the Novaredok tradition of relegating Talmud to a secondary position in the curriculum. Joffin conscientiously strove to revive Talmud study in the Białystok *yeshivah* and succeeded in this endeavor to a surprising extent.[42] First

41. Vaad Hayeshivot Archives, YIVO Institute for Jewish Research, New York, folders 1115, 1141.
42. Joffin's talmudism should be seen in the context of his personal biography. He had studied in several prominent *yeshivot* (in Slutsk, Kobryn, Malecz) before he attended Novaredok and was introduced to its unique religious life-style. In Nova-

and foremost, he presented halakhic *pilpulim* (dialectical discourses) to the student body twice a week, while also offering two weekly *Musar shmuesn*.[43] This was an important symbolic act. Joffin was thereby combining the function of a *rosh yeshivah* and *menahel*, something Hurwitz had never done. He was serving as a model for the ideal of uniting a high degree of Torah scholarship and Musar sensitivity in one personality. Moreover, the fact that he presented both his halakhic and Musar discourses twice a week put talmudic and Musar activity on equal ground; it was an implicit argument for equilibrium between the two.

By contrast, the *menahel* of the Międzyrzec center, Rabbi Dovid Bliacher, left the presentation of *shiurim* to *rashei yeshivot*, his subordinates in the *yeshivah*'s hierarchy. This rendered Talmud symbolically subordinate to Musar, there being no individual in the *yeshivah* leadership who personified both values.

By all accounts, Joffin's halakhic *pilpulim* were impressive intellectual achievements and had an outstanding reputation in the Lithuanian *yeshivot*. Their fame, according to one former student in Białystok—Rabbi Aharon Surasky—had important consequences: "His *shiurim* in Halakhah attracted young scholars of great talent. [They] extricated Novaredok, to a great degree, from its isolation

---

redok he was recognized for his talmudic talents, and Rabbi Yosef Yoizl Hurwitz appointed him to give *shiurim*. Joffin developed a close relationship with Hurwitz and eventually married one of his daughters. During the war years he assisted his aging father-in-law in directing the *yeshivah* in Homel and assumed its leadership after the latter's death. Thus Joffin was uniquely suited to alter the position of Talmud study in the Homel *yeshivah*, in its subsequent incarnation as the Białystok center. He had a solid and impressive command of talmudic literature (unlike some of Hurwitz's other disciples), and, as Hurwitz's son-in-law and successor in Homel, he had the prestige and moral authority to institute changes without being accused of "betraying" Novaredok Musarism. The final impetus for Joffin's elevating the position of Talmud study was probably provided in Homel. There he developed a close friendship with Rabbi Borukh Ber Levovitz, head of the Kamieniec (in Yiddish, Kamenits) *yeshivah*, which had likewise fled from the war front. Joffin and Levovitz were neighbors in Homel and are reported to have spent much time together. Their relationship is particularly interesting because Kamieniec was, in a sense, the very antithesis of Novaredok. It was the one major Lithuanian *yeshivah* that refused to include the study of Musar in its daily regime. Levovitz was adamant that the Talmud could provide all the religious-ethical guidance and inspiration a *yeshivah* student needed. Joffin's interaction with Levovitz apparently led him to reconsider the generations' old issue of Talmud study versus Musar and to reassess their relative weight in the *yeshivah*'s religious life. See Aharon Surasky, "Toldotav ve-kavim li-dmuto," in Avrohom Joffin, *Ha-Musar ve-ha-daat al ha-Torah*, vol. 1 (Jerusalem, 1976), pp. 9–12. On the Kamieniec *yeshivah*, see Hillel Seidman, "Yeshivat Kneset Beit Yitzhak de-Kamenits," in *Mosdot Torah be-Eropah*, pp. 307–24.

43. Hershberg, *Pinkas Bialystok*, p. 337.

and drew it closer to the mainstream of the *yeshivot*. People stopped saying that in Novaredok the study of Musar is preferred to the study of Talmud, or that the *yeshivah* values a student who fears sin more than a student who is learned."[44] Thus Joffin's *shiurim* had the effect of rehabilitating Novaredok's reputation in the Lithuanian *yeshivot,* and the Białystok center began to attract a different sort of student—young capable talmudists who were interested in hearing fine *shiurim.* Their arrival undoubtedly altered the tenor of the religious atmosphere inside the *yeshivah.*

Joffin cultivated talmudic studies in the Białystok center through other steps as well. He personally encouraged outstanding talmudic students to write down their *novellae* and publish them.[45] He chose outstanding young scholars to be his *rashei yeshivot* and helped advance their scholarly careers. Thus, shortly after the *yeshivah* settled in Białystok, he appointed a young man who had joined Novaredok during the war years, Rabbi Yaakov Kanievsky, to deliver a regular *shiur* for the most talented students. Joffin also helped Kanievsky publish his first book, *Shaarei tevunah* (1925), with the title page prominently announcing that the author belonged to the Novaredok *yeshivah* in Białystok. *Shaarei tevunah* launched Kanievsky's worldwide reputation as the Gaon from Horonstaypl or the Staypeler. After marrying the sister of Rabbi Avrohom Yeshaya Karelitz (the Hazon Ish) and emigrating to Palestine, Kanievsky became the foremost halakhic authority for non-Hasidic ultra-Orthodox circles in Bnei Brak.[46]

Kanievsky's rise to prominence was important in the history of Novaredok. For the first time a former student and now *rosh yeshivah* of a Novaredok *yeshivah* was recognized in Lithuanian rabbinical circles as an outstanding talmudic authority. The Kanievsky phenomenon played an important role in rehabilitating Novaredok's reputation among Lithuanian rabbis and *yeshivot.* This rehabilitation received its most concrete expression in the generous allocations given by the Vilna-based Vaad Hayeshivot (Council of *Yeshivot*) to the Białystok center.[47]

44. Surasky, "Toldotav ve-kavim li-dmuto," pp. 8–9.
45. Ibid., p. 23.
46. Ben Zion Bruk, "Tzidkuto ha-niflaah," special appendix in memory of Yaakov Kanievsky, in *Yated neeman,* 29 Av 5745 (1985), p. 11.
47. The allocation to Białystok was much larger than that to Międzyrzec, although the size of the two *yeshivot* was identical. See the Vaad Hayeshivot Archives, folder 1106.

In general, religious life in the Novaredok *yeshivot* became more variegated during the interwar years. While many students continued to immerse themselves in Musar, as had traditionally been the path of Novaredok, some were deeply involved in the creation of new *yeshivot,* while others delved into the pages of the Talmud. As a result of the modifications in Novaredok's value system and field of activity, its religious life was less uniform and cohesive in independent Poland than it had been in the prewar period.

Finally, a word about the position of the Novaredok movement within organized Polish Orthodoxy. On the one hand, Novaredok had virtually no political influence on the affairs of the Orthodox Jewish community. Joffin and the other *menahelim* were not active in Agudat Israel and its related bodies; they eschewed political activity as a dangerous diversion from what ought to be one's prime pursuit in life—the attainment of religious-ethical perfection.

But despite this aloofness toward the Orthodox community, Novaredok's prestige grew considerably in religious circles during the interwar years. Not only did Joffin hold a secure position on the executive committee of the Vaad Hayeshivot alongside other prominent *rashei yeshivot*—something that would have been inconceivable for Hurwitz before the war—but the Novaredokers were lauded for their steadfastness and devotion by the Gerer Rebbe himself—Rabbi Abraham Mordechai Alter (1866–1948)—the spiritual mentor of Agudat Israel.[48] This newfound respect and appreciation were due in no small measure to Novaredok's reputation for success in attracting young people to Torah and Musar. At a time when the younger generation was breaking with its parents, abandoning traditional Jewish patterns, and joining modern movements, Novaredok's aggressive efforts to "stop the epidemic"[49] were admired even in Orthodox circles that disagreed with Novaredok's religious outlook and way of life.

---

48. See the brief letter sent in the name of the Gerer Rebbe to the Novaredok periodical *Hayei ha-Musar* (reprint, Bnei Brak, 1963), 2:1.
49. The expression is that of *Or ha-Musar,* 2:96.

Ben-Zion Gold

Religious Education in Poland:
A Personal Perspective

My comments on some aspects of Jewish religious life in prewar Poland will relate to my experience in the *heder,* the Hasidic *shtibl* (prayer and study house) and the *yeshivah*—that is, to religious education in central and southern Poland, called Galicia, which were predominantly Hasidic. I am aware that the situation was different in the Lithuanian part of Poland, but it is beyond my personal experience.

I grew up in a traditional home; I went to a *heder,* then to a *yeshivah;* I prayed in a Hasidic *shtibl,* knew several Hasidic rabbis, and was close to one of them. My father, a learned merchant, represented the ultra-Orthodox political party Agudat Israel in the city council of our hometown, Radom, a city in central Poland with a population of 80,000, of which 27,000 were Jews.

I spent six years in *heder,* from 1930 to 1936. In the course of that time I learned the daily, Sabbath, and holiday prayers, a major portion of the Humash and Rashi, and a little Talmud. After my second year I also had lessons in Polish language, history, and arithmetic four times a week, two hours a day. This change was introduced by the Polish government.

One generation earlier, *hadarim* were small, consisting of a *melamed* (teacher) and his assistant, and were usually located in his home. A child would first go to the *melamed dardeki.* After he had learned to read fluently and translate some of the prayers, he would go to the *melamed* who taught Humash and Rashi, and then to the one who taught Gemora—Talmud; each stage had its own *heder.* We studied all day long, with an hour's interruption for lunch. The school year consisted of two seasons, winter and summer, with the High Holidays and Passover as vacations. Before each of them the *melamed* would recruit his students in person by visiting parents. Classes were small, and contact between the *melamed* and the parents was frequent. When a child was first brought to *heder* there was a celebration, and there was a celebration at home when he began to study Humash; each celebration had a ritual attached to it. When the child studied Talmud, the *melamed* often came on Saturday afternoon to be present when the father examined his son on what he had learned during the week.

In my time, the *heder* was regulated by the Polish government, which for sanitary reasons forbade having a *heder* in a private home. To defray the costs of rental space, the *melamed* needed more students, and often several would join together and rent a larger place and establish a graded *heder,* where a child could attend through his basic education until he was *bar mitzvah,* at which point some would either go to work or study in a *yeshivah,* a *bes-medresh* (study house), or a secular school. Under this system personal contact with the *melamed* was lost, and the ceremonies were abandoned. In my time I never was in a class of fewer than twenty until I began to study Talmud.

The *melamdim* had no professional training other than the knowledge of the subject they taught, and often that was limited. Of the five *melamdim* I had, only Reb Hendel Rosenberg stands out in my memory. He was an energetic man who used his imagination, intelligence, and considerable gift of eloquence to interest us in the study of the Bible. He addressed us as intelligent children, and we responded. His manner and bearing were dignified, and he commanded our respect. Of the other four, one was bored by his task and performed it routinely, the only excitement being provided by the students. While we recited our lesson he would pace up and down the room like a prison warden, holding a ruler ready to slap the hands of those who were caught guilty of inattention or unruliness. My first Talmud teacher was so high strung that at the slightest provocation he would tremble and stutter. In retrospect it has occurred to me that his nerves may have been frayed by malnutrition.

What we lacked was a personal relationship. We were treated as learning machines; we were there to acquire a certain amount of knowledge, and the *melamdim* did their utmost to make us learn it. It was an adversarial relationship. It was not until I went to the *yeshivah* that I was able to identify with the institution and internalize the values of the subject we studied, namely the Jewish tradition.

The teachers of secular subjects were either nonreligious Jews or Christians. They usually treated us well, and the stories and poems we read with them were interesting. Strangely enough, these teachers did not affect our general prejudice against Gentiles or secular Jews except perhaps subliminally. We thought that each teacher was an exception.

The difference between the secular teachers and the *melamdim* was not, however, lost on us. Here was a school dedicated to the preservation of a traditional way of life providing its impressionable students with attractive alternative models. But there was little that could be done about it. Secular studies were frowned upon in the ultra-Orthodox community, and no one was trained to be a licensed teacher of secular subjects. The community was ill equipped to cope with the regulations of the new Polish government.

How did these unattractive *melamdim* in the drab surroundings of a *heder* affect our learning? My *heder* education was linked directly to my life, which was centered around religion. The people among whom I lived and from whom I received personal validation prayed three times daily, read the weekly portion of the Bible, studied Talmud, Midrash, commentaries, and codes, observed the holidays and festivals, and lived by the laws. Regardless of how poorly I was taught these subjects in *heder,* they were necessary for my life and I learned them.

As our expectations were not high, we were not disappointed. I remember once overhearing my father saying to a friend, "Look who are the educators of our children, people who have failed in every other endeavor." This is not to say that there were no *melamdim* who were inspiring and whom students remembered fondly throughout life. When I was a child, an old man used to visit us periodically on the Sabbath; my father received him as an honored guest and treated him with great respect. This was his *melamed* in elementary *heder.*

After *bar mitzvah* I began to think about what to do with myself. The *yeshivah ketanah* (junior *yeshivah*) into which I had graduated from *heder* was no improvement; if anything it was worse. I was still not interested in studying Talmud seriously, and it did not help that the *melamed* was a nervous man given to shouting at the slightest provocation, which happened all too often. In the course of my year there I became a prankster, and in a fit of rage the *melamed* swore that eventually I would end up an apostate.

Some of my classmates in *heder* went on to the *gymnasium*. In Poland secular education generally meant a break with tradition. I was of the middle class, and learning a trade was out of the question. What remained was working for my father, and for that I was still too young. Besides, my father had hoped that I would become a *talmed-khokhem*, a Jewishly learned man. In my case this definitely precluded becoming a rabbi. Already my grandfather had forbidden my father to study a section of the Yoreh Deah—part of the Shulhan Arukh that is essential for a rabbi—with the explanation, ''I'm afraid that in a pinch you may become a rabbi.'' The rabbinate was in decline, often surrounded by intrigue and factional quarrels, and some middle-class, traditional, learned Jews did not wish it upon their sons. Like my father and grandfather before me, I was expected to study Talmud until marriage; then I would receive a dowry, be married, spend a few years on *kest* (supported by my in-laws), and eventually go into some business.

Before the First World War young men, upon finishing *heder,* would study in a local *bes-medresh* or *shtibl*; in Galicia these conventicles were called *kloizn*. As soon as a group of Hasidim was large enough to afford rent, they would establish a *shtibl,* furnish it with an ark, Torah scrolls, tables, and benches, and acquire a basic rabbinical library. There were Hasidic *shtiblekh* in every town and city, each bearing the name of the locality in which their rebbe resided. Rebbes with a large following, like the ones of Gur (Góra Kalwaria) and Belz, would have a network of *shtiblekh* throughout the country. In addition to being a place where the Hasidim gathered mornings and evenings to pray, the *shtibl* was also the place where they spent their free time in study and fellowship.

In the *shtibl* and *bes-medresh* you could find different age groups side by side. There were the *zaydene yunge-layt* (silken young men), as the newly married, promising scholars were called. They were on *kest* so that they could fulfill themselves in learning. Then there were the *batlonim*, those whose wives earned a livelihood to support the family while they spent their time studying. Then there were older men who no longer worked but sat and studied. Alongside these mature scholars, some of them masters in rabbinical literature, and also under their tutelage and supervision sat those who had recently finished *heder.*

It was a unique, voluntary system of higher education. There was no administration or budget. The older scholars who had achieved a reputation for their erudition and depth of learning instructed the younger ones and kept an eye out for a promising young talmudist, whom they would bring to the attention of the rabbi. Though young, some of them only thirteen, having become independent scholars they needed no further surveillance than that provided by the ethos of the *shtibl*. Studying Torah was a great *mitzvah,* and being a young scholar in the *shtibl* was a privilege few would abuse.

These young men spent the whole day from dawn to midnight studying, except for Friday afternoons, when they prepared themselves for the Sabbath. Their preparations included going to the *mikveh,* the local bath. To make up for the time lost on Friday, some of them would spend the whole of Thursday night studying. On winter evenings after supper, one could find in the *shtibl* three generations of a family sitting side by side and studying.

I would now like to relate an incident told to me by my father from the time when he was a young scholar, before the First World War. He had been studying at the large *bes-medresh* of Radom, where he had gained the reputation of a *baal masber,* that is, as having the ability to explain complex and difficult Talmud passages clearly, simply, and succinctly. Consequently, so many of the younger scholars turned to him for help that it interfered with his own studies. At that time the Hasidim of the Piaseczner Rebbe had become numerous enough to afford a *shtibl* of their own, and it was just beginning to be used, mostly by Piaseczner Hasidim. One day when the number of interruptions reached the limit, Father gathered up his books and moved into the new *shtibl.* The set of Talmud there, published in Warsaw, was not edited as carefully as the Vilna edition. When Father came across textual mistakes, particularly in the commentaries, which were printed in very small letters, he would, after careful consideration, suggest a correction on the margin. Among the people who were studying in this *shtibl* was a recently married man, Itchel Morgenbesser, with a reputation for erudition. One day Itchel came across one of Father's corrections. He called him over and asked, "Who gave you permission to make corrections in the text?" When Father tried to defend his corrections, explaining his reasons, Itchel, being a hot-tempered man, lost his patience and told him he was too young to have presumed. No one had ever before treated Father so slightingly, and, being certain of his ground, he was determined to vindicate himself. At home, in his father's library, was the Vilna edition of the Talmud. Father rushed home, pulled out the volume, and sure enough the text read as he had corrected it. Instead of eating supper, he rushed back with the volume to the *shtibl*. When Itchel saw the reading in the Vilna edition, he paled; he had insulted a young scholar, had accused him of ignorance and arrogance. Itchel was beside himself with contrition and begged Father to forgive him. That incident, my father concluded, was the beginning of a lifetime friendship between them.

The *shtibl* and *bes-medresh* produced *lomdim*—people who were thoroughly versed in Jewish traditional literature, particularly the Talmud, its commentaries, and the codes. Here the rabbis and lay leaders of Polish Jewry were educated, including many of its political leaders who were elected to represent the Jews in the Polish Sejm (House of Deputies) and Senate. The culture of ubiquitous learning also produced a language of its own—*lomdish* Yiddish, the "scholar's Yiddish." The very term *lamdn* (scholar), though from the Hebrew root *l-m-d*, is a Yiddish creation that returned into modern Hebrew in its new meaning.

This whole religious civilization, which was under attack by secular Zionism and socialism, was dealt a crippling blow during the First World War. Poland and Galicia became the battleground of Russians, Austrians, and Germans. Galician Jews fled before the Russians to Vienna and Hungary. Polish Jews were evacuated by the Russians from all the frontline towns and villages. Some towns were completely destroyed by the battling armies. People lost their moorings, their social standing, their livelihood, and along with them also their authority over their families. The German occupation, which was generally favored by Jews, introduced a Western mode of living that was attractive to many of the young who were tossed about by the war. At the same time the success of the Russian Revolution made it seem as though the messianic promises of socialism were about to be fulfilled. Indeed, for several years at least, Jews enjoyed unprecedented freedoms in the new Soviet Union. In addition the Balfour Declaration gave Zionism a measure of reality it did not have before. Under these circumstances, the traditional way of life was in decline, and the study of Torah was at an all-time low.

During the 1930s, when I was growing up, the situation had changed drastically. Of the fifteen *shtiblekh* in Radom, only one was populated by young talmudists. The others were used for daily and

Sabbath prayers and stood empty the rest of the time. Here and there one would encounter an isolated young scholar on *kest* spending the day studying in the *shtibl*, or a few older men. What only recently had been the accepted norm became in my time an exception. In the large cities like Warsaw and Łódź one could still find *shtiblekh* filled with young men studying, but on the whole the traditional community was on the defensive and losing ground. In an effort to save the remnant, *yeshivot* were organized creating supportive environments, with teachers and spiritual guides to protect students from the corrosive influences of the political and ideological movements active in the Jewish community.

By the time I was old enough for more advanced studies in Talmud—that is, during the late 1930s—there were already many *yeshivot* in Poland, including a whole network of Keter Torah *yeshivot* sponsored by the Hasidic Rebbe of Radomsko, who was independently wealthy and who used his fortune to support the *yeshivot*. At that time also, the Musar *yeshivot* spread from Lithuania into Poland. These *yeshivot*, called Beys Yosef after Rabbi Yosef Yoizl Hurwitz of Novaredok (Nowogródek), who inspired them, emphasized the study and meditation of ethical and moral literature alongside the study of Talmud. They had even set up exercises to help students break habits and character traits that made them vulnerable to outside influence or interfered with the pure service of God.[1]

In a category all by itself was Yeshivat Hakhmei Lublin. Though founded as recently as 1930, it enjoyed a reputation of excellence and distinction from its very beginning. Its founder, Rabbi Meir Shapira, one of the most gifted rabbinical leaders of interwar Poland and a renowned talmudist, was fully aware of the sociopolitical conditions in the Jewish community of his time. In 1919, at the age of thirty-two, he was already chairman of the educational committee of Agudat Israel of Poland. A year later he became its president. In 1923 he was elected deputy to the Sejm, from which he retired a year later to devote himself to his educational goals.

At that time Rabbi Shapira was already planning to establish a national *yeshivah* in Poland that would recapture for its students the dignity they deserved and needed to become the leaders of the next generation, ''a *yeshivah* that would raise the glory of Torah.'' He is

1. The Musar *yeshivot* are discussed in detail in David E. Fishman, ''The Musar Movement in Interwar Poland,'' in this volume.

quoted as saying, "I have a dream of a great *yeshivah*, more beautiful and larger than any before. In my time *yeshivah* students will no more spend their nights as watchmen in warehouses and eat like beggars every day in a different house. I'll build them a royal palace." This is what he proceeded to do. When I visited the *yeshivah* in 1937, I was impressed by the spaciousness of its halls, the attractiveness of the living quarters, and the quality of the food—not at all what one had become accustomed to expect of a *yeshivah*.

Lublin was more than a *yeshivah*; it was meant to be a model institution to raise the image and dignity of *yeshivah* studies. It was to serve as a symbol of renewed Orthodoxy. Rabbi Meir Shapira was a follower of the Rebbe of Czortków, a descendant of Rabbi Israel of Rizhin. During the *hagigat ha-Torah* celebrating the completion of the Talmud under the *daf yomi* system, which took place in the spring of 1938, I met two of Rabbi Israel's descendants, the Boyaner and the Sadegerer Rebbes, and I can testify that their bearing and manner were princely.

Rabbi Meir Shapira was concerned with *tiferet* (beauty) in its esthetic sense. Long before he was a famous rabbi and leader, when he was still a young man on *kest* in the home of his in-laws in Tarnopol, he was among the founders of a society called Tiferet Hadat (Beauty of Religion). Unlike Polish Hasidim, particularly those of the Kock (in Yiddish, Kotsk) school who had no use for esthetics, he, as a son of Galicia and a follower of Czortków, had not only a feeling for it but appreciated its significance for contemporary Jewish youth.

When the *yeshivah* opened in 1930, thousands of guests, among them the rabbinical, Hasidic, and lay leadership of religious Jewry in Poland and representatives of the government and the press were present at the opening exercises. No *yeshivah* had ever opened in such an impressive manner. During the decade of its existence, the *yeshivah* became the pride of traditional Jewry in Poland. Press coverage, particularly by *Dos yidishe togblat*, the organ of Agudat Israel, played an important role in spreading and enhancing its reputation, not only in Poland but also abroad.

The attractive building has remained intact and is now occupied by the Medical Academy of Lublin. During a visit to Poland in the spring of 1984, Chone Shmeruk of the Hebrew University, Jerusalem, protested the absence of any marker designating the origin and former use of the building. In June 1985 a celebration took place in which government and university officials and representatives of Polish Jewry dedicated a plaque stating in Hebrew, Polish, and Yiddish, "In this building was Yeshivat Hakhmei Lublin in the years 1930–1939." Even in its demise Lublin is the only *yeshivah* in Eastern Europe that has a marker.

Just about the time when I was thinking about what to do with myself, a friend of mine returned from the preparatory of the Lublin *yeshivah*. He had spent a year there and came back a changed man. He was only fifteen, one year older than I. I had known him in *heder,* where both of us were irrepressibly boisterous, but now his whole manner had changed: he had become sedate, soft spoken, almost dignified, just what I thought a *talmed-khokhem* should be. I was also impressed by the way the older and more established scholars treated him as one of their own. I liked what I saw. After questioning him about the preparatory, I made up my mind to go there.

To my surprise my father, whom I expected to leap at the idea— for this was the first sign of my becoming serious—instead rejected it saying, "Ben-Zion, if you want to study you can do so right here. I studied in a *bes-medresh* and in a *shtibl,* and I am no *am ha-aretz* [ignoramus]." My father had no use for famous brands even when it came to *yeshivot.* I know that he did not approve of the mannerisms of young Hasidim: their neglected appearance, their long *peyes* (side curls), their exaggerated piety, their wallowing in tales of miracles performed by the rebbes. Still less did he like their complete lack of concern with political and practical affairs of life. He was afraid lest I become like them. This was 1937, just after the Great Depression. At that time he had already concluded that the future of Jews in Poland was bleak and had decided to settle in Palestine. He may have had different hopes for me. Had he sat down and told me what he had in mind, most likely he would have persuaded me, but he did not, and I was already beyond being brushed off by a mere criticism questioning the seriousness of my intentions.

In a sense my father was right: I was completely taken by the idea of being a student of that famous *yeshivah.* What he did not realize was that I needed it. Like so many of my age at that time, I, too, was at a parting of the ways. The *bes-medresh* and *shtibl* had ceased to be centers for young men, and if I was to continue in the traditional path I, too, needed the added support of that attractive *yeshivah.*

In the fall of 1937, despite my father's objections, I went away to the *yeshivah*. It was located in Rachów, a small town an hour's ride by bus from Lublin. Upon arrival I met Isachar Leventhal, the *rosh yeshivah* (principal), and Rabbi Shmaryahu Fensterbush, the town rabbi, who was its president. Both had studied with Rabbi Meir Shapira in Lublin. Their dignified bearing and friendly but restrained welcome made a strong impression on me. After a short conversation, I joined the other students for supper. There were about forty of us from all over Poland and Galicia, between the ages of fourteen and seventeen, mostly sons of Hasidic families.

My transition from a boisterous boy to a serious young scholar was short, almost abrupt—an act of will. What made it possible was the supportive environment of the *yeshivah,* where I was with others who were going through a similar experience. From early childhood we were raised with the belief, which we recited in our daily prayers, that the Torah was a divine gift of love and that studying it was the greatest *mitzvah.* Once we decided autonomously to act on our beliefs, and that was the case with the vast majority of us, the result was a life dedicated to the service of God in prayer and study with a fervor only people that age are capable of. We spent all our waking hours studying and praying, careful lest we waste a precious moment of time idling. That is where I first encountered the concept of *bitl zman* (nullification of time). In our society killing time is not altogether negative, but in the *yeshivah,* time not used in either study or prayer, with the exception of tending to basic needs, was wasted, nullified. For us, time was Torah.

We began the day with independent study, and so did we end it late in the evening. I remember one night a fellow who slept across the room from me sitting up all of a sudden and reciting a page of Talmud in his sleep. In the course of one term, from after Sukkot until Passover, I underwent the biggest change in my conscious life. During the Passover vacation at home I encountered a former classmate from *heder* who had gone to the *gymnasium.* After several meetings I persuaded him to drop secular education and come with me to the *yeshivah,* for which I was granted permission from the *rosh yeshivah* only after I guaranteed that I would personally tutor my friend and bring him up to par with the rest of us. I kept my word. I remember studying with him twelve hours in one day to prepare him for an examination. David Potashnik became a devout Jew and a scholar. His interest in traditional life was kindled by my enthusiasm, and both of us were nurtured and sustained by the *yeshivah.*

Outside the *yeshivah* the world was divided between Poles and Jews and these further divided between religious and secular. We knew that only one generation ago most of the secular were religious. We felt threatened and closed ranks to protect the remnant. It is difficult to say what the face of Polish Jewry would have been had it continued. Study of the traditional community has just begun. With all of the success and strength of Agudat Israel in national, municipal, and communal elections, I am of the opinion that this strength was from the older generation awakened to the dangers threatening them. Another ten years and the polls would have registered a decline reflecting the continued flight of youth from traditional life to secure for themselves a political and economic future either in Poland or abroad. The impressive movement of return to tradition that we have been witnessing in the past fifteen years is new, and the first one since the Haskalah began to make inroads into traditional Jewish life in eighteenth-century Germany.

Literary and Cultural Creativity

Chone Shmeruk

Hebrew-Yiddish-Polish:
A Trilingual Jewish Culture

I want to preface my attempt to present a historical model of the modern trilingual culture of Polish Jewry between the two world wars with two basic points. First, I have difficulty in defining the discipline to which the following survey belongs. Demographic and sociolinguistic elements are consciously mixed within the historical perspective in an attempt to encompass heterogeneous cultural spheres such as education, literature, the theater, and the press. The necessity for an interdisciplinary approach, as opposed to the customary one, which deals with each sphere in each language separately, stems from a basic attitude that aspires to present Jewish culture in Poland between the two world wars, with all the internal contexts of its different linguistic constituents, as one entity. Second, in order to preclude the addition of new terminology, I chose to borrow the concepts "system" and "polysystem" from the literary sphere.[1] As applied to our subject, the concept of a cultural system is restricted to a cultural sphere in one language only. In contrast, the concept of a polysystem here refers to the whole range of Jewish culture in Poland, which comprises the Hebrew, Yiddish, and Polish systems together.

In addition to the traditional religious culture that was still predominant in Poland between the two world wars, three modern post-Enlightenment cultural systems existed among Polish Jewry. They were generally distinguished by linguistic and ideological characteristics. The cultural systems in the Jewish languages—Hebrew and Yiddish—were usually identified with defined Jewish nationalist ideologies. Hebrew culture relied on Zionist ideology, whereas

1. Itamar Even-Zohar, *Papers in Historical Poetics* (Tel Aviv, 1978).

modern Yiddish secular culture was built primarily by Bundists and their adherents, and to a lesser extent by Zionist socialists, Folkists, and those Jewish communists who did not advocate the assimilation of Jews. The overt ideological character of the cultural realms in the Jewish languages was often accompanied by a fanatical claim to exclusivity. The adherents of Hebrew culture brought this claim against the other two systems, and so did the adherents of Yiddish culture. Both treated with suspicion and misgiving, if not with outright rejection, the realm of Polish-Jewish culture, which in their eyes admitted the danger of assimilation. This was the case despite the preference of some Hebraists for Polish over Yiddish, and, in parallel, although less overtly, the preference of some Yiddishists for Polish over Hebrew.

What seems to be understood and natural regarding the cultural systems in the Jewish languages, which in practical terms expressed a striving for Jewish self-preservation, is less apparent regarding the Polish cultural system among the Jews. This cultural system had no well-defined overall political-ideological character. Let me point out at the outset that I am not concerned here with the thin stratum of Polish intelligentsia of Jewish descent, including renowned Polish writers, who were totally assimilated into Polish culture and identified themselves as Poles—even despite certain sporadic expressions of Jewish self-identification to which they were pushed by hostile forces over which they had no control. While their works were a component of Polish culture, they cannot be defined, either from their point of view or ours, as creators of Jewish culture. One can point within this group to an overt and declared aspiration to total assimilation within the Polish nation, even including conversion, an aspiration that totally rejected the nationalist and cultural ideologies of the Hebraists and Yiddishists. But these ideas were voiced only by a very small group of students and professionals within the Zjednoczenie Polaków Wyznania Mojżeszowego (Union of Poles of Mosaic Faith).[2] This small group is, in fact, of very minor interest, and

2. The Zjednoczenie Polaków Wyznania Mojżeszowego made its first major public appearance in independent Poland at a convention held in Warsaw, May 10–12, 1919. The proceedings were published as *Pamiętnik pierwszego wolnego zjazdu Zjednoczenia Polaków Wyznania Mojżeszowego wszystkich Ziem polskich* (Warsaw, 1919). The principal positions of Zjednoczenie expressed at the convention were further developed in its periodical organs, such as *Rozwaga* (1915–28) and *Zjednoczenie* (1931–33). On its ambivalent attitude toward conversion, see Leo Belmont, "Neo-asymilacja czyli rzecz o Semi-Polakach," *Zjednoczenie*, 1932, no. 12, p. 14; Edward Lipnik, "W obronie

only as an extreme. Most Jews in Poland whose exclusive or partial cultural language was Polish were apparently Zionist in ideology or nonaffiliated and politically apathetic. They certainly never denied their Jewish identity. To clarify the nature of this amorphous Jewish population, it can be identified with the multitude of readers of daily Jewish newspapers in Polish, which appeared in Warsaw, Lwów, and Cracow. Several of these newspapers defined themselves as Zionist, and certainly none of them advocated assimilation into the Polish nation.

We seem to be dealing with three separate cultural systems. In truth, however, the three were united by certain options—at times forced on them—and by a dynamic of interaction within an encompassing Jewish cultural polysystem, one that also included the isolationist system of traditional religious culture, by virtue of their coexistence as Jewish systems within Jewish society in Poland. By analyzing the possibilities and interrelationships of each element in this polysystem, I shall attempt to present models of the particular linguistic components with all their scope, limitations, and prospects.

The Languages

One might expect that the scope of the three Jewish cultural systems should be accurately reflected in statistics concerning the mother tongue of the Polish population as recorded in the census. The statistics of the 1921 census concerning the mother tongue were not published. The last and only census before the Holocaust that contained statistics about the mother tongue was taken in December 1931. In this census Polish citizens were asked not for their national affiliation but for their religion. According to this census, in December 1931 there were 3,113,933 people of the "Mosaic faith" in Poland. In answer to the additional question concerning mother tongue, 2,489,034—nearly 80 percent of those who declared Judaism as their religion—claimed Yiddish as their mother tongue.

---

mechesów," *Zjednoczenie*, 1933, no. 3, pp. 5–6; S. H., "Typy 'mechesów,'" *Zjednoczenie*, 1933, no. 5, pp. 7–10; Nina Hercmanówna, "W obronie mechesów," *Zjednoczenie*, 1933, no. 5, pp. 10–11; Belmont, "W obronie mechesów! List otwarty do Red. Zjednoczenia," *Zjednoczenie*, 1933, nos. 6–7, pp. 3–18.

About 12 percent claimed Polish, and about 8 percent (243,539) claimed Hebrew as their mother tongue.[3]

These statistics must not be taken, however, as accurately reflecting the linguistic situation among Jews in Poland in 1931 or as a full and faithful picture of the relationship among the linguistic "forces" within the Jewish cultural polysystem.

Prior to the census, a propaganda campaign sought to influence the Jews to declare their mother tongue in accordance with their Jewish national ideological affiliation, at times in contradiction to the facts. The nationalist Jewish camp, in all its variations, opposed Jews' declaring Polish as their mother tongue in protest against the Polish government's infringement on their rights and as a demonstration of national identity in terms of language. The Zionists demanded that their adherents declare Hebrew as their mother tongue, hence the unrealistic figure of one-quarter of a million Polish Jews declaring Hebrew. For most of these Jews, the mother tongue was probably Yiddish or Polish; the number whose mother tongue really was Hebrew was minute. And if we must add to the number of Yiddish speakers an unknown number of these declared Hebrew speakers, we must also subtract from declared Yiddish speakers a number of Jews whose mother tongue was Polish but who declared Yiddish as their mother tongue for nationalist reasons.[4]

I must emphasize that there is no possibility of using the census statistics to determine the cultural identification of the approxi-

---

3. Szyja Bronsztejn, *Ludność żydowska w Polsce w okresie międzywojennym: Studium statystyczne* (Wrocław, 1963), pp. 29–33; Jerzy Tomaszewski, *Rzeczypospolita wielu narodów* (Warsaw, 1985), pp. 146–50. Jacob Lestschinsky wrote three articles on the mother tongue of the Jews of Poland as recorded in the 1931 census: "Di mutershprakh bay yidn in Poyln," *YIVO bleter* 9 (1936): 140–43; "Di mutershprakh fun di poylishe yidn," *YIVO bleter* 15 (1940): 140–44; "Di shprakhn bay yidn in umophengikn Poyln: An analiz loyt der folkstseylung fun 1931," *YIVO bleter* 22 (1943): 147–62. In this paper I have relied primarily on the last and most detailed article.

4. On efforts to encourage the declaration of Hebrew and Yiddish as mother tongues during the census, see Lestschinsky, "Di shprakhn bay yidn in umophengikn Poyln," p. 147; Tomaszewski, *Rzeczypospolita*, p. 148. On the virulent reaction to these efforts, see "Statystyka a etyka," *Zjednoczenie*, 1932, no. 1, pp. 10–12, whose anonymous author argued that "entire Jewish families who speak neither Yiddish nor Hebrew" declared Yiddish as their mother tongue "because they were instructed to do so by the Jewish press *printed in the Polish language*" (italics in the original). Since the interest here is in general trends, specific regional differences—such as the well-known and traditional differences between former Galicia and regions of former Congress Poland—are not noted. On this subject, see Lestschinsky, "Di shprakhn bay yidn in umophengikn Poyln"; Ezra Mendelsohn, "A Note on Jewish Assimilation in the Polish Lands," in *Jewish Assimilation in Modern Times*, ed. Bela Vago (Boulder, Colo., 1981), pp. 141–49.

mately 80 percent of Jews who declared Yiddish as their mother tongue. Almost certainly more than half of the declared Yiddish speakers belonged to the traditional religious camp; evidence of this will be presented below. Among the remaining number were certainly Yiddishists of various persuasions as well as an unknown but not negligible number of Zionists of Hebraist persuasion and, for reasons already discussed, a number of Polish speakers, too.

I use the word "speakers" here deliberately, and not the terminology of the census, which recognizes only "mother tongue." Bilingualism was widespread among Polish Jews, and multilingualism existed as well. The memoirs of a Polish scholar of Jewish descent tells of his father's (born in Galicia in 1882) knowledge of languages, fairly typical of Jews in Poland.

> Father, who went only to *heder*, since there was no money for the *yeshivah*, knew five languages: Hebrew, Yiddish, German, Polish, and Ukrainian, although he apparently could not write Ukrainian. No one thought of this as anything extraordinary. I would even venture that no one even noticed. "True" foreign languages were French and English. If you had asked my father before World War I, he would certainly have answered that he knew no foreign language.[5]

Indeed, with no formal or ordered education, many Polish Jews were polyglots. Their knowledge of languages was gained through Jewish education and tradition and through contact with speakers of various languages among the local population and in dealings with local and foreign governments. To Yiddish, the primary daily language, and Hebrew, the holy tongue of prayer, traditional study, and education, were added, before World War I, Polish and Ukrainian or Belorussian of the local populace according to the ethnic geographic area. One must add to these, of course, German or Russian, the languages of the foreign governments ruling Poland from its partitions until its establishment as an independent nation after World War I.

In addition to the traditional and modern culture in Jewish languages—Hebrew and Yiddish—the spread of the Enlightenment made the cultures of the ruling states in general, and Polish culture in particular, which was dominant in the territory of ethnic Poland, very attractive. Ukrainian and Belorussian, on the other hand, served mainly for oral contact with the village population and

---

5. Roman Zimand, "Gatunek: Podróż," *Kultura* 11 (1983): 24.

lacked "higher" cultural significance. These contacts were expressed primarily in loanwords and expressions introduced into Yiddish and in influences on the level of popular culture; the exceptions only prove the rule.[6]

After 1918, Russian began to disappear gradually as a significant linguistic-cultural element among Poland's Jews, with remnants primarily in the northeastern regions of the Polish Republic. German, too, disappeared, though it retained a limited status among the Jews of Galicia even after the exodus to Germany of Germanized Jews from the western regions of Poland. The generations that grew up and were educated in independent Poland knew fewer languages than their forebears. After 1918 only Hebrew, Yiddish, and Polish continued to serve as linguistic-cultural vehicles for Poland's Jews.[7]

The census of 1931 included no questions concerning the knowledge or use of languages besides the mother tongue. For the village population of Poland, whose mother tongue was usually the sole language, the question was adequately revealing. The answers of the Jewish population to this single question, however, could at best provide a partial picture. Some knowledge of Hebrew, occasionally even a profound knowledge, was widespread among the Jews. It is also beyond question that the number of Jews whose knowledge of Hebrew was sufficient to have declared it as a second language was larger than the numbers who declared Hebrew to be their mother tongue. The knowledge of Yiddish as an everyday language, and to a lesser extent as the language of culture, was certainly widespread among those who gave Polish as their mother tongue. During the 1930s one may also assume a widespread knowledge of Polish among those who gave Hebrew or Yiddish as their mother tongue. After the traditional Ashkenazi bilingualism of Hebrew and Yiddish, Yiddish-Polish bilingualism was the most common among Polish Jews.[8] One must assume that many of those whose mother tongue

6. I know of no Ukrainian writer of Jewish origin before World War I. Shmuel Plavnik, known as Zmitrok Byadula, the well-known Belorussian writer of Jewish origin, began to publish in Belorussian before World War I. He is, however, a well-known exception. Traces of Belorussian folklore are prominent in the writings of Nisn Brusilov, *Bay di taykhn fun Polesye* (New York, 1953).

7. During the 1931 census, 6,827 Jews, or 0.2 percent of "adherents of the Mosaic faith," declared German as their mother tongue. On the insignificant numbers of Jews declaring other languages, see Lestschinsky, "Di shprakhn bay yidn in umophengikn Poyln," p. 160.

8. On traditional bilingualism among Ashkenazim, see Max Weinreich, "Ineveynikste tsveyshprakhikeyt in Ashkenaz biz der haskole: Faktn un bagrifn," *Di goldene*

was Yiddish were not identified with the Yiddish cultural system, since the Polish language, which they acquired in the course of time, established them as belonging to the Polish system.

Thus the census data provide only a shaky foundation for assessing the linguistic division of Polish Jews between the two world wars, as bilingualism and multilingualism were significant for participation in a culture that itself was by no means unilingual.

Education

Although there are no precise statistics for the number of Jewish children of elementary school age and of their distribution among the different schools, the statistics we do have shed light on education according to the various linguistic systems. At least one-half million Jewish children of school age lived in Poland in the 1930s.[9] According to the Joint Distribution Committee (JDC), for 1936 the number of students in Jewish elementary schools of all types were as shown in table 1. In a classification of education by language of

TABLE 1

Students in Jewish Elementary Schools, 1936

School organizations	Number of pupils
Tarbut	44,780
Yavneh	15,923
Shul-kult	2,343
TSYSHO	16,486
Horev	49,123
Yeshivot	15,941
Beys Yaakov	35,585
TOTAL	180,181

SOURCE: Shmuel Rozenhek, "Al maarekhet ha-hinukh ha-yehudi be-Polin bein shtei milhamot ha-olam," in *Beit Israel be-Polin: Me-yamim rishonim ve-ad li-ymot ha-hurban*, ed. Yisrael Halperin, vol. 2 (Jerusalem, 1953), p. 154.

---

keyt, no. 35 (1959): 80–88. The abundance of untranslated Polish quotations in Yiddish literature of the interwar period serves as a significant indicator of the knowledge of Polish among Yiddish speakers. See Chone Shmeruk, "Jews and Poles in Yiddish Literature between the Two World Wars," *Polin* 1 (1986): 176–95.

9. Shmuel Rozenhek, "Al maarekhet ha-hinukh ha-yehudi be-Polin bein shtei milhamot ha-olam," in *Beit Israel be-Polin: Me-yamim rishonim ve-ad li-ymot ha-hurban*, ed. Yisrael Halperin, vol. 2 (Jerusalem, 1953), p. 155. On age statistics, see Bronsztejn, *Ludność żydowska*, pp. 136–46.

instruction combined with ideological affiliation, the leader was, according to these statistics, the traditional religious educational institutions, including the Horev schools, boys' *yeshivot*, and Beys Yaakov schools for girls. Together these schools had 100,649 pupils, 55.86 percent of all the children in Jewish elementary schools. To these should apparently be added approximately 40,000 pupils who attended *hadarim* after school hours in the public schools, where the language of instruction was Polish. In the *hadarim, yeshivot*, and Beys Yaakov schools, Hebrew texts were the basis of study, but the language of instruction and translation was Yiddish. The Tarbut and Yavneh schools, where Hebrew predominated, had a total of 60,703 pupils (33.69 percent of all children in Jewish elementary schools). The Shul-kult schools, which were bilingual in Yiddish and Hebrew, had 2,343 pupils (1.30 percent), and the schools of the Tsentrale Yidishe Shul Organizatsye (TSYSHO, Central Yiddish School Organization), in which Yiddish predominated, had a sum total of 16,486 pupils (9.15 percent). In all of these schools the study of Polish was mandatory as well. We also learn from the JDC statistics, whose sum total was higher than official statistics, that of the one-half million Jewish children of school age, 64 percent studied or were supposed to study in public schools taught in Polish, some of which were intended exclusively for Jewish children.[10] These were called *szabasówki* because there were no classes on the Sabbath.

Even if these statistics are not completely accurate, we can glean from them some extremely important facts. It is clear that the traditional religious education was still ascendant among all the types of Jewish education. Moreover, one must point to the initiative of the ultra-Orthodox educational system, which founded and built an impressive system of schools for girls, the Beys Yaakov schools, to give girls an opportunity for a Jewish education and at the same time to keep them from having to attend non-Jewish public schools. Beys Yaakov schools were attended by 19.75 percent of children in Jewish elementary schools in Poland, to which should be added, as mentioned above, some 40,000 children who studied in *hadarim* after public school hours. Of children in Jewish elementary schools, 12.61 percent received a total or partial Hebrew education, and 3.8 percent received a total or partial secular Yiddish education. Most

10. Rozenhek, "Al maarekhet ha-hinukh ha-yehudi be-Polin bein shtei milhamot ha-olam," p. 153, gives 343,671 as the number of Jewish children in Polish public schools in 1934–35, according to official statistics.

Jewish children received a Polish education in the public schools, where Polish was the language of instruction and mandatory for conversation.[11]

The prospects of the various components of Jewish culture in Poland, with their varying goals, become clearer when we examine another aspect of elementary school attendance. The main reason given for most Jewish children of compulsory school age attending Polish elementary schools is that public education was free, while all Jewish schools, even publicly run schools (such as those of the Tarbut and TSYSHO networks), required some sort of fee.[12] At a time when the Polish-Jewish population was becoming progressively poorer, school fees were difficult to pay, particularly for families with many children. Sometimes parents, under the pressure of financial circumstance, sent their children to the Polish public schools. Moreover Jewish elementary schools were not considered effective in teaching the Polish language, and so many parents sent their children to public schools to learn Polish to prepare them for high school.

Indeed, the statistics on numbers of Jewish pupils in high school seem to confirm the trend toward the predominance of Polish culture and language among Jewish youth. In the school year 1930–31 the 43,583 Jewish pupils in all the high schools in the country constituted 21.1 percent of all the pupils in *gymnasiums* in Poland, a relatively high proportion explained by the fact that Jews were primarily urban dwellers.[13] The Polish high schools in which Jews studied fell into the following categories: government and communal general Polish *gymnasiums*, which were usually free, and Jewish

11. Ibid. A great deal has been written on Jewish education in independent Poland. In addition to Rozenhek, see Aryeh Tartakower, "Yidishe kultur in Poyln tsvishn tsvey velt-milkhomes," *Gedank un lebn* 4 (1946): 1–35; Tartakower, "Di yidishe shul in Poyln tsvishn tsvey milkhomes," in *Sefer ha-shanah/yorbukh*, ed. Aryeh Tartakower, vol. 2 (Tel Aviv, 1967), pp. 210–65; Hayim Kazdan, *Di geshikhte fun yidishn shulvezn in umophengikn Poyln* (Mexico City, 1947); Miriam Eisenstein, *Jewish Schools in Poland* (New York, 1950). See also bibliographical references in the articles and books as well as the section entitled "Hinukh, tarbut, dat, itonut" in the bibliography in Ezra Mendelsohn, *Yehudei mizrah-merkaz Eropah bein shtei milhamot ha-olam* (Jerusalem, 1978), pp. 28–29.

12. This is not the place to review the discrimination against the various Jewish schools that did not receive government subsidies due them according to the Minorities Treaty signed by Poland. Withholding support for the minority schools was an integral part of the government's policy of Polonization. On this subject, see the references in note 11, above.

13. Rozenhek, "Al maarekhet ha-hinukh ha-yehudi be-Polin bein shtei milhamot ha-olam," p. 147.

publicly run and private schools. The Jewish publicly run *gymnasiums* belonged to the Tarbut or TSYSHO network, and the language of instruction was therefore Hebrew or Yiddish respectively. The private schools were under Jewish auspices, and the language of instruction was Polish; although some Jewish subjects were offered, they were not mandatory and often superficial.

The number of Jewish pupils in the various non-Jewish high schools declined when quotas on Jews were instituted. The anti-semitic atmosphere of many of these schools also prevented many Jewish parents from sending their children to them notwithstanding their absence of tuition fees. A parallel decline occurred in the number of publicly run Jewish *gymnasiums*. In school year 1926–27 the Tarbut network had sixteen *gymnasiums* scattered throughout Poland (primarily in the eastern regions), while in 1938–39 only nine remained. During the same years the number of TSYSHO *gymnasiums* declined from nine to two. The number of private Jewish *gymnasiums* grew.[14] It should be pointed out that in Warsaw, which had the largest urban concentration of Jews in the country, there was not even one Jewish publicly run *gymnasium*; nor were there any Tarbut or TSYSHO high schools. In contrast, there was a fairly large network of private Jewish *gymnasiums,* generally separate for males and females, in which the language of instruction was Polish and only Jews were students.

The statistics on Jewish pupils in *gymnasiums* are confusing, as the numbers from the 1920s refer to all the grades of high school, while, after the educational reform of the 1930s, the two upper grades were separated into lyceums. It is not clear whether the numbers from the 1930s include these grades as well. It seems that after a certain crisis period in the early 1930s the number of Jewish pupils in Polish high schools in Poland was once more on the rise. In the school year 1936–37 there were a total of 33,212 Jewish high school pupils; 15,301 studied in Polish government and communal schools, and the remainder attended Jewish private and publicly run *gymnasiums*. Needless to say, the education provided in the various Polish schools was strongly Polish patriotic. In reality, the situation of the pupils of the Jewish *gymnasiums* did not differ greatly. There were a total of 2,242 pupils in publicly run Jewish *gymnasiums*, 2,059 of them studying in the *gymnasiums* of Tarbut and 184

14. Ibid.

in TSYSHO *gymnasiums*. All the rest—15,669 pupils—studied in private Jewish *gymnasiums* where, as mentioned, the language of instruction was Polish, with or without some Jewish studies. Only 6.7 percent of the students in Jewish *gymnasiums* were given instruction in a Jewish language.[15]

Nonetheless, a surprising number of Jewish pupils in Warsaw claimed Yiddish as their mother tongue. In 1936–37, 53 percent of all Jewish pupils in *gymnasiums* claimed Yiddish as their mother tongue. It is especially significant that in the Jewish private high schools in particular the percentage claiming Yiddish was only 33.2 percent.[16] These schools were called "matriculation factories" since their sole purpose was to open the doors to a higher education. It is specifically these schools that, according to Aryeh Tartakower, "increased the danger of assimilation, since they almost never thought of Jewish education there."[17]

There are those who are skeptical about the numbers of pupils claiming Yiddish as their mother tongue, suspecting that here, too, the motive was Jewish nationalism. I tend to believe that these statistics are reliable and reflect the bilingualism of Jewish youth. Evidence is also found in the statistics concerning the Jewish university students of Warsaw, where the percentage of those claiming Yiddish as their mother tongue grew from 28 percent in 1922–23 (from a total of 4,304 Jewish students) to 50.3 percent in 1929–30 (from a total of 3,189 Jewish students).[18] But these statistics, too, may reflect efforts to demonstrate a Jewish nationalist position, as opposed to the real situation in which Polish predominated. It seems, however, that the skeptics did not take into account the spread of

15. The statistical data on the 1936–37 academic year are from Menakhem Mirkin, "Yidishe talmidim in di mitlshuln in Poyln," *Yidishe ekonomik* 4–6 (1939): 257–65. For additional data on high school education, see Rozenhek, "Al maarekhet ha-hinukh ha-yehudi be-Polin bein shtei milhamot ha-olam," p. 147; Bronsztejn, *Ludność żydowska*, pp. 188–92. The small minority of students in *gymnasiums* where Yiddish and Hebrew served as the languages of instruction may be explained by the fact that these schools were not granted full "rights," which included an easing of requirements for matriculation examinations (for example, examinations held without a representative of the Polish Ministry of Education in attendance). Figures for students in Jewish teachers' seminaries need to be added to the category of high school education.

16. Mirkin, "Yidishe talmidim in di mitlshuln in Poyln," p. 265.

17. Tartakower, "Di yidishe shul in Poyln tsvishn tsvey milkhomes," p. 252.

18. Jacob Lestschinsky, "Di mutershprakh fun yidishe studentn in Varshe," *YIVO bleter* 1 (1931): 174–75; Libman Hersh, "Di shprakhlekhe asimilirtkeyt bay di yidishe studentn fun di varshever hoykhshuln," *YIVO bleter* 2 (1931): 440–44. See also Bronsztejn, *Ludność żydowska*, pp. 192–96.

high school and higher education to circles of Jews other than those classified as assimilationist in pre–World War I terms. Greater access to higher levels of education among the Jews of independent Poland suggests that the students' claim of Yiddish as their mother tongue may reflect a linguistic reality.

All of this tells us that continuous Polonization from elementary school through higher education did not cause Jewish youth to deny their Jewishness, as many who dealt in Jewish education feared. We must assume, as well, that even among those youths who spoke and declared Polish as their mother tongue there was a substantial number with a strong national Jewish identity. Nonetheless, one is forced to conclude that the educational system in Poland brought about an ever-increasing number of Jews whose main language was Polish, while Yiddish was either abandoned or preserved as a second language. Among *gymnasium* pupils, the percentage claiming Yiddish was much smaller in 1936 than it was according to the 1931 census, and, conversely, the percentage of those claiming Polish as their mother tongue grew. The schism in education, particularly in elementary schools but in *gymnasiums* as well, leaves no doubt as to the prognosis for the Jews of Poland had their future not been terminated by the Holocaust. Each cultural system placed great weight on educating the next generation, upon which continuity depends. The great advantages in this linguistic dynamic were held by the Polish cultural system, and linguistic developments among Polish Jewry must be seen in light of this dynamic, not just according to the bare statistics of the 1931 census. Moreover, statistics on Jewish education in the Jewish tongues confirm that it was at a disadvantage.

This is not the place to define and examine all the components of the Jewish cultural systems in addition to education. From here I will survey those components of the Jewish cultural polysystem in which language is the major vehicle of expression: literature, theater, and the press.

Literature

Eastern Europe, including Poland, was until the First World War the "established territory" of modern Hebrew literature. In 1941 Yosef Klausner distinguished five centers of modern Hebrew literature in Eastern Europe that were active until World War I, among them "three centers of modern Hebrew literature: the Galician center, the Volynia-Podolia center, and the Warsaw center." However, as we learned from a recent analysis, "From the end of World War I a quickened and energetic process began to turn Palestine into the center of Hebrew literature." Among the reasons given for the shift are the emigration of writers to Palestine, "the shrinking of an audience for Hebrew literature in Europe, and in contrast, the growing concentration of a population dependent on Hebrew" in Eretz Israel.[19]

In view of these developments, it is not surprising that we discern in Poland the impoverishment of Hebrew literature between the two world wars, due both to the emigration of writers (Asher Barash, Uri Zvi Grinberg, Yaakov Cohen, Yaakov Fichman, and others) and to the diminishing number of readers. The shift of the center to Palestine made the Hebrew literature created and published there dominant, and with a readership among the Hebrew readers of Poland as well. In 1940 S. Y. Pineles—the well-known critic and Hebrew teacher Isaiah Pnueyli, who emigrated from Poland to Palestine in 1935—wrote an article about the "last era of Hebrew creativity in Poland"; it suffices as confirmation of these processes. Pineles observed that "Hebrew fiction in Poland stopped giving birth to any real values" and indirectly explained its decline by commenting, "The Hebrew public also began to degenerate in Poland before the last war."[20]

Of course it is not appropriate to summarize Hebrew creativity in Poland with such generalizations.[21] Hebrew literature in indepen-

19. Yosef Klausner, "Shloshet ha-merkazim shel ha-sifrut ha-ivrit ha-hadashah be-Polanyah," *Moznayim* 11 (1940): 214–23; Itamar Even-Zohar, "Ha-sifrut ha-ivrit ha-israelit: Model histori," *Hasifrut* 4 (1973): 431. On the decline of the modern Hebrew literary centers in Eastern Europe and the growing importance of the center in Eretz Israel, see Glenda Abramson and Tudor Parfitt, eds., *The Great Transition: The Recovery of the Lost Centers of Modern Hebrew Literature* (Totowa, N.J., 1985), in particular the essays by Gershon Shaked, Yaakov Shavit, and Zohar Shavit. It is unfortunate that the Yiddish literary centers in Poland between the wars receive no particular attention in this collection of essays despite the fact that some paralleled the Hebrew literary centers in time and location, a phenomenon noted merely in passing. The composition of this collection of essays reflects the traditional perception confining cultural phenomena in the Jewish community to discussion of a single language sphere.

20. S. Y. Pineles, "Ha-tekufah ha-ahronah be-yezirah ha-ivrit," *Moznayim* 11 (1940): 312. See also Hanan Hever, "From Exile-without-Homeland to Homeland-without-Exile: A Guiding Principle of Hebrew Fiction in Interwar Poland," in this volume.

21. On Hebrew literature between the two world wars, see Abraham Levinson,

dent Poland deserves full and in-depth scholarly attention in and of itself. Nonetheless, it is doubtful that such research could deny the shift of the center of Hebrew literature to Palestine, with all the negative implications this process has for the literary center in Poland, and in particular in Warsaw, which lost its importance.

In 1926 Dovid Bergelson pointed to three centers of the extra-territorial Yiddish literature—Warsaw, Moscow, and New York—and argued for the preeminence and greatest potential of the Moscow center.[22] Now, with a historical perspective that can see the decline of Yiddish literature in the Soviet Union in the 1930s, as well as the liquidations and executions of the late 1940s and early 1950s, this claim is seen as a nightmare. Anyone following the developments in the different centers of Yiddish literature between the two wars can easily discern today that only in the Polish literary center did there exist a continuous renewal of young literary talents without any real pressures or limitations. Despite all possible criticisms (not always justified) of Yiddish literature in Poland between the two wars—whether regarding its ideological reliance on left-wing parties, its estrangement from Hebrew literature, its material poverty among the largest Jewish concentration in Europe, and so forth—this was a dynamic literary center that left us many works of high quality in a great variety of genres and themes.

We have as yet no good historical summary of the accomplishments of this literary center;[23] nor is this the place to point to specific achievements. Nonetheless, I must emphasize certain elements that stand out in the general picture. Yiddish literature in Poland served all levels of readers, from the consumers of simplistic literature called in Yiddish *shund* through the unpretentious light novel of a quite "respectable" literary standard, to the experimental and bold

---

Ha-tenuah ha-ivrit ba-golah (Warsaw, 1935); Shmuel Rozenhek, "Kavim le-toldot ha-tarbut ha-ivrit be-Polin bein milhamah le-milhamah, in *Sefer ha-shanah/yorbukh,* 2:71–111, literature on the topic is listed on p. 111.

22. D. B. [Dovid Bergelson], "Dray tsentren—kharakteristik," *In shpan* 1 (1926): 84–96. Compare Shmuel Niger, "Naye tendentsn in der yidisher literatur zint nokh der milkhome," *Oyfn sheydveg* 2 (August 1939): 167–86.

23. On Yiddish literature in independent Poland, see Isaac Bashevis, "Arum der yidisher literatur in Poyln," *Tsukunft* 8 (1943): 468–75; I. I. Trunk, *Idealizm un naturalizm in der yidisher literatur* (Warsaw, 1927); Trunk, *Di yidishe proze in Poyln in der tkufe tsvishn beyde velt-milkhomes* (Buenos Aires, 1949); Nakhmen Meisel, *Geven amol a lebn: Dos yidishe kultur-lebn in Poyln tsvishn beyde velt milkhomes* (Buenos Aires, 1951); Shloyme Shvaytser, "Dos yidishe kultur-lebn in Poyln tsvishn beyde velt-milkhomes," in *Sefer ha-shanah/yorbukh,* 2:112–209. See also the articles cited in note 22, above, and note 24, below.

innovations intended for a select intellectual elite well acquainted with the current trends of other literatures in Europe. To this original literature in Yiddish must be added numerous translations from other literatures, with original and translated children's literature filling the needs of young readers. In addition to all this, Yiddish literature within the traditional religious camp was renewed in independent Poland. It not only maintained its connections with the traditional Yiddish literature of previous generations like the Tzenah Urenah and Hasidic tales in Yiddish in numerous editions, but it also diligently established a modern religious alternative to the essentially secular modern Yiddish literature.[24]

And finally, Yiddish writers in independent Poland served as the main reserve, both before and after World War II, for the most important Yiddish literary centers across the seas, which existed and continue to exist by virtue of emigration from Eastern Europe. The most outstanding writers in today's overseas literary centers are Yiddish writers from Poland of the period between the two wars: Abraham Sutzkever from Vilna, in Israel, and Isaac Bashevis Singer from Warsaw, in the United States.

As in other places where a Jewish reading public in the national language existed, in Poland a literature in the Polish language written by Jews began to appear as early as the latter half of the nineteenth century. Again as elsewhere, in Poland we can discern an essential division between two types of writers and literary works: those who directed their works overtly and solely to the Jewish audience, as for instance those writers who published in the weekly *Izraelita* and the like;[25] and those who wrote primarily for the general

---

24. On Orthodox literature in Yiddish, see Moshe Prager, ed., *Antologye fun religyeze lider un dertseylungen* (New York, 1955). See also Prager's extensive article, *"Dos yudishe togblat,* organ fun der yidisher ortodoksye in Poyln tsvishn beyde velt-milkhomes," in *Fun noentn over,* vol. 2, ed. Jacob Pat (New York, 1956), pp. 443–534. On problems of this literature and for a critical review of Prager's anthology, see Yankev Glatshteyn, *In tokh genumen,* vol. 2 (Buenos Aires, 1960), pp. 154–60.

25. There is no survey of the literature in Polish written by Jews from its beginnings to the Holocaust. For a survey and bibliography of this literature from the end of the eighteenth century until 1918, see Wilhelm Fallek, "Twórczość Żydow na polu literatury polskiej do 1918," in *Żydzi w Polsce Odrodzonej,* vol. 2, ed. Ignacy (Yitzhak) Schiper, Aryeh Tartakower, and Aleksander Hafftka (Warsaw, n.d.), pp. 74–90. Although Fallek distinguishes in principle between "Jewish writers" and "writers of Jewish origin" (p. 81), he does not maintain this distinction consistently. See also Eugenia Prokopówna, "The Sabbath Motif in Interwar Polish-Jewish Literature," in this volume; Prokopówna, "In Quest of Cultural Identity: Polish-Jewish Literature in the Interwar Period," *Polish Review,* 32, no. 4 (1987): 415–38; Władysław Panas, "Literatura polsko-żydowska: Pismo i rana," *Akcent* (Lublin) 3 (1987): 17–26.

Polish audience, with little or no reference to a Jewish audience, such as the well-known critic and historian of Polish literature Wilhelm Feldman, who wrote novels as well, among them novels on Jewish themes.[26] The numbers of both kinds of writers increased after World War I. For Jewish writers in Polish in independent Poland, the factor distinguishing their Jewish intention was the journal in which they chose to publish. A writer who published primarily in those dailies and journals that identified themselves as Jewish (which I shall discuss further later) had no real desire—or possibility—of reaching a general Polish audience.

More complex is the range of interests among the Jewish reading public in Poland, which certainly did not limit itself to Polish literature written by Jews. This reading public undoubtedly grew noticeably toward the end of the 1930s with the ascendancy of Polish education on all levels among Jews. The specifically Jewish literature in Poland was only an *additional* and *completing* literature, nurtured primarily by Polish literature not specifically intended for Jews. It may well be that the interest of Jewish readers in Polish literature not specifically intended for Jews centered especially on material bearing some relation to Jews, either in topic or authorship. But we cannot substantiate and fully portray this phenomenon with precision. We can, however, assume that the Jewish audience was generally more interested in the works of Julian Tuwim, Antoni Słonimski, and Józef Wittlin than in other Polish writers even when these Jewish writers did not write on topics directly or indirectly connected to Judaism. I certainly do not support the contention of antisemitic Polish critics, who saw the writers of Jewish extraction as a foreign element in Polish literature.[27] On the other hand, there is no doubt that this rejection by Polish antisemites heightened Jewish interest in these writers and their works.

26. Fallek, "Twórczość Żydow na polu literatury polskiej do 1918," pp. 85–87; Ezra Mendelsohn, "Jewish Assimilation in Lvov: The Case of Wilhelm Feldman," *Slavic Review* 28 (1969): 577–90.

27. On the status of Julian Tuwim in Polish society and the attacks against him on account of his Jewish origin, see Magnus Kryński, "Politics and Poetry: The Case of Julian Tuwim," *Polish Review* 18, no. 4 (1973): 3–33. See also Chone Shmeruk, introd. to Julian Tuwim, *My, Żydzi polscy . . . We Polish Jews . . .* (Jerusalem, 1984); Madeline G. Levine, "Julian Tuwim: We, the Polish Jews . . . ," *Polish Review* 17, no. 4 (1972): 82–84. On the problematic status of Polish writers of Jewish origin in Poland to the present day, see Artur Sandauer, *O sytuacji pisarza polskiego pochodzenia żydowskiego w XX wieku* (Warsaw, 1982); Sandauer, *Pisma zebrane*, vol. 3: *Publicystyka* (Warsaw, 1985), pp. 445–529.

It can be concluded that a large Jewish reading public turned to Polish literature, including literature written for Jews and published in the various Jewish organs, as well as to Polish literature generally, apparently with a certain preference for works that related to Jewish issues. Jewish youth and the Jewish intelligentsia who read the Jewish *Nasz Przegląd, Opinja,* or other Jewish newspapers in Polish also generally read on a regular basis the literary journals *Wiadomości Literackie* and *Sygnały,* which were not addressed to Jews but apparently took this specific audience into consideration.[28]

It is difficult today to define the precise components and scope of Polish literature read by those Polish Jews who maintained a Jewish identity while spurning the Jewish languages permanently or partially and who saw Polish as the main linguistic medium of their daily life and culture. We lack even a basic survey of Polish literature written by Jews and directed at Jews. There are bound to be some surprises in this area, though one cannot expect literary achievements equal in quality to the works of Tuwim, Słonimski, and Wittlin.[29]

It is even more difficult to evaluate the scope and power of that stratum within the Jewish intelligentsia in Poland which read three literatures—Hebrew, Yiddish, and Polish—or two of them, one of which was Polish. The knowledge of languages among Jews makes this ability no isolated phenomenon, as evidenced by the links to Polish literature found among writers in Yiddish and Hebrew.[30]

---

28. On this subject, see Marek Pytasz, "Kwestia żydowska i jej konteksty w 'Kronikach tygodniowych' Antoniego Słonimskiego," in *Studia Skamandryckie i inne,* ed. Ireneusz Opacki and Tomasz Stępien (Katowice, 1985), pp. 32–45, which deals with the feuilletons of Antoni Słonimski appearing weekly in *Wiadomości Literackie* and frequently dealing with the Jewish Question. It, of course, makes no difference whether Słonimski's writing always pleased the Jewish readers of the weekly. See also Magdalena M. Opalski, "*Wiadomości Literacki*: Polemics on the Jewish Question, 1924–1939," in this volume.

29. These widely held opinions on this subject refer consistently and in particular to these three writers. See "Wśrod pism i książek," *Zjednoczenie,* 1932, nos. 7–9, p. 21.

30. On this subject, see Chone Shmeruk, *The Esterka Story in Yiddish and Polish Literature* (Jerusalem, 1985); Shmeruk, "Avrom Sutskever un poylishe poezye: Juliusz Słowacki in der poeme 'Tsu Poyln,' " in *Yihuso shel shir: Likhvod Avrom Sutskever,* ed. Dov Sadan et al. (Tel Aviv, 1983), pp. 280–91. See also Shmeruk, "Jews and Poles in Yiddish Literature between the Two World Wars." A few remarks about Hebrew literature: Yisrael Cohen argues that Matityahu Shoham was "influenced by Jerzy Żuławski and Leopold Staff." Cohen, introd. to Matityahu Shoham, *Ktavim,* vol. 1 (Jerusalem, 1964), p. 9. Yehuda Warshaviak "wrote extensively in Hebrew about Polish literature and also translated Polish literature into Hebrew." Quoted in the article on Warshaviak in Getzel Kressel, ed., *Leksikon ha-sifrut ha-ivrit be-dorot ha-*

In these brief remarks concerning the place of Polish literature in the cultural system of Polish Jewry who used the Polish language I cannot deal with all the problems the topic raises. I am certain, however, that further research will strengthen my basic contention that this complex literary area was of great importance in the cultural polysystem of Polish Jewry between the two world wars.

Theater

To the best of my knowledge, the only professional Jewish theater in independent Poland was in Yiddish. This is not the place to describe the vicissitudes of this theater or its continuous attempts at renewal. The existence of the theater as a constant feature of the Yiddish cultural system is well known and needs no further explication.[31]

There were attempts to set up amateur theater groups in Hebrew, the most significant one apparently made in Vilna in 1928. The Vilna group performed for five years in Białystok, Grodno, Łuck, Dubno, Kowel, and elsewhere. In 1933 it disbanded. A reliable contemporary source commented:

> The Vilna studio fought with the last of its strength for its existence. In order to exist at a minimal level, it sent a detailed memorandum to the World Association for Hebrew Language and Culture and to the Cultural Committee of the Eighteenth Zionist Congress, which gathered in Prague in 1933. But these efforts were in vain. Hebrew cultural sponsors did not heed their request, and the studio disbanded.[32]

It was not likely that the Hebrew theater in Poland could exist for long without massive financial support. The linguistic barrier be-

---

ahronim, vol. 1 (Merhavia, 1965), p. 708. Yehuda Warshaviak's Hebrew collection of literary criticism, Meal gdot ha-Visla (Warsaw, 1929), is wholly devoted to Polish writers and their works; the preface explains that publication of this collection was supported by the Polish Ministry of Foreign Affairs. Ber Pomerantz translated into Hebrew the famous play Wesele (The Wedding), by Stanisław Wyspiański (Warsaw, 1938). These remarks are indicative of a widespread phenomenon in Hebrew and Yiddish literature alike that warrants further study.

31. On Yiddish theater, see Itsik Manger, Jonas Turkow, and Moshe Perenson, eds., Yidisher teater in Eyrope tsvishn beyde velt-milkhomes: Materyaln tsu der geshikhte fun yidishn teater: Poyln (New York, 1968). In addition, see Marian Melman, "Teatr żydowski w latach międzywojennych," Warszawa II Rzeczypospolitej (Warsaw, 1968), pp. 361–400. There is as yet no comprehensive and methodical study of the Yiddish theater in Poland between the two world wars.

32. Levinson, Ha-tenuah ha-ivrit ba-golah, p. 246; see also p. 247. And see Rozenhek, "Kavim le-toldot ha-tarbut ha-ivrit be-Polin bein milhamah le-milhamah," p. 77.

tween the Hebrew theater and the large Jewish audience in Poland prevented a substantial income from ticket sales. Even the professional Yiddish theater fought for its life, and ticket sales did not cover its expenses, except for certain especially successful performances. In any event, an interested theatergoer could choose theater in Yiddish or Polish as well.

We can assume that here and there Jews established amateur dramatic groups in Polish, but I have found no evidence of them. They were almost certainly local sporadic phenomena, for a limited local audience such as schools and similar organizations.

We know of only one serious attempt to establish a temporary Polish-language theater in Poland for a Jewish audience—in Warsaw in 1905. This theater, in which professional actors presented a play by Sholem Aleichem, appeared during the short transitional period between the formal lifting of the ban on Yiddish theater in the tsarist regime and its actual removal. This brief experiment was very successful among the Jewish audience. This is another confirmation of the Yiddish-Polish bilingualism of the Jewish theatergoing audience, although they preferred the Yiddish performance of the same play that was soon put on in Warsaw as well.[33]

Mark Arnshteyn, who translated Sholem Aleichem's play into Polish, is well known for his active involvement in both Yiddish and Polish theater in independent Poland. He often sponsored Jewish plays in the Polish theaters, plays intended both for Jewish and Polish audiences. Sponsors of Yiddish theater and culture saw these performances as a threat to the existence of a Yiddish theater. They suspected that this Polish theater would draw Jewish audiences from the Yiddish theater and lead to the establishment of a Jewish theater in Polish,[34] a fear that can be well understood considering that Jewish inhabitants of the large cities in Poland, among them Jews in traditional garb, were a regular part of the Polish theatergoing public as early as the nineteenth century.

The Polish theater's consideration of its Jewish audience is well known, and there were performances on specifically Jewish topics

33. On this matter, see Chone Shmeruk, "*Tsezeyt un tseshpreyt* le-Sholem Aleichem ve-ha-hazagot shel ha-mahazeh ba-safah ha-polanit be-Varshah ba-shanim 1905 ve-1910," in *Studies on Polish Jewry: Paul Glikson Memorial Volume*, ed. Ezra Mendelsohn and Chone Shmeruk (Jerusalem, 1987), pp. 79–95.
34. See Michael C. Steinlauf, "Mark Arnshteyn and Polish-Jewish Theater," in this volume.

that were intended primarily for Jewish audiences.[35] While these performances cannot be thought of as a kind of Jewish cultural creativity, we must consider their function within the Jewish cultural polysystem. From this perspective, at least, this phenomenon deserves a comprehensive study starting from the Jewish plays of Gabriela Zapolska[36] and including the plays translated from Yiddish performed on Polish stages. They begin as early as the nineteenth century in Warsaw with the presentation of Abraham Goldfaden's plays in Polish.

It is not extraneous to point out here that a number of Jewish actors of the professional Polish theater acted at times in the Yiddish theater as well. This bilingualism was even more widespread among the Yiddish theatergoers. Much talk in Polish could be heard in the corridors of the Yiddish theater between the two world wars.[37]

The links between the many branches of the professional Yiddish theater and the Polish theater, through its directors and actors, as well as the influence of the Polish theater upon Yiddish theater in independent Poland, have not been researched aside from sporadic and scattered references. Such a study would help define the significance of the contacts between the Yiddish theater and the Polish theater as well as the place and function of the Polish theater in the polysystem of Jewish culture in Poland.[38]

The Press

A most significant picture emerges from an examination of the various linguistic areas of the trilingual Jewish press in independent

35. Shmeruk, *"Tsezeyt un tseshpreyt* le-Sholem Aleichem"; Michael C. Steinlauf, "Jews and Polish Theater in Nineteenth-Century Warsaw," *Polish Review* 32, no. 4 (1987): 439–58.

36. Shmeruk, *"Tsezeyt un tseshpreyt* le-Sholem Aleichem." On Gabriela Zapolska's *Małka Szwarcenkopf* (1897) and *Jojne Firułkes* (1898), see Jadwiga Czachowska, *Gabriela Zapolska* (Cracow, 1966), pp. 171–81, 201–7. *Małka Szwarcenkopf* included Yiddish dialogue and traditional Jewish garb. It was translated and performed in Yiddish in 1917. In 1928 the play in Polish was performed in Warsaw under the direction of Mark Arnshteyn, with the role of the *badkhn*—a traditional Jewish entertainer at weddings—played by a professional *badkhn*! Czachowska, *Gabriela Zapolska*, p. 173.

37. On the actor Julian Oskar, see Shmeruk, *"Tsezeyt un tseshpreyt* le-Sholem Aleichem,"* p. 93; Steinlauf, "Jews and Polish Theater," p. 456. On the attendance of Jewish Polish-speaking youth at the Yiddish theater in Cracow, see the memoirs of Henryk Ritterman-Abir, *Nie od razu Kraków zapomniano* (Tel Aviv, 1984), p. 78.

38. Reviews of Polish theater performances in the Jewish press in all three languages—Hebrew, Yiddish, and Polish—may be viewed both as an expression of the readership's interest in the Polish stage and as an avenue of contact with Polish theater of great significance.

Poland. Certainly the Yiddish press of all types, from the dailies to the wide variety of specialist periodicals, was the most impressive element of the Jewish cultural polysystem. In 1936–37, eleven dailies in Yiddish appeared in Warsaw alone, two of them afternoon papers. The Yiddish press certainly served as the broadest expression of almost all the religious, political, social, cultural, and national movements representing the Jewish community in the nation.[39] The range of the press and periodical literature in Yiddish reflects the divisions of the 1931 census, in which nearly 80 percent of Polish Jews declared Yiddish as their mother tongue.

Efforts to establish and maintain a daily Hebrew newspaper in interwar Poland failed, and even the Hebrew weekly *Baderekh*, which began publication in Warsaw in 1932, eventually lost the struggle for survival. It was forced to stop publication in 1937 due to lack of funds and readers.[40]

The Jewish press in the Polish language had its origins in 1823–24.[41] From the 1860s on it developed further, as it did in other countries where the Jews acquired the national language in the process of modernization and adaptation to the predominant culture. Also as in other countries, even to this day, a Jewish paper served as a *supplement* to the non-Jewish dailies that the Jews read along with their Polish neighbors. In Poland until just before World War I, the Polish weekly *Izraelita*, published by Jews for Jews, served this function. The old London weekly, the *Jewish Chronicle*, also illustrates the function of a Jewish weekly supplement to a generally

---

39. For a comprehensive bibliography of the Jewish press in all three languages, see Paul Glikson, *Preliminary Inventory of the Jewish Daily and Periodical Press in the Polish Language, 1823–1982* (Jerusalem, 1983), pp. viii–xv. The statistical data are from *Reshime fun di peryodishe oysgabes vos kumen on in der bibliografisher tsentrale fun YIVO, 1935–1937* (Vilna, 1938). The Center for Research on the History and Culture of Polish Jews at the Hebrew University, Jerusalem, recently published a *Preliminary Inventory of Yiddish Dailies and Periodicals Published in Poland between the Two World Wars*, prepared by Yehiel Szeintuch with the assistance of Vera Solomon (Jerusalem, 1986); 1,715 items are registered in this inventory, which also provides basic information concerning the affiliation of the publications.

40. Yohanan Pogrebinski, "Ha-itonut ha-ivrit: Sekirah bibliografit," in *Enziklopedyah shel galuyot*, vol. 1: *Warsaw*, ed. Yitzhak Grinboym (Jerusalem, 1959), p. 487. For a more detailed treatment, see Shmuel Werses, "The Hebrew Press and Its Readership in Interwar Poland," in this volume.

41. On the press in the Polish language, see Glikson, *Preliminary Inventory*. On the Polish-Jewish press in Warsaw, the major center for the Jewish press in Poland, see Marian Fuks, *Prasa żydowska w Warszawie, 1823–1939* (Warsaw, 1979); and the review of the latter by Chone Shmeruk, in *Kiryat sefer* 55 (1980): 591–602. See also Shmeruk, "A Pioneering Study of the Warsaw Jewish Press," *Soviet Jewish Affairs* 3 (1981): 35–53.

non-Jewish daily among a Jewish population that had abandoned its Jewish languages partially or altogether.

Developments in independent Poland are, however, apt to surprise those who attempt to draw parallels with the Jewish press in other countries, both in the past and in the present. Immediately upon the establishment of the Second Polish Republic, Jewish dailies in Polish began to appear, among them some that became well established and were published throughout the period until World War II. From 1918 until 1939 *Nowy Dziennik* was published in Cracow, from 1919 to 1939 *Chwila* in Lwów, from 1923 to 1939 *Nasz Przegląd* in Warsaw, and from 1931 to 1939 another Jewish daily in Warsaw, *5ta Rano*.[42] These were not Jewish supplements for regular readers of non-Jewish Polish dailies, but the regular dailies of Jews speaking Polish, for they provided general news coverage. The establishment and maintenance of these dailies in Polish are impressive and unusual in comparison to the Jewish press in other countries, where Jewish periodicals in the national language were supplements to the daily press.[43] Circulation statistics of these newspapers explain the basis of their permanence and scope. In Warsaw *Nasz Przegląd* reached a daily circulation of 50,000, and similarly *5ta Rano* sold 50,000 copies daily[44]—for a total of 100,000 newspaper purchasers in that city alone. As for numbers of readers, to the number of purchasers we can add, at the least, family members. There are no statistics on the number of readers of Jewish dailies in Cracow and Lwów, who no doubt numbered some tens of thousands if one considers both purchasers and additional readers.

Accepted ideas on assimilation, or even on acculturation, al-

42. Glikson, *Preliminary Inventory.* Fuks, *Prasa żydowska*, p. 275, includes *Głos Poranny,* which appeared from 1929 to 1939 in Łódź. It must, however, be noted that *Głos Poranny* was merely under Jewish ownership and was not directed specifically or exclusively toward a Jewish audience. I am grateful to Professor Jakub Goldberg for this information.

43. In order to substantiate this argument, I examined the comprehensive list of Jewish periodicals in "Presse," *Jüdisches Lexikon*, Band IV/I (Berlin, 1930), p. 1104. The very small number of daily newspapers in non-Jewish languages whose existence was short-lived substantiates the fact that the Jewish press in the national language was, as a matter of fact, not a daily press. The Jewish daily press in Jewish languages such as Yiddish and Judezmo served those Jews who had not yet achieved proficiency in the national language. This is further substantiated in Joseph Fraenkel, *The Jewish Press of the World* (London, 1972), pp. 125–27. In the early 1970s daily Jewish newspapers outside of Israel numbered ten—all in Yiddish.

44. Fuks, *Prasa żydowska*, pp. 263, 275. Some additional, probably more exact figures, are now available in Michael C. Steinlauf, "The Polish-Jewish Daily Press," *Polin* 2 (1987): 219–45.

though quite vague, do not explain such phenomena as the very specific Jewish culture reflected in the daily Jewish press in Polish.[45] Of course the zealous guardians of Jewish languages and others fond of traditional life saw these newspapers and their readers as a clear expression of total assimilation. But in Poland this press was specifically Jewish in character; it generally supported Zionism and expressed strong and uncompromising Jewish positions *vis-à-vis* the government in all areas touching Jewish life. Let me quote from the statement made by *Nasz Przegląd* in its first issue:

> We are establishing a Jewish platform in the Polish language and offering it to Jewish public opinion. Let it be the gate through which Jews return and come closer to their nation, and for others an expression of the thoughts and aspirations, the will and goals of Polish Jews. . . . We wish to strengthen the national feeling among our brethren and to expand the recognition of the creative power and spiritual legacy of Judaism.[46]

Even so, this Jewish press in Polish was forced to battle for recognition of its national Jewish character and from time to time even dispute against those who denied a Jewish press in the Polish language the right to exist.

In addition to the Jewish daily press in Polish, there were quite a few weekly journals that faithfully reflected the life of Jews who expressed themselves primarily in Polish. Among the best and probably most important was *Opinja* (from 1935, *Nasza Opinja*)—"the Jewish Political, Social, and Literary Weekly"—which first appeared in Warsaw in 1933 and lasted until 1939. The circulation of this Zionist weekly, intended mainly for educated readers, reached 25,000. And yet even this weekly was forced as early as 1934 to defend its right to exist on the Jewish street.

> During a press conference, one of our outstanding journalists launched a serious accusation against the Jewish press appearing in Polish. He claimed that this press is itself an instrument for the assimilation of Jewish society and therefore it has no right to inveigh against the nullification of the agreement to defend the national minorities. If no evil intention, certainly a shocking lack of knowledge motivated the author of this accusation. Is it not known that the numbers of Jewish youth leaving the Polish school, having lost their independent

45. Regarding the inexact meaning of these terms and their varying usages, see Milton M. Gordon, *Assimilation in American Life* (Oxford, 1964), pp. 60–83. See also the doubts expressed by Lloyd P. Gartner, "Assimilation and American Jews," in *Jewish Assimilation in Modern Times*, pp. 171–83.

46. Quoted in Fuks, *Prasa żydowska*, p. 261.

national character through Polonization, grow daily, and that they
therefore cannot read Yiddish, never mind Hebrew? Is it not known
that in the circles of assimilated Jews, which up to now were completely estranged from the life of the Jewish masses in Poland, the
movement of return to Judaism is gaining momentum? . . . Must one
not build a bridge for all these people to link them with Judaism? And
only a Jewish press in Polish can build such a bridge.

The author of this article was the well-known Zionist leader Moshe
Kleinbaum, later famous in Israel as Moshe Sneh.[47]

Viewed from a historical perspective, we see that those who
hoped to instill Jewish values through the Jewish dailies and periodicals in Polish were correct. By using a non-Jewish linguistic tool,
they aided those Polish Jews for whom the Polish language had
become, in the process of modernization, the partial or exclusive
means of communication. I must emphasize that the Jewish publications in Polish informed readers about the entire cultural Jewish
polysystem in all its languages, including Hebrew and Yiddish. The
periodical literature published not only the works of Jewish authors
who wrote in Polish for Jewish readers but also translations from
Yiddish and Hebrew into Polish as well. The scope and significance
of this translation effort still await a major study, but its importance
and purposes are undeniable.

The Jewish periodical literature in Polish, in particular the wide-
ranging daily press, is most worthy of serious attention by historians.
The factors that produced the daily Jewish press in Polish and that
differentiated it from the press in non-Jewish languages in other
countries should be analyzed. The first Jewish daily in Polish—
Przegląd Codzienny—appeared in Warsaw in January 1913, against
a background of strong tension between Jews and Poles following
the elections to the Russian Duma in which the Jews supported the
socialist candidate Eugeniusz Jagiełło. In addition, the Beilis trial
necessitated the detailed and comprehensive reporting that only a
Jewish newspaper could provide for those Jewish readers who read
nothing but Polish.[48]

This background may explain why from that time on Jews did not

47. Glikson, *Preliminary Inventory,* no. 342; Fuks, *Prasa żydowska,* p. 278; M. K.
[Moshe Kleinbaum], "Pro domo sua," *Opinja,* September 23, 1934, no. 38. Fuks,
Prasa żydowska, p. 279, quotes the article without designating authorship.
48. Fuks, *Prasa żydowska,* pp. 150–53. On this crucial period, see the memoirs of
Bernard Singer (Regnis), *Moje Nalewki* (Warsaw, 1959), pp. 164–69. This very talented journalist stayed on until World War II as a permanent member of the staff of
the Jewish daily *Nasz Przegląd.*

patronize the Polish press, but in interwar Poland preferred their own daily press. Research must look for those factors that brought about the flourishing of the Jewish press in Polish after World War I. What pushed the Jewish readers away from the Polish dailies and led them to establish their own Polish press? What weight did Polish attitudes toward the Jews and the lack of opportunity for Jews to participate in the non-Jewish press have in establishing the Jewish alternative? These questions do not relate to the participants or regular staff of the Jewish press in Poland alone, but first and foremost to its readers. Is it true that the Jewish newspaper in Polish was a haven for both staff[49] and readers who could not find a way to assimilate into Polish society or identify totally with its culture and values, and even for those Jews who neglected the behavioral patterns, including the language, of traditional Jewry? Once again the impression is that modernization did not affect those Jews' self-identification as Jews and their Zionist and national views.

Conclusion

If we once again examine the three cultural systems—Hebrew, Yiddish, and Polish—among the Jews of interwar Poland, it seems that none was *complete* in itself. No one system could independently and exclusively provide all the elements expected in a full cultural system.

This conclusion is particularly striking regarding most components of the Hebrew system. Hebrew literature in Poland deteriorated due to lack of both writers and readers. A local Hebrew theater did not really exist. The Jews of Poland did not maintain a Hebrew daily newspaper, and even a weekly could not survive. Only 12.6 percent of children in Jewish elementary schools received a Hebrew education; in 1936–37 only 6.2 percent of the Jews in all the *gymnasiums* in Poland were in Hebrew schools. Higher education in Hebrew did not really exist except for the Instytut Nauk Judais-tycznych (Institute for Judaic Studies) in Warsaw,[50] which was limited in the scope of its studies. Compared to the others, this system

49. Could Bernard Singer and other Jewish journalists like him have secured positions on the staff of a daily Polish newspaper not owned by Jews and not directed to the Jewish reading public?
50. Avraham Weiss and Peninah Kremer Weiss, ''Ha-mahon le-madaei ha-ya-hadut be-Varshah,'' in *Sefer ha-shanah/yorbukh*, 2:359–80.

seems to be the most culturally lacking. However, its great strength lay not in what was generally found in Poland itself but in the options provided by the Jewish settlement in Palestine. Hebrew literature from Palestine was received in Poland with much interest and even preferred to local Hebrew literary efforts. The same was also true of both the daily Hebrew press and the periodical literature from Palestine. The very successful Polish tours of the Habimah and Ohel theater troupes made up for the lack of a Hebrew theater and drew a large and enthusiastic audience even among those who did not understand Hebrew and whose language was Yiddish or Polish. The Hebrew *gymnasiums* in Palestine and the Hebrew University in Jerusalem together with the Technion in Haifa also provided Jews in Poland with the opportunity for a higher education in Hebrew. For those aspiring to a personal realization of the Hebrew-Zionist ideal, the options outside Poland were open, at least in principle, despite the curb on emigration to Palestine during the Mandate.

The Yiddish cultural system, at least according to the 1931 census, showed a stronger foundation and held out greater possibilities. Its important components—literature, theater, and the press—were the most highly developed *vis-à-vis* the other systems. In reality, however, in view of the continuing modernization of Polish Jews, this system was clearly threatened. Its minor role in Jewish elementary and high school education was bound to limit its future. For the academic year 1939–40 there were only two candidates in Poland for the fellowships of YIVO in Vilna.[51] The "mechanical" Polonization, as it was characterized by one of the scholars of Jewish education in Poland, and the transition to speech in broken Polish, which the writer Zusman Segalovitch portrayed so well in his Yiddish stories,[52] were clear signs of Jewish youth's increasing distance from Yiddish as a cultural option, a trend already apparent in Poland of the 1930s. One must add that aside from the seemingly well-developed Yiddish culture in the Soviet Union, which was attractive to only a few, Yiddish did not offer any options outside of Poland's borders. The great achievements of Yiddish literature, theater, and press in Poland could not secure the future of the language in the face of processes over which this cultural system had no control.

51. Regarding YIVO in Vilna, see the relevant articles in *YIVO bleter* 46 (1980), dedicated to the fiftieth anniversary of the institute (1925–75).

52. Tartakower, "Yidishe kultur in Poyln tsvishn tsvey velt-milkhomes," pp. 7–8. Most of the stories by Zusman Segalovitch in the collection *Shmendrikes* (Warsaw, 1930) are devoted to this phenomenon.

The Polish system found its strong basis in Polish education. It filled gaps in literature and theater in the non-Jewish environment as well as in the local Yiddish theater and in translations from Hebrew and Yiddish. Its strongest achievement was in the independent Jewish press and in the great possibilities it derived from education, which it dominated on all levels. In a negative, paradoxical way, its strength also came in great part from the lack of opportunity afforded Polish Jews who, even with a Polish education, found that social and professional advancement, outside of Jewish realms, was closed to them.[53]

Finally, it must be reemphasized that the analysis presented here for each linguistic-cultural system separately, although following current research trends,[54] does not represent the cultural scene as it existed in reality for Polish Jews between the two world wars. The true and great power of this culture lay not in the isolation of these linguistic areas but in their interaction, an interaction that included the traditional religious cultural system as well. The full picture of the culture of Polish Jews can only be perceived by approaching it as a polysystem in which the power of its components comes from the force of their mutual, dynamic interaction, and not in their isolation.

53. On this subject, see Celia S. Heller, *On the Edge of Destruction: Jews of Poland between the Two World Wars* (New York, 1977). Several years ago excerpts of archival documents dating back to the 1930s were published, revealing evidence alarming even to those familiar with the rejection of Jews who sought to assimilate into Polish society and be accepted on the basis of their contribution to Polish culture. The essential facts are these: A general meeting of a society of Polonists at the Jagiellonian University in Cracow on February 9, 1937, decided unanimously to bar Jews from membership. Furthermore, at a meeting of this same group on March 6, 1937, the announcement was made that "an evening in honor of Bolesław Leśmian will not be held, since this society is concerned with the development of Polish culture and not any other culture." Bolesław Leśmian (1878–1937), one of the greatest lyricists of Polish poetry, was of Jewish origin. I am unaware that he ever betrayed any signs of identification with Jews or his Jewish origin. These documents of a group of Polish intelligentsia that concerned itself with Polish language and culture are quoted in a complimentary review of Sandauer's *O sytuacji pisarza polskiego pochodzenia żydowskiego w XX wieku*, by Marian Stępien, "Dobrze że Sandauer tą książkę napisał," *Polityka*, July 16, 1983.

54. For an illustration of this phenomenon, see *Sefer ha-shanah/yorbukh*, vol. 2, which contains separate summaries of the different cultural systems among the Jews of Poland during the interwar period. The volume has no article on the Polish cultural system among Jews. Literary studies have for some time displayed a greater openness toward Polish culture among Jews and taken a broader view of literary-linguistic phenomena in a combined Jewish framework. See the well-known book by Israel Zinberg, *Di geshikhte fun der literatur bay yidn* (Vilna, 1929–34); Dov Sadan, *Al sifrutenu: Masat mavo* (Jerusalem, 1950).

Shmuel Werses

The Hebrew Press and Its Readership in Interwar Poland

Stages in the Development of the Daily Hebrew Press

The development of the daily Hebrew press in Poland was marked by a desperate struggle for survival. There were constant difficulties: both financial, due to limited readership, and cultural-linguistic, due to the growth of multilingualism, with competition from both a flourishing Yiddish culture and a Yiddish press and a steady rise in the use of Polish in the Zionist camp, with its demand for Polish-Jewish newspapers.[1]

Despite all these obstacles, a cyclic drama unfolds, in which periods of resurgence and hope for the future follow periods of enforced silence for lack of funds, second thoughts about continuation, and gloomy announcements of cessation of publication. As this pathetic struggle is waged, attempts are made to establish a dialogue with faithful readers and to reprove a potential public that has turned its back. The scenario comes across clearly in the pages of the Hebrew press in its various configurations, a careful study of which serves as a basis for the present discussion.

Efforts to nurture a daily Hebrew press in Poland resumed after World War I. Continued daily publication of the long-standing newspaper *Hatzefirah* (The Dawn) was not feasible in 1917, and it became a weekly. In its first issue after this change, the editors stressed the great efforts made to keep the paper going in its regular format during wartime although the closing of the borders had left the

1. For more details, see Ayzik Rembah, "Ha-itonut ha-yomit ha-ivrit be-Polin bein shtei milhamot olam," in *Itonut yehudit she-haitah*, ed. Yehuda Gotthelf (Tel Aviv, 1973), pp. 15–43.

Hebrew press with "but a tiny circle of readers and authors." The temporary discontinuation of the newspaper had had such an impact on its loyal readership that the editors had decided to continue even under such conditions, "for it would be wrong of us to withhold the Hebrew word and the Hebrew idea from those who are so eager for them." Despite the reduction in size and frequency of appearance, the editors comforted themselves with the hope that the paper's quality would thereby be improved. Unlike a daily paper, where speed is essential, contributors to *Hatzefirah* in its weekly format "will be able to review their work again and again and take care not to let something out of their hands that is not perfect."[2]

As a weekly, *Hatzefirah* was published by the Zionist Organization in Poland, and the editors promised to devote most of this new forum to the pressing problems of Zionism. However, they stated they would not overlook contemporary Jewish issues and the plight of the Jews in the Diaspora, particularly in the new state of Poland. They also promised to publish articles on Judaica and Hebrew literature, although these subjects would no longer be central.[3]

Hatzefirah continued to appear as a weekly, in the spirit the editors outlined, until the end of 1919, that is, for more than two years. Meanwhile, it seemed the time had come for reestablishing it as a daily. A large, detailed announcement to this effect was published in the paper in late 1919. The daily was to be edited by Yitzhak Gruenbaum, with regular columns by E. N. Frenk and Shmuel Rosenfeld. Their object was "to fill a great gap, the lack of a daily Hebrew newspaper in the metropolis of Poland, where there were more Jews than in all the other countries of Europe." To preserve the link with the old *Hatzefirah*, the editors expressed their hope that Nahum Sokolow, the newspaper's popular editor in its former days of glory, would also contribute.[4]

The announcement emphasized ties with the Zionist movement and current events in Palestine. While stressing the Zionist character of the paper, the editors also indicated an interest in the problems of Polish Jewry.

> Since *Hatzefirah* will appear in Warsaw, the capital city of Poland, the home of the great majority of our Jewish brethren, whose affairs are of concern to the whole of the Jewish people, this newspaper will

2. *Hatzefirah*, March 1, 1917, no. 1.
3. Ibid.
4. *Hatzefirah*, December 30, 1919, no. 52.

allocate a large section to local Jewish issues, will fight for the welfare
of the Jewish population—and will try to ascertain the state of affairs
in the country in which we live.

In the wake of this declared involvement in the problems of Jewish
political status and citizenship, readers were promised detailed, up-
to-date information on national affairs and what was being written
in the general Polish press, especially on matters of Jewish concern.
In addition to political and social material, there was to be a literary
column. The idea was to turn *Hatzefirah* of 1920 into a reliable source
of information, capable of meeting the needs of the Hebrew reader
in all spheres and making other newspapers superfluous. In the
editors' words, "One will find in it all the types of news one finds
in other newspapers, both general and Jewish, as well as things one
would find nowhere else."[5]

On January 2, 1920, several days after this plan was published,
Hatzefirah commenced as a daily. Yehoshua (Osias) Thon and Yosef
Heftman were now added to the list of editors. In a festive address
to its readers, the newspaper recounted its history.[6]

While *Hatzefirah* won encouragement from the Zionist camp, non-
Zionist parties were less receptive. A week later Gruenbaum wrote
an article on the opposition of the Orthodox Agudat Israel, whose
Yiddish newspaper had warned its young people against reading
Hatzefirah. Gruenbaum responded with a heated polemical argument, passionately restating the object of *Hatzefirah* "as a sounding
board for those who seek life, the creators of a life of renewal and
salvation. It is fighting stagnation and decline—and in this fight it
will try to rescue from stagnation and death anyone with a spark
of life still flickering in him." Gruenbaum's argument may have had
the opposite effect. Several years later, a contemporary close to the
paper testified that "most of its older readers were driven away by
the change in overall direction, the radicalism and the contrast to
the tradition of tolerance from the days of Sokolow."[7]

By the time a year had passed, the new *Hatzefirah* was already in
distress. In an open letter from the Central Committee of the Zionist
Organization in Poland, run by the newspaper several times, we

5. Ibid.
6. *Hatzefirah*, January 2, 1920, no. 1.
7. Yitzhak Gruenbaum, "Valad lo met," *Hatzefirah*, January 9, 1920, no. 7;
Ephraim Zinger, "Ha-yesh efsharut lekayem iton ivri yomi be-Polin?" *Haolam*,
July 16, 1926, no. 30, pp. 556–57.

learn of the problems encountered heretofore and the likelihood of discontinuing publication. This letter described the material and spiritual difficulty in publishing a newspaper in the postwar years, at a time when Soviet troops had invaded Poland and disturbed the normal course of life: "Since the Great War, the number of towns in this country where *Hatzefirah* is circulated has gradually decreased, and distribution has also been hindered greatly by the post office, which does not operate properly in times of emergency." Nevertheless, the newspaper continued to be printed out of nationalist sentiment: "The only Hebrew daily in the entire Diaspora is a symbol for us of the Hebrew revival for which we yearn with all our heart." Thus readers were urged to sign up new subscribers to bring readership up to ten thousand. At the same time, those who voiced their belief in the Hebrew revival but demonstrated the opposite were rebuked: "Why haven't all those thousands and tens of thousands for whom the constant call for Hebrew is a deep spiritual need arisen and come to our aid?"[8]

This emotional plea was followed by further efforts to generate interest among readers and press them into action on behalf of the Hebrew newspaper whose existence was at stake. An advertisement appeared for a public meeting "devoted to the subject of the Hebrew press"; it was organized by the Ivriyah Society, with the participation of Zionist Organization delegates. There was also a notice about a lecture under the same auspices to be delivered by E. N. Frenk, a member of *Hatzefirah*'s editorial staff, on how a newspaper is made.[9]

The open letter from the Central Committee did not seem to have much impact. Some three months later another plea issued by the Zionist Organization was reprinted in *Hatzefirah* nine times. It complained about the lack of response to the earlier call and warned that the newspaper was in danger of closing, "even though a blush of shame covers our face when we speak of such things."[10] Even this admonishment went unheeded, and at the end of 1921 *Hatzefirah* ceased publication.

8. *Hatzefirah*, December 23, 1920, no. 277; December 29, 1920, no. 282; December 31, 1920, no. 284; January 2, 1921, no. 1; January 5, 1921, no. 4; January 7, 1921, no. 6; January 9, 1921, no. 7; January 11, 1921, no. 9; January 14, 1921, no. 12.

9. *Hatzefirah*, December 24, 1920, no. 278; January 14, 1921, no. 12.

10. *Hatzefirah*, March 8, 1921, no. 54; March 9, 1921, no. 55; March 10, 1921, no. 56; March 11, 1921, no. 57; March 13, 1921, no. 58; March 14, 1921, no. 59; March 15, 1921, no. 60; March 20, 1921, no. 64; March 21, 1921, no. 65.

After three years of inactivity—from late 1921 until early 1925, during which Polish Jewry was left without a daily Hebrew newspaper—the paper reorganized and made a new start under the name *Hayom* (Today). The first issues were devoted not only to the congratulations and encouragement of institutions that promised their help but also to outlining the future path of the newspaper and probing the reasons for past difficulties and failures.

An editorial collectively blamed readers and writers of Hebrew, community activists, and political institutions "for the absence of a Hebrew press in Poland and the scarcity of the Hebrew word in our country," in spite of the long-standing journalistic tradition prior to the war.[11]

On the other hand, an article by Thon, also in the first issue of *Hayom*, was more positive in tone. Thon believed there was still justification and a future for a Hebrew daily in Poland. He called upon Hebrew readers in the Diaspora, and particularly those in Poland, who form "the largest, densest, most concentrated, and possibly the most animated and organized Jewish community in the Diaspora," to lend a hand to the renascent Hebrew press. He went on to sketch a plan for the type of newspaper he would like to see, which would include articles on "secular issues" such as sports and finance as well as on the building of Palestine. Stressing the moderate stance of *Hayom*, Thon promised readers: "We have not come to contradict or destroy but to build and restore. All that belongs to the nation is sacred to us, and we ridicule nothing, even if we are critical. Our fight is only against that which is slumbering. We will not allow our people to stagnate."[12]

In the same issue of *Hayom*, Yaakov Fichman speculated on the reasons why a Hebrew newspaper should have closed down at a time when the Hebrew book seemed to be thriving. Books, in his opinion, were not a substitute for a Hebrew newspaper, which was a living, life-giving force measuring "the pulse of the nation." From the perspective of a poet and literary critic, Fichman mourned the weakening of the bond between the Hebrew writer and the press. As for the role of the new publication, he believed it should be the mouthpiece "of liberated Judaism, of the humanist-nationalist idea, of Jewish culture." Yet it should not serve as a forum for only a

11. *Hayom*, no. 1 (January 1, 1925).
12. Yehoshua (Osias) Thon, "Tehiyat ha-hayim," ibid.

select few. While Fichman did not advocate pandering to the reader's taste, he believed "it is essential that it also have the vitality of a good popular paper."[13]

The reappearance of a Hebrew daily in 1925 was a highly significant event in the life of the Zionist community in Poland. After the printing of the first issues of *Hayom*, a public gathering was held in Warsaw. According to the report, "a large crowd filled the hall. The young people were especially numerous." The editor, Yosef Heftman, "relayed interesting details about the enthusiasm with which the paper was greeted, about the congratulatory telegrams received by the editorial staff, and about the great opportunities for Hebrew literature opened up by the newspaper." Fichman, who also spoke at the gathering, commented on "the disgrace that had been lifted from Polish Jewry at not having a Hebrew newspaper until now."[14]

Notices in the paper attest to the wide circulation enjoyed by *Hayom* in its early days: "The first issue of *Hayom* was sold out. The second issue was printed in double the number of copies, and also sold out. The excitement of readers thirsting for a Hebrew newspaper was so great that in some places newspaper vendors were offered very high prices for copies of *Hayom*, which had run out."[15]

This period of resurgence and awakening among readers of *Hayom* persisted throughout the first stages of publication. Three weeks after its first appearance, the editors placed a large notice on the front page reporting with satisfaction that their hopes had been fully borne out: "The congratulations and expressions of joy, the telegrams of thanks and appreciation, which have not ceased to arrive both from individuals and from societies and institutions, clearly indicate how pleasing *Hayom* is to all sectors of the community."[16]

The conviction that maintaining a Hebrew daily was possible was still felt in the editors' appeal to the readership six months later. With the flowering of the Hebrew language, "when the idea of Hebrew nationalism is in its glory, the Zionist dream is materializing far beyond expectations and thousands of Jews are immigrating to Palestine every month," the editors felt "it is our duty to establish a regular Hebrew forum; we must ensure the existence of a daily

13. Yaakov Fichman, "Ha-iton ha-ivri," ibid., continued in *Hayom*, no. 8 (January 9, 1925).
14. Yosef Heftman and Yaakov Fichman, in *Hayom*, no. 5 (January 6, 1925).
15. *Hayom*, no. 3 (January 4, 1925).
16. *Hayom*, no. 20 (January 23, 1925).

newspaper in Hebrew."[17] In reality, these conclusions and hopes were not justified.

The true state of *Hayom* was revealed to the public in an article by Thon a year after publication began. Focusing on the newspaper's role in the revival of the Hebrew language in everyday life, the article included circulation figures showing that in the early days, *Hayom* had had ten to twelve thousand subscribers and purchasers in Poland. While the first issue sold fifteen thousand copies, the anticipated follow-up never materialized. Thon asked in sorrow: "Why did they drop out one by one, until there were not enough to maintain the paper?" Circumstances had grown worse: "For a year, *Hayom* has been surviving on a miracle—through great sacrifice and difficulty. *Hayom* has fought a bitter war for its existence."[18]

In the very same issue there was a large editorial announcement marking the newspaper's second year of publication. Here further improvements were promised, despite the fact that the paper lacked the resources at the disposal of the widely circulated Yiddish papers. The editorial in the next issue was in the same spirit, pointing out the importance and justification of publishing a Hebrew newspaper, "which had begun to appear after years of journalistic silence due to difficult and bitter times."[19]

The hopes for the improvement of *Hayom* as it entered its second year were dashed after only a few months. For five days, February 5– 9, 1926, the newspaper was shut down for technical and financial reasons. This pause touched off a wave of speculation among readers about whether it would close permanently. This time the crisis proved temporary, however, and the editors later noted with satisfaction "that during this brief intermission we were shown how devoted our readers are to the Hebrew press. From all sides we were inundated with telegraphic queries about the state of the Hebrew organ and encouragement to go on working."[20]

The cessation of *Hayom* for this short interval also aroused much sentiment in the Palestine press. The newspaper *Haaretz* expressed sorrow and disbelief: "Has the day come when Polish Jewry is fated to live like the other parts of our nation in America, Germany, Ru-

17. *Hayom*, no. 146 (June 26, 1925).
18. Yehoshua Thon, "Zorekh ve-yekholet," *Hayom*, no. 303 (January 1, 1926).
19. *Hayom*, no. 303 (January 1, 1926); "Ha-shanah ha-shniyah le-kiyum *Hayom*," *Hayom*, no. 304 (January 3, 1926).
20. *Hayom*, no. 334 (February 19, 1926).

mania, etc.—without the ring of a Hebrew word? The idea is a terrible one, and difficult to accept."[21] The sensitivity in Palestine to the problems of the Hebrew press in the Diaspora were also expressed in the good wishes sent by the Hebrew Writers' Association convention in Tel Aviv at the time *Hayom* began to reappear: "With wonder and high hopes, we watch from afar your difficult daily struggle against apathy and alienation."[22]

The true plight of *Hayom* as it contemplated and fought for its survival was revealed in a letter from the editors that appeared several times during May 1926—one year and four months after the newspaper's inception. This emotional piece spoke of "the writhing of Hebrew journalism in untold agony, expending immeasurable amounts of energy." Readers of Hebrew were warned of the imminent discontinuation of the newspaper, despite desperate attempts to continue publication: "We have invested our blood and marrow in this modest work, in nurturing a daily Hebrew paper, in the face of apathy from all sides." Now, in contrast to the encouraging words and satisfaction voiced earlier, the editors admitted, "The months of existence of *Hayom* have been one long chain of pain and suffering for its workers, and a shameful mark of disgrace for the Jewish public desirous of the revival of Hebrew."[23]

The loyal readership of *Hayom* was called on to mount a subscription campaign to keep the paper from closing, and at first this appeal seems to have been successful. The paper announced the mobilization of new subscribers and the founding of special groups in cities and towns in support of the Hebrew press. Appended to these notices were such statements as: "Altogether, there has recently been much action on behalf of *Hayom*." There was also a report on a meeting in Warsaw at which the well-known Reuven Brainin was a guest speaker. Brainin talked about "the great value and importance of the only Hebrew organ in our country, and the terrible disgrace and loss to the entire Hebrew national movement should that organ fall." He also outlined a plan of action to ensure *Hayom*'s continued existence.[24]

21. Quoted in S. T., in *Hayom*, no. 350 (March 2, 1926).
22. Reprinted in *Hayom*, no. 370 (March 26, 1926).
23. *Hayom*, no. 391 (May 2, 1926); no. 392 (May 3, 1926); no. 393 (May 4, 1926); no. 398 (May 7, 1926).
24. *Hayom*, no. 397 (May 9, 1926); Reuven Brainin, quoted in *Hayom*, no. 398 (May 10, 1926).

But this flurry of activity ultimately made little difference; *Hayom* ceased publication on May 25, 1926. In response, Eliezer Steinman published an article entitled "Kol kore le-yehudei Polin" (An Appeal to the Jews of Poland) in the Palestinian literary periodical *Ketuvim,* giving vent to his anger and fear: "Jews of Poland! The absence of the newspaper *Hayom* for the Hebrew-speakers among you pains us here and shames you there." Steinman was concerned that "the rejected newspaper will be followed by the book, and a single tombstone will cover them both in a grave of oblivion to Hebrew in Poland."[25]

As it turned out, the discontinuation of *Hayom* was not long lived. Four months later, on September 29, 1926, following a financial reorganization and additions to the staff, it reappeared as *Hatzefirah.* Again the cycle of program outlines and declarations by the "new-old" editorial staff commenced, followed by appeals to Hebrew readers to extend their help by subscribing to the paper. Special attention was given to the symbolic importance of the name *Hatzefirah* for the renascent newspaper and to the participation of the highly reputed editor of the prewar years, Nahum Sokolow, whose new series of feuilletons and essays, called "Personalities," was widely advertised: "Readers will follow with delight the new character series to be unraveled before us by this author of genius." On this occasion *Hatzefirah* also printed a letter of encouragement from Sokolow himself, expressing the hope that the paper would be "a resuscitating force, affiliated with the past and striving toward the future, with deep roots in our national present." In his congratulatory remarks Sokolow sanctioned the use of the name "Hatzefirah" in the hope that the paper would be edited "the way I would edit it, with complete autonomy, of course, on the technical side."[26] To stress continuity with the old paper, a regular column was initiated called "*Hatzefirah* Fifty Years Ago," reproducing selections from the newspaper in those days. However, it was clear that editing the paper in the spirit of old times would be an anachronism in view of the changes experienced by Polish Jewry, with its new social and political components. In fact, the newspaper drifted away from the traditions of the old *Hatzefirah* as the years went by.

Nevertheless, Yosef Heftman, former editor of *Hayom* and now ed-

25. Eliezer Steinman, "Kol kore le-yehudei Polin," *Ketuvim,* August 24, 1926, no. 4, reprinted in *Hatzefirah,* January 2, 1927, no. 1.

26. *Hatzefirah,* September 29, 1926, no. 1.

itor of the new *Hatzefirah*, explained his ties to tradition: "We always bear in mind that the name *Hatzefirah*, which we have now dusted off, has become a symbol, and that we must exercise care; the name obligates us." He also pointed out the uniqueness of the Hebrew press, which he believed was created not only to relay information but also to teach and educate.[27]

Yitzhak Gruenbaum, who was well known in those years for his partisan and political activities in Poland, also indicated a willingness to fight for the survival of the new Hebrew newspaper, even when linguistic assimilation and the flourishing of the Yiddish press made this difficult: "The need for a Hebrew newspaper is in our bones and drives us into action. We fall and rise, fall and rise, and in our stubbornness lies our strength."[28]

Again, the early months of the newspaper in its new form were marked by reawakening and hope for the future. An evening of "live journalism" ended with a unanimous decision to assign the task of increasing readership to all members of the Hebrew camp in Poland.[29]

A month after the renewed publication of the newspaper under the name *Hatzefirah*, the editor felt the need for a preliminary report on its impact. He noted with satisfaction that "the new *Hatzefirah* has found its way into the hearts of the Hebrew reader." In his estimation the very first days were already proof that "it is progressing and improving and promises to be an attractive, good-quality paper—not a mouthpiece for empty clamor and abominable sensationalism." Reader responses reaching the editor had been favorable. In his eyes, *Hatzefirah*'s first days were therefore "days of resurgence and encouragement." He looked forward to further improvements in the paper, and, what is more, the finest Hebrew writers had promised their participation "so as not to lose a beacon for Hebrew literature and thought in the Jewish dispersion in Poland."[30]

The appearance of the fiftieth issue of *Hatzefirah* was celebrated more modestly, the editors noting matter of factly that the new path of progress and improvement would have an even greater impact on future issues. To achieve that goal, a steadiness of purpose was re-

---

27. Y. H. [Yosef Heftman], "*Hatzefirah* le-koreiha," ibid.
28. Yitzhak Gruenbaum, in ibid.
29. Yehudoni, "*Hatzefirah* ha-hayah," *Hatzefirah*, November 1, 1926, no. 27.
30. Y. H. [Yosef Heftman], "El ha-korim," *Hatzefirah*, October 29, 1926, no. 25.

quired of both writers and readers—and "not fleeting enthusiasm."[31]

This optimistic outlook on the newspaper's development continued in later appeals, when readers were asked to renew their subscriptions. Improvements in content and form were noted, with emphasis on *Hatzefirah*'s aspiration "to be the only Hebrew organ in the Diaspora to bring the Hebrew word to the Jewish masses every day."[32]

A totally different picture—one of uncertainty and hardship—emerged a year later in the editors' congratulatory message to the Third National Tarbut Convention in Poland. Now the difficulty of maintaining a Hebrew newspaper was described, "for there has been a long chain of misfortune and suffering over the past three years, as the Hebrew press in Warsaw has hovered between life and death." Aside from financial and technical difficulties, there was profound disappointment at the indifference displayed by both Hebrew writers and the Zionist establishment.[33]

In speaking to the Tarbut convention, *Hatzefirah*'s editor Yosef Heftman described an even wider range of problems encountered by the Hebrew press. Comparing Hebrew and Yiddish journalism, he found Hebrew journalism more universal, more expressive of the Jewish people as a whole. The Hebrew language was a factor of special importance: "We choose to express in it our innermost desires, as it is closest to them." Heftman elaborated here on the general significance of the newspaper in this era, and particularly the Hebrew newspaper, in its promotion of Hebrew in everyday life and in its fostering of Hebrew literature. He also protested the fact that Palestine, with its small Jewish population, had three Hebrew dailies, while the Jews in the Diaspora could barely keep up one. In this respect, Polish Jewry had a special obligation: "In the Diaspora, there is no other Jewish community so large and so responsible for tradition and attitudes toward Hebrew culture and journalism as the Polish Jewish community, which also holds the keys to the heritage of Russian and Ukrainian Jewry."[34]

31. *Hatzefirah*, November 28, 1926, no. 50.
32. *Hatzefirah*, December 24, 1926, no. 73; see also *Hatzefirah*, December 31, 1926, no. 79.
33. *Hatzefirah*, December 27, 1927, no. 295.
34. Yosef Heftman, address to the Third National Tarbut Convention, printed in *Hatzefirah*, December 28, 1927, no. 296.

Despite numerous obstacles, especially during 1927 and 1928 when the size was reduced to four pages on weekdays and eight before the Sabbath, *Hatzefirah* reached its five hundredth issue in mid-1928. The editors marked this milestone with a call to increase readership to enable the newspaper to continue publication: "Hebrew-speakers wherever they be should bear in mind the difficult fight for survival being waged by the sole Hebrew newspaper in these times of impoverishment and assimilation, when our thought and literature have been paralyzed."[35]

In spite of these continual pleas, *Hatzefirah* in its present form did not last much longer: it stopped publication on September 24, 1928. In a eulogy to the paper published in *Haolam,* contributing author Yehuda Warshaviak presented a statistical readership survey of the Hebrew press in Poland. In its first two months *Hayom* had had ten thousand readers, which later dropped to six thousand. As emigration to Palestine increased, the number dropped even more. Financial trouble led to a reduction in the size of the paper and a decrease in the range of its contents, resulting in a new exodus of readers seeking higher standards. In consequence, *Hatzefirah* was unable to employ Hebrew writers, whose fee was beyond the capacity of a newspaper fighting for its very existence. Thus a vicious cycle was initiated, whereby cutbacks "began to infuriate readers, some of whom left the paper. As the number of readers decreased, even more economizing took place and the quality of the paper deteriorated further. The paper did not meet standards because readership was small—and readership was small because standards were not met."[36]

Veteran journalist and editor Ben-Zion Katz, also reacting to the discontinuation of *Hatzefirah,* said that experience had shown there was no longer justification for a Hebrew daily in the Diaspora. He proposed turning *Hatzefirah* into a weekly. In his estimate, Hebrew readers of the old school, who had constituted a loyal following, had since disappeared. They were now accustomed to reading Yiddish or Polish newspapers, which also dealt with Jewish and Zionist matters. On the other hand, H. A. Hurwitz, responding to this proposal, believed that although the circulation of *Hayom* and *Hatzefirah* had

35. *Hatzefirah,* May 8, 1928, no. 105; May 10, 1928, no. 107; in a revised form on May 18, 1928, no. 114; May 21, 1928, no. 116.
36. Yehuda Warshaviak, "Al ha-itonut ha-ivrit be-Polanyah," *Haolam,* October 19, 1928, no. 42, p. 805.

reached a low of three thousand, the conditions necessary to support a Hebrew daily in Poland could still be attained.[37]

Optimism notwithstanding, it took more than two years for *Hatzefirah* to reappear. Publication resumed in mid-March 1931 with the help of a one-time private contribution. Thon, who had taken an active part in the various attempts to maintain a Hebrew newspaper in Poland, now recognized a repetitive cycle in the rise and fall of Hebrew journalism. In his opinion, it was the task of the new paper to accentuate even more the importance of Hebrew in Jewish life, "so that the Hebrew language becomes a language of their needs and desires, a language of their thoughts and feelings to the full extent." On the other hand, writer and Zionist activist Shimon Federbush wanted *Hatzefirah* "to raise the banner of the Hebrew revolution, to return us to Hebrew enthusiasm, to produce a movement of Hebrew pioneerism." Yitzhak Gruenbaum, well versed in the problems of Hebrew journalism in the Diaspora, cited as one source of difficulty the change in the composition of readership; it was now hard to find a common denominator and overall orientation that would satisfy the pluralistic public interested in a newspaper of this kind.[38]

After its reappearance in 1931, *Hatzefirah* only stayed open another year. With effort, it was replaced by a weekly paper called *Baderekh* (En Route), first published on September 15, 1932, under the editorship of A. L. Yakubovitz. In his opening remarks, Yakubovitz stated that the weekly format was only temporary; the goal was to turn the newspaper into a daily, which was sorely needed by the Hebrew movement at this time. In terms of contents *Baderekh* would resemble a daily paper, "and it will also be a newspaper for the Hebrew family—a political, current affairs, and literary newspaper, Jewish and general, that will include science, *belle lettres*, and criticism and offer a free forum for young people from all national parties." All this was to be accompanied by close contact with the readership and sensitivity to its requests.[39]

37. Ben-Zion Katz, "Ha-yesh kiyum le-yoman ivri ba-golah," *Haolam*, November 9, 1928, no. 45, pp. 864–65; H. A. Hurwitz, "Le-sheelat kiyumo shel iton ivri ba-golah," *Haolam*, December 7, 1928, no. 49, p. 934.

38. Yehoshua Thon, "Ki sheva yipol . . . ve-kam," *Hatzefirah*, March 15, 1931, no. 1; Shimon Federbush, "Ha-mered ha-ivri," *Hatzefirah*, March 22, 1931, no. 7; Yitzhak Gruenbaum, "Ve-ha-derekh mahi?" *Hatzefirah*, March 15, 1931, no. 1.

39. A. L. Y. [Yakubovitz], "Le-hofaat *Baderekh*," *Baderekh*, September 15, 1932, no. 1.

Gruenbaum, who had already seen a number of good starts and disappointments in the sphere of Hebrew journalism, again contemplated the crisis resulting from changes in Hebrew readership in Poland. This public was now so varied that he did not advocate adapting the newspaper to the taste of its conservative readers. He called for a different pace, stating resolutely, "Let us have no fear of shaking up the reader, shocking him with our description of life and probing of its issues. If he is shocked and fearful—then he will find our paper interesting and desire to read it."[40]

Even after the daily press had shrunk to a weekly, circulation and finances were no better. The visions of a rapid shift to daily publication were quickly set aside. Within two months the editors announced that since the paper could not cover expenses and the number of readers-subscribers was continually declining, it would have to cut back from eight to six pages—or raise the price. This juncture afforded an opportunity to appeal to the remaining readers: "Know, *Baderekh* readers, that those of you who have been faithful until today, are the most loyal of Hebrew-speakers. Each and every one of you is a chosen individual to whom the Hebrew word is dear. You are bound in soul to Hebrew, not with noise and clamor, but out of inner love and spiritual need."[41]

Baderekh continued publication, but two years later, when the editors marked the appearance of the 150th issue, they again pondered aloud the paradox of a flourishing Yishuv (Jewish community in Palestine) and rising emigration to Palestine while a Hebrew weekly in the Diaspora had to fight for survival: "Is it conceivable to any Hebrew-speaker that in our state, with its millions of Jews, this modest Hebrew organ should collapse?" A campaign to double the number of readers and subscribers was now launched with this emotional appeal: "Hebrew-speaker, will you indeed deafen yourself to the sound of your conscience, which calls upon you to nurture every living bud of Hebrew culture in the Diaspora?"[42]

With the same melancholy, writer Yosef Babitsch surveyed the history of Hebrew journalism, commemorating the founding of the first Hebrew daily, *Hayom,* in 1886. He expressed his amazement that one Hebrew weekly was desperately gasping for life while the Jewish community in Poland supported twenty-five Yiddish and

40. Yitzhak Gruenbaum, "Ve-shuv nisayon," ibid.
41. "El korei *Baderekh,*" *Baderekh,* November 3, 1933, no. 43.
42. "Et laasot," *Baderekh,* September 2, 1935, no. 31.

three Polish papers: "And all this in the country considered the most Zionistic and the most Hebrew-oriented in the Diaspora."[43]

Despite the broken spirit emerging from these various assessments, the author and cultural activist Abraham Levinson believed that a daily Hebrew paper still had a chance, provided that former errors and shortcomings were rectified. In 1935, after describing the fate of earlier papers, he stated:

> Yes, there is room for a daily Hebrew newspaper in Poland, a public-oriented paper suited to the requirements of the time and the needs of the generation; a newspaper that will serve as a mouthpiece for the revolutionary spirit and content of our Zionist and Hebrew movement. But such a paper will arise when an association of readers from all levels of society has faith in its existence and recognizes its essentialness, and when it is properly edited and organized.[44]

Faith in the future of a Hebrew newspaper for Polish Jewry never materialized. *Baderekh* shut down two years after Levinson's forecast, at the end of 1937. Before its cruel annihilation, Polish Jewry would never again have a general Hebrew periodical of its own.

The Character of Hebrew Newspaper Readership

One of the key problems facing the daily Hebrew press in Poland, aside from financial and organizational difficulties, was its relationship with a diverse, unstable readership. Indeed, throughout the existence of the Hebrew press between the two world wars much attention was devoted to probing the character and essence of this readership. Occasionally readers were asked to share responsibility for the fate of the newspaper and to engage in activities on its behalf. Sometimes they were asked to express an opinion about the size, price, and content of the paper.

Among the investigations into the social and cultural makeup of this public, with its interlinguistic mobility among Hebrew, Yiddish, and Polish, Gruenbaum's inquiries, based on direct observation, are particularly notable. In 1926, after publication of *Hatzefirah* was resumed, he described the multilingualism common among potential purchasers of a Hebrew newspaper in Poland. Initially, families would buy two papers, one in Hebrew and one in a language understood by the whole family—Yiddish or Polish. When the budget

43. Yosef Babitsch, "Hag ha-itonut ha-ivrit," *Baderekh*, April 30, 1936, no. 18.
44. Abraham Levinson, *Ha-tenuah ha-ivrit ba-golah* (Warsaw, 1935), p. 227.

became tighter, the Hebrew newspaper, which only some family members could read, was dispensed with first. A similar process took place in the decision between a newspaper in Yiddish or Polish; as Polish Jews became more and more assimilated, the Yiddish paper was given up. Gruenbaum also pointed out the paradox accompanying the crisis of the Hebrew press. The Hebrew language had become more firmly rooted than before the war as a result of the broad network of Hebrew schools. The emphasis was, however, on speaking Hebrew rather than attachment to the Hebrew book. In his opinion, the habit of reading in Hebrew was not sufficiently fostered, as reflected in the dwindling cadre of young Hebrew newspaper readers.[45]

Other aspects of this readership were sketched by Gruenbaum in 1931, when *Hatzefirah* was renewed for the last time. Examining the makeup of readers from a social standpoint, he noted the homogeneity they had once exhibited. *Hatzefirah*'s former public had been more uniform in its tastes and desires, with the head of the household, full of longing for the religious life-style of his youth, being its chief representative. When the new state of Poland emerged, changes took place in this public. It was joined by young people from the Hasidic community, for whom a Hebrew daily was the only window onto the outside world, as well as by young people from the modern secular community. In the early 1920s, Gruenbaum perceived a further change: the dominant older readership was disappearing, and one sensed a move toward the flourishing Yiddish press. Hasidic readers had now found an answer to their needs in their own Yiddish newspaper, while those who had begun to assimilate read Polish papers and no longer needed a Jewish paper at all. Unfortunately, when this public ceased to be a natural readership cadre for the Hebrew press, young people from the Zionist youth movements did not move in. They had their own periodicals in Hebrew or were accustomed to reading the Hebrew press from Palestine. The problem facing *Hatzefirah* was thus which readership to cater to: "To the remnants of our former readership, the enlightened or nearly enlightened heads of households, or the younger generation. The demands of the two camps differ, and it is difficult for the newspaper to satisfy them both." On the other hand, catering only

45. Yitzhak Gruenbaum, "Od nisayon ehad," *Hatzefirah*, September 29, 1926, no. 1.

to one camp did not ensure enough readers to meet minimum circulation requirements.[46]

When *Baderekh* was first published, Gruenbaum continued his portrayal of the Hebrew reading public. This time he emphasized the keen competition from the Yiddish press, which had actually assumed several of the functions of the Hebrew paper and drawn away some of its readers. Now "the Hebrew press no longer has an environment of its own where only it is needed, as was the case in the generation before the war." Gruenbaum further lamented that out of the large population of Hebrew school graduates, no regular body of readers had formed. The new enlightened Jews were reading foreign language papers: "The enlightened Hebrew speaker has not shown solidarity with his newspaper, with Hebrew literature, especially in the Diaspora. In Palestine, this solidarity is a function of the place." This being the case, Gruenbaum believed it necessary to find a way back to the readers: "The reader must again find in the Hebrew newspaper all that he found when he emerged from the *besmedresh* [study house] and *yeshivah*—spiritual nourishment, news of the world, an answer to life's questions."[47]

Readers of the Hebrew newspaper were not always characterized by division into cultural and political camps; sometimes there was unity and partnership, too. In 1926, Heftman described the reading public of the renascent *Hatzefirah* in this light. He found "a heartwarming, close relationship, like in a family." From this perspective, readers were seen as "not just news-hungry people spending money to read information printed on a piece of paper; they are also friends and supporters, who have feelings of affection and passion for it, who rejoice at every positive innovation and are pained by any failure or mockery that peers from between the lines."[48]

Readers representing both generations came together at the evening of "live journalism" in Warsaw when *Hatzefirah* resumed publication in 1926. According to the report:

Old people, quite a few of them in velvet caps and brought up on Hayim Selig Slonimsky and Nahum Sokolow, now came to see who their heirs were in continuing the beautiful, responsible tradition of *Hatzefirah*: just "plain" people, the most devoted of Hebrew speakers,

46. Gruenbaum, "Ve-ha-derekh mahi?"; see also Chone Shmeruk, review in *Kiryat Sefer* 55 (1980): 594–98.

47. Yitzhak Gruenbaum, "Ve-shuv nisayon."

48. [Heftman], "*Hatzefirah* le-koreiha."

girls and boys from the Hebrew schools and seminaries, and a very small number of official Zionists.[49]

This ideal alignment of the two groups of *Hatzefirah* readers was not long lived in the face of the Zionist movement in Poland. Among the reasons cited by Hurwitz for the discontinuation of *Hayom* and *Hatzefirah* was the split with its potential, natural reading public—members of the pioneering youth movements. These young people found these papers too conservative in character for their taste and too moderate and restrained in general orientation, for the papers shied from the sharp political contrasts in the Zionist movement. Hurwitz described the state of affairs in 1928 as follows: "The Halutz and Hashomer Hazair movements were always complaining that *Hayom* and *Hatzefirah* were too 'middle class.' These youngsters, upholders of the Hebrew language, wanted a Hebrew newspaper that smelled of them. Since neither of these two papers had any 'odor,' they rejected them altogether."[50]

In 1935, Levinson described the distance between the Hebrew newspapers and the Zionist youth movements in a similar vein: "*Hatzefirah* did not perceive the changes wrought by time or the shift in guard. It pegged its hopes chiefly on its distinguished 'middle-class' readers. *Hatzefirah* did not see the younger generation."[51]

Despite this rift with the younger generation, the Hebrew press did attempt to develop contacts with its readership. *Hayom*, for example, tried to activate readers by carrying out surveys and publishing letters to the editor on cultural affairs. Of particular note is the survey among readers as to how much coverage the newspaper should devote to events in Palestine. This survey showed "that the overwhelming majority of our readers want extensive letters from writers living in Eretz Israel." The interest this question generated is evident in some of the replies. As one reader wrote: "News from Eretz Israel is as vital as the air we breathe, and this is our only way of maintaining contact with our brethren there. The least bit of information from Eretz Israel is more important than entire articles on dry politics."[52]

49. Yehudoni, "*Hatzefirah* ha-hayah."
50. Hurwitz, "Le-sheelat kiyumo shel iton ivri ba-golah."
51. Levinson, *Ha-tenuah ha-ivrit ba-golah*, p. 227.
52. *Hayom*, no. 347 (February 25, 1926); and the responses in no. 346 (February 24, 1926); no. 348 (February 26, 1926); no. 355 (March 8, 1926); no. 359 (March 12, 1926).

Readers were also concerned about the Zionist camp's lack of interest in the Hebrew newspaper. Angry letters of protest appeared in the pages of *Hatzefirah* in 1931, citing Zionist activists and Hebrew educators who did not buy the paper. One loyal reader even proposed "allocating a special place in the newspaper for a 'column of disgrace' which would publicize the names of any Zionist association or national youth movement not subscribing to *Hatzefirah*" as well as "the names of individuals who speak so high and mighty about the revival of Hebrew at Zionist assemblies and celebrations."[53]

In light of the frustrated attempts to keep a Hebrew daily alive, and the gap between reader expectations and newspaper content that sometimes emerged, *Baderekh*, which hoped one day to become a daily, made a more concerted effort to maintain a close relationship with its readership. This effort was evidenced in the editor's declaration on the first day of publication in 1932: "Our reader cannot be just an ordinary reader, a mute reader. The Hebrew newspaper cannot survive unless the reader takes part in creating, i.e., editing, it. It is his duty to assist the editor through his advice, instructions, requests, and complaints." A constant dialogue of this type was seen as productive and useful for both parties: "By reading all your complaints and requests, we will learn about the nature and attributes of most of our readers, and this in itself will make it easier for us to penetrate their heart."[54]

Thon, who had followed the daily Hebrew press in its various configurations over the years, tried to speak on behalf of the *Baderekh* reader, articulating his demands and explaining his indifference. In Thon's opinion, in addition to the love of Hebrew that led the reader to the paper in the first place, the reader "wants to find in it what he finds in any other language he knows. The newspaper is not an external compilation of articles and information but an organic entity. Thus he demands a clear orientation, for there is 'no newspaper without a flag.'"[55]

In response, *Baderekh*'s editor rejected the idea of a "flag" and continued to uphold a newspaper marked by pluralism in content and philosophy. On the other hand, he spoke at length of the ma-

53. *Hatzefirah*, June 9, 1931, no. 69; June 17, 1931, no. 76; July 29, 1931, no. 112; July 15, 1931, no. 100.

54. [Yakubovitz], "Le-hofaat *Baderekh*."

55. Yehoshua Thon, "Ha-kore ha-ivri ve-taanotav," *Baderekh*, February 16, 1933, no. 7.

terial difficulties encountered by the weekly and the drop in subscribers for financial reasons. This drop reduced the possibility for
improvements even he felt were needed. As for the financial plight
of readers, he stated: "I know a number of readers in Warsaw and
the provinces who genuinely cannot afford to spend 25 *groshy* a week
on a Hebrew newspaper, but who get together in twos and threes
to buy one, just so they have a Hebrew paper to read." The economic
situation was also reflected in the letters of faithful readers, who
complained to the editor about people "who do not buy *Baderekh*,
but pay the vendor a small sum so that one copy is read secretly by
a whole group. In the end, the vendor returns the paper to the
publisher."[56]

As part of the campaign to stimulate readers, *Baderekh* began to
run a column called "Beineinu le-vein koreinu" (Between Ourselves and Our Readers) that dealt, among others, with issues of
content and circulation. When the question of cutting the number
of pages or raising the price came up, a reader survey showed a
difference of opinion between those who were well off and those
who were poor. One reader explained his strong opposition to an
increase in price as follows: "Raising the price is a dangerous step
nowadays because the number of unemployed is increasing daily,
and even a few *groshy* must be taken into account."[57] As there was
a draw between the two views, it was decided to put out a smaller
paper without raising the price. Another decision clearly supported
by the readers was separate publication of the children's supplement.

The correspondence in "Between Ourselves" was also indicative
of the diversity of readership taste and opinion. One reader thought
"historical investigations" had no contemporary value; another requested more material on Zionist history. One reader lodged a complaint against the serialized novel that had been appearing for some
time. Sensitivity to linguistic and stylistic problems is also evident.
An elderly reader protested the idiom and spelling in *Baderekh*, which
he found hard to adjust to, and expressed longing for the biblical
style of Hebrew newspapers in the past. The editor's reply was unequivocal: "Such a thing can no longer be, especially in a newspaper
dealing with all aspects of life and current affairs. Biblical Hebrew

56. A. L. Y. [Yakubovitz], "Sodot min ha-maarekhet," *Baderekh*, February 23,
1933, no. 8; "Le-gilion ha-meah shel *Baderekh*," *Baderekh*, September 10, 1934,
no. 32.
57. "Beineinu le-vein koreinu," *Baderekh*, December 29, 1933, no. 51.

is fine for poetry and rhetoric, but in describing political and scientific life, it is quite imperative to use language which is simple, clear, and precise." As for the spelling the reader complained about, there was no choice because the use of vowels was technically impossible.[58]

One of the issues that interested both editors and readers at this time was the balance of power within the Zionist camp. In response to readers who claimed that one party was being preferred over another in the newspaper, the editors restated their sincere desire to allow each party to express its views. They urged readers to cure themselves of "that fatal disease of partisanship" and to rally around the common goal of cultivating the Hebrew language. On the other hand, the editors tried to focus the reader's interest on emigration to Palestine, even sponsoring an essay competition on "My Opinion on *Aliyah* to Eretz Israel." The idea was to allow each reader to express himself, for "the uproar created by the partisan battle in our national camp is slowly blocking out the vital wishes of the individual."[59]

Another issue raised from time to time was the loosening of ties between the educational system and the Hebrew press. In 1928, M. Berenholtz, who wrote for *Hatzefirah*, proposed that the Hebrew newspaper be introduced as part of the curriculum of the higher grades in Hebrew secondary schools. He even set out a didactic plan of action to put this idea into practice. He argued that "the Hebrew newspaper, in its very being and purpose, is free of the cheap sensationalism and filth that other newspapers are concerned with, and thus it is particularly suitable for schoolchildren."[60]

This idea of using the Hebrew newspaper for educational purposes was also suggested by the readers of *Baderekh*. One of them, the chief inspector of the Tarbut school network, reported that *Baderekh* had been successfully introduced as a mandatory part of the curriculum and that "the students are very excited about this and anxiously await each new issue of *Baderekh*." A Hebrew teacher described his experience with the newspaper in similar terms: "The students are

58. "Beineinu le-vein koreinu," *Baderekh*, January 19, 1934, no. 3; on language problems, see January 26, 1934, no. 4.
59. "Beineinu le-vein koreinu," *Baderekh*, January 12, 1934, no. 2; September 16, 1935, no. 33.
60. M. Berenholtz, "Ha-iton ha-ivri be-veit ha-sefer: Homer le-vikuah," *Hatzefirah*, January 24, 1928, no. 21.

interested in the paper, wait anxiously to receive it every week, and respond to everything that happens in our Hebrew world. Each article serves them as a basis for discussion."[61]

But all of these efforts of improvement were in vain. The decline of the Hebrew press in Poland was unavoidable, for it was caught in the tragic circumstances of Polish Jewry. It was in Eretz Israel that the Hebrew press found its vivid and dynamic continuation.

61. Y. E. Shpirt, "Ha-iton be-veit ha-sefer," *Baderekh,* October 1, 1935, no. 40. On this subject, see also A. H. Shifer, "Ha-iton be-veit ha-sefer," *Hatzefirah,* February 2, 1928, no. 29; A. Einstein, "Hankhu korim le-iton ivri!" *Baderekh,* March 9, 1934, no. 10.

Hanan Hever

From Exile-without-Homeland to Homeland-without-Exile: A Guiding Principle of Hebrew Fiction in Interwar Poland

I

Writing about Hebrew fiction in interwar Poland entails examining an entity whose prominent feature is void or nothingness. The twenty years that elapsed between Poland's independence in 1918 and collapse in 1939 witnessed the decline of that country's Hebrew literature, a process portrayed in the harshest terms by its own readers and writers. In renewing the publication of *Luah Ahiasaf* in 1923, Dr. Yehoshua (Osias) Thon wrote about the hopes aroused by the revival of the literary annual. In the same breath, however, he went on to stress that the publication lacked writers of stature, and he forecast the criticism it could anticipate in consequence. At the same period, Z. Z. Weinberg, one of the last Hebrew writers in Poland, described the desolate condition of Hebrew literature in that country, concluding with the somber proclamation that "the time has come for grave digging and burial."[1]

The broader causes of this decline have been widely considered. Overwhelmed by a sense of defeat, members of the interwar generation continually speculated about its causes. The unstable regime of post–World War I Poland subjected its Jewish citizens to physical and spiritual tribulations—persecutions, pogroms, and official restrictions such as Władysław Grabski's tax laws and the anti-Jewish *numerus clausus* applying to university admissions—that hastened

This essay has been translated from Hebrew by Peretz Kidron.
1. [Yehoshua (Osias) Thon], ed., "Sifrut ve-shaar ha-ksafim . . . ," *Luah Ahiasaf: Measef sifruti* 13 (1923); Michael Sternberg [Z. Z. Weinberg], in *Kolot*, 1923, no. 7, p. 242.

the decline of the country's Hebrew intelligentsia, who often opted for emigration, particularly to Palestine. In fact during these years the Hebrew cultural center in Palestine grew and flourished, sometimes at the expense of Hebrew cultural centers in the Diaspora. The emergent center of Hebrew culture in Palestine now proved capable of offering an alternative that endangered the survival of the Hebrew center in Poland.

The golden age of Hebrew culture in Poland coincided with the early years of the twentieth century, which produced a profusion of eminent periodicals such as *Hatzefirah* (The Dawn), *Hatzofeh* (The Observer), and *Hador* (The Generation). Pre–World War I Warsaw attracted numerous Hebrew writers, including Y. L. Peretz, H. D. Nomberg, H. N. Bialik, Yaakov Fichman, David Frishman, Yaakov Steinberg, Zalman Shneor, Yaakov Cohen, and Baal Makhshavot.[2] Even after the devastation that befell the Jews during World War I, attempts were made to resuscitate Poland as a center of Hebrew culture. A not inconsiderable number of Hebrew writers, fleeing the Russian Revolution, settled in neighboring Poland. Leaving Moscow, Abraham Stiebel transferred his publishing house to Warsaw; prominent among Hebrew periodicals, *Hatekufah* (The Era) likewise moved to the Polish capital, where it was edited by David Frishman, Yaakov Cohen, and Fishel Lachover. The journal's editorial policy sought to elevate *Hatekufah* into the principal outlet for the works of leading Hebrew writers, whether in the Diaspora or in Palestine. But in this, *Hatekufah* was exceptional; most of the Hebrew journals appearing in Warsaw were characterized by an awareness of the secondary place they occupied in relation to the Palestinian center. In spite of all efforts, Poland failed to regain its former position as a center of Hebrew culture.

The Russian Revolution also contributed to the decline of Hebrew culture in newly independent Poland. The enforced separation of Poland from the Hebrew-reading public in the Soviet Union gave a further boost to Yiddish culture and literature, to which many readers of Hebrew now turned. In the first edition of *Baderekh* (En Route), the Hebrew weekly that commenced publication in Warsaw in the early 1930s, Yitzhak Gruenbaum diagnosed "an important rule in our cultural life."

---

2. Dan Miron, "Ha-sifrut ha-ivrit be-reshit ha-meah ha-esrim," *Measef le-divrei sifrut, bikoret, ve-hagut,* vol. 2 (Jerusalem, 1961): 463–64; Gershon Shaked, *Ha-siporet ha-ivrit, 1880–1980,* vol. 2: *Ba-aretz u-ba-tefuzah* (Tel Aviv, 1983), pp. 249–50.

The educated portion of the [Jewish] people, the Hebrew[-reading] portion, which in large part is likewise numbered among the educated portion, is incapable of supporting any cultural institution uniquely unto itself alone, neither a genuine theater in the spoken tongue nor a Hebrew press. This may be because it cannot resort to them exclusively, being both able and obliged to resort to the press in other languages, [and] to cultural institutions of other peoples. The Hebrew intellectual is unable, so to speak, to enter into exclusive communion with his press, [or] with his Hebrew literature, particularly in the Diaspora. In Palestine, such communion is facilitated by local conditions, and behold, a strong foundation for the Hebrew press and for Hebrew literature is coming into being [there].

Gruenbaum concluded that it was vitally important to increase the number of consumers of Hebrew culture, which should be extended to broader classes, to "ordinary readers" who read for pleasure. This broadening should be done even if it meant employing "simple Hebrew"—a concession reflecting the powerful competition the waning Hebrew culture faced from its Yiddish and Polish rivals. Without doubt, Gruenbaum was also referring to the graduates of the Hebrew Tarbut school network, who failed for the most part to become consumers of Hebrew books or papers, and certainly not exclusively of Hebrew works published in Poland.[3]

In a review of a recent issue of *Hatekufah*, L. Eliav noted that, with the exception of Stiebel, Hebrew publishers in Poland had ceased to function. Three years later the manager of Ever, Warsaw's Hebrew bookstore, pointed out the disgraceful decline in purchases of Hebrew books in Poland, going on to add that his store was now the only one in the country devoted entirely to Hebrew books and papers. A few years later A. Urinovsky wrote that, aside from a few textbooks, not a single Hebrew book had been published in Poland during the preceding year.[4]

The dwindling number of Hebrew readers, particularly among the less elitist classes, was reflected in the pitiful state of the Hebrew novel in Poland. A not inconsiderable portion of the novels published in Poland during this period were by Hebrew authors writing in Palestine, who were forced by their precarious circumstances to fall

3. Yitzhak Gruenbaum, "Ve-shuv nisayon," *Baderekh*, September 15, 1932; Leib Hazan, "Min ha-mezar," *Hatzefirah*, October 28, November 4, 11, 1927.

4. L. Eliav, "Sefarim hadashim (reshimot bibliografiot): Kerekh hadash shel *Hatekufah*," *Hayom*, November 27, 1925; A. Zemer, "Le-takanat shuk ha-sefarim ha-ivri," *Hatzefirah*, June 25, 1928; A. Urinovsky, "Ha-tenuah ha-ivrit bi-shnat 1932–33 be-Polanyah," *Baderekh*, October 13, 1932.

back upon the generosity of Warsaw's Stiebel publishing house.[5] A humorous piece written at the time by Nachman Mifelev featured a Hebrew writer who, having pursued a wearisome and hopeless courtship of the publishers, only to find that they preferred translations to original Hebrew manuscripts, concluded that his sole hope of a literary future lay in working as a translator.[6] Indeed, an examination of *Hatzefirah*, the veteran Hebrew daily that defied difficulties to continue its sporadic appearance through the interwar period, reveals that translations provided the bulk of its literary material.

The bleak state of Hebrew fiction in interwar Poland was attested to by the well-known critic Benzion Benshalom, who, after serving as a lecturer at the renowned university of his native Cracow, reached Palestine in 1940. Three years later he wrote a summary of Hebrew literature in interwar Poland, focusing exclusively upon poetry because, as he noted, "in the sphere of fiction, Hebrew literature in Poland in the period under discussion did not produce significant talents."[7]

This somber description of the decay of a splendid cultural center has, however, another side to it. In the long view that reaches up to the present day, one tends to gauge the achievements—and, equally, the failures—of the decaying Polish center against those of its emergent Palestinian counterpart. It is important to recognize here that Zionist ideology has colored attitudes toward modern Hebrew literature, and a historiography resting upon Zionist teleology naturally tends to overlook manifestations of cultural vitality in the Diaspora. The brutal eclipse of these manifestations, moreover, has led to their being portrayed as marginal to the creation of the cultural center in Palestine. Looking only at Hebrew fiction in Palestine, one cannot help but endorse Benshalom's assertion that its Polish counterpart was insignificant. A similar view can be found in the comprehensive "Al ha-sipur ha-ivri" (About the Hebrew Story), published in 1930 by the Palestinian critic Yaakov Rabinovitch.[8] Nonetheless, in our recollection of the terrible tragedy that befell

---

5. For example, A. Reuveni, *Ha-oniot ha-ahronot* (The Last Ships) (Warsaw, 1923); Reuveni, *Shamot* (Devastation) (Warsaw, 1925).

6. Nachman Mifelev, "Sipur ivri mekori," *Hatzefirah*, June 1, 1928.

7. Benzion Benshalom, *Ha-sifrut ha-ivrit bein shtei milhamot ha-olam* (Jerusalem, 1943), p. 13.

8. Yaakov Rabinovitch, "Al ha-sipur ha-ivri," *Almanakh mitzpeh* (Tel Aviv, 1930), pp. 81–101.

Jewish culture in Poland, and in our awareness that its physical destruction was preceded by a progressive decline, we run the risk of overlooking its unique inner dynamism.

II

This working hypothesis of an inner dynamism is best examined at the intersection of the spiritual complex delineated as "exile-homeland," which stands out among the themes explored by Hebrew fiction in interwar Poland. Indeed, the contrast between an increasingly impoverished Diaspora and the renascent homeland provided the spiritual focus for those who, while languishing in the Polish Diaspora, regarded themselves as citizens of the world of Hebrew culture.

A most characteristic example is Leib Hazan's *Geulah* (Redemption), one of the few Hebrew novels written in interwar Poland.[9] It was published in Kowel in 1930, at the very epicenter of the period under discussion. The book relates the story of a group of Jewish revolutionaries who dreamed of redemption in the form of a workers' uprising. Throughout, the novel depicts their revolutionary aspirations in analogy and, indeed, in genetic relation to Jewish religious hopes. Their Marxist conviction that the economic crisis which marked the early years of Polish independence would undermine a decaying capitalism and replace it with a new and just society is exhibited as a further expression of the traditional Jewish yearning for redemption.

In more specific terms, the novel's cast of characters features an apparent contrast between Reb Abraham Joseph, the simple Jewish beadle whose entire existence is given over to hopes of religious redemption, and his hardworking neighbor Hannah Leah, who dedicates her life totally to dreams of redemption arising from her revolutionary faith. Her home serves as a meeting place for the Jewish members of a revolutionary party.[10] When Hannah Leah's pretty younger sister, the pleasure-seeking Rivka, moves into the apart-

9. Leib Hazan, *Geulah* (Kowel, 1930).
10. These revolutionaries are apparently adherents of the Bund and, specifically, of its left-wing faction, which strove for collaboration with the Komunistyczna Partia Polski (KPP, Polish Communist Party), while dismissing the Polska Partia Socjalistyczna (PPS, Polish Socialist Party) as reformist. See, for example, Ezra Mendelsohn, "Poland," in *Ha-tefuzah: Mizrah Eropah*, ed. Yaakov Zur (Jerusalem, 1976), p. 196.

ment, she intensifies the erotic pressures imbuing and confounding the activities of the revolutionaries. The group's political failure is highlighted by the revelation that Berish, the most enthusiastic and dogmatic of their number, is an informer who has betrayed his comrades to the police. The book's intellectual code, which cautions Jews against the perilous delusion of seeking to reform a society to which they do not belong, is illustrated, in the story as in real life, by the antisemitism of the non-Jewish revolutionaries. On the personal plane, success falls to Rivka, who marries a factory owner, a representative of the opposing side. Rivka's triumph stands out against the setback Hannah Leah suffers in her romantic relations with Comrade Stach, who is more moderate than she in political views. On the other side, too, personal and political themes merge when the decline of revolutionary ferment, leaving time for intimate concerns, permits Rivka's industrialist lover to marry her. Hannah Leah's emotional sacrifice in dedicating her entire life to revolutionary redemption is almost compounded by personal disaster when she comes within inches of falling into the trap laid for her by Berish; her suicide terminates a life of illusions, personal no less than political. After the disintegration of the revolutionary cell, the reader is left with the character of Stach, who, having discarded his revolutionary illusions, now seeks a positive outlet for his ideological convictions.

But what, in concrete terms, is Stach's plan—which also, coincidentally, represents the ideological solution proffered by the novel? In Gershon Shaked's historiographical study of modern Hebrew fiction, approached largely from the Zionist perspective, *Geulah* is presented as a novel whose literary structure reflects its author's Zionist ideas; it is described as a "Zionist ideological novel."[11] Indeed, certain aspects of the story possibly allow Stach's ultimate decision to leave Poland to be depicted as a Zionist choice. Hazan's narrator, however, who never relinquishes his critical ideological identity, signally refrains from an unambiguous affirmation to this effect. It is only within the standard context of accusations and imprecations directed against Stach by his adversaries on the Left that he is described as a "Zionist"—an appellation that could be interpreted as derogatory, coming as it did from those who took a poor view of what they regarded as Stach's constructivist deviations. Moreover,

---

11. Shaked, *Ha-siporet ha-ivrit*, 2:286.

the precise national identity of the new society Stach hopes to establish "there in that distant land" is not specified; it could be interpreted as referring to the socialist colonies in Palestine, but Hazan leaves the specific identity open.[12]

The basic plot structure contrasts Jewish hopes of religious redemption, as expressed by the beadle, with the parallel aspirations of the Jewish revolutionaries; this contrast is highlighted in the dialogue between the old man and Stach, when the two examine the various paths to redemption. The beadle propounds the traditional Jewish doctrine of "I wait for the Lord, my soul doth wait, and in his word do I hope" (Ps. 130:5), rejecting despair and seeing himself duty bound to hope for succour even when the sword is at his throat. On this occasion, Stach presents his views in unequivocal terms, as he proclaims his universalist quest "to find happiness for myself and for the whole of humanity."[13]

A resolution so ambiguous and open-ended in a work that, in all its other formal characteristics, is a *roman à thèse*, clearly calls for thorough explanation. Defying our natural expectations of this genre, which typically presents a clear ideological position, the book takes us back to the methodological point of departure, with its stress on void and nothingness. That the writing and publication of a Hebrew novel were relatively rare in interwar Poland ultimately shaped *Geulah*'s literary structure. The open-ended plot, avoiding clear ideological definitions, can be largely explained by the broad range of cultural and social functions undertaken by Hebrew fiction in Poland. On the other hand, any attempt on the part of Zionist historiography to fill the gaps left by the novel's failure to make an ideological choice is liable to overshadow the inner developments unique to the environment in which it was written. Like the few other Hebrew stories appearing in Poland at that time, *Geulah* should be judged in light of the fact that most of the Hebrew writers still living in the country wrote and published little or nothing. The ideological ambiguity evident in *Geulah* can be interpreted as representing a reluctance to offer its readers a coherent ideological message. The literary ruse of an "open ending" may also reflect a kind of ambivalence toward the ideological task of representing, or influencing, reality by means of a literary text. It is noteworthy that, in

12. Hazan, *Geulah*, p. 228.
13. Ibid.

literature as elsewhere, such an ideological task is generally performed by subjects who convert their particular viewpoint of the social or economic situation in which they find themselves into a total, overall portrayal that is presented as both self-evident and unavoidable.[14] The common ideological pattern whereby a social vision is transformed into a coherent literary reality is, however, sometimes replaced by an ambivalent and critical attitude toward the real-life conditions and factors constituting and influencing that vision. As in other works written at the time in Poland, Hazan's novel makes extensive use of lacunae, inexplicable jumps, silences, and a refusal to make literary decisions, which together proffer a soberly critical message.

The Hebrew writer in interwar Poland was confronted by cultural options in a state of tension that was capable of moving to antagonism. In view of the rapid emergence of Hebrew culture in Palestine, the very decision to continue writing Hebrew in the Polish center-in-decline entailed an evident paradox. The nigh-automatic assertion of creative activity in Hebrew Zionist ideology made Hebrew writing in the Polish Diaspora an endeavor inclined to perceive itself as nothing more than a means or a preparation, subsidiary to authentic creativity in the Palestinian center. This tension found expression in the controversy aroused throughout the Zionist movement by the decisions of the Helsingfors Conference in 1906. Polish Zionists were divided between supporters of "work for the present" and disciples of "work for the future." On the political plane, the debate was reflected in the disagreements between the *et livnot* (time to build) faction, which held that the principal task of the Zionist movement was to organize mass emigration of Polish Jews to Palestine, and the *al ha-mishmar* (on watch) faction headed by Yitzhak Gruenbaum, which argued that emigration to Palestine should be selective and that parallel efforts should be made to foster Jewish national existence in Poland and to cultivate the Zionist consciousness of the potential emigrants to Palestine.[15] Gruenbaum's strenuous activity within the Minorities Bloc formed in the Polish Sejm (House of Deputies) during the early years of the country's independence reflected his determination, as far as possible, to seek

14. See, for example, Terence Eagelton, "Ideology, Fiction, Narrative," *Social Text* 1, no. 2 (1979): 62–80; Tony Bennet, *Formalism and Marxism* (London, 1979).
15. See, among others, Mendelsohn, "Poland," p. 198.

equal rights and a dignified existence for the Jews within the multi-national patchwork of the Polish state.

Zionism's *shelilat ha-golah* (denial of the Diaspora) branded Hebrew cultural activity in Poland as secondary, thereby largely eroding the motivation of writers—and, equally, readers—to recognize Hebrew writings as effective ideological weapons. The double pressure exerted by a hostile environment and the absence of a steady audience for such works led to a marked decline in Hebrew literature as a channel of communication. Paradoxical was the predicament of a literature—composed in a language bearing a clear ideological label and on behalf of a well-defined ethnic group—that effectively set itself the task of diminishing the numbers of its own readers. When the writer Z. Z. Weinberg left Poland and set out for Palestine, the ambivalent comments of his colleagues sharply reflected this inner tension.[16]

Given the historical situation of a stricken Diaspora and a blossoming Hebrew homeland, Hebrew writings were inevitably drawn to national themes. But efforts to produce ideological utterances capable of resolving, or at least moderating, the inner contradictions of the society within which they were generated became progressively more arduous and well-nigh hopeless. On top of the unequal battle it was obliged to wage against popular Yiddish culture, with its broad appeal and its intensive backing by the Bund and others, Hebrew literature in Poland also became the target of a kind of pincer movement by its Palestinian counterpart. First and foremost, the latter robbed it of readers and writers who elected to express their Hebrew interests in their ideological homeland in Palestine rather than in what they perceived as an extremely precarious temporary shelter. In addition, Palestine also offered Hebrew writers and readers still residing in Poland an alternative form of literary creation and consumption that was far more attractive. Palestine's Hebrew press and literature made persistent efforts to establish direct contact with the Hebrew-reading public in Poland. Whether on ideological grounds, or due to a lack of high-quality material, the Hebrew press in Poland was likewise in the habit of reprinting material from its Palestinian counterparts or publishing the works of Hebrew writers living in Palestine. Matters were exacerbated by the incli-

16. See, for example, Z. Zohar, "Le-aliyat Z. Z. Weinberg le-Eretz Israel," *Baderekh*, July 6, 1934.

nation of Hebrew writers in Poland to publicize their works through Palestinian periodicals and publishing houses.

III

The ideological and creative blind alley depicted here was perplexing for some of those Hebrew writers who wished to continue their creative activity in Poland. The inability to choose between emigrating to Palestine or exchanging the dismal Polish Diaspora for exile in another form, as in Hazan's novel, had been preceded by a solution of a different kind, which achieved relative prominence in the Hebrew literature produced during the early years of Polish independence. Only a close scrutiny of the dynamics of Hebrew writing in Poland can reveal the significance of this intriguing phase, when Hebrew culture grappled with the sense of its own decline and with the inner contradictions threatening to destroy it. Along with a shared awareness of its own decay, Hebrew literature in post–World War I Poland also developed an opposing frame of mind that endeavored to think in more positive, though nevertheless sober, terms. Alongside a bewailing of the prevalent disintegration and decay, there is evidence of literary and journalistic activity aimed at making the best of the situation. Economic and political constraints, together with restrictions on immigration, severely limited the feasibility of finding a solution in Palestine. Consequently, one possible way of resolving the dilemma lay in attempting to preserve and reinforce the unique nature of the Diaspora, in contrast with the new homeland in Palestine and in spite of the blossoming of the latter; in other words, to transform weakness into a measure of strength.

This school was largely represented by the Warsaw periodical *Kolot* (Voices) and its moving spirit Eliezer Steinman. Steinman reached Poland shortly after its liberation, remaining in the country four years before his emigration to Palestine in 1924. "Here, in one of the cities of the exile," he wrote in the third issue of *Kolot*, "it is necessary to build a center of Hebrew culture, an electric power station to distribute light. This center is the observant eye of the pulsing Hebrew heart, the voice heralding, in [all] lands, the existence and resurgence of our culture, the unifying telegraph." Drawing an unusual distinction, Steinman in effect proposed a Hebrew version of S. M. Dubnov's autonomist views, differentiating between a cultural center in the Diaspora and its periphery that, as he defined it, could be taken to include Palestine. In another issue of *Kolot*, Steinman criticized the cultural pretensions of the new Palestinian center while simultaneously conceding his own dependence upon it: "Woe unto us from the construction and renewal of the Israeli center after the manner of the existence of all the false centers of our society; and woe unto us from its total destruction." Steinman presented the Hebrew language as a kind of national ontology capable, on the linguistic plane at least, of offering a genuine alternative to the emerging Palestinian entity.

> We, who shall not despise the Diaspora, and shall not flatter the He-
> brew language by dispatching it to be the [sole] heritage of the one
> hundred thousand strong Jewish community in the land of our fore-
> fathers, but shall, instead, aspire to see it flourishing in the mouths of
> seventeen million Children of Israel in all the [lands of] exile through-
> out the world; we who contemplate the whole existence by way of the
> twenty-two Hebrew letters, we shall uphold the tradition.[17]

The historical and conceptual analysis proposed by Yitzhak Baer in his well-regarded *Galut* (Exile) illustrates clearly that as far back as the period of the Second Temple, when the Jewish state and the Temple were still in existence, the Diaspora was not regarded in purely negative terms as a form of political enslavement; moreover, the Diaspora also played a positive role in teaching and propagating the true faith throughout the world.[18] The sharp awareness of the decay, physical and spiritual, that overcame the Polish Diaspora between the two world wars also produced an ephemeral blossoming in spite of the unfavorable conditions.

Steinman's proclamation was reflected in the emergence—albeit limited—of daily papers such as *Hatzefirah*, and *Hayom* (Today) and of periodicals such as *Kolot* and, later, *Zeramim* (Currents), *Hasolel* (The Trailblazer), and *Galim* (Waves), all of which aimed at providing platforms for discussion of the problems and dilemmas peculiar to Hebrew culture in Poland. Likewise, Steinman's views were reflected in an upsurge of genres like sketches and seminarrative essays, which achieved great prominence in Hebrew writing during the early years of Poland's independence. The wide disparities in

17. Eliezer Steinman, "Hearot ketanot, merkaz," *Kolot*, 1923, no. 3, p. 117; Steinman, "Mahshavot bi-zmanan: Ha-yahas el ha-merkaz," *Kolot*, 1923, nos. 5–6, p. 204; Steinman, "Mahshavot bi-zmanan: Mi-saviv la-medurah ha-yetomah," *Kolot*, 1923, nos. 5–6, p. 31.
18. Yitzhak Baer, *Galut* (Jerusalem, 1980), pp. 9–19.

prevalent historical codes, the pressures of everyday reality increasingly demanding literary expression, and the profound contradictions underlying Hebrew cultural activity in a renascent Poland all combined to demolish coherent narrative structures. They were replaced by the feuilleton and the sketch, with their particular interpretation of the relationship between Diaspora and homeland. A characteristic example is "Levado nishar: Ziyur" (Alone He Remained: A Sketch) by Nachman Mifelev. It sings the praises of Yosef, the son of Hayim Reuven, and his obstinacy in clinging to the soil of his devastated Lithuanian township. After the death of the father, the rest of the family moves to America, where one of the brothers has already put down roots. But Yosef, foreseeing a rosy future in Lithuania, stays on in the town to rebuild the family home destroyed during the war. In this story the conflict between homeland and exile is removed from the Zionist context, with the Eastern European Diaspora legitimized by its own vitality and persistence. In Steinman's "Ba-nekhar" (In Foreign Lands), published about the same time, a similar set of opposites is presented. The decadent "foreign land" is Belgium, depicted by the Jewish immigrants settled there in contradistinction to their native Poland, which, in spite of being a form of Diaspora, is the object of their yearnings and thus achieves the status of virtual homeland.[19]

In contrast with later texts, which highlight the hopelessness of Jewish existence in Poland, the travel notes published by Yakir Warshavsky in 1926 constitute a hymn of praise to Poland's landscapes, its culture, and its history. The writer's Jewish identity quickly comes to the fore through the imagery used to compare Poland's vistas and the landscape of Palestine. "Vavel!" Warshavsky exclaims while describing his tour of Cracow, "How uplifting is that name to the heart of any son of Poland, how it carries within it Poland's joys and sorrows! This mountain is linked with the course of Poland's history as Mount Zion is with that of the Jew. It penetrates the very depths of the people's soul, blending into it in a single amalgam." Referring to the Vistula, he writes, "This river is the heart's artery of this land, like the river Volga of Russia's soil, and the Jordan of the Land of Israel." But Warshavsky's ideological motivation emerges in full force when his tour of Jewish Cracow arouses him to exclaim

---

19. Nachman Mifelev, "Levado nishar: Ziyur," *Hatzefirah*, March 31, 1921; Eliezer Steinman, "Ba-nekhar," *Hatekufah*, 1922, no. 12, pp. 117–44.

over the mere fact of existence in a universal exile. In consequence, he does not feel himself to be a stranger in Cracow: "And I, a strange wayfarer, from a distant city, nevertheless am not alien in any way. I am among brothers, sensing myself linked and united with those about me, with those dispersed among the nations and states, and with all the generations which preceded me."[20]

Whereas Hazan's novel and its open-ended ideological conclusion reflect the instability of the historical situation it depicts, the stories published a decade earlier, just after World War I, present a clear ideological message whose unambiguous formulation was sometimes accomplished at the expense of balanced narrative development. The immediate need to publicize a specific viewpoint, which headed the list of priorities in Hebrew writing in Poland at that time, ultimately affected the literary structures that became prevalent. The want of literary talent and the decline of creative writing undermined standards of quality and compelled the dwindling ranks of Hebrew writers to assume a multiplicity of roles as publicists and creators of *belles lettres* alike.[21] The pressure to produce an immediate ideological response was exemplified in the seminarrative pieces, characterized by their intellectual shortcuts. In ever-increasing measure, narrative development was subjugated to the ideological positions the stories were expected to represent and exemplify. Referring to Yakir Warshavsky's *Maalot u-mordot* (Ups and Downs), subtitled *Sipurim u-ziyurim* (Stories and Sketches) and published in Warsaw in 1925, a critic wrote that fortuity has a central role and described the transitions as overabrupt.[22] Indeed, one of the more prominent pieces in the collection, "Yaldei ha-Visla" (Children of the Vistula), illustrates the manner in which the Polish-Jewish conflict is handled, with the narrative mechanism secondary to the story's philosophical message. The piece stands out for its balanced development of the symbiosis between the two peoples. The crisis arising from the romantic relations between a Jewish youth and a Polish girl induces the former to commit suicide. Subsequently, however, the two sides make a marked effort to maintain their symbiotic relationship in mourning the calamity. Nevertheless, at the conclu-

20. Yakir Warshavsky, "Be-merhavei Polin: Reshmei over orakh," *Hatzefirah*, October 4, 13, 1926.
21. See the remarks of A. L. Y. [A. L. Yakubovitz, the editor], "Le-hofaat *Baderekh*," *Baderekh*, September 15, 1932.
22. B. Kahin, "Me-olam ha-sifrut," *Hatzefirah*, January 28, 1927.

sion of the story, its narrative mechanism unexpectedly breaks down. In stark contradiction to what has hitherto transpired, the dead boy's father finds an exclusively Jewish solution that he is unable to share with his Polish friends. This denouement conveys the impression of serving to propagate a notion without foundation either in the characters portrayed or in the story's plot structure.[23]

At the same time Warshavsky published, in serialized form, his story "Etim hadashot" (New Times). The first installment, composed as an essay, describes the antisemitic ferment in Poland. Reb Yitzhak, known as Panie Itsheh—a standard Polish nickname for the Jewish stereotype—serves to demonstrate how antisemitism grants legitimacy to one individual Jew who is acknowledged as being different from the other members of his race. This literary device highlights racist generalizations by focusing the plot upon a character who proves the rule by constituting an apparent exception. The composition of the fragment restores the "deviant" example to the level of generalization by means of a sentence attributing overall historical significance to Reb Yitzhak's fears as he senses that the upsurge of anti-Jewish discrimination will ultimately undermine the foundations of his own existence. The second installment expands this illustrative plot by depicting the sorrow of a father when his son decides to quit Poland and sets off to study in Switzerland. The father is anxious about the future of Poland; yet he grieves over his son's departure. As far as he is concerned, the central conflict is between continuing his existence in Poland and the fate of his son "in an alien land, seating himself to dine at the table of strangers." As all of Reb Yitzhak's children leave him and go their separate ways, he is left in his empty home to reflect over their aims. The younger generation exchanges one exile for another, with Zionism making its sole appearance in the form of orations by Zionist leaders, and even they are coupled with similar speeches by socialists.[24]

In playing down the role of Zionism, Warshavsky reflected Steinman's opinions, which were, in turn, influenced by the philosophy of David Frishman. Frishman was well known for his reservations about Zionism and his espousal of the esthetic qualities of Hebrew literature. Leaving Moscow for Warsaw not long after the October

23. Yakir Warshavsky, "Yaldei ha-Visla," in Warshavsky, *Maalot u-mordot: Sipurim u-ziyurim* (Warsaw, 1925), pp. 19–35.

24. Yakir Warshavsky, "Etim hadashot: Perek mi-sipur," *Hayom*, December 25, 1925, January 4, 1926.

Revolution, Frishman proceeded to dedicate himself to editing, and particularly to translation. He died in 1922, at the commencement of the era under discussion; right up to his death he continued to publish his series of biblical tales, *Ba-midbar* (In the Desert) (1909–21). These stories exercised little influence on Hebrew fiction in Poland, but it is worth noting the ideological link between his interest in the desert wanderings of the Children of Israel and his view that the Diaspora, far from being merely a preparation for emigration to Palestine, existed as an autonomous entity that shaped the Jewish people's culture and guiding principles. Frishman's story "Ha-mekoshesh" (The Wood Collector), composed in his characteristic biblical style, endowed the exile in the desert with the status of a normative form of existence. The story traces the political and judicial institutionalization experienced by the Children of Israel during their wanderings. To illustrate the powerful punitive aspect of biblical law at that time, it describes the execution of a poor man who had the audacity to collect firewood on the Sabbath.[25]

An instructive illustration of a highly developed narrative solution, depicting an exile self-sufficient and unconnected with the homeland, is provided in "Be-hararei Karpat" (In the Carpathian Mountains) by Reuven Fahn. Set in a hamlet in Red Reissen in Eastern Galicia, among the Carpathian Mountains, the narrative juxtaposes the "palace," the home of the local feudal landlord, and the nearby inn, inhabited by Yisrael the taverner. This contrast, heightened by the comment that the taverner's forefathers "came to Poland and Ukraine in freedom, a freedom which was not bequeathed to later generations," effectively sketches the lines of the conflict and the potential scope for its predictable resolution. The wanderings of the young family from Starona, the Carpathian Mountain village, to the Ukrainian town that is the home of the young husband, Rabbi Moshe Solotviner, are depicted in the story as enforced exile to a place of learning (following the traditional Jewish precept, quoted in the story: "Be exiled unto a place of learning"). The story expresses this theme in concrete terms when the rabbi tells his bride that "the time has come to distance ourselves from the table of your father and draw near to the table of our Father in Heaven. . . . Here, there is a laxity of learning, and that is a great

---

25. David Frishman, "Ha-mekoshesh," *Hatekufah,* 1921, no. 12, pp. 7–12.

sin. Let us then make preparations to journey to *our state!*"[26] The traditional motif of Jews separated from their community unfolds here to a miraculous resolution whereby the discovery of some pearls provides the taverner's daughter with a dowry that rescues her from the threat of sexual conquest by the feudal lord. The supernatural elements of this story in effect stress and embellish the inner richness and validity of life in the Diaspora. The difficulties and crises endured collectively by the Jews on account of their national and religious identity are resolved here by means of miraculous connections and legendary characters. Matching the account of the rabbi's magical links with the Baal Shem Tov, in similar fashion the Ukrainian bandit leader Dobush is transformed into the rabbi's faithful servant and vows that he will never again harm a Jew.

To add further prominence to this modern imitation of Hasidic legend, Fahn relates the story of a blood libel, presented as an example of "one of those arduous times to which Israel is accustomed throughout the generations." The corpse of a young maidservant, whom her master the priest murdered and flung at the door of the Jewish taverner in one of the villages, provides the standard pretext for expulsion of the Jews from the Carpathians to the Lwów community. Calling upon his mystical gifts, Rabbi Moshe Solotviner invokes the spirit of the murdered girl, which unmasks the real murderer, thereby fending off the calamity that threatens his coreligionists. Here again, it is noteworthy that Fahn puts the rhetoric of his account to unusual use in depicting exile as a permanent condition characterized by conflicts that are nevertheless capable of solution. When the Jews are ordered to be expelled, the narrator offers his interpretation: "Behold, another exile is added, from one land to another, on top of all the other exiles."[27] In this manner the narrative progressively strips the concept of exile of its normal binary opposite, the Land of Israel. To Rabbi Moshe Solotviner, the Ukraine is "our state" rather than "our homeland"; likewise, the story depicts expulsion from the Carpathians as the replacement of one land of exile by another. In any case, this is not exile from a homeland: rather, it is exile-without-homeland. The rabbi's endeavors to refute the blood libel are analogous to the chronicle of

---

26. Reuven Fahn, "Be-hararei Karpat," in Fahn, *Mivhar ketavim*, ed. Nurit Govrin (Givatayim, 1969), pp. 189–213, quotations on pp. 189, 197, italics mine. The story was first published in serialized form in *Hayom*, February–March 1926.

27. Ibid., pp. 207, 209.

his wanderings, from the house of his father-in-law in the Carpathian home and, from there, after years of service to his people, back to the region where he had lived previously with his father-in-law, in the nearby town of Solotvina. In essence this journey represents the renewal of those spiritual and mystical links with the Carpathian landscape that had accompanied him throughout the course of his life. In terminating the exile the rabbi had undertaken for the purpose of study and his religious duties, Fahn's story rests content with restoring him to his spiritual and mystical origins, which are linked to the Carpathian landscape. In a similar manner, the mystical event succeeds in abrogating the expulsion decree in the analogous subplot relating to his ethnic community. Admittedly, this is not exile from a perfect homeland, for, as already cited, the freedom of the taverner's forefathers had not been "bequeathed to later generations"; nevertheless, the homeland-exile opposition is transferred *into* Eastern Europe, where one pole offers direct and vital contact with a land and its landscape (Fahn set his story in his native village of Starunia). In this manner exile becomes a prolonged and vital form of existence in which the absence of a homeland is soberly taken into account.

It is nevertheless noteworthy that this ideological pattern displays a singular sensitivity toward the Zionist option. When the omnipotent Dobush offers to lead his friend, Rabbi Moshe Solotviner, by way of hidden tunnels and caverns, to Palestine, the rabbi rejects the offer "because he did not wish to employ venality for the purpose of holiness."[28] In other words, the Land of Israel is not a realistic option in the context of the exile, but even if Zionism is not a genuine way out, it does exercise a tangible hold on the drab, painstaking historical process. Though invoked to resolve conflicts and crises throughout the course of the story, mystical motivation is rejected outright in relation to the Land of Israel. Departing from the kabbalistic outlook, the rabbi refuses to countenance a temporary alliance with evil, not even for the sacred goal of redemption. Even at the furthest extremities of exile-without-homeland, messianic and mystical semantics are barred from trespassing into areas dominated by an antimessianic orientation.

Fahn's story, the narrative form of which draws largely upon the fantasy of traditional Hasidic tales, may be regarded as a connecting

28. Ibid., p. 207.

link between the seminarrative genre so prevalent at the beginning
of the period and the novelistic forms that gained prominence halfway through it, around 1930. The early works of Steinman, Warshavsky, Mifelev, Yehoshua Heschel Yevin, and others were largely
limited to sketches, feuilletons, essays, or longer works that avoided
the ideological issues of their time.[29] In this they responded to the
pressures later to find expression in Hazan's *Geulah*, which, like
traditional romances and intrigue literature, relied on fortuity and
coincidence to unmask the villain. Even when the novel traces a
process of ideological disillusionment, manipulating the reader in
relation to the "good guys" and the "bad guys," no fundamental
change comes about. Stach's constructivism is a basic component
of the novel. In direct, almost mechanical response to the dramatic
events he experiences—the suicide of his lover and the disintegration of the revolutionary cell—he resolves to leave Poland. It should
be recalled, however, that given the circumstances of the time of the
novel's composition, the ideological foundations supporting the cast
of characters are not sufficiently firm to lead them to an unambiguous adherence to Zionism.

But how could one move from the personal essay, the sketch, or
even the longer story that patches its plot together by means of
miracles, to the larger narrative framework that would provide an
ideological response to the pressures exerted by real life? Hazan
encountered difficulties of composition that stemmed from the disparity between his desire for ideological expression within the broad
framework of the realistic novel—which naturally seeks to integrate
the individual into his background—and the linguistic possibilities,
in the spiritual and ideological sense of the term. An intriguing
solution to Hazan's difficulties is to be found in Z. Z. Weinberg's
Bayit u-rehov: Shnot 1918–1926 (House and Street: The Years 1918–
1926), published in 1931, at about the same time Hazan's novel
appeared. The book was issued by Stiebel, whose removal from
Warsaw to Tel Aviv and Berlin reflected—concretely no less than
symbolically—the disintegration of the Hebrew center in Poland. At
the time Weinberg was regarded as one of the most prominent Hebrew writers in Poland. Like Hazan, whose novel was also written
halfway between the two world wars, Weinberg directs his attention—as indicated by the work's subtitle—above all to the formative

29. For example, Eliezer Steinman's novel *Esther Hayot* (Warsaw, 1923).

early years of Polish independence. The book traces the sufferings of the Jews of Poland as the country becomes a battlefield.

As in the fiction composed at the beginning of the period, this novel, too, harshly relates the tribulations the Jews endured in the Polish Diaspora. These sufferings emerge with particular clarity in the funeral of the priest who had protected the Jews from their tormentors. During the early days of the war, he defended young Jews against the Russians who accused them of espionage. When the Germans invaded, he stood up to them, too, whereupon he was harassed and sent to a detention camp. When the town was taken by the Poles, the priest again defended the Jews against their enemies and protested the restrictions to which they were subjected. When the town was occupied by the Bolsheviks, he defied them side by side with the rabbis. Finally, when the Poles returned and began mistreating the Jews, he threatened to give up his position as spiritual leader of the community if the Polish soldiers harmed the Jews. "Holy soul!" the narrator exclaims, addressing the dead priest,

> Hearken unto the throbbing of hearts and the flow of sentiments and the pulse of life aflame within the spirits of your mourners, and be an honest witness before God's throne, for them and for their vanities and for their battles and for their lunacies on this dismal soil, the unhappy soil of Poland, which is powerless to extend maternal wings, the wings of a homeland, over all those born upon it and seeking shelter in its shade.[30]

Insofar as it was called upon to propose any direct solution to Jewish existence in Poland, the novel left such issues unanswered. Nevertheless, they were raised by the very fact of the story's being written in Hebrew as well as by the historical circumstances of its composition and, above all, by its own intensive preoccupation with the basic principles underlying the reality it portrayed. Moreover, these issues affected the book's structure, primarily in Weinberg's choice of a genre closely approximating a documentary chronicle. The fact that the narrator is presented as having personally experienced the events he relates both explains, and is explained by, the book's composition. Its account of Jewish sufferings is presented from the personal viewpoint of the narrator, Michael Sternberg— the pen name Weinberg used in the pieces he published in *Kolot* and other periodicals. The book's autobiographical form provides a pre-

---

30. Z. Z. Weinberg, *Bayit u-rehov: Shnot 1918–1926* (Warsaw, 1931), p. 140.

text for its avoidance of any clear ideological solution. The plot's motifs and conflicts, which draw upon the most highly charged of historical materials, are processed through the personal filters of the narrator, who takes shelter behind his subjective viewpoint to evade the necessity of proffering overall solutions to the ideological issues posed by his personal experience.

It may have been this broad span of ideological interpretation and commitment that induced one critic to summarize the novel on an optimistic note. Overlooking Weinberg's explicit references to Poland's cruelty—past and prospective—toward its Jewish citizens, the critic's comments were characteristic of those who clung to their belief in exile-without-homeland. After recommending that the book be translated into Polish, he added that the book depicts "the grief of a faithful citizen of Poland, who sees his beloved country in its waywardness. The author is bound by thousands of bonds to the soil of Poland upon which his fathers and forefathers lived and died. . . . And the author believes in a fairer tomorrow, and that hatred of nation for nation shall not dishonor the state of Poland."[31] It is no accident that a review written in Palestine should give the novel an outright Zionist interpretation, depicting it as "denying the exile" with the rootless and hopeless existence it offered the Jews. The Palestinian critic complained about the book's quasi-documentary character, which he blamed for its failure to grasp the fateful and fundamental dimension of the events it portrays.[32]

The narrator depicts Jewish existence in a turbulent Poland, commencing with his arrival in Warsaw immediately after the country's independence and concluding with his return, at the end of the period of upheavals and pogroms, to his native village and the nearby provincial town. By opting for a narrative in chronicle form, presented by a narrator who claims to be nonfictional, Weinberg was free to depict Polish antisemitism in its naked form, not forced to weave it into a "closed" ideological plot. In this manner he made use of the ramified tradition of the essay and the sketch, transforming them into the organizing principle for a long and unified work. The narrator-chronicler, whose presence generates this stream of memoirs, liberates the seminarrative genres from the forced and artificial character they sometimes adopted under the weight of their

31. G. Elkes, "Iton va-sefer," *Reshit,* September 1932, no. 1, pp. 24–25.
32. Shmueli, "Bikoret sefarim *Bayit u-rehov,*" *Moznayim,* July 2, 1931, p. 13.

ideological message. In passing, it is interesting to note that at the same time Reuven Fahn was likewise drawn to the documentary form. In a letter to Bialik he sought counsel about the composition and publication of a book that, drawing upon his personal experience in an important political post, would present the annals of the Jewish community of Eastern Galicia during the critically fluid situation "when the world war ended, and the Ukrainians took over the government in that country. At that time, the Jewish community was perplexed by the complexity of events: it organized, defended itself, demanded national autonomy etc., etc."[33]

The Jews' hopes of acquiring full rights as Polish citizens, irrespective of their religious and national identity, as aroused by Józef Piłsudski, are dispelled in Weinberg's book, which describes the crude antisemitism of Piłsudski's soldiers. The context of personal testimony within which the ideological generalizations are presented, however, gives Weinberg's work a most potent human dimension that makes examination of the generalizations in a broader historical perspective thoroughly unnecessary. Similar is the ironical reaction to the Jewish hopes of integration into Polish society in view of the pogroms accompanying the victories of the Polish army. These hopes are reexamined in the light of fundamental categories drawn largely from the reconstructed consciousness of the characters taking part. The latter appear in the story, however, not from the choice of an author characterized by a highly developed historical awareness, but due to their fortuitous encounter with the narrator, in a variety of bizarre ways. It is by this literary device that Weinberg examines the Zionist option. Recalling the ambivalence evident in Hazan's novel, Weinberg, too, leaves the issue unclear: the narrator's young friend and neighbor, the enthusiastic Zionist Tzali Freiman, comes to tell him that he has been released from the Polish army and is "a free Jew who wishes to savor the taste of a homeland." The war against the Germans and Russians had aroused the young Zionist to nationalist fervor, for "Poland, which was trampled under the foot of the tsar, and torn by the hoofs of the Prussian, has been restored to life. I am a Zionist. The dream of renaissance— is my dream! Poland's banner—is my banner! . . . Let the Poles know—a voice whispered to me—that the Jews, too, are a nation.

The Jew is linked to his homeland."[34] The brutal antisemitism that subjects him to humiliation and imprisonment has ultimately brought him, in his disillusionment, to seek discharge from the Polish army. Even here, however, there is no clear alternative to the much-disparaged Polish Diaspora. In addition, it should be recalled that, within the literary context created by Weinberg, the collapse of Jewish hopes of joining in Polish identity likewise casts a heavy shadow over the Zionist motivation of the naïve volunteer.

IV

The ideological hesitation evident in Hazan's *Geulah* can be interpreted both as reflecting the difficulty of presenting an unambiguous position and, equally, as attempting to give a unique ideological form to the paradoxical and hopeless situation of Hebrew literature in Poland. In considering the Hebrew literature produced in Poland, the stress on void and nonexistence as a substantial and structural element proves to be an equally effective point of departure with regard to more conventional plot solutions, such as that proposed by Yehuda Warshaviak's *Orot me-ofel* (Lights from Darkness), published in Warsaw in 1931.[35] As noted at the conclusion of the book, it was composed in 1928–29, when the economic crisis sweeping the country produced an upsurge of economic antisemitism. Like Hazan's *Geulah* and Weinberg's *Bayit u-rehov,* Warshaviak's work portrays the final days of World War I, the liberation of Poland from Russian occupation, and the rebirth of its independence, all blending as the formative experience of an entire generation. All three books highlight the hopes of young Jews for a dignified existence in a sovereign Poland. Similarly, anticipation of an imminent workers' revolution, so prominent in the novels of Hazan and Warshaviak, in the final account represents Jewish hopes of national equality and the elimination of antisemitism under the future socialist regime.

In an interesting blend of the hero of the *Zeitsroman* and the *Bildungsroman,* Warshaviak's Margolin undergoes a progressive process of personal and ideological maturation. The process commences with a Jewish soldier's returning from the battlefields of the world war to seek his way in life and concludes with his finding shelter in

34. Weinberg, *Bayit u-rehov,* pp. 117, 118.
35. Yehuda Warshaviak, *Orot me-ofel* (Warsaw, 1931).

Zionist ideals, which he goes on to put into practice. In delineating Margolin as a character typical of the generation of young Jews who grew to maturity in interwar Poland, Warshaviak was obliged to lead him, step by step, along the arduous path to the Zionist solution. When Margolin returns from the war, his rootlessness induces him to seek asylum in the arms of a Polish waitress employed at a railway station snack bar. In the early sections of the novel, Margolin displays an alienated reserve toward the Jewish world in which he is expected to find his place. His first encounter with Zionism, in his native town, leaves him totally indifferent; by contrast, heroic tales of the Polish Uprising of 1863 ignite his enthusiasm. Margolin is invited to visit the estate of Czortinski, the duke's son, and his acceptance likewise is presented as a symbolic act of alliance with the Polish elite, which he achieves by overcoming mental and cultural obstacles. Even if he displays ambivalence toward Polish aspirations for national redemption (as reflected in his response to the tale of Antosh, the disillusioned disciple of Piłsudski, who exacted private vengeance upon the Germans), Margolin finds that his visit to the Czortinski estate leads him to outright rejection of the Zionist option and to temporary relief from his despondency working at his father's flour mill. Here, too, he finds an ephemeral vitality in sexual relations with a Polish woman, Yasha, the younger daughter of his father's employee. The next and decisive phase of Margolin's personal and ideological development occurs as he begins to respond to the revolutionary ideas implanted in his mind by Czortinski. Margolin's sense of disgrace and guilt over his abuse of the trust placed in him by Yasha's father puts an end to his attempts to settle down in his parents' township, and he sets off for Warsaw, to his friend Czortinski, now a political activist. Hoping to find substance for his life and convinced that proletarian unity requires the Jews to take part in the revolution, Margolin is drawn into active work for the party (apparently the Polish Socialist Party). His political activity, however, progressively exposes him to contradictions and pressures arising from his Jewish origins. Along with his party colleagues, he joins the Socialist National Legion formed by the party to defend the Polish homeland against the Bolsheviks. The internal contradictions experienced by the Polish revolutionaries, torn between their loyalties to their class and to their nation, pale when compared with the profound inner conflict Margolin experiences as a Jew. He soon finds himself involved in a national conflict that expands until his disillusionment leads him to question, "What is in all this for us?" His tragic encounter with the Jewish victims of abuse by Polish soldiers intoxicated by their triumph over the Soviets leads him to make his choice: he abandons the Diaspora in favor of the Zionist solution.

In the novel's concluding paragraph, Warshaviak rejects the concept of cultivating and developing the Diaspora, a school of thought that went so far as to criticize the Zionists for regarding Palestine as their homeland. Undoubtedly, the novel is imbued with the general conviction that the Polish Diaspora could hold out few prospects. After the initial hopes inspired by the Polish government in its Jewish citizens, disillusionment was now general. The physical confrontation with antisemitism and the legal enactment of economic restrictions had shown the vision of the early days of Polish independence to be totally illusory. During the early 1930s, those who hoped to benefit from the collapse of Palestinocentrism, to pursue the idea of exile-without-homeland, were vigorously attacked by the Hebrew poet Malkiel Lusternik.[36] Indeed, Warshaviak dedicated considerable efforts to a *rapprochement* with Polish culture, with which he hoped to construct a symbiotic relationship.[37] In *Orot me-ofel*, Warshaviak's fluctuating attitude toward the relationship between the Diaspora and the new homeland took a new tack. The hero's departure for Palestine is depicted as a *total* relinquishing of the exile, toward which there is now no trace of any positive sentiment: "The train hastened to leave behind the expanses of the soil of exile, as though fleeing from them in disgust. . . . The eastern horizon began to don a bracing and invigorating light. The dawn began to break. Margolin pushed his hands out of the window, and along with his hands, his eyes were drawn forward."[38]

But the emergence of this new polarity, representing a Zionism based upon homeland-without-exile, was not accomplished without difficulty. In numerous and intriguing ways, the novel continues to depict the Diaspora, with its strength and promise, as the focus of

36. Malkiel Lusternik, "Ve-od . . . ," *Reshit*, October 1933, no. 2, p. 23.
37. For example, the two volumes of *Meal gdot ha-Visla* (Over the Banks of the Vistula) (Warsaw, 1929, 1933), were published with Polish assistance; they comprise essays on Polish authors and on Jews in Polish literature. Likewise, Warshaviak showered praise on one work for the mere fact of its cultural uniqueness as a Polish novel about Palestine. "Roman polani me-hayei Eretz Israel ba-hoveh," *Hatzefirah*, May 21, 1931.
38. Warshaviak, *Orot me-ofel*, p. 188.

a powerful attraction. In opting unequivocally for a *Zeitsroman* to trace the ideological development of a young Jew in interwar Poland, Warshaviak highlighted the weaker points of his chronicle of the personal and ideological turnabout that led Margolin to Zionism. One reviewer expressed his dissatisfaction with the superficiality, the fortuity, and the emptiness characterizing Margolin and his path to Zionism.[39] The turn at the end of the novel is explained, *inter alia*, by the mysterious illumination of a crucifix, leading Margolin to perceive the current historical situation as a renewed crucifixion of Jesus the Jew, who is required yet again to oil the wheels of historical change in the Gentile world. This mystical event underlines the *leitmotif* of darkness and light that makes its first appearance in the novel's title and, after numerous repetitions and variations, returns in the final lines, where the light is represented as a metaphor for Zionist hope brightening the gloom of exile. This systematic development, which stresses the antagonism between Diaspora and homeland by associating it with the contrast between darkness and light, helps create the final effect of spurning exile in favor of the hope for a new homeland.

But alongside these interesting motifs, the novel also develops an analogous story line whose grotesque configuration highlights the existential predicament of Poland's Jews. When the duke's daughter complains that the Jews, for all their sharpness of wit, find difficulty in drawing a distinction between humor and reality, Margolin responds, "For us, a lighthearted jest has often been transformed into a cruel and merciless reality—the Jew dreads them both."[40] His reply constitutes a link in a grotesque series that foreshadows his encounter, toward the end of the novel, with the demented laughter of the Jewish *halutzah* (Zionist pioneer woman) who has fallen victim to the cruel abuse of Polish soldiers.

Margolin's disillusionment with his former revolutionary ideals is underlined when the enthusiastic slogans lauding the vision of universal revolution punctuate the insane mouthings of the *halutzah*, now deranged after the rape. However, the Zionist solution, meant to resolve, or at least draw a sharp distinction between, the poles of the grotesque—the comic and the nightmarish—is not characterized adequately to place it upon an existential, personal, or social par

39. G. Goldberg, "*Orot me-ofel*: Rishmei keriah," *Hatzefirah*, July 24, 1931.
40. Warshaviak, *Orot me-ofel*, p. 95.

with the pressures that, according to the novel, exile exerts upon the Jews. On the other hand, one cannot help being impressed by the rhetoric of the grotesque whereby the novel displays the complexity and ambivalence of its ideological perception of the interplay of exile and homeland. Czortinski, the Gentile, recalls how his Jewish artist friend Lebovitz showed him a painting of a Jew with his mouth open wide with laughter; Czortinski himself was struck by what he perceived as the subject's tragic expression. Czortinski elaborates the anecdote into an allegory illustrating the contrast between the Jews, with their candid eyes that reflect their genuine feelings, and the Gentiles, whose artful eyes conceal their inner mood. Margolin's turn to Zionism, depicted as his return to Jewish authenticity, is part of his efforts to contend with manifestations of the grotesque. Early in the novel Margolin is impressed by the Gentile workman whose behavior blurs the distinction between the sublime and the ridiculous. Toward the end of the novel, this grotesque confusion of feelings is revived by the horrifying spectacle of the Pole Marginski, the venerable member of the workers' party, who, in time of war, emerges as a hysterical nationalist; his absurd laughter reminds Czortinski of the grotesque portrait painted by his friend Lebovitz. These changing responses further emphasize the personal and ideological metamorphosis Margolin has undergone: in the first case, when he is caught up on the horns of his grotesque dilemma, it is the solemn and sublime side that predominates; now, as he approaches the realization that there is no future for Jewish life in Poland, horror and disgust gain the upper hand. Czortinski's analogy between Marginski and Lebovitz's portrait also highlights the profoundly tragic element of this conclusion.

The novel's recourse to the grotesque, with the inner conflict characterizing it, is a symptom of the sharp ideological ambivalence that the grotesque leaves unresolved. The disparity between the questions the novel poses and the answers it provides emphasizes the fact that it is, in many ways, torn between the stark ideological conviction that there is nothing more to expect from a despicable Diaspora and the feeling that, for all its pathological contradictions, the Diaspora still retains its vital energy. As in the works of Hazan and Weinberg, this novel's ideological ambivalence repeatedly illustrates the intellectual division and confusion of its audience. The grotesque pattern of Warshaviak's novel, and the contradictions so characteristic of it, left it open to a variety of interpretations in Poland and elsewhere. These inner conflicts and divisions detracted from the integrity of the novel; its esthetic flaws did indeed draw harsh criticism.[41]

In this connection it should be reiterated that, in flagrant contrast to the thin trickle of literary creativity seeking to convey a coherent ideological utterance, there stretched an expansive void of emptiness and nothingness. Warshaviak's work is perhaps the most striking example of an attempt to revive Hebrew literature at a time when the potential—whether collective, in relation to the audience, or individual, with regard to the talent available—was limited. He and others were the continual target for criticism that, at a time of cultural decline, positions of unwarranted importance were occupied by all kinds of honor seekers and "graphomaniacs" who should properly be relegated to a marginal literary status.[42]

As depicted in the novel, Margolin's anguished path of disillusionment stretches from a Diaspora with no longings for the Zionist homeland to a sense of homeland reinforced by disgust toward the Polish Diaspora. In his concluding Zionist address, delivered at the town assembly hall, he encapsulates his ideological message within his life's story. In other words, through the biographical format that provides the novel's structural foundation, Warshaviak characterizes Jewish life in the Diaspora, with its illusory hopes, revolutionary and otherwise, as being adrift in a world of legends. Margolin's Zionist phase is thus depicted as a response to the traditions of exile-without-homeland. In similar fashion Warshaviak depicts Margolin's wonder at the patience and the submission to nature he detects in a homespun Polish peasant. Resembling the admiration for the simple Poles that can be found in Warshaviak's earlier stories,[43] this feeling enables Margolin, at an earlier stage of his development, to formulate his criticism of the Zionists' endeavors. His comments sound like a minor variation on the theme of exile-without-homeland, whose advocates voiced their criticisms of the Palestinian "Diaspora."

41. Y. Goldberg, *"Orot me-ofel*: Y. Warshaviak," *Reshit,* November–December 1933, nos. 3–4, pp. 38–39.
42. A. Riv, "Gahelet ha-yezirah ha-ivrit: Le-hofaat *Amudim,"* *Baderekh,* June 12, 1936. See also Yehuda Warshaviak, "Be-shulei hitnaplut ahat: Meein teshuvah ke-zarah," *Amudim,* July 1936, p. 15.
43. For example, Yehuda Warshaviak, "Beli emunah" (Without Faith), in the collection bearing the same name, *Beli emunah* (Warsaw, 1928), pp. 5–27. The story traces the fundamental religious doubts of a farmer's son.

You are too frantic and urgent, your garrulity overflows the deeds and enterprises; and who knows whether even the men of the Land of Israel have succeeded in extricating themselves from this Diaspora destiny, as Benyamin the coachman describes it: no matter how much a Jew hastens, he will always be late, and he will hasten nevertheless, even though he knows full well that he will be late, he will be late.[44]

Margolin's view that "this Diaspora destiny" overshadows Zionist endeavors in Palestine, which is presented in the novel in a sober context, similarly disparages the attitudes still characteristic of the Hebrew center in Poland.

Admittedly, at this advanced stage that center no longer voiced pretentious declarations after the manner of Steinman's radical views from the early 1920s. However, a residue of the ideal of exile-without-homeland was still evident in the heroic effort to maintain *Baderekh* as a Hebrew weekly in Poland during the 1930s. The desire to preserve an organ of Hebrew cultural activity separate and distinct from the periodicals published by the Zionist pioneer movements, such as *Heatid* (The Future), was supported by the demand that the Hebrew press in the Diaspora should serve as a common platform, with Hebrew providing a basic common denominator adequate for expressing all the nationalist factions in Poland. An awareness of the cruel fate in store for Hebrew culture in Poland evoked repeated calls to close ranks, to play down disagreements, and soberly to endeavor to defend every Hebrew outpost—in this case, *Baderekh*.[45]

A further echo of the survival of the concept of exile-without-homeland is found in G. Goldberg's review of Warshaviak's novel. In spite of his awareness of the work's flaws, the reviewer commended it equally for exploring the life of the Polish people and for the mere act of writing and publishing a book "in the neglected field of our [Hebrew] literature in Poland."[46] In a lecture published in Lwów in 1933, Simon Rawidowicz reiterated these notions: "Just as the Diaspora needs the Land of Israel, the Land of Israel needs the Diaspora." On a similar note, Rawidowicz responded enthusiastically to Asher Barash's harsh criticism of the contemptuous at-

44. Warshaviak, *Orot me-ofel*, p. 81.
45. A. Urinovsky, "Reshimot A: Miflagtiut o daat ha-zibur ha-ivri," *Baderekh*, September 15, 1932. For a detailed discussion of efforts to maintain the Hebrew press in Poland, see Shmuel Werses, "The Hebrew Press and Its Readership in Interwar Poland," in this volume.
46. G. Goldberg, "*Orot me-ofel*: Rishmei keriah."

titude toward the Diaspora displayed by the Palestinian center.[47] Barash, one of the leading Hebrew writers in Palestine, had voiced his criticism in a controversial lecture entitled "Sifrut shel shevet o sifrut shel am?" (Literature of a Tribe, or Literature of a People?). Endorsing similar views expressed by Rawidowicz in *Haolam* (The World), the organ of the World Zionist Organization, Barash criticized Hebrew literature in Palestine for its dismissal of Diaspora literature and for its tribalism, thereby questioning both the cultural roots and significance of Palestinian Hebrew literature. Barash elaborated the concept of a legitimate and vital Diaspora existing side by side with a predominant metropolitan homeland and urged Hebrew literature in Palestine to grant a share in its own development to the Hebrew Diaspora.[48]

In response, Yaakov Rabinovitch affirmed that he was not concerned about the emergence of a tribe in Palestine; on the contrary, he hoped for such a development. He believed that adherence to Hebrew had constituted a force for salvation throughout Jewish history. At this time it would also save the Diaspora from perdition and ultimately foster Palestinian culture to achieve the breadth and depth it deserved.[49] Writing in Palestine in 1931, Rabinovitch thereby advocated a view astoundingly similar to the national ontology attributed to the Hebrew language by Steinman and his colleagues during the immediate postwar period. By contrast, it was the Warsaw periodical *Hatzefirah* that now proceeded to publish an article condemning Rabinovitch for his conviction that the Hebrew language *alone* could offer salvation both to the Diaspora and to the homeland.[50] Some three years later, Lusternik, writing in another Warsaw periodical, *Reshit*, attacked the Palestinian center for referring to itself under the demeaning term of "tribe." By his reproof, he showed himself to be more Palestinian than the Palestinians.[51]

47. Simon Rawidowicz, *Im lo kan—Heikhan?* (If Not Here—Where?) (Lwów, [1933]). Rawidowicz's response to Asher Barash is "Shtei sheelot she-hen ahat," *Moznayim*, March 12, 19, 1931.

48. Asher Barash, "Sifrut shel shevet o sifrut shel am?" *Moznayim*, January 22, 1931; Simon Rawidowicz, "Le-shem hidush sifrutenu," *Haolam*, December 2, 9, 16, 1930.

49. Yaakov Rabinovitch, "Al am va-shevet," *Moznayim*, April 30, 1931.

50. R. Zeligman, "Al lashon ve-tarbut," *Hatzefirah*, June 12, 1931.

51. Malkiel Lusternik, "Mi-saviv la-nekudah," *Reshit*, January–March 1934, nos. 4–6, pp. 33–34.

V

With the passage of the years, a growing sense of dread and desperation became evident. The Nazis' advent to power in Germany in 1933 inspired Polish antisemitism to a rising frenzy. In a programmatic article entitled "Yahadut Polin—Heikhan" (Polish Jewry—Whither?) Leib Hazan wrote that Palestine was now the only lifeline, whereas in Poland "a chasm has opened up at the feet of the rising generation of an entire people!"[52] Gone was the ideological ambivalence of Hebrew literature, but concurrently that literature itself was on the wane. What had still been feasible in 1930—the preservation, in literature at least, of a measure of uncertainty, complexity, and sobriety—became anachronistic in 1935 with the death of Piłsudski, who, notwithstanding the bitter disappointments he had inflicted upon Poland's Jews, was still regarded as a ray of light in the terrifying gloom prevailing all about.[53] Piłsudski's demise signaled the onset of a new and savage phase of persecution, which reached its peak in 1936–37.[54]

In the sphere of literary genres, the most striking illustration of the change was the disappearance of the Hebrew novel, a literary form that, by its very nature, could at least have attempted to contend with the wealth of material provided by everyday reality and the ideological pressures it generated. As the Zionist interpretation of Jewish existence in Poland grew more somber and unambiguous, the novel was progressively replaced by the short story and the novella. As the arena of struggle narrowed and its prospects grew dimmer, there was a return to the shorter and pithier forms prevalent in Hebrew fiction in Poland in the period immediately after the war. It is interesting to note that this was the precise reverse of the trend evident during the same period in Palestinian Hebrew literature. In the controversy that unfolded in Palestine at that time with regard to the desirable literary genres, there were demands for an increased share of short stories at the expense of novels. In his contribution to the debate, Yaakov Fichman pointed to the novel's capacity to respond to variegated materials conveying a clear ideological mes-

---

52. Leib Hazan, "Yahadut Polin—Heikhan?" *Baderekh*, January 18, 1935.

53. See, for example, the eulogy entitled "Gibor Polanyah" (Poland's Hero), dedicated to him by Y. L. Meizel, *Baderekh*, May 17, 1935.

54. Emanuel Melzer, *Maavak medini be-malkodet: Yehudei Polin, 1935–1939* (Tel Aviv, 1982), pp. 39–162.

sage (a novel about life in the *kibbutz,* a novel about the war years), in contrast with the greater formal flexibility of the novella. Like Rabinovitch some years before, Fichman recognized the genuine national-ideological need fulfilled by the wealth of novels (while simultaneously looking forward to the development of the novella).[55]

This opposing emphasis highlighted the contrast between the Polish center-in-decline and its flourishing Palestinian counterpart. It also points to the particular relation of dependence between the Polish center and its counterpart in Eretz Israel. The fear, evinced by Barash, that the Eretz Israel center might become merely "tribal" amounts to a recognition that this relation was one of mutual dependence. While the Hebrew center in Poland was obviously dependent on Eretz Israel, it is equally possible to discern the latter's need for the Diaspora's special contribution to its development. Now this pattern of mutual complimentarity between the two cultural-territorial systems was actualized to some degree in the distribution of narrative genres. The short story and the novella, much vaunted literary goals for leading critics in Eretz Israel, were, as already noted, the principal narrative genres practiced during the last years of the Hebrew center in Poland. Conversely the Hebrew realistic-ideological novel, which had virtually disappeared in Poland, was already prominent in Eretz Israel.

As Hebrew fiction in Poland progressively fell silent, it threw off all hope of survival in the Polish Diaspora. "Av antishemi" (Anti-semitic Father), written by Warshaviak in the anecdotal manner of Gershon Shofman's stories, portrays antisemitism as a natural phenomenon, indestructible, and unaffected by environment or history. The antisemite, identified on the train solely by his movements and facial expressions, is depicted as relentless in his hatred of Jews. His display of tender feeling, brought on by the sight of his son's reflection through the sunlit carriage window, is an ironic device designed to bring out the deep-rootedness of the man's ill-will toward Jews.[56]

55. Yaakov Fichman, "Mikhtavim al ha-sifrut ha-ivrit: Mikhtav shevii," *Moznayim,* April 7, 1938, pp. 98–103; Rabinovitch, "Al ha-sipur ha-ivri," pp. 98–99.
56. Yehuda Warshaviak, "Av antishemi," in *Afilot* (Late Blossoms) (Warsaw, 1935), pp. 115–18. For the link between Warshaviak's early works and Gershom Shofman's stories, see Shaked, *Ha-siporet ha-ivrit,* 2:270. The view expressed here differs somewhat from Shaked's view, which applies to Warshaviak as well and which suggests that the "Shofmanian influence is particularly characteristic of writers whose themes are non-Israeli, because the documentary-ideological requirement does not apply to this reality and Shofman's devices are adequate for the small acts of memory typical of such works."

At the same time, Hebrew fiction in Poland showed a growing inclination toward the Palestinian homeland. *Sefer ha-shanah le-yehudei Polanyah* (The Polish-Jewish Yearbook) published by the Miflat publishing house in 1938, contains a story by Mifelev, significantly entitled "Hu lo yireh et ha-aretz" (He Shall Not See the Land).[57] Miflat set itself the sober objective of printing one or two Hebrew books per year and distributing a few hundred copies, as its "effort to maintain the outpost and the line" even though "the people of the Land of Israel may perhaps not understand the matter."[58] At the beginning of the volume its editorial board pointed out that the yearbook was being published "at a difficult period for Polish Jewry, at a time of increasingly aggressive antisemitism, at a time when despair is gaining control of the Jewish streets, during a time of the spiritual and material decline of Polish Jewry."[59]

Mifelev's story describes the growth and expansion of Polish Zionism during the interwar period. The process is depicted in contrast to the progressive eclipse of Zvi Green, an old-fashioned Hebrew teacher and one of the earliest active Zionists. His want of political gifts and absence of leadership qualities, which lead to his decline, highlight the changed nature of Zionist work and the new attributes required for its pursuit. The fact that he finds his place in cultural activity stresses the futile nature of "work for the present." It gradually emerges that Green serves Mifelev as a satirical butt and an allegory for Hebrew endeavor in Poland. Green's deteriorating economic status, contrasting with his persistence in his cultural work, particularly those aspects lacking any real significance, are part of a broader canvas that also includes barbed criticism of the deceit implicit in the aid Polish Zionists receive from Palestine. The story reaches its climax when Green realizes that, precisely because of his naïve Zionist integrity, he will not be able to fulfill his dream of emigrating to Palestine. Unlike those who, in spite of their indifference to the Zionist ideal, manage to find underhand ways of acquiring immigration certificates, Green is condemned to remain in Poland, robbed of the reward he deserves for his efforts.

The new homeland in Palestine was now in the process of shaking off the Zionist Diaspora with its outmoded values. Caught between

---

57. Nachman Mifelev, "Hu lo yireh et ha-aretz," *Sefer ha-shanah le-yehudei Polanyah*, vol. 1 (Cracow, 1938), pp. 200–214.

58. Z. Zilberpfennig, "Mei Miflat?" in ibid., p. 356.

59. The editorial board, in ibid., p. 6.

the efforts of the Polish government to solve its Jewish Question by encouraging emigration to Palestine and the restrictions on immigration into that country imposed by the British mandatory authorities, Poland's Jews experienced a sense of entrapment that contributed to a decline in the Zionist parties. This process was hastened by the campaign mounted in the late 1930s by the Bund, which launched scathing attacks on what it depicted as a community of interests and policies between the Zionists and the Polish antisemites and their shared view of Poland's Jews as second-class citizens.[60] In this atmosphere the hopelessness of Green's personal predicament reflects the cruel triumph of homeland-without-exile. Mifelev's satirical allegory, whose form stresses its unambiguous ideological message, illustrates the great distance traversed by Hebrew fiction in Poland: from the seminarrative genres whose ideas clashed with the pattern of their narrative mechanism, by way of the dialectical attempt to develop ideological utterances, through the realistic novel of ideas that somehow conveys its statement in an ambiguous form, to the unbalanced satire that colors its heroes in ideological hues of an untempered harshness. In an expanding void of literary creativity, a certain lassitude informed the ideological and poetical structures of Hebrew fiction as it endeavored to extract whatever possible from a hopeless predicament.

VI

This tangled mass of tensions—manifestations of strength and weakness, whether conscious or not—was, as we all know, ultimately torn apart in the most vile and brutal manner imaginable. Like so many Hebrew writers in Poland, the tireless disciples of "work for the present," who had sought to preserve a proud and vital Diaspora, ultimately fell victim to the not always tacit alliance of domestic Polish antisemitism and German Nazi invaders. But during those final years before World War II, the stubborn defenders of the residual shreds did not shut their eyes to the imminent disaster. As the hour of decision approached, Hebrew literature in Poland, exhibiting an unflinching sobriety, expressed and recorded the conviction that the Palestinian homeland would soon be alone, left without the Polish Diaspora. Nevertheless, names like *Baderekh* (En

60. Melzer, *Maavak medini be-malkodet*, pp. 140–63, 196.

Route) (1932–37), *Reshit* (Beginning) (1933), and *Tishrei* (the first month in the Hebrew calendar) (1938), chosen as titles for periodicals, underline the optimism—albeit waning—that characterized Hebrew culture in Poland. In 1937, some two years before the calamity, when the Hebrew periodical *Tehumim* (Spheres) was launched, its editors wrote that "at a time of terrible desolation and prolonged drying up of sources, as in our times, the mere preservation of a platform of Hebrew expression in the Diaspora is a desirable and favorable purpose."[61]

Toward the end of the interwar epoch, the Hebrew poet Ber Pomerantz published a powerful literary essay in which he depicted tribulations and lingering resentments accompanying the agonizingly complex transition from exile-without-homeland to homeland-without-exile.

> The horror of the situation even exceeds its disgrace. The disgrace cries: Silence! The horror demands: Raise your voice, and hark.... The exile remains, doubly orphaned. Somewhere in the world, there may be such a father who requests his children's permission to leave the house for a moment, promising to bring them bread, and goes out and abandons the children in their place of concealment for all eternity. If there is somewhere in the world such a father, he could be a fitting model for the Hebrew writers and poets. Our good mentors and fine friends, one by one, abandoned us in the Diaspora and closeted themselves somewhere in Tel Aviv. And even though they have yet to succeed in creating *a center*, in the singular, they have already created *forums*, in the plural, and undertake to influence the Diaspora from afar, from beyond the seas.[62]

61. The editors, in *Tehumim*, 1937, no. 1, pp. 1–2.
62. Ber Pomerantz, "Eyma, Masuot," *Reshit*, January–March 1934, nos. 4–6, p. 38.

Dan Miron

Uri Zvi Grinberg's War Poetry

I

Uri Zvi Grinberg, the great Hebrew-Yiddish modernist, was a poet born twice. Making his *début*, at the age of fifteen, in the year 1912, he soon established himself as a late and minor romanticist. He produced mainly short, mostly strophic lyrical poems in which the conventional themes of romantic love, the beauty of nature, and the loneliness of the poet were involved with equally conventional moods of autumnal melancholy and elegiac *Weltschmerz*. The poems offered sentiments curbed by a sense of form and emotionalism controlled by resignation. They aimed at a combination of sincerity and elegance and exercised the effects of a soft and rich euphony, of lilting rhythms and a delicate, professedly poetic diction. Actually, they conveyed a semiconscious sense of incompleteness, of a self barred from full realization by some hidden obstacles. The poet, however, did not investigate these obstacles. Accepting his limitations rather than confronting them, he sought refuge in an undefined idea of a poetic mission, which endowed his experiences with esthetic permanence. With this mission as the core of his being, the poet could indulge in a self-image of the unrecognized chosen one, the prince in tatters.

All these attributes hardly singled Grinberg out from his literary contemporaries, Yiddish and Hebrew poets who made their appearance in the years immediately preceding World War I. As a Yiddish poet Grinberg shared his melancholic moods as well as his mellifluous effects with some of the other members of the so-called Galician or Lemberg school, a basically conservative group that flourished at the time under the tutelage of the poet S. I. Imber. Imber, the author of graceful, well-crafted but conventional Heinesque lyrics, taught his disciples the virtues of purity—in diction as well as in sentiment—and of form. As a Hebrew poet, Grinberg belonged to the first post-Bialik wave, which at the time separated itself from the great poet and his immediate followers by rejecting the prophetic postures, the grand public rhetoric, and the mimetic-descriptive solidity so characteristic of the Bialik school. It practiced a deliberately minor and private mode and a low-keyed descriptive attitude somewhat informed by the then-current impressionist trend. It, too, found one of its main centers in Galicia and particularly in Lemberg (in Polish, Lwów), Grinberg's hometown.

In 1921, with the publication of his third Yiddish book, *Mefisto*, Grinberg abruptly shed this poetic persona. It still controlled most of the poetry he wrote throughout the war and during the years immediately following it, which was collected in 1922 in his major Yiddish collection, *Farnakhtngold* (Evening Gold). But when *Farnakhtngold* appeared, it already belonged to Grinberg's romantic-impressionist past, while the present and the future were totally conditioned by the poet's new allegiance to expressionism as well as other modernist, postsymbolist poetic creeds. Grinberg became one of the chief prophets of radical modernism in Yiddish and Hebrew literature. The poetry he now wrote completely broke away from his earlier work, deviating in at least six central points:

1. The poet now strove for a poetry of knowledge or of a heightened self-awareness (which he called *hakarat ha-yeshut*, the knowledge of one's mode of being, of one's existence) rather than for a poetry of estheticized emotionalism. Setting free his pent-up emotions, he used them for an intellectual-analytical attack on the secrets of the self and the ambiguities of the objective world.

2. Instead of limiting himself to individual expressions, Grinberg wanted to express humanity *en masse*. Eventually he settled for a smaller constituency—the Jewish people—but his blurred self-image as a chosen or marked person, from now on, became conditioned by a clear, ideologically controlled idea of a specific public mission. This soon led to his reenactment of H. N. Bialik's prophetic role.

3. Grinberg now discarded the notion of the poet-prince with his golden harp and instead developed a down-to-earth egalitarian self-image. He completely rejected the notion of poetry as an independent, autonomous realm. This meant giving up the esthetic norm that controls poetic expression and separates it from other, nonpoetic discourses.

4. Grinberg also renounced his quietism, which had indicated a static conception of reality as a solid, permanently structured entity. Against such a reality defiance stood no chance. Now Grinberg conceived reality as explosively dynamic—either apocalyptically entropic or eschatologically reformulable. Such a reality prescribed an active rebellious *modus operandi* in society as well as in art.

5. All these characteristics led to drastic changes in Grinberg's diction, prosody, and euphony. Rhyme became rare in his new poetry; meter, although not altogether discarded, was replaced by free verse; the soft, lilting sequences gave way to jolting, deliberately inelegant rhythms. Pleasing musicality was renounced. "Pure" poetic diction was replaced by an "impure" and grating diction. Grinberg's early short strophic lyrical structures were pushed aside, at least for the time being, by vast and seemingly formless structures, even as his short verses grew into long lines obliterating accepted demarcations separating verse from prose. In every way, Grinberg's poetry closely resembled the patterns of rhetorical prose.

6. With the passing of poetic-esthetic ideals, fierce naturalism invaded Grinberg's poetry, evoking deliberately ugly images intended to shock rather than please. Figurative language now avoided all organic, romantic metaphors, favoring metaphorical mixtures that were discordant and unacceptable to the traditional decorum of poetic language.

II

Thus Grinberg the poet was reborn in 1921, and his rebirth coincided with the heyday of Yiddish and Hebrew literary modernism. It was, of course, much commented on, seriously discussed, and differently evaluated by various critics and scholars. Challenging all the accepted poetic norms of its day, Grinberg's new poetry inevitably became the center of stormy polemics, where conflicting attitudes toward the esthetic and ontological status of literature were brought into sharp focus.

There was, however, one aspect of the poet's artistic rebirth that did not seem to call for any disagreement, and consequently this aspect—the genetic one—was never seriously debated and investigated. When faced with the questions of how and why this new development in Grinberg's poetry had been triggered, a seemingly self-evident answer suggested itself: the war, or, to be exact, the poet's exposure to its horrors brought about the radical changes. The changes indicated nothing but the new sense of reality that forced itself upon the poet's mind when he served as a soldier in Serbia during fall and winter of 1915–16.

On the surface this explanation seems to make perfect sense. When the war broke out, Grinberg, on the eve of his eighteenth birthday, was not mobilized because Lemberg, situated on the eastern frontier of the Austro-Hungarian Empire, was occupied by the Russian army. The young poet was given almost a full year to watch the war and suffuse himself with fear and anxiety from a distance. But then in June 1915 the town was liberated, and the Austrian authorities, perhaps fearing a Russian counteroffensive, quickly mobilized its entire youth, in large part Jewish. The boys were packed in livestock wagons and shipped to the Hungarian countryside, where they were given six weeks' basic military training. Then they were shipped to the Serbian front as cannon fodder for the projected fall onslaught on the Serbian positions blocking the way to Belgrade. Fighting took place near the River Sava, which had to be crossed under heavy fire. Reaching Serbian positions on the opposite bank, the troops, cutting through rolls of barbed wire, had to resort to fierce face-to-face combat. It was a veritable carnage, which completely shocked the poet-boy, striking him with fear and desolation for many years.

One scene in particular burned its imprint in Grinberg's memory. After crossing the river and losing many soldiers who were hit by bullets and fell into the water, the troops, reaching the soggy bank, got entangled in barbed wire. Suddenly the poet found himself alone, facing the dead bodies of his fellow soldiers, who, hit while attempting to get through the wire, hung on to it with heads dropping down and legs pointing up. At that moment the moon appeared in a clearing of the cloudy, autumnal sky. It shone brightly and was reflected in the metal cleats on the upturned boots of the dead soldiers. Grinberg never forgot this sight, which eventually represented to him the very essence of a fear of cosmic dimensions. *Eimah gedolah ve-yareah* (Great Fear and the Moon) (1925), the title of his first Hebrew collection of poems, indicated, in its combination of horror and moonlight, the death of the moon as a romantic symbol of beauty, spirituality, and otherworldliness. In its framework the moon became the portent of imminent death and decomposition, as well as the expression of heaven's (i.e., God's) indifference to human misery. Although the poem "Eimah gedolah ve-yareah" it-self did not directly refer to the scene on the banks of the River Sava, this scene informed its atmosphere and message.

This scene, endowed with haunting reality, kept recurring in Grinberg's poetry. First, immediately after the war, it was recorded in Grinberg's poetic war memoir *In tsaytns roysh* (In the Rush of Time) (1919); then the poet returned to it in *Mefisto* (1921), then in various other works up to his late lyrical cycles written in the 1950s. Its most poignant expression was achieved in 1928, in his Hebrew memorial poem to the war dead included in *Anakreon al kotev ha-itzavon* (Anacreon at the Pole of Sorrow).

> Ah! If I could but raise up now the bitter cup
> And drink to fear with eyes turned inward
> For the sake of brothers-soldiers, in whose company I reached the
>   banks of River Sava,
> Where legs-upward they dropped against the wire,
> The whimper of their expiring life-essence lasting for a mere minute,
> And very darkly they died.
> Alone I stood, the last member of a fighting human race,
> And watched my brothers growing upward with their legs
> Until they could, dead already, kick the heavens.
> I saw the moon like an animal rubbing its silvery face
> Against the outworn cleats on the soles of upside-down soldiers,
> And this terrible shine on the cleats in the boots of dead people kicking
>   against the sky
> Electrified my life with fear—fatally luminous.
> With my eyes of flesh I saw a divinity in the mystery of fear and in
>   the fallen human carcass,
> And then and there I wept like I were the last weeper upon earth,
> And I shall never weep again as I did on the banks of River Sava.[1]

Does not this poem, by its sheer force, convince us of the correctness of what might be called the war-impact hypothesis in the origin of Grinberg's modernity? The poet himself maintained that the hor-rendous experience "electrified" his life, charging it with its current high voltage. The metaphor of electrification served in all contem-porary European literatures as, among other things, a symbol of modernization.

The critics and more recently the Grinberg scholars never doubted the correctness of this war-impact hypothesis. Admirers and de-tractors alike referred to it as self-evident and not calling for further proof. The former enthusiastically asserted that Grinberg's wartime

---

1. Uri Zvi Grinberg, "Hazkarat neshamot," in *Anakreon al kotev ha-itzavon* (Tel Aviv, 1928), p. 49.

shock amounted to a revelation.[2] The latter—mainly critics from the Zionist Left—maintained that the shock slackened the poet's moral fiber, and undermined his already fragile personality to such an extent that he was morally paralyzed. Thus, they said, his modernist poetry, though showing much talent, expressed a sick mind so overwhelmed by fear of death and physical decomposition as to be completely bereft of the integrity necessary for a moral view of the self and the place of the self in society. Hence the poet's admiration of brute force and his fascist chauvinism.[3] Bialik, who struck a middle ground, said, while confirming the essential poetic quality of Grinberg's modernist poetry, that the poet must, nevertheless, be given time "to come to his senses." His poetry is that of a person who had just emerged from a *koshmar* (nightmare), and as he disentangled himself from his nightmarish experiences, his poetry would mellow.[4] Thus Bialik, too, predicated a causal connection between the war *koshmar* and Grinberg's new poetics.

Grinberg himself never cited the war as the exclusive, or even as the main, explanation for his artistic development. Nevertheless he, too, resorted to it several times, especially when in a polemical mood. He would refer then to the reality of the war as one of the origins, and hence as a possible justification, of his poetry. Here, for example, is this argument as it was phrased in the manifestolike "Proklamirung" (Proclamation) with which Grinberg launched the first issue of his literary journal *Albatros*.

> That's how it is. Whether we want it or not.
> We stand as we are: with open-lipped wounds,
> With rolled-up arteries, with screwlike bones, after cannon bombard-
>   ments, "hurras" and gassing—
> Hence the horrible in the poem.
> Hence the chaotic in the image.
> Hence the outcry of the Blood.[5]

III

It is my intention here to question the validity and tenableness of the war-impact hypothesis as providing for a possible dynamic con-

2. See, e.g., Perets Markish "Uri Zvi Grinberg," in *Farbaygeyndik* (Vilna, 1921), pp. 71–74.

3. See, e.g., David Kenaani, *Le-nogah ez rakav* (Merhavia, 1950).

4. H. N. Bialik, "Al ha-sifrut ha-ivrit ha-zeirah," in Bialik, *Devarim she-be-al peh* (Tel Aviv, 1938), 2:20.

5. Uri Zvi Grinberg, "Proklamirung" (1922), in Grinberg, *Gezamlte verk*, ed. Chone Shmeruk (Jerusalem, 1979), 2:422.

text within which the modernist shift in Grinberg's poetry can be understood. Since, to some extent, this shift represents the eruption of the entire modernist revolution in our literature, the investigation of its psychic and cultural origin seems significant and worthwhile. Was this eruption the result of a mental shock? Was Jewish modernism, as Bialik maintained, a mere response to a historical *koshmar*?

My difficulties with the war-impact hypothesis begin with a reading of Grinberg's war poetry, that is, those parts of his bilingual poetry where the war experience is expressed, described, or referred to. To my mind, this part of the poet's work, just like its other parts, breaks sharply into two units, the poems written before *Mefisto* of 1921 and those written after it. This deep cleavage indicates that the wartime experience, as such, does not explain the development of the poet's art. Rather, the varying expressions of this experience are explained by this development. In other words, the horrors to which Grinberg was exposed, like any other experience that occupied his mind and stirred his soul, were not the origin of his abrupt and revolutionary turn to modernism but, rather, its illustrative material. Before the shift, the poet treated and expressed these experiences in a certain poetic way. After the shift the treatment drastically changed, but the experience *per se* remained neutral so far as the cause of the shift is concerned.

This explanation proves true by whatever examples we might choose from Grinberg's pre-*Mefisto* and post-*Mefisto* war poetry. Even when the two examples record exactly the same situation, the total difference between the two poetic modes they indicate strongly suggests the lack of any connecting link between the situation itself and its respective poetic rendering. Here, for instance, is the recording of the River Sava incident in *In tsaytns roysh*.

We travel across a wide boiling body of water. Over our heads whimpering bird beaks fly . . . someone cries U-ah and writhes. Suddenly a warm wave hits the face: somebody's blood. The boats are perforated. Do I know where I am now? I hear shouts of "hurra." I shout "hurra" myself. Already at the bank the legs sink into a bog. The rucksack pulls me down. I shout "hurra." In the meantime people somehow fall back into the water: bll . . . what do I know? I shout "hurra." On the bank lines of barbed wire are spread. I know that the slightest touch is enough to twist in two one's . . . And when a moon swam out of the clouds and beamed at the bank I wanted to cry loudly but was unable to. The eyes watched as if covered by a cataract. Something warm dripped down the cheeks, and I saw human bodies hanging on the wire with downward dropping heads and upturned legs, and on the worn-out soles the cleats and horseshoe nails glistened and sh . . . sh . . . Where am I actually?[6]

On the surface this description resembles in every detail the 1928 memorial poem in *Anakreon al kotev ha-itzavon,* but upon a closer examination the two renderings of the same horrendous experience turn out to be diametrically opposed to each other in at least five ways:

First, the passage from *In tsaytns roysh* reflects a consciousness swimming in a vortex of impressions completely at its mercy. Hence the blurry contours, the question "Where am I actually?", the references to eyes not seeing and mind not grasping. Things happen here "suddenly" and "somehow," and unexplained gaps are left between them. In *Anakreon,* the poet's vision, which reflects an inner reality rather than actual sensory data ("with eyes turned inward"), is endowed with absolute clarity. Hence the sharply etched contours of each detail and the poet's unfaltering grasp over space and time. In that poem there are no gaps; no connecting links are missing. The description is solid because the poet knows exactly where he is and what he sees, with no "suddenly" or "somehow."

Second, in the 1919 passage we are supposed to absorb the various details as they occur. One impression after the other hits us, and they all seem strangely equal. None is more significant than another—the rucksack tearing at the speaker's back, his dumbfounded shouts of "hurra," the shining cleats—they are all equal, and their equality indicates the speaker's mental blankness. In the 1928 poem, we find a perfect hierarchy that organizes all the details according to their significance. Everything leads to the clash between the "upward growing" legs of the dead soldiers and the moon coming down from heaven to rub its face against them. The interaction between the boots and the moon is developed into a high drama of man's rebellion and protest *vis-à-vis* God's indifference. In *In tsaytns roysh,* by contrast, there is no meaningful interaction between the descriptive details.

Third, the 1919 passage includes some striking metaphors that vividly convey the speaker's sensory impressions. Thus the rushing waters of the river are "boiling," and the bullets overhead are "whimpering bird beaks." The passage as a whole, however, is not

---

6. Uri Zvi Grinberg, *In tsaytns roysh* (1919), reprinted in ibid., 1:41.

organized within a metaphorical framework. The 1928 poem is organized within such a framework. The metaphor in that poem is rather simple, and there is nothing particularly striking or vivid about the relationship between its tenor and vehicle. Rather, by fitting into the situation as a whole, it is striking, almost overwhelming. The speaker is a boy among his older and bigger brothers. As a younger brother, he is used to watching them growing up toward heaven, getting taller and towering above him. Only now that they are dead, they do that with their upturned boots rather than with their heads, and now they kick heaven. Their position does not hinder heaven's cat, the moon, from rubbing its face against their steel-enforced shoes. No matter how much they kick it, it still manages to get the little rubbing pleasure it craves out of their dead bodies.

Fourth, in *In tsaytns roysh*, the dying soldiers are "somebody" and "someone," and they die "somehow." They are anonymous, unknown, extrinsic to the speaker's sense of being. In *Anakreon*, they are "brothers-soldiers," and their death is real and fully explained. The speaker raises the bitter cup to the memory of his family members. Accordingly, the 1919 passage is fitted into a private diary, a record of the poet's individual impressions, while the 1928 poem is a memorial dirge, part of a chapter in a poetic sequence expressing the poet's empathy with any suffering human being.

Finally, in the 1919 passage the horrible occurrences have no causes and no far-reaching consequences. The speaker is too overwhelmed to learn anything from them. In the 1928 poem there is a whole series of ideational consequences. The poet actually represents the experience as a mystical, prophetic revelation. With his eyes of flesh, he says, he saw a new divinity, that which dwells in the mystery of fear and in the fallen human carcass. In other words, the divine essence is displaced here; wrenched out of heaven, it is located in the bodies of the dead soldiers as well as in the poet's own emotions, that is, his fears.

Grinberg's two renderings of the River Sava experience reveal superficial resemblances and deep structural differences. Poetically and ideologically, they are so far removed from each other as to represent not only two different poetic systems but also two conflicting, mutually exclusive literary cultures.

IV

Grinberg's direct exposure to the war horrors occurred, as stated before, in the fall and winter of 1915–16. His modernist poetic rebirth took place a full five years later. To those who regard the poet's frontline experience as the psychic source of his eventual modernity, this time gap poses a question that might be explained by the poet's needing time to "chew" on his experiences. Thus the war-impact hypothesis leads to another one—the hypothesis of the gestation or incubation period, which, by necessity, is also understood as a transition period.

How do we know that a poet is undergoing a transition? We might start by discovering in his works hints, some telltale changes, that, even if not completely coherent, point in the direction in which we assume the transition was leading. Thus, works by Grinberg from the years 1917–18, and particularly his book *In tsaytns roysh*, were interpreted as rife with such telltale hints. The intergeneric composition of *In tsaytns roysh*, which included both poetry and prose, as well as its passages of rough, disjointed prose descriptions, were cited as clear indications of the new directions in the development of Grinberg's art.

But this interpretation leads to a misinterpretation of Grinberg's war poetry and particularly of *In tsaytns roysh*—its structure, its poetic assemblage, and its meaning. All Grinberg's work up to 1921 follows the same poetic pattern. That is not to say that it is monolithic and static; it is a living, developing body of a poet's *oeuvre*. Its development flows directly from its initial, original sources, however; it entails nothing but further, more advanced realizations of a set of inherent patterns.

The central pattern of Grinberg's prewar poetry can be described as a progress that stops at four stations:

1. The first is a tragic state of decline and impending doom usually represented by a somber and glowing sunset, its abundant red colors often compared to the flow of blood from an open wound.

2. There is also a sense of drifting, of being carried away by uncontrollable forces. This sense is often conveyed through the description of a boat aimlessly floating or even sinking into the glowing-red sunset sea. The boat represents both the poet and, more important, his human connections, such as the girl he loves, who seems to be drifting away from him.

3. This sense of drifting leads to a phase of loneliness and desolation. Nevertheless, the poet's loneliness also entails an affirmation of his poetic mission, which is to estheticize his sorrow into an independent poetic kingdom.

4. With his esthetic mission confirmed, the poet can achieve a serenity indicating both his resignation and his sense of superiority. The poet is now both subjugated to the forces he cannot control and superior to them.

Thus, the pattern as a whole, which, of course, emerges only from the combination of many short poems into cycles and sequences, involves a gradual distancing and counterbalancing following an initially upsetting experience. Its goal is the regaining of equilibrium through a quiet affirmation of the poet's esthetic prerogative.

In Grinberg's works written between 1915 and 1920, this pattern endlessly repeats itself. Most of these works, as we can learn from *Farnakhtngold* or from the Hebrew poetic sequences published right after the war in *Hatekufah,* are not at all connected with the experience of war, but even those that are—and perhaps they more than the others—depend on this pattern for their structure and meaning.

Thus, *Ergets oyf felder* (Somewhere in the Fields) (1915), the poet's first collection, which contains two cycles of short war poems, repeats in each the same progress from an initially tragic encounter to resignation and equilibrium. The first cycles start with an account of the death of young soldiers in the fields, which are covered by the red colors of blood and flowers. Then the poet remains all alone in the fields, which had become one large cemetery. Then the process of distancing begins. The poet knows that there is "one mouth" that can, by saying "enough," stop the carnage. But the "mouth" remains silent, and the poet does not quarrel with it. Instead he turns to the gods, Amor and Jesus, for their help, but both are as helpless as he is, and he identifies himself with them, especially with Jesus. By now his pain has largely subsided. In a mellow mood he turns to "the dream path that leads to the Orient" and enjoys the golden reflection of the sunshine on the thorny crown of God's sweet son. In the second cycle, the same progress repeats itself in an even softer version. A girl bewails her lover, who, she intuitively knows, died on the battlefield. The tragic intuition is here swiftly moderated by folkloric motifs and balladic techniques. The girl accepts her loneliness and resigns herself to a lifetime of bittersweet memories. Soon she sees herself playing the role of an old woman telling *mayselekh* (stories) and *blutike legendn* (bloody legends) by the fireside.[7]

7. Uri Zvi Grinberg, *Ergets oyf felder* (1915), reprinted in ibid., pp. 17–22.

In *In tsaytns roysh*, in spite of its more complex structure and its by far more direct exposure to the actual experience of war, the same pattern is reaffirmed. This book, the most enduring achievement of Grinberg's preexpressionist phase, should be seen as a major attempt on the part of the poet to domesticate the devastating reality of war, blunt its edge, and finally absorb its shocking impact into the habitual quietist patterns of his poetry.

For a full realization of this pattern, one should read the original edition of 1919 rather than the much-altered edition published in 1923 under the new title, *Krig oyf der velt* (War in the World). The new edition reflects, both in its omissions and in its additions, the poet's new poetics. The entire focus of the book shifts in a new direction. As the new title suggests, the focus is now the war and the horrors of war. The focus of the first edition was, again as suggested by the original title, the poet's sense of the flow of time, rushing and all-engulfing. Thus, such a poem as "Kh'ver veyniger alts yedn tog un ver ful yedn tog" (I Diminish by the Day and Fill Up by the Day), which figured as the very core of the first edition, was deleted from the second one. In this poem the poet is presented as a moon, constantly diminishing but, just as constantly, waxing and growing. The meaning of this metaphor within the context of the book as a whole was clear: reality and its horrors may diminish and shrink the poet's existence, but his poetic mission rebuilds and brings it back to a state of fullness.

This simultaneous waning and waxing was the central message of *In tsaytns roysh*. Starting with the word *amol* (once) and with a reconstruction of an idyllic past and ending with the ecstatic love song "Hanuma," it encompassed the horrors of war it was to describe with a soft web of bittersweet lyricism. The structure suggests careful balancing. Thus the opening section, a war diary in prose with the title "Ba mir in pinkes" (In My Notebook) is counterbalanced by the closing section, also in prose, with the title "Farnakhtn un nekht" (Evenings and Nights). The devastation of innocence and the ravages of war recorded in the diary were mellowed into the melancholy of a postbellum existence. This existence is projected as the rustic, simple, and beautiful world of the Adriatic Coast, full of sad, hot-blooded Bosnian women, gusla music, and fragrant eroticism. In spite of the painful memories, this world breathes life, acceptance of loss, rekindled fertility and hope. "In vaytn veg" (On the Faraway Road), the intermediate poetry section, also leads from poems of doom and gloom to poems of regained equilibrium, indicative of the poet's will and ability to turn his face from war to nature and to hope.

Even in "Ba mir in pinkes" the war experience, as direct as its recording might seem, is instantly softened. This section represents the high point in young Grinberg's commitment to impressionism. Everything here is rendered in terms of accumulating sensory data, and the entire section bathes in a welter of visual, acoustic, and tactile details. Contours are blurred and hazy, and the reporting is done by a person whose perceptions are constantly conditioned by pathetic fallacies and who has only a tentative grasp of the dimensions of time and space. When we compare "Ba mir in pinkes" to Grinberg's "Royte epl fun veybeymer" (Red Apples from the Trees of Pain),[8] another war-diary type of story, we watch impressionism and expressionism clash with each other. "Royte epl fun veybeymer" is full of quotations from and allusions to "Ba mir in pinkes" because the story is meant to serve as a parody and critique of the impressionist sensibility. This sensibility is represented by the speaker of "Ba mir in pinkes," a romantic poet with a triangle-shaped face and calflike eyes. The poet is methodically undermined by his counterpart, a down-to-earth, rude, and cynical observer, the representative of expressionism. "Royte epl," written in 1922 and published in Grinberg's *Albatros*, is the best proof of the poet's own awareness of what, at the height of his modernist revolution, he regarded as the insufficiency and inadequacy of his prerevolutionary art as represented in *In tsaytns roysh*.

V

Let me now draw some conclusions:

First, the war-impact hypothesis fails to provide a viable explanation of Grinberg's growth as one of the leading Jewish modernists. To start with, it obfuscates the nature of the change in Grinberg's art. This change was abrupt and revolutionary rather than evolutionary and accumulative. It was triggered by a revelation rather than by a growing understanding of one's past experiences. The war experience in itself did not either enhance or hinder it. What con-

8. Uri Zvi Grinberg, "Royte epl fun veybeymer" (1922), reprinted in ibid., 2: 436–44.

stituted the change was not the experience *per se* but the methods and aims of its poetic rendering. An earlier rendering aimed at containment through impressionistic softening of line and a blurry mixing of colors. The later rendering aimed at direct impact through expressionistic sharpening of contours and the use of vivid, primary colors. The first rendering was intended to enable the poet to regain esthetic equilibrium. The later rendering was intended to change the reader's mind and possibly also his behavior through shock and insight. The change was triggered then by an intellectual and esthetic conversion rather than by any exposure on the part of the poet to reality.

Second, on the individual-psychic level, the war-impact hypothesis grossly oversimplifies the issue by presenting a physical and emotional shock, a *koshmar,* as the sole or main origin of an esthetic and intellectual discovery. In fact, Grinberg's modernist shift was caused by a complex psychological process in which the overwhelming effect of the war experience might have played its part. But it could not come into being until the entire process was refashioned and reorganized by the victory of an analytical mind over an emotional temperament. Only when Grinberg, seeking knowledge and understanding, learned to use the momentum of his intense emotionalism for the benefit of his new intellectual purposes could he create a new kind of poetry characterized by an emotionally charged intellectualism and didacticism. This learning how to use one's upsurge of feelings for the purpose of sharpening one's mind and rendering one's insights more accurate and more penetrating could not have been caused only or mainly by such an emotional crisis as the one recorded in "Ba mir in pinkes."

Third, on the sociocultural level the war-impact hypothesis fails to interpret correctly the nature of the interaction between historical occurrences and concurrent intellectual and artistic developments. It is based on a simplistic, untenable model that predicates a direct, causal connection between the historical event and the artistic or intellectual event, and such direct connections simply do not exist. For the proper understanding of the various possible correlations between political and social history and the development of art and poetry, a more complex model is needed, a model that can function without positivistic cause-and-effect mechanisms.

Finally, Grinberg's modernism, as we can learn from its earliest manifestations such as the cycle *Mefisto,* follows from the poet's need for knowledge of the self and of the world. In *Mefisto,* for instance, he investigates the vitiation of human eroticism as much as he investigates, in a part of *Eimah gedolah ve-yareah* and in *Anakreon,* the vitiation of one's moral existence by the fear of death. In all these great works, the search for insight is systematic and unflagging. The poet uses his own being as a laboratory animal which he dissects again and again from every possible direction for the enhancement of a general objective knowledge that, once achieved, can be put to actual human use. Grinberg's definition of the term "expression," and hence of expressionism itself, connects the use of pointed, intensified language with revelatory insight. The true expression is the sudden formation of such insight in a blazing linguistic combination. Thus expressionism amounts to the use of combustive language, rather like a series of blinding magnesia flashes, in order to penetrate the darkness of human existence.

What triggered Grinberg's modernism was not the war or any other personal and historical experience as much as it was the discovery of expressionism—the art and the philosophy it entailed. Expressionism as a revelation opened the way for a recapitulation of the meaning of existence, a meaning Grinberg's earlier poems strove to escape and circumvent. The case of Grinberg's conversion was not the one of the discovery of an art through experience but, rather, that of the discovery of experience through art.

Abraham Novershtern

Yung Vilne: The Political Dimension of Literature

I

After the Nazis had murdered about two-thirds of Vilna's Jews during the first months of the German occupation, the Vilna ghetto entered a period of shaky, fragile order in the shadow of destruction. Cultural activities played a central role in the struggle to maintain a feeling of apparent normalcy, and, among the impressive list of concerts, theater performances, and conferences, one literary evening in July 1942 was devoted to Yung Vilne (Young Vilna), the group of Yiddish writers who had emerged in that city, in those very streets, in 1929.

Among the members of Yung Vilne, only two were trapped in the ghetto that evening: Shmerke Kaczerginsky, whose dynamic personality and organizational abilities had energized the group, and Abraham Sutzkever, the delicate lyric poet whose work underwent dramatic changes during the Holocaust. Other members of Yung Vilne had fled the city during the first days of the German attack and had since become refugees in the Soviet Union. Among them were Leyzer Wolf, a man with wild talent and pronounced inclinations to the grotesque, and Chaim Grade, acknowledged by both critics and general readers to be the most prominent figure in the group. The literary evening in the ghetto was meant to recall better days and, at the same time, to provide an opportunity for sending a symbolic greeting to the absent members of the group, whose fate was then unknown to the inhabitants of the ghetto.

The evening opened with a speech by the director of the ghetto library, Herman Kruk, in which he sketched a collective portrait of the members of Yung Vilne.

They are all the sons of workers and simple folk. As young men they all received secular education in Yiddish, in a secular Yiddish school, and the main point is that they are all workers who live from their labor. . . . Artistically they are realists, as real as their own lives, true realists, 100 percent. The central topics of Yung Vilne are motifs with social content. The poets and artists of the group are strongly linked with the life of the Jewish masses, placing their talents at their disposal.[1]

It might seem as if I have begun this essay on Yung Vilne in the wrong way, in that Herman Kruk was neither a professional literary critic nor a native of Vilna. He was a Bund activist in the area of culture who had served as the head of the central Bundist library in Warsaw and arrived in Vilna with the great influx of refugees at the beginning of the war. Moreover, why begin a discussion of a literary group active in the 1930s with an episode that took place during the Holocaust?

Kruk's comments on Yung Vilne in the extreme circumstances of that summer evening demonstrate, however, the staying power of long-held positions. We may wonder whether the gist of his observations had much relevance to the Vilna ghetto on the verge of destruction. Yet they are certainly the final echo of the prevailing views about Yung Vilne during its formative years in the 1930s. It goes without saying that after the Holocaust, an approach like Kruk's was never taken again.

Herman Kruk painted Yung Vilne in broad outlines that fail to do justice to the complex individual backgrounds and poetical tendencies of the group. His remarks, which might sound simplistic to us today, combine a clearly pragmatic, even utilitarian concept of the function of literature with underlying romantic notions. Kruk's point of departure is the writers' biographies; he implies that if they only remained faithful to themselves, their work would be imbued with the proper content and would serve the desired social and political aim, expressed in a formulaic fashion. If the writings of Yung Vilne *truly* expressed all the conditions of its members' lives, which were representative of their generation, then there would be no disparity between their creative impulses and the needs of their audience. As writers they would avoid the danger of bias as well as the temptation to treat literature as an end in itself; they would be constantly aware of their purpose: "to serve the Jewish masses."

---

1. Herman Kruk, *Togbukh fun vilner geto* (New York, 1961), pp. 321–22.

II

From the start, it must be noted that the biographical background presented by Herman Kruk does not fit the facts: two of the central poets of the group did not spring from the soil of Yiddishism. Chaim Grade (b. 1910) came to Yung Vilne from the world of the Lithuanian Musar *yeshivot*; and Abraham Sutzkever (b. 1913) was educated in a Talmud Torah and a Polish-Jewish *gymnasium*. He, who was to become the virtuoso of Yiddish poetry, never attended a secular Yiddish school.

Although the members of the group brought a mixed bag of traditions with them, there can be no doubt concerning the social context in which their writing emerged. Within the rich cultural and human mosaic of which Jewish Vilna was proud, those young men had to depend upon the only sector that encouraged them when they entered the world of literature: the Yiddishist intelligentsia, which extended over a broad political spectrum from the Center leftward. Five Yiddish dailies were published in Vilna in the 1930s.[2] Only one of them, however, could be considered a proper forum for the publications of the group. That was the *Vilner tog*, which took a Yiddishist line, was aloof from Zionism, and favored the Soviet Union, although, with the heavy pressure of Polish censorship, it could not express that attitude openly and unequivocally. The establishment of Yung Vilne in 1929 was indeed marked by the formal publication of the group's work in the *Vilner tog*, whose editor, Zalmen Reisen, considered that his cultural outlook obligated him to develop the literary talents of young Yiddish writers.[3]

Both contemporary critics and later memoir writers hold that Yung Vilne cannot be regarded as a literary group in the full sense of the word because the cohesive force of an explicit literary or ideological credo was lacking. Thus it is interesting that the only collective publication by its members, three issues of *Yung Vilne* (1934–36), did not attempt to formulate common principles that defined the group as a whole. Even then, as the members of the

---

2. For a list of Yiddish periodicals in Vilna in this period, see Ephim Jeshurin, "Di yidishe un algemeyne prese in Vilne hayntikn tog," in *Vilne: A zamlbukh gevidmet der shtot Vilne*, ed. Ephim Jeshurin (New York, 1935), pp. 357–60.

3. "Der araynmarsh fun 'Yung Vilne' in der yidisher literatur" ("Yung Vilne" Marches into Yiddish Literature), *Vilner tog*, October 11, 1929, p. 4. This section of the paper was reprinted in a special issue of *Di goldene keyt* devoted to the jubilee of Yung Vilne, no. 101 (1980): 66–76.

group took their first steps, they recognized that the differences among them outweighed what they held in common. One of the central obstacles in this regard was the issue of social radicalism and the demand that it be implemented in literature.

The cover of the first issue of *Yung Vilne* was meant to solve that problem in some respects, and it should be considered as a true expression of the group's ideological drift. The crooked lines of the alleys of Jewish Vilna fill the lower and more modest portion. The drawing of the factory played another role; it was not intended to stand for an actual element in the geography of the city itself, which had almost no significant industry, but was to represent modern society in general. Finally, above these images the rising sun stands out, a profession of faith in the world of tomorrow. The cover thus attempts to combine representation of the actual environment with utopian symbols. It in fact gives the latter a more prominent place and creates a parallel between the vertical movement and the course of time, in which a splendid future will take the place of the deteriorated present. Taken together, these elements provide a clear indication of the radical views prevailing in Yung Vilne.

Critics have identified Yung Vilne with the city of Vilna, or, more precisely, they have viewed that group of young writers as the first fruits of modern Jewish Vilna. The group's emblem, designed by Ben Zion Michtom, the same artist who drew the cover of their magazine, was indeed a tree growing over the gates of Vilna's Jewish quarter; it symbolized youthful vitality rising up but nevertheless rooted in a concrete historical background. After the Holocaust each of the group's surviving members viewed himself as the spokesman of the ruined city, describing and weeping for it. Sutzkever, who moved to Israel, came to symbolize the link between the Jerusalem of Vilna and Jerusalem. Grade assumed the task of commemorating the characters, streets, and atmosphere of Jewish Vilna in detail, as though obligated both to the generation wiped out and to the generation succeeding it. That decision had powerful effect on his choice of literary genre: though before the war he had written only poetry, after settling in the United States he also wrote prose, and today the reader in English, for instance, has access to Grade almost solely as a novelist.

However, the indissoluble bond between Yung Vilne and Jewish Vilna was mainly forged *after* the Holocaust. During the 1930s, when those writers lived and created in Vilna, the city, with its human variety, played only a secondary role in their works, just as, among the three elements on the cover of the first issue of *Yung Vilne*, the alleys of the city were given a rather modest place.

Jewish Vilna occupied a significantly different place in the prose than in the poetry of the group's members. In Shmerke Kaczerginsky's journalism and in the volume of stories by Moyshe Levin, *Friling in kelershtub* (Spring in a Basement Room) (1937), local color is much in evidence. Prose did not, however, figure prominently in the output of Yung Vilne; in the poetry of the 1930s by Sutzkever and Grade, the most important representatives of the group, the human landscapes of Jewish Vilna are far from central. Though it is difficult to describe Grade's poetry and prose after the Holocaust without reference to the background of the Vilner Shulhoyf (Vilna Synagogue Yard), in the 1930s that symbol of Jewish Vilna seldom appears in the works of the members of the group. When it does, it represents primarily the world of yesterday from which the young poet must detach and distance himself.

One might well ask why the group's poets did not give the near and familiar world a central place in their early poetry. That literary decision would seem to have many implications for our understanding of the complex connections between the Yiddish writer and the ground from which he sprang, and it also indicates the dramatic reversal in Yiddish literature after the Holocaust.

The members of Yung Vilne refused to bear the standard of localism both within Yiddish literature in Poland and within the broader context of Yiddish literature throughout the world. They certainly felt that the quality of Vilna as a *locus actionis* did not suit their artistic intentions and that the danger of provincialism lurked at the gate.[4]

Another reason for that antilocal attitude is inherent in the literary affiliations of the group: the early poetry of Yung Vilne, including that of Grade, is implicitly set in a big city, for that is the landscape preferred by expressionism, one of the poets' central inspirations in the early stages of their development. Longing for the

4. Mikhoel Natish, a young poet of Święciany, near Vilna, noted the lack of any specific local color in his review of the first issue of *Yung Vilne*. " 'Yung Vilne' un ir zamlheft," *Literarishe bleter* 11, no. 34 (August 24, 1934): 560. In a discussion of stories by Moyshe Levin, even the Vilna writer A. Y. Grodzenski, a conservative in literary taste, differentiated between "local color," which is of lesser and dubious value, and "general significance." "Di shrayber-grupe 'Yung Vilne' un ir araynmarsh in der yidisher literatur," *Di tsukunft* 42 (1937): 685.

large dimensions of a metropolis is also related to leftist ideological inclinations, which held the huge factory and the industrial proletariat as leading factors in the social struggle, and those were hardly the strong points of Jewish Vilna. Indeed it would seem that their ideological orientation was central in impelling the poets of Yung Vilne to view themselves as obligated to raise the flag of rebellion against their immediate environment during the 1930s. Characteristically, before the Holocaust, Chaim Grade's major poem about the streets of Vilna treats them as a setting for revolutionary action.[5]

Thus it is not accidental that Leyzer Wolf, a poet with pronounced leanings toward the grotesque, made greater use of his immediate surroundings than did his associates. His ironic attitude combined reservations concerning the life he was describing with a slight tinge of nostalgia.[6] In the thematics of the group, Jewish Vilna did not, therefore, represent the spiritual atmosphere with which they were imbued. Leyzer Wolf himself expressed the cosmopolitan spirit that inspired his comrades by concluding the autobiography he sent to YIVO in 1932 with the following words:

> Mayn vayter ideal iz: di mentshhayt—eyn folk.
> Di velt—eyn land.[7]

> My distant ideal is: mankind—a single nation.
> The world—a single land.

III

We possess a good deal of biographical information about Yung Vilne.[8] After the Holocaust the surviving members of the group

5. Chaim Grade, "Dos gezang fun undzer gas bay der nakht" (The Song of Our Street by Night), *Di tsukunft* 42 (1937): 563–64. A revised version was included in Grade's *Farvoksene vegn* (Overgrown Paths) (Paris, 1947), pp. 74–78. See also his "Yatkever gas" (The Street of the Butchers), in *Toyznt yor Vilne*, ed. Zalmen Shik (Vilna, 1939), pp. 162–64. I have been unable to locate the first publication of this poem.

6. See, for instance, Leyzer Wolf's poems "Ayzik Meir Dik un di almone Rom" (Ayzik Meir Dik and the Widow Rom), "Der vilner goen un der Besht" (The Vilna Gaon and the Besht), "Vilner shulhoyf" (The Vilna Synagogue Yard), "Bite" (Please), "Montefiore in Vilne," in his posthumous collection *Lider*, ed. Leyzer Ran (New York, 1955), pp. 114–19, 133–43.

7. "Oytobyografye" (Autobiography), in ibid., p. 42.

8. See *Literarishe bleter* 14, no. 9 (February 26, 1937), a special issue devoted to Yung Vilne; Elias Schulman, *Yung Vilne, 1929–1939* (New York, 1946); Leyzer Ran, ed., *Finf un tsvantsik yor "Yung Vilne"* (New York, 1955); *Di goldene keyt*, no. 101 (1980).

sought to memorialize their past on many occasions and with various means of expression, though none of them wrote a complete autobiography. But at many points there are significant gaps in our information, perhaps the most central of which touches upon the question of the political orientation of the group's members. That is not surprising; as the cultural and ideological world of the members of Yung Vilne in particular, and of Yiddish writers in general, underwent far-reaching change in the wake of the Holocaust, the establishment of the State of Israel, and the destruction of Jewish culture in the Soviet Union, the writers themselves were not inclined to speak freely of what they viewed retrospectively as the "sins of their youth."

That is not, however, the only reason for the paucity of our information on political orientations; members of Yung Vilne moved in a variety of circles in the Center and anti-Zionist Left, between territorialism and communism, but only Shmerke Kaczerginsky, whose literary contribution to the group was rather modest, is known to have been active in the illegal Komunistyczna Partia Polski (KPP, Communist Party of Poland) and in other quasi-legal groups close to it.[9] He also wrote for the New York communist paper, *Morgn frayheyt,* and, significantly, two of his poems, set to his music, were widely sung in leftist youth movements.

Therefore one may speak only of the left-wing sympathies of Yung Vilne and not of actual activism in a political party. One detail, though it might seem secondary, is in fact quite revealing concerning the group's tendencies. Hebrew words in the issues of *Yung Vilne* were spelled the way they are pronounced in Yiddish and not in their original Hebraic form, a system of spelling that was adopted in the Soviet Union and procommunist publications outside that country.[10]

The fact that we are speaking merely of attitudes determines the place of Yung Vilne on the political map of Yiddish literature in

9. During the 1930s, after Shmerke Kaczerginsky's arrest, his active participation in the Komunistyczna Partia Polski probably came to an end, and he was considered as a kind of "fellow traveler." See *Shmerke Kaczerginsky ondenkbukh* (Buenos Aires, 1955), p. 9.

10. Only a handful of Polish-Yiddish periodicals adopted this system of spelling Hebrew; among them must be mentioned the magazine associated with the communists, *Literarishe tribune* (printed in Łódź, edited in Warsaw, 1930–33), which inaugurated the new writing system in 1931. Shmerke Kaczerginsky published his first story in this magazine: "'Alts in bestn ordenung'" ('Everything's in Good Shape'), *Literarishe tribune,* nos. 18–19 (1931): 9–11.

Poland between the world wars. In Warsaw during the 1930s a group of Yiddish writers with procommunist tendencies included, among others, Kalmen Lis, Binem Heler, Dovid Mitsmakher, Dovid Sfard, Binyomen Shlevin, and Moyshe Shulshteyn, and writers elsewhere in Poland also joined that group.[11] The writers of Yung Vilne were never directly identified with the Warsaw group, though contemporary critics placed them alongside it as occupying a position to the left of center in the literary-political spectrum.[12]

Not all the members of the group, however, shared the same political convictions or took the same approach regarding the proper relationship between literature and radical ideology. The poetry of Abraham Sutzkever was entirely out of step with the thinking of the other members, and for that reason he had a secondary, even precarious status within the group, especially at the start. The central role played by nature in his poetry and its personal, lyrical tone seemed to detach it completely from actual events.

Kaczerginsky's memoirs tell of the disputes that raged around Sutzkever's first poems: "I would argue against him: 'Abrashke, maybe your poems aren't bad, but we're not living in a crystal age, but in an age of steel. . . . Who can understand, grasp poems like that?' But he couldn't write differently."[13]

As the noose of historical reality was drawn tighter in Poland in the late 1930s, the distance between it and Sutzkever's poetry grew wider. That tension received its highest expression in his second book, *Valdiks* (Of Forests), which appeared in early 1940, during that short twilight period when Vilna was part of independent Lith-

---

11. In 1936 an anthology of these writers was published in the Soviet Union, including primarily their work in poetry and prose on social themes: Avrom Damesek, ed., *Lebn un kamf: Zamlbukh fun der yidisher linker literatur in Poyln* (Life and Struggle: Miscellany of Yiddish Leftist Literature in Poland) (Minsk, 1936). The descriptive "Yiddish leftist literature" is, of course, highly significant and shows a desire for a broader common denominator. It might also indicate that the descriptive "proletarian literature" had become less common. The significance of the subtitle stands out in contrast to the collection previously published in the Soviet Union, including works from many countries: Avrom Veviorke, ed., *In shotn fun tliyes: Almanakh fun der yidisher proletarisher literatur in di kapitalistishe lender* (In the Shadow of Gallows: Almanac of Yiddish Proletarian Literature in the Capitalist Countries) (Kiev, 1932).

12. Yoysef Teper, "Yung Vilne," *Literarishe bleter* 14, no. 9 (February 26, 1937): 134.

13. Shmerke Kaczerginsky, "Mayn khaver Sutzkever," in Abraham Sutzkever, *Fun dray veltn* (Buenos Aires, 1953), p. 59. See also Mikhoel Astur, "Sutzkevers poetisher onheyb," in *Yoyvl-bukh tsum fuftsiksstn geboyrn-tog fun Avrom Sutzkever,* ed. Zalmen Shazar, Dov Sadan, and Moyshe Gros-Tsimerman (Tel Aviv, 1963), pp. 28–29.

uania. Almost every critic who wrote about the poems felt obliged
to call attention to their uniqueness: a book consisting mainly of
nature poetry and the aspiration toward monumentality written
while war had already broken out all around. In their congratulatory
message upon the publication of *Valdiks* the members of Yung Vilne
actually asked Sutzkever not to ignore the life around him in his
poetry: "Sing of it or weep for it as it appears today with its bare,
bloodied face. Perhaps the poem will vanquish the bayonet."[14]

Sutzkever's exceptional estheticism brings out what the other
members of Yung Vilne had in common. The question thus arises,
What did it mean for a young Yiddish writer to express sympathies
for the Left without being openly *engagé*?

Herman Kruk's remarks were quoted above because they offer
insight into this problem. Although he made them during the Holocaust, they reflect one of the central aspirations of that branch of
Yiddish literary criticism connected with leftist political ideologies
in Poland during the 1930s. Those critics sought to bring out the
harmony between apparently competing demands: the norms of realism, the romantic claim of self-expression, and the view that literature must be committed to a message of social radicalism. That
very aspiration for harmony, however, also impelled them to take a
dim view of political poetry as a distinct genre. Their position, deriving from the Marxist tradition and influenced by the current
trends in official Soviet criticism, was that the ideological message
could not be confined within any borders and ought to emerge naturally from "within" any type of literary work.

Therefore, in the context of Yiddish poetry in Poland during the
1930s, the possibility of poems responding immediately to current
events and intended to arouse a reaction to them was not entertained, not even as a genre to be considered "lower" than personal
lyric poetry. In any case, Polish censorship would have severely constrained open political expression. Social and political content was
thus supposed to appear in two central genres of poetry. One was
the short lyric, which did not, however, enjoy great prestige among
the writers of the Left because, for them, it symbolized *a priori* the
private world of the *petite bourgeoisie*.[15] They favored the second genre,

14. Quoted in Abraham Novershtern, *Avrom Sutzkever tsum vern a ben-shivim* (Jerusalem, 1983), p. 122.

15. See, for instance, Moyshe Litvin, "Der problem fun tematik bay undzere pro-
let-shrayber" (The Question of Thematics in Our Proletarian Writers), *Literarishe tribune*, no. 32 (1932): 4–7.

poetry interwoven with balladic or epic elements, such as a dialogue between a mother and her children who suffer because the head of the family is unemployed, or long poems recounting the story of workers during a strike or demonstration or the fate of a political prisoner.

Despite the striking quantity of so-called *social* motifs in Yiddish poetry in Poland between the wars, the range of *political* themes expressed could not fail to be severely limited. Here we must consider the Procrustean bed that censorship imposed upon all Polish literature, limiting the possibilities for direct political expression. Fear that publications would be confiscated and fear of the arrests and trials that would follow haunted writers at every step.[16] But in the case of Yiddish literature, it would seem that censorship was an external factor acting in concert with other influences of equal weight.

Beyond general remarks about the oppressive atmosphere in Poland (such as reference to political prisoners, the conduct of the police during demonstrations, or to censorship itself) the Yiddish writer refrained from reacting to specific issues in national politics that did not have a direct impact on the Jews. One basic reason for this restraint is self-evident: since Yiddish writing was meant only for internal Jewish consumption, any discussion of the Polish government, parties, or national political issues could have no possible influence and thus could never be viewed as a significant political act.

Another aspect of the question, however, seems more significant to me: in most cases Yiddish writers did not believe that political struggles and tensions *within* the Jewish community were appropriate materials for literature. Therefore we confront a surprising phenomenon: in those publications that served as the organs of leftist political parties on the "literary front," such as *Vokhnshrift far literatur kunst un kultur* published by the Bund (1931–35) and the procommunist *Literarishe tribune* (1930–33), belletristic content is not related to the journalistic polemics that appear on the very same pages. In contrast to the factionalism, the bitter divisions, and the

16. In this context, it is sufficient to recall that the first two issues of *Yung Vilne* were confiscated. See *Yung Vilne*, no. 3 (1936): 95. The second issue was seized because of Chaim Grade's poem "Velt in nayntsn fir un draysik" (The World in 1934); the issue later appeared in a revised edition in which that poem was replaced by another.

virulence of the political struggles characterizing Jewish politics in Poland between the two world wars, Yiddish literature at that time (implicitly, if not explicitly) displayed a surprising degree of unity and basic agreement regarding the ideological picture of the world it expressed. Although adhesion to one group or another immediately gave a writer a political label, in the actual writing, that political affinity found little expression.

The causes of that phenomenon lie in various areas. Even those who demanded the unequivocal political mobilization of literature shared, without acknowledging it, the view that appropriate esthetic distance must be preserved regarding current events, which must be expressed at the fitting level of generalization. As a result even literary material published in leftist journals reflected *current concerns* without being bound to specific *current events*.

In retrospect we can propose yet another explanation, of which the authors themselves were probably only dimly aware at the time: internal Jewish political struggles seemed too trivial, particularly when the entire structure of Jewish communal life was increasingly threatened from without and seemed about to crumble. If both the national political context and the internal Jewish political context were eschewed in Polish-Yiddish literature between the wars, particularly in poetry, what background was considered appropriate for presentation of its political message?

IV

To answer that question we should analyze the political aspects of Chaim Grade's poetry in the 1930s. His work met the expectations of a broad spectrum of readers, both those who demanded a close bond between literature and social radicalism and those who advocated an autonomous status for poetry. Grade was accepted as the poet of a broad literary consensus, leading one to ask how his poetry came to satisfy the claims of both wings at the same time, incorporating radical contents but without arousing the opposition of critics who feared political bias.

If we look closely at the thematic clusters of Grade's early poetry, we can conclude that he avoided any subject which could be a bone of contention among his potential readers. It is significant that, of all the central ideological and political tensions for a young Polish Jew at that time—observing religion or abandoning it, Zionism and anti-Zionism, socialism and communism—Grade chose to deal with only the first. Both for him and for most of his readers, the break with tradition was a sealed chapter, an issue no longer in dispute and certainly not one that might take on political coloring. From that point of view it is significant that the long poem *Musernikes,* which presents a variegated gallery of students at a Musar *yeshivah,* is not only devoid of any political or social thematics, but the speaker also indicates the chronological distance separating him from the world he describes,[17] thus relegating its spiritual quandaries to the biographical past.

As described above, the two main genres that were supposed to bear the political and social message in poetry were the personal lyric and the epic-balladic poem. One of the major differences between the members of Yung Vilne and members of the so-called proletarian group in Warsaw was that, while the latter preferred to present their message in epic or balladic form, Chaim Grade sought to express it in personal lyric poetry.

Grade's early poem, "Hey, khaver Grade" (Hey, Comrade Grade), printed in the first issue of *Yung Vilne* (1934), can serve as an example of the aspiration to combine personal lyric expression with explicit political content. Grade's decision not to include that poem in his first book, *Yo* (Yes) (1936), and certainly not in the later collections appearing after the Holocaust, is, of course, quite significant, whether it is attributed to fear of censorship (when he put out his first book) or reservations about the coarse language and rough diction (especially after the Holocaust), or to the two factors together.

"Hey, khaver Grade" would certainly have aroused the opposition of critics who feared political bias in literature. The poem is shallow, posterlike in quality, with frequent reiterations of the color red as contrasted to the black of the old world, the worn-out religious books providing fodder for mice. Because of the poem's apparent simplicity, it must be pointed out that only the speaker himself is a target for political mobilization. The poem begins with an outright call for political action.

Hey, khaver Grade, hey, khaver Grade,
kum, shlis zikh on on der royter brigade.[18]

17. Chaim Grade, *Musernikes: Poeme* (Vilna, 1939), p. 11.
18. Chaim Grade, "Hey, khaver Grade," *Yung Vilne,* no. 1 (1934): 22.

Hey, comrade Grade,
Come, join the Red Brigade.

But the text is mainly an interior dialogue in which the speaker takes an ironic and distant attitude toward his aspirations and fears as a typical *petit bourgeois* intellectual, aspirations and fears that are judged and found wanting. Neither here, in this poem, nor in most of Grade's other poetry of the 1930s do we find a rhetorical appeal to the outside world, to potential readers and listeners, and *a fortiori* we do not find poems in which Grade holds a debate with an ideological or political opponent of any kind. Even when he assumes a prophetic pose, inspired by the models of H. N. Bialik's poetry, the poet emphasizes the prophet's refusal to bear a message and to accept the role of one who admonishes the people at the gates.[19]

It would seem that the poets of the group felt intuitively that the political struggle which could nourish their works was taking place neither within the confines of Jewish society nor in the Polish arena. Grade's poetry on political themes was thus nurtured mainly by the ongoing struggle in the larger European capitals. In 1935 they were Vienna and Berlin, from which the poet was drawn by a chain of associations to Paris and the French Revolution, to Moscow and St. Petersburg.[20] After some time, Spain became the focus of meaningful political action for Grade.

"Shpanye" vel ikh onrufn mayn zun,

. . . .
"Shpanye"—vel ikh im a nomen gebn
oyb ikh vel nokh hobn mut a zun der velt tsu brengen.[21]

"Spain" is what I'll call my son,

. . . .
"Spain"—is the name I'll give him
If I have the courage to bring a son into the world.

Not long ago that poem in praise of the Spanish Republic, first published in 1936, became a *corpus delicti* in a minor squabble concerning Grade's leftist sympathies in the 1930s.[22] Therefore, we

---

19. Chaim Grade, "Yekhezkl" (Ezekiel), in Grade, *Yo* (Vilna, 1936), pp. 67–82, reprinted in Grade, *Doyres: Lider un poemes* (New York, 1945), pp. 63–76.

20. Chaim Grade, "Velt in nayntsn fir un draysik" and "Vin" (Vienna), in *Yo*, pp. 31–38, reprinted in *Doyres*, pp. 33–38.

21. Chaim Grade, "Shpanye" (Spain), in Grade, *Farvoksene vegn*, pp. 85–86.

22. Ruth R. Wisse, "Religious Imperatives and Mortal Desires" [review of *Rabbis and Wives*, by Chaim Grade], *New York Times Book Review*, November 14, 1982, p. 3; letter from Inna Hecker Grade, *New York Times Book Review*, March 27, 1983, p. 46.

must bear in mind that in the context of its publication, Grade would have expected none of his readers to oppose a principled stand in favor of the Spanish Republic. The poem rested on a broad consensus in values;[23] at most it might have been expected to arouse opposition not for its political principles but for the harshness of the poet's stand.

Actually, if any part of the poem ought to have encountered opposition, it is the conclusion, which one might have expected to arouse the Left because of the evident passivity it advocates—and this in one of the few cases in which Grade addresses readers with shared values.

> Khaveyrim, lomir zikh tsezetsn in a rod,
> vi holtsheker arum a fayer, ayngebrokhene un mid,
> un lomir opvartn dos faln fun der letster shtot—
> dos faln fun der letster shtot Madrid.[24]

> Comrades, let us sit in a circle,
> Like woodcutters around a fire, broken and tired,
> And let us await the fall of the last city—
> The fall of the last city, Madrid.

These lines illustrate a significant feature of Grade's poetry that is also found in the works of his colleagues in Yung Vilne. The powerful emotional force lying in the substrate of most of the poems that incorporate social or political themes is more than a rhetorical device to arouse the reader's sympathy. Poems such as "Velt in nayntsn fir un draysik" (The World in 1934) or "Vin" (Vienna), or "Shpanye" (Spain) were meant to bridge the gap between two tendencies that sometimes pulled in opposite directions. On the one hand, the members of Yung Vilne had absorbed romantic assumptions regarding the centrality of personal experience as the basis of poetry, and thus Grade, as pointed out earlier, expressed the political thematics in personal lyric. On the other hand, Grade's own intuitive vision of politics obliged him to place significant events at a considerable physical and cultural distance from himself. Therefore most of his poetry on political themes revolves around the emotional reaction to things taking place far from the speaker, while he ex-

23. The *Vilner tog* tells that when the poet Moyshe Broderzon visited Vilna and asked his audience for themes for extemporaneous poems, "The entire hall shouted out: The march on Madrid. The heroic struggle of the Spanish masses is indeed a theme which inflames many freedom-loving writers." "Poezye fun hayntikn tog," *Vilner tog*, December 25, 1936, p. 6.

24. Grade, "Shpanye," p. 86.

presses his feeling of being shut in and helpless in the face of dramatic events that he cannot influence. The distance between the constrained speaker and the wide world for which he yearns builds the dramatic tension of the poems, the rhetorical power of which is nourished by his inability to take part in the decisive struggle. That thematic cluster accords with one of the primary focuses of Grade's early poetry: the struggle between the individual's natural urges, which wish to burst out, and his feeling of physical and spiritual confinement.

Thus it should become clear why the central vehicle embodying the radical message in Grade's poetry is the political prisoner, the one who has dedicated his life to the revolutionary ideal and suffers on that account.[25] There can be no doubt that once the political prisoner bore the standard of political action, but a prisoner behind bars changes from an active subject to a kind of passive object unable to exert any real influence on events. He need not bear any explicit political message, and thus in most of young Grade's poetry that figure had neither a name nor identifiably Jewish traits. Hence the poet was also spared the need of choosing between emphasizing the national or the international aspect of the struggle.[26]

The motif of the political prisoner in Grade's poetry is a kind of junction where the historical reality of Poland between the world wars encounters the romantic tradition of the suffering hero, a tradition that, at the time, was being transformed in Yiddish poetry into the widely accepted theme of the suffering victim in H. Leivick's poetry. It would seem that the political prisoner could arouse the greatest empathy without reservations or controversy. From the widespread use of this motif we may infer that the political message considered most effective was one blurred enough to be accepted by the largest number of readers without arousing internal dissent.

25. See the following poems by Grade: "Kratn" (Bars), in *Yo*, p. 30, reprinted in *Doyres*, p. 32; "In der fremd" (Abroad), in *Yo*, pp. 16–20, reprinted in *Doyres*, pp. 21–24; and the section "Khaveyrim" (Comrades) in *Farvoksene vegn*, pp. 73–96. This theme also appears in poems not included in Grade's books, such as "Tsvey khaveyrim" (Two Comrades), *Yung Vilne*, no. 3 (1936): 65–66 (not to be confused with another poem with the same title printed in *Farvoksene vegn*), and "A royter tsetl" (A Red Notice), *Baginen*, January 1934, no. 1, p. 12, reprinted with minor stylistic changes under the title "Bakant-makhung" (Notice), *Di tsukunft* 41 (1936): 648. Regarding Sutzkever's poems on the same theme, with or without political overtones, see Abraham Novershtern, *Avrom Sutzkever biblyografye* (Tel Aviv, 1976), nos. 34, 63, also nos. 47, 66.

26. The poem "Bakant-makhung" is an exception, for it explicitly states that the man condemned to death is a *dorfs-goy* (Gentile villager).

If the literary critics sympathetic to the Jewish Left in Poland had been more aggressive in their demands, they would have accused Grade of passivity and the glorification of martyrdom, accusations frequent at that time in the Yiddish literary scene in the Soviet Union. But from the material at our disposal it appears that even the Jewish Left reacted positively to Grade's poetry, voicing only weak protests.[27]

In contrast, there is much testimony that these poems completely fulfilled the demands made upon literature by the radical readership. During an evening held in honor of the publication of Grade's first book, *Yo*, Zalmen Reisen proclaimed: "Grade thoroughly satisfies the demands: national in form and socialist in content [*natsyonal loyt der form, sotsyalistish loytn inhalt*]. Grade has found the artistic means of expressing the sorrow and anger of our period."[28] If in 1936 Grade's poetry could receive such unreserved praise from a radical intellectual, the following years provided even stronger impetus for maintaining the broad consensus. The bitter antisemitism in Poland, on the one hand, and the slogan of the popular front, on the other, both tended to blur the unequivocal character of the message the radical intelligentsia insisted on hearing from literature.

The path taken by Grade in the 1930s, against the background of Yung Vilne, is thus an excellent example of the constraints gradually narrowing the channels of political expression available to Yiddish literature in Poland. I leave it to historians to draw whatever inferences may be drawn from poetry about the intrinsic problems of Jewish leftist radicalism in Poland between the world wars.

27. Avrom Leyb Germanisky, "A kreftiker talent" (A Powerful Talent), *Vilner tog*, June 5, 1936, p. 4. An editor's disclaimer was appended to this article, published after the author's death. The poet Kalmen Lis also made some diffuse objections to Grade's "passivity" in his review of *Yo* in *Shriftn* (Warsaw) 2, no. 2 (February 1937): 46–47.

28. Quoted in "Der ovnt lekoved Khaim Grades liderbukh *Yo*," *Vilner tog*, April 17, 1936, p. 4.

Michael C. Steinlauf

Mark Arnshteyn and Polish-Jewish Theater

One of the striking features of the development of modern Jewish culture in Poland was its relative isolation from the surrounding Polish culture. For Poles, linguistic and traditional psychological and social barriers, compounded by increasing antisemitism, created a situation in which, as the Polish critic Tadeusz Boy-Żeleński noted in the 1920s, one had to "voyage" to see Yiddish theater,[1] even though the "voyage" amounted to nothing more than a walk or trolley ride. On the Jewish side, the situation was much more complex: one measure, indeed, of our gradual increase in knowledge about this period is our increasing appreciation of its complexity. It is possible to say that by the interwar period the vast majority of Jews knew some Polish, many were fluent in Polish and well acquainted with Polish literature, and numerous Jewish writers and artists were hardly indifferent to Polish culture. Furthermore, there existed certain areas of Polish culture—and theater is a good example—with which Jewish audiences had already developed a tradition of contact. At the same time, in certain circles, the notion of developing *Jewish* cultural creativity in the Polish language began to be entertained as well. On the other hand, most of Jewish—and most particularly, Yiddish—culture, involved, like any youthful culture, in a struggle for autonomy and authenticity, had to keep Polish influences, to a certain extent, at arm's length. Moreover, certainly in the "higher" realms of culture, the lines of national and linguistic division were sufficiently strong that for a Jew, for example, to begin

I would like to express my warmest thanks to Professor Chone Shmeruk, who first suggested the career of Mark Arnshteyn to me as a field worthy of investigation.

1. Tadeusz Boy-Żeleński, "W teatrze żydowskim," *Kurjer Poranny,* October 10, 1928, no. 296, reprinted in his *Pisma,* ed. Henryk Markiewicz (Warsaw, 1956–75), 22:518.

to write literature in Polish often marked his departure from Jewish society and his identification as a "Polish writer of Jewish origin."[2]

The career of Mark Arnshteyn[3] (born in Warsaw about 1879 and died probably in the Warsaw ghetto in 1943) is a curious, instructive, and forgotten exception to the "Chinese wall" often said to separate Polish and Jewish cultures from each other. In a time and place characterized by intense national preoccupation and the increasing linkage of cultural, linguistic, and national issues, Mark Arnshteyn, known in the Polish world under the pseudonym Andrzej Marek, managed steadfastly to pursue a literary and theatrical career devoted in equal measure to creation in Polish and Yiddish. A disciple of Stanisław Przybyszewski, high priest of Polish romantic modernism, Arnshteyn gained renown in turn-of-the-century Warsaw with his play *Pieśniarze* (Singers),[4] which he later translated into Yiddish as *Der vilner balebesl* (The Little Vilna Householder).[5] It was based on the legendary life of the nineteenth-century Vilna cantor said to have been destroyed by his success on the Warsaw opera stage. Inspired by Y. L. Peretz and his circle, Arnshteyn also pioneered as the first modern director in the history of Yiddish theater, working with the Ester Rokhl Kaminska Troupe in its early efforts at "literary" theater.[6] Arnshteyn never ceased to concern himself with Jewish themes, and he devoted his life to a beautiful, but under the historical circumstances naïve, dream: "to bring about

2. Artur Sandauer, *O sytuacji pisarza polskiego pochodzenia żydowskiego w XX wieku* (Warsaw, 1982).

3. Instead of using any of the extant Polish spellings of Arnshteyn's name (Arnstein, Arenstein, Arnsztejn), I have chosen to transliterate his name from Yiddish using the YIVO system. This seemed particularly appropriate because the Polish world knew him, after all, as Andrzej Marek. Sources for Arnshteyn's life and career are scattered and sometimes unreliable. By far the most complete biographical source is the long article in Zalmen Zilbercweig, *Leksikon fun yidishn teater*, vol. 5 (Mexico City, 1967), cols. 4414–67, with bibliographies in vol. 1 (New York, 1931), cols. 101–2, vol. 5, cols. 4464–67. These must be supplemented by *Bibliografia Literatury Polskiej "Nowy Korbut,"* vol. 15 (Warsaw, 1978), pp. 33–36, for Arnshteyn's work in the Polish theater and press.

4. *Pieśniarze* premiered in 1902 in Łódź and the following year in Warsaw. It was first published in *Izraelita* 38, nos. 1–9, 11–16 (January 2–February 27, March 13–April 24, 1903).

5. *Der vilner balebesl* premiered in 1905 in Warsaw. It was published as *Der vilner balebesl: Drame in 4 aktn* (Warsaw, 1908).

6. See A. Mukdoyni [Aleksander Kappel], "Zikhroynes fun a yidishn teater-kritiker: Yidisher teater in Poyln fun 1909 biz 1915," *Arkhiv far der geshikhte fun yidishn teater un drame*, ed. Jacob Szacki (Shatzky), vol. 1 (Vilna, 1930), pp. 345, 360–61; Avrom Taytlboym, "Mark Arnshteyn: Tsum 40stn yor fun grindn durkh im di ershte yidishe literarishe trupe in Varshe—1907," *Yidishe kultur* 9, no. 1 (1947): 44–45.

an intellectual Jewish-Polish *rapprochement*," "to build a bridge between Polish and Jewish societies" on the basis of dramatic art.[7]

In this essay, I will briefly focus on one aspect of a career well worth further investigation: Arnshteyn's project in the interwar period to bring Yiddish plays to the Polish stage and the reaction that this activity aroused, particularly in Yiddish cultural circles.

In interwar Poland, the Jewish theatergoer encountered an *embarras de richesse*. Yiddish dramatic theater had come of age: without public or private funding, operating on a shoestring with actors whose poverty and idealism became legendary, the new Yiddish art companies staged serious productions of Yiddish classics, as well as William Shakespeare, Jean Baptiste Molière, Eugene O'Neill, and Theodore Dreiser, artistically on a par with any in Europe. Unlike most of their Western European counterparts, however, the creators of this theater inevitably linked their art to a national "mission": Yiddish dramatic theater perceived itself as a moral force in the struggle for survival of Jewish society in Poland.[8] Simultaneously, the well-established and extremely creative Polish theater attracted a large Jewish audience as well. By the late nineteenth century, not only upper-class assimilators but Yiddish-speaking Jews in traditional dress regularly attended Polish theater.[9] Moreover, before World War I, when national antagonisms were considerably less inflamed than during the interwar period, Polish theater had responded to this audience and produced plays translated from Yiddish and on Jewish themes.[10] Furthermore, there was at least one case of a Yiddish play staged in Polish by Jews and specifically intended for a Jewish audience: this was the 1905 Warsaw premiere of Sholem Aleichem's *Tsezeyt un tseshpreyt* (Scattered and Dispersed), translated and directed by Mark Arnshteyn.[11] During the interwar

7. Mark Arnshteyn, "Vi azoy ikh bin gekumen tsu der bine," *Teater tsaytung un fervaylungs-blat,* December 7, 1928, no. 6; Arnshteyn, "Ir zent gerekht, Khaver Weichert," *Literarishe bleter,* August 3, 1928, no. 31, pp. 603–4.

8. See, e.g., Zygmunt Turkow, *Di ibergerisene tkufe* (Buenos Aires, 1961); Michał Weichert, *Zikhroynes,* vol. 2: *Varshe (1918–1939)* (Tel Aviv, 1961).

9. Michael C. Steinlauf, "Jews and Polish Theater in Nineteenth-Century Warsaw," *Polish Review* 32, no. 4 (1987): 439–58.

10. Polish productions of Abraham Goldfaden's *Shulamis* and *Di kishef-makherin* (The Sorceress) were staged in Warsaw as early as the 1880s. See also note 14, below.

11. Chone Shmeruk, "*Tsezeyt un tseshpreyt* le-Sholem Aleichem ve-ha-hazagot shel ha-mahazeh ba-safah ha-polanit be-Varshah ba-shanim 1905 ve-1910," in *Studies on Polish Jewry: Paul Glikson Memorial Volume,* ed. Ezra Mendelsohn and Chone Shmeruk (Jerusalem, 1987), pp. 79–95.

period, despite the tense national climate, Jewish attendance at Polish theater continued to grow. Indeed, in both Polish and Jewish theater circles, it seems to have been common knowledge that Jews made up the *majority* of the Polish theater audience.[12]

In 1924, Mark Arnshteyn, who had spent a decade working in Yiddish theater abroad, returned to a greatly changed Warsaw, discovered that the new, nationally minded Yiddish theater had little place for him, and turned "temporarily" to "a different work that is, I am convinced, not less important and necessary than Yiddish theater . . . a work that must be done and that no one else besides me, for the time being does—or perhaps can do."[13] Between 1925 and 1929 Arnshteyn produced on the Warsaw stage Polish versions of five major works of Yiddish theater: S. Anski's *Der dybbuk*, Sholem Asch's *Got fun nekome* (God of Vengeance), H. Leivick's *Der golem*, and Jacob Gordin's *Mirele Efros* and *Got, mentsh, un tayvl* (God, Man, and Devil).[14] On artistic grounds, both Arnshteyn's Polish *Dybbuk* and his *Got fun nekome* were highly praised.[15] Critics noted the

12. In an interview published in *Literarishe bleter,* Juliusz Osterwa, director of Teatr Reduta, a major Polish drama company, stated that his theater was "supported primarily by the Jewish theatergoer" and, based on a current tour, provided the following statistics on the Jewish proportion of his audience: Vilna, 60 percent; Białystok, 80 percent; Brześć nad Bugiem (in Yiddish, Brisk), 90 percent. Aaron Alperin, "Juliusz Osterwa, rezshiser fun 'Reduta,' vegn yidishn teater-oylem," *Literarishe bleter,* December 9, 1927, no. 49, p. 960. Osterwa's observations are supported by a letter to the editor of a Polish newspaper, which, referring to Vilna Jewish society, declares that "without it, the [Polish] theater could save itself the expense of turning on the lights." "Polak wyznania mojżeszowego" (Pole of the Mosaic Faith), "Żydzi wileńscy wobec *Murzyna Warszawskiego,*" *Kurjer Wileński,* 1929, no. 24, cited in Joanna Godlewska, "Komedie Słonimskiego a prasa," pt. 1, *Dialog,* 1982, no. 3, p. 102. The situation was apparently similar in Warsaw, where Mark Arnshteyn reported that more than half the audience at Stefan Jaracz's celebrated Teatr Ateneum was Jewish. "Leon Schillers toes," *Literarishe bleter,* February 23, 1934, no. 8, p. 120. See also the account of the Polish-Jewish theater debate below; Michał Weichert, "Undzere taynes tsu Mark Arnshteyn," *Literarishe bleter,* July 13, 1928, no. 28, pp. 539–40.

13. Arnshteyn, "Ir zent gerekht, Khaver Weichert."

14. *Dybbuk* premiered May 29, 1925, at Teatr Szkarłatna Maska; it had been produced earlier that year at the Łódź municipal theater. *Bóg zemsty* premiered July 6, 1926, at Teatr Nowości (the second production of Arnshteyn's new Teatr Niezależny [Independent Theater]). *Golem* premiered May 26, 1928, at the Warsaw Circus Arena; it had been produced on January 6, 1928, in Lublin. *Mirla Efros* premiered July 21, 1929, at Teatr Elizeum; it had been produced earlier that year in Łódź. *Bóg, Szatan, i Człowiek* premiered November 19, 1929, at Teatr Elizeum. Significantly, in 1928 Arnshteyn also staged a revival of Gabriela Zapolska's *Małka Szwarcenkopf,* a prime example of a Polish play aimed at a Jewish audience. First produced in Warsaw in 1897, in the years before World War I *Małka Szwarcenkopf* was one of the most popular plays on the Polish stage. On *Małka Szwarcenkopf,* see Steinlauf, "Jews and Polish Theater in Nineteenth-Century Warsaw."

15. See reviews by Eyner [Aaron Einhorn], *Haynt,* June 5, 1925, no. 128; N. M.

reverence with which Arnshteyn approached the original, the artistic "purity" of the productions, and his ability to elicit powerful
performances from Polish actors not by "disguising [them] as
Jews"[16] but by permitting them to discover a way to perform true
to their own cultural traditions. Thus, for example, Arnshteyn
shifted the aura of the *Dybbuk* from Jewish folk mysticism to Polish
romanticism. Arnshteyn's version of Leivick's *Golem*, which had previously been staged only in Hebrew,[17] was more controversial and
characteristic of Arnshteyn's sensibility. Leivick's dramatic poem,
based on the famous Jewish legend about the Maharal of Prague,
who was said to have created out of clay a superhumanly powerful
being, the Golem, to defend Jews against the blood libel, was set
amid the narrow streets and catacombs of the medieval ghetto and
presented a Golem symbolic of the perilous attempt to bring messianic national redemption through violence.[18] Arnshteyn radically
altered Leivick's conception, discarding much of the philosophy,
introducing a motif of love between the Golem and the Maharal's
daughter, and, most of all, turning Leivick's claustrophobic setting
inside out to create a spectacle of movement and sound. He staged
his production in the circular arena of the Warsaw Circus amid a
constructivist set built by the Polish stage designers Andrzej Pronaszko and Szymon Syrkus,[19] and he enlisted the participation of
the 150-member choir of the Great Tłomacki Synagogue. Thereby
he created a spectacle akin to Greek theater and medieval mystery
plays, yet one in which, in the words of a reviewer in the Polish-

---

[Nakhmen Meisel], *Literarishe bleter,* June 19, 1925, no. 59, p. 5; Michał Weichert,
Teater un drame, vol. 2 (Vilna, 1926), pp. 172–73; Tadeusz Boy-Żeleński, in *Kurjer
Poranny,* June 10, 1925, no. 158, reprinted as "Anski *Dybbuk,*" in his *Pisma,* 21:319–
23; Karol Irzykowski, in *Robotnik,* July 9, 1926, no. 186, reprinted in *Recenzje teatralne*
(Warsaw, 1965), pp. 173–76.

16. Weichert, *Teater un drame,* 2:172–73.
17. The Habimah production reached Warsaw in 1926.
18. H. Leivick, *Der golem* (New York, 1921).
19. Andrzej Pronaszko (1888–1961) later designed sets for the Yiddish dramatic
theater, collaborating with the directors Jakób Rotbaum and Michał Weichert. See
Rotbaum and Weichert's reminiscences, "Współpraca Pronaszki z Teatrami Żydows-
kimi: Wspomnienia," *Pamiętnik Teatralny* 13 (1964): 53–62. The Jewish architect
Szymon Syrkus (1893–1964) also designed sets for both the Yiddish and Polish
productions of Michał Weichert's play *Boston* (about the Sacco and Vanzetti case) in
1933–34. Faina Burko, "The Yiddish Theater in Interwar Poland," in *Poles and Jews:
Myth and Reality in the Historical Context,* ed. Harold B. Segal (photoduplicated by the
Institute on East-Central Europe, Columbia University, New York, 1986), p. 381.
This article contains a number of valuable observations on Polish-Jewish contacts in
theater in the interwar period.

language Jewish press, "out of a great circle gaping with abysses, across the amphitheater's steps, moved Jewish crowds. Ancient crowds, calling for help, for rescue from the bloody slanders of ritual murder . . . cries even to this day still ringing, nor scattered by the winds of time." Amid great fanfare, the production was attended by foreign ambassadors and correspondents and high Polish government officials.[20]

In the highly charged national atmosphere of interwar Poland, however, to produce Jewish plays on the Polish stage was much more than an artistic event; it was to stride unavoidably into the political arena. With respect to the Polish reaction, Arnshteyn understood this. When the *Dybbuk* was staged in 1925, he and his collaborators announced that the production was a "political act" furthering Polish-Jewish understanding, a kind of artistic complement to the political agreement or Ugoda then being negotiated between the Polish government and the Galician Zionist leaders of the Koło Żydowskie (Jewish Parliamentary Club).[21] Major Warsaw theaters and the Polish actors' union refused to stage the play, and there were even rumors of an attack planned, presumably by nationalist Polish hooligans, on the small new theater that agreed to stage it.[22] Interestingly enough, however, it was precisely on the Polish side that Arnshteyn's initiative found its most stalwart supporter. Tadeusz Boy-Żeleński, translator, publicist, and theater critic, was one of the last defenders of the rationalist, liberal, and democratic tradition of nineteenth-century Polish Positivism, and therefore also something of an anomaly in interwar Poland.[23] Boy followed with great interest all of Arnshteyn's Polish-Jewish productions and, indeed, was also one of the few Poles to draw attention to Yiddish theater. He praised

20. Saul Wagman, in *Nasz Przegląd*, May 31, 1928, no. 149. See also Bożena Frankowska, " 'Golem' na Arenie i 'Daniel' w Teatrze Kolistym," *Pamiętnik Teatralny* 11 (1962): 520–38.

21. Weichert, *Teater un drame*, 2:170. On the Ugoda, see Ezra Mendelsohn, "Reflections on the 'Ugoda,'" in *Sefer Raphael Mahler: Kovez mehkarim be-toldot Israel*, ed. Shmuel Yeiven (Merhavia, 1974), pp. 87–102.

22. But note that Weichert, who reports this (*Teater un drame*, 2:171), implies the rumor was started by the theater management as a publicity ploy. Three years later, Arnshteyn's Polish *Golem* in Lublin "aroused a scandal" in the local Polish press, including denunciations of the play as "provocation" and "blasphemy" in *Głos Lubelski*, cited in *Literarishe bleter*, January 20, 1928, no. 3, p. 61.

23. Jan Kott, "Dziennik Boya w osiemnastu tomach," in Boy-Żeleński, *Pisma*, 19:27. In English, see Czesław Miłosz, *The History of Polish Literature* (Berkeley, Calif., 1983), pp. 361–62; Julian Krzyżanowski, *A History of Polish Literature* (Warsaw, 1978), pp. 651–53.

Arnshteyn's "energy" and "consistency" and repeatedly pointed out the social importance of his work.[24]

Another source of consistent support for Arnshteyn's productions was the Polish-language Jewish press.[25] The Warsaw daily *Nasz Przegląd,* the largest in circulation and most influential of these publications, had little more than language in common with its pre–World War I assimilationist predecessors. Espousing an aggressive Jewish national perspective whose cornerstones were Zionism and support for Jewish civil and national minority rights, *Nasz Przegląd* strongly supported Yiddish (and Hebrew) culture and, for example, regularly printed translations from Yiddish literature and reviews of Yiddish theater. Yet in interwar Poland choice of language was hardly an incidental matter, and in itself necessarily led to specific politics. Most obviously, employing the same language as the surrounding Polish nation meant that one was also speaking *to* it; *Nasz Przegląd* was therefore involved, as no Yiddish paper could or wanted to be, in the endeavor of offering Polish society "an understanding of our national self, its laws and ideals,"[26] an orientation similar to Arn-

24. Boy's theater criticism appeared in Warsaw throughout the 1920s and 1930s, primarily in *Kurjer Poranny,* and has been collected in the twenty-eight volumes of his *Pisma.* His numerous reviews of and reflections on Jewish theater staged in Polish, Yiddish, and Hebrew are worthy of further attention. These writings are as follows (articles on Arnshteyn's productions marked with an asterisk): vol. 21: *"An-ski *Dybbuk,"* pp. 319–23; "An-ski *Dzień i Noc,"* pp. 357–62; vol. 22: *"Zapolska *Małka Szwarcenkopf,"* pp. 485–89; "W teatrze żydowskim" [Y. L. Peretz's *Bay nakht oyfn altn mark*], pp. 518–20; "Teatr hebrajski 'Habima'"[*Dybbuk*], pp. 577–78; *"Niedyskrecje teatralne" [Arnshteyn's Teatr Niezależny], pp. 603–4; *"Golem,"* pp. 682–83; vol. 23: *"Gordin *Bóg, Szatan, i Człowiek,"* pp. 149–51; *"Teatr 'Elizeum': Występy Wandy Siemaszkowej" [*Mirla Efros*], pp. 515–17; "Teatr hebrajski 'Habima'" [*Dybbuk* and Sholem Aleichem's *Dos groyse gevins*], pp. 531–32; vol. 25: "Blume *Boston"* [Yung Teater], pp. 92–97; *"Munzer-Marek *Żyda na Stos,"* pp. 134–36; "[I. J.] Singer *Boris Sawinkow,"* pp. 175–79; "Wizyta w żydowskim 'studio' Teatru Młodych" [Yung Teater's *Trupe Tanentsap*], pp. 575–76; vol. 26: "Wizyta w żydowskim studio 'Teatru Młodych'" [Yung Teater's *Mississippi*], pp. 552–54; "Moris Szwarc w teatrze żydowskim," pp. 598–99; "Z żydowskiego studio 'Teatr Młodych'" [Yung Teater's *Simkhe Plakhte*], pp. 630–31; vol. 28: "Teatr 'Habima' w Warszawie" [*Uriel Acosta*], pp. 497–99; "*Korona Dawida* w Teatrze 'Habima,'" pp. 511–12. Along with a large group of Polish intellectuals, Boy was murdered by the Nazis in Lwów in 1941.

25. A monograph on the influential interwar Jewish daily press in the Polish language—*Nasz Przegląd* in Warsaw, *Nowy Dziennik* in Cracow, *Chwila* in Lwów—is sorely needed. As a preface to such a study, see Michael C. Steinlauf, "The Polish-Jewish Daily Press," *Polin* 2 (1987): 219–45.

26. Jakób Appenszlak, "Pietnastolecie *Naszego Przeglądu,"* *Nasz Przegląd,* September 18, 1938, no. 263. In this fifteenth-anniversary issue, Appenszlak, the editor of the paper, cites these words from his own editorial in the founding issue. Appenszlak's article is followed by congratulations and reminiscences from many public figures including Andrzej Marek, whose article, entitled "Misja *Naszego Przeglądu"* (The Mission of *Nasz Przegląd*), appears immediately below Appenszlak's.

shteyn's "mission." Furthermore, alongside its support of Yiddish culture, *Nasz Przegląd* was also sympathetic to the idea of Jewish cultural creativity in the Polish language. And even *Nasz Przegląd*'s support of Yiddish culture amounted, of course, to bringing this culture to linguistically assimilated Jews through the medium of the Polish language. Understandably, therefore, *Nasz Przegląd*'s readers, primarily middle- and upper-middle-class Jews including many professionals, made up a large proportion of Arnshteyn's audience.

The most revealing perspective on the entire enterprise, however, was the increasingly negative, and for Arnshteyn doubtless quite unexpected, reaction of the Yiddish press. With his first production, Yiddish critics were quite explicit about distinguishing between the praise it deserved on artistic grounds and the political claims it engendered. Thus, a reviewer for the daily *Haynt* begins his review: "Let's not make a political event out of it, and let's not think that the *Dybbuk* on the Polish stage signifies a break in the Chinese wall which divides the two peoples who live side by side for hundreds and hundreds of years, yet are still so totally strange to each other. . . . If only it were so, but it would be very naïve to think that it already is so."[27]

Increasingly, reaction to Arnshteyn in the Yiddish press focused on the political implications of his work, and the tone of this criticism became heavy with sarcasm. Y. M. Nayman, reviewing Arnshteyn's *Golem*, derides the notion that it demonstrates the "wealth" of Yiddish culture and ridicules it as old-fashioned servility to the omnipotent Gentile: "Here is proclamation. Here are invited the Sejm and the Senate and the City Hall, and what Jews possess is shown, everything. Oh—what a rich people are these neighbors of the 'Mosaic faith.' All that they possess! A *Dybbuk* and a *Golem*.— And *tsitselekh* [ritual fringes] and *peyelekh* [side curls], see—see what Jews possess, and temper your hearts."[28] Nayman's reaction is partly, as he explicitly admits, the result of envy: the contrast between what is possible in a financially solvent Polish theater and on the poverty-stricken Yiddish stage.[29] There is also a sense of violation here: a

27. Eyner [Aaron Einhorn], *Haynt,* June 5, 1925, no. 128.

28. Y. M. Nayman, "Der golem po polsku," *Haynt,* June 1, 1928, no. 128. Nayman begins his review with a bilingual pun: "For some days now, we've been enjoying in Warsaw *ryba po żydowsku* [fish Jewish-style, i.e., gefilte fish prepared as a Polish delicacy] and *der 'Golem' po polsku* [*Der golem* in Polish or Polish-style]."

29. Nayman is specifically bitter about the appearance of a lavish Polish *Golem* while the Yiddish original had not yet been staged. Arnshteyn, who replied directly

fragile young Jewish culture is being offered up to the Gentiles. But beyond all this, there is a graver matter: Arnshteyn's endeavor must be fought because, given the precarious position of Yiddish culture among *Jews*, it presents a threat to that culture.

This issue came to a head in 1929 and received its most uncompromising expression in the pages of the major Yiddish literary weekly, *Literarishe bleter*. Warsaw Yiddish theater was in the throes of a crisis. Kaminski's Theater, built before World War I specifically to perform Yiddish plays, was being transformed, it was rumored, into a parking garage. The Varshever Yidisher Kunst-Teater (VIKT, Warsaw Yiddish Art-Theater), Warsaw's only resident Yiddish dramatic company, had been unable to find a theater in which to perform and had disbanded. And the Elizeum, where in 1920 Yiddish theater history had been made with the Vilner Trupe (Vilna Troupe) premiere of the *Dybbuk*, had stopped playing Yiddish theater and was now presenting a Polish company performing, with huge commercial success, Mark Arnshteyn's Polish version of *Mirele Efros*, one of the most popular plays in Yiddish theater history.[30] Furthermore, *Nasz Przegląd*'s reviewer chose to praise Arnshteyn's "bold experiment" as the makings of "a new type of Jewish theater: a Polish-Jewish theater," which "responds to a vital need and can maintain itself beside Yiddish theater, just as a Polish-Jewish paper exists beside the Yiddish press." Advanced as the avatar of "a new type of theater," and doubtless aware of the provocative nature of such a role, Arnshteyn immediately sent a "clarification" to *Nasz Przegląd*

---

to this criticism ("Among other nations, such an occurrence would be an occasion for joy and pride" [Mark Arnshteyn, "Vi ikh ze dos . . . ," *Literarishe bleter*, August 30, 1929, no. 35, pp. 688–89]), also responded by staging the first Yiddish *Golem* several months later. Nayman's expression of envy is implicitly shared by Aaron Einhorn in his review of Arnshteyn's *Dybbuk*, where he points to one "great virtue" of the Polish production over the Yiddish one: "that great measure of old artistic culture, to whose level our young theater has not yet been able to attain." *Haynt*, June 5, 1925, no. 128.

30. *Mirele Efros* is about the undoing of a powerful, greathearted, and old-fashioned businesswoman by her coarse and ruthless daughter-in-law. The play, whose American subtitle was *Di yidishe keynign Lir* (The Jewish Queen Lear), ends, however, on a happy note—reconciliation on the occasion of the *bar mitzvah* of Mirele's grandson. On the situation of Warsaw Yiddish theater in 1927–29, see the following: N. M. [Nakhmen Meisel], "Glaykhgiltikeyt oder boykot," *Literarishe bleter*, January 28, 1927, no. 4, p. 60; I. Milejkowski, "Czyja to wina?" *Nasz Przegląd*, January 13, 1929, no. 13; Menakhem Kipnis, "A shpatsir iber di teatern," *Haynt*, August 6, 1929, no. 177; "Kaminskis teater vert a garazsh far oytomobiln?" *Haynt*, August 9, 1929, no. 180; "In untergang fun Kaminskis teater iz shuldig der yidisher artistn-fareyn," *Haynt*, August 11, 1929, no. 181; K. Tsher., "Tsi veln mir nokh hobn in Varshe a yidish teater?" *Haynt*, August 27, 1929, no. 195; Turkow, *Di ibergerisene tkufe*, pp. 207–22.

disavowing any such intentions. His dream, he insisted, was neither a "Jewish-Polish" nor a "Polish-Jewish" theater, but a theater of peace, tolerance, and brotherhood, which would, of course, produce a certain number of "Jewish" (*zydonawcze*) plays. Unfortunately for Arnshteyn, he attracted further "support" from an unlikely source: the Yiddish writer Yoel Mastboym, who, in a letter to the editor of *Nasz Przegląd*, praised Arnshteyn's commitment to a Polish-language Jewish theater that would "strengthen the position of Yiddish culture in the eyes of Polish society."[31]

Directly responding to Mastboym's letter, Jonas Turkow, a key figure in the new Yiddish art-theater, launched the attack against Arnshteyn with an article entitled "Yidish teater on yidish" (Yiddish Theater without Yiddish).[32] The whole subject of a Polish-Jewish theater, declares Turkow, has taken on a serious character, and doubtless very soon "a whole new 'ideology' will be created around it." The real question, however, is not whether one "should" or "can" stage Yiddish theater in foreign languages, but rather, "To be or not to be?" with respect to Yiddish theater itself. "At a time when we do not have any theater at all, at a time when we stand before a catastrophic theater decline, at a time when in Jewish Warsaw with a population of 350,000 there is not one [permanent] Yiddish theater . . . you arrive with your 'project': to create a theater that would stage Yiddish plays in the Polish language." Moreover, asks Turkow: "Who attends your *Mirele Efros* and *Golem* productions in Polish if not 99 percent Jews?" and, he continues, "the same Jews who in any case constitute the majority of the theater audience in [Polish] theaters." Arnshteyn's project would effectively pull this Jewish audience even farther away from the "unclean" (*treyfener*) Yiddish language and theater, strengthen assimilation, and "lead to the collapse (not much is lacking!) of the Yiddish theater."[33]

31. "Zastępca" [Substitute], "Scena polsko-żydowska," *Nasz Przegląd*, July 26, 1929, no. 203; Andrzej Marek, "Wynaśnienie p. A. Marka," *Nasz Przegląd*, July 30, 1929, no. 207; Yoel Mastboym, letter to the editor, *Nasz Przegląd*, August 7, 1929, no. 215.

32. It is important to note that the single Yiddish word *yidish* signifies both "Yiddish" and "Jewish." Thus, the term *poylish-yidish teater* around which the polemic turns may be rendered in English as "Polish-Jewish theater" or "Polish-Yiddish theater." Because of its ambiguity, the term is clumsy even in Yiddish, a fact that Turkow exploits when he claims the only appropriate term for Arnshteyn's theater is "*not-yidish-poylish*, *not-poylish-yidish* theater." For convenience I have chosen the translation "Polish-Jewish," but in the discussion that follows the slipperiness of the term should be kept in mind.

33. Jonas Turkow, "Yidish teater on yidish," *Literarishe bleter*, August 16, 1929, no. 33, p. 641.

Until this point Arnshteyn had consistently justified his enterprise by insisting that his productions were intended for a Polish audience. Now, however, confronted by Turkow's unassailable argument based on the actual makeup of his audience, Arnshteyn replied with a new and highly significant defense. Since, argued Arnshteyn, as Turkow says, Jews constitute the majority of Polish theater audiences anyway—is it not better for them at least to see a play with Jewish content that might awaken in them "interest and curiosity to see plays performed *precisely in Yiddish,*" and, indeed, "perhaps bring more than one back to Jewishness in general?"[34] Carefully skirting a possible challenge to Yiddish culture, Arnshteyn's argument is nevertheless a justification for a role, however secondary, for a Jewish culture in the Polish language.

Arnshteyn's cautious defense—coupled with the continuing appearance in *Nasz Przegląd* of articles unambiguously advocating the need for a permanent Polish-Jewish theater[35]—was to no avail. Responding on the front page of *Literarishe bleter,* Turkow derided the notion that Arnshteyn's productions could reinterest Jews in Yiddish culture: "Not the Yiddish theater, not the Yiddish school, not the Yiddish printed word, but precisely Yiddish plays performed in Polish?! I consider this a joke." Nakhmen Meisel, the editor of *Literarishe bleter,* had already referred to "Mark Arnshteyn or more rightly— Andrzej Marek" and accused him of "pouring oil on assimilation fires." Now Turkow concluded that blame for the decline of Yiddish theater must be shared by those sectors of Jewish society that will not fulfill their responsibility to Yiddish culture and, among them, "those who help in widening the abyss that separates Jewish society from the Yiddish theater—I mean the builders of the Polish-Jewish theater."[36] Mark Arnshteyn had hoped to reach a Polish audience and "build a bridge between Polish and Jewish societies." Instead, his audience filled with Jews seeking a bit of Jewishness in the Polish language, he found himself accused of "widening an abyss" within Jewish society itself.

34. Arnshteyn, "Vi ikh ze dos . . . ," Arnshteyn's italics.
35. M. Friszlender, "Czy potrzebny jest teatr polsko-żydowski? Artykuł dysku-syjny," *Nasz Przegląd,* August 28, 1929, no. 236; Pierrot [Jakób Appenszlak], "Między wierszami: Czy powinien istnieć teatr 'polsko-żydowski,'" *Nasz Przegląd,* September 2, 1929, no. 245; J. Podskocz, "Czy potrzebny jest teatr polsko-żydowski: Artykuł dyskusyjny," *Nasz Przegląd,* September 16, 1929, no. 256.
36. Jonas Turkow, "Di 'kemfer' far yidisher kultur" (The 'Fighters' for Yiddish Culture), *Literarishe bleter,* September 6, 1929, no. 36, pp. 695–97; Nakhmen Meisel, in *Literarishe bleter,* August 30, 1929, no. 35, pp. 675–76.

Although Arnshteyn's *Mirele Efros* was enormously successful, the Polish *Got, mentsh, un tayvl* was not. As a result of this failure and doubtless also because of the controversy provoked by his work, Arnshteyn lowered the curtain on his Polish-Jewish theater—at least in the overheated atmosphere of Warsaw.[37] In Łódź he found, it seems, a more hospitable environment in which to work, and for a number of years he continued to stage "Jewish plays" on the Polish stage. And behind the walls of the Warsaw ghetto, putting to work a number of fine Jewish actors from the Polish stage, Mark Arnshteyn founded the Nowy Teatr Kameralny (New Chamber Theater), a Polish-language dramatic theater devoted to Polish-Jewish theater.[38]

How shall we look at the phenomenon of Polish-Jewish theater? Shall we employ the notion of "assimilation" used by Turkow and Meisel, and thereby interpret the polemic around Polish-Jewish theater as one skirmish in an ongoing struggle between the defenders of a Jewish national culture and the proponents of linguistic and perhaps cultural assimilation? This implies that one side was somehow "less Jewish" than the other—and as soon as we accept this notion, we condemn that side, from the perspective of Jewish history, to obscurity. And this, indeed, has been the fate of Mark Arnshteyn. Furthermore, more generally speaking, the notion of assimilation as used polemically in the Polish-Jewish theater debate, and often by historians as well, is based on a Western European model of modern Jewish culture and may not, in fact, apply to interwar Poland.

Elsewhere in this volume, Chone Shmeruk advances an alternative and more fruitful way of looking at this situation. Shmeruk defines interwar Polish-Jewish culture in its broadest sense—encompassing education, literature, theater, and press—as a "polysystem" composed of three linguistic subsystems: Jewish cultural

---

37. A Grafman, in "A ridl zamd" (A Spadeful of Sand), *Literarishe bleter,* December 6, 1929, no. 49, p. 958, intends his caustic words on the "tragic" demise of the "Mirla-culture" to be the spadeful of sand that Jewish Warsaw throws on her grave.

38. Eli Baruchin, "Sztuka żydowska na polskiej scenie: Na marginesie sztuki *Pieśniarze Ghetta* Andrzeja Marka w Teatrze Miejskim w Łodzi," *Nasz Przegląd,* October 1, 1931, no. 269; Ruta Sakowska-Pups, "O działalności teatralnej w getcie warszawskim," *Biuletyn Żydowskiego Instytutu Historycznego,* no. 69 (1969): 47–70.

creativity in Hebrew, Yiddish, and Polish.[39] This model allows us to move beyond ideologically or nationally inspired polemics and to affirm, first of all, that Jewish cultural creativity in interwar Poland did in fact exist in all three languages. Second, it follows that no one linguistic subsystem stood alone; that is, neither Hebrew- nor Yiddish- nor Polish-language Jewish culture alone could fully meet the needs of all sectors of interwar Polish-Jewish society. Finally, it also follows that each linguistic subsystem interacted in a variety of ways—both positively and negatively, supportively and competitively—with the other subsystems. To approach the complexity of Jewish culture in interwar Poland is to begin to trace, therefore, the many-layered interplay between cultural creation in Hebrew, Yiddish, and Polish.

The perspective that in interwar Poland Jewish culture developed simultaneously in three different linguistic realms enables us to view the subject of our study in an entirely new way. Polish-Jewish theater, its defenders and its critics, as well as its reluctant avatar, Mark Arnshteyn, emerge as players within a broad and complex web of relationships between authentic—however prolific or modest—*Jewish* cultural creativity in Yiddish and in Polish. While the notion of assimilation limits the scope of Jewish history, here its scope expands to recover the achievements of a Mark Arnshteyn, and no doubt others like him still forgotten.

39. Chone Shmeruk, ''Hebrew-Yiddish-Polish: A Trilingual Jewish Culture,'' in this volume. For an earlier suggestion of a similar approach, see Max Weinreich's concluding remarks on ''internal trilingualism'' in ''Ineveynikste tsveyshprakhikeyt in Ashkenaz biz der haskole: Faktn un bagrifn,'' *Di goldene keyt,* no. 35 (1959): 80–88.

Eugenia Prokopówna

The Sabbath Motif in Interwar Polish-Jewish Literature

The idea of a Polish-Jewish literature will not surprise a reader from the West, who is familiar with classifications like American-Jewish literature or Russian-Jewish literature.[1] In Poland, however, the notion is a great novelty. Only at the beginning of the 1980s did Jan Błoński write in Poland about the possible existence of Jewish literature in Polish, calling to mind "a poetic dream" of Adam Mickiewicz, who prophesied a brotherly relationship between the two nations in which each would retain its spiritual autonomy. Błoński's famous essay, "Autoportret żydowski" (Jewish Self-Portrait), played, however, an equivocal role in establishing the idea of a Polish-Jewish art. According to Błoński, cultural and sociological conditions in interwar Poland were such that Polish-Jewish literature could have developed—but did not.[2] I should like to take issue with his opinion.

Let me begin with some basic assertions.[3] Polish-Jewish literature is an artistic and a sociological phenomenon. Both these dimensions closely correlate, since this literature is determined by both esthetic and biographical factors. The metaphor "self-portrait," used by Błoński, renders perfectly this peculiar intertwining of art and biography. We should keep this interrelationship in mind as we define

This essay has been translated from Polish by Abraham Shenitzer.

1. See Abraham Chapman, ed., *Jewish-American Literature: An Anthology of Fiction, Poetry, Autobiography* (New York, 1974); Irving Malin, ed., *Contemporary American-Jewish Literature* (Bloomington, Ind., 1973); Vasily Lvov-Rogachevsky, *A History of Russian-Jewish Literature*, ed. and trans. Arthur Levin (Ann Arbor, Mich., 1979).

2. Jan Błoński, "Autoportret żydowski," in Błoński, *Kilka myśli co nie nowe* (Cracow, 1985), p. 118.

3. For the description of Polish-Jewish literature that follows, I owe much to the work of Lvov-Rogachevsky.

412

Polish-Jewish literature: works written in Polish on Jewish themes by authors who identify themselves as Jews.

The basic feature of Polish-Jewish literature is its cultural syncretism. If the Polish language serves to record the specific character of Jewish life, we may expect two systems of tradition and literary convention—Polish and Jewish—to be present in Polish-Jewish works. The association of the two systems creates a new quality that is this literature's peculiar mark. Moreover, the language determines the circle of potential readers: they are Polish-speaking Jews as well as Poles and thus different, so far as culture is concerned, from the readers of Yiddish and Hebrew literatures. The readership of Polish-Jewish literature is closely correlated, in fact, to the readership of Polish literature.

As a literary phenomenon, Polish-Jewish literature may be viewed from two different perspectives. On the one hand, it may be treated as an integral, though peculiar, part of Polish literary output. On the other hand, it may be treated as a part of the polysystem of Jewish culture in Poland, a polysystem consisting of the creative activity in all the languages spoken by Polish Jews.[4] Thus, we may talk about the "Jewish School" in Polish literature or, alternately, the "Polish School" in Jewish literature. It seems rather obvious that both these approaches are equally valid and not mutually exclusive. In this essay I will approach Polish-Jewish literature from the perspective of Polish literature only.

Literature in which the Polish and Jewish cultural traditions "interface" could develop only in the post-Enlightenment period, as the precondition for its development was advanced acculturation combined with modern Jewish national awareness. The question of self-identification is of great importance here: a Pole of Mosaic faith and a Jew feeling at home in Polish culture are two entirely distinct models of Jewish identity.[5] On literary grounds a Polish writer of Jewish origin and a Jewish writer who writes in Polish correspond to these models. As a sociological phenomenon, Polish-Jewish literature is the result of those processes taking place in the Jewish

4. Chone Shmeruk explains the polysystem of Jewish culture in Poland in the period between the wars in "Hebrew-Yiddish-Polish: A Trilingual Jewish Culture," in this volume.

5. See Lucy S. Dawidowicz, "Jewish Identity: A Matter of Fate, A Matter of Choice," in Dawidowicz, *The Jewish Presence: Essays on Identity and History* (New York, 1977), pp. 30–31.

population since the beginning of the nineteenth century that gave rise to the Polish-speaking Jewish intelligentsia. This group, situated on the borderline between the two nations, played the role of intermediary between them. Polish-Jewish literature's primary readers were undoubtedly Polish-reading Jews, readers for whom Polish was the language of their thoughts, yet for whom their Jewishness remained precious.

Here we touch on another important precondition of Polish-Jewish literature. If two cultural traditions are to coexist in artistic creativeness, they must have equal rights. To manifest one's Jewish identity in literature written in Polish presupposes an affirmation of the values and ideals of Jewish culture as well as an approval of its individual character.

Błoński is right that sociocultural factors in Poland between the two world wars were conducive to the formation of a ''Jewish School'' of Polish literature. During this period the two processes mentioned above were particularly dynamic in shaping Jewish society in Poland. On the one hand, the process of acculturation affected broad strata of the Jewish population, which now absorbed Polish culture on a scale unmatched in the past. At the same time, however, there was an equally intensive erosion among Jews of a Polish national identity. Assimilation, if it did occur, rarely entailed an effective integration into Polish society.[6] What is extremely significant is the fact that Eastern European Jewish culture was no longer regarded as anachronistic, inferior to the European heritage. These phenomena had important consequences for Polish literature: never before had Jews participated in Polish literature on such a scale, and never before had they manifested their own autonomy in it so firmly.

There is one final factor that must not be overlooked in the development of Polish-Jewish literature in interwar Poland. The creativity of the Polish-Jewish writers was not simply an authentic, spontaneous affirmation of Jewishness. It was also a response to antisemitism; the outburst of antisemitism of the period made Polish writers of Jewish origin become Jewish writers who wrote in Polish. The new level of Jewish participation in Polish literature must have been significant and interesting if Kazimierz Czachowski and Ignacy

6. Celia S. Heller, ''Poles of Jewish Background: The Case of Assimilation without Integration in Interwar Poland,'' in *Studies on Polish Jewry, 1919–1939,* ed. Joshua A. Fishman (New York, 1974), pp. 242–76.

Fik, the authors of the first syntheses of the literature produced in the Second Polish Republic before 1939, gave attention to it.[7]

If we think of literary history as treating only masterpieces, then we cannot speak of a Polish-Jewish literature. But if we consider also second-rate, or popular, literature, then Polish-Jewish literature has a distinctive place in literary history. Its practitioners include poets and prose writers connected with the flourishing Polish-Jewish press—with the dailies *Chwila* (The Moment) (Lwów, 1919–39), *Nowy Dziennik* (New Daily) (Cracow, 1918–39), and *Nasz Przegląd* (Our Review) (Warsaw, 1923–39), as well as with the weeklies *Opinja* (Opinion) (Warsaw, 1933–35), *Nasza Opinja* (Our Opinion) (Lwów, 1935–39), and *Ster* (The Helm) (Warsaw, 1937–38). The group of Polish-Jewish authors includes poets Fryderyk Bertisch: *Kwiaty na ugorze* (Flowers on a Fallow) (1939); Roman Brandstaetter: *Królestwo trzeciej świątyni* (Kingdom of the Third Temple) (1933) and *Jerozolima światła i mroku* (Jerusalem of Light and Darkness) (1935); Karol Dresdner: *Heine i nieznajoma* (Heine and a Stranger) (1928); Anda Eker: *Na cienkiej strunie* (On a Thin String) (1936) and *Melodia chwili* (Melody of the Moment) (1937); Hersz Awrohem Fenster: *O tym, co opuszczam* (About What I'm Leaving) (1932); Daniel Ihr: *Pożegnanie młodości* (Farewell to Youth) (1934); Jakub Lewittes: *Posthumus* (The Posthumous) (1930); A. B. Mayer: *Pieśni chaluca* (Songs of Halutz) (1934); Stefan Pomer: *Elegie podolskie* (Elegies of Podolia) (1931); Karol Rosenfeld: *W ciszy łez: Poezje golusu* (In a Silence of Tears: Poetry of Galut) (ca. 1920); Maurycy Schlanger: *Idę* (I'm Going) (1936); Minka Silberman, *W cieniu życia* (In the Shadow of Life) (1936); Maurycy Szymel: *Powrót do domu* (Return Home) (1931), *Skrzypce przedmieścia* (The Suburban Violin) (1932), and *Wieczór lirczyny* (Lyric Evening) (1935); and prose writers Henryk Adler: *Ariela i Jubal: Palestyńskie opowieści romantyczne* (Ariela and Jubal: Palestinian Romantic Tales) (1931); Jakób Appenszlak: *Piętra: Dom na Bielańskiej* (Stories: A House on Bielańska Street) (1933); Rubin Feldszuh: *Noce palestyńskie* (Palestinian Nights) (1928) and *Czerwone dusze* (Red Souls) (1932); Józef Hartblaj: *Jehoszua* (Yehoshua) (1928); Adam Madler: *Falista linia* (A Wavy Line) (1932); Czesława Rosenblattowa: *Ludzie, którzy jeszcze żyja* (People, Who Are Still Alive) (1934); Emil Tenenbaum: *Tła* (Backgrounds) (1935);

---

7. Kazimierz Czachowski, *Obraz współczesnej literatury polskiej, 1884–1934*, vol. 3: *Ekspresjonizm i neorealizm* (Warsaw, 1936), pp. 319–20; Ignacy Fik, *Dwadzieścia lat literatury polskiej, 1918–1938* (Cracow, 1949), pp. 31–34.

Bernard Zimmermann: *Tirsa: Powieść z życia współczesnej Palestyny* (Tirsa: A Tale of Modern Palestinian Life) (1930). I have mentioned here only those writers who managed to publish their works in book form. The list would be much longer if it included also those writers who did not publish separate books but whose works appeared in the Polish-Jewish press.

As we can see, these are not isolated cases of Polish-Jewish creativity in the interwar period. On the contrary, there was a relatively large group of Polish-Jewish writers, recognized by at least one critic as "flocks of Polish-Jewish poets, growing in number every day."[8] What is more important is the fact that these writers were clearly aware of their literary distinctiveness. Indeed, we may speak of a "literary circle"—a group of writers responding to a particular situation, perhaps even temporarily advancing a particular program. The activity of literary critics associated with the circle such as Izydor Berman, Wilhelm Fallek, and Chaim Löw, was fairly important here. Most significant in creating these writers' group awareness was, however, undoubtedly a stormy discussion that took place in the columns of the Warsaw weekly *Opinja* in 1933. Viewpoints on Polish-Jewish poetry and literature as well as Polish-Jewish culture as such—its model and the way of its existence—were expressed not only by poets and prose writers (Roman Brandstaetter, Adam Madler, Maurycy Szymel), but also by literary critics (Izydor Berman, Chaim Löw), Polish-Jewish journalists, and readers of the magazine.[9] This most interesting polemic deserves a separate de-

---

8. Ben-Hillel, "O kulturze polsko-żydowskiej słów kilka," *Opinja*, September 10, 1933, no. 32, p. 6.

9. See Roman Brandstaetter, "Sprawa poezji polsko-żydowskiej: Artykuł dyskusyjny," *Opinja*, July 9, 1933, no. 23, p. 5, July 16, 1933, no. 24, p. 6, July 23, 1933, no. 25, p. 6; Maurycy Szymel, "Kij w mrowisku: W sprawie artykułu Romana Brandstaettera o poezji polsko-żydowskiej," *Opinja*, August 5, 1933, no. 27, p. 6, August 12, 1933, no. 28, p. 6, August 20, 1933, no. 29, p. 6, September 3, 1933, no. 31, p. 6; Chaim Löw, "Czy możliwa jest poezja polsko-żydowska," *Opinja*, September 10, 1933, no. 32, p. 6; Ben-Hillel, "O kulturze polsko-żydowskiej słów kilka," *Opinja*, September 10, 1933, no. 32, p. 6; Izydor Berman, "Dużo racji-trochę przesady," *Opinja*, September 17, 1933, no. 33, p. 6; Adam Madler, "O szerszy punkt widzenia," *Opinja*, September 17, 1933, no. 33, p. 6; Roman Brandstaetter, "Neofita," *Opinja*, September 17, 1933, no. 33, pp. 5–6; Leopold Rosner, "Kultura polsko-żydowska? Na marginesie dyskusji w sprawie poezji polsko-żydowskiej," *Opinja*, September 24, 1933, no. 34, p. 6; Maksymilian Boruchowicz, "O polsko-żydowską poezję: Na marginesie pewnej dyskusji," *Nowy Dziennik*, September 25, 1933, no. 263, pp. 8–9. The same problem enlivened the Polish-Jewish press again with the publication of Chaim Löw's *Smok w słowiczym gnieździe: Żydzi w poezji Odrodzonej Polski* (A Dragon in a Nightingale's Nest: Jews in the Poetry of Renascent Poland) (Warsaw, 1934): Maurycy Szymel, "Krajobraz duszy żydowskiej w liryce polskiej,"

tailed analysis, for which there is unfortunately no room here. Among the many different opinions, one conclusion seemed beyond doubt—that Jewish national life was expressed in Polish poetry and literature. As Roman Brandstaetter asserted in his manifesto:

> We express our own Jewish longing in the Polish language, we set the pain of a Jewish heart in the sound of [Jan] Kochanowski's words for the first time on Polish land, we associate the words of Mickiewicz with the holy words of the Bible. . . . We are a group that rehabilitates with its output the activity of the apostate [Julian] Klaczko, which contradicts [Wilhelm] Feldman's ideology with existence. . . . The soul of a Polish Jew speaks through us for the first time.[10]

And Maurycy Szymel, while briefly describing the development of Polish-Jewish poetry in the years 1918–33, concluded:

> Today we are quite a large group, and even though we are scattered all over Poland, we perform our service honestly and joyfully.[11]

Chaim Löw added the following gloss to their opinions:

> Presenting the idea of Polish-Jewish poetry and developing it into a program in the columns of *Opinja* should not surprise those who have followed the participation of Jews in Polish poetry for any length of time. Anybody could have noticed that a sizable group stands apart from the large group of Polish poets of Jewish origin and that this group differs fundamentally from all the others in attitudes toward the problems of its nation.[12]

The discussion of 1933 clearly indicates that Polish-Jewish literature was not at the time a phenomenon of minor importance, disregarded by critics. On the contrary, it aroused considerable interest, and even passionate controversies. This literature was connected with groups that belonged to a cultural borderland between the Polish and Jewish worlds, yet it was forgotten after the Holocaust, which consumed so many of its practitioners and readers.

Seen from the broader perspective of the Polish literary tradition, the writers in the Jewish literary group were hardly doing anything new or unusual when they sought and explored Jewish themes.

Opinja, March 10, 1935, no. 9, p. 9, March 17, 1935, no. 10, p. 10; April 14, 1935, no. 14, p. 10; Löw, "O 'uświadomionym żydostwie' i nie uświadomionych Żydach," *Opinja*, May 2, 1935, no. 18, p. 9; Izydor Berman, "O tzw. cechach narodowych w literaturze pięknej," *Nasza Opinja*, August 25, 1935, no. 2, p. 7, September 1, 1935, no. 3, p. 10, September 8, 1935, no. 4, p. 6.

10. Brandstaetter, "Sprawa poezji polsko-żydowskiej," *Opinja*, July 23, 1933, no. 25, p. 6.

11. Szymel, "Kij w mrowisku," *Opinja*, August 20, 1933, no. 29, p. 6.

12. Löw, "Czy możliwa jest poezja polsko-żydowska," p. 6.

What was new, however, was their literary approach to the Jewish world.

In Polish literature, the Jewish theme is always presented as a tale of "strangers," a tale in which "the reality presented differs culturally from the reality of the reader."[13] The cultural barrier in the works with this theme arises from the simple fact that the language of the text describes a cultural realm that is not its own. Thus the text must be a kind of cultural translation; it must specify and explain the cultural values, categories, and notions that constitute this different reality.

The format of this tale of strangers is interesting. In its simplified form, the storyteller is a guide to a land unknown to the reader. The storyteller is distanced from the reality he presents but has considerable knowledge of it. Put briefly, the storyteller presents a world where he is not at home, which is not his own. There is usually a clearly defined distinction between "we" and "they": "we" includes the storyteller, his reader, and their common world; "they" is the strange world that is presented. That model can clearly be seen, for instance, in *Lejbe i Sióra* (Lejbe and Siora) (1821) by Julian Ursyn Niemcewicz, *Meir Ezofowicz* (1878) by Eliza Orzeszkowa, and *Getto potępione: Powieść o duszy żydowskiej* (The Condemned Ghetto: A Novel of the Jewish Soul) (1934) by Kazimiera Alberti.

With the emergence of the Polish-Jewish literary group in the interwar period, this format, in which the familiar and alien stand opposed in this way, was radically redrawn. The autobiographical touch transformed the earlier "we" (the common world shared by the storyteller and his reader), into a "we" that united the writer and the world of his narrative, a world that is familiar to him. It also transformed the earlier "we–they" opposition into a new one: "we–you." "You" are the readers, who may be culturally distanced from the world described. Returning to Błoński's metaphor, "portrait" was replaced by "self-portrait." Polish-Jewish literature turns out to be a peculiar encounter between art and biography.

I would now like to turn to the Sabbath motif, one of the most important and most interesting motifs in this literature. In the remainder of this essay I shall examine the use of the Sabbath motif as an example of a specific image of the Jewish world in Polish-Jewish literature against the background of Polish literary tradition.

13. Kazimierz Cysewski, "Bariera kulturowa i dzieło literackie," *Ruch Literacki* 1–2 (1984): 47.

Through the Eyes of a Stranger: Ritual and Time

In Polish literary portrayals of the Jewish world, the Sabbath motif is used primarily to provide local color. When describing the Sabbath ritual, authors focus on two different scenes—the Sabbath feast and the attendant prayer. Two relevant examples are Aleksander Groza's depiction of the Sabbath feast in his romantic tale *Starosta Kaniowski* (The *Starosta* of Kaniów) (1855) and Kazimiera Alberti's image of the Sabbath in her poem "Wieczór piątkowy" (Friday Evening) (1934). In Groza's novel we are shown a room flooded with light, a table laden with Jewish delicacies, and a feasting crowd. In Alberti's poem:

> Shadows cling to the purplish curtains stiff with starch—
> The polished candlesticks shine,
> The wilted, old, creased faces nod
> Beards and shoulders bend down: the candles! the candles are burning!
> Bow-shaped backs. Flutter of dry hands. Smacking sounds.
> All I know is that they are praying! grieving!
> That theirs is a call to the awesome Jehovah,
> A voiceless call that comes from the bones, the blood, and every nerve!
>
> . . . .
> They pray to their God as old as the world,
> The oldest of all Gods.[14]

The Sabbath ritual is not a family celebration but rather a mystery celebrated by old men, a mystery of complaints, sorrows, laments, and prayers. It is a national and religious ecstasy in which despair takes the place of rejoicing. The narrator emphasizes his role as a spectator peeping at what he regards as exotic scenes behind the window shades of Jewish homes in a small town. This perspective lends the scene a theatrical air, full of strange and troubling currents, but, paradoxically, the scene's mysterious and menacing picturesqueness also makes it attractive. The poet's basic intention is to disclose the profound and tragic national essence of the holiday, to render its inner meaning that is hidden from strangers. In this way the stereotypes of the Jewish world characteristic of the Enlightenment and the Positivist period (small-town Jewish poverty and backwardness) merge with clichés prevalent in romantic Polish historiosophy (Jews perceived as a tragic nation of wanderers), which play a particular role in ennobling this play of shadows.

14. Kazimiera Alberti, "Wieczór piątkowy," *Nowy Dziennik*, July 23, 1934, no. 202, p. 8.

In the treatment of the Sabbath in Polish literature, the metaphysical and realistic dimensions are usually combined. This is the case in, say, Ignacy Hołowiński's *Rachela* (Rachel) (1845), in Józef Ignacy Kraszewski's *Żyd* (The Jew) (1866), and in Eliza Orzeszkowa's *Meir Ezofowicz* (1878). What makes Kraszewski's treatment of the holiday especially interesting is his juxtaposition of the observance of the Sabbath by an Orthodox, patriarchal family and by superficially assimilated Jews. The traditional rite, highly valued by the narrator, is at once a family feast and a form of prayer. In *Żyd*, Kraszewski provides a detailed description of the customs underlying the holiday and chooses talmudic parables and extensive quotations from prayers to emphasize its national character. Samuel Orgelbrand's *Encyklopedia powszechna* (General Encyclopedia) was not the only source that provided Kraszewski with information on the metaphysical and national significance of the Sabbath[15] and the link the Talmud establishes between strict observance of the Sabbath and the Jews' return to the Promised Land. These layers of meaning explain Kraszewski's use of the romantic stereotype that drew a parallel between Israel ("the older brother" of the Poles) and Poland as two chosen, persecuted, and suffering nations. In *Żyd* the Sabbath is not only a day of rest in memory of God's creation of the world but also a commemoration of the Jews' exodus from Egypt.

Despite Michał Grabowski's claim, following the period of sentimentalism the Sabbath—and more precisely its religious dimension—was not satirized in works of "high art." In fact even in early romantic prose Jewish prayer scenes were marked by solemnity (see, for example, *Pierwsza młodość, pierwsze uczucie* [Early Youth, Early Emotion] [1829] by Elżbieta Jaraczewska). In poetry Jewish figures were stylized along biblical lines and lifted to poetic heights. The Jew at prayer, performing the Sabbath rites, is an established literary type. Grabowski, who as late as the middle of the nineteenth century assigned Jewish literary motifs the same place and function assigned them by classicist esthetics, overlooked the metaphysical ennoblement of the praying Jew characteristic of postclassicist Polish literature.[16]

15. Samuel Orgelbrand, ed., *Encyklopedia powszechna*, vol. 24 (Warsaw, 1867), p. 513.
16. Michał Grabowski to Aleksander Groza, February 18, 1842, *Korespondencja literacka Michała Grabowskiego*, vol. 1 (Vilna, 1942), letter 3, pp. 75–79. On poetry, see Mieczysław Inglot, "Obraz Żyda w polskiej prozie fabularnej okresu romantyzmu," typescript, pp. 12–13.

So powerful was the emphasis on the Jews' religious elevation that the religious context frequently transformed otherwise negative Jewish characters, who would be mere caricatures when depicted in a nonreligious context, into idealized literary figures. This kind of metamorphosis often occurred on the Sabbath, a holiday whose unique status in Jewish life gives it the power of spiritually transforming the community. In his description of a noisy *shtetl*, Juliusz Brincken, the author of the novel *Józef Frank* (1845), stresses:

> It is different on the Sabbath: the town looks quiet and deserted. The children of Israel pray or sleep on the holy day. If you come across a Jew in the street, his steps are grave and he is deep in thought as if half the world's trouble were upon his shoulders.[17]

An example of the ennobling effect of the Sabbath on the otherwise negative character is also found in Hołowiński's *Rachela*. Here religious ecstasy refines the innkeeper Abramek, father of the heroine, and erases the ugliness of his facial features.

Jakub Hammon, the protagonist of Kraszewski's *Żyd*, claims that the Sabbath detaches the Jew from worldly concerns, brings him closer to God, and transports him by an act of memory to the lost fatherland. It is therefore not surprising that the Sabbath—viewed as a day of transcendence, of metaphysical speculations and patriotic reflections—is sometimes monumentalized as an existential and national discourse, a debate with God. The transcendental dimension imparted to characters chanting *zemirot* (Sabbath melodies) accord with the traditional Jewish belief (recalled by Gabriel in Wilhelm Feldman's *Cudotwórca* [The Magician] [1901]) that on Friday night Jehovah gives to every Jew an extra soul that He takes back at the end of the holiday.

Biblical models appear to have played an important role in the Sabbath elevation of Jewish characters, which assumes the form of their religious, metaphysical emancipation. The adaptation of biblical patterns to modern works was made possible by the gradual rejection of the norms of classicist esthetics. First sentimentalism abolished the classicist convention of representing Jewish characters as comical, plebeian figures and extended literary emancipation to Jewish heroes. Then romanticism brought together two previously

---

17. Juliusz Brincken's *Józef Frank: Powieść historyczna z drugiej połowy XVIII wieku przełożona z nie wydanego rękopisu przez Aleksandra Bronikowskiego,* was published in *Biblioteka Warszawska* (Warsaw) 3 (1845): 101.

incompatible clichés—that of the contemporary Jew (before sentimentalism, invariably negative or comical) and that of the biblical
Jew (invariably sublime). Romantic historicism established a connection between the ancient people of Moses and contemporary
Israelites and thus created a new cliché, a palimpsest in which the
degenerate present overlays a sublime past.

There are reasons to believe that biblical stylization also played
an important part in forming the image of the Sabbath. Viewed from
the outside, the Sabbath holiday is usually a solemn, masculine
ritual. One obvious reason for this is that men, rather than women,
could be religiously idealized by being associated with patriarchs
and prophets. In the works of Hołowiński, Groza, Kraszewski, and
Orzeszkowa (and in the interwar period in the works of Maria Kuncewiczowa and Alberti) men are the crucial figures in the Sabbath
ritual; in fact, in *Meir Ezofowicz* even the blessing over the candles is
recited by a man. A stranger viewing the Sabbath scene would see
lighted candles, large figures of soulful men, and small figures of
women in the far background. Such a scene has been superbly depicted by Michał Andriolli in his illustration of the Sabbath for Orzeszkowa's *Meir Ezofowicz*. It depicts a patriarchal old man with
raised arms at the center of the group gathered around a festive
table. The figures surrounding the old man are distinctly depicted
as men. The tight group of female figures on the left side of the
composition gives the impression of having been pushed aside. This
nineteenth-century cliché of the Sabbath remained relevant in the
interwar period, as seen in Alberti's poem quoted above and in the
description of Kazimierz, a very picturesque and "literary" *shtetl*,
from Kuncewiczowa's *Dwa księżyce* (Two Moons) (1933): "On Friday
evenings the windows shuddered with the frenzy of beards, prayer
shawls, and the aroma of spices."[18]

In addition to using the Sabbath to effect elevating metamorphoses
of Jewish characters and to provide local color, writers used it for
compositional ends. A turning point or a crucial development in the
lives of the characters frequently occurs on the Sabbath. The Sabbath
provides an ideal opportunity for the clash between the solemn
mood of the holiday and events that shatter idyllic homelife and
destroy the established order. For example, in Hołowiński's *Rachela*
the heroine's escape from home, an escape that ultimately leads to

18. Maria Kuncewiczowa, *Dwa księżyce* (1933; reprint, Warsaw, 1960), p. 29.

her conversion, takes place on Friday evening. In Orzeszkowa's *Meir Ezofowicz* the complications in Meir's life set in on the Sabbath. Accused of violating the Sabbath, he embarks on a fight with the town's religious fanatics that ends with his *herem* (excommunication) and expulsion.

Jerzy Ficowski's "Co jest" (Whatever There Is) deals with the time of the Sabbath.

> At Sabbath
> time the coachman
> climbs down from the coach box
> you can find him
> at the mullein candlestick
> that butts the sky
> black and blue with clouds
> you can meet him
> the cabalist of the twelve numbers
> armed with the spears of the clock's hands
> and shielded behind its face.[19]

The time of the Sabbath recalls Erich Fromm's mythical time of cosmic harmony and order.[20] It is a suspended time. It is also a vanquished time, for cosmic peace rules over all beings and all action has ceased.

The Sabbath in the Sentimental Mode: Idyllic Jewishness and the Harmony of the Universe

The Sabbath is one of the major motifs in the works of those Polish-Jewish writers in the interwar period who viewed the existing Jewish world as a ruined version of the former traditional and harmonious one, as a disintegrating once-ideal form. In other words, the Sabbath theme became a favored motif of those writers who adopted the sentimental perspective.[21] Understandably, the senti-

---

19. Jerzy Ficowski, "Co jest," in Ficowski, *Odczytanie popiołów* (Warsaw, 1983), p. 22.

20. Erich Fromm, *Zapomniany język: Wstęp do rozumienia snów, baśni i mitów,* trans. Józef Marzęcki (Warsaw, 1977), p. 232.

21. Sabbath motifs are extremely popular, particularly in poetry: Roman Bandstaetter, "Ballada o rabinie z Płocka," in *Królestwo trzeciej świątyni* (Warsaw, 1934), pp. 19–20; Karol Dresdner, "Piątek," in *Heine i nieznajoma* (Warsaw, 1928), p. 18; Anda Eker, "Bajka o sobocie," in *Ojców dzieje* (Lwów, 1937), pp. 40–42; Eker, "Wiersz o sobocie," in *Na cienkiej strunie* (Lwów, 1935), pp. 100–101; H. A. Fenster, "Elegia o sobotnim wieczorze," in *O tym, co opuszczam* (Warsaw, 1932), pp. 17–18; Daniel Ihr, "Sambation," *Chwila,* no. 5321 (January 15, 1934): 22; Stefan Pomer, "Moja matka," in *Elegie podolskie* (Warsaw, 1931), p. 24; Karol Rosenfeld, "Sabbat,"

mental Jewish self-portrait did not entirely refrain from using those literary clichés that marked the outsiders' approach to the Sabbath theme. For instance, the slice-of-life approach to the holiday repeatedly surfaces in the poetry of Maurycy Szymel, a writer who delighted in describing Sabbath scenes set in poor suburbs and in small towns and villages ("Notatki autobiograficzne" [Autobiographical Notes] [1931], "O staruszku tęskniącym" [A Nostalgic Old Man] [1932], "Świąteczny wieczór na wsi" [A Holiday Evening in the Country] [1929]). Szymel's tendency to dwell on the minutiae of customs was likely inspired by the poets in the Skamander group, who rehabilitated the province of everyday life as an appropriate subject for literature. In addition, Szymel's pictures betray the influence of that Positivist tradition which made it possible for Wiktor Gomulicki to introduce the motif of Jewish rites into nineteenth-century Polish poetry ("El mole rachmim" [God Full of Compassion] [1879]). Critics persistently classified Szymel's depictions of Jewish customs as Positivist, a label they also attached to similar descriptions in the poetry of other members of the Jewish group. Here is a typical description from Szymel's "Świąteczny wieczór na wsi":

> Soon the hammer will strike three times upon the low wooden door,
> Time to pray at Jankiel's old inn,
> Time for a hasty farewell. Supper is steaming on the table:
> Plaited bread and wine blessed and holy.

Such Sabbath scenes are not limited to poetry. Similar examples are found in prose works by Polish-Jewish writers such as Szymel's short story "Krawiec z Białegokamienia" (The Tailor from Białykamień) (1934) and Adam Madler's novel *Falista linia*. Interestingly, the Sabbath motif appears far less frequently in prose than in poetry.

Polish-Jewish writers also employed the compositional device of

---

in *W ciszy łez: Poezye golusu* (Cracow, ca. 1920), p. 27; Horacy Safrin, "L'cha dodi . . . ," *Chwila*, no. 6691 (November 6, 1937): 10; Minka Silberman, "Opowieść o starym Mendlu," in *W cieniu życia* (Stanisławów, 1937), pp. 20, 22; Maurycy Szymel, "Gdy w małym miasteczku zapada sobota," in *Wieczór liryczny* (Warsaw, 1935), p. 61; Szymel, "Matka w mroku," in *Powrót do domu* (Warsaw, 1931), p. 13; Szymel, "Notatki autobiograficzne," in *Powrót do domu*, p. 9; Szymel, "O sobocie utraconej," in *Skrzypce przedmieścia* (Warsaw, 1932), p. 29; Szymel, "O staruszku tęskniącym," in *Skrzypce przedmieścia*, p. 18; Szymel, "Sobota," in *Powrót do domu*, p. 10; Szymel, "Świąteczny wieczór na wsi," *Nowy Dziennik*, November 11, 1929, no. 302, p. 8; Szymel, "Żydowscy trubadurzy," *Nowy Dziennik*, November 25, 1929, no. 316, p. 8. Brief excerpts from some of these poems are quoted in the remainder of the essay; dates indicate first publication in the press or a collection.

contrasting the tranquil mood of the Sabbath with intensely dramatic events. For example, in Emil Tenebaum's novel *Tła* a pogrom that occurs on the Sabbath ends the peaceful existence of a small border town. On a Sabbath a tailor, the hero in Szymel's "Krawiec z Białegokamienia," becomes obsessed with the idea of the coming of the Messiah and begins to sew clothes for him, thus violating the prohibition of work on the Sabbath. Postwar prose writers also used this technique. Thus in Julian Stryjkowski's *Przybysz z Narbony* (The Visitor from Narbonne) (1978) Sabbaths are the days when the novel's hero is severely tested. Instead of being days of ritual joy, Stryjkowski's Sabbaths are days of fasting, awe, and death.

Sabbath as a ritual and Sabbath as a special holiday were frequent elements of the earlier, "external" depictions of Jewish life. In the Jewish self-portrait, the Sabbath motif is fundamentally transformed by acquiring new symbolic meanings. These new symbolic dimensions of the Sabbath relegate to the background the theme's former basic function as a source of local color. In the first place, the Sabbath now becomes a symbol of a specific conception of the Jewish tradition, of the heritage that the sentimental subject-storyteller tries to repossess. Such Jewish returns are depicted in European art as early as the beginning of the twentieth century. The anecdote inherent in Wilhelm Wachtel's well-known painting *W piątek wieczór* (Friday Evening) reappears in the sentimental Jewish self-portrait in a number of variants. The painting shows a lonely, elegantly dressed man nostalgically looking through the window of a poor man's home that glows with the lights of Sabbath candles.

This symbolic significance of the Sabbath—which becomes synonymous with Jewishness—is emphasized by writers belonging to the Jewish group. In Szymel's "Żydowscy trubadurzy" (The Jewish Troubadours) (1929) the severing of community ties and the return to the community are equated, respectively, with the passing and the approach of the Sabbath.

> Through glowing windows Sabbaths beckoned us
> With eyes of golden flickering candles.

The Sabbath as the synonym of tradition also appears in postwar literature. In Stryjkowski's *Syriusz* (Sirius) (1974) the American Jews' attempt to reconstruct the Eastern European way of life is described in a scene that depicts the clumsy and even sacrilegious enactment of the ritual.

In Szymel's "Żydowscy trubadurzy," quoted above, Jewishness—identified with the Sabbath—constitutes a kind of "archaic home." The sentimental subject-storyteller, anxious to return to the harmonious and gentle forms of existence that he associates with childhood, home, and tradition, characteristically identifies the idyllic "archaic home" with the Sabbath. Although on rare occasions the place of the Sabbath may be taken by Passover or Hanukah, in the literature under study the Sabbath remains the most private and intimate part of the Jewish heritage. Frequently, in works of the sentimental self-portrait variety, it is the only mark of Jewishness of the main characters. In "Piątek" (Friday) (1928) Karol Dresdner writes, "The glow of Sabbath lights is not entirely extinguished in me."

Anticipating the discussion below, we can say that the Sabbath represents a very special part of the Jewish tradition, its special form invested with the power of creating harmony in humankind and in its environment. The Sabbath provides the evidence that there is a core of sense and peace in the disturbed individual and in the chaotic world. Associated with home and mother, the Sabbath becomes an archetype of the idyllic state and of idyllic Jewishness.

Rootedness in Jewish tradition is one way of escaping alienation. By embracing tradition one finds a key to universal order, an explanation of the universe and the individual's place in it. In Adolf Rudnicki's *Lato* (Summer) (1938) tradition enables the former ghetto dwellers to befriend the outside world. The sentimental image of the Jewish world tradition—a source of profoundly human values—forms the idyllic core that can cure those who return to it. In particular, in Szymel's poetry ("Biblia na stole" [Bible on the Table] [1931] and "Dziadowie Biblii" [Forefathers of the Bible] [1931]) immersion in tradition is a therapeutic procedure, and tradition provides refuge for the weary hero. The identification of Jewishness with the Sabbath idyll is an act of substantial symbolic importance: the holiday idyll extends to all things Jewish, making them look harmonious and gentle. By returning to the Jewish home, the sentimental subject-storyteller returns to an archaic, carefree world.

In Jewish tradition the Sabbath is often associated with a young woman—a queen, princess, or bride. Anda Eker's "Bajka o sobocie" (The Sabbath Fairy Tale) (1937) and Stryjkowski's *Syriusz* are among the many examples of this symbolism in Polish-Jewish literature.[22] Horacy Safrin's paraphrase of the ritual song "L'cha dodi . . ." (Come, My Beloved . . .) (1937) also portrays the original association of the Sabbath, bride, and princess. The encounter with the Sabbath has the emotional tension of the encounter of lovers.

> Come, my beloved, to meet your princess
> Let us greet Sabbath eve with song!
> . . . .
> Enter your husband's chamber, you, his crown,
> Your friends await you.

In the sentimental self-portrait, the metaphor of the Sabbath as bride and princess, and thus as a young woman, is frequently replaced by the metaphor of the Sabbath as a mother and thus as an old woman. This metaphor is found in Maurycy Szymel's poem "Sobota" (Saturday) (1931). The images used by Szymel are those of a waiting old woman-Sabbath, of a waiting old woman-mother, and of a mother whose eyes reflect the light of Sabbath candles, of mother-Sabbath. In this context the blessing of the candles is the melancholy gesture of an old woman.

> All too often we are late on Friday evenings,
> And keep old woman-Sabbath waiting in the glimmer of candles.

Old mother-Sabbath signifies the intimacy and antiquity of the home tradition. The Sabbath is synonymous with the past; to submit to modernity is to destroy the Sabbath ritual.

At times other images are associated with the figure of mother-Sabbath. In a fairy tale for children by Anda Eker, "princess Motherland will stand on a mountain top, and, stretching her hands like a mother blessing the Sabbath, will utter just three words: God bless you."[23] Here the image of the princess-Sabbath merges with that of the mother-motherland, thereby giving the blessing of the candles a touch of patriotic pathos. The connection between the figure of mother and the Sabbath frequently goes beyond a simple personification. In Anda Eker's "Wiersz o sobocie" (Poem about the Sabbath) (1935) only the mother, the sole priestess of the ritual, is capable of recreating the holiday idyll.

22. A. J. Heschel, *The Sabbath: Its Meaning for Modern Man* (New York, 1984), pp. 53–55, 59–62.
23. Anda Eker, "O Teodorze Herzlu gdy był małym chłopczykiem . . ." (Theodor Herzl as a Little Boy . . .), in Eker, *Ojców dzieje* (Lwów, 1937), p. 87.

We recall that, viewed by outsiders such as Kraszewski and Orze-szkowa, the Sabbath was presented as a colorful feast or religious mystery presided over by patriarchal graybearded old men. Unlike this "external" approach, the sentimental image of the Sabbath ritual invariably places at its center the figure of the mother blessing the candles. It is striking that the Kiddush ritual appears in a Polish-Jewish work just once, in Szymel's poem "Gdy w małym miasteczku zapada sobota" (Sabbath Evening in a Small Town) (1935). In this poem, however, the blessing is recited by the lyrical subject-narrator, and neither father nor grandfather enters the mother-dominated realm of the Sabbath. While the "external" perspective tended to monumentalize the Sabbath and, at times, invested the ritual with national and patriotic meanings, in the interpretation prevailing among Polish-Jewish writers the Sabbath is a small-scale, intimate holiday. Unlike the crowded scenes found in the works of Orzeszkowa and Alberti, the sentimental Sabbath is usually restricted to the mother-child realm. The narrator depicting the Sabbath is most likely to assign to himself the role of a child (as in the poems of Eker, Dresdner, Rosenfeld, Szymel, and Fenster), a device that considerably strengthens the "archaic home" idealization. The child's perspective repeatedly appears in the postwar prose of Julian Stryjkowski. In two large scenes in *Głosy w ciemności* (Voices in the Dark) (1956) and *Przybysz z Narbony,* the Sabbath is described through the eyes of small boys who accompany their mothers during the blessing of the candles. In *Austeria* (The Inn) (1966) the Sabbath description is a fragment of the childhood memories of old Tag.

In the sentimental self-portrait the image of the Sabbath ceremony is frequently just a metaphor for the Sabbath ritual: a description of the mother, poised over the candles in the ritual gesture of blessing. Saturated with an aura of tenderness, the vision of the Sabbath as a kingdom of mothers and lights appears in Polish-Jewish poetry with such frequency that it finally attains the status of a key image.

I can still see you in the glory of candlelight
Blessing the Sabbath, your hands covering your face.
    (Stefan Pomer, "Moja matka" [My Mother] [1931])

Mother, your form wrapt in a veil of memories
Approaches me slowly—an airy, tender image.
The thin muslin of your hands is woven around the two lights,
The soundless prayer of your lips opens the gates of heaven,

With a pair of snow-white wings, like a bird in sky-high flight,
You bless us both, the Sabbath and your son.

(Dresdner, "Piątek")

The poems of Szymel ("Matka w mroku" [Mother in the Darkness] [1931]), of Eker ("Wiersz o sobocie"), and of Rosenfeld ("Sabbat" [Sabbath] [ca. 1920]), as well as the prose works of Stryjkowski, offer numerous examples of this cliché. According to Itzik Manger, the maternal blessing of the candles is a colorful and moving scene that no Jewish child will ever forget.[24] Manger's psychological interpretation of the ritual underlies—with various degrees of explicitness—the imagery characteristic of the sentimental Jewish self-portrait. Characteristically, the scene of lighting the candles (briefly mentioned in Kraszewski's *Żyd* as well as in the novel *Ziemia nasza* [Our Country] [1859] by Władysław Chodźkiewicz and depicted in more detail in Hołowiński's *Rachela*) only occasionally appears in Polish writers' depictions of the Jewish world.

The motif of light is one of the most important elements in the depiction of the Sabbath in the works of writers of the Jewish group. At times the metaphorical images of the ritual are composed exclusively of light, glow, and shimmer. Their components are explicitly chosen to maintain unity of predominantly bright colors such as white, gold, and silver. In Eker's poems dealing with the holiday, the whiteness of the hands coincides with that of the tablecloth; in addition to the whiteness of the light of the candles with which Eker fills her Sabbath scenes are the silver of the candlestick and the pink of the flame. Similarly, Rosenfeld's "Sabbat" is saturated with the silver of tears and the shimmer of candlesticks. The brightness and shimmer of objects and the nuances of light are also brought out in realistically depicted scenes of the ritual. For instance, in the poem "O sobocie utraconej" (On the Lost Sabbath) (1932), in spite of the wretchedness of the milieu typical of most of his works, Maurycy Szymel uses the brightest possible colors.

The polished candlesticks absorbed the liquid gold
Of the evening glow that flowed down the wet window panes.

The motif of light can even dominate the description of the Sabbath landscape at night. In Szymel's "Świąteczny wieczór na wsi" the night landscape is a luminous mixture of silver and gold. Rep-

24. Itzik Manger, "The Poetry of Our Holy Days," in *An Anthology of Modern Yiddish Literature*, ed. Joseph Leftwich (The Hague, 1974), p. 175.

resented as a young woman, the Sabbath is a luminous figure, her dress composed of shiny elements like an opalizing crown (Eker's "Bajka o sobocie"). Light and brightness are so closely associated with the Sabbath that in the end all light, as opposed to darkness, is identified with friendly Sabbath glimmers. To the hero of Roman Brandstaetter's "Ballada o rabinie z Płocka" (Ballad about the Rabbi of Płock) (1934):

> The starry sky is the golden Sabbath
> And the stars in the sky are golden candlesticks.

When associated with the mother figure the Sabbath is the realm of feminine gentleness that is both friendly and motherly.

> In the small *bes-medresh* the sky opened for me,
> The old Sabbath sky of mother, warm and womanly.
> (Szymel, "Gdy w małym miasteczku zapada sobota")

Thus the Sabbath stands for something at once festive and intimate. Stanisław Vincenz wrote that the experience of the Sabbath is one of the most significant spiritual experiences of the Jewish child, for it combines sublimity with coziness and quiet.[25] To carry Vincenz's thought a bit further, we might say that the word "Sabbath" is synonymous with the words "safe" and "homelike." Understandably, the realm of Jewishness symbolized in the sentimental self-portrait of the Sabbath is the realm of homeliness reminiscent of Gaston Bachelard's description of the "realm of happiness."[26]

In Polish-Jewish literature the Sabbath is not only the symbol of idyllic Jewishness but also of mythical time and the mythical harmony of the world. This traditional idea, found in the Zohar's description of the special Sabbath order of the universe, is likewise present in twentieth-century Jewish thought. In particular, we find it in the works of A. J. Heschel and Erich Fromm. In Polish-Jewish literature, the Sabbath aura of quiet and peace has been glorified by writers as different as the postwar prose writer Artur Sandauer (*Zapiski z martwego miasta* [Notes from a Dead City] [1963]) and the interwar elegist of the Sabbath, Maurycy Szymel. For Anda Eker in "Wiersz o sobocie" the Sabbath world is already the idyllic world-home, described with fondness and delight.

> And I don't know why, suddenly, the world is so quiet.
> Bright and good as our home on the Sabbath.

25. Stanisław Vincenz, *Barwinkowy wianek* (Warsaw, 1956), p. 314.
26. Gaston Bachelard, *La poètique de l'espace* (Paris, 1958), pp. 57–58.

. . . .
I don't know why the world is different
At the Sabbath evening hour: why it is so honest, serene and pure.

In *Głosy w ciemności*, Stryjkowski makes an interesting use of Sabbath symbolism by combining the motifs of paradise and Sabbath happiness to describe the spring orchard seen by Aronek. The impressionistic picture (luminous and throbbing with splashes of white, silver, and pink) is used to evoke delight in the visible world. When it recurs in the protagonist's dream, it becomes his private image of the paradise of a never-ending Sabbath.

> It was quiet and festive. The Sabbath stood among the trees and would not budge. It seemed that mirrors were hung everywhere. Silver light was reflected from them and penetrated the branches. . . . All vibrated with the sun's brightness. Rocked by the wind, the trees rustled softly. They were silently reciting the prayer of the Eighteen Benedictions.[27]

The sense of harmony of the world brought by the Sabbath is a barely remembered childhood experience, for sentimental Sabbaths are largely recollections of past ceremonies and even imaginary rituals rather than a real rite. Frequently the theme of the Sabbath takes on an elegiac aspect and assumes the form of a melancholy contemplation of the bright and mild image of the holiday reconstructed in the knowledge that the former idyll cannot be resurrected. Elegies about the Sabbath evening and poems about the "lost Sabbath" were written in the interwar period by Szymel, Fenster, Eker, and Dresdner. In Polish-Jewish literature the return home, to the small town, to tradition, are returns to ruins. All idyllic dimensions in which the subject-narrator tries to set down new roots are in ruins: the house has collapsed, the small town is devastated, and tradition turns out to be incapable of creating order in the universe. The Sabbath can no longer generate a sense of harmony. The collapsed home is at once the death of the mother and the loss of the sense of the cosmic order experienced in childhood. In Eker's "Wiersz o sobocie," the idyll of the Sabbath remains an image dear to the writer's memory, but irrevocably lost in the distance.

While the Sabbath symbolism provides the means to render the spiritual harmony of the subject-narrator, to convey love, happiness, and delight in the world, it is also used in very different contexts. The motif of the Sambation, the legendary turbulent river that comes

27. Julian Stryjkowski, *Głosy w ciemności* (Warsaw, 1956), p. 131.

to rest only on the Sabbath, is used to reflect the protagonist's inner chaos or the menacing lack of order in the universe. In Daniel Ihr's "Sambation" (1934) the Sambation is the threatening world-river that terrifies the individual. Liberation and peace will come only with death, which is compared to the Sabbath. The archetypal idyll cannot be realized in such a world. This background betrays the therapeutic and escapist character of the efforts to build the sentimental utopia of the "archaic home" of Jewishness.

The latter idea is expressed most clearly in Fenster's "Elegia o sobotnim wieczorze" (Elegy on a Sabbath Evening) (1932). The poem is a request to the mother to tell soothing Sabbath tales. The author-narrator's quest for a soothing utopia is mixed with his inability to believe in it, and his desire to immerse himself in a soothing tradition is accompanied by his realization that such therapy is doomed to failure. The symbol of the Sambation is clearly outlined, and the clash between the past and the present is explicit. The author-narrator has experienced the pain of expulsion from the idyllic world, which is on the point of falling apart.

> . . . tell me why the old and tired Sambation does not rest even on the Sabbath?
> I know that we are the Sambation but why is our path so slippery and steep
> That our bones never know peace. . . .

It is intriguing that the interpretation of Bruno Schulz, the most outstanding interwar Polish prose writer of Jewish origin, works in a similar direction toward destruction of the Sabbath idyll. In Schulz's "Genialna epoka" (The Epoch of Genius) (1937) Szloma, the son of Tobias, paraphrases Genesis: "The first six days of creation were divine and bright. But on the seventh day his hands sensed a foreign web and, horrified, he withdrew his hands from the world although he had enough creative zeal left for many days and nights."[28] Thus, far from being the time of peace and rest or of esthetic contemplation, the Sabbath is the time of alienation, for "on the seventh day" the Creator experienced his creation as alien. Thus the basis of the universe is not harmony and happiness but alienation. Schulz's conclusion completes the total destruction of the idyllic meanings of the Sabbath.

---

28. Bruno Schulz, "Genialna epoka," in Schulz, *Proza*, ed. Artur Sandauer and Jerzy Ficowski (Cracow, 1964), p. 143.

As the case of the Sabbath motif clearly indicates, the image of the world created by writers of the Jewish group is fashioned in a distinct and original language of literary conventions. Their vision of the intimate maternal Sabbath, which enables the child to experience universal order, differs substantially from the cliché of the Sabbath deeply rooted in Polish literary tradition: the monumental masculine ritual invested with national symbolism. This striking difference in interpretation makes it legitimate to question Jan Błoński's denial of a distinctly Jewish literary school in any of the interwar European literatures.

Magdalena M. Opalski

Wiadomości Literackie: Polemics on the Jewish Question, 1924-1939

The first of the 829 issues of *Wiadomości Literackie*, published in interwar Poland under the editorship of Mieczysław Grydzewski, appeared in January 1924.[1] Originally designed to financially secure *Skamander*, yet another of Grydzewski's publishing ventures, *Wiadomości* quickly established itself as the leading journal specializing in cultural and literary matters. Until its career was abruptly halted by the outbreak of World War II, *Wiadomości* was one of the most prestigious cultural institutions in interwar Poland. The journal's own literary prizes—Nagroda *Wiadomości Literackich*, established in 1934 and soon followed by Nagroda Czytelników *Wiadomości*—successfully competed with the prizes awarded by the official Polska Akademia Literatury (Polish Academy of Literature). The privileged status of *Wiadomości*, which for almost a decade remained Poland's only literary journal with a nationwide circulation, was also illustrated by its role as ambassador of Polish *belles lettres* abroad. *Wiadomości*'s French-language subsidiary, *La Pologne littéraire*, which was published with the financial assistance of the Ministry of Foreign Affairs, served to promote Polish culture in the West.

Wiadomości quickly outgrew its French prototype, *Les nouvelles littéraires*, evolving from a narrowly literary journal into a periodical covering a wide range of cultural, social, and political issues, both domestic and international. However, its monopoly of the literary scene—characteristic of the 1920s—came to an end in the following decade. In the 1930s Grydzewski's weekly faced competition from

1. Mieczysław Grydzewski (1894–1970) was the editor of *Pro Arte et Studio, Skamander* (a journal devoted to modern poetry, 1920–39), and *Wiadomości Literackie* (1924–39). After World War II he published in London *Wiadomości Polskie*, later renamed *Wiadomości*.

new cultural and literary journals such as the government-backed *Pion*, the Endecja's *Prosto z mostu*, and the church-sponsored *Kultura*. Their emergence between 1933 and 1936 reflected the growing demand for information on cultural matters, a trend exemplified by the greater attention now paid by the Catholic church to the specific needs of its intellectual elite. The new journals, which explicitly aimed at undermining *Wiadomości*'s influence and offsetting its liberalism,[2] also echoed the growing political radicalization of the Polish press. Cultural matters were no longer excluded from the political warfare in which the Jewish Question occupied a central place.

In other words, the shift to the right in Polish politics in the 1930s, a trend clearly encouraged by political developments in Germany, had a profound effect on *Wiadomości*'s standing. In those years *Wiadomości* became the target of massive attacks, mainly from the rightist and church-controlled press. This trend coincided with the erosion of the support the journal traditionally enjoyed in the ruling Sanacja camp. Particularly pronounced in the years following Józef Piłsudski's *coup* of 1926, this support was seriously undermined during the Brześć Purges, in which *Wiadomości* broke with its custom and took a position against the government. The publication of *La Pologne littéraire* was discontinued in 1936 when governmental subsidies were withdrawn. In this deteriorating political climate *Wiadomości*, a journal that had been characterized by the absence of a clear-cut political line, became more articulate in its opposition to fascism.

Despite its importance to Poland's intellectual elite and the impressive panoply of intellectual stars among its contributors, *Wiadomości* expressed the views of a fairly narrow stratum of the Polish intelligentsia. In the fifteen years of the journal's existence, its readership did not widen significantly. Andrzej Paczkowski appears to be correct in linking this narrowness of *Wiadomości*'s social basis— best illustrated by the weekly's circulation, which rarely exceeded ten thousand—with its relatively unorthodox cultural and political views as compared to the views of most of the Polish intelligentsia. Describing *Wiadomości* as the product of a "specific intellectual formation whose liberalism was deeply rooted in the philosophical

2. Andrzej Paczkowski, *Prasa polska, 1918–1938* (Warsaw, 1980), p. 263. See also Wiktor Weintraub, "O redaktorze *Wiadomości Literackich*," in *Książka o Grydzewskim, Wiadomości* (London, 1971), p. 321.

tradition of the Enlightenment," Paczkowski also takes note of *Wiadomości's* image as the organ of "free-masons, Jews, and crypto-bolsheviks."[3]

In fact, *Wiadomości's* image as a "Jewish" institution, serving the specific needs of the most "Judaized" strata of the Polish intelligentsia, was not limited to groups politically opposed to the weekly. This widespread perception, well illustrated by *Wiadomości's* popular nickname "Jado Mośki Literackie" (Here Come the Literary Moshes), was substantiated by the prominent role of assimilated Jews among *Wiadomości's* editors and regular contributors. Among them were Mieczysław Grydzewski, Antoni Borman (the journal's coeditor and financial manager), Julian Tuwim, Józef Wittlin, Antoni Słonimski, Marian Hemar, Bruno Schulz, Stefan Eiger-Napierski, Emil Breiter, and Henryk Adler—to mention only the most obvious. Many Polish nationalists perceived *Wiadomości* as a symbol of the Jewish "infiltration" of Polish culture, a process over which they grew increasingly alarmed. This concern was, of course, hardly a new phenomenon. The 1921 press campaign, aimed at splitting the poets' circle Skamander along ethnic lines, provides a telling early example of this trend.[4] As the issue of "infiltration" continued to gain visibility in the following years, the debate became increasingly tainted by racism.

On the one hand, *Wiadomości* responded to these perceptions by vigorously defending the assimilated Jews' right to participate fully in Polish culture. Although hardly generous in granting them certificates of satisfactory Polonization, *Wiadomości* opposed ideologies that questioned the Jews' ability to assimilate. On the other hand, anxious to avoid accusations of a pro-Jewish bias, *Wiadomości* eagerly demonstrated its "evenhandedness" in dealing with the broader Jewish Question in Poland. It remained open to both pro- and anti-Jewish views, carefully balancing the former with the voices of such notorious antisemites as Adolf Nowaczyński, who in 1939 exhorted his readers to burn all books written by Jews.[5] Grydzewski's own

3. Paczkowski, *Prasa polska*, p. 260.

4. Alina Kowalczykowa, *Liryki Słonimskiego, 1918–1935*, vol. 20 of *Historia i teoria literatury* (Warsaw, 1967), p. 159. An open letter published in *Kurjer Polski* 72 (1921) and signed by ten poets associated with the group protested: "Przeciwstawianie poetów *Skamandra* aryjczyków kolegom ich pochodzenia żydowskiego [które] przybierać zaczyna charakter prowokacji" (Playing the Jewish and non-Jewish poets of *Skamander* against each other increasingly assumes the form of provocation).

5. Joseph Marcus, *Social and Political History of the Jews in Poland, 1918–1939* (New

stand on Jewish issues was ambiguous and evasive.[6] Although he stubbornly downplayed the importance of antisemitism—treating it as a painful but peripheral issue with no direct impact on the journal—*Wiadomości*'s handling of Jewish matters hardly supports its claim to complete "detachment." On the contrary, its own vulnerability to antisemitism cast a deep shadow over the journal's treatment of the Jewish Question in Poland.

The statement of *Wiadomości*'s goals published in its first issue declared the journal's artistic and political neutrality. The editors stressed their dedication to pluralism and expressed the desire that *Wiadomości* become the forum for an open exchange of views. They also emphasized their universalist understanding of a European culture rooted in an optimistic view of social evolution and—in the name of the underlying idea of progress—declared war on "parochialism," backwardness, and narrow-minded particularism. The editors did not, of course, specify the position of various manifestations of Jewish culture on the scale between "universalism" and "parochialism."[7] This pattern, however, can be easily observed by studying *Wiadomości*'s editorial practices.

The journal's coverage of the Jewish contribution to various non-Jewish cultures was extensive. *Wiadomości*'s readers were well acquainted with men of letters and artists such as Isaac Babel, H. N. Bialik, Max Brod, Marc Chagall, Lion Feuchtwanger, Joseph Roth, Baruch Spinoza, and Israel Zangwill. Grydzewski's weekly took note of the prominent role that Jewish authors played in the birth of Soviet literature. It was the first Polish journal to promote Franz Kafka, a writer who enjoyed popularity among Poland's Jewish in-

---

York, 1983), p. 418. Among antisemitic writers frequently appearing in *Wiadomości* also were Andrzej Niemojewski, Aleksander Świętochowski, Józef Weyssenhoff, and Konstanty Hubert Rostworowski, who initiated the campaign against "Marranos" of Polish literature.

6. The portrait of Grydzewski that emerges from the more than sixty essays devoted to his memory is that of an ardent Polish nationalist with some antisemitic leanings. Proud to be called *faktor literatury polskiej* (a factor of Polish literature), he denied that the Jews were a separate nation. A former director of the Instytut Badań Spraw Narodowościowych (Institute for Research on Nationalities' Affairs) remembers his giving up membership in a discussion club in protest against extending an invitation to a lecturer who defended the idea that Jews *were* a separate nation. Stanisław Paprocki, "Mieczysław Grydzewski we wspomnieniach kolegi uniwersyteckiego," *Książka o Grydzewskim*, pp. 205–6, 69–70, see also pp. 121, 137–38, 358.

7. "Od redakcji," *Wiadomości Literackie* (hereafter *WL*), January 6, 1924, no. 1, p. 1.

telligentsia while remaining virtually unknown to Polish readers.[8] *Wiadomości*'s recognition of the "universalism" of distinctly Jewish authors depended on the language in which they wrote (Yiddish being a serious disadvantage), their attitude toward tradition, and the place of non-Jewish topics in their work. The journal's "deparochialization" of Jewish authors was best illustrated by its sympathetic profile of Shaul Tchernichowsky, who was introduced as "a Hebrew poet and Hellenist." Likewise, a Polish anthology of Yiddish-language writers was reviewed under the characteristic title "Prowincja i nacjonalizm" (Provincialism and Nationalism). Interestingly, a certain degree of "universalism" characterized the cultural life of Jewish immigrants to Palestine, to which *Wiadomości* devoted a fair amount of attention. Artur Sandauer is, of course, correct in pointing to a strong emphasis on the settlers' Polish patriotism and their attachment to Polish culture.[9] Nevertheless, emigration to Palestine appeared to move the Jews closer to the "universalist" end of the scale.

Wiadomości's concept of "universalism" was, however, too narrow to include the Yiddish-language culture of the overwhelming majority of Polish Jews. Although *Wiadomości* sporadically reviewed Polish translations of Yiddish-language authors,[10] published short articles taking note of such cultural phenomena as the Vilna Yiddish theater,[11] Sholem Asch,[12] and "Jewish literature in Poland," and occasionally discussed publications on the Jewish Question in Poland, the space devoted to the cultural life of Polish Jews was an insignificant fraction of *Wiadomości*'s impressively detailed and worldwide coverage of cultural matters. Its commitment to Yiddish-

8. Eugenia Prokopówna, "Kafka w oczach dwudziestolecia," *Pamiętnik Literacki* 76, no. 4 (1985): 89–132.

9. Henryk Adler, "U poety żydowskiego—hellenisty," *WL*, July 4, 1926, no. 27, p. 2; Andrzej Stawar, "Prowincja i nacjonalizm," *WL*, July 12, 1925, no. 28, p. 4; Artur Sandauer, *O sytuacji pisarza polskiego pochodzenia żydowskiego w XX wieku* (Warsaw, 1982), p. 32. See also Henryk Adler's interview with Natan Bistrycki, "Wizyty pisarzy obcych: Prozaik hebrajski," *WL*, April 10, 1927, no. 15, p. 2.

10. For example, *Wiadomości* reviewed Sholem Asch's *Motke Ganef, WL*, May 10, 1925, no. 19, p. 4; Urke Nachalnik's *Żywot własny przestępcy, WL*, March 12, 1933, no. 2, p. 4; I. J. Singer's *Josie Kalb, WL*, February 4, 1934, no. 5, p. 3; the previously mentioned Polish anthology of Yiddish-language writers, *WL*, July 12, 1925, no. 28, p. 4; and a few other works.

11. Zygmunt Tonecki, "Teatr żydowski w Polsce," *WL*, August 23, 1933, no. 33, p. 3.

12. Sholem Asch's status as *Wiadomości*'s most frequently and most positively discussed Yiddish-language writer seems to be partially a result of his courtship of the Christian readership.

language culture could not compare with the space, energy, and talent it devoted to denouncing—in the name of "universal" values—the anachronistic "parochialism" and cultural emptiness of ghetto life.

The treatment of the latter theme provides the best illustration of *Wiadomości's* indebtedness to the traditions of Positivism and the Enlightenment. Its criticism of Jewish society was first initiated by Antoni Słonimski's belligerent article "O drażliwości Żydów" (On Jewish Oversensitivity). Published in 1924, the article found a resounding echo in both the Jewish and Polish press and helped consolidate Słonimski's status as the *bête noire* of the former.[13] Its fame survived World War II and provided Władysław Gomułka with anti-Jewish arguments in his campaign against "revisionists and Zionists" in 1968.[14] The "Jewish" themes outlined in the article subsequently became a *spécialité de la maison* of Słonimski's "Kronika tygodniowa" (Weekly Chronicle)—yet another influential institution within *Wiadomości*—and remained prominent on its agenda until the outbreak of World War II. Słonimski later claimed that he stopped harassing the beleaguered Jewish community in the late 1930s.[15] In contrast to earlier writings on Słonimski, which failed critically to examine this contention, a recent study of "Kronika tygodniowa" describes the change in Słonimski's attitude as a matter of tone and frequency rather than substance. It also emphasizes the pride that Słonimski—himself under heavy fire from Polish nationalists—took in exercising his right to criticize Jews "objectively," no matter what the historical circumstances.[16]

"O drażliwości Żydów" accused the Jewish community of being oversensitive to criticism, a response that Słonimski saw as rooted in the Jews' self-image as the Chosen People. Why did they make

13. Antoni Słonimski, "O drażliwości Żydów," *WL*, August 31, 1924, no. 35, p. 3; Słonimski, "Prasa żydowska o wybryku *Wiadomości Literackich*," *Nasz Przegląd*, 1924, no. 251.

14. Władysław Gomułka, "Przemówienie do aktywu warszawskiego," quoted in Yisrael Gutman, *The Jews of Poland after World War II* (Jerusalem, 1985), pp. 155–57.

15. This claim is repeated in a number of places in Antoni Słonimski, *Alfabet wspomnień* (Warsaw, 1975).

16. Marek Pytasz, "Kwestia żydowska i jej konteksty w 'Kronikach tygodniowych' Antoniego Słonimskiego," in *Studia skamandryckie i inne* (Katowice, 1985), p. 41. In November 1938 Słonimski wrote: "Wiem, że w prasie żydowskiej powstanie mała wrzawa, że w 'takiej chwili' sprzymierzam się z czarnym antysemityzmem, ale ja po prostu nie zdradzam mojego przymierza z ludźmi walczącymi o wolność sumienia" (I know the Jewish press will raise hell that at "such a moment" I ally myself with the black antisemitism, but I am not giving up an alliance with those who struggle for freedom of conscience). "Kronika tygodniowa," *WL*, November 6, 1938, no. 46, p. 7.

so much fuss about Kazimierz Wierzyński's reference to a theater "stuffed with horrible Jews" or Tuwim's poem "Srulki," he wondered. Since they were unable to accept even the most legitimate criticism, the Jews, "the world's most chauvinist nation," had no moral right to complain about Polish nationalism. It would be foolish, Słonimski argued, to dismiss as entirely unfounded the criticism of Jewish society inherent in the general dislike of Jews. Słonimski's own receptiveness to antisemitic clichés was evident in his depiction of Jewish society as morally degenerate, culturally unproductive, and totally alienated from "the most noble spiritual achievements of mankind."[17]

On the other hand, Słonimski denounced the Polonization of some strata of the Jewish intelligentsia as superficial, hypocritical, and ethically questionable.[18] In view of these Jewish shortcomings, the anti-Jewish mood of some Poles was hardly surprising. Antisemitism was an integral element of social reality in Poland, and as such was part of a "package deal." Those oversensitive Jews who could not tolerate the criticism of their non-Jewish surroundings faced a "take-it-or-leave-it" alternative. The choice was between coming to terms with antisemitism in Poland or voluntarily emigrating to Palestine. Słonimski's recipe for the solution of the Jewish Question in Poland—as outlined in "O drażliwości Żydów—remained basically unchanged until 1939.[19]

Initiated by Słonimski, *Wiadomości*'s criticism of traditional Jewish society culminated in Wanda Melcer's series on Jewish life in Warsaw. Despite fierce opposition from Jewish quarters, Grydzewski ran the articles with the series title "Czarny ląd—Warszawa" (The Dark Continent—Warsaw) in 1934 and 1935. Written in the form of reports from a journey to an exotic land, Melcer's articles traced the successive stages in the life of ghetto dwellers, with Jews portrayed as victims of their own oppressive tradition. In her reports, Jewish Warsaw of the 1930s—desperately poor, backward, and intolerant—appeared to be a "continent" darker and more savage than the unexplored heart of Africa to which the series' title alluded.[20] In

---

17. Słonimski, "O drażliwości Żydów," p. 3.

18. Słonimski's *Murzyn warszawski* (The Warsaw Negro), a box-office hit of the 1920s, generated a lively debate on this issue. Joanna Godlewska, "Komedie Słonimskiego a prasa," pt. 3, *Dialog*, 1982, no. 5, pp. 100–106. *Murzyn warszawski* was originally published by Grydzewski in *Skamander.*

19. Słonimski, "O drażliwości Żydów," p. 3; Pytasz, "Kwestia żydowska," p. 44.

20. Wanda Melcer, "Czarny ląd—Warszawa": "Dziecko żydowskie rozpoczyna

1936, shortly before the Przytyk pogrom, *Wiadomości* found it appropriate to reaffirm its full support of Melcer by welcoming the book edition of *Czarny ląd*. Published on the journal's first page, the review reiterated *Wiadomości*'s support for such enlightened measures against Jewish "obscurantism" as the proposed ban on ritual slaughter. It is hardly surprising that for Samuel Hirszhorn, who reviewed Melcer's book for the Jewish press, *Czarny ląd* exemplified the process of a topical and ideological "specialization" in the Polish criticism of Jews. While the most reactionary circles attacked the Jews' drive toward modern education and culture, Hirszhorn wrote, the liberals campaigned against the allegedly incurable backwardness of Jewish society.[21]

Traditional Jewish culture was not alone, however, in mocking *Wiadomości*'s enlightened standards of "universalism." In fact, the concept of a Polish-language Jewish culture taking shape in interwar Poland was equally as incompatible with *Wiadomości*'s understanding of universalism. While *Wiadomości* rarely took note of what it referred to as the "prasa żargonowa" (jargon press; i.e., Yiddish-language press), Grydzewski's journal became a persistent irritant to the Jewish press, which—as Słonimski ironically observed in "O drażliwości Żydów"—depended on the Polish language to spread Jewish nationalism. The journal's polemics with the Polish-Jewish press reached a peak of intensity in 1934–36, when several of *Wiadomości*'s contributors joined the discussion on the Jewish cultural renewal initiated by Roman Brandstaetter.[22] Brandstaetter was not,

ziemską wędrówke," *WL*, April 8, 1934, no. 14, p. 1; "Młodzieniec żydowski wstępuje w świat," *WL*, June 3, 1934, no. 22, p. 2; "W mykwie i pod baldachimem," *WL*, September 30, 1934, no. 40, p. 1; "Żona i matka," *WL*, January 27, 1935, no. 4, p. 2; "Business Is Business," *WL*, April 7, 1935, no. 14, p. 2; "Religia i befsztyk," *WL*, April 14, 1935, no. 15, p. 2; "Modlitwa i umieranie," *WL*, September 8, 1935, no. 36, p. 2. The series was published in book form as *Czarny ląd—Warszawa* (Warsaw, 1936). Melcer's introduction to the book discusses the Jews' massive and overwhelmingly negative response to her reports in *Wiadomości*, which Grydzewski chose to ignore.

21. Stanisław Rogoż, "Sprawy żydowskie," *WL*, March 1, 1936, no. 9, p. 1; S. H. [Samuel Hirszhorn], review of *Czarny ląd—Warszawa*, by Wanda Melcer, in *Nasz Przeglad*, 1934, no. 278. See also Antoni Słonimski, "Kronika tygodniowa," *WL*, March 8, 1936, no. 10, p. 7; Słonimski, "Kronika tygodniowa," *WL*, March 15, 1936, no. 11, p. 7.

22. Słonimski, "O drażliwości Żydów," p. 3; Roman Brandstaetter, "Pluję! Deszcz pada!" *Opinja*, 1935, no. 6; Brandstaetter, "Popas w Mechesówce," *Nasza Opinja*, 1935, no. 5; Brandstaetter, "Narodowi hemar-frodyci," *Nasza Opinja*, 1935, no. 20, p. 8. See also Brandstaetter, "Kilka słów o człowieku, który ułatwił sobie życie: Na marginesie Antoniego Słonimskiego *Wierszy zebranych*," *Opinja*, 1933, no. 17, p. 6. I am indebted to Eugenia Prokopówna for bringing these articles to my attention.

however, concerned about "infiltrating," "spoiling," or even contributing to Polish culture. He was attempting to define a concept of Polish-language Jewish culture and to work out a corresponding literary program. Responding to this initiative, *Wiadomości* did not hesitate to describe it as "pathological," and Brandstaetter himself as a racist and "Jewish Nazi." Dismissing his concept of Jewish culture as the product of a fascist mentality—characteristic of equally distasteful German, Polish, or Jewish nationalisms—"Kronika tygodniowa" accused Brandstaetter of depriving the Jews of the blessings of the European tradition.[23]

Apart from engaging in polemical exchanges, the journal also addressed the Polish-Jewish press and its readers in a less direct way. They were often the specific target of *Wiadomości*'s criticism of Jewish assimilation. The journal delighted in ridiculing the Polish-language works produced in these circles by putting together lists of horrible "Yiddishisms" and making fun of their narrowly nationalistic ideas. Such writings were frequently satirized in *Wiadomości*'s delightful section devoted to the worst book of the month, in Tuwim's satirical "Camera obscura," and even in serious book reviews.[24]

The discussion of Brandstaetter's concept of Jewish culture was interesting from yet another point of view. It clearly revealed the importance of *Wiadomości* to the Polish-Jewish press's quest for its own cultural profile. The attitudes of Jewish participants toward *Wiadomości* in that discussion played a significant role in the polemical exchange. Their unhappiness with the way in which *Wiadomości*'s Jewish "universalists" approached the Jewish Question in Poland was coupled with a criticism of those Jews who, as a Polish writer put it, "deserted the Bible for *Wiadomości Literackie*."[25] Julian Tuwim wrote, not without satirical overtones:

23. Antoni Słonimski, "Kronika tygodniowa," *WL*, May 10, 1936, no. 20, p. 5; Słonimski, "Kronika tygodniowa," July 12, 1936, no. 30, p. 5; Stanisław Rogoż, "Patologiczna publicystyka," *WL*, July 19, 1936, no. 31, p. 6. At the same time, in a conciliatory move, *Wiadomości* positively reviewed Brandstaetter's poem "Jerozolima światła i mroku" (Jerusalem of Light and Darkness), which appeared in *W drodze*. See K. W. Zawodziński, "Poeci Eretz Izraelu i ghetta," *WL*, June 14, 1936, no. 26, p. 4.

24. See, for example, "Quidam" [W. Weintraub], review of *Polacy-chrześcijanie pochodzenia żydowskiego*, by Mateusz Mieses, *WL*, August 14, 1938, no. 35, p. 6.

25. Roman Brandstaetter, "Palestyna potem i krwią płynąca: Kartki z okrętowego dziennika," *Opinja*, 1935, no. 25; Mojżesz Kanfer, "Fałszerz w potrzasku," *Nowy Dziennik*, 1934, no. 209. The formulation by Zygmunt Kubiak—"Żydzi którzy porzucili Biblię dla *Wiadomości Literackich*"—has been quoted to me by Aleksander Leyfell.

Panna Mimosenduft z Tarnowa
Omdlewające ma spojrzenie
I głośno mówi z panem Pimplem
O *Wiadomościach Literackich*.[26]

Miss Mimosenduft from Tarnów
Looks as if she were fainting
And loudly discusses with Mr. Pimple
Wiadomości Literackie.

In fact, *Wiadomości* enjoyed a substantial Jewish readership, and Grydzewski was understandably reluctant to acknowledge its importance to the journal. Moreover, there was no clear dividing line between the Jewish milieu that crystallized around the journal and the readers of the *narodowożydowska* (national-Jewish) press in the Polish language. As Eugenia Prokopówna has observed, the gray zone between the two was further obscured by a few writers and critics who, like Mieczysław Braun, Izydor Berman, Roman Brandstaetter, Artur Prędzki, Aleksander Dan, and Mieczysław Jastrun, published in both *Wiadomości* and the Polish-Jewish press.[27] The Polish-Jewish press's obsessive preoccupation with *Wiadomości* did not result in any consistent "strategy." Mojżesz Kanfer's article "Czy *Wiadomości Literackie* są pismem żydowskim?" (Is *Wiadomości Literackie* a Jewish Journal?) is hardly exceptional in the Polish-Jewish press in asking—and failing to offer an unequivocal answer to—this question. Kanfer's openly expressed resentment of *Wiadomości*'s treatment of Jewish matters (and Jewish cultural achievements in particular) is moderated by concern about the antisemitic attacks against *Wiadomości*, and a clear—albeit selective—feeling of cultural affinity with the journal.[28] On the whole, Miss Mimosenduft and her Jewish interlocutor, as well as the broader category of "Mośki literackie," emerge from the Brandstaetter debate as the object of ideological competition between the two circles of Polish-speaking Jewish intelligentsia.

Wiadomości's position with respect to the Brandstaetter discussion

26. Julian Tuwim, "Pierwsza kolacja w pensjonacie," in Tuwim, *Dzieła*, vol. 3 (Warsaw, 1958), p. 17.
27. Eugenia Prokopówna, private communication to author.
28. Mojżesz Kanfer, "Czy *Wiadomości Literackie* są pismem żydowskim?" *Nowy Dziennik*, August 1932, no. 219, p. 9. See also W. Berkelhammer, "Nekrolog dla panny Racheli," *Nowy Dziennik*, October 10, 1925, no. 226, p. 7; and the discussion "Kultura polska a Żydzi" in *Przegląd Poranny*: Karol Irzykowski, "Żyd to jest Polak z rezerwą," August 12, 1937, no. 222, p. 8; Irzykowski, "Udział Żydów w literaturze polskiej," August 14, 1937, no. 224, p. 8.

sheds more light on the journal's understanding of "evenhanded-ness." Calling Brandstaetter a "fascist" was more than a slip of the tongue. Słonimski's accusation echoed *Wiadomości*'s reluctance to acknowledge a qualitative difference between Jewish, German, and right-wing Polish nationalisms. Until World War II the theme of their structural similarity continued to surface in the context of the dis-cussion of Jewish separatism, providing a justification for *Wiado-mości*'s unwillingness to give in to Jewish calls for restraint in criticizing Jewish society. By the end of 1938, *Wiadomości* gave the following response to those voices, which pointed to the extraor-dinary political circumstances:

> Luckily Jewish chauvinism does not have the use of prison cells. Like patients in a hospital, the Jews provide us today with an opportunity clinically to examine the gangrene caused by their greed for power, the blindness spreading from the rabbinates, the cramps of their tribal megalomania, the blood clots of racial hatred and their gold fever. Defying the (thank God toothless) anger of would-be Jewish censors, we should call the political leaders of the Jews by the names they deserve to be called—be they the *Führers* of hundreds of thousands—and denounce their risky political games. Arriving at a diagnosis of the disease would benefit all of us. The Jews serve today as a modern laboratory and in this sense play a messianic role. Whoever considers himself a member of the greater human family should take advan-tage—wherever possible—of the freedom of speech.[29]

Indeed, Grydzewski seized every opportunity to emphasize the journal's equal distaste for all "militant nationalisms." A front-page article, "Norwid a Żydzi" (Norwid and the Jews), provides another typical example of this approach. The article appeared in response to a press campaign by Polish nationalists who, on the occasion of the fiftieth anniversary of Cyprian Norwid's death, presented the poet as a Jew-hater and precursor of the antisemitic movement. At the same time, however, the article attacked *Nasz Przegląd* for trying to promote the image of Norwid as a Jew-lover and accused it of dishonestly manipulating the quotations from his work. *Wiadomości*'s own account of Norwid's attitude toward Jews characteristically fo-cused on the broader context in which the Jewish Question ap-peared in Norwid's work. Although the article was, as usual, evasive on the issue of his pro- or anti-Jewish bias, the evidence it presented supported the nationalist view rather than the interpretation offered

29. Mariusz Dawn [M. Morska], "Londyn-Grochów-Częstoniew: Hitler dobrze zasłużył się Żydom," *WL*, November 6, 1938, no. 46, p. 4.

by *Nasz Przegląd*. Similarly, *Wiadomości* defended the authenticity of the legend surrounding Berek Joselewicz, the Jewish hero of the Kościuszko Uprising. The Endeks and the Zionists (the latter represented by Nathan Michael Gelber) were equally blamed for attempting to downplay this symbol of Polish patriotism.[30]

"Evenhandedness" also marked Ksawery Pruszyński's coverage of the Przytyk trial. Responsibility for the pogrom was symmetrically divided between two unenlightened and primitive groups suffering from comparable economic hardships. Although Pruszyński also blamed the government for its failure to ease the latter, he passed over in silence the authorities' handling of the trial and by and large ignored the defensive nature of Jewish involvement in the riots.[31] *Wiadomości's* search for a "balanced" approach to Poland's Jewish Question was not facilitated by the political situation, which grew increasingly "unsymmetrical" during the 1930s.

In general, Grydzewski's journal was marked by a striking scarcity of information on Poland's "Jewish" politics and rarely provided more than a weak echo of political developments. It is true that, apart from the above-mentioned article by Pruszyński, the Przytyk pogrom was briefly discussed in "Kronika tygodniowa." Similarly, the article on the anti-Jewish university riots in Vilna in 1936 was not alone in taking note of and condemning anti-Jewish violence. Beside Melcer's *Czarny ląd*, the parliamentary debate on ritual slaughter was echoed by a delightful caricature of Mrs. Prystor portrayed as a kosher meat vendor. In 1938 *Wiadomości* devoted some attention to the Zbąszyn affair, in which thirty thousand Jews deported by Nazi Germany were detained at Zbąszyn, and reviewed press reactions to the beating of Father Puder by Polish nationalists. Finally, the responses to *Wiadomości's* 1937 questionnaire on antisemitism contained references to the question of Jewish loyalties during the Polish-Soviet War of 1920 and the heatedly debated issue of *numerus clausus*.[32] On the whole, however, in its coverage of Po-

30. M. H. Piątkowski, "Norwid a Żydzi," *WL*, September 15, 1933, no. 39, p. 1; Ernest Łuniński, "Legenda o Berku," *WL*, November 28, 1926, no. 48, p. 1.

31. Ksawery Pruszyński, "Podróż po Polsce: Przytyk i stragan," *WL*, July 12, 1936, no. 30, p. 1.

32. Antoni Słonimski, "Kronika tygodniowa," *WL*, June 28, 1936, no. 28, p. 5; Jerzy Wyszomirski, "List z Wilna [December 1936]" *WL*, January 16, 1937, no. 3, p. 7; "Jam" [Mieczysław Grydzewski], "Przegląd prasy: Napad na księdza Pudra," *WL*, July 17, 1938, no. 30, p. 7; K. W. Zawodziński, "Apel do serca i rozumu," *WL*, May 2, 1937, no. 19, p. 2. The questionnaire was titled "Pisarze polscy w kwestii żydowskiej" (Polish Writers and the Jewish Question).

land's policy toward its Jewish minority, *Wiadomości* remained uncharacteristically docile and faithful to its initial promise of political neutrality.

Although frequently ambiguous in its treatment of Jewish matters, *Wiadomości* opposed antisemitism on its own terms. Its involvement in the defense of the Jews can be divided into three separate but interrelated themes.

The first theme was represented by *Wiadomości*'s continuous harassment of the "nationalist" press. Publishing some of Poland's best satirical authors, the journal pitilessly ridiculed the anti-Jewish program of the Right. It denounced its irrationality, anti-Christian character, and intellectual clumsiness. At the same time, the use of satire as the main polemical weapon enabled *Wiadomości* to downgrade the importance of the issue. Until 1933 *Wiadomości*'s treatment of the Nazi movement in Germany was marked by a similar refusal to discuss the problem "seriously."[33] Słonimski was not alone among *Wiadomości*'s contributors in considering the latter too "absurd" to represent a real threat. The most frequent target of *Wiadomości*'s attacks was the Endecja's own "Jewish connection." The journal delighted in tracing and exposing the nationalist press's ideologically embarrassing dependence on Jewish advertising. Similarly, it eagerly researched the Jewish ancestry of prominent Endek leaders. *Wiadomości*'s half-Jewish arch-enemy, Stanisław Piasecki of *Prosto z mostu* ("Stasiek prosto spod mostu," as Słonimski called him), was the favorite target of its mockery. Among the funniest products of this brand of investigative journalism was a long report entitled "Czy malarz Józef Buchbinder był Żydem?" (Was the Painter Józef Buchbinder a Jew?). Written in the form of a classical detective story, the report not only revealed the Jewish roots of the Wasiutyński family but, in great detail, documented the family's desperate efforts to get rid of its Jewish connection.[34]

This genealogical "research," however, was one of the many ways in which Grydzewski approached a broader theme. *Wiadomości* consistently reminded its readers of the presence of a Jewish component

33. Kowalczykowa, *Liryki Słonimskiego*, pp. 189–91.

34. M. S. ["Mędrzec Syjonu," a pseudonym meaning Wise Man of Zion], "Żydowska bezczelność," *WL*, May 31, 1936, no. 24, p. 5; Antoni Słonimski, "Kronika tygodniowa," *WL*, July 9, 1939, no. 18, p. 5; Słonimski, "Kronika tygodniowa," *WL*, July 17, 1939, no. 30, p. 5; M. G. [Mieczysław Grydzewski], "Czy malarz Józef Buchbinder był Żydem?" *WL*, May 23, 1937, no. 22, pp. 6–7.

within the fabric of Polish society and culture. By doing so the journal targeted one of Endecja's basic myths: the myth of "genuine Polishness" in both its racial and cultural dimensions. In the final analysis, investigating the Jewish origins of Mr. Buchbinder served a purpose similar to that of Tadeusz Boy-Żeleński's essays on Adam Mickiewicz, which subsequently gained a lasting place in Polish literary scholarship. The essays, printed in *Wiadomości* for several years in a row, focused on the multicultural dimension of Poland's greatest romantic poet (including the Jewish influence) and his unorthodox religious concepts.[35]

The second "pro-Jewish" theme was *Wiadomości's* defense of selected aspects of the Jewish heritage as an integral part of the broader "universal" tradition. While denouncing the "parochialism" of the Eastern European ghetto, *Wiadomości* repeatedly engaged in polemics with theories denying—or at best minimizing—the Judaic roots of Christian civilization. One of them was generated by Tadeusz Zieliński's study on Judaism, Hellenism, and Christianity. In an attempt to prove the Hellenic origins of Christianity and to minimize its Judaic component, Zieliński constructed an idealized mode of the former while systematically denigrating the latter. In a discussion that was printed in several issues, Zieliński's views were challenged by Paweł Hulka-Laskowski, one of the most consistent defenders of the Jews in *Wiadomości*.[36] An exchange between Henryk Ułaszyn and his "genuinely Polish" opponents on the Christian roots of antisemitism served a similar purpose.[37]

The last of the three themes focused on racism and German-style state-sponsored antisemitism. Unlike the earlier satirical approach to fascism, this theme surfaced only after 1933 and tended to be deadly serious. It concentrated primarily on Germany and generally avoided tracing parallels between the German and Polish varieties

35. Tadeusz Boy-Żeleński's essays, which appeared in *WL*, 1929–30, were published as *O Mickiewiczu* (Warsaw, 1949).

36. Tadeusz Zieliński, *Hellenizm a Judaizm* (Warsaw, 1927); and the polemic: Ignacy Wieniewski, "Sąd nad judaizmem," *WL*, September 18, 1927, no. 48, p. 3; Paweł Hulka-Laskowski, "Nieprawidłowości proceduralne w sądzie nad judaizmem," *WL*, October 2, 1927, no. 40, p. 2; Wieniewski, "Cios w próżnię," *WL*, October 16, 1927, no. 42, p. 3; Hulka-Laskowski, "Dyskusja, nie dysputa," *WL*, November 13, 1927, no. 46, p. 3; Wieniewski, "Dalsza charakterystyka judaizmu," *WL*, March 11, 1928, no. 11, p. 3.

37. Henryk Ułaszyn, "Chrześcijanizm a Żydzi," *WL*, January 10, 1932, no. 2, p. 3; "Prenumerator" [Subscriber], "O stosunek do Żydów," *WL*, February 7, 1932, no. 6, p. 6; Ułaszyn, "Jeszcze z powodu artykułu 'Chrześcijanizm a Żydzi,'" *WL*, March 12, 1932, no. 11.

of antisemitism. In the 1930s *Wiadomości* published several series of firsthand accounts of the Jews' situation in Adolf Hitler's Germany. Reporting on Jewish emigration, *Wiadomości* realistically depicted the tragic fate of those trying to escape.[38] Mariusz Dawn's enthusiastic report on youth undergoing agricultural training before emigrating to Palestine presented their efforts as the noblest of Jewish responses to Hitler.[39] Finally, on the philosophical level, *Wiadomości* confronted various racist ideologies and patiently, one by one, denounced their arguments as dangerous intellectual nonsense. Its "Konkurs rasistowski" mocked the widespread ethnic stereotypes.[40] The aspect of antisemitism most opposed by *Wiadomości* was "psychological" racism and corresponding concepts of the Jewish role in non-Jewish cultures. The journal's emphasis on this particular ideology overshadowed many other dimensions of the problem. In its polemical zeal *Wiadomości* went so far as to praise Stanisław Cat-Mackiewicz, editor of Vilna's *Słowo*, for his rejection of "psychological antisemitism" in favor of the "consistent" Hitlerite understanding of race.[41] However, the 1937 questionnaire on antisemitism, which devoted more attention to the specifically Polish aspects of the situation, was conducted with the usual evenhandedness. In addition to the voices that defended the Jewish contribution to Polish culture (Andrzej Stawar, Ksawery Pruszyński, Józef Łobodowski, Paweł Hulka-Laskowski), other voices emphasized the "organic" nature of Polish-Jewish antagonism (Aleksander Świętochowski) and defended *numerus clausus* as a temporary necessity (K. W. Zawodziński).[42]

38. Antoni Sobański, "W Niemczech po przewrocie: Żydzi a kultura," *WL*, July 2, 1933, no. 29, p. 3; Sobański, "W Niemczech po przewrocie: Kwestia żydowska," *WL*, July 16, 1933, no. 31, p. 2; Marjusz Dawn [M. Morska], "Wrażenia z Anglii: Immigracja Żydów do Imperjum," *WL*, June 18, 1939, no. 26, p. 3; Dawn, "Wrażenia z Anglji: Tragedia hotelu Bloomsbury," *WL*, August 27, 1939, no. 36, p. 3; Zbigniew Grabowski, "Kwestia żydowska na cenzurowanym," *WL*, July 31, 1938, no. 31, p. 4.
39. Dawn, "Londyn-Grochów-Częstoniew," p. 4.
40. Mieczysław Choynowski, "Rozprawa z rasizmem," *WL*, April 3, 1936, no. 19, p. 1; Paweł Hulka-Laskowski, "Przesilenie antysemityzmu," *WL*, April 23, 1933, no. 18, p. 1; Hulka-Laskowski, "Rozkład nacjonalizmu," *WL*, September 11, 1938, no. 38, p. 1; Mariusz Dawn [M. Morska], "Piekło w domu rodzinnym," *WL*, February 27, 1938, no. 9, p. 1; "Konkurs rasistowski *Wiadomości*," *WL*, April 12, 1936, no. 16, p. 1.
41. "Jam," "Przegląd prasy," p. 7.
42. The questionnaire "Pisarze polscy w kwestii żydowskiej": Andrzej Stawar, "Jeszcze o antysemityzmie," *WL*, May 23, 1937, no. 22, p. 2; Ksawery Pruszyński, "W największym skrócie," *WL*, May 16, 1937, no. 21, p. 3; Józef Łobodowski, "Tra-

In conclusion, *Wiadomości*'s record in dealing with the Jewish Question in Poland is best described as mixed. Its wars on the Jewish Question were fought on two fronts: against the Jewish as well as the Endecja press. Paradoxically, in the first decade of *Wiadomości*'s existence, its attacks on Jewish separatism and backwardness both outweighed and outnumbered its exchanges with the Endeks. In the late 1930s, as the focus gradually shifted toward ideological confrontation with fascism, *Wiadomości* became more articulate in condemning anti-Jewish violence. On the whole, the journal's polemics on the Jewish Question were strongly conditioned by the specific social situation of the group that shaped its profile: the *crème de la crème* of the Polonized Jewish intelligentsia. Under constant pressure to provide proofs of their "genuine Polishness" and defending their increasingly questioned membership in Poland's cultural elite, the editors and contributors of the journal were doomed to compromise on "Jewish" matters. In their discussion of one of Słonimski's plays, some reviewers described Słonimski as a living "proof" that environment and not race was the deciding factor in shaping human personality.[43] If this was one of the roles *Wiadomości* aspired to play, it had its price. Although the best literary journal Poland has ever had scored splendid victories in its verbal and intellectual duels with its opponents, tragically its global vision of society remained out of step with the trends that were winning an upper hand in interwar Europe.

---

gedia żydowska," *WL*, February 27, 1938, no. 9, p. 2; Paweł Hulka-Laskowski, "Na marginesie sprawy żydowskiej," *WL*, June 13, 1937, no. 25, p. 2; Aleksander Świętochowski, "Antysemityzm," *WL*, April 11, 1937, no. 16, p. 3; K. W. Zawodziński, "Apel do serca i rozumu," *WL*, May 2, 1937, no. 19, p. 2. See also Emil Zegadłowicz, "Poza dyskusja," *WL*, May 16, 1937, no. 20, p. 2; Mieczysław Wardziński, "Antysemityzm—daltonizmem państwowym," *WL*, July 4, 1937, no. 28, p. 3; Henryk Dembinski, "Europejskie poczucie godności," *WL*, July 11, 1937, no. 29, p. 3; Antoni Sobański, "Kwestii żydowskiej nie ma," *WL*, August 29, 1937, no. 36, p. 3; Wanda Wasilewska, "Szukam antysemityzmu," *WL*, September 26, 1937, no. 40, p. 3; Manfred Kridl, "Przypomnienie starych i prostych prawd," *WL*, October 31, 1937, no. 45, p. 2.

43. "Wieczór dyskusyjny o *Rodzinie*," *Czas*, 1934, no. 27, as quoted in Godlewska, "Komedie Słonimskiego," pt. 3, p. 140; see also Emil Breiter, "Nowa komedia Słonimskiego," *WL*, January 10, 1934, no. 2, p. 4.

Historiography

Artur Eisenbach

Jewish Historiography in Interwar Poland

The history of historiography not only explains concrete research problems and trends in the writing of history but indirectly throws light on many aspects of the life of a given national community. For Jewish history in particular, the scientific works of Jewish historians also exert a considerable influence upon the shaping of the social and historical consciousness of the Jewish people.

A history of Jewish historiography in Poland has yet to be written, although a number of critical studies deal with the activities of particular scholars and theories of the development of historical writing.[1] I regard this essay as a review of various research currents in the interwar period and, therefore, as a prelude to a much greater understanding. It is, after all, impossible to present a complete analysis of the accomplishments of the Jewish historians of that time in a single article.

The beginnings of modern Jewish historiography in Poland date to the end of the nineteenth century, when the number of scholars was still small and the state of research into the history of the Jews in Poland still inadequate. The pre–World War I period saw increased work in this field, but the basic breakthrough in the Jewish historical sciences took place with the rebirth of the sovereign Polish state, when the Jewish community flourished in a variety of ways.

The integration of Polish lands, until 1918 divided among three political states, gave rise to a number of difficulties. The Partition areas varied considerably in economic development and population

1. Filip Friedman, "Pokłosie historiografii żydowskiej lat ostatnich w Polsce," *Miesięcznik Żydowski*, 1935, nos. 3–4, pp. 182–94, which includes a review of accomplishments and trends in Jewish historiography; Friedman, "Polish-Jewish Historiography between the Two World Wars (1919–1939)," *Jewish Social Studies* 11 (1949): 373–408; Isaiah Trunk, "Le-toldot ha-historyografyah ha-polanit ba-shanim ha-aharonim," *Gal-Ed* 3 (1976): 245–68, which discusses the works of Jewish historians in three centers—the Congress Kingdom, Galicia, and Poland—in 1918–39.

structure. For some time after 1918 each retained its political and cultural traditions, and modern society emerged only gradually. At the same time, profound changes were taking place among the Jews; internal migration, for example, reached considerable dimensions, particularly to the central regions of the country, and an awareness of belonging to a single state began to emerge.

In the first years of the Second Republic, a network of Jewish elementary and secondary publicly run schools was established. Compulsory requirements specified that those teaching history in the secondary schools, as well as those teaching other subjects, had to possess university diplomas. The prospect of obtaining teaching jobs inclined many Jewish university students to study history and to select topics in the history of the Jews in Poland for master's or doctoral dissertations.

The growing interest in Jewish history also stemmed from trends in the Jewish community itself. The First World War, revolutions and political changes in Central and Eastern Europe, the expansion of political activity and national consciousness, and the flourishing of Jewish culture in renascent Poland all increased interest in contemporary Jewish economic and social problems and in the long history of the Jews in Poland. Despite economic and social difficulties, the interwar years were a time of great activity in the area of Jewish culture and science, including history. While the old generation of historians continued to be active, new trends and research centers emerged, and increasing numbers of scholars developed new methods in areas until then practically uncultivated.

At the very beginning I would like to note that this review does not provide a full picture of Jewish historiography in the interwar period because it does not include works published after World War II, though written before it. Scholars of the middle and younger generations who survived the war and had been able to save their materials or works published them after 1945, mainly abroad. These works are not surveyed here.

The development of Jewish historiography was considerably influenced by Polish historians and the general progress of scientific research. Polish historical sciences entered into a new stage with the new political conditions of the postwar period. There were changes in the organizational structure and functions of the historical sciences. New universities were founded, and scientific research centers expanded. New central and regional societies emerged; the Polskie

Towarzystwo Historyczne (Polish Historical Society) had, for example, fifteen regional branches in 1925. Prewar historical periodicals continued to be published, and new ones came into being. Historians gained access to manuscript collections, and the opening of archival sources was of enormous importance for those embarking on new kinds of investigations. The Archiwum Oswiecenia Publicznego (Archives of Public Enlightenment) had been founded in 1915. In March 1916 the Archiwum Skarbowe (Treasury Archives), which contained an enormous collection of manuscript materials dating from the beginning of the fifteenth century, was opened. Soon afterward the Archiwum Akt Nowych (Archives of Old Acts) began operations, making available acts from 1807 on concerning administrative and police affairs in the Duchy of Warsaw and the Kingdom of Poland. After the unification of the three former Partition areas, historians had easier access to the central collections of the Archiwum Akt Nowych, the army archives, and the archives in Lwów as well as the regional archives in Cracow, Poznań, Łódź, and other provincial administrative centers. Historians could now make use of manuscripts in a number of libraries, including the Zamojski and Krasiński libraries, the Czartoryski Archives, and the Jagiellonian Library. All those organizational changes had an enormous impact on the development of the historical sciences.

These favorable conditions encouraged Jewish historians of the older and middle generations to undertake research in the history of the Jewish population in Poland. An additional stimulus was the fact that Polish historians showed little interest in the history of this national group, which for centuries had inhabited Polish lands and at the end of the nineteenth century was the largest group of Jews in the world. One can refer to only a small number of publications, which pertain more to the Jewish Question than to a comprehensive history of the Jewish community: the fundamental work by Władysław Smoleński on the Jewish population; articles by Wacław Tokarz, Henryk Mościcki, and Natalia Gąsiorowska; and Stanisław Kutrzeba's remarks on Jewish self-government in his history of the political system of Polish lands and his book on the Jewish Question, which examined only certain aspects of the history of the community.[2]

2. Władysław Smoleński, *Stan i sprawa żydów polskich w XVIII wieku* (Warsaw, 1876); Wacław Tokarz, "Z dziejów sprawy żydowskiej za Księstwa Warszawskiego,"

From the beginning of the twentieth century, as political and social struggles intensified, the Narodowa Demokracja (National Democracy, its adherents the National Democrats, or Endeks) re-examined the past of the Jewish population in Poland in order to provide a theoretical foundation for its ideology concerning the Jewish Question. Antoni Marylski and Zygmunt Balicki published openly anti-Jewish articles on this subject, and Andrzej Wojtowski and Władysław Tatarzanka studied the economic role of Polish Jews. Many of their essays were published in *Przegląd Narodowy* and *Przegląd Judaistyczny*. The journalistic works by Teodor Jeske-Choiński were of a similar nature. Other antisemitic works, displaying little scientific objectivity, include Jan Ptaśnik's publications on the role of the Jews in Polish towns and Rudolf Korsch and Father Marjan Morawski's descriptions of the destructive role of the Jews in Polish economic life.[3]

It is not my intention to review Polish historical literature on Jewish topics. I only wish to point out certain works that exemplify the political function of history, in this case the stirring of a nationalistic spirit in Polish society. This spirit of nationalism created obstacles to institutional integration; in 1912, for example, a separate scientific periodical on the history of Polish Jews was published in Warsaw.[4] Moreover, there were differences of opinion on various historical approaches. Hence, even before the First World War, and

Kwartalnik Historyczny 16 (1902): 262–76; Henryk Mościcki, "Żyzdzi litewscy pod berłem Katarzyny II," *Kwartalnik Poświęcony Badaniom Przeszłości Żydów w Polsce*, 1912, no. 1; Natalia Gąsiorowska, "Cenzura żydowska w Królestwie Kongresowym," *Kwartalnik Poświęcony Badaniom Przeszłości Żydów w Polsce*, 1912, no. 2, pp. 55–64; Stanisław Kutrzeba, *Historia ustroju Polski w zarysie* (Lwów, 1925); Kutrzeba, *Sprawa żydowska w Polsce* (Lwów, 1918).

3. Antoni Marylski, *Dzieje sprawy żydowskiej w Polsce* (Warsaw, 1912); Zygmunt Balicki, "Apolityczny wpływ Żydów," *Przegląd Narodowy*, 1912, no. 4, pp. 337–55; Balicki, "Żydowszczyzna w polityce," *Przegląd Narodowy*, 1913, no. 9, pp. 225–40; Andrzej Wojtowski, "Polityka rządu pruskiego wobec Żydów polskich od 1793–1806," *Przegląd Judaistyczny*, 1922, no. 2, pp. 96–107, no. 3, pp. 182–97, nos. 4–6, pp. 304–321; Władysław Tatarzanka, "Przyczyni do historii Żydów w Królestwie Kongresowym 1815–1830," *Przegląd Judaistyczny*, 1922, nos. 4–6, pp. 274–99; Teodor Jeske-Choiński, *Historja Żydów w Polsce* (Warsaw, 1913); Jeske-Choiński, *Neofici polscy* (Warsaw, 1905); Jan Ptaśnik, *Miasta w Polsce* (Lwów, 1922); Ptaśnik, *Miasta i mieszczaństwo w dawnej Polsce* (Cracow, 1934); Ptaśnik, "Żydzi w Polsce w wiekach średnich," *Przegląd Warszawski*, 1922, no. 2, pp. 215–37; Ptaśnik, "Zalew miast polskich przez Żydów w XVI do XVIII w.," *Przegląd Narodowy*, 1924, no. 35, pp. 26–40; Rudolf Korsch, *Żydowskie ugrupowania wywrotowe w Polsce* (Warsaw, 1925); Marjan Morawski, *Stanowisko Kościoła wobec niebezpieczeństwa żydowskiego w dawnej Polsce* (Włocławek, 1938).

4. *Kwartalnik Poświęcony Badaniom Przeszłości Żydów w Polsce* (Warsaw) (1912–13). Only three numbers were published.

subsequently in the Second Republic, separate institutions undertook independent analytical and theoretical research on the history of Jews in Poland.

I shall not present extensive biographies of the large group of Jewish historians in Poland in the last half century. It is, however, my intention to describe three generations of historians who were active in the interwar period. The majority of the older and middle generation worked in Jewish secondary schools. Teaching was their main source of income and probably kept them from embarking on more extensive research. Nevertheless, from the very beginning of the Second Republic, the chronological range of research expanded to include the formerly neglected Enlightenment era and the nineteenth century. At the same time, there developed a dynamic current aimed at combining economic history, the history of social movements, the emancipation of the Jews, and Jewish education and culture. Works on these topics were written in Polish, Yiddish, Hebrew, German, Russian, and French.

The Older Generation of Historians

One should mention at least three names important for Jewish historiography in Poland during the period under examination. All three historians came from Galicia, began their research between 1898 and 1903, and continued their work through the interwar period. Pioneers in research into the Jewish past in Poland, they investigated primarily the pre-Partition era.

Mojżesz (Moses) Schorr (1874–1941) was born in Przemyśl, studied in Vienna, and from 1910 taught as a docent and from 1916 as a professor at the University of Warsaw. He lectured on philology and the history of the East, especially Assyriology. This outstanding Orientalist was interested mainly in the pre-Partition history of the Jews of Przemyśl and in the history and organization of Jewish self-government in that period.[5]

Majer Bałaban (1877–1942) was born in Lwów. He studied at the University of Lwów, where courses by Ludwik Finkel and Szymon Askenazy to a large degree influenced his scientific interests.

5. Israel Ostersetzer, "Prof. Mojżesz Schorr: W 60-lecie urodzin," *Miesięcznik Żydowski*, 1934, no. 5, pp. 460–67; *Księga Jubileuszowa ku czci Prof. Dr. Mojżesza Schorra* (Warsaw, 1935).

Bałaban became a doctor of history in 1904, and in 1928 he was named a docent in the Instytut Nauk Judaistycznych (Institute for Judaic Studies) at the Wolna Wszechnica Polski (Polish Free University) and at the University of Warsaw, where in 1935 he was nominated professor.

Bałaban laid the foundations for the history of Polish Jews. Although he devoted himself primarily to the seventeenth–nineteenth centuries, the chronological range of his scientific interests was impressive. He dealt basically with the internal processes at work in Jewish history and based his research on a wide variety of sources. He carried out investigations in many domestic and foreign archives, and, after critically examining many kinds of materials, he reconstructed the life of the Jewish community. Bałaban wrote in a highly descriptive manner, and he colorfully described figures and events from Jewish history, paying more attention to cultural trends and religious movements than to the everyday economic life of the masses. Hence his works lack a thorough analysis of the social dynamics of historical process.

Bałaban wrote several hundred works, and his monographic studies, essays, and reviews are a great contribution to the history of Polish Jews. He also taught a whole generation of young historians, the majority of whom followed his example and employed the idiographic method. His scholarly interests included: (1) the bibliography of the literature and the history of the Jews in Poland; (2) the history of the *kahals*; (3) the organization and structure of self-government in the Commonwealth; (4) the history of Jewish dissident groups and the mystical movement in Poland; (5) descriptions of Jewish historical monuments (cemeteries, synagogues, sacral objects, and works of art); (6) Jewish customs and education; (7) Jewish biographies and genealogical studies of rabbinical families, elders, and medical doctors.[6]

6. See bibliographies of Majer Bałaban's publications in *Miesięcznik Żydowski*, 1933, no. 4, pp. 346–51, and of his articles published in *Nasz Kurjer* and *Nasz Przegląd* in 1920–39 in *Biuletyn Żydowskiego Instytutu Historycznego* (hereafter *BŻIH*), no. 103 (1977): 49–73. On Bałaban, see Filip Friedman, "Prof. Majer Bałaban: W 30-lecie pracy naukowej," *Miesięcznik Żydowska*, 1933, no. 4, pp. 340–46; Krystyna Pieradzka, "Majer Bałaban," *Kwartalnik Historyczny* 53 (1939–45): 414–15; Emanuel Ringelblum, "Majer Bałaban," *BŻIH*, no. 25 (1958): 16–18; Isaiah M. Biderman, *Majer Bałaban, Historian of Polish Jewry: His Influence on the Younger Generation of Jewish Historians* (New York, 1976); Raphael Mahler, "Majer Bałaban: Der nestor fun yidisher geshikhte shraybung in Poyln," *Yidishe kulture* 5, nos. 8–9 (1943): 56–59; Maurycy Horn, "Profesor Majer Bałaban jako badacz przeszłości Żydów dawnej rzeczpospo-

Ignacy (Yitzhak) Schiper (1884–1943) was born in Tarnów and studied philosophy and law at the University of Lwów. In 1907 he was nominated doctor of law, and from 1934 he held the post of docent in the Instytut Nauk Judaistycznych. For many years Schiper was one of the leading figures in the central organs of Poalei Zion and later in the General Zionists, whom he represented in the Sejm (House of Deputies). He was also an energetic social activist.

Schiper demonstrated great vitality in scientific research. He represented a totally different type of scholar from Bałaban, who was only a few years older. Schiper perceived history as a scientific discipline that was supposed to throw light on patterns of social development, and he worked out a number of hypotheses to explain some of the key problems in the historical development of the Jews in Poland and elsewhere. Although some of these hypotheses were impossible to defend, their significance lay in the fact that they encouraged a verification of the facts and the use of specific cognitive methods.

Schiper's broad interests were focused not so much on the static aspect of history but on the dynamic processes of development that shaped the Jewish community. From the very beginning of his career, he was interested primarily in economic history, and he is considered the founder of the economic and social history of the Jews. Although he was not a consistent materialist, he believed that socioeconomic relations, to a large degree, determined other sectors of national life. He published analytical, synthetic, and popular works that deal with the economic relations of the Polish Jews and with the development of trade and credit. For many years Schiper conducted research on the history of Jewish self-government, and he wrote on the organization and structure of the Sejm of the Four Provinces, emphasizing especially the financial reasons Polish authorities had for establishing this institution. That which appeared in print was actually only a fragment of his larger work.[7] He also dealt with broader problems concerning Jewish culture, such as language, literature, the theater, and customs. He was interested in the

---

litej," *BŻIH,* no. 103 (1977): 3–14; Michał Szulkin, "Prof. Majer Bałaban: W stulecie urodzin," *BŻIH,* no. 101 (1977): 3–16; Isaiah Trunk, "Majer Bałaban: Der forsher fun der koolsher organizatsye un oytonomye in amolikn Poyln (Draysik yor nokh zayn toyt in varshever geto)," *YIVO bleter* 44 (1973): 198–206.

7. Emanuel Ringelblum, in his description of Ignacy (Yitzhak) Schiper as a historian, recalled seeing a manuscript in German of more than six hundred pages. Ringelblum, *Kronika getta warszawskiego* (Warsaw, 1983), p. 547.

political history of the Jews in Poland and their participation in the November Uprising. His works concerning the historical demography of Jews in Poland should also be mentioned.[8]

The Middle Generation of Historians

The second generation of historians occupies a special place in Jewish historiography in Poland. These scholars grew up under the influence of the social revolutions in Europe, with their many new ideological currents, and they matured while Jewish culture flourished in Central and Eastern Europe, especially Jewish literature, journalism, theater, and education. Influenced by this atmosphere, these new scholars introduced into the historical sciences the national and social approaches of secular Jewish culture. Their interests found expression in intensive investigations into economic and social activities as well as in a search for the roots of modern Jewish culture. Research on the Jewish Enlightenment against the background of that general intellectual trend was initiated; attention was paid to the Hasidic movement, particularly its social aspects; and studies on the Jewish working-class movement were inaugurated. Moreover, the legal problems and organization of self-government of the Jewish communities were also examined. A characteristic feature of the second generation of scholars and, under their influence, of the younger historians as well was a gradual extension of the range of research to include the life of nineteenth-century Jews in Poland and the application of various research methods. Certain scholars remained under the influence of Szymon Askenazy; others turned to the methods of historical materialism. All of them engaged in a high level of theoretical reflection within a well-developed framework. They also did research in little-known or totally new state and communal archives and public manuscript collections.

This middle generation of historians included Raphael Mahler,

8. On the life and works of Ignacy Schiper and for a bibliography of his published monographs, studies, and reviews, see Jechiel Hirszhaut, "Dr. Yitzhak Schiper, zayn lebn un shafn," and "Bibliografye fun verk un arbetn fun Dr. Yitzhak Schiper," in *Fun noentn over,* vol. 1, ed. Jacob Pat (New York, 1955), pp. 185–256, 257–63. This bibliography was supplemented by Jacob Szacki, in *YIVO bleter* 39 (1955): 352–54. See also Emanuel Ringelblum, "Dr. Yitzhak Schiper: Der pioner fun moderner yidisher visnshaft," *Sotsyale meditsin/Medycyna Społeczna,* 1934, nos. 11–12; Ringelblum, *Kronika getta warszawskiego,* pp. 544–52; Raphael Mahler, "Yitzhak Schiper," *YIVO bleter* 25 (1945): 19–32.

Emanuel Ringelblum, and Filip Friedman in Poland, and abroad, Nathan Michael Gelber, Jacob Szacki (Shatzky), Mark Wischnitzer, and Bernard Dov Weinryb. The first four came from Galicia, as did the representatives of the older generation. The majority of these historians combined their scholarly work with political activity in national and working-class movements. Their main source of income was teaching in secondary schools or working in libraries and publishing houses. Certain members of this generation moved abroad and managed to save their material and works begun before the war. It was only during the war or many years later that their synthetic studies on the history of the Polish Jews were published.

Raphael Mahler (1899–1977) was born in Nowy Sącz. He was a graduate of a secondary school in Cracow and of the historical and philological departments at the University of Vienna, where in 1922 he wrote his Ph.D. dissertation. Upon returning to Poland, Mahler settled in Warsaw, where he worked as a secondary school teacher. In 1937 he emigrated to the United States; in 1951 he left the United States for Israel. In 1959 he was nominated a docent and in 1961 a professor at Tel Aviv University.

Mahler was an erudite man of extensive knowledge. His scientific interests and talent for comparative interpretations were impressive. Theoretical and methodological reflection is characteristic of his works. He was a consistent supporter of Marxism, and his works were written from a Marxist position. Like Schiper, his predecessor, he emphasized the significant role of economic factors in the history of the Jewish people. He dealt with the economic, demographic, professional, and social structure of the Polish Jews, with the self-government of *kahals* in the eighteenth century, and with social and cultural movements such as Hasidism and the Haskalah. After World War II Mahler prepared a history of the Jews in modern times beginning with the era of enlightened absolutism and the French Revolution; only seven volumes appeared in print.[9]

Emanuel Ringelblum (1900–44) was born in Buczacz. He grad-

9. Raphael Mahler, *Divrei yemei Israel: Dorot ahronim* (Tel Aviv, 1952–80). On Raphael Mahler's seventy-fifth birthday, a commemorative volume appeared, containing studies by his friends, colleagues, and students, as well as a bibliography of his works from 1925 to 1973. See Shmuel Yeiven, ed., *Sefer Raphael Mahler: Kovez mehkarim be-toldot Israel* (Merhavia, 1974). See also Isaiah Trunk, "Raphael Mahler: Der historisher materyalist," in Trunk, *Geshtaltn un gesheenishn* (Tel Aviv, 1983), pp. 32–51; hereafter cited with date of publication to distinguish it from another book by Trunk with the same title.

uated from a secondary school in Nowy Sącz in 1919 and studied history at the University of Warsaw, where he attended a seminar held by Jan Kochanowski and Marceli Handelsman. Ringelbum received his Ph.D. in 1927, with a dissertation on the·history of Jews in medieval Warsaw.

Ringelblum was enthralled by the tumultuous social and political ideas of the postwar period. He became one of the leading and most culturally active figures in the Jewish community of Warsaw. A greatly talented organizer, he founded a seminar of Jewish historians in 1923 in the Żydowski Dom Skodewicki (Jewish Students' Hostel), whose publication, *Yunger historiker,* he co-edited. He was also a member of the Historical Section of YIVO in Vilna and of its branch in Warsaw. During the German occupation, Ringelblum helped organize social aid in the Warsaw ghetto and subsequently maintained a clandestine archives of Jewish activities during this period.

Like Bałaban, Ringelblum dealt exclusively with the history of Polish Jews. His method is characterized by a tendency to prepare every problem as a monographic study based on archival source materials. He was interested primarily in the history of Warsaw Jews. The first volume of his study was published in 1932, and until his death he was engaged in preparing the second volume (up to the end of the eighteenth century), sections of which appeared during his lifetime. His work, partially extant in manuscript form, examined the history of the Jews of Poland against an extensive comparative background.

Ringelblum also investigated the economic, social, and cultural aspects of the history of Polish Jews, differentiating among the large elements of this population and examining its inner social antagonisms and the harm inflicted by the landowners and the *kahal* oligarchy. In a separate study, Ringelblum described attempts during the reign of Stanisław August to restratify the Jews and to include them in industrial production. He wrote about the beginnings of the Enlightenment among the Jews and published brief studies on the history of Jewish books and publishing in eighteenth-century Poland. Ringelblum was also interested in Polish-Jewish relations under Nazi occupation.[10]

10. On Emanuel Ringelblum, see Raphael Mahler, "Emanuel Ringelblum," *YIVO bleter* 24 (1944): 307–17; Jacob Szacki, "Menakhem ben Fayvish Ringelblum," in *Kapitlen geshikhte fun amolikn yidishn lebn in Poyln fun Emanuel Ringelblum* (Buenos Aires, 1953), pp. 11–49; Artur Eisenbach, introd. to Ringelblum, *Kronika getta warszaw-*

Filip Friedman (1901–59) was born in Lwów, where he finished secondary school. In 1925 he wrote a Ph.D. dissertation in Vienna on the struggle of Galician Jews for civil equality. That same year he returned to Poland and worked as a secondary school teacher in Łódź. Friedman became interested in the archival materials available in Łódź, which inspired fundamental works on the relations and development of that town and on the history of the local Jewish population, its social and professional structure and its structural transformations in the context of the economic development of Polish Jews up to 1914. Friedman was concerned with more than economic and social problems; he also wrote about conflicts between the supporters of the Enlightenment and Hasidism. Characteristic of his works is a striving to explain patterns of historical development and synthetically to interpret the problems under examination.

Friedman spent the war years in Lwów. In 1945 he was nominated director of the Centralna Żydowski Komisja Historyczna (Central Jewish Historical Commission) in Łódź, and in 1947 he emigrated to France, and later to the United States, where he was a lecturer at Columbia University in New York. From 1945 he studied the Second World War and the German occupation in Poland, publishing many works on this subject as well as a bibliography of Jewish history for the years 1939–45.[11]

In reviewing the Jewish historians in Poland, one cannot overlook those scholars who emigrated from Poland and conducted extensive research on the history of Polish Jews in the United States, Germany, the Soviet Union, and Palestine. Jacob Szacki worked in New York from 1922 on, while Raphael Mahler, Bernard Weinryb, Mark Wischnitzer and his wife Rachela Wischnitzer-Bernstein, and others arrived in the city in the 1930s. Up to 1933 the small but significant group of Jewish historians in Berlin included Simon Dubnov, Jacob Lestschinsky, the Wischnitzers, Elias Tcherikower and Joseph Meisl. In Germany certain periodicals contained many studies and material

---

skiego, pp. 5–27; Eisenbach, "Araynfir," in Emanuel Ringelblum, *Ksovim fun geto,* vol. 1 (Warsaw, 1961), pp. 7–23; Michał Szulkin, "Dr. Emanuel Ringelblum: Historyk i organizator podziemnego archivum getta warsawskiego," *BŻIH,* nos. 2–3 (1973): 111–25; Isaiah Trunk, "Emanuel Ringelblum: Der historiker un gezelshaftlekher askn," in Trunk, *Geshtaltn un gesheenishn* (1983), pp. 52–65.

11. Isaiah Trunk, "Dr. Filip Friedman," in Trunk, *Geshtaltn un gesheenishn: Historishe esayen* (Buenos Aires, 1962), pp. 35–46. See also Salo Wittmayer Baron's introduction to Friedman's collected works, *Roads to Extinction: Essays on the Holocaust,* ed. Ida Jane Friedman (New York, 1980), pp. 1–8.

on the history of Polish Jews, such as the *Zeitschrift für Demographie und Statistik der Juden* (sixteen volumes published 1905–20 and three volumes 1924–26), the Yiddish *Bleter far yidishe demografye un statistik* (1923–25), and Martin Buber's *Der Jude* (1916–28).

An important group of historians worked in the Soviet Union: J. I. Gessen, Israel Sosis, Tobiah B. Heilikman, R. Aleksandrow, Ilya Galant, and Simon Ginzburg, who published their works in Kiev, Moscow, and Leningrad. They continued the *Evreiskaia Starina* and introduced new periodicals such as the *Evreiskaia Letopis* (1923–26) and the *Evreiskie Vestnik* (1928); *Tsaytshrift*, the Yiddish-language periodical for research into Jewish history, demography, economics, literature, philology, and ethnography (Minsk, 1926–31); the *Visnshaftlekhe yorbikher* (1929); and annals of the Jewish Historical and Archeological Commission.

N. M. Gelber, Israel Halperin, and Israel Klausner worked in Palestine and stayed on after the founding of Israel. The scientific journal *Zion*, published in Jerusalem, contained works concerning the history of Jews from various countries.

Among those who emigrated from Poland are several historians whose contributions to the research into the history of Polish Jews were particularly significant. Jacob Szacki (Shatzky) (1893–1956) was born in Warsaw. In 1913 he passed his final secondary school examinations in Cracow, where he was awarded a scholarship by the Polska Akademia Umiejętności (Polish Academy of Sciences). In 1914 he attended a seminar held by Szymon Askenazy, and in 1914–17 he served in the Piłsudski Legions as lieutenant. In 1917 Szacki won the Kasa Mianowskiego scholarship, and in 1922 he wrote his Ph.D. dissertation on "The Jewish Question in the Kingdom of Poland under Paskiewicz" (unpublished). In the same year he emigrated to the United States and settled permanently in New York.

Szacki was active in many fields of the social sciences, but his main interest lay in the history of the Jews in Poland. In this context he dealt with the history of Jewish education, theater, literature, philosophy, folklore, bibliography, and the Jewish press. The list of his works—monographic studies, articles, and reviews—published in New York in 1939 contains 580 items, while a list for the period 1940–56, posthumously published, includes 267 works. His monumental three-volume *Geshikhte fun yidn in Varshe* (The History of Jews in Warsaw), which treated the subject up to the end of the nineteenth century, appeared in 1947–53. Szacki was an outstanding expert on the history of the Polish Jews in all three Partition areas. He defined his research method as historical realism and sought to explain the opinions and attitudes of various groups by referring to their economic interests. In doing so he revealed the elements of the social struggle within the Jewish population.[12]

Mark Wischnitzer (1882–1955) was born in Równe (Volynia province) and graduated from a secondary school in Brody. He studied history at the universities of Vienna and Berlin. In 1906 he presented his Ph.D. dissertation entitled "The University in Göttingen and the Development of Liberalism in Russia in the First Quarter of the Nineteenth Century" (published in 1907). In 1907 he settled in St. Petersburg, where in the years 1908–13 he was the editor of the section on Jewish history in the *Evreiskaia Encyklopedia* and published a number of articles. He also published historical works, based on archival sources, in the *Evreiskaia Starina, Perezhytoe,* and *Minuvshye gody,* and, for *Istoriya Evreiskogo Naroda,* Wischnitzer wrote on the Frankists, the guilds in Crown Poland, Lithuania, and Belorussia, and the economic history of Polish Jews in the seventeenth and eighteenth centuries. In 1918 he left the Soviet Union for Berlin and after 1933 emigrated to the United States, where in 1948 he became professor at Yeshiva University in New York.

Bernard Dov Weinryb was born in Turobin (Lublin province) in 1900. He studied at the University of Wrocław, where in 1931 he received his doctorate and became the head librarian in the Jüdisch Theologisches Seminar (Jewish Theological Seminary). He was also a member of the editorial board of the *Encyclopedia Judaica.* From 1936 to 1938 Weinryb was professor of economics at the Hebrew University in Jerusalem. In 1940 he emigrated to the United States and lectured at Yeshiva University in New York and at Dropsie College in Philadelphia, where he settled after the war. Weinryb published sources for the history of the Jewish communities in Poznań, Cracow, and Lublin. He is also the author of studies on the economic history of the Jews in Poland and Russia in the nineteenth century.

Nathan Michael Gelber (1891–1966) was born in Lwów. A graduate of a secondary school in Brody, he studied history in Vienna

---

12. See the commemorative volume, I. Liftshitz, ed., *Szacki-bukh: Opshatsungen vegn Dr. Jacob Szacki un Dr. Szackis zikhroynes, briv, referatn un essayen* (New York, 1958), with articles by Filip Friedman, Joseph Tenenbaum, Leibush Lehrer, and others. See also Isaiah Trunk, "Jacob Szacki," in Trunk, *Geshtaltn un gesheenishn* (1983), pp. 29–34.

and Berlin; in 1914 he wrote his Ph.D. dissertation in Vienna. In 1932 Gelber arrived in Jerusalem, where he was an active Zionist and headed the Polish branch of the Keren Hayesod (Foundation Fund). He began publishing in 1910. In the interwar period and after World War II he published a number of studies and several books in which he dealt with certain aspects of the political history of Polish Jews in the eighteenth and nineteenth centuries.

The Young Generation

The much more numerous young generation was concentrated mainly in Warsaw. Its members studied in the 1920s or even in the 1930s, and they created a dynamic, although fluid, milieu. Many of them attended meetings held by the Warsaw branch of the Historical Section of YIVO; some published their works in *Yunger historiker* or periodicals such as the *Miesięcznik Żydowski*. Since it would be difficult to characterize this group as a whole, I would like to mention the most active young historians whose works, published before 1939, are discussed below: Lipman Comber, Artur Eisenbach, Rafal Gerber, Aaron Sawicki, Isaiah Trunk, Esther Tenenbaum, Moshe Kremer, Bela Mandelsberg, Józef Kermisz, Szymon Szymkiewicz, David Wurm, Jehuda Warszawski, Szymon Zajczyk, Israel Ostersetzer, and Pinkhas Kon.

The Organization of Research

From the earliest postwar years, Jewish historians were involved in the organizational aspects of their discipline. The establishment of institutions that would direct and coordinate historical research and prepare new historians for utilizing the archival collections of the Jewish communities and the state and town archives became an urgent task. Another important undertaking was inventorying art relics and publishing source materials, historical works, and bibliographical reviews. Gradually a few centers for the study of Jewish history were established in Warsaw and Vilna. In 1923 the Żydowski Dom Skodewicki organized a seminar on the history of Jews at the initiative of Emanuel Ringelblum, then a student at the University of Warsaw. The purpose of this self-education group was to encourage Jewish students of history to embark upon subjects connected with the history of the Jews of Poland and to acquaint them with the appropriate source materials, scientific bibliography, and methodology. The patrons of the group were Majer Bałaban and Ignacy Schiper. Despite the founding of new research centers, the seminar continued to function. After 1928, when a branch of YIVO opened in Warsaw, the seminar became the Warsaw Historical Commission, later the Historical Commission for All of Poland, which flourished in 1928–39. Meetings took place once a month, and the attendance reached thirty. The tasks of the group were modified as an increasing number of students and doctoral candidates preparing works on the history of Jews made it necessary to explain certain theoretical and methodological problems.[13]

In 1925 the Yidisher Visnshaftlekher Institut (YIVO, Jewish Scientific Institute) was established in Vilna. It soon became an important scientific center in which a numerous group of historians worked or cooperated. YIVO's purpose was to develop scientific research in the humanities; research, conducted in Yiddish, served as a basis for national education. YIVO wanted to expand its activities primarily in Poland and in other European Jewish communities with a history and intellectual heritage that extended back for centuries. It also maintained scientific posts in Paris and New York. YIVO was divided into four sections—Historical, Philological, Economical-Statistical, and Psychological-Pedagogical—which by no means possessed a uniform ideological profile; the same holds true for its methods of scientific research. It attracted the cooperation of Marxist historians as well as the adherents of other theories and trends. The Historical Section, headed by Simon Dubnov, represented various historical schools and emphasized modern history and the history of Polish Jews.

Each of the four sections issued monographs in which representatives of various disciplines could present their works. The Historical Section published three volumes of *Historishe shriftn* (1929–39). Studies, historical documents, and reviews were also published in the chief periodical issued by the institute, *YIVO bleter,* which contained four departments corresponding to the institute's four sec-

---

13. Members of those groups published their works in their own publication, *Yunger historiker.* The first volume appeared in 1926, dedicated to Simon Dubnov, and the second in 1928, dedicated to Ignacy Schiper. The growing activity and membership of the group resulted in a change in the title to *Bleter far geshikhte,* of which two volumes appeared, in 1934 and 1938. For a complete discussion of the historical work of YIVO, see Lucjan Dobroszycki, "YIVO in Interwar Poland: Work in the Historical Sciences," in this volume.

tions. The historical department included studies, archival material for the history of Jews in Poland, and works dealing with archives in general, bibliographies, museums, and reviews of and information about foreign scientific publications.

The Łódź branch of the Society of the Friends of YIVO had its own publication, *Lodzer visnshaftlekhe shriftn*. Volume 1, published in Łódź in 1938 and edited by Filip Friedman, presented works on the history of the Jews in Poland. Apart from these publications, YIVO itself published two extremely valuable sources: Nathan Nata Hanover's *Yeven mezulah* (The Abyss of Despair) edited by Jacob Szacki (Vilna, 1938), and Yosef Perl's collected works, edited by Israel Weinlös and Zelig Kalmanowicz (Vilna, 1937). In the years from 1935 to 1938 YIVO organized a few postgraduate courses on Jewish history and culture.

In 1927 the Wolna Wszechnica Polski in Warsaw created the Instytut Nauk Judaistycznych, in which Majer Bałaban lectured on the history of the Jews, with particular emphasis on the Jews of Poland. Following his nomination in 1928 as docent in the institute and at the University of Warsaw, and in 1935 as professor, Bałaban gave monographic lectures and held a seminar on the history of Polish Jews that produced more than fifty M.A. theses and Ph.D. dissertations based on source material.[14]

In 1928 the Instytut Nauk Judaistycznych began training rabbis and teachers of Judaic subjects in public secondary schools. The institute was also concerned with research work concentrated in a separate faculty. It included a department of the history of Jews in general and in Poland, including economic history and sociology. Lectures were given by Mojżesz Schorr, Majer Bałaban, Ignacy Schiper, Abraham Weiss, Edmund Stein, Israel Ostersetzer, Aryeh Tartakower, and others. The results of the research conducted by the institute were published in twelve volumes.

YIVO and the Instytut Nauk Judaistycznych quickly won wide recognition in the scientific world. Thanks to its efforts, Jewish historians were able to participate in the International Congress of the Historical Sciences held in Warsaw in 1933. At first their attendance met with considerable difficulties, since the bylaws of that international organization permitted the participation only of representa-

14. The Żydowskiego Instytuty Historycznego Archives in Warsaw contains a number of dissertations by graduates of Warsaw University, an overwhelming majority of which were written under the guidance of Majer Bałaban.

tives of states and countries, not of national groups. These obstacles were overcome at the urging of, among others, Marceli Handelsman and Tadeusz Manteuffel, the secretary of the congress. The congress recognized, although informally, the separate YIVO delegation and the Instytut Nauk Judaistycznych in Warsaw. Papers on Jewish history were read at two sessions, on August 22 and 27.[15] Jewish historians attending the congress held a number of meetings on further cooperation with the International Congress of the Historical Sciences. They rejected the creation of a separate section on Jewish history, arguing that Jewish history should be treated as an integral part of other fields of general history—social, economic, political, and so forth—of a given country. There was considerable discussion of a project proposed by Filip Friedman to organize a world conference of Jewish historians from various states and cultural centers. Friedman outlined a detailed plan for a number of sections and presented the themes and methods of research to be pursued in each. He also sought to establish a temporary organizational committee of Jewish historians.[16]

The Main Trends and Methods of Research

Jewish historiography developed considerably in the interwar period. Progress was achieved primarily in research methods. Even before 1919 certain Jewish historians employed the critical method that was one of the achievements of the modern scientific workshop, and it was subsequently perfected further. Moreover, these historians expanded the base of source materials and the chronological scope of investigation, making use of newly accessible collections of primary materials, especially documents from central state and municipal archives as well as acts from the archives of Jewish communities and other public and private collections. This new approach was particularly evident in the work of the middle and younger generations.

15. Emanuel Ringelblum, "Historia Żydów na VII Miedzynarodowym Zjeździe Nauk Historycznych w Warszawie," *Miesięcznik Żydowski*, 1933, nos. 11–12, pp. 258–60; Majer Bałaban, "Historycy Żydzi i historycy żydowscy na Wszechświatowym Kongresie Historycznym w Warszawie 21–28 sierpnia 1933," *Nasz Przegląd*, February 26, 1933, no. 57; Bałaban, "Po 7 Kongresie historykow w Warszawie: Pokłosie historii żydowskiej," *Nasz Przegląd*, September 9, 1933, no. 247.
16. Filip Friedman, "O zjazd historyków żydowskich i wszechświatowa organizację żydowskiej nauki historyznej," *Miesięcznik Żydowski*, 1933, no. 3, pp. 275–84.

In the field of methodology, the idiographic, descriptive method was abandoned, as well as the gathering and evaluation of individual facts. The new trend opposed traditional historiography and the cult of facts, although the importance of factual accuracy was never ignored. The new approach emphasized that the task of the historian was not merely to present or ascertain facts but to explain their causal relation and their place in the general historical process. This approach added depth to scientific research, revealing the changes that occurred among the Jews of Poland in the context of the country's general economic and political development. Transformations in the opinions and attitudes of various groups in the Jewish community were recognized and explained. In this context, the development of comparative research became an urgent need.

In the period under examination the range of scientific research was considerably broadened. Primary importance was ascribed to such fields as the history of economic relations, education and culture, social trends, daily customs, and dissident currents. Considerable attention was devoted to historical demography and structural changes within the Jewish community in the context of the socio-economic development of the country as a whole. Historians observed the development of new classes and their political activities, and research into the history of the Jewish working-class movement was initiated. These new trends were reflected in a number of books, studies, and polemics.

A characteristic feature of Jewish historiography of the interwar period was a departure from the history of the Commonwealth and a transition to the history of Jews in the nineteenth century, particularly in Galicia and the Kingdom of Poland. The pursuit of modern history led to greater interest in various forms of political activity of the Jewish population in its struggle for civil rights and its participation in Polish independence movements and national uprisings. In this effort a considerable role was played by the atmosphere in the department of Jewish history at the University of Warsaw and in the branch Historical Section of YIVO in Warsaw. These two centers fulfilled an important function not only in training a new generation of historians concerned with the history of Polish Jews but also in moving beyond traditional methods, stimulating methodological interests, and placing changes within the Jewish community in a wider historical context.

The theory and methodology of research became a very attractive field. New ideas were expressed in monographic studies (Schiper), but more often in smaller studies and polemics (Bałaban, Mahler), and sometimes also in reviews (Szacki). Theoretical problems were usually discussed within the context of a concrete field of the historical sciences. Methodological and theoretical reflection was also stimulated by the Marxist understanding of the historical process. As a result, new research problems were posed and examined in the context of a global process at a certain time and place. Some scholars, such as Majer Bałaban, touched upon the problems of evaluation and periodization and the relation of history to other social sciences.[17] The articles and essays written by Mahler are worthy of special mention, since in dealing with the methodological problems of the history of Jewish culture and social movements, particularly the Jewish Enlightenment and the Hasidic movements, Mahler introduced a number of schools of Jewish historiography. From the point of view of methodology and theoretical reflection, these were pioneering works. Mahler used a comparative method to identify the driving forces behind the development of Jewish communities in various countries and the factors that contributed to the retention of Jewish national distinctiveness throughout the Diaspora. Mahler polemized with Yehezkel Kaufman and his nationalistic conception of the development of the history of the Jews, and with Otto Heller and his *Der Untergang des Judentums* (Twilight of Jewry) (1931), written from a seemingly Marxist, but actually an ultra-Left position. Mahler also polemized with Simon Dubnov, who interpreted religious trends as factors in national development. In reality, Mahler claimed, such trends reflected the social differences among the Jews.[18]

17. Majer Bałaban, "Zagadnienia historiozofii żydowskiej w stasunki do historii Żydów w Polsce," *Miesięcznik Żydowski,* 1932, nos. 11–12, pp. 369–82; Bałaban, "Zadania i potrzeby historjografji żydowskiej w Polsce," in *Pamiętnik v Zjazdu Historyków w Polsce* (Lwów, 1931), pp. 225–28; Bałaban, "Kiedy i skąd przybyli Żydzi do Polski," *Miesięcznik Żydowski,* 1930, no. 1, pp. 1–2, no. 2, pp. 112–21. Bałaban polemized with Ignacy Schiper, who perceived the first Jewish settlements as Khazar agrarian colonies.

18. Raphael Mahler, "Vegn teoryes fun der yidisher kultur-geshikhte," in *Yunger historiker,* vol. 1, ed. Yaakov Berman, Raphael Mahler, and Emanuel Ringelblum (Warsaw, 1926), pp. 21–40, also published in an expanded version as "Teorje żydowskiej historjografii o rozwoju dziejowym kultury żydowskiej," *Miesięcznik Żydowski,* 1933, nos. 11–12, pp. 208–26; Mahler, "Ahad Ha-Ams filosofye fun der yidisher geshikhte un kultur," in *Yunger historiker,* vol. 2, ed. Yaakov Berman, Raphael Mahler, and Emanuel Ringelblum (Warsaw, 1928), pp. 5–23; Mahler, "A religyez-natsyonalistishe teorye fun der yidisher geshikhte," in *Bleter far geshikhte,* vol. 1, ed. Yaakov Berman,

Mahler postulated a "realistic" history of the Jews, maintaining that the idealization of history does not explain anything and that a realistic approach is the only correct one both for general history and for the history of the Jews. He wrote, "Only by way of a thorough analysis of individual, unique, and concrete economic and social relations, both in the history of the Jews and in the history of the countries of their settlement, can we reach a scientific explanation of the specific, although by no means exceptional, basic issues in the history of Jewish culture."[19]

The *Kahal* and the System of Jewish Self-Government

A number of scholars concentrated on the important subject of the history of the Jewish urban population. At the end of the nineteenth century several studies appeared in Hebrew on the Jewish *kahal*, primarily biographies and genealogies of rabbis and leaders of *kahals* in Cracow, Lwów, Żółkiew, Vilna, Brześć nad Bugiem, and Grodno. At the beginning of the twentieth century short monographic studies dealt with the history of the Jews in the towns of Great Poland—Inowrocław, Bydgoszcz, Leszno, Jarocin, Gniezno, and others.[20] These were not thorough works, and Schorr's publication on the Jews in Przemyśl was the first to meet this requirement.[21] Bałaban wrote monographic studies on Jews on Lwów, Lublin, and Cracow.[22] His work on Lwów was a Ph.D. dissertation presented in 1904; two years later it appeared in print, and is superior to the publication by Jacob Caro on the same subject.[23] Bała-

Raphael Mahler, and Emanuel Ringelblum (Warsaw, 1934), pp. 5–49; Mahler, "Tsi zenen yidn alemol geven a handlsfolk," *YIVO bleter* 7 (1934): 20–35; Mahler, "Ven un vi azoy zenen yidn gevorn a handlsfolk," *YIVO bleter* 8 (1935): 27–43; Mahler, "Simon Dubnov," in Mahler, *Historiker un vegvayzer* (Tel Aviv, 1967), pp. 68–99.

19. Mahler, "Vegn teoryes fun der yidisher kultur-geshikhte."

20. A. Hepner and I. Herzberg, *Aus Vergangenheit und Gegenwart der Juden und der jüdischen Gemeinde in den Posner Landen* (Kosmin and Bydgoszcz, 1909–29); Herzberg, *Geschichte der Juden in Bromberg* (Frankfurt a.M., 1903); Louis Lewin, *Geschichte der Juden in Lissa* (Pinne, 1904); Lewin, *Geschichte der Juden in Inowrocław* (Posen, 1900); St. Simon, *Żydzi inowrocławscy za czasów Księstwa Warszawskiego (1807–1815)* (Inowrocław, 1939).

21. Mojżesz Schorr, *Żydzi w Przemyślu do końca XVIII wieku* (Lwów, 1903).

22. Majer Bałaban, *Żydzi lwowscy na przełomie XVI i XVII wieku* (Lwów, 1906); Bałaban, *Die Judenstadt von Lublin* (Berlin, 1919); Bałaban, *Dzieje Żydów w Krakowie i na Kazimierzu (1304–1868)*, vol. 1: *1304–1655* (Cracow, 1913). A considerably enlarged version pertains to the 1304–1868 period: *Historja Żydów w Krakowie i na Kazimierzu (1304–1868)* (Cracow, 1931–36).

23. Jacob Caro, *Geschichte der Juden in Lemberg* (Cracow, 1894).

ban presented the life of the Jews only at the end of the sixteenth century, but he also took into consideration their legal status and economic relations. Bałaban's work on Lublin pertained to another large community. Cracow, too, was a town to which Bałaban devoted many years of work. In the copious two-volume monographic study that covers practically six centuries, Bałaban used municipal acts as well as those of the Jewish community. All these studies, based upon various sources analyzed in detail, were excellent in construction. Bałaban also examined smaller Jewish communities.[24]

Emanuel Ringelblum wrote about Warsaw, which had the largest concentration of Jews in Poland. His Ph.D. dissertation, completed in 1927, discussed the history of Warsaw Jews in the Middle Ages. He also prepared a second volume of the study, taking it up to the end of the eighteenth century, but managed to publish only a few sections of it.[25] Certain aspects of economic life of the Jews of Warsaw in the eighteenth century were examined by Esther Tenenbaum and in the nineteenth century by Isaiah Warszawski.[26]

Filip Friedman wrote *Dzieje żydów w Łodzi* (The History of the Jews of Łódź) upon the basis of archival material; another study dealt with the proletarization of the Jewish population in that town. Friedman, Aaron Alperin, and Z. Elenberg also published studies on other aspects of the life of the Jews in Łódź.[27]

24. Majer Bałaban, "Żółkiew," in Bałaban, *Z historii Żydów w Polsce: Szkice i studia* (Warsaw, 1920), pp. 42–65; Bałaban, "Żydzi w Olkuszu i gminach parafjalnych," in Bałaban, *Studia historyczne* (Warsaw, 1927), pp. 151–66.

25. Emanuel Ringelblum, *Żydzi w Warszawie*, vol. 1: *Od czasów najdawniejszych do ostatniego wygnania w r. 1527* (Warsaw, 1932); Ringelblum, "Yidn in Varshe in akhtsntn yorhundert un zeyer rekhtlekh-gezelshaftlekhe lage," in *Historishe shriftn*, vol. 2 (Vilna, 1937), pp. 248–69; Ringelblum, "Dos ineveynikste lebn fun di varshever yidn in akhtsntn yorhundert fun der farkerter tsayt," *Fun noentn over,* 1937, no. 1, pp. 179–88, 275–81; Ringelblum, "Der yidisher opshoym in akhtsntn yorhundert," *Fun noentn over,* 1938, no. 1, pp. 275–80, no. 2, pp. 119–30; Ringelblum, "Yidishe doktoyrim in Varshe," *Sotsyaler meditsin/Medycyna Społeczna*, 1931, nos. 9–10, pp. 127–31; Ringelblum, "Pruv fun a reshime fun yidishe doktoyrim in Poyln," *Sotsyaler meditsin/Medycyna społeczna*, 1932, nos. 7–8, pp. 107–11; Ringelblum, "Shmuel Zbytkower: Askan ziburi-kalkali be-Polin be-yemei halukatah," *Zion* 3, no. 5 (1938): 246–66, 337–55.

26. Esther Tenenbaum, "Dos varshever birgertum un di yidn in der tsveyter helft fun akhtsntn yorhundert," in *Yunger historiker,* 1: 41–57; Isaiah Warszawski, "Struktura społeczna i gospodarcza żydowstwa warszawskiego w 1840 roku," *Miesięcznik Żydowski*, 1931, no. 9, pp. 245–62.

27. Filip Friedman, *Dzieje żydów w Łodzi: Od początków osadnictwa żydów do r. 1863* (Łódź, 1935); Friedman, "Di industrializatsye un proletarizatsye fun di lodzer yidn in di yorn 1860–1914," in *Lodzer visnshaftlekhe shriftn*, vol. 1, ed. Filip Friedman (Łódź, 1938), pp. 63–132; Friedman, "Łódzka Chewra Kadisha i jej dzieje," in *Stary cmentarz żydowski w Łodzi,* ed. J. Szper (Łódź, 1938); Aaron Alperin, "Żydzi w Łodzi:

Israel Klausner wrote a richly documented history of the Jews in Vilna. Pinkhas Kon published several contributions on interrelations in that community during the eighteenth and nineteenth centuries.[28] Works dealing with other Polish towns include A. S. Hershberg on Białystok,[29] Isaiah Trunk on Kutno and Płock,[30] David Wurm on Brody, Jacob Schall on Żółkiew, Ephraim Sonenschein on Czortków, and Mojżesz Steinberg on Jarosław.[31] Less valuable were the works on Łask by P. Z. Gliksman, on Piotrków by Mojżesz Feinkind, and on Słonim by G. A. Goldberg.[32] Finally, let me mention the essays and source materials pertaining to Łęczyca, Kalisz, Konin, Kowel, and Tykocin.[33]

The origin of self-government among the Polish Jews, and its various organizational levels, met with great interest among historians. Alongside the governing bodies of the various *kahals*, which had strictly defined duties and powers, higher self-government structures

Początki gminy żydowskiej, 1780–1822," *Rocznik Łódzki* (Łódź, 1928), pp. 151–78; Z. Elenberg, *Żydzi i początki szkolnictwa powszechnego w Łodzi* (Łódź, 1930); P. Z. Gliksman, "Tsvey alte hevres in Lodz," in *Lodzer visnshaftlekhe shriftn*, 1:267–76; Mojżesz Feinkind, "Di hevre kedishe in Piotrkow," in *Lodzer visnshaftlekhe shriftn*, 1:55–62.

28. Israel Klausner, *Toldot ha-kehillah ha-ivrit be-Vilna*, vol. 1 (Vilna, 1938); Pinkhas Kon, "Fun vilner arkhivn un bibliotekn," in *Historishe shriftn*, vol. 1 (Warsaw, 1929), pp. 753–78, continued in 2:605–14, which concerns social controversies between the plebs and the *kahal* oligarchy in Vilna. See also Zalmen Reisen, ed., *Pinkes far der geshikhte fun Vilne in di yorn fun milkhome un okupatsye* (Vilna, 1922); Moshe Schalit, ed., *Oyf di khurves fun milkhomes un mehumes: Pinkes fun gegnt-komitet EKOPO* (Vilna, 1931).

29. A. S. Hershberg, *Pinkas Bialystok*, vol. 1 (New York, 1949). This publication was prepared in 1934–35 and ultimately published by the author's son after the war.

30. Isaiah Trunk, "A yidishe kehile in Poyln baym sof akhtsntn yorhundert—Kutno," in *Bleter far geshikhte*, 1:87–140; Trunk, "Di rekhtlekhe lage fun di yidn in Plock in zekhtsntn yorhundert," in *Bleter far geshikhte*, vol. 2, ed. Yaakov Berman, Raphael Mahler, and Emanuel Ringelblum (Warsaw, 1938), pp. 89–105; Trunk, *Di geshikhte fun yidn in Plock, 1237–1657* (Warsaw, 1939). Ignacy Schiper also wrote a popular monograph on Płock entitled *Siedemset lat gminy żydowskiej w Płocku* (Lwów, 1938).

31. David Wurm, *Z dziejów żydowstwa brodzkiego* (Brody, 1935); Jacob Schall, *Dawna Żółkiew i jej Żydzi* (Lwów, 1939); Ephraim Sonenschein, *Perakim mi-toldot ha-yehudim be-Czortkow* (Warsaw, 1939); Mojżesz Steinberg, *Żydzi w Jarosławiu* (Jarosław, 1933).

32. P. Z. Gliksman, *Ir Lask ve-hakhmeiha* (Łódź, 1926); Mojżesz Feinkind, *Dzieje Żydów w Piotrkowie i okolicy* (Piotrków, 1936); G. A. Goldberg, *Z dziejów miasta Słonimia* (Słonim, 1934).

33. Filip Friedman, "Materyaln tsu der geshikhte fun di yidn in Letshits [Łęczyca]," in *Lodzer visnshaftlekhe shriftn*, 1:239–46; N. M. Gelber, "Di yidn in Kalish [Kalisz] in der oyfshtand in 1830–31," in *Lodzer visnshaftlekhe shriftn*, 1:258–63; Eliezer Feldman, "Tsvey alte yidishe kehiles in lodzer kant: Kalisz un Konin," in *Lodzer visnshaftlekhe shriftn*, 1:3–31; Raphael Mahler, "Tsu der geshikhte fun yidn in Kowel," in *Landkentenish*, vol. 1 (Warsaw, 1933), pp. 26–46; Israel Halperin, "Toldot ha-yehudim be-Tiktin," *Hatzofeh* 15 (1931): 287–98.

appeared around 1579. The representatives of the *kahals* who gathered at the provincial Sejms of Little Poland and Great Poland, Volynia, Podolia, and Lithuania selected a *vaad* (council of elders), which conferred with state authorities in various cases relating to the entire Jewish community in the Commonwealth.

This system was largely influenced by Polish self-government and parliamentary structures. Recognition of the autonomy of the *kahals* was in keeping with the principle of self-government accorded to all religious communities in Poland. The self-government of the *kahals* was closely connected with the legal status of Polish Jews, which determined their relations with the Christian population. The Statue of Kalisz in 1264 laid the foundations for the self-government of the *kahals* as regards the powers of the elders, arbitral courts, and so forth. Self-government was guaranteed in the general privileges issued by the Polish monarchs and in edicts given to certain towns. In private towns, where from the middle of the sixteenth century the Jewish population was subject to the jurisdiction of the owners, these relations sometimes took on a different form. Financial motives played a considerable role in the provincial governors' determination of the *kahal* leaders' functions.

The legal status of Jewish self-government in pre-Partition Poland had been discussed by Ludwik Gumplowicz and Mojżesz Schorr, who based their work almost exclusively on the royal privileges and edicts mentioned above.[34] These privileges and edicts, however, did not reflect the actual relations within the *kahals*. Bałaban was the first to continue research in this field, and he expanded the base of source materials by making use of the subprovincial ordinances and municipal acts. He thus could propose an outline of the actual relations in the *kahal*, the limits to the powers of its organs, and the relations with the *starosta* (district head) and *wojewoda* (provincial governor). In his monographic works on the *kahals* and in special studies, Bałaban presented genealogies, which sometimes reached a few generations back, of famous rabbis, leaders of the *kahals*, doctors,

---

34. Ludwik Gumplowicz, *Prawodawstwo polskie względem Żydów* (Cracow, 1867); Mojżesz Schorr, "Organizacja Żydów w Polsce od najdawniejszych czasów do 1772: Głównie na podstawie źródeł archiwalnych," *Kwartalnik Historyczny* 13 (1899): 482–520, 734–75, published in German as *Rechtstellung und innere Verfassung der Juden in Polen* (Berlin, 1917). On the activity of the provincial courts, see Zbigniew Pazdro, *Organizacja i praktyka żydowskich sądów podwojewodzińskich w okresie 1740–1772: Na podstawie lwowskich materyałów archiwalnych* (Lwów, 1903).

and pharmacists. In doing so, he used tombstone inscriptions and extant correspondence.

Bałaban gave the problems of self-government a central place in his scientific research. In monographic studies on the *kahals* in Lwów and Cracow, he devoted much time to explaining the range of powers of the organs of the *kahals*, the election and tax systems, the rabbinate, and the court system. He also broached these problems in a number of studies published in Russian, Polish, and German.[35]

A few years later Bałaban proposed an impressive plan for a monographic study on the development of Jewish self-government in Poland and its organizational structure throughout five centuries. Sections of this work, which was to include the Partitions and the Second Republic, were published in 1937–39 in *Głos Gminy Żydowskiej*.[36] In this study, Bałaban expanded the range of topics he treated. Although the organizational aspects of the many levels of the *kahals*, their finances, and their election system still dominated, he gave much more attention to the work of the *kahals* in the fields of culture, education, health care, charity, protection of morality, and so on. In the published material there is no mention of the higher organs of Jewish self-government. Bałaban did not include this topic, nor did he explain the essence of the social conflicts within the *kahals* or the general economic and political reasons for the disintegration of the higher structures of self-government at the beginning of the reign of Stanisław August.

These gaps were partially filled by Schiper and Mahler, who did

35. Majer Bałaban, "Pravoy stroy Evreiov v Polshe v sredniye i noviye vieka," *Evreiskaia Starina*, 1910, pp. 39–60, 161–91, 1911, pp. 40–51, 180–96; Bałaban, "Ustrój kahału w Polsce XVI–XVII wieku," *Kwartalnik Poświęcony Badaniom Przeszłości Żydów w Polsce*, 1912, no. 1, pp. 17–54. In *Istoriya Evreiev v Rossii*, vol. 11 of *Istoriya Evreiskogo Naroda* (Moscow, 1914), Bałaban published a number of contributions: "Kahal," pp. 132–60; "Evreiskiy Seym v Polshe ili vaad Korony i seymiki ili vaady okrugov," pp. 161–80; "Organizatsiya Evreiskogo Suda," pp. 211–32; Bałaban, "Die krakauer Judengemeindeordnung aus dem Jahre 1595 und ihre Nachtrage," *Jahrbuch der jüdischen Literaturgesellschaft in Frankfurt a/M.*, vol. 10 (Frankfurt a.M., 1915), pp. 296–360, vol. 11 (Frankfurt a.M., 1916), pp. 88–114; Bałaban, "Ze studjów nad ustrojem prawynym Żydów w Polsce: Sedzia żydowski i jego kompetencja," *Pamietnik trzydziestolecia pracy naukowej Prof. Dr. Przemyslawa Dabkowskiego* (Lwów, 1927), pp. 245–80; Bałaban, "Stan kahału krakowskiego na przełomie XVII i XVIII wieku," *Miesięcznik Żydowski*, 1931, no. 11, pp. 413–428; Bałaban, "Za zagadnień ostrojowych żydowstwa polskiego: Lwów a ziemstwo Rusko-Bracławskie w XVII w.," in *Studja Lwowskie* (Lwów, 1932), pp. 41–65.

36. Majer Bałaban, "Ustrój gminy żydowskiej w Polsce w XVI–XX wieku," *Głos Gminy Żydowskiej*, published in installments 1937–39.

not limit themselves to a description of the central organs of self-government. By seeking out official revenue acts, they examined the relations of those organs with the Polish treasurer. Schiper published several studies that, besides attempting to reconstruct the central organs of Jewish self-government, explained the reasons for the breakdown of the whole structure. Moreover, he provided a description of the activity of the Warsaw Commission, established in 1666 by the General Sejm of the Crown to negotiate with the commissars of the undertreasury on financial matters and Jewish debts.[37] Mahler also examined the complicated financial problems of the central self-government organs.[38] Ringelblum's synthetic outline of the history of Jewish self-government in pre-Partition Poland and Eisenbach's articles on the attempted restitution of the central organs of Jewish autonomy in the Duchy of Warsaw are also worthy of mention.[39]

Several valuable source materials and studies concerning this broad problem were published abroad. Simon Dubnov, who was a pioneer in this field, published a collection of protocols of the general Sejm of Lithuania, and Israel Halperin published essays on the structure and activity of the *vaad* of the central provinces of the Crown and its relations with the Lithuanian Sejm.[40] Louis Lewin contributed to the subject of the general history of the provincial Sejm of

37. Ignacy Schiper, "Beitrage zur Geschichte der partielen Judentage in Polen," *Monatsschrift für Geschichte und Wissenschaft des Judentums* 52 (1912): 458–77, 602–11, 736–44; Schiper, "Der tsuzamenshtel funem Vaad Arba Arazot," in *Historishe shriftn*, 1:73–82; Schiper, "Poylishe regestn tsu der geshikhte funem Vaad Arba Arazot," in *Historishe shriftn*, 1:83–114; Schiper, "Samorząd żydowski w Polsce na przełomie wieku 18 i 19-go.," *Miesięcznik Żydowski*, 1931, no. 6, pp. 513–29; Schiper, "Finantseyler khurban fun der tsentraler un provintseyler oytonomye fun yidn in altn Poyln," in *Ekonomishe shriftn*, vol. 2, ed. Jacob Lestschinsky (Vilna, 1932), pp. 1–19; Schiper, "'Komisja warszawska': Przycznek do dziejów autonomji Żydów w dawnej Polsce," *Księgo jubileuszowa ku czci D-ra Markusa Braudego*, vol. 4 of *Pisma Instytutu Nauk Judaistycznych w Warszawie* (Warsaw, 1931), pp. 147–57.
38. Raphael Mahler, "Dokumentn tsu der geshikhte fun di vaadey hagliles in Poyln," in *Historishe shriftn*, 2:639–49; Mahler, "A budzshet fun Vaad Arba Arazot in akhtsntn yorhundert," *YIVO bleter* 15 (1940): 63–86.
39. Ringelblum's essay serves as an introduction to I. Bornstein, *Budzety gmin żydowskich w Polsce* (Warsaw, 1929); Artur Eisenbach, "Di tsentrale reprezentants-orgonen fun di yidn in varshever firshtntum (1807–1815)," in *Bleter far geshikhte*, 2:33–88; Eisenbach, "Dokumentn tsu der geshikhte fun di departament-vadim un geplante tsentrale vadim in varshever firshtntum," in *Bleter far geshikhte*, 2:127–45.
40. Simon Dubnov, *Pinkas ha-medinah (o pinkas vaad ha-kehillot ha-rashiot be-medinat Lita)* (Berlin, 1925); Israel Halperin, *Tosafot u-miluim le-pinkas medinat Lita* (Jerusalem, 1935); Halperin, "Zur Frage der Zusammensetzung der Vierlandesynode in Polen," *Monatsschrift für Geschichte und Wissenschaft des Judentums* 76 (1932): 519–22; Halperin, "Reshito shel. Vaad Medinat Lita ve-yahaso el Vaad Arba Arazot," *Zion* 3, no. 5 (1938): 51–57; Halperin, "Der Vaad Arba Arazot un zayne batsiungen mit oysland," in *Historishe shriftn*, 2:68–79.

Great Poland and Weinryb to the financial history of the *kahals*.[41] Israel Sosis discussed the social activity of the Jewish Sejm of the Belorussian province.[42]

Economic and Social History

Economic history stimulated great interest. In this field, and in social history, a pioneering role was played by Ignacy Schiper, who in 1906 and 1911 published two large works on the economic history of medieval Jews in the context of the general economic development of the society of that period. Both works were based on various archival sources.[43] The central problem Schiper examined was the origin of the accumulation of capital, the political and economic reasons for the gradual transition of Jewish economic activity from trade to credit in different countries, and the reasons for the abnormal economic structure of the Jewish population. Schiper polemized with Werner Sombart on the role of Jews in the development of capitalism. He was also the first to attack and destroy the notion of Jewish predilection toward trade and usury.

Twenty years later Schiper published a four-volume study of all domains of Jewish economic activity in various European countries, mainly in the Middle Ages. Here Schiper touched upon certain key issues and proposed a number of hypotheses, one concerning the Khazar lineage of the Polish Jews at the beginning of their settlement in Poland.[44] Some of Schiper's theses were questioned by other scholars, giving rise to a lively polemic that engaged the attention of Majer Bałaban, Mateusz Mieses, Jacob Szacki, and Filip Friedman.

41. Louis Lewin, "Neue Materialen zur Geschichte der Vierlandersynode," *Jahrbuch der jüdischen Literaturgesellschaft in Frankfurt a/M.*, vol. 2 (Frankfurt a.M., 1904), pp. 1–26, vol. 3 (Frankfurt a.M., 1905), pp. 79–130, vol. 11 (Frankfurt a.M., 1916), pp. 141–208; Lewin, *Die Landessynode der grosspolnischen Judenschaft* (Frankfurt a.M., 1926), with supplements in *Dubnow Festschrift* (Berlin, 1930), pp. 124–35; B. D. Weinryb, "Beitrage zur Finanzgeschichte der judischen Gemeinden in Polen," *Monatsschrift für Geschichte und Wissenschaft des Judentums* 82 (1938): 248–63.

42. Israel Sosis, "Der yidisher seym in Lite un Vaysrusland in zayn gezetsgeberisher tetikeyt (1623–1761)," *Tsaytshrift* (Minsk) 2–3 (1928): 1–72. One should also mention D. B. Teimanas, *L'Autonomie des communautés juives en Pologne en XVI et XVII siècles* (Paris, 1933).

43. Ignacy Schiper, *Die Anfange des Kapitalismus bei den abendländischen Juden* (Vienna, 1906); Schiper, *Studja nad stoscinkami gospodarczymi Żydów w Polsce podczas średnowiecza* (Warsaw, 1911), published in Yiddish as *Die virtshaftsgeshikhte fun di yidn in Poyln baysn mitlelter* (Warsaw, 1926).

44. Ignacy Schiper, *Yidishe geshikhte: Virtshaftsgeshikhte* (Warsaw, 1930).

Schiper also published a synthetic work on the economic history of the Jews in Poland up to the end of the eighteenth century. In another large monographic study he outlined the role of Jews in the development of trade relations in Poland from antiquity to the twentieth century.[45] A weakness in his work is the failure to establish a connection between Jewish trade and the economic history of the country as a whole. M. Brilling, Marcus Breger, and Mark Wischnitzer also wrote about the trade activity of Polish Jews.[46]

Another particularly noteworthy sector of economic life was the crafts. Much was written on the organization of the Jewish craftsmen, their separate guilds, and the participation of Jewish artisans in general town guilds. Moshe Kremer's Ph.D. dissertation, published in three installments, seems to be especially valuable.[47] Much new information concerning the history of Jewish craftsmen is provided by Perla Kramerówna's article on Jewish guilds and by Bela Mandelsberg's article on the mutual relations between Jewish tradesmen and town guilds in Lublin.[48] Ringelblum published protocols of the tailors' guild in Płock, and Rivke Notik published an article on Jewish artisans in Lithuania.[49]

One should also mention works issued abroad, of which the most important seem to be Mark Wischnitzer's study of the organization of Jewish guilds in the Crown and Lithuania, Israel Sosis's study of Jewish tradesmen in Poland and Lithuania, and Israel Halperin's study of Jewish guilds in Poland.[50]

45. Ignacy Schiper, "Dzieje gospodarcze Żydów Korony i Litwy w czasach przed-rozbiorowych," in *Żydzi w Polsce Odrodzonej*, vol. 1, ed. Ignacy Schiper, Aryeh Tarta-kower, and Aleksander Hafftka (Warsaw, n.d.), pp. 111–210; Ignacy Schiper, *Dzieje handlu żydowskiego na ziemiach polskich* (Warsaw, 1937).

46. M. Brilling, "Jüdische Meesegaste und Marktsbesucher in Breslau in XVII Jahrhundert," *Jüdische Familienforschung* 6–8 (1930–32): five installments; Marcus Breger, *Zur Handelsgeschichte der Juden in Polen währen des XVII Jahrhundert* (Berlin, 1932); Mark Wischnitzer, "Die Stellung der Brodyer Juden in internationalen Handel in der zweiten Halfte des XVIII Jahrhundert," in *Dubnow Festschrift*, pp. 113–23.

47. Moshe Kremer, "Le-heker ha-melakhah ve-hevrot baalei melakhah ezel ye-hudei Polin," *Zion* 2, no. 5 (1937): 294–325; Kremer, "Der onteyl fun yidishe baley-melokhes in di kristlekhe tsekhn in amolikn Poyln," in *Bleter far geshikhte*, 2:3–32; Kremer, "Yidishe baley-melokhes un tsekhn in amolikn Poyln: 16–18 yorhundert," *YIVO bleter* 40 (1956): 86–119.

48. Perla Kramerówna, "Żydowskie cechy rzemieślnicze w dawnej Polsce," *Mie-sięcznik Żydowski*, 1932, nos. 9–10, pp. 259–98; Bela Mandelsberg, "Lubliner yidishe hantverker un di shtat-tsekhn in der ershter helft fun XVII yorhundert," in *Yunger historiker*, 2:54–66.

49. Emanuel Ringelblum, "Der pinkes fun der plotsker 'hevre khayatim,' " in *Historishe shriftn*, 1:20–31; Rivke Notik, "Tsu der geshikhte fun hantverk bay litvishe yidn," *YIVO bleter* 9 (1936): 107–19.

50. Mark Wischnitzer, "Die jüdische Zuntwerfassung in Polen und Lithuania in

A number of historians wrote about agricultural settlements. Among the most noteworthy are Lipman Comber's article on the policy of the Prussian government regarding Jewish colonization, Jacob Szacki's larger study on colonization in the Kingdom of Poland, and Filip Friedman's work on the settlements of the Galician Jews.[51] Ethnographic studies were accompanied by more extensive works on the general economic history of the Jewish population. An example is Bernard Dov Weinryb's economic history of Jews in Poland, which included a history of Jews in the Polish lands of the Russian Partition in various sectors of economic life (trade, industry, and agriculture) during the nineteenth century. This research was based on exceptionally rich archival sources and publications of source materials. It attempted a synthesis, but Weinryb's interpretation of the sources and his statistical methods were criticized by certain scholars. A few years later Weinryb published a considerably expanded version of his economic history of the Jews of Poland.[52] Research was also undertaken on the cooperative movement that Polish Jews began developing early in the nineteenth century. In this interwar period a number of cooperatives were functioning, including credit cooperatives, crafts cooperatives, and production cooperatives. These were studied in works by Abraham Prowalski and A. Szmosz.[53]

17- und 18-ten Jahrhundert," *Vierteljahrschrift für Sozial- und Wirtschaftsgeschichte* 20 (1928): 33–51, published in Yiddish as "Di struktur fun yidishe tsekhn in Poyln, Lite un Vaysrusland inem zibetsntn un akhtsntn yorhundert," *Tsaytshrift* 2–3 (1928): 73–88; Israel Sosis, "Di yidishe bal-melokhes un zeyere arbeter in Lite, Vaysrusland, un Ukrayne," *Tsaytshrift* 4 (1930): 1–29; Israel Halperin, "Hevrot baalei melakhah yehudiim be-Polin ve-Lita," *Zion* 2, no. 5 (1937): 70–89.

51. Lipman Comber, "A mekloymershter pruv tsu kolonizirn yidn oyf erd in iber-gang fun XVIII–XVIII yorhundert," in *Yunger historiker,* 2:109–30; Jacob Szacki, "Tsu der geshikhte fun der yidisher kolonizatsye in Kinigraykh Poyln," *YIVO bleter* 4 (1934): 209–32; Filip Friedman, "Landvirtshaft, kolonizatsye un gruntbazits bay di galitsyanishe yidn arum der helft fun dem nayntsntn yorhundert," in *Yunger historiker,* 2:131–42.

52. B. D. Weinryb, *Neueste Wirtschaftsgeschichte der Juden in Russland und Polen, 1772–1881* (Breslau, 1934), published in a new edition (Hildesheim, 1972); Weinryb, *Mehkarim be-toldot ha-kalkalah ve-ha-hevrah shel yehudei Polin* (Jerusalem, 1939). See the review by Filip Friedman, "Referatn un retsenzyes," *YIVO bleter* 8 (1935): 258–63; and the polemic: Weinryb, "A por bamerkungen tsu a retsenzye," *YIVO bleter* 9 (1936): 152–54; Friedman, "Nokh amol vegn B. Weinryb's *Nayste vertshafts-geshikhte fun di yidn in Rusland un Poyln,*" *YIVO bleter* 11 (1937): 387–93.

53. Abraham Prowalski, "Ruch spółdzielcy wśród Żydów w Polsce," *Miesięcznik Żydowski,* 1932, no. 6, pp. 546–56, nos. 7–8, pp. 146–58, nos. 11–12, pp. 477–502, 1933, nos. 1–2, pp. 111–29; Prowalski, *Spółdzielczość żydowska w Polsce* (Warsaw, 1933); Prowalski, "Spółdzielczość żydowska w Polsce Odrodzonej," in *Żydzi w Polsce Odrodzonej,* vol. 2, ed. Ignacy Schiper, Aryeh Tartakower, and Aleksander Hafftka

A special publication of the YIVO Economical-Statistical Section in Vilna was devoted to economic issues. The two large volumes of *Ekonomishe shriftn* (volume 1 in 1928; volume 2 in 1932, both edited by Jacob Lestschinsky) contained articles concerning the role played by Jews in industry and trade. The volumes also dealt with the demographic structure of the Jewish population and with migrations, and they published school statistics for Poland and other Central and Eastern European countries. Finally, let me mention the publications of the Economic-Statistical Bureau of the CEKABE (Central Organization of Societies for the Support of Noninterest Credit and Promotion of Productive Work) (nonprofit loaning banks).[54]

During this period historians also began studying the structural changes and processes of restratification experienced by the Jewish population in the eighteenth and nineteenth centuries. Ringelblum examined the pre-Partition period in a copious source material study discussing attempts at introducing Jews into production through employment in agriculture and manufactures belonging to Jewish and magnate entrepreneurs in the second half of the eighteenth century. In examining the history of Jews in the new and rapidly growing industrial center of Łódź, Filip Friedman studied aspects of socioeconomic transformations in both Łódź and the whole Congress Kingdom in the nineteenth century. While speaking of structural changes, one should mention the works by Georges Gliksman and Jacob Lestschinsky.[55]

Historical demography was a new field of research, although at the beginning of the twentieth century in the Crown and in Lithuania in the eighteenth century, statistics concerning the Jewish population met with considerable interest. Ferdynand Bostel, A.

(Warsaw, n.d.), pp. 590–617; A. Szmosz, "Yidishe kooperatsye in Poyln," *Kooperative bavegung*, 1927, no. 4.

54. *Biuletyn Ekonomiczno-Statystyczny: Materiały i Cyfry z Życia Ludności*, (Warsaw, 1936–37).

55. Emanuel Ringelblum, *Projekty i próby przewarstwowienia Żydów w epice Stanisławowskiej* (Warsaw, 1934); Friedman," Die industrializatsye un proletarizatsye fun di lodzer yidn," pp. 132–63; Friedman, "Wirtschaftliche Umschichtungsprozesse und Industrialisierung in der polnischen Judenschaft 1800–1870," in *Jewish Studies in Memory of G. A. Kohut* (New York, 1935), pp. 178–249; Friedman, "Powstanie żydowskiego proletariatu przemysłowego i początki konfliktów społecznych w Łodzi," *Miesięcznik Żydowski*, 1935, nos. 1–2, pp. 60–68; Georges Gliksman, *L'aspect economique de la question juive en Pologne* (Paris, 1929); Jacob Lestschinsky, "Przesiedlenie i przewarstwowienie Żydów w ostatnim stuleciu," *Miesięcznik Żydowski*, 1933, nos. 11–12, pp. 236–57.

Czuczyński, F. Kleszczyński, and Majer Bałaban analyzed some of the archival materials.[56] Ignacy Schiper made the first attempt to determine the number, geographical location, and structure of the Jewish population in the Commonwealth in the eighteenth century. Mahler gave a full source material presentation of statistical material from the 1764–65 fiscal census. Before the war, he was able to publish only sections of this work; the study in its entirety appeared after the war. Eliezer Feldman was also interested in historical statistics.[57] Works also appeared dealing with contemporary demography—the natural mobility of the Jewish population, its death rate, behavior, and their causes. This group of works includes books and articles by Jacob Lestschinsky, Libman Hersch, Cemach Szabad, J. Koralnik, and Artur Eisenbach.[58] Lestschinsky, Aryeh Tartakower, and Menaham Linder studied the emigration of Polish Jews to various European and overseas destinations and Jewish migrations in general.[59]

An important area of historical research was the origin and history of various currents and dissident sects among the Polish Jews in the seventeenth and eighteenth centuries. Here a particularly significant contribution was made by Majer Bałaban, who first published a study on the Frankist movement, based on archival sources, and a few years later prepared two volumes on the history of the

56. For an analysis of these works, see Artur Eisenbach, *Z dziejów ludności żydowskiej w Polsce w XVIII i XIX wieku* (Warsaw, 1983).

57. Ignacy Schiper, "Rassieleniye evreiev v Polshe i Litvie," in *Istoriya Evreiev v Rossii*, vol. 11 of *Istoriya Evreiskogo Naroda*, pp. 105–31; Raphael Mahler, "Statistik fun yidn in der lubliner voyevodstve in di yorn 1764–65," in *Yunger historiker*, 2:67–108; Mahler, "Di yidishe bafelkerung oyfn shetakh fun der lodzer voyevodshaft in yor 1764," in *Lodzer visnshaftlekhe shriftn*, 1:32–54; Mahler, *Yidn in amolikn Poyln, in likht fun tsifern: Die demografishe un sotsyal-ekonomishe struktur fun yidn in Kroyn-Poyln in XVIII yorhundert* (Warsaw, 1959); Eliezer Feldman, "Do statystyki Żydów w dawnej Polsce," *Miesięcznik Żydowski*, 1933, nos. 1–2, pp. 130–35.

58. Jacob Lestschinsky, *Probleme der Bevolkerungsbewegung bei den Juden* (Padua, 1926); Libman Hersch, "Vegn di problemes fun der natirlekher bafelkerungbavegung bay yidn," in *Ekonomishe shriftn*, vol. 1, ed. Jacob Lestschinsky (Vilna, 1928), pp. 249–53. Other works were published during 1931–39 in *YIVO bleter, Yidishe ekonomik, Ekonomishe shriftn,* and *Sotsyale meditsin/Medycyna Społeczna.*

59. Jacob Lestschinsky, *Die Anfange der Emigration und Kolonisation der Juden im 19 Jahrhundert* (Berlin, 1929); Lestschinsky, "Die Umsiedlung und Umschichtung des judischen Volkes im letzten Jahrhundert," *Weltwirtschaftliches Archiv* 30 (1929): 131–56, 32 (1931): 569–99; numerous smaller studies by Lestschinsky in *Yidishe ekonomik*, 1937–39; Aryeh Tartakower, *Yidishe emigratsye un yidishe emigratsye politik* (Vilna, 1939); Tartakower, *Yidishe vanderungen* (Warsaw, 1939); Menaham Linder, "Emigracja Żydów z Polski w okresie kryzsu (1929–33)," *Miesięcznik Żydowski*, 1935, nos. 3–4, pp. 142–72; Linder, "Yidishe vanderungen far di letste tsen yor," *Yidishe ekonomik* 2, nos. 7–8 (1938): 338–65.

Frankists (in Hebrew). Bałaban recalled that the Hebrew volumes were destroyed during the war. He also wrote a synthetic work on mysticism and messianic movements and a separate study on the Sabbatean movement.[60]

Bałaban also dealt with the Karaite sect, which seceded from the Jewish community in the Commonwealth and created separate *kahals*, although formally their legal standing was identical. The only exception was the Karaites in Troki, near Vilna, whose status was based on the Magdeburg Law. At the end of the eighteenth and in the first half of the nineteenth centuries this division was sanctioned by the Austrian and Russian authorities, and the Karaites were excluded from legislation that discriminated against the remaining Jews. During the Second World War, Nazi authorities decided that, from a racial point of view, the Karaites were members of a Turkish-Mongol group, and that saved the sect from extermination. On the basis of archival material, Bałaban wrote a monographic study on the Karaite groups in Łowicz, Halicz, Łuck, and Troki, analyzing their relations with the Jewish population and the attitude toward them of the Polish authorities and, after the Partitions, the Austrian and Russian authorities as well.[61]

In the interwar period the problem of the origin of the Karaites was the source of a heated polemic involving Jewish historians, such as Majer Bałaban, Julius Brutzkus, and Gedo Hecht, and Karaite historians, such as Ananiasz Zajączkowski, Szymon Firkowski, A. Mordkowicz, and A. Szyszman.[62]

The Neophyte movement interested Polish and Russian scholars. Before the First World War, Ignacy Schiper wrote about the Neophytes in Jagiellonian Poland. The most important works from the

60. Majer Bałaban, "Studien und Quellen der frankistischen Bewegung in Polen," in *Studies in Memory of A. S. Poznanski* (Warsaw, 1927), pp. 25–75; Bałaban, "Praca mojego życia," in *Księga jubileuszowa dla uczczenia 60-lecia profesora Majera Bałabana* (Lwów, 1938); Bałaban, "Mistyka i ruchy mesjańskie wśród Żydów w dawnej Rzeczypospolitej," in *Żydzi w Polsce Odrodzonej*, 1:255–81; Bałaban, "Sabataizm w Polsce," in *Księga Jubileuszowa ku czci Prof. Dr. Mojżesza Schorra*, pp. 47–90.

61. Majer Bałaban, "Karaici w Polsce," *Nowe Życie* 1 (1924): 1–23; Bałaban, "Lekorot ha-karaim be-Polin," *Hatekufah* 16 (1923): 293–307, 21 (1924): 226–35, 25 (1929): 450–87; Bałaban, "Karaici w Polsce," in *Studia historyczne*, pp. 1–92.

62. Julius Brutzkus, "Di opshtamung fun di karaimer in Lite un Poyln," *YIVO bleter* 13 (1938): 109–23; Gedo Hecht, *Karaimi: "Synowie Zakonu"* (Warsaw, 1938); Ananiasz Zajączkowski, *Na marginesie studium Bałabana: Karaici w Polsce* (Vilna, 1928); Zajączkowski, *Karaimi na Wołyniu* (Równe, 1933); Zajączkowski, *Elementy tureckie na ziemach polskich* (Zamość, 1935); Szymon Firkowski, *O Karaimach w Polsce* (Troki, 1938); A. Mordkowicz, *Ogniska karaimskie* (Łuck, 1934); A. Szyszman, *Osadnictwo karaimskie na ziemach Wielkiego Księstwa Litewskiego* (Vilna, 1936).

interwar period included those by Shmuel Loeb Zitron, E. N. Frenk, N. M. Gelber, and Mateusz Mieses. The Neophytes were also discussed by Ludwik Korwin (Piotrowski), Stanisław Didier, and Leon Białkowski, who accused Mieses's work of being shaped by political ideology.[63]

Sociocultural movements such as Hasidism were also studied, and here a pioneering role in research was played by Simon Dubnov, who published a history of Hasidism in Yiddish, Hebrew, and German. In Poland this was the domain of Yermiyahu Frenkel, the author of a compendium on Hasidism.[64] Historians were also interested in studying the Haskalah (Jewish Enlightenment) in Galicia and the Kingdom. Israel Weinlös, S. Katz, and Filip Friedman published documents from the newly discovered archives of Yosef Perl from Tarnopol, a leading representative of the intellectual movement in Galicia. Friedman and Raphael Mahler also wrote about the conflicts between the supporters of the Haskalah and Hasidism in Galicia, and Ringelblum wrote about the subject in Warsaw.[65] These thorough works are well grounded in archival sources. A number of historians perceived factors that formed the profile of cultural and

63. Ignacy Schiper, "Żydzi neofici i prozelici w Polsce do. r. 1569," *Kwartalnik Poświęcony Badaniom Przeszłości Żydów w Polsce,* 1912, no. 2; Shmuel Loeb Zitron, *Meshumodim* (Warsaw, 1923); E. N. Frenk, *Meshumodim in Poyln in nayntsntn yorhundert;* N. M. Gelber, "Die Taufbewegung unter den polnischen Juden in 18-tem Jahrhundert," *Monatsschrift für Geschichte und Wissenschaft des Judentums* 68 (1924): 225–41; Mateusz Mieses, *Polacy-chrześcijanie pochodzenia żydowskiego* (Warsaw, 1938); Mieses, "Judaizanci we wschodnej Europie," *Miesięcznik Żydowski,* 1933, nos. 7–8, pp. 41–62, nos. 9–10, pp. 169–85, 1934, no. 2, pp. 147–59, no. 3, pp. 241–60, no. 4, pp. 342–58, no. 6, pp. 566–76; Ludwik Korwin (Piotrowski), *Szlachta polska pochodzenia żydowskiego* (Cracow, 1933); Korwin, *Szlachta mojżeszowa* (Cracrow, 1938–39); Stanisław Didier, *Rola neofitów w dziejach Polski* (Warsaw, 1934); Leon Białkowski, *Żyd o neofitach polskich* (Warsaw, 1938).

64. Simon Dubnov, *Geshikhte fun khasidizm* (Vilna, 1930), published in Hebrew as *Toldot ha-hasidut* (Tel Aviv, 1930–32), and in German as *Geschichte des Chassidismus* (Berlin, 1931–32); Yermiyahu Frenkel, "Chasydyzm wśród Żydów dawnej Rzeczypospolitej," in *Żydzi w Polsce Odrodzonej,* 1:281–88.

65. The writings of Yosef Perl were published by YIVO as *Yidishe ksovim gefunen in der tarnopoler Perl-bibliotek,* ed. Israel Weinlös (Vilna, 1937), with a philological analysis by Zelig Kalmanowicz; Filip Friedman, "Yosef Perl vi a bildungs-tuer un zayn shul in Tarnopol," in *Pedagogishe shriftn,* vol. 2 (Vilna, 1940), pp. 28–87, reprinted in *YIVO bleter* 31–32 (1948): 131–91; S. Katz, "Naye materyaln funem Yosef Perl arkhiv," in *Wachstein-bukh: Zamlung tsum ondenk fun Bernhard Wachstein, 1868–1935* (Vilna, 1939), pp. 557–77; Filip Friedman, "Di maskilim in Galitsye onheyb XIX yorhundert," *Fun noentn over,* 1938, no. 2, pp. 90–102; Friedman, "Di ershte kamfn tsvishn haskole un khasidizm," *Fun noentn over,* 1937, no. 1, pp. 259–74; Raphael Mahler, *Der kamf tsvishn haskole un khasides in Galitsye in der ershter helft fun nayntsntn yorhundert* (New York, 1942); Emanuel Ringelblum, "Khasides un haskole in Varshe in akhtsntn yorhundert," *YIVO bleter* 13 (1938): 124–32.

social movements. Ignacy Schiper wrote about the Jewish Enlightenment at the end of the eighteenth century; Hillel Zeitlin wrote on the Hasidic movement. Majer Bałaban discussed new publications pertaining to that movement; and S. A. Horodezky wrote on the Hasidic movement and its leaders.[66]

Jewish historians in the Soviet Union such as Tobiah B. Heilikman, Israel Sosis, and Abraham Yuditski were interested in other aspects of the social history of the Polish Jews. One should also mention the publication by A. Gomer on the cultural and social history of the Jews in Lithuania in the seventeenth and eighteenth centuries.[67]

Political Life

The considerable interest in political life was concentrated on Jewish participation in the independence movements. Majer Bałaban preferred to present the part played by Jews in the defense of the country in the sixteenth and seventeenth centuries, particularly in wars against the Tatars; he also wrote about Jewish engineers in the field operations conducted by the Polish armies. Bałaban edited a separate publication devoted to the participation of Jews in the Kościuszko Uprising and on Berek Joselewicz, which included a number of interesting essays.[68]

Emanuel Ringelblum devoted a separate monographic study to Jews in the Kościuszko Uprising, making use of numerous archival sources. He wrote about the participation of the Jews in the incidents of April 1794 and in the citizens' militia and about mutual Polish-Jewish relations. Ignacy Schiper's book on the situation of the Jews and their part in the November Uprising was criticized by Filip Friedman, Rafal Gerber, and particularly by Jacob Szacki. N. M. Gelber

66. Ignacy Schiper, "Początki haskali na ziemiach centralnej Polski," *Miesięcznik Żydowski*, 1932, no. 4, pp. 311–27; Hillel Zeitlin, *Khasides* (Warsaw, 1922); Majer Bałaban, "Hasidut: Al sifrut ha-hasidut ba-tekufah ha-ahronah," *Hatekufah* 18 (1923): 488–502; S. A. Horodezky, *Ha-hasidut ve-ha-hasidim* (Berlin, 1922).

67. Tobiah B. Heilikman, *Geshikhte fun der gezelshaftlekher bavegung fun di yidn in Poyln un Rusland* (Moscow, 1926); Israel Sosis, *Di geshikhte fun di yidishe gezelshaftlekhe shtremungen in Rusland in tsvantsikstn yorhundert* (Minsk, 1929); Abraham Yuditski, *Yidishe burzshuazye un yidisher proletaryat in ershter helft nayntsntn yorhundert* (Kiev, 1931); A. Gomer, *Beitrage zur Kultur- und Sozialgeschichte des Litauischen Judentums in 17 und 18 Jahrhundert* (Cologne, 1930).

68. Majer Bałaban, ed., *Album pamiątkowy ku czci Berka Joselowicza Polkownika wojsk polskich* (Warsaw, 1934).

wrote extensively about the Jews in the 1846 Revolution and the Uprising of 1863, and certain essential additional information was provided by Szacki, who indicated new sources and presented a new approach to the subject.[69]

Roman Brandstaetter described the plan proposed by Adam Mickiewicz to create a separate Jewish legion in the Turkish army fighting against the Russians in the Crimean War. Brandstaetter cited the correspondence between Mickiewicz and Armand Levy and the representatives of the Turkish government and the Jewish circles, explaining the organizational, financial, and political difficulties connected with the founding of such a military formation. Smaller works on the subject include Meir Rozenblat's article on the Jewish presence in the patriotic movement in the Kingdom of Poland in the early 1860s, and Filip Friedman's doctoral dissertation, printed in 1929, on the struggle for civil emancipation waged by Galician Jews in 1848 and 1867–68.[70]

Mateusz Mieses wrote a study about Jews in the Polish independence struggle, a section of which he managed to publish in *Nasz Przegląd* (1938 and 1939). Majer Bałaban published the correspondence between O. L. Lubliner, a member of the Great Emigration, and Joachim Lelewel, about his mission in Frankfurt am Main in 1848.[71]

The history of the Jewish working-class movement in Poland had not yet become the subject of much interest. Nevertheless, before 1931 there appeared a number of valuable monographic studies and contributions. These included primarily the works of A. Wolf Jasny (Yasni), Aryeh Tartakower, and studies published in the third vol-

69. Emanuel Ringelblum, *Di poylishe yidn in oyfshtand fun Kosciuszko* (Warsaw, 1937); Ignacy Schiper, *Żydzi królestwa polskiego w dobie powstanie listopadowego* (Warsaw, 1932); review by Jacob Szacki, in *Historishe shriftn*, 2:355–89; N. M. Gelber, "Die Juden und die polnische Revolution 1846," in *Aus zwei Jahrunderten: Beitrage zur neueren Geschichte der Juden* (Vienna, 1924); Gelber, *Die Juden und der polnischen Aufstand 1863* (Vienna, 1923); Jacob Szacki, "Yidn in dem poylishn oyfshtand," in *Historishe shriftn*, 1:423–68; Szacki, "Di amerikaner yidn un der poylisher oyfshtand fun 1863," *YIVO bleter* 4 (1932): 407–18.

70. Roman Brandstaetter, *Legion żydowski Adam Mickiewicza* (Warsaw, 1931), reprinted in *Miesięcznik Żydowski*, 1932, nos. 1–2, pp. 20–45, no. 2, pp. 112–32, no. 3, pp. 225–48, nos. 7–8, pp. 26–41; Jacob Szacki, "Referatn un retsenzyes" [review of Brandstaetter's *Legion żydowski*], *YIVO bleter* 7 (1934): 248–53; Meir Rozenblat, "Der onteyl fun di varshever yidn in di politishe demonstratsyes fun di yorn 1861–1862," in *Bleter far geshikhte*, 2: 104–26; Filip Friedman, *Die galizischen Juden im Kampfe um ihre Gleichbereichtigung* (Frankfurt a.M., 1929).

71. Majer Bałaban, "Korespondencja Lublinera z Lelewelem," *Miesięcznik Żydowski*, 1933, no. 4, pp. 289–321.

ume of *Historishe shriftn* (1939), which dealt with the shaping of the
Jewish socialist movement in Poland. Several Jewish historians in
the Soviet Union devoted much attention to the history of the Jewish
working-class movement in Poland, especially Nahum A. Buchbinder, Abraham Kirshnitz, and A. Moses Rafes.[72]

The History of Culture and Education

A distinct field that attracted much attention in the interwar period was the history of education and culture. Among the larger
synthetic works on this topic is Ignacy Schiper's study of Jewish
culture in Poland during the Middle Ages, which examines both the
intellectual life of the Jews and the history of Yiddish.[73]

Several authors outlined the development of Jewish literature.
Israel Zinberg wrote a copious history of Jewish literature in Poland
up to the end of the eighteenth century. Max Weinreich published
studies on this subject, and Zalmen Reisen published a lexicon of
Yiddish literature, press, and philology. Ignacy Schiper wrote a synthesis on the development of Jewish literature in post-Partition Poland up to 1918. Isaac Lewin wrote about rabbinical literature from
the same period, and Yermiyahu Frenkel wrote on neo-Hebrew literature in Poland. Monographic studies and smaller works on modern Jewish and Hebrew literature, in which much attention was paid
to its development on Polish soil, were also published abroad, including studies by Meir Weissberg, Yosef Klausner, and A. A. Roback. Other literary historians, such as Karol Dresdner, Wilhelm
Fallek, and Chaim Löw, dealt with Jewish influence upon Polish
literature.[74]

---

72. A. Wolf Jasny (Yasni), *Geshikhte fun der yidisher arbeter-bavegung in Lodz* (Łódź,
1937); Aryeh Tartakower, "Zur Geschichte des jüdischen Sozialismus," *Der Jude*,
1923–24, in four installments, published in Hebrew as *Toldot tenuat ha-ovdim ha-yehudit*
(Warsaw, 1929–32); Elias Tscherikower, Franz Kursky, Abraham Menes, and
A. Rosin, eds., *Di yidishe sotsyalistishe bavegung biz der grindung fun Bund* (Vilna, 1939);
Nahum A. Buchbinder, *Di geshikhte fun der yidisher arbeter-bavegung in Rusland* (Vilna,
1931); Abraham Kirshnitz and A. Moses Rafes, eds., *Der yidisher arbeter* (Moscow,
1928); *Revolutsyonnoe dvizheniye sredy Evreiev* (Moscow, 1920). Abraham G. Duker,
"Notes on the Bibliography of the Jewish Labor Movement in Europe," *Jewish Social
Service Quarterly* 2 (1935): 267–69, includes references to the labor movement in
Polish lands.

73. Ignacy Schiper, *Kultur-geshikhte fun di yidn in Poyln baysn mitlalter* (Warsaw,
1926).

74. Israel Zinberg, *Di geshikhte fun der yidisher literatur bay yidn* (Vilna, 1935–36);
Max Weinreich, *Bilder fun der yidisher literatur-geshikhte: Fun di onheybn biz Mendele*

A valuable contribution to the subject of Jewish education is Jacob Szacki's monograph on educational policy toward the Jews in the Kingdom of Poland during the nineteenth century. Aaron Sawicki wrote a doctoral dissertation on the rabbinical school in Warsaw in the nineteenth century. Józef Bero also described Jewish schools in the Kingdom, while Majer Bałaban examined the Jewish school system in pre-Partition Poland. Filip Friedman investigated the school system introduced by Yosef Perl in Galicia in the nineteenth century, and the topic of Jewish publicly run schools was variously treated by Aryeh Tartakower, Gedo Hecht, and Hayim Kazdan. Saul Langnas's study concerned Jewish students in Polish schools of higher learning. Many articles dealt with the theory of education and the pedagogical problems encountered in Jewish schools in Poland. Much attention was also devoted to psychology and the new tasks faced by Jewish scholars in this field.[75]

Mokher Seforim (Vilna, 1928); Zalmen Reisen, *Leksikon fun der yidisher literatur, prese un filologye* (Vilna, 1926–30); Ignacy Schiper, "Rozwój literatury żydowskiej w Polsce porozbiorowej (do 1918)," in *Żydzi w Polsce Odrodzonej*, 2:91–102; Isaac Lewin, "Literatura rabiniczna Żydów polskich w czasach porozbiorowych," in *Żydzi w Polsce Odrodzonej*, 2:103–13; Yermiyahu Frenkel, "Literatura nowohebrajska w Polsce," in *Żydzi w Polsce Odrodzonej*, 2:60–73; Meir Weissberg, "Die neuhebraische Aufklerungsliteratur in Galizien," *Monatsschrift für Geschichte und Wissenschaft des Judentums* 57 (1913): 513–26, 735–49, 71 (1927): 54–62, 100–109, 371–87, 72 (1928): 71–88, 184–201; Joseph Klausner, *Historiyah shel ha-sifrut ha-ivrit ha-hadashah*, vols. 1–3 (Jerusalem, 1930–39); A. A. Roback, *The Story of Yiddish Literature* (New York, 1940); Karol Dresdner, "Żydzi w poezji polskiej XIX w.," *Miesięcznik Żydowski*, 1932, no. 5, pp. 399–426; Wilhelm Fallek, "Twórczość Żydów na polu literatury polskiej do 1918 r.," in *Żydzi w Polsce Odrodzonej*, 2:74–90; Fallek, "Motywy biblijne w 'Panu Tadeuszu' Mickiewicza," *Miesięcznik Żydowski*, 1931, no. 11, pp. 400–12; Chaim Löw, "Żydzi w poezji Odrodzonej Polski," *Miesięcznik Żydowski*, 1933, nos. 7–8, pp. 27–35, nos. 9–10, pp. 145–68, 1934, no. 1, pp. 54–67, no. 3, pp. 225–40, no. 4, pp. 326–41; Löw, "Rodowod Jankiela w 100-lecie 'Pana Tadeusza,'" *Miesięcznik Żydowski*, 1934, no. 6, pp. 385–401; Löw, "Stanisław Wyspiański i Żydzi," *Miesięcznik Żydowski*, 1932, nos. 9–10, pp. 221–37.

75. Jacob Szacki, *Yidishe bildungs-politik in Poyln fun 1806 biz 1866* (New York, 1943); Aaron Sawicki, "Szkoła Rabinów w Warszawie (1826–1863)," *Miesięcznik Żydowski*, 1933, no. 3, pp. 244–74; Józef Bero, "Z dziejów szkolnictwa żydowskiego w Królestie Kongresowym," in *Minerva Polska*, ed. Ignacy Schiper, Aryeh Tartakower, and Aleksander Hafftka (1930), pp. 77–106; Majer Bałaban, "Szkolnictwo żydowskie w dawnej Rzeczypospolitej," in *Żydzi w Polsce Odrodzonej*, 1:337–44; Filip Friedman, "Yosef Perl vi a bildungs-tuer un zayn shul in Tarnopol"; Aryeh Tartakower, "Batei ha-sefer shel ha-zibur ha-yehudi be-Polin," in *Księga Jubileuszowa ku czci dla Markusa Braudego* (Warsaw, 1931), pp. 136–67; Gedo Hecht, "Di nets fun yidishe shuln in Poyln," in *Yidisher gezelshaftlekher leksikon* (Warsaw, 1939), 1:247–98; Hayim Kazdan, *Di geshikhte fun yidishn shulvezn in umophengikn Poyln* (Mexico City, 1947); Saul Langnas, *Żydzi a studia akademickie w Polsce w latach 1921–1931* (Lwów, 1933); *Pedagogishe un psikhologishe shriftn fun YIVO*, vol. 1 (Vilna, 1933). A complete list of articles and reviews published in *YIVO bleter* appears in *YIVO Bibliography* (New York, 1943), nos. 1537–1615.

Emanuel Ringelblum, Chaim D. Friedberg, and Majer Bałaban wrote about the history of Jewish printing, and Shmuel Loeb Zitron and Aleksander Hafftka wrote about the Jewish press.[76] Valuable monographic works and smaller studies dealt with the history of Jewish theaters in Poland. Ignacy Schiper published a large monographic study; Jacob Szacki wrote several studies; while Zalmen Zilbercweig and Jacob Mestel prepared a lexicon of artists and people of the theater.[77]

Studies were also undertaken and published on the architecture of synagogues and the plastic arts in Poland. Before World War I, Majer Bałaban published an essay on Jewish historical monuments. Subsequently, he expanded his studies and published their results in several works, devoting attention to descriptions of synagogue interiors as well as to cemeteries and tombstones. In this context, Bałaban also examined artistic crafts and objects not only of religious significance but also of a secular nature.[78] Ignacy Schiper and Otto Schneid dealt with the beaux arts; Mateusz Mieses, Szymon Zajczyk, and Andrzej Szyszko-Bohusz examined the architecture of synagogues; while scholars abroad such as Rachela Wischnitzer-Bernstein, A. Breier, C. Aronson, and Georges Loukomski studied the architecture of wood and brick synagogues.[79]

76. Emanuel Ringelblum, *Tsu der geshikhte fun yidishn bukh un druk in Poyln in der tsveyter helft fun akhtsntn yorhundert* (Vilna, 1936), published in Polish as "Z dziejów księzki i drukarstwa żydowskiego w Polsce w drugei nabowie XVIII w.," and "Drukarz ksiąg żydowskiej w nowym dworze," *BŻIH*, no. 41 (1962): 20–44, no. 42 (1962): 45–60; Chaim D. Friedberg, *Toldot ha-defus ha-ivri be-Polanyah* (Antwerp, 1932); Majer Bałaban, "Zur geshichte der hebraischen Druckerein in Polen," *Soncino Blatter* (Berlin) 3, no. 1 (1929): 1–51; Bałaban, "Drukarstwo żydowskie w XVI wieku," in *Pamiętnik Zjazdu Naukowego im J. Kochanowskiego* (Cracow, 1931), pp. 102–16, also in *Z historii Żydów w Polsce: Szkice i studja* (Warsaw, 1920), pp. 66–84; Shmuel Loeb Zitron, *Di geshikhte fun der yidisher prese fun yor 1863–1889* (Vilna, 1923); Aleksander Hafftka, "Prasa żydowska w Polsce do 1918," in *Żydzi w Polsce Odrodzonej*, 2:148–61.

77. Ignacy Schiper, *Geshikhte fun der yidisher teater-kunst un drame fun di eltste tsaytn biz 1750*, vols. 1–4 (Warsaw, 1923–28); Jacob Szacki, *Arkhiv far der geshikhte fun yidishn teater un drame*, vol. 1 (New York, 1930); Zalmen Zilbercweig, ed., *Leksikon fun yidishn teater* (New York, 1931).

78. Majer Bałaban, "Evreiskiye istoricheskiye pamiatniki v Polshe: Viedeniye v istoriyi Evreiskogo isskustva," *Evreiskaia Starina*, 1909, pp. 55–71; Majer Bałaban, *Zabytki historyczne Żydów w Polsce* (Warsaw, 1929); Bałaban, "Bóżnice obronne na wschodnich kresach Rzeczypospolitej," *Nowe Zycie* 1 (1924): 197–203, reprinted in *Die Juden in Polen* (Vienna, 1927); Bałaban, *Przewodnik po żydowskich zabytkach Krakowa* (Cracow, 1935).

79. Ignacy Schiper, "Sztuka plastyczna u Żydów w dawnej Rzeczypospolitej," in *Żydzi w Polsce Odrodzonej*, 1:308–36, including a large bibliography; Schiper, "Zydzi polscy a sztuki piękne (muzyka i śpiew-teatr-malarstwo, grafika, rzeźba-przymysł

Synthetic Histories

The interwar period was dominated by analytical monographs on all the various topics mentioned above. Nevertheless, a second trend, whose intention was to present a synthetic outline of the history of the Jewish community in Poland, was also evident. Early syntheses were complex, and it was not until many years later, especially after the war, that scientific or popular works appeared, many of them abroad.

The first synthetic approaches include Samuel Hirszhorn's history of the Polish Jews from the reign of Stanisław August to the First World War. The author was a publicist; he did not explore archival material or the works existing on the subject of the post-Partition period. Jacob Schall's publication on the history of the Jews in Poland and Lithuania was of an analogous nature. Despite the title the book lacks many aspects of Jewish history and remained a popular digest and a textbook for secondary school.[80]

A collective history of Jews in Poland and Lithuania, which appeared in 1914 in Russian, was the first to meet the requirements of a scientific synthesis. Only one volume was published, containing studies by Simon Dubnov, Majer Bałaban, Ignacy Schiper, Mark Wischnitzer, B. A. Katz, P. S. Marek, J. I. Gessen, E. N. Frenk, and S. L. Zinberg. In a series of Russian works, one should also mention J. I. Gessen's history of Jews in Russia, covering the eighteenth and nineteenth centuries, several chapters of which refer to the Jews in Polish lands.[81]

---

artystyczny) do 1918," *Żydzi w Polsce Odrodzonej*, 2:114–47; Otto Schneid, "Yidishe kunst in Poyln," in *Yidisher gezelshaftlekher leksikon*, 1:334–58; Mateusz Mieses, "Podziemne synagogi," *Miesięcznik Żydowski*, 1938, no. 8, pp. 145–52; Szymon Zajczyk, *Architektura barokowych bóżnic murowanych w Polsce* (Warsaw, 1936); Andrzej Szyszko-Bohusz, *Materiały do architektury synagog w Polsce* (Warsaw, 1927); Rachela Wischnitzer-Bernstein, *Synagogen in ehemaligen Königreich Polen: Das Buch der polnischen Juden* (Berlin, 1916); A. Breier, M. Eisler, and M. Grunwald, *Holzsynagogen in Polen* (Vienna, 1934); C. Aronson, "Wooden Synagogues of Poland," *Menorah Journal* 25 (1937); Georges Loukomski, "Old Polish Synagogues," *Journal of the Royal Institute of British Architecture* (London) (1935); Loukomski, "Wooden Synagogues in Poland," *Burlington Magazine* 66 (1935): 14–21; Loukomski, *Jewish Art in European Synagogues from the Middle Ages to the 18th Century* (London, 1947); Karol Dresdner and Maximilian Goldstein, *Kultura i sztuka ludu żydowskiego na ziemach polskich* (Lwów, 1935).

80. Samuel Hirszhorn, *Historia Żydów w Polsce: Od Sejmu Czteroletniego do wojny europejskiej (1788–1914)* (Warsaw, 1921), published in Yiddish as *Geshikhte fun yidn in Poyln* (Warsaw, 1923); Jacob Schall, *Historja żydów w Polsce na Litwie i Rusi* (Lwów, 1934).

81. *Istoriya Evreiev v Rossii*, vol. 11 of *Istoriya Evreiskogo Naroda*; J. I. Gessen, *Istoriya Evreiskogo naroda w Rossii* (Leningrad, 1925–27), vol. 2.

An attempt at a synthetic presentation of the history of Polish Jews throughout the centuries can be found in the collection of essays *Żydzi w Polsce Odrodzonej* (Jews in Renascent Poland). Only two volumes of this publication appeared in print, although the next ones were already prepared. It was the work of a group of historians and experts on affiliated subjects including Majer Bałaban, Ignacy Schiper, Emanuel Ringelblum, Filip Friedman, Isaac Lewin, Mateusz Mieses, and Aryeh Tartakower. Separate chapters deal with the history of Jews in various periods of the Commonwealth, the three Partitions, and the 1918–33 period. Each author presented a separate aspect of economic, social, political, and cultural history, as well as the history of customs, the problem of Jewish emancipation, and the policy of the partitioning authorities toward the Jewish population. The publication as a whole is not of an academic character but was intended to be a popular work.[82] Other studies on the same subject include N. M. Gelber's work on the Jewish Question in the Four-Year Sejm, Lipman Comber's work on the Prussian government policy toward the Jews, Artur Eisenbach's work on Jews in the Duchy of Warsaw, Majer Bałaban's work on the Jewish population of Galicia, and Isaiah Warszawski's essays on Jews during the constitutional period of the Kingdom of Poland.[83]

One should also mention a number of publications that appeared abroad, although they are of varying merit. The most valuable are the three volumes by S. M. Dubnov on the modern history of the Jews, from the French Revolution to the First World War, in which much discussion is devoted to the situation of the Jewish population in the three Partition areas. Aaron Eisenstein wrote about the legal status of Polish Jews in the thirteenth and fourteenth centuries, and Jacob Meisl wrote three volumes on the history of Jews in Poland and Russia.[84]

82. Volumes 1 and 2 of *Żydzi w Polsce Odrodzonej* appeared in Warsaw in the early 1930s; the volumes carry no date of publication.

83. N. M. Gelber, "Żydzi a zagadnienie reformy żydów na sejmie czteroletnim," *Miesięcznik Żydowski*, 1931, no. 10, pp. 326–44, no. 11, pp. 429–40; Lipman Comber, "Di batsiung fun der praysisher makht tsu di yidn in Poyln fun der tsveyter biz der driter khaluke (1793–95)," in *Bleter far geshikhte*, 1:78–85; Artur Eisenbach, "Yidn in varshever firshtntum," *YIVO bleter* 10 (1936): 91–99; Majer Bałaban, *Historia Żydow w Galicji i w Rzeczypospolitej Krakowskiej (1772–1868)* (Lwów, 1916); Isaiah Warszawski, "Yidn in di nay-oysgeboyte shtet in Kongres Poyln, 1822–1831," *YIVO bleter* 2 (1933): 28–35; Warszawski, "Yidn in Kongres Poyln, (1815–31)," in *Historishe shriftn*, 2: 322–54.

84. Simon Dubnov, *Di nayste geshikhte fun yidishn folk, 1789–1914*, vols. 1–3 (Vilna,

Bibliography

A number of Jewish scholars worked in the field of bibliography, and the greatest accomplishments in preparing a synthetic bibliography for the history of Jews in Poland were those of Majer Bałaban. From the very beginning of his scientific activity, Bałaban dealt with bibliography. In 1903 he published several general and specialized bibliographies for the history of Jews in Poland in the *Kwartalnik Historyczny, Przegląd Historyczny, Evreiskaia Starina, Miesięcznik Żydowski,* and other periodicals. Moreover, his bibliographies also dealt with select subjects such as the history of *kahals* and the Hasidic movement, in which he was especially interested. Just before the Second World War, Bałaban published the first part of his bibliography of the history of the Jews in Poland and neighboring countries from 1900 to 1939, which included three thousand works. He did not manage to publish the second part, which was a regional bibliography.[85]

Other authors mentioned in this essay prepared bibliographies on a number of occasions, including Mark Wischnitzer, Edward Poznański, Filip Friedman, and, abroad, Salo Wittmayer Baron.[86] The Vilna-based YIVO kept a systematic bibliographical section and published bibliographies of the contents of all periodicals published by

---

1938); Aaron Eisenstein, *Die Stellung der Juden in Polen im XIII und XIV Jahrhundert* (Cieszyn, 1934); Jacob Meisl, *Geschichte der Juden in Polen und Russland,* vols. 1–3 (Berlin, 1921–25). The best synthesis of the history of the Jews in Poland is Abraham Menes, Raphael Mahler, Jacob Szacki, and Wiktor Shulman, *Di yidn in Poyln fun di eltste tsaytn biz der tsveyter velt milkhome* (New York, 1946).

85. Majer Bałaban, "Przegląd literatury historyi żydów w Polsce," *Kwartalnik Historyczny,* 1903, pp. 475–86, 635–40, 1908, pp. 494–524; Bałaban, "Przegląd literatury historyi żydów w Polsce," *Przegląd Historyczny* 15 (1912): 231–48, 369–85, 16 (1913): 243–56; Bałaban, "Bibliographicheskiye zametki po istorii Evreiev v Polshe," *Evreiskaia Starina,* 1909, pp. 309–17, 1910, pp. 141–47, 305–17, 442–53; Bałaban, "Przegląd literatury dotyczacej żydowskich gmin wyznaniowych w Polsce," *Miesięcznik Żydowski,* 1931, no. 10, pp. 374–81; *Wydawnictwa Instytutu Nauk Judaistycznych* (Warsaw, 1939), a photocopy published by the World Federation of Polish Jews in Jerusalem in 1978. According to Trunk, *Geshtaltn un gesheenishn* (1983), p. 20, the second part of Bałaban's regional bibliography was saved by Polish friends.

86. Mark Wischnitzer, "Bibliografia po istorii Evreiev w Polsze i Litwie," in *Istoriya Evreiev v Rossii,* vol. 11 of *Istoriya Evreiskogo Naroda,* pp. 505–16; Edward Poznański, "Zagadnienia bieżącej bibljografji żydowskiej," *Miesięcznik Żydowski,* 1931, no. 7, pp. 28–42; Poznański, *Sefer ha-shanah le-bibliografyah yehudit be-Polanyah* (Warsaw, 1936); Filip Friedman, "Pokłosie historjografii żydowskiej lat ostatnich w Polsce," *Miesięcznik Żydowski,* 1935, nos. 3–4, pp. 182–94; Friedman, "Historishe literatur vegn yidn in der lodzer voyvodshaft (1918–1937)," in *Lodzer visnshaftlekhe shriftn* 1:133–48; Salo Wittmayer Baron, *A Social and Religious History of the Jews* (New York, 1937), vol. 3, with a large bibliography and critical notes pertaining to the history of the Jews in Poland.

YIVO or scientific institutions affiliated with it in the years 1925–41.[87]

In an overall survey of Jewish historiography during the interwar period, one can detect the shaping of new trends based on new methodological premises and the pursuit of little cultivated fields as well as the expansion of chronological range. All this scholarly activity took place despite the fact that the political situation and pauperization of the Jewish population did not create a favorable atmosphere for the flourishing of the historical sciences.

87. *Roczinski Bibliograficzne,* vol. 1 (Vilna, 1926); *YIVO Bibliography,* which included 2,523 items.

Lucjan Dobroszycki

YIVO in Interwar Poland:
Work in the Historical Sciences

Like other interdisciplinary institutions, the Yidisher Visnshaft-lekher Institut (YIVO, Jewish Scientific Institute) in interwar Poland was divided into various sections, each specializing in a given area of study and for which there is an extensive collection of archival materials. Consisting of, among other things, minutes of the meetings of the Historical Section and its committees and subdivisions, reports, memorandums, questionnaires, and correspondence, the archival collection covers YIVO's years of operation in Poland, from 1925 through 1939. These materials, collected and safeguarded by Elias Tcherikower, are now in the archives of the YIVO Institute for Jewish Research in New York.[1]

YIVO's scholarly achievements in all fields are well known, and the works of its staff members have been regularly cited in the bibliographies of a variety of disciplines. Less well known, perhaps, is YIVO's activity in promoting and organizing research in Jewish history, both inside and outside of academia. YIVO's historians were not only amassing a fund of historical data and scholarly research, but they were also defining many of the terms of their discipline for the first time. Before 1925, Jewish historiography simply had no institutional base in Poland.

The Historical Section, or Di Historishe Sektsye as it was called

1. Records of YIVO's activity in the field of history conducted in Poland or related to the history of Jews in Poland were, as a matter of institutional protocol, systematically sent to Berlin, then to Paris, where the main office of YIVO's Historical Section was located. Were it not for this arrangement, the records would not have survived. When Elias Tcherikower was forced to leave Germany in 1933, he moved to France. Seven years later, when France was invaded by Germany, he managed to hide these papers before fleeing the country. Recovered after World War II, the Tcherikower Collection (hereafter TC) constitutes file numbers 2070–2415 of the archives of the YIVO Institute for Jewish Research in New York.

in Yiddish, was set up at a meeting in Berlin on October 31, 1925, two months after YIVO itself was founded. The inaugural meeting of the section was chaired by Simon Dubnov, the prominent Jewish historian and theoretician of the Diaspora, and among its participants were people whose names were already well known in Jewish scholarly and intellectual circles: Elias Tcherikower, Jacob Lestschinsky, Mark Wischnitzer, and Nakhum Schtiff.[2]

The capital of the Weimar Republic seemed to be an ideal place for the newly formed Jewish historical center as the postwar turbulence began to subside in the mid-1920s. The founders of the section had, after all, made plans to organize and conduct historical research throughout Europe and America; for them Germany was convenient both geographically and politically. Actual circumstances, unfortunately, proved otherwise. Neither the German-Jewish community of the late 1920s nor its intellectual elite was particularly interested in East Central European Jewish studies. Moreover, the possibility of maintaining headquarters for YIVO's Historical Section in Germany was completely ruled out by the rise of the Nazi movement and Adolf Hitler's seizure of power.[3]

Paris was selected as the new site for the main office of the Historical Section, and its chairman, Tcherikower, moved there to commence work. Yet Paris was no better suited for the task. Ultimately, Western Europe in the 1920s and 1930s, with its assimilated and acculturated Jewish communities, could not serve as a center for YIVO; the social and the academic milieus necessary for the institute's activities were apparently to be found in Eastern Europe, above all in Poland.

To establish YIVO headquarters in Poland was not easy either. As Yosef Hayim Yerushalmi and Ismar Schorsch have recently reminded us, Jews in the Diaspora entered into modern historiography almost simultaneously with their emancipation in the second part of the nineteenth century.[4] In Congress Poland and Galicia this development came later, much later than in Germany—or even in Russia, where, at least from the 1870s on, Jewish historical scholarship was

---

2. Also invited but unable to attend the inaugural meeting was Joseph Meisl, historian and archivist. Minutes of the meeting, October 31, 1925, TC, 142873–76.

3. For an evaluation of work done by the Historical Section in Berlin, see report, n.d. [1928], TC, 142856–58.

4. Yosef Hayim Yerushalmi, *Zakhor: Jewish History and Jewish Memory* (Seattle, Wash., 1982), pp. 81–133; Ismar Schorsch, "The Emergence of Historical Consciousness in Modern Judaism," *Leo Baeck Institute Yearbook* 28 (1983): 413–37.

emerging and producing such publications as *Russkii Evreiskii Arkhiv,* *Evreiskaia Biblioteka, Voskhod, Evreiskaia Starina,* and *Perezhytoe.* On Polish soil, on the other hand, not until the first decade of the twentieth century was there a single Jewish historical journal, either in Yiddish or in Polish. Poland also lacked the associations that were forming in Germany, England, France, and Russia to bring together those who wrote on historical topics, issued their own publications, or were simply interested in the history of the Jews. The first Polish-Jewish journal, *Kwartalnik Poświęcony Badaniom Przeszłości Żydów w Polsce,* which appeared in Warsaw in 1912, expired shortly thereafter, an early casualty of World War I.[5]

Polish-Jewish historiography developed slowly, and for a long time there was a paucity of initiatives in this field. Although historical scholarship was well advanced in Poland[6] and was represented internationally by a number of recognized historians, history was not a subject of study by Jews. As in other countries, it was a non-Jew, Tadeusz Czacki, who was to write the first history of Jews in Poland.[7] Jewish students did not attend history classes, even years after they had first been admitted to Polish schools of higher learning. At the turn of the century Jews constituted about 18 percent of the student body at both the Lwów and Cracow universities, yet not until 1899 was a Jew—Mojżesz (Moses) Schorr—first awarded a doctorate for a dissertation on a Jewish topic. His "Organizacja Żydów w Polsce od najdawniejszych czasów do 1772" (The Organizational Struc-

5. Among the contributors to *Kwartalnik Poświęcony Badaniom Przeszłości Żydów w Polsce* were three great historians: Majer Bałaban and Ignacy (Yitzhak) Schiper, both of whom specialized only in Jewish history, and Szymon Askenazy, who devoted himself to Polish and general history. Askenazy was the founder of one of the most distinguished historical schools in Poland; his two studies on the history of the Jews in the Duchy of Warsaw and Congress Poland are, perhaps, his only contributions on Jewish topics.

6. The Polskie Towarzystwo Historyczne (Polish Historical Society) was established in 1886, nearly simultaneously with the formation of similar societies in France and England.

7. Among the prominent non-Jewish writers on Jewish history were Jacques Basnag, an eighteenth-century French Huguenot, and the nineteenth-century Russian historian Sergei Aleksandrovich Bershadskii. Tadeusz Czacki's work, *Rozprawa o Żydach i Karaitach* (A Treatise about Jews and Karaites), was first published in Vilna in 1807. Later, in the second part of the nineteenth century, other books on Jewish history of a popular character were published. The most notable, and not without cognitive value, were Ludwik Gumplowicz, *Prawodawstwo polskie względem Żydów* (Polish Legislation concerning the Jews) (Cracow, 1867); Aleksander Kraushar, *Historia Żydów w Polsce* (History of the Jews in Poland) (Warsaw, 1866–67); Kraushar, *Frank i frankiści polscy* (Frank and the Polish Frankists) (Cracow, 1895).

ture of Jews in Poland from the Earliest Years until 1772) was soon published by the prestigious Polish quarterly, *Kwartalnik Historyczny.*[8]

Schorr was also the first Jew to present a paper on Jewish history at the Third Convention of Polish Historians in Cracow in 1900. He addressed the issue of developing Jewish historiography in Poland— which, as he candidly stated, had to be created virtually out of nothing.[9] Schorr's entrance into academia, while a distinctive personal accomplishment, did not signal an immediate breakthrough in Polish-Jewish historiography. Schorr himself became more interested in Assyriology than in Polish-Jewish history, although his inspiring role as a university professor, rabbi, and founder of the Instytut Nauk Judaistycznych (Institute for Judaic Studies) in Warsaw should not be overlooked. More than a quarter of a century after Schorr presented his paper in Cracow, another great Jewish scholar, Majer Bałaban, while mindful of the gains in Polish-Jewish historiography in the interim, could say, not without sarcasm:

> Only here [in Poland], in a country with about three million Jews, where the [Jewish] printing press has been functioning since 1534, in the field of [collecting and preserving] Jewish historical monuments, as in other fields, there is a kind of stagnation and resignation. State libraries collect neither Jewish nor Hebrew materials, sometimes justifying this policy by their inability to catalog them. None of the large book and manuscript repositories, such as the Ossolineum, the libraries of the Czartoryskis, Krasińskis, Przeździeckis, Zamojskis, Raczyńskis, and Mielżyńskis, or the library of the Poznańskie Towarzystwo Przyjaciół Nauk [Poznań Society of the Friends of Science], collect Jewish materials either. Jews in Poland themselves have formed only three, perhaps four collections worthy of the name. . . . Were historians to rely only on Jewish libraries and archives, it would be advisable to resign from any work at all.

When YIVO was built in 1925, literally from the ground up, it was generally recognized among Jewish intellectuals of all disciplines that the gap needed to be filled. The time and conditions were ripe

8. Stanisław Grudziński, *Materiały do kwestii żydowskiej w Galicji* (Lwów, 1910), p. 53; Mojżesz Schorr, "Organizacja Żydów w Polsce od najdawniejszych czasów do 1772: Głównie na podstawie źródeł archiwalnych," *Kwartalnik Historyczny* 13 (1899): 482–520, 734–75.

9. Sektsya I—Historia Żydów w Polsce: Referent Dr. M. Schorr, in *Pamietnik III zjazdu historyków polskich w Krakowie urzadzonego przez Towarzystwo Historycene Lwowskie w dniach 4, 5 i czerwca 1900* (Cracow, 1901), pp. 1–3. In a panel discussion of Schorr's paper—with Professor Tadeusz Korzon, Dr. Aloyzy Winiarz, Dr. Adolf Sternschus, and Dr. Adam Chmiel as participants—it was pointed out that more sources from which to study Jewish history existed in Polish archives and in the synagogues than might be supposed (pp. 47–48).

for the founding of a Jewish "academy" that, as it was visualized by its founders, "would embrace all the various branches of human knowledge."[10]

During its fifteen years of existence, from 1925 until 1939, YIVO in Poland amassed a unique collection of records and books, one that compensated, at least in part, for decades of neglect. This was accomplished in several ways, among them: (1) voluntary arrangements, modeled after state law, with Jewish publishers, printers, institutions, and associations, requiring them to send free copies of all their printed matter (books, brochures, posters, leaflets, and so forth) to the YIVO library or archives; (2) the efforts of *zamlers* (voluntary local collectors) throughout Poland, from Zbąszyn in the west to Łuniniec in the east, and Kołomyja in the south to Druja in the north;[11] and (3) responses to questionnaires on specific topics, such as the current situation of Jews in towns and villages or the activities of the Jewish workers' movement.[12]

Another significant way in which YIVO accumulated materials was by sponsoring writing contests. In one contest Jews recounted their experiences during World War I. In contests held in 1932, 1934, and 1939, Jewish youths ages sixteen to twenty-two wrote their autobiographies. These three contests were patterned largely on the methods of collecting personal accounts for sociological study developed by William Isaac Thomas and Florian Witold Znaniecki.[13] Of the 620 autobiographies entered, 410—or nearly 35,000 manuscript pages—were rescued from YIVO in Poland and are preserved at the YIVO Institute for Jewish Research.[14]

10. Majer Bałaban, *Zabytki historyczne Żydów w Polsce* (Warsaw, 1929), pp. 32–33, 44; report, n.d. [1928], TC, 143734.

11. It could be said, without exaggeration, that the archives of YIVO in Vilna was created by its *zamlers*. Some of the materials contributed, together with the typical Polish envelopes of the time in which they were sent to Vilna, have survived and are now at the YIVO Institute for Jewish Research.

12. The first questionnaire, issued in 1927 by the Historical Section of YIVO and signed by Simon Dubnov, Elias Tcherikower, I. Chernikov, Emanuel Ringelblum, Jacob Szacki (Shatzky), and Ignacy Schiper, is given in the appendix, no. 2.

13. It was William Isaac Thomas who supported Max Weinreich's application to the Rockefeller Foundation for a grant to carry out YIVO's Jewish Youth Project. Weinreich's findings from the project were published by YIVO, in *Der veg tsu undzer yungt: Yesoydes, metodn, problemen fun yidisher yungt-forshung* (Vilna, 1935). An essay by Weinreich, "Studium o młodzieży żydowskiej: Program i metoda Wydziału Badań Młodzieży Żydowskiego Instytutu Naukowego," appeared in the same year in *Przegląd Socjologiczny* 13 (1935): 30–82, the prestigious journal founded by Florian Witold Znaniecki.

14. Of the 302 entries for which statistical data were available, 236 were written

YIVO's library and archives, along with its bibliographical and publishing workshops, were housed in a newly constructed building in Vilna. The institute's officers and directors, including Max Weinreich, lived in Vilna. Its training center—the Aspirantur—and virtually all of its sections had their offices there. In such areas as linguistics, literature, folklore, ethnography, and psychology, the institute's headquarters in Vilna was very much the center of activity. However, Vilna and its university, which had just reopened after a long hiatus, were unlikely places for the study of Jewish history.[15] Very few, if any, of YIVO's historians had studied in the history department of the University of Vilna. The place for historiographical scholarship had traditionally been the University of Warsaw. Its alumni included Jacob Szacki (Shatzky), Emanuel Ringelblum, Isaiah Trunk, Artur Eisenbach, David Wurm, Moshe Kremer, Józef Kermisz, Janina Szafran, Bela Mandelsberg, and Esther Tenenbaum. Between 1919 and 1939 some seventy Jewish students had earned master's degrees at the University of Warsaw with theses on the history of Polish Jewry.[16] Many of these theses were written under the guidance of Majer Bałaban, who received an appointment in Jewish history at the university in 1928. It was also in Warsaw that a student could best profit from YIVO's Economical-Statistical Section, as well as from the Instytut Nauk Judiastycznych, which was established there in 1927. Finally, a major factor drawing Jewish students to Warsaw was the liberal atmosphere within the university's department and institute of history, undoubtedly due to a great extent to Professor Marceli Handelsman, founder and mentor of one

---

by men and 66 by women; 223 of them were in Yiddish, 71 in Polish, and 8 in Hebrew. Entries averaged fifty-nine pages in length, thirty-four more than was required under the contest rules (the average was no doubt tilted by one entry that ran a mammoth eight hundred pages long!). Moses Kligsberg, "Child and Adolescent Behavior under Stress: An Analytical Topical Guide to a Collection of Autobiographies of Jewish Men and Women in Poland (1932–1939) in the Possession of the YIVO Institute for Jewish Research," mimeograph (New York: YIVO, 1965), pp. 3, 10. The value of the preserved autobiographies as a resource is immense.

15. Founded by King Stefan Batory in 1578, the University of Vilna was shut down by the tsarist government after the Polish national Uprising of 1830–31. The university reopened after World War I. Its division of Eastern European history was headed, until 1931, by Feliks Koneczny, well known for his antisemitic prejudices and theories.

16. Fortunately, most of the dissertations written at the University of Warsaw are preserved in its archival files. These papers cover a great variety of topics. Their value for anyone doing research on Polish Jewry cannot be overlooked, particularly because, in many instances, the archival sources on which they were based have either been destroyed or are now inaccessible to scholars outside of Eastern Europe.

of the most prominent schools in Poland and a historian widely respected outside his own country.

In Warsaw, YIVO managed to gather around itself the major Polish-Jewish historians, as well as students and lovers of history, and to interest ever-wider groups of the Jewish community in its programs. All activities were concentrated initially in its Warsaw Historical Commission, which was transformed, as work expanded, into the Historical Commission for All of Poland.[17] Ignacy (Yitzhak) Schiper was named chairman, while Artur Eisenbach, Filip Friedman, Pinkhas Kon, Raphael Mahler, Emanuel Ringelblum, Isaiah Trunk, Leon Ringelblum, Shaul Feldman, Nathan Michael Gelber, and Lipman Comber were elected officers. Although Schiper, as the senior historian, was the scholarly authority and mentor of the entire team, it was Ringelblum who was the true architect of the commission's activity. A man of extraordinary organizational skills, never-failing inventiveness, and personal magnetism, Ringelblum was behind nearly every aspect of YIVO's work in the field of history.

It is interesting, even striking, to note that all but four of the Warsaw Jewish historians came from Galicia, that region of partitioned Poland distinctive in culture from the rest of the country as well as in the emancipated legal status of its Jews. The combination in Galicia of the Haskalah movement and the easy access to secular education for Jews on all levels—elementary schools, high schools, and the universities—made the difference.[18] This combination enabled Jews not only to enter Polish universities, where they could study history in general, but also to undertake specifically Jewish studies.

Connected formally and informally with the academic community, the commission became a forum for lectures and discussion as well as an advisory body for the historical sections of various Jewish social and cultural organizations, among them the Gezelshaft tsu Farshpreytn Kunst tsvishn Yidn (Society for the Dissemination of

17. The transformation took place at a meeting of the Warsaw Historical Commission held on November 17, 1934, in the home of Ignacy Schiper on the occasion of his fiftieth birthday. The minutes of that meeting are given in the appendix, no. 4.

18. Fluency in Polish among Jews in partitioned Poland was nowhere so common as in Galicia, where Polish was the language of instruction in state schools at every level, including the universities in Lwów and Cracow. Thus, the 1931 census shows that, whereas 98.2 percent of Jews in Vilna (Pale of Jewish Settlement) declared Yiddish as their mother tongue, and in Warsaw (Congress Poland) the percentage was 95.8, only 73.7 percent in Cracow and 68.0 percent in Lwów claimed Yiddish as their mother tongue. *Statystyka Polski,* ser. C (Warsaw, 1936–38).

Art among Jews) and the Gezelshaft far Landkentenish (Sightseeing Society). The commission also maintained contacts with business and industrial organizations, primarily to encourage the preservation of the archives of Jewish enterprises.[19]

As the number of organizations and people interested in Jewish history grew, both the Warsaw Historical Commission and, later, the Historical Commission for All of Poland were able to undertake certain projects that, by their very nature, could be accomplished only through collective effort.[20] Among these was the project to investigate and restore Jewish antiquities in Poland, which the commission had long considered one of its most urgent tasks and, in many instances, its last chance to save many precious items from dilapidation. Under the auspices of the commission, a central body, Komisye tsu Forshn Yidishe Altertimlekhkaytn (Jewish Antiquities Commission), was established to carry out the work.[21] It included people from many fields of endeavor, including Szymon Zajczyk, the well-known specialist in the history and architecture of synagogues: Otto Schneid, the art historian; E. Herstein, the architect; and A. Mintz, the art collector.[22] There were, however, too many objects and too few qualified people to help conserve them. As a remedial measure, though a very modest one, the commission organized a course on preservation with twenty-five participants. Bałaban, Schiper, and Zajczyk were among its instructors. Another step was a plan to publish a kind of *vade mecum,* which, as Ringelblum projected it, would provide a forum for information about conservation work done in Poland and abroad, instructions in the organization of archives, reprints of historical records and documents, and discussions of the significance of antiquities for Jewish historiography.[23]

19. Report on the activities of the Historical Commission, January–May 1937, TC, 143152.

20. See the appendix, nos. 4, 5.

21. In a letter to Emanuel Ringelblum, dated February 25, 1930, Tcherikower expressed great satisfaction that YIVO's Warsaw Historical Commission was to oversee the Jewish Antiquities Commission. TC, 135698–99.

22. The son of Benjamin Mintz, one of the major Judaica collectors in Poland, A. Mintz was involved in the commission's project to catalog Judaica art items in private collections.

23. Minutes of the Warsaw Historical Commission meeting, November 8, 1929, TC, 143028–29. History classes were held primarily in the Aspirantur, YIVO's teaching and training division. Of the sixty-eight students in the program between 1935 and 1939, nineteen were history students, outnumbering the enrollment in the six other offered disciplines: language, literature, economics, folklore, sociology-psychology, and pedagogy.

The commission had to be highly selective in identifying the items that needed immediate attention or that, at the very least, deserved priority on a list of future restoration projects. In a series of meetings and discussions, it was decided that such a list should focus on the provinces of Poznań and Pomorze, from which once-sizable Jewish communities had nearly entirely disappeared following Poland's Partition, leaving behind an abandoned Jewish quarter, cemeteries, and former synagogues, study houses, and prayer houses.[24] Because these areas yielded no local Jewish organizations to which the commission could appeal for help, it was hoped that former residents or their children in the United States would supply funds to enable on-site research and restoration to begin.[25]

Another region in which Jewish antiquities of great historical value were concentrated was eastern Poland, including both the Lithuanian and Polish parts of the former Commonwealth. Here the commission selected several towns to be investigated, among them Włodawa, originally a privately owned town, established in the sixteenth century; Krasnystaw, by the Wieprz River, chartered as a town in 1394; Odelsk, a townlet in Białystok province, where the wooden synagogue, erected in the eighteenth century, was in the final stages of disrepair; Chełm, established in the twelfth century and believed to be the home of one of the oldest communities in Poland; and Lublin, the major medieval and modern center of Jewish scholarship and self-government.[26]

In each case the commission tried to enlist the cooperation and financial support of local Jewish communities and their executive boards, the town rabbis and the Agudat Harabbanim (Association of Rabbis) in Poland, the municipal councilmen, and the office in

24. Some Jews from these provinces, which had fallen under Prussian rule, emigrated deep into Germany or to America, while others were fully assimilated and left the Jewish community entirely. Others moved east, to Russian-ruled territory, where Jewish communities remained more traditional. Because of these movements, and a lower birthrate among Jews in the provinces of Poznań and Pomorze, the percentage of the Jewish population declined from 6.7 percent in 1831 to .5 percent in 1921. The decline is dramatically apparent when one compares census figures in individual towns: the percentage of Jews in Chodzież, Inowrocław, Szamotuły, Szubin, Łabiszyn, and Wolsztyn in 1808 was 64.2, 84.5, 48.9, 42.7, 56.1, and 41.6, respectively. By 1921 the same figures had dropped to 1.6, 1.0, 3.9, 3.3, 4.7, and 1.6. Bogdan Wasiutyński, *Ludność żydowska w Polsce w wiekach XIX i XX: Studium Statystyczne* (Warsaw, 1930), pp. 160–71.

25. Minutes of the Warsaw Historical Commission meeting, March 29, 1930, TC, 143039–40.

26. Minutes of the Warsaw Historical Commission meetings, March 22, 29, 1930, TC, 143035–37, 143039–40.

charge of the conservation of landmarks. However, the results of such efforts were, with a few notable exceptions, insignificant, despite the many interventions personally undertaken by Schiper and Ringelblum. Eventually the commission decided to sponsor expeditions of its own to each of these locations, beginning with Lublin. Raphael Mahler, accompanied by two architects, E. Herstein and A. Eisenberg, investigated Lublin's synagogues, including the famous Maharshal and Maharam, the old *bes-medresh* (study house), and the cemetery. They took pictures (large glass photonegatives), made maps and recorded the measurements of structures, and compiled bibliographical notes on old religious books and items of Judaica art found in the *bes-medresh* and the office of the *kehillah* (Jewish community council). There were plans eventually to collect these materials in a monograph on the Jewish community in Lublin.[27]

Another project, of much greater significance, was the so-called *pinkeysim* campaign. Carried out by the Historical Commission for All of Poland, it was an effort to retrieve the record books and chronicles traditionally kept by local Jewish communities in Poland and their various religious, occupational, social, and charitable organizations. Indeed, with each passing year their number was shrinking, and very little was known even about their whereabouts.

Simon Dubnov, who himself was perhaps the most successful collector of *pinkeysim*, initiated the campaign. YIVO's search for *pinkeysim* could be fruitful only if the scholarly, general, and local Jewish communities joined and turned it into a nationwide effort. In preparation, thousands of questionnaires were sent out to virtually every Jewish settlement. Of great help was the central and local Jewish press, which widely publicized the undertaking and published an appeal signed, on behalf of the Historical Commission, by Dubnov, Bałaban, Schiper, Ringelblum, and Mahler.[28] As a result of the campaign a total of 293 *pinkeysim* from nearly two hundred Jewish towns and cities were located, described, and, in many instances, copied. The oldest *pinkes*, dated 1601, was from the *kehillah* of Opatów. The most recent one was compiled by a religious association in 1916.

27. Report on activities, January–May 1937, TC, 143149–50; minutes of the Warsaw Historical Commission meeting, June 27, 1930, TC, 143157; report on the expedition to Lublin, 143159–63.
28. "Anketes vegn yidishe historishe mekoyrim in Poyln," *Yediyes fun YIVO* 1–3 (1937): 18–19. For the questionnaire, see appendix, no. 2.

Altogether, 101 of the *pinkeysim* were kept by burial associations, 28 by *kehillot*, 25 by professional guilds, 43 by philanthropical societies, 85 by religious organizations, and 11 by synagogues and houses of prayer.[29]

By the mid-1930s, the Warsaw Historical Commission, or the Commission for All of Poland, had turned into a stable institution with a well-known address, its own budget, regular office hours, and a secretarial staff. Minutes of the commission's plenary meetings indicate that it was involved in organizing both individual and collaborative research projects. It also served as a forum for the presentation of papers and lectures by invited speakers on various topics of Jewish history. Moreover, the numerous reports and correspondence generated by the commission reveal a level of collaboration and activity among its elected officers that was in accordance with its position as an established research organization. The report on activities between January and May 1937, for example, relates that the

> Historical Commission for All of Poland . . . which includes Dr. I. Schiper, chairman, Dr. R. Mahler, Dr. E. Ringelblum, and others, had four plenary meetings and a number of meetings of the presidium during the period of the report. The members of the presidium are in constant contact with the administration and participate in its daily activities. Until March 1, the secretary of the commission was Mr. A. Eisenbach; from March 1, Mr. S. Zalel. The office of the commission is open three days a week in the afternoon, from five to eight, in the office of the Fraynd fun Yidishn Visnshaftlekhn Institut in Varshe [Friends of YIVO in Warsaw]. Since March 1, in addition to questionnaires, circulars, minutes, press releases, replies to submitted questionnaires, etc., the administration sent out 68 letters. During the same time, 31 letters were received.[30]

The apparently harmonious teamwork among the officers of the Historical Commission aside, relations among the institute's historians were not, of course, entirely free of occasional friction or misunderstandings. Some tension existed between the commission in Warsaw and the home office in Vilna on the one hand, and its Historical Section in Paris on the other, but this was mostly manifested in routine reminders to commission members that each new

29. Report on the *pinkeysim* campaign, TC, 142470–72; report on activities, January–May 1937, 143149–53; minutes of the Historical Commission meeting, September 11, 1937, TC, 143068–69. See also "Anketes vegn yidishe historishe mekoyrim in Poyln."

30. Report on activities, January–May 1937, TC, 143153, p. 5.

project had to be approved by the Historical Section, a policy that in principle, the commission did not question.[31]

Whether in Warsaw or Vilna, or in Paris, YIVO's historians were in agreement on the important goals: to establish a base for Jewish historiography and to define its unique characteristics. YIVO in interwar Poland shared a kind of consciousness-raising mission with many other major centers of Jewish life. It was not merely coincidental that three remarkable Jewish academic institutions—the Hebrew University of Jerusalem, YIVO, and the Instytut Nauk Judaistycznych of Warsaw—came into being at the same time. Initiatives taken in Kiev and Minsk in the 1920s, though short-lived, should also not be overlooked.[32] Each of these institutions was a product of the growth of national and cultural self-awareness among the Jewish people, a process that started at the turn of the century and accelerated in the years following World War I. Despite differences in aims, philosophy, language of preference, and methodology, these newly formed institutions cooperated closely with each other.

The Warsaw Commission, which played the major role in preparing the historical sessions of YIVO's general conferences in Vilna, was also planning an international conference of Jewish historians. Filip Friedman, who was in charge of the commission's contacts with Jewish historians abroad, had been in the process of organizing this conference when World War II broke out. In 1933, however, the commission had secured the participation of Jewish historians from Poland and abroad in the International Congress of the Historical

31. A more serious incident took place in connection with the *Unvayzungen*, a manual on how to write popular town histories prepared by Emanuel Ringelblum and Lipman Comber. In a postcard sent to the commission in Warsaw, Zalmen Reisen and Zelig Kalmanowicz in Vilna classified the *Unvayzungen*, in a rather unpleasant manner, as not being up to YIVO's standards. Ringelblum, with unanimous support from the commission's members, threatened to resign as vice-chairman of the Historical Commission and to publish nothing from YIVO that was "edited by Reisen and Kalmanowicz." The dispute was quickly brought to a satisfactory close for both sides, however, when Max Weinreich and Zalmen Reisen, in a letter to Ringelblum, apologized for the tone of the criticism and suggested that the entire correspondence on the matter be withdrawn as if it had not existed. Ringelblum acquiesced and took back his resignation. Minutes of the Historical Commission meeting, April 29, 1938, TC, 143072; Reisen and Kalmanowicz to Historical Commission, February 15, 1938, TC, 143103; Ringelblum, Artur Eisenbach, Isaiah Trunk, and Comber to YIVO, February 27, 1938, TC, 143106; Weinreich and Reisen to YIVO, March 6, 1938, TC, 143100.

32. For a discussion of the institutions in Minsk and Kiev, see Alfred Abraham Greenbaum, *Jewish Scholarship and Institutions in Soviet Russia, 1918–1941* (Jerusalem, 1978).

Sciences, meeting in Warsaw. Previously Jewish historians had been admitted to the congresses only as members of national delegations, not as members of a distinguished Jewish panel. That Jewish historians were received as a Jewish delegation was owing largely to the work of Emanuel Ringelblum, YIVO's spokesman in both Jewish and Polish historical circles.

At the First YIVO Conference, held in Vilna in October 1929, Ringelblum had urged that the congress's rules governing the admission of delegations be changed, and he won the support of Marceli Handelsman, a member of the congress's board in Geneva, and Handelman's disciple, Tadeusz Manteuffel, the secretary of the convention. They saw to it that a joint Jewish delegation was able to attend the Seventh International Congress of the Historical Sciences opening on August 21, 1933. YIVO was represented by Ringelblum, as well as Schiper and Mahler. Simon Dubnov, Jacob Lestschinsky, Julius Brutzkus, Rachela Wischnitzer-Bernstein, and Elias Tcherikower were also supposed to attend, but, following Hitler's takeover, they were unable to get out of Germany. Résumés of their papers were, however, included in the convention proceedings. Mojżesz Schorr, Menachem Emanuel Stein, and Majer Bałaban represented the Instytut Nauk Judaistycznych of Warsaw. The group of historians from abroad included Salo Wittmayer Baron and Abraham G. Duker from New York, and Mayer A. Halevy of Bucharest.[33]

It is noteworthy that the integration of Polish and Jewish historians was already a great deal stronger than that among other fields of YIVO. Many of the institute's historians were members of the Polskie Towarzystwo Historyczne (Polish Historical Society). Though the degree of contact with outside scholars was, of course, determined by the attitudes of individual scholars or the policy of the department of history at a given university, many historians at YIVO could count on the guidance and cooperation of colleagues in the field. In fact, one might say that the strength of YIVO's historians derived from their broader base.[34]

33. Minutes of a joint meeting of YIVO's Economical-Statistical Section and Historical Section, Berlin, May 26, 1932, TC, 143991; Tcherikower to Ringelblum, September 17, 1932, March 17, 1933, TC, 135766–67, 135777–78; Ringelblum to Tcherikower, November 23, 1932, TC, 135772–73. See also Emanuel Ringelblum, "Historia Żydów na VII Miedzynarodowym Zjeździe Nauk Historycznych w Warszawie," *Miesięcznik Żydowski,* 1933, nos. 11–12, pp. 258–60; *La Pologne an VII Congres International des Sciences Historiques Résumés des Communications Presentées an Congres* (Warsaw, 1933), vols. 1–2.

34. See appendix, no. 3.

It goes without saying that YIVO's medium was Yiddish. It was the mother tongue, the language the great majority of Polish Jews spoke. Therefore, the study of Yiddish in all its aspects was one of the most important goals of YIVO in Poland. There was, however, among some members of YIVO an overinsistence on the use of Yiddish, a fetish a scholarly institution can ill afford. Some at YIVO questioned whether books or articles should be published simultaneously in Yiddish and Polish, or even in Hebrew, or whether to give a foreign publisher permission to translate something in which he was interested before it appeared in the original Yiddish. At one point the question was whether to perform *visnshaft* in Yiddish or to do *yidishe visnshaft*.[35] Yet YIVO's historians published their works in many languages, including Yiddish, Hebrew, German, and Polish.

YIVO was open to all historians; scholarship was the only criterion. There were always sharp differences of opinion on various topics, but, as Filip Friedman recalled:

> In Vilna, YIVO not only gathered an imposing collection of materials on Jewish history but became, in a short time, an important center of scientific work and training school for new scholars. . . . YIVO never attempted to impose a unified ideological approach or methodology upon historians grouped around it. Simon Dubnov was a sort of intellectual godfather to the historical section. But representatives of various historical schools published their work in YIVO publications. It was outspokenly Yiddishist in its direction, and also aimed to bring the Jewish masses into the orbit of Jewish scientific activity.[36]

Indeed, YIVO's Historical Commission was known as a place where historians of such differing views as Majer Bałaban and Ignacy Schiper, or Raphael Mahler and Filip Friedman, could work together in harmony.

YIVO occupied a distinct place in Jewish scholarship in general and in the field of history in particular. It aimed at and to a great extent succeeded in gathering primary traditional and secular Jewish sources, and in systematically examining materials in state and municipal archives, in order to study both the internal history of Jews in Poland and their history in relation to the society in which

35. Whether Yiddish should be the only medium for YIVO's publications and the issue of Yiddish as a language in general were discussed at a number of meetings and in correspondence between the Historical Section and the Historical Commission.
36. Philip (Filip) Friedman, "Polish Jewish Historiography between the Two Wars, 1918–1939," in Friedman, *Roads to Extinction: Essays on the Holocaust,* ed. Ida Jane Friedman, introd. Salo Wittmayer Baron (New York, 1980), p. 468.

they lived. YIVO's historians distinguished themselves by their broad consideration of the Jewish experience, with a special emphasis on the daily life of the people. As Ignacy Schiper once put it:

> We know the Sabbath Jew with his festive spirit, but it is now high time to become acquainted with the history of the workday Jew, and his workday ideas and to turn the spotlight on Jewish labor. They [the early historians] gave us a splendid picture of the spiritual leaders of Diaspora Jewry. We are, however, left completely in the dark about the history of the untold hundreds of thousands whose claim to recognition rests not on the riches of the spirit but on their toil and labor.[37]

The accomplishments of YIVO in interwar Poland are ineradicable. Today, after the destructions of World War II, it is difficult to conceive of studying the history of Polish Jewry without turning to the publications prepared by YIVO's historians—*Historishe shriftn, Yunger historiker, Bleter far geshikhte, Lodzer visnshaftlekhe shriftn, Ekonomishe shriftn, Yidishe ekonomik,* and *YIVO bleter*—and to the archival resources that were rescued from Vilna.

37. Quoted in Isaiah M. Biderman, *Majer Bałaban, Historian of Polish Jewry: His Influence on the Younger Generation of Jewish Historians* (New York, 1976), pp. 236–37. For more of Schiper's views on historiographical work at YIVO, see his letter to Tcherikower, November 5, 1926, in the appendix, no. 1.

Appendix

Tcherikower Collection, Archives of the YIVO Institute for Jewish Research, New York. These documents have been translated from Yiddish by Chana Mlotek.

No. 1
Ignacy (Yitzhak) Schiper to Elias Tcherikower, November 5, 1926 (copy)
TC, 136309–11

Dear Mr. E. Tcherikower,

This time I am not writing about Emig-direkt,* but about the Historical Section of the institute. First of all, I want to tell you that you will receive my article for the volume** in about a week. Regretfully, the article will be in German. I am taking it from my German manuscript on Jewish autonomy and do not have the time to translate it myself. It is, however, a minor thing that you will be able to take care of.

*Emigrationsdirectorium, an international committee for Jewish emigration from Eastern Europe established in Prague in 1921, headed by Miron Kreinin, J. Berenstein, and Oscar Cohn.
**Ignacy Schiper, "Der tsuzamenshtel funem Vaad Arba Aratzot," in *Historishe shriftn,* vol. 1 (Warsaw, 1929), pp. 73–81.

I want to take this occasion to impart a few of my thoughts on the work of the Historical Section. I do this in accordance with the request of the Vilna friends, with whom I had a small conference yesterday during my stay in Vilna.

I subscribe to writing history insofar as it relates to present-day problems. I feel that we should make a conscious effort to adhere to this principle, namely of supporting and organizing only those studies that have a direct or indirect bearing on vibrant Jewish life and can effect to some extent the deeper comprehension of present-day problems. With this viewpoint in mind, I must first form an image of the dynamic of the present; that is, in which the activity of a modern Jewish person reveals itself. I see this activity in the following areas: the question of migration, cultural universalism, that is, the aspiration to commingle specific cultural values with universal cultural aspirations. From this it follows that our historical research encompasses the following areas: history of Jewish migration, economic history (particularly the study of class differentiation of Jews, historical causes of Jewish mass poverty in Eastern Europe, the rise of class organizations, namely guilds, *kehillot* as organs of economic struggle, modern proletarian organizations, artisan unions, merchants' associations, etc.), historical statistics, the history of Jewish autonomous aspirations, Jews as diplomats and members of legislatures, the role of Jews as intermediaries in transplanting the accomplishments of Oriental culture to Europe, European cultural achievements in Jewish culture, particularly, in the culture of the Jewish common man, and the like.

Naturally, this plan is very broad and would exceed the capabilities of a whole generation of scholars (which, incidentally, is not large), let alone the capabilities of our institute. I therefore feel that we could restrict the program, so to speak, geographically and place the main thrust of the study of the aforementioned problems on the communities of Eastern Europe. In this respect, we might make a further delimitation. Inasmuch as the medieval history of Jews in Poland and Lithuania has already been adequately researched according to the mentioned points of departure, it would be expedient to place emphasis on lesser researched eras—notably the period after 1569, since up to that date there are adequate collections of historical sources. In other words, we need studies that pertain to Jewish mass-life of Eastern European areas, primarily during the seventeenth and eighteenth centuries, and of course the nineteenth century. (This last period would require different methods from the previous periods as we are dealing with sources that necessitate a different organization of study.) I leave out the question as to the way research work of the nineteenth century should be dealt with (I will write you about it on another occasion) and will give you a brief outline of my viewpoint as to the feasible ways to organize the research work with respect to the period from ca. 1569 to approximately the end of the eighteenth century. The first consideration is the gathering of sources. In this connection the type of source will decide the plan of organization. As far as I perceive, we are concerned with three types of sources:

First, the type that is most easily accessible. These are the responsa of contemporary rabbinic authorities. They should be copied (especially the relevant responsa) from the pertinent collections and compiled in editions chronologically. Also relatively easily accessible are such semihistorical sources as, for instance, Hebrew and Yiddish prayers that were written in connection with specific historical events, chronicles, songs of conflagrations, and plain folksongs with a historical motivation or on a historical subject. We have a precise list of these sources in the noted work by [Moritz] Steinschneider on the historical literature of the Jews, and it would be worthwhile to prepare critical editions of these sources, or at least of the most important or hitherto unpublished ones.

The study of Hebrew-Yiddish sources would necessitate the formation of a special subcommittee, and inasmuch as a large number of these sources (particularly of the second type) are found in Western European libraries, notably in Oxford, Frankfurt am Main, and Berlin, etc., Western European correspondents could be helpful in this regard.

Second, Hebrew-Yiddish sources that are found in various *kehillot*, synagogues, study houses, artisan organizations, and the like, come under consideration. Here I particularly have in mind the *pinkeysim*. From experience I know that many *pinkeysim* preserved in various places have not been registered to this day by our scholars. Thus, for example, I became aware only recently that some local artisan organizations in Poland still use the guild *pinkeysim* from the seventeenth and eighteenth centuries, which include very interesting notations. It would be worthwhile to register these *pinkeysim* and copy them if possible. However, this work would have to be done by a special subcommittee on various sources, whose seat would have to be in Poland (most advantageously, in Warsaw).

Finally, the immensely important so to speak Judaic-Christian material that has been preserved in Polish-Jewish archives is to be considered. For the time being, we would have to put aside the smaller town archives that are found in practically every larger town and proceed with the central and provincial archives; that means organizing the work in the Archiwum Akt Nowych [Archives of Old Acts] in Warsaw, which houses the records of the royal chancellery, the Lublin Trybunał Koronny [Royal Tribunal] (which judged blood libel accusations and conducted political trials), the Radom Koronny Trybunał Skarbowe [Royal Financial Tribunal], as well as the records of the Mazowsze [blank]. Simultaneously, work in the provincial archives in Cracow, Lemberg, Poznań, Lublin, and Vilna, where land and city records of the areas mentioned are found, might also be conducted. Work in all the cited archives would be under the supervision and direction of a separate committee working with groups of students, teachers, and more or less qualified amateurs, who could copy documents of a given type according to predetermined directives, or at least prepare short lists. In this connection, we would be able to avail ourselves in Warsaw and Lemberg, for instance, of already existing seminaries of young Jewish students who stand very close to the goals of our institute and would willingly be subject to our supervision. We could also organize a few historical seminars in Vilna, Cracow, and possibly Poznań. A special periodical would be the best instrument for publishing the results of such a collective project.

I am satisfied with proposing, for the time being, the above program. Naturally, all results in the three areas mentioned would have to be centralized in a Polish-Jewish central archives. If we would, for example, furnish the central archives with two copies of each historical document and separate duplicates of each of our archival descriptions, I believe we might easily enlist the support of the Hebrew University's committee in Jerusalem to finance our work to a certain extent, in return for furnishing copies of the duplicates to them, to enable them to create an analogous central archives at the Jerusalem University. I believe that for a similar trade, in the form of copies and duplicates, we might also be able to receive certain subsidies from societies that support large Judaic seminaries and institutions, particularly in America (Philadelphia, New York). In general, it would also be worthwhile to conduct propaganda among the Joint [Distribution Committee] people to appropriate certain sums for this project and thereby help us create aid through work for needy students, unemployed teachers, and generally unemployed intellectuals. We could point out that the Joint has already participated in several such projects of allocating funds for literary anthologies, to secure a livelihood for poor Jewish writers. If you will be able to extract a few thoughts from this already lengthy letter for the upcoming work of the Historical Section, I will be most gratified.

With cordial regards,

Yours,

Yitzhak Schiper

No. 2

Yidisher Visnshaftlekher Institut, Historical Section, Questionnaire 1, February 25, 1927
TC, 142434

The history of the Jewish settlement in Eastern Europe is still far from completely studied, and a whole series of materials that could have primary significance for Jewish history are lying around neglected and scattered, inaccessible to the Jewish historian and cultural researcher. During the last tempestuous period, a trove of documents was destroyed that would have helped illumine whole epochs of Jewish life. It is the obligation of Jewish people to gather and preserve from destruction whatever has remained.

In order to determine our holdings, YIVO is issuing a series of questionnaires. The present questionnaire is the first. All institutions and individuals for whom Jewish culture is dear are requested to reply to the following questions; in so doing they will be making an important contribution to Jewish scholarship.

1. How large is your city? How many Jews live there, and is there any information as to when Jews settled there?

2. Does your community have an archives?

3. Do you have a municipal or state archives, museum, etc., and does it house Jewish materials, and what kinds? Give the address of the pertinent institution.

4. Do you have a burial society, care of the sick society, free-loan society, society for dowries for poor girls, consoling mourners society, and is there any information as to whether such societies ever existed in your community?

5. How long has each of these societies existed?

6. Have there remained any written materials about these societies: minute books, statutes, etc.? Indicate the years that each of these documents covers, and copy at least the title page of the document.

7. In whose possession is each of these documents? Indicate an exact address of the individuals or societies where the record books or other materials are located.

8. Does your city have archives of parties, cultural societies, trade unions, etc.?

9. Are there historical materials in the possession of private individuals, such as genealogical papers, memoirs, old volumes, etc.? Indicate their names and addresses and as far as possible at least a short summary of these documents.

10. Did you have documents that were lost or removed? How long ago and under what circumstances were they lost or removed?

11. Are there any information and written materials about former artisans' societies? Have houses of worship for artisans remained, and what are their names?

12. Do you have old synagogues? What are their names, and how old are they? Are they wooden or brick? Do they have any old books, holy ark curtains, candelabra, and other objects, and how old are they?

13. Do you have other old communal buildings?

14. How many cemeteries are there in your city? What are their names? What well-known deceased are interred there (martyrs, saints, communal leaders, writers)? Are there interesting tombstones? As far as possible, send us photographs of them or else precise descriptions.

15. Give us information about the surrounding *shtetlekh* that were entirely destroyed (in the Poznań region; during the recent catastrophe in the Ukraine, etc.) and have ceased to exist as Jewish settlements. In which of them were the record books and private archives saved, and where are they located?

16. Was your city ever written about, and where was this printed? Indicate the exact author, title of book, city, publisher, and year of publication, or the name and year of the periodical, in which the materials about your city were published.

17. What can you add to the aforementioned questions? If you have anything to add, you are requested to do so.

The Historical Section of the
Jewish Scientific Institute
Professor S. Dubnov, Chairman;
E. Tcherikower, I. Chernikov,
E. Ringelblum, Dr. J. Szacki,
Dr. I. Schiper.

Address for all shipments: Towarzystwo Przyjaciół Żydowskiego Instytutu Naukowego, Wilno. W[ielka] Puhulanka 18

Offprint from *Literarishe bleter,* February 25, 1927, no. 8, p. 149. Drukarnia B-ci Wojcikiewicz, Warsawa, Pawia 10.

No. 3
Minutes of the Warsaw Historical Commission meeting, November 11, 1929
(copy)
TC, 143032

Present: Dr. Schiper, Dr. Mahler, and Dr. Ringelblum.

Inasmuch as Mr. Tcherikower informed Dr. Schiper that a conference on matters concerning the Historical Section will take place at Professor Dubnov's house within the coming weeks, most of the matters were postponed pending the receipt of Mr. Tcherikower's report. It was resolved: (1) to write to Mr. Trunk asking him to send his whole paper concerning the Jews in Mazowsze, so that Dr. Schiper may become acquainted with it and select chapters for inclusion in the Dubnov volume;* (2) to inform the Historical Section in Berlin that the Warsaw Commission still maintains its proposal about publishing an annual devoted to the history of Jews in Poland, with the inclusion also of studies of a more local nature, while studies of a general character would go into the [Historical] Section's publications. The Historical Commission also maintains its previous year's proposal that (a) in order to establish contact with the Polish scholarly world, and (b) to strengthen our position in seeking [state] subsidies, our annuals should be issued simultaneously in the Polish language, according to financial means available. It was also decided to appeal to the Historical Section in Berlin to send, through our mediation, approximately ten copies to leading scholars of Poland and leaders of the Polish democratic circles like Thugutt,** Kalinowsky,*** and others; to the remainder of Polish scholars and institutions, to distribute the Polish summary with a suitable letter. The Historical Commission has decided to request the Ethnographic Commission in Vilna to copy materials with historical content for the Historical Commission.

Notice was taken of the fact that the research expedition of the Jewish Antiquities Commission will take place on the 25th of November with the participation of Dr. Mahler, E. Herstein and Eisenberg.

---

*The first volume of *Historishe shriftn*, which appeared in 1929.

**Stanisław August Thugutt (1873–1941), leader of the Polskie Stronnictwo Ludowe–Wyzwolenie (Polish Peasant Party–Liberation). In the years 1922–24 he was a deputy to the Sejm (House of Deputies), and, from 1925, chairman of the Instytut Badań Spraw Narodowościowych (Institute for Research on Nationalities' Affairs) in Warsaw and vice-chairman of the Polish Liga Obrony Praw Czlowieka Obywatela (Human Rights League).

***Stanisław Kalinowski (1873–1946), physicist, rector of the Wolna Wszechnica Polski (Polish Free University).

No. 4
Minutes of the Warsaw Historical Commission meeting, November 17, 1934
TC, 143062–63

On November 17, 1934, a meeting of the Historical Commission of YIVO in Warsaw took place in the home of Dr. Schiper with the participation of the following members: E. Tcherikower, Dr. Schiper, Yitzhak Giterman (Warsaw branch of YIVO), Dr. Mahler, Dr. Ringelblum, and Messrs. Isaiah Trunk and Shaul Feldman.

Dr. Schiper opened the meeting. Mr. Tcherikower warmly greeted Dr. Schiper on his fiftieth birthday. E. Tcherikower gave a report on the activities of the Historical Section, particularly with respect to the volume devoted to the labor movement and the Dubnov volume.* The content of these volumes and the treatment of subjects were discussed, particularly regarding the Dubnov volume. Those present have promised to prepare their papers for the Dubnov volume within three months.

Historical Commission

Everyone present agreed on the absolute necessity to create a commission in Warsaw that would serve all of Poland. It was emphasized that the Historical Section, which had always been located in foreign countries, had been unable to execute important projects that should be undertaken in Poland. The members expressed dissatisfaction that such important projects as registering and copying *pinkeysim*, gathering historical materials, and the like have hitherto been utterly neglected. Those present expressed a categorical demand that once and for all this work be started. Subsequently dealt with were the questions of (1) the composition of the Commission for All of Poland; (2) the functions of the commission; (3) the finances of the commission; as well as (4) the *Bleter far geshikhte*.

Regarding point 1: The following composition was decided: Dr. Schiper, Dr. Mahler, Dr. Ringelblum, Messrs. I. Trunk and Feldman.

Regarding point 2: A broad discussion developed around the duties of the commission. There were two opinions: one favored broad research functions, the second placed emphasis on organization of the research work such as gathering and copying *pinkeysim* and other documents in various cities and towns of Poland, conducting various surveys, studying Jewish antiquities, and the like. The majority were

---

*Elias Tcherikower et al., eds., *Di yidishe sotsyalistishe bavegung biz der grindung fun Bund: Forshungen, zikhroynes, materyaln*, vol. 3 of *Historishe shriftn* (Vilna and Paris, 1939); Elias Tcherikower, ed., *Simon Dubnov lekoved zayn finf um zibetsikstn yoyvl*, vol. 2 of *Historishe shriftn* (Vilna, 1937).

in favor of the second view, without dismissing the first idea, and when the means are available, it will also be considered.

Regarding point 3: Mr. Tcherikower reported that the Historical Section had forgone material aid from the Center [in Vilna] for the benefit of the Warsaw Commission. The commission will have at its disposal the amount of 100 *złotys* monthly, to be appropriated for research and organizational activities; the secretary of the Warsaw office will henceforth conduct the purely routine administrative work.

Regarding point 4: The question of the publication *Bleter far ge-shikhte* evoked a broad discussion, concerning its advisability, frequency, etc. All present spoke in favor of such a publication as constituting an organic component of the work of the Warsaw historians' circle. As for the projected frequency, the majority spoke in favor of semiannual publication. With respect to finances, Dr. Schiper pledged to raise the amount of 150 *złotys* for each issue; if the Historical Commission will save money left over from the sum allocated by the Central Office, it will have the right to appropriate it for the *Bleter.*

Dr. Schiper declared that he was prepared to serve on the editorial board of the *Bleter.* The editorial board of the *Bleter* pledged to communicate with the Historical Section in Paris and elicit its approval of the contents, before publishing each volume.

No. 5
Minutes of the Historical Commission meeting, November 20, 1936, in Academic House.
TC, 143065

Present: A. Eisenbach, I. Trunk, Dr. R. Mahler, Dr. E. Ringelblum, Dr. I. Schiper and Dr. Schneid. The meeting was chaired by Dr. Schiper.

Agenda: 1. Membership of the Historical Commission
2. Forthcoming projects of the Historical Commission

Dr. Ringelblum takes the floor. Ringelblum states that wishing to take advantage of Dr. Schneid's visit to Warsaw, he invited him and S. Zajczyk to the meeting in order to take up the subject of the conservation of Jewish antiquities in Poland. A. Eisenbach then reads a letter of the Central Administrative Committee of YIVO approving the appropriation of 100 *złotys* monthly for the Historical Commission.

Regarding agenda item 1: On the suggestion by Dr. Mahler, with emendations by a few members, the commission will consist of the following members: Dr. Schiper, Dr. Mahler, Dr. Ringelblum, Dr. Comber, I. Trunk and Dr. F. Friedman (Łódź), P. Kon (Vilna), Dr. N. Gelber. A. Eisenbach of Warsaw is named secretary.

After the secretary reads the work plan that was prepared at the conference of the 25th of this month, Dr. Ringelblum takes the floor. Ringelblum is of the opinion that the first projects of the Historical Commission should be devoted to organizing the *pinkeysim* campaign and preparing guidelines for awarding prizes for the best papers on Jewish history in Poland and publishing them. Dr. Ringelblum then dwells on the need to undertake a publicity campaign for the restoration of Jewish art antiquities in Poland. He holds, however, that the invited cultural historians should first have the opportunity to voice their opinions. Mr. Ringelblum also proposes to the commission to establish contact with the board of the Gezelshaft far Landkentenish [Sightseeing Society]. The Historical Commission would be able to serve and direct the historical-ethnographic circles of the provincial departments of this association. The board would also have its representative on the commission and would financially support our work. The last proposal is immediately approved of and the meeting moves to appeal to the Gezelshaft far Landkentenish concerning cooperation.

Dr. Schiper states that he is of the opinion that the most important and urgent function of the Historical Commission should now be to undertake a wide scope of archival studies in the central Polish archives, in order to prepare a publication of sources on the history of Jews in Poland. The materials should initially pertain to the nineteenth century. As for the earlier eras, archival research should be directed to the preparation of registries of unpublished records of the Polish part of the Polish-Lithuanian Commonwealth since the middle of the sixteenth century. Dr. Schiper contends that monographs by provincial authors are of small value, in general, and that they should not be the most important projects of the commission. Mr. Schiper proposes that before proceeding with the *pinkeysim* campaign we should first communicate with Professor Dubnov, who has already utilized many of them.

In view of the late hour, it is decided first of all to discuss the question of the conservation of Jewish antiquities. Dr. Schneid speaks about the importance of the conservation of Jewish antiquities at the present time. He tells of the destruction of Jewish antiquities in Przemyśl and other cities and proposes the establishment of a central agency, with headquarters in Warsaw or Vilna, that should be engaged in preserving Jewish antiquities. Mr. Zajczyk supports the proposal of Mr. Schneid. He proposes the establishment of a museum council, composed of, in addition to YIVO, representatives of Jewish communities and clergy. The council should be in contact with the boards of Jewish synagogues and generate interest among them in restoring Jewish antiquities and museum artifacts. In that way it will also be easier to procure the *pinkeysim*. In the ensuing discussion Dr. Schiper declares himself in agreement with the proposal in principle, to organize an agency for conserving Jewish antiquities. He feels, however, that the actual work can and should be undertaken by the Jewish communities, but they are, however, still in the hands of black reactionaries [*shvartser reaktsye*]. Only when new [elected] boards of the *kehillot* begin working will it be possible to proceed to organize the proposed agency. Such a specific project should first be proposed to the Warsaw community. It is resolved to suggest such a project to the Warsaw community in due time.

The meeting is thereby closed.

Jack Kugelmass and Jonathan Boyarin

Yizker Bikher and the Problem of Historical Veracity: An Anthropological Approach

The nearly one thousand memorial books—called variously *yizker bikher, pinkeysim,* or *sifrey zikorn*—written primarily by Polish Jews to commemorate their destroyed communities, constitute a vast source of information about the world the survivors had known. For scholars, the questions generated by such books are many. These are not primary sources as the term is used in historiography; that is, they are not contemporaneous documents that have been passed down to us intact. Nor is their general character that of proper secondary sources or monographs. Virtually none of those devoted to Eastern European communities constitute "objective" or academic reconstitutions of the social world and the events with which they are concerned.

The practical problem addressed in this essay concerns the variety of possible uses or readings of the *yizker bikher*—for example, by survivors of the communities themselves, by their descendants and other Jews born after the war, or by scholars of twentieth-century Polish Jewry. In order to suggest the outlines (but not dictate the content) of authentic readings, we examine the distinctive character of these books as a textual genre. This genre is marked by, first, the production of the books as an expression of the survivors' cultural creativity, and, second, the extraordinarily intimate original relation between the books' collective authorship and the collective readership.[1]

---

1. For information on the Jewish literary antecedents of these books, see the introduction to Jack Kugelmass and Jonathan Boyarin, eds. and trans., *From a Ruined Garden: The Memorial Books of Polish Jewry* (New York, 1983). Although the phenomenon of commemorating the dates of deaths through *yizker bikher* is a common Jewish activity, Jews are not the only people who have created books to commemorate the destruction of their culture in general. Memorial books now exist for East Germans uprooted since the Second World War and for Armenians massacred at the time of the First World War.

Until the *yizker bikher* are understood as a genre, they are subject to a variety of misreadings. They may be taken to represent the Jewish community "as it was" rather than as it is remembered and recreated. They may be decried as inadequate, amateurish accounts. They may also be mistrusted as a *post hoc* myth having little to teach us about the world the survivors knew. Learning what is specific about the memorial books may not only remove these barriers to historical comprehension but also teach us something about our own conventions.

Some scholars have found little of value in these books. The historian Jacob Szacki (Shatzky), in a review of several memorial books published in the 1950s, regretted that they were not organized as professional historical monographs. Thus he sums up his comments on the Rokiškis (in Yiddish, Rakishok) book: "In general there is no editorial hand to be seen. Everything is vague, chatty, and unverified (for example, the history of the town and its Jews)." He complains of the inclusion of an article on the Chełm-story genre in a book for Chełm that such stories "reveal nothing new, and are generally inappropriate in a book about the Holocaust, because the Chełm story was not destroyed, and the genre actually has only a slim connection to the city of Chełm." In his remarks on the Ostróg (in Yiddish, Ostre) book, he offers a straightforward solution to such deficiencies.

> Perhaps all of the materials sent in should have been handed over to a professional, who could rework them into his narrative and give credit to everyone who sent in materials. This would result in the books' being of smaller proportions, more easily read and remembered. The way they are assembled now, they are for the most part gravestones, not books. As is well known, no one reads gravestones.[2]

We wish to argue that Szacki was quite wrong. Gravestone inscriptions are read. These "gravestones" are moving and informative. Szacki's critical reviews do have cautionary value; at several points he notes serious factual errors, and we can only wish we had more such careful reviews to refer to. It is true that the books are not always reliable as sources for chronology or detailed biography. Nevertheless, studying the historical process by which the books were assembled enables us to understand why the Ostróg book

2. Jacob Shatzky (Szacki), *"Yizker bikher,"* YIVO bleter 39 (1955): 340, 345, 351.

would not be better if it were shorter and why the Chełm stories have a place in a book occasioned by the destruction of Chełm.

The main question is not the qualifications of those who produced *yizker bikher* but rather their motivations. The terms used to designate the books tell us much about the intention of their creators. The term *yizker bikher* hints at a connection to the earlier *Memorbücher* of Ashkenazi Jewry. Like them, the books' main function is preservation of the names and the recording of acts of martyrdom. Not surprisingly, many memorial books conclude with unadorned lists of such names. The designation *pinkes,* on the other hand, suggests a replacement of the community chronicle, and hence one source for the typical emphasis on remarkable events and outstanding personalities. At least one memorial book writer explicitly draws this analogy: "Now, in connection with the publication of this *Pinkes Kovel,* I remembered . . . the old *pinkes* of our town."[3] Finally, in traditional Eastern European Jewish usage the word *sefer* refers to a religious text bearing rabbinical approval. Hence *sefer zikorn* is almost a term for a ritual object, a vessel in which the holy memory of the martyrs and the community they constituted will be preserved. Thus the books represent the fulfillment of a folk conception of history (elaborated in the related modes of martyrology, moral example, common origin, and lost childhood ideal), and at the same time—as Szacki correctly observed but incorrectly interpreted, and as is often stated in the introductions to the books—the establishment of a surrogate tombstone.[4] The *yizker bikher* are not inadequate academic histories but the often eloquent voices of simple people determined to preserve a glimpse of a world they knew, loved, and lost. Our insistence on this point is the crux of our disagreement with Szacki.

It is not surprising that an urge we may call historical would appear in the wake of such annihilation. Yosef Hayim Yerushalmi has discussed the phenomenon with regard to the expulsion from Spain, arguing, "The primary stimulus to the rise of Jewish histo-

---

3. Leybl Shiter, "What Is a *Pinkes*?" in *From a Ruined Garden,* p. 25.
4. One book's editors, trying to point out its distinctiveness, confirmed this last point: "It is generally said that a memorial volume is a monument in memory of a city or small town. But this does not apply to Wołożyn. . . . The Book of Wołożyn is not a graveyard or the mark of a last kindness. It sets out to record life." Eliezer Leoni et al., eds., *Wołożyn: Sefer shel ha-ir ve-shel yeshivat Etz Hayyim* (Tel Aviv, 1970), English sec., p. 7. In fact, since the surrogate tombstone is essentially built of narrative, all the books necessarily "record life" as well.

riography in the sixteenth century was the great catastrophe that had put an abrupt end to open Jewish life in the Iberian Peninsula at the end of the fifteenth."[5] This urge entails a certain sense of responsibility for describing the community in its fullness, "as it was." The unexpectedly realistic analysis in Nathan Nata Hanover's martyrology of the Chmielnicki pogroms is another case in point. There was also, of course, a compelling counterurge, as David G. Roskies notes in the case of individual modern Jewish chroniclers of catastrophe: namely, the need to "reshape the ancient archetypes in its wake."[6] This affects the memorial books as well. But those who wrote as part of an actual community of mourners were motivated toward faithful recreation of reality. Unlike fiction writers or even some autobiographers, for whom the expression of the individual self as distinct from the group is a paramount value, the urge for accuracy on the part of *yizker bukh* contributors is necessarily reinforced by the collective character of the undertaking. Those responsible for the memorial books constituted, *grosso modo,* so many eyewitnesses to all the events described in the books and could to some degree serve as verifiers or supplements to one individual's account of an aspect of the community.

This should not be taken to mean that all groups are equally represented in the *yizker bikher,* or even that the process of compiling the books was uneventful. Countless examples prove the opposite. In the case of the Zwoleń book, the Israeli *landslayt* balked at the notion of a project not centered in Israel. The Paris *landslayt* were reluctant to reveal their leftist agitation in the town before the war for fear of being associated with the communists. Hence the political aspect of life in Zwoleń is poorly represented. At the opposite end of the spectrum, religious life in the town is also underrepresented, since the Orthodox preferred not to participate in a project that was largely in the hands of secularists.[7]

It would be wrong to conclude that those who did not work on particular books were not concerned with commemoration. It is entirely likely that religious *landslayt* were involved in efforts to com-

---

5. Yosef Hayim Yerushalmi, *Zakhor: Jewish History and Jewish Memory* (Seattle, Wash., 1982), pp. 58–59.

6. Nathan Nata Hanover, *The Abyss of Despair,* trans. Abraham J. Mesch (Bloch, N.Y., 1950); David G. Roskies, *Against the Apocalypse: Responses to Catastrophe in Modern Jewish Culture* (Cambridge, Mass., 1984), p. 259.

7. Miriam Hoffman, "Memory and Memorial: An Investigation into the Making of the Zwoleń Memorial Book" (M.A. thesis, Columbia University, 1983), p. 83.

memorate particular saintly individuals from Zwoleń and elsewhere—a different strategy reflecting a different understanding of their community's life and death.[8]

To take another example, an interview with the president of the Lublin *landsmanshaft* in Paris revealed the following: In the late 1940s, a Lublin *landsmanshaft* was established in Poland for the purpose of publishing the Lublin *yizker bukh*. Two members of that group, Meir Szildkrojt and Khale Marder, arrived in Paris with the first materials. By 1951 the book was assembled and the necessary money had been raised. However, the communists in the *landsmanshaft* raised problems. The book, in principle, was intended to represent the full range of Jewish life in Lublin. A Bundist in Paris, Khiel Najman, contributed a piece on the Bund, but the communists did not allow his name to be printed at the end of it, claiming that he was a "social fascist."[9] The communists also rejected the idea of a contribution by Yankev Glatshteyn, claiming that he had advocated the use of the atom bomb on Japan. An article was commissioned from Yitzhak Gruenbaum, in Israel, on the Jewish resistance in Poland; the communists wanted another article, reflecting their viewpoints. Certain concessions were made to the communists because the book was printed on the presses of the *Naye prese*, the communist Yiddish newspaper.[10] The book was published in 1952, and shortly afterward the *landsmanshaft* split along political lines. It may be assumed that, in this case, the task of commemoration did not serve in the long run to promote ideological tolerance within the *landsmanshaft*.

Interviews with editors of memorial books point to similar cases where the circumstances of a book's production resulted in specific lapses. One editor pointed to the example of the Nowy Sącz (in Yiddish, Sandz) memorial book, edited by a professional historian, Raphael Mahler.

> He was the editor of the memorial book for his town, Sandz. And there they had bitter complaints against him, and they were justi-

8. Writing about the portrayal of a synagogue attendant who was said to have died rescuing a Torah scroll during the 1903 Kishinev pogrom, Roskies notes: "The one heroic death of the *shames* [beadle] expiated the involuntary death of the many." *Against the Apocalypse*, p. 280.

9. However, the memorial book editor, himself from Lublin, states that the reason the Bund is underrepresented in the Lublin memorial book was that the surviving Bundists failed to send in materials. Anonymous, interview with Jonathan Boyarin, Tel Aviv, July 1986.

10. Szmuel Spiro, interview with Jonathan Boyarin, Paris, November 1982.

fied. . . . He virtually excised the Bund from the book; it is absent. And there was a Bund in Sandz. And Mahler, as a historian, a true historian—he himself failed. He should have made every effort to see that there was something, one or two articles about the Bund. And he didn't see to it.

For my part, when I make a memorial book . . . I say every group, every movement, everything must be there. I search for, I inspire the people to bring me [someone]: "Bring me someone here who has something to say about the *linas hatsedek* [hospice for the poor], about another philanthropic institution, about . . . whatever there was, that has to be. . . . I have the conception of a book.[11]

This mention of "the conception of a book," however, raises a problematic issue: Is there a set image of the *shtetl* that predetermines the eventual representation of a particular community in a *yizker bukh*? This "conception" may be part of what made Szacki and other historians wary of memorial books, why they were so concerned about the sacrifice of accurate facts in favor of mood and sentiment. The problem is made more acute by the fact that some editors undertake work on volumes devoted to communities of which they had no knowledge before the destruction. Revealingly, in an essay on memorial books the historian Abraham Wein criticized the editor we have just quoted, implying that his factual knowledge could not be sufficient to the task of editing books "from widely-scattered communities . . . Kazimierz, Kutno in central Poland, Rohatyn in Podolia, and others."[12]

All this information should not be seen as damning. Any account is necessarily partial, and distortion is an integral aspect of communication. The question here is the nature of the preconception. The answer lies only partly with the issue of editorship. Perhaps to a greater degree, we should consider the books in the light of the ethnographic tendency in modern Yiddish literature—especially Sholem Aleichem's work—and its impact on the Yiddish-speaking public.

Whether or not the urge to record in what academic specialists might consider a fair and balanced way can be successfully achieved is also a political question. Given the fragmentation of the Jewish community both now and in interwar Poland, there remains within

11. Anonymous, interview with Jonathan Boyarin, Tel Aviv, July 1986.
12. Abraham Wein, " 'Memorial Books' as a Source for Research into the History of Jewish Communities in Europe," *Yad Vashem Studies* 9 (1973): 255–72, quotation on p. 260.

the *yizker bikher* nonetheless a remarkable determination to elevate and distill the moral legacy of all members of the community, designated as martyrs. It is at death, as Walter Benjamin points out, that the life of an individual becomes the stuff of stories.[13] And the memorial books—again in their most characteristic style, that of the personal reminiscences of *folksmentshn*—are mosaics of stories, not monographs.

It follows that the need to sanctify the vanished community entails demands which conflict with standards of factual veracity. How can one be both accurate and reverent? The answer could not be a retreat to free allegory, unrelated to the persons and events the survivors had known. The survivors were still too shaped by their particular experiences, and there were too many of them to accept an idealized version of pious *shtetl* unity.[14] Yet the stark realism characterizing *gvies eydes*—eyewitness testimonies of Holocaust survivors—seemed insufficient as a rhetorical mode. The book had to do more than convey destruction and sorrow. It had to embody something of the texture of life before the destruction.

Discord was very much part of *shtetl* reality during the interwar period. The *yizker bikher* note the existence of vicious poverty and class distinctions; helpless, crippled, or mentally ill individuals; struggles for communal power and mutual betrayal to the Gentile authorities in the course of these struggles; the ridicule of the Orthodox by radicals and the excommunication of radicals by the Orthodox.

How were the contributors to the books to deal with these issues, given the need to create monuments on paper? To a large degree they proved adept at sanctifying that which in context would have been considered impure or trivial.

An almost ubiquitous example is the way town fools and other eccentrics are treated in the books. They are pictured as emblems of the community. Since they are impartial and belong to everyone,

---

13. Walter Benjamin, *Illuminations* (New York, 1969), p. 94.

14. The anthropologist James Clifford has recently argued that all cultural description is allegory, in the loose sense that "this is a (morally charged) *story* about that." "On Ethnographic Allegory," in *Writing Culture*, ed. James Clifford and George E. Marcus (Berkeley, Calif., 1986), pp. 98–121, quotation on p. 100. We note, first, that Clifford's focus is on ethnography as cultural description across cultural boundaries rather than as retrospective accounts of a destroyed world by those who knew it; and, second, that, even in Clifford's formulation, there exists a prior referent—he does not mean to argue that ethnography is unconditioned by experience.

they help to constitute the community's *identity,* something that could not be taken for granted. Their depiction is heightened in vignettes that conclude with their martyrs' death; the reader is generally left with the impression of these madmen, cripples, and simpletons as holy innocents.

The strategy is not always successful. Sometimes the characters remain too real. One character sketch, which appeared in a memorial book, is particularly striking.[15] We translated it with the intention of including it in our book *From a Ruined Garden.* It is a portrait of T—— the coachman.

> T—— the coachman was known throughout the entire region of N——, both by those who rode with him from N—— to S—— and by those who didn't. Everyone knew him. When he was still far distant, one heard shouts in Polish from C—— Street: *"Uwaga! Pan T—— edze!"* (Look out, here comes Mr. T——!) Above average height, with sunken cheeks and a crooked nose, with large eyeglasses in a white frame, his pants baggy and his jacket open, carrying a short whip in his hand, he walked behind the wagon holding the reins in his hand and calling: "Pan T—— is coming!" The peasants recognized him and were happy to give him the right of way. T——'s wagon was upholstered like a taxi: four places in back and three in front. The stuffing was straw, and it was covered with a Gentile-style fur. The stuffing in back was higher than in front, so that the passengers in back would have some place to put their feet.
>
> T—— was a gentleman. He used to help the passengers on and off the wagon. Especially young women and newlywed wives, to whom he would shout: "Quick, down from the wagon, young goats!" The road from N—— to S—— remained unpaved until the years before the Second World War, and T—— and his passengers used to trudge sluggishly along the sandy road.
>
> His horse wasn't the strongest, nor was it very well fed. If T—— came to a hill, he would jump down from the wagon. Seeing this, the other passengers also had to climb down and walk up the hill by foot; if not, he would yell until even old women got down from the wagon. And T—— would shout even more: "Who asked you to get out of the wagon? Now it will take you a half hour to get back in with your old paws." T—— had a very high opinion of himself. Everyone had to ride with *him*—or else he would stand in the middle of the street in N—— and shout: "You, young bitch! You don't want to ride with T——! Just wait, pretty soon I'll tell the world who you're spending your nights with!" And that was enough to make the young woman ask her parents and all of her aunts and uncles in S—— to ride exclusively with T—— so that, God forbid, she wouldn't be prevented from making a good match.
>
> T—— also used to cause such a ruckus in the synagogue that the

15. For reasons of privacy, references to personal names and geographic places have been deleted.

reading of the Torah had to be stopped; and if a dispute broke out there, T—— would shout louder than anybody else. He himself didn't know what he was screaming about, but when it was time for screaming, he screamed. . . . The only one who could calm him down was F——, his wife. When she would stick her head out from the women's section, people would say to him: "T——, F—— is looking . . ." and T—— would quiet down of his own accord.

The second coachman in S—— was popularly called "Y.M.," although his name was S——. He came from another town. When he arrived as a bridegroom in town, his in-laws attempted to cheat him out of the promised dowry. So he yelled, "If you give me the dowry, fine; and if not, I'll give you a Y.M. and an M.Y. (a Russian curse), and I'll go back home and leave the bride here."

The mother and father-in-law, being afraid of the curse, paid the dowry.

But T—— wasn't afraid of the "Y.M." and allowed no one to travel with him. The "Y.M." used to wait until T—— had filled up his wagon; only then would he set off.

Eventually T—— got used to the idea that the "Y.M." was also a coachman and had the right to take passengers to N——, but the burghers of S—— usually traveled with T——.

Later a new trouble arose: a bus route was started between S—— and N——. The rich men of S—— were ashamed now to ride in a humble wagon and took the bus. Then a second bus began to travel between the two towns.

Virtually the whole town began to ride the bus, and T—— was left with almost no livelihood. . . .

Meanwhile the Second World War broke out. The Soviets entered the town. All trade stopped and no one had any reason to leave town.

The last time I met T—— was on that Monday, December 8, 1941. The Germans drove all the Jews into the district court at the end of K—— Street. All of the buildings were packed with the rounded-up Jews. Soon there was no longer any more room, and the Jews were driven into a wooden building, the woodshed of the court. Over 500 people were pressed together in the shed.

At first the Germans selected those who were to die, but when they came to the storeroom, the Germans shouted, "Typhus!" and all of the Jews of S—— were driven in automobiles which brought them to their deaths. T—— began to remonstrate with the Germans: he wanted to live, he was still young, he'd work, anything but death. He shouted, hollered, and still shouting, he was led away to the graves at K——.

On one hand the story stands as an allegory of the experience of the mass of Polish Jews between the two wars. A simple man, *amkho*, is well known and liked even by non-Jewish peasants. He has a living that he manages to protect through his personal knowledge of his clientele and judicious threats of gossip. He is the craftsman of sorts, about to be made redundant as new technology makes its way into the *shtetl* economy. But the Jewish *shtetl* shares the craftsman's fate. It, too, is made redundant by modern means of production and the elimination of the traditional economy based on ethnicity and custom. Finally, T—— suffers the fate of his community at the hands of the Nazis, and this in the course of a few brief pages.

But there is a problem with this story, which indicates the limitations of the strategy of sanctification. When we asked permission of the mutual aid society to publish our translation of it, the request was denied. A representative from the society arrived in New York with a firm refusal in one hand and a pile of his own papers in the other—material that, he explained, had been left out of the memorial book for one reason or another but deserved, he thought, publication in our book. T——, he explained, was a real figure, and his relatives who survived him are living today in New York. They had objected vehemently to his portrait in the memorial book and threatened a lawsuit. Reluctant to stir up old trouble, the editorial committee was adamant that we leave the story out.

It is not hard to see why T——'s family found the portrait objectionable. If we accept the division within *shtetl* culture between *sheyne layt* (elite) and *proste* (common people), this coachman belongs in the latter category. He is coarse, vulgar, and lacks self-restraint. The problem with this portrait is that T—— comes through too vibrantly as real *boser vedom*, flesh and blood. Also, given his remonstrance with the German soldiers, he does not ultimately appear as a martyr. For survivors determined to see their brother as an exemplary Jew, one of the six million *kedoyshim* (holy martyrs), this irreverent portrait will not do.

T——'s fate is archetypal, but the fate of his story is a revealing anomaly. It was considered appropriate for inclusion as part of the communal self-portrait but not as the portrait of a blood relative whose image remained alive in personal memory. Here is an unusual example in folk literature (whether oral or written) in which the struggles to establish conventions are still transparent. Despite a preponderance of vignettes focusing on individuals, events, and facets of social life, the books are studded with striking and unusual entries. One example is the highly Christological allegory "Dear God!" from the memorial book for the town of Nowogródek (in Yiddish, Navaredok).[16] Significantly, that story is credited to Dovid Kahan, a professional writer whose biography appears in the *Lek-*

16. *From a Ruined Garden*, pp. 154–57.

sikon fun der yidisher literatur (Lexicon of Yiddish Literature). Another fragment, about an apprentice ritual slaughterer, may well recount an actual incident. While the literary device of a disrupted festival harks back to Sholem Aleichem and is typical of the *yizker bikher,* the moral of self-sacrifice as atonement is hardly a classic Jewish lesson.

> I recall an extraordinary story. The day before Shevues, 1919, I was on my way to the rabbi, Ha-rav Stashevski. It was 6:00 A.M. when I passed by the house of the slaughterer, Moyshe Binyomin, from whose door there flowed a river of blood. It turned out that the slaughterer's son-in-law had committed suicide. He killed himself with the ritual knife. The whole town grieved. Shevues became not a holiday but a time of mourning. The reason for the suicide is as follows. The father-in-law had taught him the methods and laws of slaughtering and he, a gentle soul, could not bear it. The day before he had slaughtered a goat, which cried so much that it caused him much grief. Unwilling to be a slaughterer, he had taken his own life.[17]

Roskies argues that recourse to archetypes as an essential strategy of the modern Jewish literary response to catastrophe means that the actual experience of persons who have lived is thereby relegated to what he calls "myth": "All past divisions would ultimately cease to have meaning. . . . Liberated from their physical reality, the Jews of eastern Europe entered the realm of myth." What Roskies means by "myth," however, is apparently reference to ancient Jewish literary figures, as in the fragment from Yitzhak Katzenelson that Roskies quotes on the same page: " 'A wailing Jeremiah, Job afflicted, Kings despairing, all in one—it's they!' "[18] The amateur contributors to the *yizker bikher* found their neoclassical models in Yiddish literature from the turn of the twentieth century. And though that may warn us to beware of the memorial book portrait as sentimentalized, overly retrospective toward an imagined classic *shtetl,* the books appear on the whole to be well grounded in actuality. Whereas a wholehearted surrender to archetype may have been possible in the commemorative esthetic of an individual writer such as Katzenelson (to whom Roskies refers), the balance of objective reference and allegory in the memorial books is more tightly determined by the intimate community of authors and readers.

Given the unsettled nature of the material, the *yizker bukh* editors had a critical role in shaping the finished products. Moreover, they

17. *Sefer yizkor shel kehillat Dzialoszyce* (Tel Aviv, 1973), p. 73.
18. Roskies, *Against the Apocalypse,* p. 224.

had to tread a fine line in order to arrive at a result that was both authentic and acceptable to the *landslayt*.

Nor were the editors always successful. While researching her master's thesis on the production of the Zwoleń memorial book, Miriam Hoffman discovered deep animosity among the *landslayt* toward the editor. It was charged that he was responsible for inaccuracies, had cut texts without authorization, and—the most bitter charge—had eliminated the personal, subjective aspects of both painful and warm memories. The resentment of this outsider was expressed by one Zwolener thus: "He is not a *mentsh*. And a *Litvak* at that, rigid and obstinate. He left out the essence and what remained has no *yidishn tam*, no Jewish essence."[19]

Believing that the process of creating the *yizker bikher* is important both to students of Ashkenazi culture and those concerned with survivorship, we recently began distributing a questionnaire to memorial book editors. Although the information we have received in response is sketchy, we expect more substantial data as we are able to conduct intensive face-to-face interviews. Yet even the few responses we have thus far received are revealing. One is from the aforementioned editor of the Zwoleń book, a Lithuanian Jew living in New York who has edited four books all told. The second is from a Polish Jew living in Israel who has edited some twenty books on his own and coedited several others. Both are in their mid-seventies; both left Europe in the late 1940s.

Essential to the questions we are raising here are the editors' answers to this question: "Do you consider the individual articles and the overall picture as constituting a historically valid record? If it is distorted in certain respects, how so and why?"

Significantly, the editor from New York responded to this question by dividing the material in the *yizker bikher* into three parts: Holocaust, "research essays," and the firsthand accounts of interwar *shtetl* life. Holocaust material in the memorial books leans toward a focus on the individual rather than on the community. The research essays are accounts of the long-term history of the *shtetl*, predating the living memory of the survivors and *émigrés* who contributed to the books. They appear in most books and are quite often written by the professional editor, if one has been hired, or by another individual who is a recognized historian. Regarding the accounts of *shtetl*

---

19. Quoted in Hoffman, "Memory and Memorial," p. 88.

life, which are our main concern, however, this editor wrote that "they are of less value [than the Holocaust accounts]. They are generally of worth only for the survivors and their families and friends."

The response of the Israeli editor to this question also expresses doubt about the historical veracity of the *shtetl* memoirs. He wrote: "Certainly there are many imprecisions, but time has erased from memory a multitude of dates, figures, facts. Also, the minimal education of most of the writers did not afford precise description."

Although this comment may seem to echo Szacki's judgment, albeit from a more sympathetic perspective, for this editor, such imprecisions are of secondary importance. Clearly he values subjective, personalistic narration above impersonal information.[20]

> I am against the contention that the memorial books do not contain genuine historical material. On the contrary. The authentic material, very close to the truth, can be found only in the memorial books, I would say perhaps even more than in the historical books. Why? Because they are written by living witnesses, people who experienced it themselves.
>
> [The imprecisions and distortions] in no way diminish the deeply thought out, and also objective descriptions, even if they are personally expressed. . . . The future historian must decide, must choose, must segregate, and because so many memorial books have appeared, he can compare them. That is his task. The task of these people is to tell what they remember. What these Jews tell—is what comes from their hearts.

Apparently the personal memories contained in the books were never intended as sources of facts, dates, and figures. In fact, the nonprofessional editors of one memorial book—*landslayt* of the town themselves in this case—state explicitly in their introduction that when the facts of one account conflicted with those stated in another they printed both as they stood. Their justification bears on the question of precision and balance versus the production of a generally acceptable collective portrait.

> The Editorial Board did not wish to correct one or the other, therefore contradictory accounts of the same event might possibly be found. Let the reader know that we are conscious of the fact and still have left it without comments. What matters most is that in spite of the contradictions integrity is being preserved. This or that episode does not make a difference as long as the whole atmosphere is there. The

---

20. Compare Benjamin, *Illuminations*, pp. 88–89.

same is to be said about descriptions of people, spiritual leaders and communal workers.[21]

What is essential to the contributors—and what we should in turn grasp as central—is the affective quality of their memories and the names and moral qualities of the dead (whether individuals, groups, or entire communities). Their need was first for a focus of catharsis (a gravestone) and only then for an objective record. Given such popular momentum, even those editors who were inclined to steer the books toward a more objective presentation could hardly have done so. Here, for example, are the words of another editor, who writes, in "Instead of an Introduction" to the Kozienice book, that though he has never seen all of its characters, artisans, and *yeshivah* students, "Yet I see them with my *spiritual* eyes alive, creative, just as if we were good, old acquaintances."[22] He thus articulates the *landslayt*'s goal of providing not so much a record of the past as the sensation of reliving, through a vehicle for mourning and a resting place for the "homeless souls."[23]

The memorial books can indeed serve as a great resource for those who want to study Jewish life in twentieth-century Poland. There is much they reveal about social and educational institutions, political parties, and sports clubs. They are particularly useful for studying the culture of Jewish adolescence in Polish towns between the wars, since most of the survivors were young adults at the war's end. We might at this point briefly suggest some examples of how the books may be used most reliably and effectively. One such way is to provide local details on general phenomena. This has been done, for instance, by Isaiah Trunk in his book on the *Judenrat* and by Nakhman Blumental in his study of Holocaust folklore.[24]

21. Hillel Harshoshanim et al., eds., introd. to *Radomysl rabati ve-ha-sevivah: Sefer yizkor* (Tel Aviv, 1965), English sec., n.p.

22. Borukh Kaplinsky, ed., "Instead of an Introduction," in *Sefer zikaron le-kehillat Kozienice* (Tel Aviv, 1969), n.p.

23. The term comes from Robert Jay Lifton, *The Broken Connection: On Death and the Continuity of Life* (New York, 1979), in which he writes: "The great problem for survivors in all cultures is to convert 'homeless souls,' particularly those of the recent dead, into comfortably enshrined or immortalizing souls. Funeral ceremonies are rites of passage precisely for this purpose. *What is involved is the symbolic transformation of a threatening, inert image (of the corpse) into a vital image of eternal continuity (the soul)— or of death as absolute severance to death as an aspect of continuous life*" (p. 85, Lifton's italics).

24. Isaiah Trunk, *Judenrat* (New York, 1977); Nakhman Blumental, *Verter un vertlekh fun der khurbn-tkufe* (Tel Aviv, 1981).

Given the preponderance of vignettes and anecdotes in the *yizker bikher,* the books are best used for studying *topics,* not *towns.* We will provide a few brief examples of the kind of topics for which the books contain especially rich information, with references and with the advice that such information is often found buried within more general memoirs.

Certain types of information—fascinating to anthropologists precisely because of the "changes" entailed in "transmission"—may be important to historians because, while problematic, they may be the only data available on a given topic. An apt example is the town maps often included in the books. These are schematic, usually drawn from memory, and occasionally fanciful, with little stick animals drawn in the section labeled "pasture" and so forth. But they are equally likely to show, as the map of Dzisna (in Yiddish, Disna) does, the location of the town's Nazi ghetto—"superimposed" on memory, as it were. Or they may provide information about the ethnic makeup of a *shtetl;* the same map of Dzisna shows near the Dwina River the Russian and the Polish cemeteries, near the town square the "old [Jewish] *bes-oylem"* (cemetery) and on the other side of town altogether, the "new *bes-oylem."*[25] From the standpoint of historiography, the information is at once graphic and conceptual, suggesting not only the physical layout of a town but its inhabitants' sense of space. It may help us detect the sociocultural clues shaping an individual's experience of his or her daily reality.

Weddings receive considerable attention in the *yizker bikher.* Details can be found on such questions as engagements and arrangement of marriages. In the middle of a description of a market day in Czortków (in Yiddish, Tchortkov), the author relates:

> The annual market had another very important purpose. Jewish families would agree upon making *zeungen* [meetings] between young people, resulting in discussions and even *tnoyim* [coming to terms]. The completion of the matchmaking was a boon to business since the in-laws would buy presents for the couple.[26]

Other quotations are tantalizing and suggest the urgency of interviewing memorial book contributors while there is still time. One example is the comment that the towns around "Łosice [in Yiddish,

25. Aron Beilin et al., eds., *Disna: Sefer zikaron le-kehillah* (Tel Aviv, 1969), n.p.
26. Meir Loker Druk, "Der yor-yarid in Tchortkov," in *Sefer yizkor le-hanzahat kedoshei kehillat Czortkow,* ed. Yeshayahu Austri-Dunn (Tel Aviv, 1967), pp. 180–82, quotation on p. 182.

Loshits] were also connected by family ties, because they contracted marriages between each other."[27]

Market days receive a good deal of attention in the books, as is fitting since the *shtetlekh* were in essence market towns. These descriptions shed light on the towns' relations to the larger regions and on their economic ties to the surrounding peasant population. Sometimes there are surprises, as in this description of an especially lively fair.

> A variety of jugglers, organ grinders, and "magicians" would also come and they were a special attraction for children. As part of their trade all these tricksters would wear Turkish hats, speak various languages and grow hoarse from screaming "hocus-pocus." When it was time for *minkhe* [afternoon prayers] all these "Turks" would go to the synagogue. It turned out that they were really Jews—even *Litvaks*.[28]

To make these books fully useful for researchers of Polish-Jewish life, a vast project of indexing is called for. Such a project will require a team of scholars from a range of disciplines with knowledge of

27. Dovid Ruzal, "Dos iz geven undzer shtetl," in *Loshits,* ed. Mordkhe Shner (Tel Aviv, 1963), pp. 26–31, quotation on p. 26.

28. Zvi Shtutshko, "Der vekhntlekher mark tog un der groyser yarid," in *Sefer Jadow,* ed. A. Wolf Jasny (Yasni) (Jerusalem, 1966), pp. 46–47, quotation on p. 47. For more examples of town maps, see, *inter alia,* David Shtokfish, ed., *Sefer Niewsiez* (Tel Aviv, 1976), first leaf; Shimon Kanc, ed., *Przedborz—33 shanim le-hurbanah* (Tel Aviv, 1977), pp. 8–9; Max Mermelstein (Weidenfeld), ed., *Skala* (Tel Aviv, 1978), end papers; Yitzhak Ganuz, ed., *Ayaratenu Stepan* (Tel Aviv, 1977), p. 4; Hayim Rabin, ed., *Voronova: Sefer zikaron le-kedoshei Voronova she-nispu ba-shoat ha-nazim* (Israel, 1971), first page; Mark Schutzman, ed., *Sefer Wierzbnik-Starachowitz* (Tel Aviv, 1973), pp. xx–xxi. For more on weddings, see Jacob Meshulam, "Af a yidisher khasene," in *Sefer Kalish* (Tel Aviv, 1964), pp. 483–84; Borukh Shimkovitsh, "Shabeysim, yomim toyvim, un khasenes," in *Sefer Klobutsk,* ed. A. Wolf Jasny (Tel Aviv, 1960), pp. 50–59; Tsirke Urshteyn, "Af di vegn fun nekhtn," in *Przedborz,* pp. 237–44, esp. pp. 242–44; Sore Hamer-Zhaklin, "A khasene in Przedborz," in *Przedborz,* pp. 245–52; Zev Sobotowsky, "A khasene afn beys-hakvures," in *Sefer yizkor le-kehillat Radomsk ve-hasevivah,* ed. L. Losh (Tel Aviv, 1967), pp. 154–55; Jacob Fuks, "A khasene in shtetl," in *Yizker bukh Ratne,* ed. Yakov Botoshansky and Yitshak Yanasovitsh (Buenos Aires, 1954), pp. 441–43; M. Chazan, "A khasene afn beys-oylem," in *Szumsk: Sefer zikaron le-kedoshei Szumsk,* ed. Hayim Rabin (Tel Aviv, 1968), pp. 382–86. On markets and traveling peddlers, see Dov Gozhaltshani, "An iberblik ibern oyfkum un vuks fun yidishn yishuv in Czyzewo," in *Sefer zikaron Czyzewo,* ed. Shimon Kanc (Tel Aviv, 1961), pp. 76–108, esp. pp. 87–99; "Parnoses fun gliner yidn," in *Megiles Gline,* ed. Henoch Halpern (New York, 1950), pp. 28–44; Zvi Shtutshko, "Der vekhntlekher mark tog un der groyser yarid," in *Sefer Jadow,* pp. 46–47; Arye Margolit, "A shpatsir iber di shtot," in *Sefer ha-zikaron le-kehillat Ostrow-Mazowieck,* ed. Abba Gordin et al. (Tel Aviv, 1960), pp. 129–49, esp. pp. 136–41; Yakov Vronski, "Arum mark," in *Pinkes Nowy Dwor,* ed. Arye Shamri et al. (Tel Aviv, 1965), pp. 248–50; Moshe Zayants, "Sokolow tsvishn beyde velt-milkhomes," in *Sefer ha-zikaron: Sokolow Podlaski,* ed. M. Gelbart (Tel Aviv, 1962), pp. 72–88, esp. pp. 78–83; Leybush Vaysleder, "Zhelekhov vi ikh gedenk," in *Yizker bukh fun der zhelekhover yidisher kehile,* ed. A. Wolf Jasny (Chicago, 1953), pp. 89–95, esp. pp. 91–95.

Yiddish and Hebrew. It will take years to formulate properly, let alone complete.

At the moment, there is a more urgent task to be accomplished. It is almost too late to begin and must be scaled down to what is still possible. That project is to document the great process that resulted in these books and then to detail the vital tensions that left their marks on the character of each one. This is an anthropologist's task, requiring a tape recorder, legwork, and the patience to track down editors and contributors to the memorial books. Interviewing them will enable us to assess the process of creation and the place the books now hold in the lives of survivors. We will undoubtedly find unexpected reflections, distortions, and transformations of interwar Jewish life in the culture of survivors and especially in the creation of *yizker bikher.*

Yet the goal of such a study is not to reduce the memorial books to one correct reading or to deduce the "real" Jewish community from them. As we have seen, accuracy of detail was not the major concern of those who produced the books, let alone a one-to-one maplike correspondence of points in the books' narrative with points in the towns' history. Again: "This or that episode does not make a difference as long as the whole atmosphere is there."

The *yizker bikher* thereby stand as a model for a genre that the anthropologist Stephen A. Tyler has called "post-modern ethnography." Remarkably, he finds no existing examples of this genre, which he describes as "a cooperatively evolved text consisting of fragments of discourse intended to evoke in the minds of both reader and writer an emergent fantasy of a possible world of commonsense reality, and thus to provoke an aesthetic integration that will have a therapeutic effect."[29]

The word "evoke" here means something quite particular. Tyler argues that it is a distortion to see an ethnographic text as "a presence that calls into being something that was absent." Rather, "it is a coming to be of what was neither there present nor absent."[30] This suggests that we should not view the memorial books statically, as more or less acceptable reflections or representations of the reality of Polish-Jewish communities. Rather they are artifacts bearing a certain relation to those who created them, to those who read them,

29. Stephen A. Tyler, "Post-Modern Ethnography: From Document of the Occult to Occult Document," in *Writing Culture,* pp. 122–40, quotation on p. 125.
30. Ibid., p. 130.

and to the "possible world" they evoke. That relation remains to be discovered and made explicit.

Those who come together to create a *yizker bukh* collectively evoke fragments of several towns bearing the same name. These are the *shtetlekh* that continue to exist in the minds of survivors. But the writers of the *yizker bikher* have completed their task, while we, the anthropologists and historians who come after them, seeking to know a vanished world, must now begin our work. Until we document the historical, social, and political context in which the memorial books were created, we will never be able to distinguish between folk history and history, and so we will forever run the risk of rejecting one in the name of the other.

Contributors

Gershon C. Bacon is Senior Lecturer in Jewish History at Bar-Ilan University, Ramat Gan, Israel. He is the co-author, with Gershon D. Hundert, of *The Jews in Poland and Russia: Bibliographical Essays* (1984) and the author of *Agudat Yisrael in Poland, 1916–1939: The Politics of Tradition* (forthcoming).

Jonathan Boyarin is Post Doctoral Fellow at the Max Weinreich Center for Advanced Jewish Studies, YIVO Institute for Jewish Research, New York. He is the author of "Waiting for a Jew: Marginal Redemption at the Eighth Street Shul," in *Between Two Worlds: Ethnographic Essays on American Jews,* ed. Jack Kugelmass (1988). He also edited, with Kugelmass, *From a Ruined Garden: The Memorial Books of Polish Jewry* (1983).

Abraham Brumberg is Visiting Fellow at the Johns Hopkins University School of Advanced International Studies, Washington, D.C. A contributor to *Foreign Affairs,* the *New York Review of Books,* and the *Times Literary Supplement,* he is also the editor of *In Quest of Justice: Protest and Dissent in the Soviet Union Today* (1972) and *Poland: Genesis of a Revolution* (1984).

Lucjan Dobroszycki is Professor of History at the Max Weinreich Center for Advanced Jewish Studies, YIVO Institute for Jewish Research, and at Yeshiva University, New York. He edited *The Chronicle of the Lodz Ghetto, 1941–1944* (1984) and, with Barbara Kirshenblatt-Gimblett, prepared *Image before My Eyes: A Photographic History of Jewish Life in Poland, 1864–1939* (1977).

Artur Eisenbach is Professor Emeritus of Social History at the Institute of History of the Polish Academy of Sciences, Warsaw, where he specialized in the history of Polish Jewry. Until 1968 he was also the Director of the Jewish Historical Institute, Warsaw. His publications include *Kwestia równouprawnienia Żydów w Królestwie Polskim* (1972) and *Emancypacja Żydów na ziemiach polskich 1785–1870 na tle europejskim* (1988).

David E. Fishman is Assistant Professor of Jewish History at the Jewish Theological Seminary of America and Research Associate at the YIVO Institute for Jewish Research, New York. The translator of *Kiddush Hashem: The Warsaw Ghetto Writings of Rabbi Shimon Huberband*

(1987), he is currently working on a cultural history of Belorussian Jewry in the early modern period.

Frank Golczewski is Professor of Modern History at the Universität der Bundeswehr, Hamburg, Federal Republic of Germany. He is the author of *Polnisch-jüdische Beziehungen 1881–1922: Eine Studie zur Geschichte des Antisemitismus in Osteuropa* (1981) and, with W. Reschka, of *Gegenwartsgesellschaften: Polen* (1982).

Rabbi Ben-Zion Gold is Director of B'nai B'rith Hillel at Harvard University, Cambridge, Massachusetts.

Yisrael Gutman is Professor of Contemporary Jewish Studies at the Hebrew University and Director of Research at Yad Vashem, Jerusalem. He is the author of *Anashim va-efer: Sefer Auschwitz-Birkenau* (1957) and *The Jews of Warsaw, 1939–1943: Ghetto, Underground, Revolt* (1982).

Hanan Hever is Lecturer in the Department of Hebrew Literature at the Hebrew University, Jerusalem. He is the author of ''Reshito tisgeh: Iyun be-shirav ha-rishonim shel Ben-Yitzhak le-or homer min ha-arkhiyon,'' *Siman Keriah* 12–13 (February 1981) and ''Hebrew in an Israeli Arab Hand: Six Miniatures on Anton Shammas's *Arabesques*,'' *Cultural Critique*, no. 7 (Fall 1987).

Samuel D. Kassow is Professor of History at Trinity College, Hartford, Connecticut. He is the author of several articles, including ''Trotsky and the Bulletin of the Opposition: A Study of the Left in the 1930s,'' *Studies in Comparative Communism* 10 (Summer 1977) and of *Students, Professors and the State in Tsarist Russia, 1884–1917* (1988).

Jack Kugelmass is Assistant Professor of Anthropology at the University of Wisconsin, Madison. He is the author of *The Miracle of Intervale Avenue* (1986). With Jonathan Boyarin, he edited *From a Ruined Garden: The Memorial Books of Polish Jewry* (1983).

Emanuel Melzer is Editor of *Gal-Ed: Studies on the History of the Jews in Poland*, published by Tel Aviv University, Tel Aviv, Israel. His publications include ''Ha-diplomatyah ha-polanit u-beayat ha-hagirah ha-yehudit ba-shanim 1935–1939,'' *Gal-Ed* 1 (1973) and *Maavak medini be-malkodet: Yehudei Polin, 1935–1939* (1982).

Ezra Mendelsohn is Chairman of the Institute of Contemporary Jewry and Professor of Jewish History at the Hebrew University, Jerusalem. His publications include *Zionism in Poland: The Formative Years, 1915–1926* (1981) and *The Jews of East Central Europe between the World Wars* (1983).

Dan Miron is Professor of Hebrew Literature at Columbia University, New York, and the Hebrew University, Jerusalem. His publications include *Ha-preidah min ha-ani–he-ani: Mahalakh be-shirato* *ha-mukdemet shel Hayim Nahman Bialik* (1986) and *Bodedim be-moadam: Le-dyokanah shel ha-republikah ha-sifrutit ha-ivrit be-reshit ha-meah ha-esrim* (1987).

Moshe Mishkinsky is Professor Emeritus of Tel Aviv University, Tel Aviv, Israel. He served as Editor of *Gal-Ed* from 1972 to 1986. He is the author of *Reshit tenuat ha-poalim be-Rusyah: Megamot yesod* (1981) and "Did the Russian Jacobins (Blanquists) Have a Special Attitude toward the Jews?" in *Jewish History: Essays in Honour of Chimen Abramsky* (1988).

Abraham Novershtern is Senior Lecturer in Yiddish Literature at the Hebrew University, Jerusalem. He prepared *Avrom Sutzkever biblyografye* (1976) and is the author of *Avrom Sutzkever tsum vern a ben-shivim* (1973).

Magdalena M. Opalski is Adjunct Professor at the Institute of Soviet and East European Studies, Carleton University, Ottawa, Canada. She is the author of *The Jewish Tavern-Keeper and His Tavern in Nineteenth Century Polish Literature* (1986). In 1987 she edited a special issue of the *Polish Review,* vol. 32, no. 4, devoted to Polish-Jewish cultural relations.

Antony Polonsky is Reader in International History at the London School of Economics and Political Science, London. He is the author of *Politics in Independent Poland* (1970) and, with Bolesław Drukier, of *The Beginnings of Communist Rule in Poland* (1980).

Eugenia Prokopówna is Assistant Professor of Literature in the Institute of Polish Philology at the Jagellonian University, Cracow. Her publications include "Kafka w Polsce międzywojennej," in *Pamiętnik Literacki: Czasopismo Kwartalne Poświęcone Historii i Krytyce Literatury Polskiej* 76 (1985). She also contributed "In Quest of Cultural Identity: Polish-Jewish Literature in the Interwar Period," to the *Polish Review* 32, no. 4 (1987).

Jehuda Reinharz is Richard Koret Professor of Modern Jewish History and Director of the Tauber Institute for the Study of European Jewry at Brandeis University, Waltham, Massachusetts. His publications include *Fatherland or Promised Land: The Dilemma of the German Jew, 1893–1914* (1975) and *Chaim Weizmann: The Making of a Zionist Leader* (1985).

Chone Shmeruk is Professor of Yiddish Literature at the Hebrew University, Jerusalem. He is the author of *Prokim fun der yidisher literatur-geshikhte* (1988) and the editor, with Irving Howe and Ruth R. Wisse, of *The Penguin Book of Modern Yiddish Verse* (1987).

Shaul Stampfer is Lecturer in the Department of Jewish History at the Hebrew University, Jerusalem. He is the author of *Shalosh yeshivot litaiyot* (1982) and contributed "Ha-mashmaut ha-hevratit shel nisuei-boser be-Mizrah-Eropah ba-meah ha-19'' to *Studies on Polish Jewry: Paul Glikson Memorial Volume* (1987).

Michael C. Steinlauf is Post Doctoral Fellow at the Ukrainian Research Institute, Harvard University, Cambridge, Massachusetts. He is the author of "Jews and Polish Theater in Nineteenth-Century Warsaw," *Polish Review* 32, no. 4 (1987) and "The Polish-Jewish Daily Press," *Polin* 2 (1987).

Jerzy Tomaszewski is Professor of Economics and History at the Institute of Political Science, Warsaw University, Warsaw. His publications include *Rzeczpospolita wielu narodów* (1985) and, with Zbigniew Landau, *The Polish Economy in the Twentieth Century* (1985).

Ephraim E. Urbach is Professor Emeritus of the Hebrew University, Jerusalem. His publications include *Hazal: Pirkei emunot ve-deot,* 5th ed. (1982) and *Halakhah: Mekoroteiha ve-hitpathutah* (1984).

Shmuel Werses is Professor of Hebrew Literature at the Hebrew University, Jerusalem. He is the author of *Sipur ve-shorsho: Iyunim be-hitpathut ha-prozah ha-ivrit* (1971) and *Mi-Mendele ad Hazaz: Sugiot be-hitpathut ha-siporet ha-ivrit* (1987).

Edward D. Wynot is Professor of History at Florida State University, Tallahassee, Florida. His publications include *Polish Politics in Transition: The Camp of National Unity and the Struggle for Power, 1935–1939* (1974) and *Warsaw between the World Wars: Profile of the Capital City in a Developing Land, 1918–1939* (1983).

Index

Titles of works are indexed under author's name only; m = map, n = note, t = table.

130; archives, 455; commerce in, 143t, 145t, 147t; demonstrations and pogroms in, 100, 109–25; elections of 1928 in, 114–15; in Hebrew fiction, 349; historians in, 463; history of, 472, 476; marital patterns in, 178t, 180t, 182t, 185t, 186t, 188t, 191t, 193t, 194t, 195t; mother tongues in, 122, 500n; Polish-Ukrainian war in, 112–13; Polytechnic, 130; and press, 115–22, 287, 306, 405n, 415; as publishing center, 361; Reformed Temple, 113; university, 457, 459, 496, 500n. *See also* Lemberg
Lwów province: commerce in, 144t, 147t, 148m; marital patterns in, 178t, 180t, 182t, 185t, 186t, 188t, 190t, 191t, 193t, 194t, 195t
Lwowski Kurjer Poranny, 115–16, 117–18

Madagascar, 94
Madler, Adam, 416; *Falista linia,* 415, 424
Magdeburg Law, 483
Maggid of Kozienice, 231
Maharam Synagogue, 503
Maharshal Synagogue, 503
Mahler, Raphael, 460, 461, 463, 471–72, 482, 484; Marxism of, 461, 471; as memorial book editor, 523–24; studies of antisemitism, 102; studies of self-government, 461, 476–77; and YIVO, 500, 503, 504, 506, 507, 514, 515, 516–17
Maimonides, 231, 238
Makhshavot, Baal. *See* Baal Makhshavot
Maków, 261t
Malecz, 244, 268n
Mały Dziennik, 153
Manchester Guardian, 123
Mandelbaum, Yehiel Reuven, 245
Mandelsberg, Bela, 466, 479, 499
Manger, Itzik, 429
Manteuffel, Tadeusz, 469, 506
Marchlewski, Julian, 68, 71, 99; *Antisemityzm a robotnicy,* 68, 68n, 71
Marcus, Joseph, 77n, 171, 171n–72n, 214
Marder, Khale, 523
Marek, Andrzej. *See* Arnshteyn, Mark
Marek, P. S., 490
Mariawites, 111–12
Marital patterns, 173–97, 233–36, 237–38, 533–34; age at marriage, 173, 175–87, 196–97, 218, 218n; age at widowerhood or widowhood, 173, 189, 191t, 192–94, 195t, 197;

mixed marriages, 234–35; proportion never married, 173, 187–89, 190t, 218n. *See also* Marriage laws; Weddings; Widows
Mark, Bernard (Berl), 224n
Markets and market days, 149, 162; in *shtetlekh,* 200–201, 205, 206n, 215, 533, 534
Marriage laws, 238. *See also* Marital patterns; Weddings
Marxism, 75, 75n, 78, 92; in literature, 338, 391; and historians, 461, 467, 471
Marylski, Antoni, 456
Mastboym, Yoel, 408
Material aid: communal, 192, 197, 202, 204, 205, 206n, 210, 211–16, 220, 237–38, 462, 476, 512, 528; from *landsmanshaftn,* 202–3, 204, 204n, 213–14, 215, 220, 232, 502; and marital patterns, 189, 192; to pogrom victims, 134; to poor in Palestine, 237; to war victims, 203n, 212, 227. *See also communal institutions by name*
May Day demonstrations, 85, 87–88, 92n
Mayer, A. B.: *Pieśni chaluca,* 415
Mazowsze, 511, 514
Meir Arik, Rabbi, 230, 236, 237–38
Meisel, Nakhmen, 409, 410
Meisels, Dov Berish, 26
Meisl, Jacob, 491
Meisl, Joseph, 463, 495n
Mekabzael, 245
Melamdim. See Teachers, *hadarim*
Melcer, Wanda, 440–41; *Czarny ląd—Warszawa,* 440–41, 445
Memorial books, 3, 198, 200n, 205, 224, 519–36
Menahem Yosef, 230
Mendel (Shtokfish), Hersh, 59n
Mendelsohn, Ezra, 23, 187
Merchants, 77n, 84, 141–57, 197, 272; organizations, 9, 27, 153, 509; Polish, 134, 153–54, 200, 214–15; in *shtetlekh,* 42, 102, 142–43, 147–57, 179, 206, 206n, 214–16, 218n, 220; and Sunday rest, 162, 168, 169, 169n, 170, 171, 171n–72n. *See also* Boycott; Businessmen; Commerce; Peddlers
Messianism, 64, 247, 350, 483
Mestel, Jacob, 489
Metalovetz (Bekerkunst), H., 59n
Metivta, 228, 244
Mezritsh. *See* Międzyrzec
Micewski, Andrzej, 107